ECOLOGY

ECOLOGY

The experimental analysis of distribution and abundance

CHARLES J. KREBS

Institute of Animal Resource Ecology
The University of British Columbia

Harper & Row, Publishers
NEW YORK EVANSTON SAN FRANCISCO LONDON

To Charles Elton and Dennis Chitty

Contents

Preface

One of the mysteries of university education is the way in which dynamic and engrossing subjects are transformed into boring, static, and tedious courses. Since my undergraduate days I have been interested in ecology and simultaneously disappointed by the level at which it is presented in textbooks. If a person interested in ecology is bored by books on the subject, what hope is there for students in liberal arts, agriculture, or chemistry?

This book is my own attempt to present modern ecology as an interesting and dynamic subject. Beneath the variety of approaches that characterizes modern ecology lie a few basic problems that I have attempted to sketch. I have placed special emphasis on problems, and have illustrated them by examples chosen as diversely as possible from the plant and animal kingdoms. This book is not an encyclopedia of ecology, but an introduction to its problems. It is not descriptive ecology, and will not tell students about the ecology of the seashore or the ecology of the alpine tundra. It approaches ecology as a series of problems, problems that are confined neither to the seashore nor to the alpine tundra, but are sufficiently general to be studied in either area.

To understand the problems of ecology, students must have some background in biology and college algebra. Students will find that they can understand ecology without knowing any mathematics, but that mathematics is necessary for those who wish to proceed beyond the simplest level of analysis. Ecology is not a haven for people who cannot do mathematics, and in this respect it is no different from chemistry and physics. Statistics and calculus are useful but not essential for an understanding of this book. I present mathematical analyses step by step and illustrate them with graphs. Those who cannot follow the mathematics should be able to get the essence of the arguments from the graphs.

The problems of ecology are *biological* problems and will be solved not by mathematicians but by biologists. Students will find that, contrary to the impression they get from other sources, the problems of ecology have not been solved. A start has been made in solving ecological problems, but only a start, and I cannot give *the answer* to any of the problems I discuss. Controversies are common in ecology, and an important part of ecological training is appreciating the controversies and trying to understand why people may look at the same data and yet reach opposite conclusions.

Students can learn far more about ecology by analyzing one of its controversies than by reading textbooks. To lead in this direction and to provide more depth, I have included at the end of each chapter a list of selected readings and a list of questions and problems. The questions often are quotations from the writings of ecologists, and they may be used as a focal point for a few moments of private meditation or as a starting point for a short essay or group discussion. Eminent ecologists sometimes make stupid statements, and so you should not be surprised if you find yourself disagreeing with some of the statements quoted. Problems are included because no one can appreciate the quantitative aspects of ecology without going through some of the calculations. Most of the calculations are simple, but I have tried to leave some of them open-ended so that interested students can carry on under their own steam.

If there is a message in this book it is a simple one: Progress in answering ecological questions comes when experimental techniques are used. The habit of asking *What experiment could answer this question?* is the most basic aspect of scientific method that students should learn to cultivate.

Technical terms are kept to a minimum; labeling with words should not be confused with understanding. The glossary of technical words, together with the indexes, should be adequate to cover technical definitions.

I thank many friends and colleagues who have contributed to formulating and clarifying the material presented here. In particular, Dennis Chitty, William Murdoch, Joseph Connell, David Mertz, Conrad Istock, Henry Horn, Neil Gilbert, Peter Larkin, Judy Myers, Conrad Wehrhahn, John Krebs, Tom Reynoldson, Bill Wellington, Eric Pianka, Robert MacArthur, D. P. Clark, Ian Efford, and Rudi Drent have helped me with their comments. Judy Rowell helped by typing the manuscript from my rough notes. The errors are mine, and I would appreciate hearing about them. My students at Indiana University provided an intellectual background in which the ideas in the book became formulated. The Institute of Animal Resource Ecology at the University of British Columbia provided me with a year of leisure to finish this book. Whether they did a wise thing you can judge for yourself.

Charles J. Krebs

PART ONE

WHAT IS ECOLOGY?

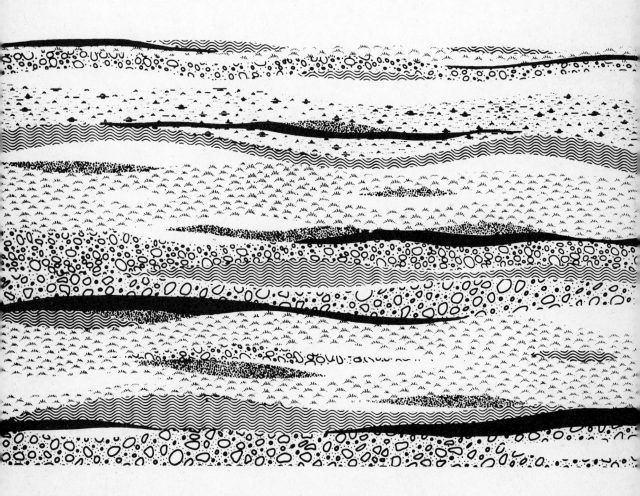

1 Introduction to the science of ecology

Ernst Haeckel in 1869 coined the word *ecology* and defined it as the total relations of the animal to both its organic and its inorganic environment. This very broad definition has provoked some authors to point out that, if this is ecology, there is very little that is *not* ecology. Since four biological disciplines are closely related to ecology—genetics, evolution, physiology, and behavior—the problem of defining ecology may be viewed schematically in the following way:

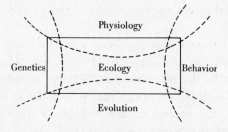

Broadly interpreted, ecology overlaps each of these subjects; hence we need a more restrictive definition.

Charles Elton (1927) in his pioneering book *Animal Ecology* defined ecology as *scientific natural history*. Although this definition does point out the origin of many of our ecological problems, it is again uncomfortably vague. Eugene Odum (1963) has defined ecology as the study of the *structure and function of nature*. This statement has the merit of emphasizing the form-and-function idea that permeates biology, but it is still not a completely clear definition.

A clear definition of ecology is this: *Ecology is the scientific study of the distribution and abundance of organisms* (Andrewartha 1961). This definition is static and leaves out the important idea of *relationships*. Ecology is about relationships, and we can modify Andrewartha's definition as follows: *Ecology is the scientific study of the interactions that determine the distribution and abundance of organisms*. This definition of ecology restricts the scope of our quest to a manageable level and forms the starting point for this book. We are interested then in *where* organisms are found, *how many* occur there, and *why*.

HISTORY OF ECOLOGY

The roots of ecology lie in natural history, which is as old as man himself. Primitive tribes, which depended on hunting, fishing, and food gathering, needed detailed knowledge of where and when their quarry might be found. The establishment of agriculture increased the need to learn about the practical ecology of plants and domestic animals.

Spectacular plagues of animals attracted the attention of the earliest writers. The Egyptians and Babylonians feared locust plagues, and supernatural powers were often believed to cause these outbreaks. The Book of Exodus (7:14–12:30) describes the plagues that God called down upon the Egyptians. In the fourth century B.C. Aristotle tried to explain these plagues of field mice and locusts in his *Historia Animalium*. He pointed out that the high reproductive rate of field mice could produce more mice than could be reduced by their natural predators, such as foxes and ferrets, or by the control efforts of man. Nothing succeeded in reducing these mouse plagues, Aristotle stated, except the rain, and after heavy rains the mice disappeared rapidly.

Ecological harmony was a guiding principle basic to the Greeks' understanding of nature, and Egerton (1968a) has traced this concept from ancient times to the modern term "balance of nature." This concept of "providential ecology," in which nature is designed to benefit and preserve each species, was implicit in the writings of Herodotus and Plato. The assumptions of this world view were that the numbers of every species remain essentially constant. Outbreaks of some populations might occur, but these could be traced usually to divine intervention for the punishment of evil-doers. Each species had a special place in nature, and extinction did not occur because it would disrupt this balance and harmony in nature.

Little conceptual advance occurred until students of natural history and human ecology began to focus the ideas of ecology and provide an analytical framework. Graunt (1662), who described human populations in quantitative terms, can be called the father of demography (Cole 1958). He recognized the importance of measuring in a quantitative way the birth rate, death rate, sex ratio, and age structure of human populations, and he complained about the inadequate census data available in England in the seventeenth century. Graunt estimated the potential rate of population growth for London and concluded that even without immigration, London could double its population in 64 years.

Buffon in his *Natural History* (1756) touched on many of our modern ecological problems and recognized that populations of man, other animals, and plants are subjected to the same processes. Buffon discussed, for example, how the great fertility of every species was counterbalanced by innumerable agents of destruction. He believed that plague populations of field mice were checked partly by diseases and scarcity of food. Buffon did not accept Aristotle's idea that heavy rains caused the decline of dense mouse populations but thought that control was achieved by biological agents. Rabbits, he stated, would reduce the countryside to a desert if it were not for their predators. Buffon thus dealt with problems of population regulation that are still unsolved today.

Malthus published one of the earliest controversial books on demography. In his *Essay on Population* (1798) he calculated that although the numbers of organisms can increase geometrically (1, 2, 4, 8, 16, . . .), their food supply may never increase faster than arithmetically (1, 2, 3, 4, . . .). The arithmetic rate of increase in food production seems to be somewhat arbitrary, and Malthus may have presented this rate as a reasonable maximum supposition (Flew 1957). The great disproportion between these two powers of increase led Malthus to infer that reproduction must eventually be checked by food production. The thrust of Malthus' ideas was *negative*—what prevents populations from reaching the bare subsistence level that his theory predicts? What checks operate against the tendency toward a geometric rate of increase? Two centuries later we still ask these questions. These ideas were not new, since Machiavelli had said much the same thing about 1525, and Buffon in 1751 and several others had anticipated Malthus. It was Malthus, however, who brought these ideas to general attention. Darwin used the reasoning of Malthus as one of the bases for his theory of natural selection.

Other workers questioned the ideas of Malthus. For example, in 1841 Doubleday brought out his true law of population. He believed that whenever a species was threatened, nature made a corresponding effort to preserve it by increasing the fertility of its members. Human populations that were undernourished had the highest fertility; those that were well fed had the lowest fertility. Doubleday explained these effects by the oversupply of mineral nutrients in well-fed populations. Doubleday thus observed a basic fact that we recognize today, although his explanations were completely wrong.

Interest in the mathematical aspects of demography increased after Malthus. Quetelet, a Belgian statistician, suggested in 1835 that the potential ability of a population to grow geometrically was balanced by a resistance to population growth. In 1838 his student Verhulst derived an equation describing the course of growth of a population over time. This S-shaped curve he called the *logistic curve*. This work was overlooked until modern times and we shall return to it later in detail.

Farr (1843) was one of the earliest demographers concerned with mortality. He discovered that in England there was a relation between the density of the population and the death rate (Farr's rule), such that mortality increased as the sixth root of density:

$$R = cD^m$$

where
R = mortality rate
D = density of the population
c, m = constants (m = approx. $\frac{1}{6}$)

Farr returned in 1875 to further consideration of the human population of England. He pointed out that even though the death rate had been steadily declining in England during the 1800s, this did not automatically lead to a population increase, since the birth rate might fall an equivalent amount. Farr pointed out that Malthus' postulate that food supply increases arithmetically was not true at least in the United States, where food production had increased geometrically at a rate even greater than that of the human population.

During most of this time the philosophical background had not changed from the idea of harmony of nature of Plato's day. Providential design was still the guiding light. In the late eighteenth and early nineteenth centuries two ideas that undermined the idea of balance of nature gradually gained support: (1) that many species had become extinct and (2) that competition caused by population pressure is important in nature. The consequences of these two ideas became clear with the work of Malthus, Lyell, Spencer, and Darwin in the nineteenth century. Providential ecology and the balance of nature were replaced by natural selection and the struggle for existence (Egerton 1968b).

Many of the early developments in ecology came from the applied fields of agriculture, fisheries, and medicine. Work on the insect pests of crops has been one important source of ideas. The regulation of population size in obnoxious insects is a basic problem that has long been under study. In 1762 the mynah bird was introduced from India to the island of Mauritius to control the red locust. By 1770 the locust threat was a negligible problem (Moutia and Mamet 1946). Forskål wrote in 1775 about the introduction of predatory ants from nearby mountains into date palm orchards to control other species of ants feeding on the palms in southwestern Arabia. In subsequent years an increasing knowledge of insect parasitism and predation led to many such introductions all over the world in the hope of controlling introduced and native agricultural pests (Doutt 1964). We discuss this problem of *biological control* in Chapter 17.

Medical work on infectious diseases such as malaria around the 1890s gave rise to the study of epidemiology and interest in the spread of disease through a population. Before malaria could be controlled adequately it was necessary to know in detail the ecology of mosquitoes. The pioneering work of Ross (1908, 1911) attempted to describe in mathematical terms the propagation of malaria, which is transmitted by mosquitoes. In an infected area the propagation of malaria is determined by two continuous and simultaneous processes: (1) The number of new infections among people depends on the number and infectivity of mosquitoes; (2) the infectivity of mosquitoes depends upon the number of people in the locality and the frequency of malaria among them. Ross could write these two processes as two simultaneous differential equations:

$$\text{Rate of increase of infected humans} = \left(\underset{\underset{\substack{\downarrow \\ (\textit{depends on number of} \\ \textit{infected mosquitoes})}}{}}{\text{new infections per unit time}} - \text{recoveries per unit time} \right)$$

$$\text{Rate of increase of infected mosquitoes} = \left(\underset{\underset{\substack{\downarrow \\ (\textit{depends on number of} \\ \textit{infected humans})}}{}}{\text{new infections per unit time}} - \text{deaths of infected mosquitoes per unit time} \right)$$

This type of mathematical approach is a paradigm we shall see again later. It helps us to clarify the problem—we can now analyze these components— and to predict new situations (see Lotka 1923).

Production ecology had its beginnings in agriculture, and Egerton (1969) has traced this back to the eighteenth-century botanist Richard Bradley. Bradley recognized the fundamental similarities of animal and plant production, and he proposed methods of maximizing agricultural yields (and hence profits) for vineyards, trees, poultry, rabbits, and fish. The conceptual framework that Bradley used—monetary investment vs. profit—could be applied to any organism. This *optimum-yield problem* is an important part of applied ecology (see Chapter 16).

Recognition of communities of living organisms in nature is very old, but specific recognition of the interrelations of the organisms in a community is relatively recent. Edward Forbes in 1844 described the distribution of animals in British coastal waters and part of the Mediterranean Sea, and he wrote of zones of differing depths which were distinguished by the associations of species they contained. Forbes noted that some species are found only in one zone and that other species have a maximum of development in one zone but occur sparsely in other adjacent zones. Mingled in are stragglers that do not fit the zonation pattern. Forbes recognized the dynamic aspect of the interrelations between these organisms and their environment. As the environment changed, one species might die out, another might increase in abundance. Similar ideas were expressed by Karl Möbius in 1877 in a classic essay on the oyster-bed community as a unified collection of species. Möbius coined the word *biocoenosis* to describe such a community.

S. A. Forbes (1887), in a classical paper on "The Lake as a Microcosm," suggested that the species assemblage in a lake was an organic complex and that by affecting one species we exerted some influence on the whole assemblage. Thus each species maintains a "community of interest" with the other species, and we cannot limit our studies to a single species. Forbes believed that there was a steady balance of nature, which held each species within limits year after year, even though each species was always trying to increase its numbers.

Studies of communities were greatly influenced by the Danish botanist Warming (1895, 1909). Warming raised questions about the structure of plant communities and the associations of species in these communities. The dynamics of vegetation change was emphasized first by North American plant ecologists. In 1899 H. C. Cowles described *plant succession* on the sand dunes at the southern end of Lake Michigan. This aspect of the development of vegetation was analyzed by Clements (1916) in a classic book that began a long controversy about the nature of the community (see Chapter 19).

Thus by about 1900 ecology was started on the road to becoming a science with the recognition of the broad problems of populations and communities. The roots of ecology lie in natural history, human demography, biometry (mathematical approach), and applied problems of agriculture and medicine.

BASIC PROBLEMS AND APPROACH

We can approach the study of ecology from either a *descriptive* or a *functional* point of view. The descriptive point of view is mainly natural history and proceeds by describing the vegetation groups of the world, such as the temperate deciduous forests, tropical rain forests, grasslands, and tundra, and by describing the animals and plants and their interrelationships for each of these ecosystems. The functional point of view, on the other hand, is oriented more toward *relationships* and seeks to analyze general problems common to most or all of the different areas. Both approaches have shortcomings. The primary difficulty with the descriptive approach is that one can get entirely lost in it. We could use all the space in this book just to describe the temperate deciduous forests of North America. With the functional approach there is a tendency to get far removed from reality, in the absence of detailed biological knowledge. In this book I shall use a functional approach and emphasize the general problems of ecology.

Distribution and abundance
The basic problem of ecology is to determine the causes of the distribution and abundance of organisms. Every organism lives in a matrix of space and time that can be considered as a unit. Consequently, these two ideas of distribution and abundance are closely related, although at first glance they may seem quite distinct. What we observe for many species is this:

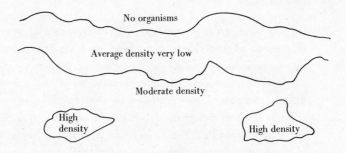

Thus we can view the average density of any species as a contour map, with the provision that the contour map may change with time. Now, throughout the area of distribution, the abundance of an organism must be greater than zero, and the limit of distribution equals the contour of zero abundance. Thus distribution may be considered as a facet of abundance, and distribution and abundance may be said to be reverse sides of the same coin (Andrewartha and Birch 1954). Thus the factors that affect the distribution of a species may also affect its abundance.

The problems of distribution and abundance can be analyzed at the level of the single species population or at the level of the community, which contains many species. The complexity of the analysis may increase as more and more species are considered in a community, and consequently in this book we shall consider first the simpler problems involving single species populations.

There is considerable overlap between ecology and its related disciplines which we cannot cover thoroughly in this book. Environmental physiology has developed with a wealth of information that impinges on problems of distribution and abundance. Population genetics and ecological genetics are two additional foci of interest that we shall touch only peripherally. Evolutionary ecology is another interdisciplinary area that has implications for the study of distribution and abundance.

Levels of integration

In ecology we are dealing primarily with the three starred levels of integration:

Biosphere
*Ecosystems
*Communities
*Populations
Organisms   decreasing
Organ systems   scientific
Organs   understanding
Tissues
Cells
Subcellular organelles
Molecules

On one side, ecology overlaps with environmental physiology and behavior in studies of individual organisms, and on the other side, ecology fades into meteorology, geology, and geochemistry when we consider the biosphere, the whole-earth ecosystem. The boundaries of the sciences are not sharp but diffuse, and nature does not come in discrete packages.

Each level of integration involves a separate and distinct series of attributes and problems. For example, a population has a *density* (e.g., number of deer per square mile), a property that cannot be attributed to an individual organism. A community has a *species diversity*, which is an attribute without meaning at the population level. In general, a scientist dealing with a particular level of integration seeks his explanatory mechanisms from lower levels of integration and his biological significance from higher levels. Thus to understand mechanisms of changes in a population an ecologist will study mechanisms that operate on individual organisms and will try to view the significance of these population events in a community and ecosystem framework.

Some ecologists have suggested that the ecosystem, the biotic community and its abiotic environment, is the basic unit of ecology (Tansley 1935, Rowe 1961, Evans 1956). There may be a particular significance attached to the ecosystem level from the viewpoint of human ecology, but it is only one of the levels of organization at which ecologists operate. There are meaningful and important questions to be asked at each level of integration, and none should be neglected.

The extent of scientific understanding varies with the level of integration. We know a good deal about the molecular and cellular levels of organisms; we know something about organs and organ systems, and about whole organisms; but we know relatively little about populations and even less about communities and ecosystems. This point is illustrated very nicely when you look at the levels of integration—ecology comprises about one-third of biology from this viewpoint. But no basic biology curriculum could be one-third ecology and do justice to *current* biological knowledge. The reasons for this are not hard to find—they include the increasing complexity of these higher levels and the inability to deal with them in the laboratory.

Whatever the reasons for this decrease in knowledge at the higher levels, it has serious implications for the study we are about to undertake. You will not find in ecology the strong theoretical framework that you find in physics, chemistry, molecular biology, or genetics. It is not always easy to see where the pieces fit in ecology, and we shall encounter many isolated parts of ecology that are well developed internally but are not clearly connected to anything else. This is typical of a young science. Many students unfortunately think of science as a monumental pile of facts that must be memorized. But science is more than a pile of precise facts—it is a search for systematic relations, for explanations to problems, and for unifying concepts. This is the growing end of science, which is so evident in a young science like ecology. It involves a lot of unanswered questions and a good deal more of controversy. A scientific discipline like ecology can be viewed as a mine—to the casual observer what is obvious and important is the increasing pile of facts on the ground surface; to the more serious student what is less obvious but probably more important is the actual working area at the bounds of knowledge.

The theoretical framework of ecology may be weak at the present time, but this must not be interpreted as a terminal condition. Eighteenth-century chemistry was perhaps in a comparable state of theoretical development as ecology at the present time. Sciences are not static and ecology is in a strong growth phase.

Methods of approach Ecology has been attacked on three broad fronts: the *mathematical*, the *laboratory*, and the *field*. These three approaches are interrelated, but some problems have arisen when the results of one approach fail to verify those of another. For example, mathematical predictions may not be borne out in field data. We are primarily interested in understanding the distribution and abundance of organisms in *nature*, that is, in the *field*. Consequently, this will always be our criterion of comparison, our basic standard.

Some authors divide ecology into *autecology*, the study of the individual organism in relation to its environment, and *synecology*, the study of groups of organisms in relation to their environment. Synecology may then be further subdivided into population, community, and ecosystem ecology. This subdivision of ecology has the bad feature of suggesting that the environmental factors relevant to individuals are somehow different from the environmental factors relevant to groups of organisms. Much of what is traditionally considered as autecology is really environmental physiology and may or may not be necessary for answering specific questions about distribution and abundance.

Plant and animal ecology have tended to develop along separate paths. Historically, plant ecology got off to a faster start than animal ecology. Since animals are highly dependent on plants, many of the concepts of animal ecology are patterned on those of plant ecology. *Succession* is one example. Also, since plants are the ultimate source of energy for all animals, to understand animal ecology we must also know a good deal of plant ecology. This is illustrated particularly well in the study of community relationships.

There are, however, some important differences separating plant and animal ecology. First, animals tend to be highly mobile, whereas plants are stationary. Thus a whole series of new techniques and ideas must be applied to animals, for example to determine population density. Second, animals fulfill a greater variety of functional roles in nature—some are herbivores, some are carnivores, some are parasites. This distinction is not complete because there are carnivorous plants and parasitic plants, but the possible interactions are on the average more numerous for animals than for plants.

Historically, plant ecology has been mostly community ecology, and animal ecology has been mostly population ecology. This distinction has fortunately broken down during the last 15 years, so that population ecology is a strong area of development in plant ecology, and zoologists are increasingly dealing with problems of community ecology. Many plants are long-lived and further complicate their study as populations by being very large and producing dormant seeds. These problems are well illustrated in forests, which change slowly and often imperceptibly over many years. Other plants are often vegetative reproducers, which makes it difficult to define an individual plant. By contrast, the complex interrelationships among animals has slowed community analysis in the past, and zoologists typically have begun with the study of single-species populations rather than multispecies communities.

In spite of these differences, I shall attempt to integrate plant with animal ecology. The problems of ecology, of distribution and abundance, are common to all organisms.

SELECTED REFERENCES

ALLEN, K. R. 1955. The growth of accuracy in ecology. *Proc. New Zeal. Ecol. Soc.* 1:1–7.

MCMILLAN, C. 1954. Parallelisms between plant ecology and plant geography. *Ecology* 35:92–94.

MAJOR, J. 1958. Plant ecology as a branch of botany. *Ecology* 39:352–363.

MILLER, R. S. 1957. Observations on the status of ecology. *Ecology* 38:353–354.

ODUM, E. P. 1964. The new ecology. *BioScience* 14(7):14–16.

PLATT, J. R. 1964. Strong inference. *Science* 146:347–353.

POPPER, K. R. 1963. *Conjectures and Refutations.* Chap. 1, pp. 33–65. Routledge & Kegan Paul, London.

ROWE, J. S. 1961. The level-of-integration concept and ecology. *Ecology* 42:420–427.

TANSLEY, A. G. 1935. The use and abuse of vegetational concepts and terms. *Ecology* 16:284–307.

QUESTIONS AND PROBLEMS

1 "The definition . . . 'ecology is the branch of biological science that deals with relations of organisms and environments' would provide the title for an encyclopaedia but does not delimit a scientific discipline" (Richards 1939, p. 388). Discuss.

2 Is it necessary to define a scientific subject before one can begin to discuss it? Contrast the introduction to several textbooks of ecology with those of some areas of physics and chemistry, as well as other biological areas, such as genetics and physiology.

3 Is it necessary to study the methodology and philosophy of science in order to understand ecology? Consider this question before and after reading the essays by Popper (1963) and Platt (1964).

PART TWO

THE PROBLEM OF DISTRIBUTION: POPULATIONS

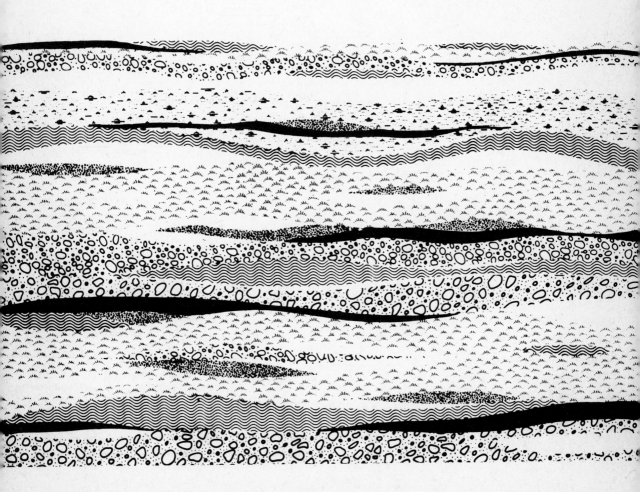

Methods of explaining distributions

The distribution of any species can be analyzed on a series of levels from the worldwide and continental to the local. We consider here only the range of the species based on the criteria of presence or absence. We shall not be concerned here with the pattern of arrangement of the organisms within the zone of occupation.

Why are organisms of a particular species present in some places and absent from others? To answer this question, we look for differences between areas occupied and areas not occupied. This can be done in several ways, and one method of attack is to proceed sequentially through the following steps (Macan 1963):

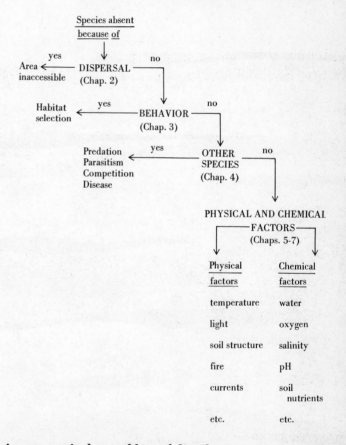

To explain any particular problem of distribution, one proceeds down this chain, eliminating things one by one.

2 Factors limiting distributions: dispersal

The absence of an organism may be due to the species having failed to reach the area being studied. This simple possibility should be examined before more involved possibilities.

The transport or *dispersal* of organisms is a vast subject, which has been of primary interest not only to ecologists but also to *biogeographers,* who wish to understand the historical changes in distributions of animals and plants. There are some very difficult problems associated with the study of dispersal. For one thing, the detailed distribution is known for so few species that most dispersals are probably not noticed. Second, an organism may disperse to a new area but not colonize it because of biotic or physical factors.

The most spectacular examples of transport affecting distribution are those species which are introduced by man and explode to occupy a new area. Let us look into a couple of these situations.

EUROPEAN STARLING *(Sturnus vulgaris)*

The European starling has spread over the entire United States and much of Canada within a period of 60 years. Originally it occurred in most of Eurasia, from the Mediterranean to Norway and east to Siberia. Many early attempts were made to introduce the starling into the United States. One attempt was made at West Chester, Pennsylvania, before 1850, the next at Cincinatti, Ohio, in 1872–1873, but nothing came of these or several other importations. In 1889 twenty pairs were released in Portland, Oregon, but these gradually disappeared.

The permanent establishment of the starling dates from April 1890, when 80 birds were released in Central Park, New York City. In March of the following year 80 more were released. About 10 years were required for the starling to become established in the New York City area (Cooke 1928). It has since expanded its range across North America (Figure 1). This

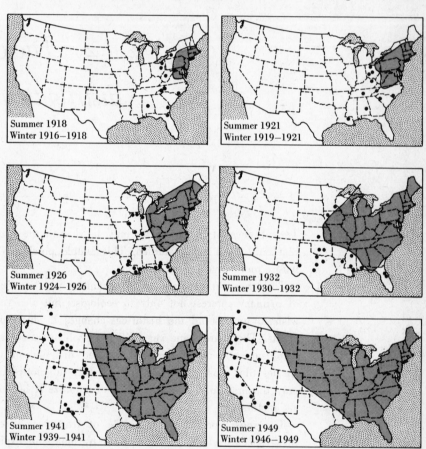

FIGURE 1

Westward expansion of the range of the starling. The shaded area shows the approximate breeding range for a given summer; dots indicate winter occurrences outside the breeding range for the same and two or three previous years. The star indicates an unusually advanced breeding record, in 1934, at Camrose, Alberta. (After Kessel 1953.)

rapid extension of the breeding range has been due to the irregular migrations and wanderings of nonbreeding juvenile birds 1 and 2 years of age. Adult birds typically use the same breeding area from year to year and thus do not colonize new areas (Kessel 1953). The usual pattern of colonization has involved migration in and out of new areas for 5 to 20 years before taking up permanent residence. For example, the starling was first reported in California in 1942 and first nested there in 1949, although large-scale nesting of starlings in California did not occur until after 1958 (Howard 1959). About 3 million square miles were colonized by the starling during the first 50 years after introduction.

CHESTNUT BLIGHT *(Endothia parasitica)*

The American chestnut *(Castanea dentata)* was an important component of many deciduous forests of the eastern United States from Maine to Georgia and west to Illinois (Figure 2). Chestnut made up more than 40% of the overstory trees in the climax forests of this area. In 40 years this species has been virtually eliminated from its entire range by chestnut blight.

The chestnut blight is a fungal disease that attacks chestnut trees. The disease was first noticed about 1900 in the area around New York City, where it killed all its hosts. The fungus was apparently introduced on

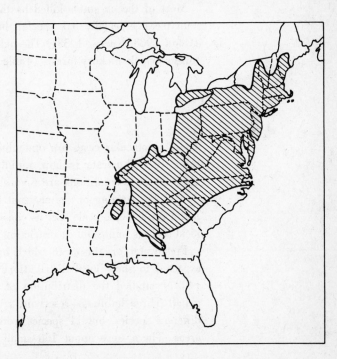

FIGURE 2

Original distribution of the American chestnut tree, Castanea dentata. *(After Grimm 1967.)*

nursery stock from Asia. Although found on other species of trees, *Endothia parasitica* is lethal only to the American chestnut. The fungus enters the host tree through a wound in the bark, grows chiefly in the cambium, penetrates only short distances into the wood, and kills the tree by girdling. Once a chestnut tree is attacked, it is 2 to 10 years until it is killed.

Closely-related native species of *Endothia* are usually saprophytic on chestnuts and do not harm their host tree. *Endothia parasitica* is a very weak parasite on closely-related species of oaks and never seems to attack the closely-related American beech (Shear, Stevens, and Tiller 1917).

The U.S. Department of Agriculture sponsored an expedition to China, Japan, Korea, and Taiwan from 1927 to 1930 to collect Asiatic chestnut seed. The purpose of importing seeds was (1) to determine if blight-resistant Oriental chestnuts could replace the vanishing American chestnut and (2) to establish Oriental chestnuts for crossbreeding with the American species. Both Chinese chestnuts (*Castanea mollissima*) and hybrid trees have been successful in areas of the central Appalachians and the Ohio Valley, but not in northern New York and southern New England, where the American chestnut once lived in abundance (Diller and Clapper 1969). There has also been a search for a native blight-resistant American chestnut. Large surviving native trees are found on occasion but none has proved blight resistant. They appear to have been lucky individuals that somehow escaped infection (Jaynes 1968) and are examples of how the fungus may be absent because of insufficient dispersal of spores.

Most of the chestnuts killed by the blight have been replaced by codominant trees, especially oak species, but also beech, hickories, and red maple (Good 1968, Keever 1953). The oak–chestnut forests have now become oak forests or oak–hickory forests (Table 1).

OTHER STUDIES

These spectacular cases are undoubtedly a biased sample, but the important thing they illustrate is how rapidly some organisms can spread to new areas if other conditions are favorable. Dispersal did not limit the distribution of the starling or the chestnut blight fungus on a local scale, although it did on a global scale. Let us consider a few cases in which transport on a local scale is important in restricting distribution.

Freshwater organisms to which both land and sea are barriers might be expected to show local distributions strongly affected by dispersal. Boycott (1927) studied the distribution of aquatic snails of a small area in England. Three habitats—reservoir, river, and ponds—contained snails of 20 different species, but 11 species were found only in the river and reservoir areas. There were about 150 small ponds in this area, 84 of which were

TABLE 1

Basal areas[a] of dominant tree species in a watershed area of western North Carolina[b]

Tree species	Basal area (sq. ft)		
	1934 (Before severe chestnut blight damage)	1941	1953 (After chestnut blight)
Chestnut	53.3	38.5	0.9
Hickory	18.8	16.1	20.7
Chestnut oak	10.5	10.1	14.2
Northern red oak	9.8	9.7	5.2
Black oak	9.6	10.7	17.9
Yellow poplar	2.9	5.5	13.0
Red maple	2.0	2.5	3.7
Scarlet oak	1.5	2.2	6.9
Total basal area	129.0	117.3	103.4

[a] Basal area is the cross-sectional area at a point 4.5 ft above ground. All trees 0.5 in. in diameter or more at this point were measured. Not all minor tree species are included in the table.

[b] This area was first attacked by chestnut blight in the late 1920s.

SOURCE: After Nelson (1955).

completely cut off from any other pond or stream; these were artificial cattle ponds approximately 100 to 200 years old. Two species of snails absent from these isolated ponds were artificially introduced by Boycott into 14 ponds that appeared suitable for the snails but lacked them. About 100 snails were introduced in each case, with the following results:

	No. successful populations of 14 introductions
Planorbis corneus	10–12
Bithinia tentaculata	0

Planorbis is apparently absent because of a lack of dispersal to these isolated ponds, and *Bithinia* is absent for some other reason. Boycott (1936) pointed out that many species of mollusks were able to colonize these ponds. He surveyed 69 ponds in 1915 and again in 1925. During this decade there were 64 disappearances of species and 93 fresh appearances, which suggests considerable overland dispersal for some species and a high rate of extinction. On the average each pond got one new species every

9 years. Boycott (1936) concluded that, although a few species of fresh-water mollusks (e.g., *Planorbis corneus*) are limited in distribution by dispersal or competition with other mollusks, most species are limited only by their physical and chemical tolerances, chiefly those tolerances concerned with calcium content and the turbidity of the water.

Ruffed grouse (*Bonasa umbellus*) were originally found only on three Michigan islands in the Great Lakes, all three within 0.5 mile of the mainland. All other islands more than 0.5 mile from shore were uninhabited by this bird. Palmer (1962) suggested that lack of dispersal explained this island pattern of distribution, and he tested the flight capacity of several grouse over water. None could fly as much as 800 yards (about 0.5 mile) over water, and Palmer concluded that ruffed grouse are not capable of flying across 1 mile of open water to colonize offshore islands. Some of the offshore islands were artificially stocked with ruffed grouse, and populations have been very successful (Moran and Palmer 1963).

Mysis relicta is a large freshwater crustacean that is widely distributed in the Northern Hemisphere (Figure 3) but inhabits few areas, such as Labrador, Baffin Island, or western Greenland, in which suitable lakes seem to occur (Holmquist 1959). The dispersal powers of this crustacean are poor, and lack of dispersal is suggested as the cause of its limited distribution. A successful introduction of *M. relicta* has been recorded for one lake in southeastern British Columbia (Sparrow, Larkin, and Rutherglen 1964), and it could probably be introduced successfully into many other lakes.

Even on a global scale, dispersal may not limit distribution because introduced species may be unable to survive. Phillips (1928) lists some of

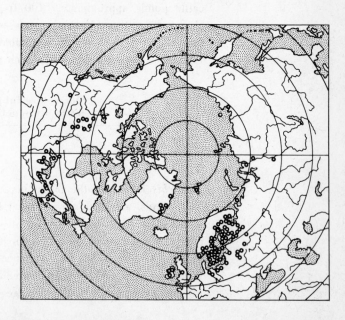

FIGURE 3

Geographical distribution of the crustacean Mysis relicta. *(After Holmquist 1959 and Ricker 1959.)*

the early attempts to introduce foreign birds to North America. He concluded that there were few species that could gain a foothold in North America. Unfortunately, failures to establish a species are rarely studied to obtain an explanation, and accidental introductions are often recorded only when they are successful. The wool trade has been responsible for the introduction of 348 plant species into England, but of these only 4 species have become established (Salisbury 1961). Few plant species introduced into continental areas are able to become established except in disturbed areas.

There have been many attempts to establish populations of fish species in areas outside their original distribution. Estimates of the fraction of introductions that have been successful are difficult to obtain. Dymond (1955), for example, discusses the introduction of fishes in Canada. Rainbow trout (*Salmo gairdneri*), native to western North America, have been widely introduced in eastern North America waters. Rainbow trout are now well established in all the Great Lakes. But a number of introductions into Clear Lake in southern Manitoba have failed (Rawson 1945), and little success has been achieved in trying to establish rainbow trout in Alberta lakes and rivers (Miller 1949). Atlantic salmon (*Salmo salar*) have been extensively introduced from eastern Canada to British Columbia, but none of the introductions to Pacific waters has been successful (Dymond 1955).

Bird introductions into continental areas are usually failures (Mayr 1964). In North America only 4 species of introduced birds are common, although 50 species were introduced. In Europe only 13 successful establishments of birds are recorded from 85 species introduced. There are about 204 species of breeding birds around Sydney, Australia, and 50 or more bird species were introduced to this area. Only 15 species got established and only 8 species are common. Thus a rough estimate of 10 to 30% success is obtained in continental bird introductions.

Many species of game birds have been introduced into North America in the hope of providing food and sport. Between 1883 and 1950 there were 23 attempts to introduce four species of grouse into North America (Bump 1963). All these ended in failure; the reasons are not known.

Other game-bird introductions, however, have been very successful. Ringed-neck pheasants (*Phasianus colchicus*) were introduced into North America from Asia in the 1880s. Many earlier attempts to introduce this bird had been unsuccessful. Pheasants have established large populations in the northeastern and north central United States and in scattered areas of the western states. In Illinois pheasants are abundant only in the northeastern third of the state, and the southern limit of distribution coincides with the outer boundary of the Wisconsin glaciation (Figure 4). Why do pheasants not occur south of this boundary in Illinois?

Numerous attempts have been made to establish pheasants south of the

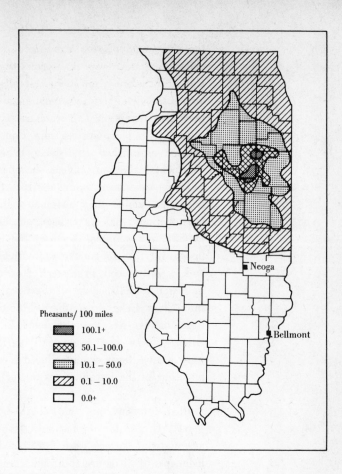

FIGURE 4

Distribution and abundance of pheasants in Illinois, April 1957 and 1958. Neoga and Bellmont are two areas south of the present range at which pheasants were released and studied. (After Ellis and Anderson 1963.)

Pheasants/ 100 miles

100.1+

50.1–100.0

10.1 – 50.0

0.1 – 10.0

0.0+

glacial boundary in Illinois and all have failed (Ellis and Anderson 1963). Thus dispersal cannot be the factor limiting distribution. Pheasants introduced south of their present range reproduce effectively, but survival from late summer until the breeding season the following spring is too low to maintain numbers. Deficiency of calcium in the diet was suggested as a cause, but Harper and Labisky (1964) were unable to find any calcium deficiency in the pheasants introduced south of their present range.

Plants disperse primarily by means of their seeds and spores, and transport is rarely an important factor limiting distributions of plants on a local scale. Few experimental data are available to substantiate this general conclusion. *Rumex crispus* var. *littoreus* is a British plant confined to a narrow zone of the seashore at the level of the highest tides. Cavers and Harper (1967) sowed seed of this species in a variety of nonmaritime habitats and found that seedlings became established in large numbers but most did not survive the first year. The local distribution of this plant is thus not limited by dispersal or by seed-germination requirements. Salisbury (1961, p. 100) discusses the invasion of weeds into bombed areas of

London during World War II. Seeds and spores that were wind dispersed colonized these areas very quickly.

Plant species obviously vary enormously in their dispersal powers and the adaptations they show for dispersal (Pijl 1969). Is the distribution of a species related to its dispersal ability? This question has been considered in very few cases, and the conventional view is that little of the great variation one sees in the distribution ranges of plants can be explained by dispersal powers. In some cases we may question this conventional view. There are four species of poppies (*Papaver* spp.) in Britain, all of which live in open weedy fields and disperse seeds by wind from a seed capsule. Salisbury (1942) analyzed the relationship between geographical range and seed output in this group, with the following results:

Species of *Papaver*	Mean no. capsules per plant	Mean no. seeds per capsule	Mean percentage germination	Mean reproductive capacity
Uncommon species				
P. argemone	6.81	314	63	1,347
P. hybridum	7.28	230	91	1,529
Common series (widespread)				
P. dubium	6.83	2,008	42	5,757
P. rhoeas	12.5	1,360	64	10,928

Thus the reproductive capacities of the two common species are greater than those of the two rare species. The seed weights of these species are very similar, and the effective dispersal distance of seeds is largely controlled by the height of the seed stalk above ground.

Species of *Papaver*	Height of seed capsule pores above ground	
	Mean (cm)	Range of heights of capsule pores (cm)
Uncommon species		
P. argemone	35	14–65
P. hybridum	26	16–43
Common species (widespread)		
P. dubium	56	21–98
P. rhoeas	58	32–88

Thus the common, widespread species are those with the greater dispersal capacity.

Small animals often have a stage in the life cycle that can be transported by wind, and these species resemble plants in that their distributions are rarely limited by lack of dispersal. Many insect species are transported by wind for long distances. Mosquitoes are a good example. The flight patterns of disease-carrying mosquitoes have been studied so that adequate control measures can be set up. The distances mosquitoes disperse determine the limits to which a given breeding location may be dangerous and the area where control work must be done if a given human habitation is to be protected from diseases like malaria. Eyles (1944) summarized the flight ranges of several important *Anopheles* mosquitoes:

	Range (miles)
Maximum observed flight	0.11– 8.0
Maximum seasonal flight	3.7 –12.0

Hocking (1953) calculated the maximum flight range of four species of northern mosquitoes to be between 13.7 and 32.9 miles.

The dispersal of salt-marsh mosquitoes, severe insect pests in Florida, was followed by radioactive tagging of *Aedes taeniorhynchus* larvae with ^{32}P (Provost 1957). This was done on a coastal island in southwestern Florida, and radioactive adults were collected by traps. Dispersal occurs only in days 1 to 4 after adult emergence, and during this short period radioactive females were found up to 25 miles downwind from the release point, whereas males did not disperse beyond 3 miles.

Maguire (1963) showed that small aquatic organisms could rapidly colonize bottles of artificial lake water placed up to 400 yards from small ponds. Protozoa, diatoms, and algae appeared within a few days after the bottles were set out.

I would like to finish this discussion of transport by describing a striking natural experiment which suggests how the problem of transport could be attacked experimentally. On August 26, 1883, the small volcanic island of Krakatau in the East Indies was completely destroyed by a volcanic eruption. Six cubic miles of rock was blown away, and all that remained of the island was a peak covered with ashes. This sterilized island was in effect a large natural experiment on dispersal. The nearest island not destroyed by the explosion was 25 miles away. Nine months after the eruption only one species—a spider—could be found on the island. After only 3 years the ground was thickly covered with blue-green algae, and 11 species of ferns and 15 species of flowering plants were found. Ten years after the explosion coconut trees occurred on the island. After 25 years there were 263 species of animals on the island, which was covered by a dense forest. Within 50 years there were 47 species of vertebrates on the island, 36 bird species, 5 lizards, 3 species of bats, a rat with 2 subspecies, a crocodile, and a python (Hesse, Allee, and Schmidt 1951, pp. 68–69). There is some controversy about the methods of transport, but the majority of the plants and animals were probably transported by wind. Larger vertebrates probably arrived on driftwood rafts or in a few cases by swimming. The suggestion that emerges from these observations is that when there is a vacant space, animals and plants are not long in finding it.

SUMMARY

A species may not occur in an area because it has not been able to disperse there. This hypothesis can be tested by artificial introductions of the organism into unoccupied habitats. Some species introduced from one continent to another, such as the starling, have spread very rapidly. Other introduced species (the majority) die out and are not successful in new areas. On a local scale few species seem to be restricted in distribution by poor powers of dispersal, but more experimental work is needed to test this general conclusion.

Thus dispersal is rarely an important factor limiting the *local* distribution of plants and animals. Organisms have many special adaptations for dispersal, and this results in rapid colonization of new areas. On a *global* scale, however, dispersal is a critical factor in biogeography, and barriers to dispersal help to determine distribution patterns among continents and islands.

There are other aspects of dispersal relevant to population problems and to community considerations, and these will be treated later.

SELECTED REFERENCES

ANDREWARTHA, H. G., and L. C. BIRCH. 1954. *The Distribution and Abundance of Animals.* Chap. 5, Dispersal. University of Chicago Press, Chicago.

ELTON, C. S. 1958. *The Ecology of Invasions by Animals and Plants.* Methuen, London.

GOOD, R. 1964. *The Geography of the Flowering Plants.* Chap. 19, The Factors of Distribution: IV. The Dispersal of Plants. Longmans, London.

HESSE, R., W. C. ALLEE, and K. P. SCHMIDT. 1951. *Ecological Animal Geography.* Second ed., Part 1, The Ecological Foundations of Zoogeography. Wiley, New York.

MACAN, T. T. 1963. *Freshwater Ecology.* Chap. 4, Transport. Longmans, London.

UDVARDY, M. D. F. 1969. *Dynamic Zoogeography with Special Reference to Land Animals.* Chap. 2, The Ecology of Dispersal. Van Nostrand Reinhold, New York.

1 The *Biological Flora of the British Isles* is published irregularly in the *Journal of Ecology* and includes for each species discussed a distribution map and some statement of the suspected factors limiting distribution. Analyze a set of species to determine what factors are considered to limit distribution.

2 Salisbury (1961, p. 82) states:

The geographical distribution of weeds can usually be expressed in general terms but for them, as indeed for most categories of plants, any attempt to map their distribution with great precision could be wholly misleading and unscientific, since the area and density of occupation is not static but dynamic.

Explain why you agree or disagree with this.

3 One of the recurrent themes in studying introduced species such as the starling is that several unsuccessful introductions have often preceded the successful introduction. Are there cases of successful introductions by man on the first attempt? What might account for this pattern?

4 The Dutch elm disease is a virus disease spread by bark beetles and lethal to the American elm (*Ulmus americana*). Compare the American chestnut–chestnut blight interaction to that of the American elm–Dutch elm disease interaction. Discuss in particular the factors promoting the spread of the two diseases. Banfield (1968) provides some literature references on Dutch elm disease.

5 In discussing dispersal and colonization in birds, Mayr (1964, p. 32) states: "The history of faunal changes on islands proves that island faunas offer far less resistance to immigrants than mainland faunas." Refer to Mayr's paper, and obtain some data on island and mainland faunas to evaluate his conclusion. List some possible reasons for these facts.

3 Factors limiting distributions: behavior

The distribution of a species may be limited by the behavior of individuals in selecting their habitat. Either the species *could* or *could not* survive in the areas that it does not inhabit. We are not interested here in the second case (which will be covered in subsequent chapters), but we are interested in the first case, in which the species effectively limits its own distribution by habitat selection.

In many invertebrates habitat selection is accomplished in a simple manner. For example, when the isopod *Porcellio scaber* is placed in a humidity gradient, it moves at random with respect to the gradient, but it moves much more rapidly in dry air than in moist air. An individual that in the course of its random movements happens to find moist air will slow down and become motionless. The result is that most of the animals eventually come to rest at the moist end of the gradient, a very simple form of habitat selection (Fraenkel and Gunn 1940).

A more complex form of stereotyped behavior is involved in the choice of oviposition sites by many insects. In certain species of dragonflies the males occupy territories that determine where females will oviposit (Macan 1963). The European corn borer larva will feed on a wide variety of plants. It occurs mainly on corn because the ovipositing females are attracted by an odor produced by the corn plant (Schoonhoven 1968).

Anopheline mosquitoes are often important disease vectors, and their ecology has been studied a great deal because of the practical problems of malaria eradication. Each mosquito species is usually associated with a particular type of breeding place, and one of the striking observations that a student of malaria first makes is that large areas of water seem to be completely free of dangerous mosquitoes. Large areas of rice fields in Malaya are free of *Anopheles maculatus,* and so are the majority of shallow pools in some breeding grounds of *Anopheles gambiae* (Muirhead-Thomson 1951). Why are some habitats occupied by larvae and others not? Early workers assumed that something in the water prevented the larvae from surviving, and they neglected to study the behavior of females in selecting sites in which to lay eggs. More recent work has emphasized the role of habitat selection in female mosquitoes and shown that larvae can develop successfully over a much wider range of conditions than those in which eggs are laid. Thus, although we presume that the female selects a type of habitat most suitable for the larvae, many of the places she avoids are suitable for growth and development.

In South India the mosquito *Anopheles culicifacies* (a malarial vector) does not occur in rice fields after the plants grow to a height of 12 inches or more, even though these older rice fields support two other *Anopheles* species. Russell and Rao (1942) could find no eggs of *A. culicifacies* in old rice fields, yet when they transplanted this mosquito's eggs into old rice fields, the larvae survived and produced normal numbers of adults. The absence of *A. culicifacies* from this particular habitat is apparently due to the selection of oviposition sites by the females. In a series of simple experiments Russell and Rao were able to show that mechanical obstruction of the rice plants was the main limiting factor. Glass rods vertically placed in small ponds deterred female *A. culicifacies* from laying eggs, and so did barriers of vertical bamboo strips. Shade did not influence egg laying. This mosquito oviposits while flying and performing a hovering dance, never touching the water but remaining 2–4 inches above it. Mechanical obstructions seem to prevent the female mosquitoes from the free performance of this ovipositing dance and thereby restrict the species to a habitat range less than that it could otherwise occupy.

Anopheles gambiae in Africa is always associated with bare-edged pools in direct sunlight. The absence of this malaria vector from shaded areas has prompted the idea of using shade plants to control potential breeding sites. Absence of the species from shaded areas has no simple explanation (Muirhead-Thomson 1951). As many eggs were laid in artificially shaded pools as in sunlit pools. However, shade alters other aspects of these small pools. Thick vegetation around the pool edge seems to offer mechanical obstruction to *A. gambiae* females and reduces egg counts. Most anopheline mosquitoes are very sensitive to polluted water, and shady pools that become stagnant are unattractive to *A. gambiae*. Throwing green vegetation into breeding places of this species may thus keep a pool free of mosquitoes for several months.

Habitat selection in birds has been studied in more detail than in most other groups. Two kinds of factors must be kept separate in discussing habitat selection: (1) evolutionary factors, conferring survival value on habitat selection and (2) behavioral factors, giving the mechanism by which birds select areas. We shall be concerned here with behavior that is the result of stimuli from (1) landscape and terrain, (2) nest, song, watch, feeding, and drinking sites, (3) food, and (4) other animals. The list is that of Hilden (1965), who suggests that birds respond to a summation of these factors and that habitat selection thus has some variability within a species. Landscape features are important: Categories such as open/closed, flat/undulatory, continuous/discrete, and amount of water seem to be important. For example, the lapwing *Vanellus vanellus* selects by color the meadows in which it breeds. It avoids green meadows and prefers gray-brown meadows, which are poor meadows that support only the low grasses to which the lapwing is adapted. Other birds search primarily for a nest site. Some hole-nesting birds, for example, will nest in any type of forest (even where they would not normally occur) when provided with nest boxes (von Haartman 1956). Food, by contrast, does not seem to have an immediate effect on habitat selection in most birds. But some specialized feeders, such as the snowy owl, which feeds on lemmings, will nest only in areas or years of high food abundance. Other individuals of the same species will affect habitat selection either positively, as in colonial-nesting seabirds, or negatively, as in many passerines, in which high density deters individuals from settling.

The wheatear (*Oenanthe oenanthe*), a common bird of open heaths in Britain, nests in old rabbit burrows and was not found in newly forested heaths that were devoid of rabbits (Lack 1933). It was therefore excluded from an otherwise suitable habitat by its nesting-site selection.

The tree pipit (*Anthus trivialis*) and the meadow pipit (*Anthus pratensis*) have similar requirements except that the tree pipit breeds only in areas having one or more tall trees. For this reason the tree pipit is absent from many treeless areas in Britain which the meadow pipit inhabits. Both pipits are ground nesters and feed on the same variety of organisms. Lack (1933) found tree pipits breeding in one treeless area close to a telegraph pole. The only use to which the tree or pole is put by the tree pipit is as a perch on which to land at the end of its aerial song. The meadow pipit has a similar song but ends it on the ground. Thus the tree pipit is excluded from colonizing heathlands only because it needs a perch to sing from.

Lack (1933) concluded that the distribution of bird species in the Breckland heaths of England and their associated pine plantations was largely a result of specific habitat selection restricting each bird to a habitat range less than that which it could occupy.

Habitat selection in birds is partly a genetic trait, although it can be modified somewhat by learning and experience. The genetic basis of habitat selection is probably responsible for a slow response by some birds to man-made changes in the environment. The original habitat selected by a bird is often reinforced by site tenacity. Many old birds return year after year to the same nesting site, even if the habitat at that site is deteriorating. Unfortunately, there has been little experimental analysis of habitat selection in birds. Klopfer (1963) has shown that chipping sparrows (*Spizella passerina*) raised in the laboratory preferred to spend their time in pine rather than oak leaves, just as wild birds do. However, laboratory birds reared with oak leaves showed a decreased preference for pine as adults. Thus the innate preference for staying in pine could be modified somewhat by early experience:

| Chipping sparrows | % time spent in: | |
	"Pine"	"Oak"
Wild-caught adults	71	29
Laboratory-reared, no foliage exposure	67	33
Laboratory-reared, oak foliage exposure only	46	54

Other good examples of habitat selection can be found in mammals. The deer mouse, *Peromyscus maniculatus*, has received the most attention from this point of view. The deer mouse is very widespread, found over most of North America, and can be divided into two ecologically adapted types: (1) the long-tailed, long-eared forest form and (2) the short-tailed, short-eared prairie form. The prairie form that has been most intensively studied is the subspecies *bairdi*. This subspecies avoids forested areas, even those with a grassy substratum, as can be readily seen from the results of trapping lines (Harris 1952).

It was first necessary to show that *bairdi* could live in woody areas, and this was done in field enclosures. Other studies with *Peromyscus* have shown little difference in the food preferences or temperature requirements of grassland subspecies compared with forest subspecies. Harris (1952) therefore concluded that *bairdi's* absence from forested areas is due to its behavior, not to the unsuitability of the habitat.

Experiments in which the mice were given a choice between "woods" and "grassland" showed that *bairdi* usually chose the grassland. This behavior might be either *genetically determined* or *learned* from early experiences, and an attempt was made to separate these. Early experience can play an important part in the development of adult behavioral characteristics, and perhaps the early experience of young mice in a particular habitat could determine the adult reactions to different habitats.

Wecker (1963) used laboratory stock and field animals in three types of situations: (1) direct testing of adults, (2) testing of offspring reared in field habitat, and (3) testing of offspring reared in woodland habitat. The results are given in Table 2. The wild-caught field animals showed an overwhelming preference for the field habitat. The laboratory stock, held in laboratory conditions for 12 to 20 generations, had apparently lost some of its preference for field habitat. Exposure of this stock to early experience in a field greatly increased the preference for the field habitat, but the same exposure to a woods did not cause the mice to select woodland.

TABLE 2

Habitat selection in prairie deer mice
(Peromyscus maniculatus bairdi)[a]

| | Time spent in field part of pen | |
Treatment	% of active time	% of inactive time
Laboratory stock		
Tested directly	**48**	**40**
Offspring reared in field	85	97
Offspring reared in woods	59	44
Field animals		
Tested directly	**84**	**86**
Offspring reared in field	72	61
Offspring reared in woods	77	53

[a] Mice in each group were placed in a pen 100 ft × 16 ft that was half in a grassy field, half in an oak–hickory woodlot. The time spent in each half of the pen was recorded both for the part of the day in which mice were active and the part in which they were inactive. Test results for adult controls are shown in boldface type.

SOURCE: After Wecker (1963).

The conclusion was that habitat selection in the prairie deer mouse is normally predetermined by heredity and results in the animal occupying a more restricted range of habitats than is theoretically possible.

SUMMARY

If individuals are introduced into areas not occupied by the species and are able to survive, grow, and reproduce in their new habitat, the distribution of the species must be restricted either by lack of dispersal or by behavioral reactions. The behavior of individuals in selecting their habitat may thus restrict the distribution of some species of animals. Habitat selection of ovipositing insects provides some good examples in which a species can survive in a wider range of habitats than it usually occupies. Birds have also been studied from this point of view, although little experimental work has been done so far to find out why birds select some habitats for breeding and avoid others.

Behavioral limitations on distribution are usually subtle and may be the hardest to study. At present few animal distributions are believed to be restricted by behavioral reactions. Plants do not have this mechanism available, and plant distributions must be limited in other ways.

SELECTED REFERENCES

ANDREWARTHA, H. G., and L. C. BIRCH. 1954. *The Distribution and Abundance of Animals.* Chap. 12, A Place in Which to Live. University of Chicago Press, Chicago.

HILDEN, O. 1965. Habitat selection in birds: a review. *Ann. Zool. Fennici* 2:53–75.

LACK, D. 1937. The psychological factor in bird distribution. *Brit. Birds* 31:130–136.

MACAN, T. T. 1963. *Freshwater Ecology.* Chap. 5, Behaviour. Longmans, London.

WECKER, S. C. 1964. Habitat selection. *Sci. Amer.* 211(4):109–116.

QUESTIONS AND PROBLEMS

1 After an analysis of the distribution of birds in a tropical African area, Moreau (1935) states: "In conclusion I can only say that after all this talk, and after observing and meditating upon bird distribution in a limited area for more than five years I am still hardly any nearer to a rational explanation of it than I was at the beginning." Review Moreau's findings, and discuss why he might have reached the conclusion quoted.

2 Discuss the evolution of habitat selection and try to relate your conclusions to some of the examples presented in this chapter. How can natural selection maintain the particular ovipositing dance of *Anopheles culicifacies*, for example, if it results in suitable habitats being left unoccupied? Does natural selection always favor the broadest possible habitat range for a species?

4 Factors limiting distributions: interrelations with other organisms

Up to now we have discussed cases in which the organism could actually live in places that it did not occupy. From now on we shall be dealing with cases in which the organism *cannot* complete its full life cycle if transplanted to areas it did not originally occupy. One reason for this inability to survive and reproduce could be the actions of other organisms.

PREDATION

The local distribution of some species seems to be limited by predation. Work on intertidal invertebrates has provided some graphic examples of the influence of predation on distribution. Kitching and Ebling (1967) have summarized a series of studies at Lough Ine, on the south coast of Ireland, and their studies are an excellent example of ecological work on distribution. Lough Ine is connected to the Atlantic Ocean by a narrow channel called the Rapids, through which the tide ebbs and flows approximately twice a day (Figure 5).

The common mussel (*Mytilus edulis*) is a widespread species on exposed

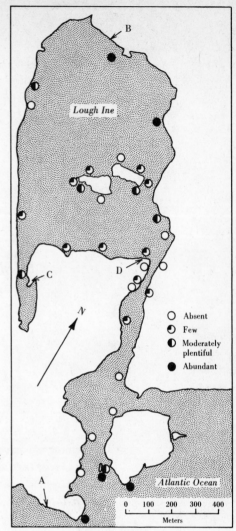

FIGURE 5

Distribution of the mussel Mytilus edulis *in Lough Ine and the adjacent Atlantic coast of Ireland, July 1955. For an explanation of points A to D, see Figure 6. (After Kitching and Ebling 1967.)*

rocky coasts in southern Ireland and throughout the world. Small mussels (less than 25 mm in length) are abundant on the exposed rocky Atlantic coast, but within Lough Ine and the more protected parts of the coast this mussel is rare or absent (Figure 5). The only exceptions are populations in the northern end of the Lough, but these animals are typically very large (30 to 70 mm in length).

Kitching and his co-workers transferred pieces of rock with *Mytilus* attached from various parts of the Lough to others. Figure 6 gives some typical results. Small *Mytilus* disappeared quickly from all stations to which they had been transferred within the Lough, the Rapids, and the protected bays; they survived only on the open coast. The rapid loss, shown in Figure 6, suggested that predators were responsible. Large mussels that were transplanted around the Lough also disappeared rapidly from most stations except those places where they occurred naturally. Continuous observations on the transplanted mussels showed that three species of crabs and one starfish were the principal agents of destruction. By placing mussels of various sizes and crabs of the three species together in wire cages, Kitching and Ebling were able to show that one of the smaller crabs (*Carcinus maenas*) could not kill large *Mytilus*, but that the other crabs could open all sizes of mussels. The areas of the Lough where large *Mytilus* survive have few large crabs, and where the large crabs are common, *Mytilus* is scarce or absent.

The distribution of this mussel in the intertidal zone at Lough Ine is thus controlled as follows: On the open coast, heavy wave action restricts the size of mussels and prevents predators from eliminating small mussels. In sheltered waters predators eliminate most of the small mussels, and

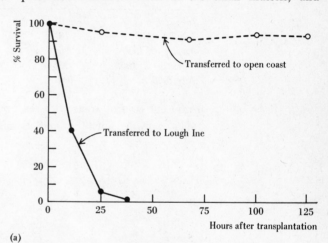

(a)

FIGURE 6

Percentage survival of mussels in transplant experiments. Small mussels (a) disappear rapidly when transplanted anywhere in Lough Ine, but do not disappear if transplanted to the open coast (A in Figure 5). Large mussels (b) disappear if transplanted to some parts of Lough Ine such as the southeastern part (D in Figure 5), but do not disappear if transplanted to other parts of the Lough such as the southwestern part (C in Figure 5), where they are found naturally. (After Kitching and Ebling 1967.)

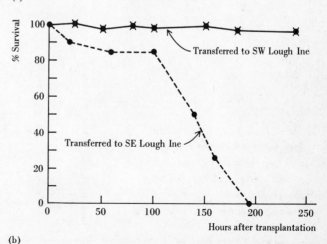

(b)

Mytilus survive only in areas safe from predators (such as steep rock faces), where they may grow to large sizes.

In a second set of experiments, Kitching and Ebling (1961) studied the relationship between the sea urchin *Paracentrotus lividus* and the algae on which it grazes. *Paracentrotus* lives in the shallow part of the sublittoral zone, just below the tide level, and is common in Lough Ine, although nearly absent from the open coast. One of the most extensive beds of this sea urchin occurs on the north side of Castle Island in the center of the Lough, and this area is practically free from obvious algal growth. By contrast, algae are abundant in areas where this sea urchin is less common (Figure 7).

On July 1959 an area of 290 sq. m was completely cleared of sea urchins by the removal of 1957 *Paracentrotus*. Algae immediately began to colonize the area as follows:

	Algal cover (%) on experimental area
July 7, 1959	*0*
July 23, 1959	*10*
August 10, 1959	*25*
September 3, 1959	*50*
July 1960	*100*

Adjacent control areas with sea urchins continued to have almost no visible algal growth. Kitching and Ebling transferred the sea urchins removed

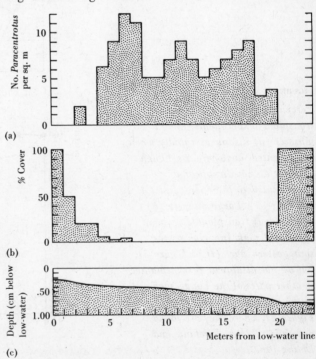

FIGURE 7

Transect from tidal zone toward deeper water off Castle Island in Lough Ine, Ireland: (a) sea urchins, (b) algal cover, and (c) bottom depth profile. Note that algal abundance is almost zero where sea urchins are common. (After Kitching and Ebling 1961.)

from this area into several areas of dense algal growth and found that they began to clear these areas of algae as well. There is thus an inverse relationship between the occurrence of *Paracentrotus* and algae.

Kitching and Ebling (1967) proposed four criteria to be fulfilled before one could conclude that a predator restricts the distribution of its prey:

1 Prey individuals will survive when transplanted to a site where they do not normally occur, if they are protected from predators.

2 The distributions of prey organisms and suspected predator(s) are inversely correlated.

3 The suspected predator is able to kill the prey, and this can be observed in the field or in the laboratory.

4 The suspected predator can be shown to be responsible for the destruction of the prey in transplantation experiments.

The lake trout (*Salvelinus namaycush*) is unique among North American fishes; it is the only freshwater species that ranges into the far north of Canada and Alaska but does not occur westward across the Bering Strait into Siberia (Lindsey 1964). Why has the lake trout failed to cross this narrow barrier? One suggestion is obtained from Figure 8: There is an inverse relationship between the distribution of large predatory lampreys and the distribution of lake trout. Lake trout have not crossed the narrow sea barriers to Newfoundland or Vancouver Island, nor have they crossed the Bering Strait. In contrast, they have crossed to Banks Island, Victoria Island, and other islands in the Canadian high arctic, all areas that seem to be beyond the range of marine lampreys. Evidence for this example thus satisfies criteria 2 and 3, but information on 1 and 4 is missing.

In the cases just discussed, the predator is believed to restrict the distribution of its prey; consequently, the reasons for the predator's distributional limits must be sought elsewhere. In these situations the predator may

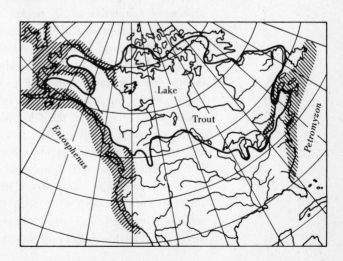

FIGURE 8

Distribution of the lake trout Salvelinus namaycush *(heavy outline) and of large lampreys (hatched area). Limits of* Petromyzon *are before entry to upper Great Lakes. (After Lindsey 1964.)*

feed on a variety of prey species, and each prey species may in turn be fed upon by many predatory species. The relationship may also operate in the other direction, and the prey may restrict the distribution of its predator. The prey may be a food plant and the predator a herbivore; alternatively, the prey may be a herbivore and the predator a carnivore. But if the prey is to restrict the predator's range, the predator must be very specialized and feed on only one or two species of prey. Such a predator is called "obligate." Many insect predators are obligate, but most vertebrate predators are not.

One example of a species that is limited in its distribution by its food source is *Drosophila pachea*, a rare fruit fly, which breeds only in the stems of senita cactus (*Lophocereus schottii*) throughout the Sonoran Desert of the southwestern United States and northern Mexico. This fly will not breed on the standard laboratory medium for *Drosophila* unless the medium is supplemented by a cube of fresh or autoclaved senita cactus. Conversely, medium supplemented by the cactus is toxic in varying degrees to the adults and larvae of other local species of *Drosophila*. The preliminary hypothesis is that the senita cactus contains a factor that is necessary for the development of *D. pachea* and a factor that is toxic to other species.

Heed and Kircher (1965) demonstrated that a unique sterol, schottenol (Δ^7-stigmasten-3β-ol), is the factor required by *D. pachea* for growth and reproduction. Every insect that has been investigated requires a sterol in its diet. Cholesterol satisfies this requirement for every insect studied except *D. pachea*. The function of sterols in the diet is probably twofold: (1) They are precursors for the molting hormone ecdysone, and (2) they affect female fertility in some way. *Drosophila pachea* is somewhat unusual in depending on this unique sterol for these requirements.

The substance of the senita cactus that is toxic to other local species of *Drosophila* is probably part of the alkaloid fraction of the cactus. The process of adaptation of *D. pachea* to this habitat has been possible only because of its tolerance of this potentially toxic substance.

The leaf-feeding beetle *Chrysolina quadrigemina* was introduced into the United States to control the klamath weed (*Hypericum perforatum*). In any introduction of this type to control weeds it is important that the insect should eat only the weed, not crop plants. Holloway (1964) discusses this problem for the *Chrysolina* beetle. The feeding habits of the beetle are very specific. Adult and larval beetles will not feed and will die when confined with plants other than those of the genus *Hypericum*. Adult beetles often refuse to stand on the leaf surfaces of those plants which have leaves of different surface texture than that of *Hypericum*. The adults explore the leaf edges with the antennae, and if they encounter a serrated (toothed) leaf edge rather than a smooth one, they drop off the plant. The life history of this beetle is synchronized with that of its host plant and includes a summer (dry season) aestivation of the adults and subsequent response to fall rains. Thus the feeding habits, behavior, and life history of this leaf-eating beetle restrict it to a single host plant, and the range of distribution of *Chrysolina* is thereby restricted.

There are a few British moths whose distribution is very limited because they feed upon a rare plant species (Ford 1967, p. 120).

The red tree mouse (*Phenacomys longicaudus*) is an arboreal mouse which has the most restricted diet of all North American mammals (Hamilton 1962). It feeds almost entirely on the needles and new twigs of Douglas fir (*Pseudotsuga menziesii*). Its distribution is limited to coastal California (north from San Francisco Bay) and coastal Oregon and is geographically congruent with the distribution of coastal Douglas fir up to the Columbia River. The coastal Douglas fir, however, extends north into Washington and British Columbia, whereas the red tree mouse is apparently stopped by the barrier of the Columbia River; it has never been captured in Washington State. Howell (1926) pointed out that this mouse was often absent from isolated patches of Douglas fir within its zone of distribution, presumably because it has not dispersed to them.

Parasites and diseases are, of course, limited in their distribution by the distribution of their hosts, but unless they are very host specific this may not be the explanation for their distribution. One good example of parasite limitation by host distribution is the white pine blister rust (*Cronartium ribicola*), a fungus that attacks the bark of white pine trees and is often fatal. This fungus is limited to areas supporting both of the hosts necessary for its life cycle: the white pine (*Pinus strobus*) and several species of *Ribes* (gooseberries). This fact was used in controlling this disease; all one had to do was to eliminate the *Ribes* from the white pine areas.

ALLELOPATHY

Some organisms, plants in particular, may be limited in distribution by "poisons," "antibiotics," or *allelopathic agents*. The action of penicillin among microorganisms is a classical case (Brock 1966, p. 127). Other good examples of this occur in the algae. *Chlorella,* a common alga often used in botany classes, produces a bactericide that not only kills bacteria but also retards the growth of *Daphnia,* which feed on *Chlorella* (Ryther 1954).

Interest in toxic secretions of plants arose from a consideration of "soil sickness." It was observed in the nineteenth century that as one piece of ground was continuously cropped to one plant the yields decreased and could not be improved by additional fertilizer. As early as 1832 DeCandolle suggested that the deleterious effects of continuous one-crop agriculture might be due to toxic secretions from roots. Several cases were also observed of detrimental effects of plants growing with one another: for example, grass and apple trees (Pickering 1917). Experiments of the general type shown in Figure 9 were performed. Apple seedlings were grown with three different sources of water: a primary source, a secondary source passing through grass and soil, and a secondary source passing through soil only. The growth of the young apple trees was apparently inhibited by something produced by the grass and carried by the water.

In the early 1900s several agronomists commented on the effect of black walnut trees (*Juglans nigra*) on nearby grass and alfalfa plants. Massey (1925) observed that the zone of dead alfalfa around a walnut tree extended over an area 2 to 3 times greater than that covered by the tree canopy and suggested that this zone was determined by the outer limits of walnut roots. The roots were suspected of secreting a toxin to which some plants, for example alfalfa (lucerne) and tomatoes, were susceptible; other plants, for example corn (maize) and beets, showed no ill effects. Schneiderhan (1927) showed that black walnut trees injured and killed apple trees up to 80 ft away. The average limit of the toxic zone was about 50 ft in radius from the walnut trunk. In every case the toxic zone was greater than the area covered by the walnut canopy, but larger walnut trees did not necessarily have much larger toxic zones.

Davis (1928) extracted from the roots and hulls of the black walnut a crystalline substance called juglone (5-hydroxy-α-napthaquinone) and

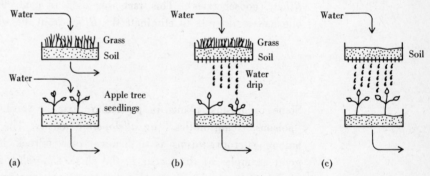

FIGURE 9

Experiments that demonstrated the detrimental effects of grass on apple-tree seedlings. Grass and tree seedlings are grown in separate flats in a greenhouse. Water is provided either independently (a) to both grass and trees, or as a single source to the grass and soil (b) or soil alone (c). Water drip provides moisture for the apple seedlings in (b) and (c). Apple-tree seedlings do not grow properly when the water has passed through grass first (b).

showed that this chemical would kill tomato and alfalfa plants. Brooks (1951) found no evidence of antagonism between walnut and other timber tree species that normally occurred together with black walnut in forest stands, and he emphasized the selective effects of the walnut toxin: Some species like alfalfa are killed; others like Kentucky blue grass become more abundant than usual near walnut trees. Not all walnut species secrete toxic chemicals. The closely-related English walnut (*Juglans regia*) and the California walnuts (*Juglans hindsii* and *Juglans californica*) apparently do not secrete growth inhibitors (Garb 1961).

Agriculturalists have recognized the action of "smother crops" as weed suppressors. These smother crops include barley, rye, sorghum, millet, sweet clover, alfalfa, soybeans, and sunflowers. Their inhibition of weed growth was assumed to be due to competition for water, light, or nutrients. Barley, for example, is rated as a good smother crop and has extensive root growth.

Overland (1966) showed that barley (*Hordeum vulgare*) inhibited the germination and growth of several weeds, even in the absence of competition for nutrients or water. Growth experiments with barley and chickweed (*Stellaria media*) gave the following results:

| | Average dry weight per plant (g) after 2 months of growth | | No. of chickweed flowers |
	Barley	Chickweed	
Controls (each grown alone)	4.15	3.20	100+
1 barley:1 chickweed mixture	4.85	1.43	10

Extracts of living roots were more inhibitory than extracts of dead roots. The active inhibitory agent was found to be an alkaloid, but its specific chemical nature is not known. Thus the adverse effect of barley is partly due to the secretion by their roots of chemicals that reduce growth and germination of nearby weeds.

Many fruit trees will grow poorly if planted in soil that has previously grown the same kind of fruit tree. This has given rise to a variety of agricultural problems, which is illustrated by the "peach-replant" problem. In 1922 at Davis, California, peach and apple orchards were planted; in 1942 these trees were removed, and the whole area was planted in Faye Elberta peach trees in the spring of 1943. Within one year it was clear that the peach trees succeeding apples were growing better than the peach trees succeeding peaches. Proebsting (1950) records the yields for these two treatments as follows:

	Average yield of fruit (lb per tree) in 1949
Field A	
Peach following peach	92.6
Peach following apple	212.5
Field B	
Peach following peach	145.0
Peach following apple	220.2

This is one notable characteristic of the replant problem: It is highly specific. Not all subsequent crops do poorly. Börner (1960) reviews the soil-sickness problem in higher plants and cites many cases in which crop residues in some way affect subsequent crops. The causal mechanism for these effects is not understood.

The "replant problem" is not restricted to agricultural plants. Some timber trees of the tropical rain forest will not grow in monocultures. Pure plantations of some of these trees have been set out by foresters, but the trees fail to grow properly and they die. Webb, Tracey, and Haydock (1967) studied the tree *Grevillea robusta* in the subtropical rain forest of northern Australia and found that seedlings of this tree could not grow under older trees of the same species. When seedling roots make contact with the roots of older trees, the leaves of the seedlings blacken and they die, even in the laboratory with adequate light and abundant water and nutrients. Water percolated through the soil of older trees contains a factor toxic to seedlings. Thus parent trees of *G. robusta* kill their own seedlings chemically, and commercial production of this tree could only be obtained in mixed forest plantings.

Some natural plant communities show superficially similar effects. The distribution of annual plants in desert areas is not random, and early observations indicated that some shrubs were rarely associated with annual herbs, whereas other shrub species harbored large numbers of annuals. Went (1942), for example, observed this pattern in the deserts of the southwestern United States:

Shrub species	Condition	No. annual herbs living under shrub
Encelia farinosa	Living	Few to none
	Dead	Some to many
Franseria dumosa	Living	Some to many

Went suggested that two factors might be involved in the reduction of certain annuals: (1) Organic detritus might be lacking, and (2) toxic chemicals might be present. Gray and Bonner (1948) demonstrated that *Encelia farinosa* leaves contained a chemical that would inhibit growth of tomato plants growing in sand in the laboratory. Water extracts of leaves were also inhibitory, and Gray and Bonner were able to isolate the toxic substance, 3-acetyl-6-methoxybenzaldehyde. This inhibitor was shown to have no effect on *Encelia* itself. Dried *Encelia* leaves retained their toxicity for several months. Gray and Bonner noted that this toxic effect was less striking on tomato plants grown in rich garden soil, perhaps because soil microorganisms destroyed the chemical inhibitor.

Muller (1953) confirmed the basic observation that *Encelia farinosa* harbored few annuals whereas *Franseria dumosa* harbored many. But he showed that water extracts of *Franseria* leaves were also highly toxic to tomato seedlings and even more toxic than *Encelia* leaf extracts! Muller suggested that herbs do not grow beneath *Encelia* because of its growth form (Figure 10); it is short lived and does not accumulate organic matter around its base. *Franseria*, on the other hand, is long lived and branches in such a way as to trap a mound of soil and organic matter around its base (Figure 10). The production of these toxic substances by these plants does not seem to have any effect on most field populations, perhaps because the inhibitors are broken down by soil microorganisms or absorbed onto soil particles.

The chaparral of southern California is a mixture of shrubs with a sparse understory of herbaceous vegetation. Recurrent fires at intervals of 10 to 40 years destroy this dense shrub cover, and in the first growing season after the fire a luxuriant growth of herbs is produced. The shrubs regenerate principally by root sprouting. As the shrubs regenerate, seeds stop germination, usually about 5 to 6 years after the fire, and herbs again become sparse. Even in open stands of shrubs with 50% of the ground bare and adequate rainfall, there is no seed germination. Muller, Hanawalt, and McPherson (1968) cleared some chaparral stands by clipping close to the

FIGURE 10

Generalized habit sketches of desert shrubs. (a) Franseria dumosa, *each rhizomatous shoot independently rooted and the intricate system of branching accumulating a mound of windblown soil and debris above the general soil level. (b)* Encelia farinosa, *the branches appearing above soil level and not independently rooted. (After Muller 1953.)*

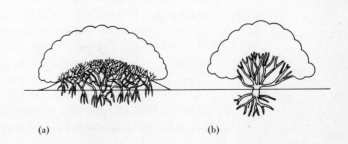

(a)   (b)

soil surface and removing the shrubs without disturbing the soil litter. In the next growing season these clipped plots showed rapid germination of 30 herb species and appeared like an area 1 year after a fire; adjoining uncleared areas again produced no germination. Thus the fire cycle of the California chaparral is a sequence of events that follow from the destruction of toxic chemicals and the shrubs that produce them (Muller, Hanawalt, and McPherson 1968).

In southern California, chaparral shrubs such as the aromatic *Salvia leucophylla* and *Artemisia californica* are often separated from adjacent grassland by a bare area 1 to 2 m wide (Figure 11). Apparently volatile terpenes, which are released from the leaves of these aromatic shrubs, are able to inhibit growth in nearby grasses. To demonstrate this aerial transmission, Muller (1966) grew cucumber (*Cucumis sativus*) seedlings in a closed chamber with beakers containing 2 g of plant leaves so that there

FIGURE 11

The shrub Salvia leucophylla *producing differential composition in annual grassland: (1) to the left of A,* Salvia *shrubs 1 to 2 m tall; (2) between A and B, a zone 2 m wide bare of all herbs except a few minute inhibited seedlings of the same age as the large herbs to the right (the root systems of the shrubs, on the average, failing to reach B); (3) between B and C, a zone of inhibited grassland consisting of small plants of* Erodium cicutarium, Bromus rubens, B. mollis, *and* Festuca megalura *(lacking* Avena fatua *and* B. rigidus*); (4) to the right of C, uninhibited grassland, with large plants of* E. cicutarium, Festuca megalura, B. rubens, B. mollis, B. rigidus, A. fatua, *and other herbs. (After Muller 1966.)*

was no physical contact between the growing seedlings and the test leaves; in one experiment he obtained these results:

	Length of seedlings (mm) after 48 hr
Control (no leaves)	28.6
Salvia apiana leaves	11.4
Salvia leucophylla leaves	2.9
Salvia mellifera leaves	2.3

Grasses were even more drastically suppressed in growth. Muller (1966) suggested that the deterioration of old *Salvia* stands might be caused by autointoxication.

Other chaparral shrubs, such as the common "chamise" *Adenostoma fasciculatum,* secrete allelopathic agents from their leaves. McPherson and Muller (1969) reported a series of experiments designed to explain why chamise stands harbored few herbs. Competition for light, for mineral nutrients, for soil moisture, and for oxygen were eliminated as possible causes by field experiments. Another suggestion was that grazing by small rodents and rabbits might be responsible for the shortage of herbs in the brushy areas of the chaparral. To test this idea, McPherson and Muller placed small screened exclosures in *Adenostoma* stands and found that some of the effect was in fact caused by animal damage, but most of it was produced by leaf toxins:

	No. seedling herbs per square meter	No. herb species
Unprotected area within chamise (grazing + toxins)	11	6
Screened plot within chamise (no grazing + toxins)	70	6
Clearing outside chamise stand (grazing + no toxins)	>1000	ca. 30

The leaves of mature *A. fasciculatum* shrubs accumulate a toxin on their surfaces during the dry season. This toxin is water soluble and is carried to the soil in rain; its chemical nature is unknown. In the soil the toxin reduces germination and growth of the various herb species and produces the noticeable lack of herbs in these chaparral stands, while adjacent grasslands and woodlands have dense herb populations.

The study of such allelopathic agents is currently a very active field of research in plant ecology, and it is too early to say how much the distributions of plants are determined by interactions involving toxins.

The presence of other organisms may limit the distribution of some species through "competition." Such competition is usually confined to closely-related species which eat the same types of food and live in the same sorts of places. The first indication of possible competition is usually the observation that the geographical distributions of two closely-related species do not overlap. A second indication may be the observation that when species A is absent, species B lives in a wider range of habitats. The principal difficulty in dealing with these situations is that competition is only one of several hypotheses that will account for these facts. Some examples illustrate this difficulty very well.

The distribution of the two crustaceans *Gammarus pulex* and *Gammarus duebeni* in the British Isles is shown in Figure 12. *Gammarus pulex* occurs in fresh waters throughout most of Britain but not on islands off the coast; it is absent from Ireland. *Gammarus duebeni,* by contrast, is a brackish-water species occurring all around the coast of Britain; it also occupies freshwater habitats in most of Ireland and many of the islands off the British coast. The preliminary indication of competition is quite clear: *G. duebeni* lives only in brackish water unless *G. pulex* is absent. Where *G. pulex* is absent, as in Ireland, *G. duebeni* lives in both fresh and brackish water.

The two *Gammarus* species occur together in only a single locality, in fresh water on the Isle of Man (between England and Ireland). Hynes (1954) thought that *G. pulex* may have been recently introduced to this locality by fishermen. Everywhere else the two species do not occur in the same habitat. The detailed local distribution of these two *Gammarus* species was analyzed by Hynes (1954). Figure 13 gives one example from south-

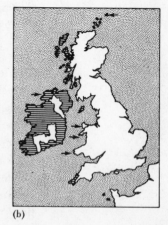

FIGURE 12

Distribution of (a) Gammarus pulex *and (b)* G. duebeni *in the British Isles. Arrows indicate small islands on which the species also occur. (After Hynes 1954.)*

(a)   (b)

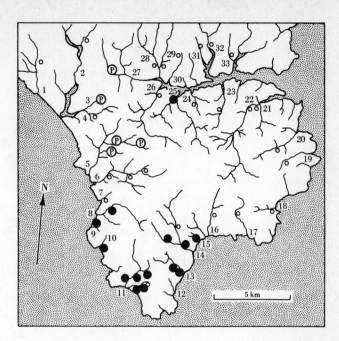

FIGURE 13

Distribution of Gammarus pulex *(Ⓟ)*
and G. duebeni *(●) on the Lizard*
Peninsula in extreme southwestern
England. ○ = *localities without*
Gammarus. *Separate streams are*
numbered. (After Hynes 1954.)

western England. *Gammarus duebeni* lives in streams on the southwestern
tip of Cornwall only and was absent elsewhere except for one brackish-
water population. There was no zone of contact or overlap between these
two species.

Hynes considered two hypotheses to explain this distribution. (1) *Gammarus pulex* is a superior competitor and has replaced *G. duebeni* from
Britain by gradually eliminating it from fresh water. *Gammarus duebeni*
remains only in marginal brackish habitats and is successful in colonizing
fresh water only in the absence of *G. pulex*. (2) There are two physiological
races of *G. duebeni*, one adapted to brackish water, another to fresh water.
The distribution of these forms depends upon their physiological tolerances
to salt and not upon competition from other forms.

Hynes (1954) could find no evidence of distinct physiological races of
Gammarus, but he recognized some difficulties with the first explanation. The
distribution from the Lizard Peninsula (Figure 13) was not suggestive of
competition, because there are unoccupied habitats between the distributional limits of the two species, and the mechanism by which competition
was supposed to act was not known. In four field experiments Hynes introduced *G. pulex* to streams occupied by *G. duebeni*, but the introduced
G. pulex completely disappeared.

The sodium regulation of *Gammarus* is crucial to the second hypothesis
and was studied by Sutcliffe (1967a, b). The physiological differences
between the races of *G. duebeni* living in fresh water and brackish water
are very subtle. *Gammarus duebeni* continuously loses sodium when in a

dilute medium. This loss is countered by active transport of sodium from the water by a system probably in the gills. Two distinct physiological races of *G. duebeni* were described by Sutcliffe:

| Source of *G. duebeni* | Sodium transport system (mg/liter Na) | |
	Fully saturated[a]	Half saturated
English brackish water	230[b]	23–46
Irish fresh water	23–46	12

[a] The sodium transport system is fully saturated when further increases in sodium content of the water do not show up as increased uptake by the organism.
[b] Approximately 2% seawater.

As the concentration of sodium in the water falls below the half-saturation level, the transport system is more and more strained to pick up sodium at the necessary rate to hold the blood concentration up, so the animals die. The sodium transport mechanism is temperature sensitive, and in a very dilute medium the warmer the water, the more difficult is sodium uptake. Sutcliffe showed that *G. duebeni* from English fresh waters (e.g., Figure 13 area) was physiologically equivalent to animals in brackish waters and not like the Irish form.

Sutcliffe (1967c) reanalyzed the distributional data on *G. duebeni* and showed that the brackish form of this species occurs on peninsulas and islands exposed to southwestern gales from the Atlantic Ocean. The sodium content of these fresh waters is high, usually above 23 mg/liter sodium, owing to sea spray and salty rain. He suggested that the brackish form of *G. duebeni* might be a recent colonizer of fresh water in Britain, a complete reversal of the previous hypothesis that it was being eliminated from fresh water by competition with *G. pulex*.

Thus *G. pulex* is a freshwater species present in Britain but absent in Ireland, probably because it has not been able to disperse there. *Gammarus duebeni* is a species originally adapted to brackish waters and has evolved a race tolerant of fresh waters in Ireland but not in Britain. The present distributional limits of the two species are not set by competition but probably are a result of dispersal ability and salt tolerances. *Gammarus pulex* cannot tolerate salt water, cannot withstand dessication, and has no resting stage of the life cycle for possible dispersal.

A second example of a closely-related group whose ranges do not overlap occurs in the pocket gophers of North America. Pocket gophers are rodents with numerous adaptations for an underground, burrowing existence: massive skulls, small eyes and ears, and enlarged forefeet. They excavate burrow systems of feeding tunnels and nesting chambers and are solitary except when mating. An effective barrier to the general distribution of the pocket gophers is a lack of suitable soils; particular species are limited in local distribution by soil type, climatic factors, and competition with other species of pocket gophers (Miller 1964).

When the ranges of two species of pocket gophers meet, the two populations do not overlap but abut at a sharp boundary. Four species meet in Colorado with very little overlap (Figure 14). Vaughan (1967) studied a population boundary in Colorado in detail and confirmed the abruptness of the boundaries. The feeding habits of all species are very broad, and there is no indication that the boundaries of these distributions coincide with vegetational changes in suitable food plants.

Soil depth and soil texture seem to be the most critical ecological factors for pocket gophers. The four Colorado species all prefer deep sandy loam soils which are easily burrowed and well drained. Their ranges of tolerance, however, are markedly different (Figure 15). *Geomys bursarius* will live only in a narrow range of deep and fine soils; *Thomomys talpoides* will live in almost any soil that could possibly be dug into.

Whenever two of these species come into contact, one species clearly seems to dominate the other. Durrant (1946), for example, in the Oquirrh Mountains of Utah found only *Thomomys bottae* up to 5000 ft and only *T. talpoides* above 6000 ft. Between 5000 and 6000 ft either species might occur, *T. bottae* in the deepest soils and heaviest vegetation, *T. talpoides* in areas of rocky soils and sparse vegetation. These four species can thus be ranked in competitive ability:

G. bursarius > *C. castanops* > *T. bottae* > *T. talpoides*

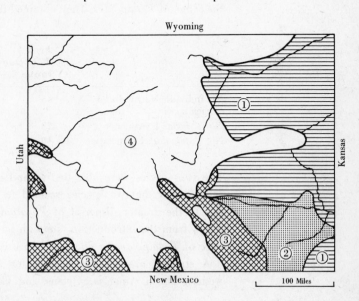

FIGURE 14

Geographic distributions of the pocket gophers (1), Geomys bursarius *(2),* Cratogeomys castanops *(3),* Thomomys bottae *and (4)* T. talpoides *in Colorado. (After Miller 1964.)*

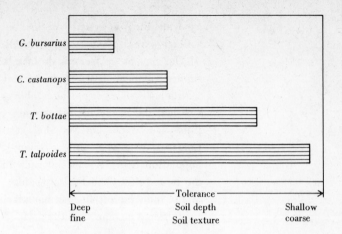

FIGURE 15

Relative tolerances of pocket gophers to soil depth and soil texture. (After Miller 1964.)

Miller (1964) concluded that interspecies competition limits the distribution of pocket gophers in some areas. The eastern limit of *T. talpoides* is determined by competition with *G. bursarius*. The mechanism by which this competition acts is not known. Pocket gophers are highly territorial and aggressive during most of the year, and Vaughan (1967) suggests that the different species react aggressively in the same way, not only to members of their own species but to members of the other species as well. In some respects pocket gophers thus behave as though they were one species, and they compete for space.

Few experiments have been done to analyze this pocket gopher situation. Vaughan and Hansen (1964) introduced *T. bottae* and *T. talpoides* into two areas 0.5 mile apart, one within the range of *T. bottae* and another within the range of *T. talpoides*. They obtained these results:

	Area A, *T. bottae* range	Area C, *T. talpoides* range
No. individuals introduced of each species	45	35
No. *T. bottae* 1 year later	29	11
No. *T. talpoides* 1 year later	10	19

The two species were able to live and reproduce side by side, but in each case one of the two species seemed to be dominant. This was apparently due to the greater dispersal of *T. talpoides* in the first case (which caused a loss from the introduction site with no replacement) and the greater tolerance of *T. talpoides* to poor soil types in the second case.

A striking case of competition for space occurs in the blackbirds of western North America. Orians and Collier (1963) describe competition for breeding space between the closely-related redwing blackbird (*Agelaius phoeniceus*) and the tricolored blackbird (*A. tricolor*). Male redwings establish territories in marshy areas in the winter much before the colonial nesting tricolored blackbirds begin to establish a colony. Figure 16 shows one marsh completely occupied by male redwing territories in early spring. When large numbers of tricolors move into a marsh inhabited by redwings, the male redwings show strong aggression but tricolors win out by virtue of overwhelming numbers (Figure 16). No successful redwing nests have been found in large tricolor colonies. A similar interaction occurs between the redwing and the yellow-headed blackbird (*Xanthocephalus xanthocephalus*) in western North America (Orians and Willson 1964).

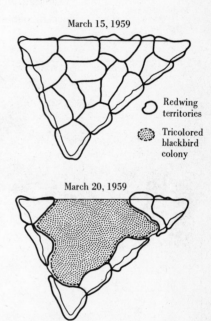

March 15, 1959

Redwing territories

Tricolored blackbird colony

March 20, 1959

FIGURE 16

Interactions between redwing and tricolored blackbirds at the Hidden Valley Marsh, Ventura County, California, in 1959. (After Orians and Collier 1963.)

The two salamanders *Plethodon cinereus cinereus* and *Plethodon richmondi shenandoah* are closely related and have similar habitat preferences. Moreover, their geographic distribution is almost mutually exclusive (Jaeger 1970). *Plethodon cinereus* is more widely distributed in eastern North America, and *P. richmondi* occurs in isolated pockets within the general range of *P. cinereus*. These distributions suggest competitive interaction, which Jaeger studied in an area of overlap in the Shenandoah National Park of Virginia.

Plethodon richmondi in this area in the Appalachian Mountains occurs almost exclusively in talus slopes, whereas *P. cinereus* occurs in all the other

habitats but not in talus areas (Figure 17). In nearby areas where only
P. cinereus occurs, it again fails to colonize talus slopes. Within talus areas,
P. richmondi is most common in small pockets of soil surrounded by talus.
From these observations Jaeger concluded that

1 *Plethodon cinereus* is prevented from colonizing the talus areas by an environmental factor, probably lack of moisture (Jaeger 1971).
2 *Plethodon richmondi* is excluded from the soil outside of talus slopes by competition with *P. cinereus*.
3 *Plethodon richmondi* in this area is likely to become extinct, because of the gradual erosion of the talus slopes and subsequent replacement by *P. cinereus*.

The mechanism by which this exclusion occurs is not known.

Competition between closely-related forms is important in affecting abundance in populations and communities, as will be discussed later.

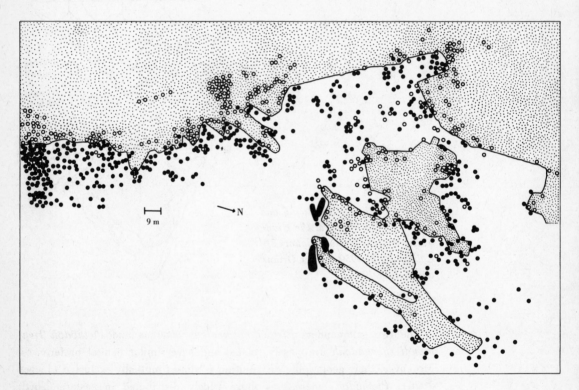

FIGURE 17

*Portion of the talus–soil interface on Hawksbill Mountain, Virginia.
Solid lines indicate the interface, stippled areas are talus, and the
white area is deep soil. Hollow circles* (P. r. shenandoah) *and solid
circles* (P. c. cinereus) *represent the positions of all collected
salamanders in this area. Large dark objects are large boulders.
(After Jaeger 1970.)*

Many animals and plants are limited in their local distribution by the presence of other organisms—their food plants, predators, diseases, and competitors. Experimental transfers of organisms can test for this factor, and cages or other protective devices can be used to determine the critical interactions.

Predators can affect the local distribution of their prey, and studies on intertidal organisms have illustrated this influence. The converse can also occur, in which the prey's distribution determines the distribution of its predators, but this is not common. In some cases an animal is dependent on a single food source and may have its distribution limited by the distribution of the food. Few such cases have been described.

Some organisms poison the environment for other species, and local distributions may be affected by these chemical poisons, or allelopathic agents. The action of penicillin is a classical example. Chemical interactions have been described in a variety of crop plants and in native vegetation.

Competition between plants and animals for food and space may also restrict local distributions. Some species drive others out by aggressive interactions. In other examples the distributions of closely-related species do not overlap, and this suggests possible competitive interactions. Little experimental work has been done to determine the mechanisms that keep distributions of closely-related species from overlapping.

SELECTED REFERENCES

BÖRNER, H. 1960. Liberation of organic substances from higher plants and their role in the soil sickness problem. *Bot. Rev.* 26:393–424.

KITCHING, J. A., and F. J. EBLING. 1967. Ecological studies at Lough Ine. *Advances Ecol. Res.* 4:197–291.

MULLER, C. H., R. B. HANAWALT, and J. K. MCPHERSON. 1968. Allelopathic control of herb growth in the fire cycle of California chaparral. *Bull. Torrey Bot. Club* 95:225–231.

ORIANS, G. H., and M. F. WILLSON. 1964. Interspecific territories of birds. *Ecology* 45:736–745.

PICKERING, S. 1917. The effect of one plant on another. *Ann. Bot.* 31:181–187.

QUESTIONS AND PROBLEMS

1 One criterion of interspecies competition is this: Closely-related species having mutually exclusive ranges are in competition at their zones of contact. Discuss this criterion in relation to the factors limiting distribution.

2 The Plains pocket gopher *Geomys bursarius* extends east in North America to approximately the Mississippi River (Hall and Kelson 1959, p. 451). What limits the eastern distribution of this species? Design experiments sufficient to test any suggestions you make.

3 Vaughan and Hansen (1964) released pocket gophers of two different species into the same plots in Colorado to study interspecific competition. Compare and contrast their experimental design and results with that of Kitching and Ebling (1967), who transplanted mussel populations around the Lough Ine area to study predation.

4 Macan (1963, p. 114), in discussing aquatic organisms, states: "All species are probably limited to places that offer refuges from predators, unless they live in waters which, because they are temporary or offer extremes of some factor such as salinity, harbour no predators." Can you suggest any exceptions to this generalization? Does it apply to terrestrial organisms? To plants?

5 The sea urchin *Paracentrotus lividus* is nearly absent from the open coast of Ireland (page 38). Look up the natural history of this marine organism and suggest some possible reasons for this limitation of distribution.

5 Factors limiting
distributions: temperature

There is an immense amount of literature on the effects of temperature on organisms, principally because temperature is a critical environmental factor, but partly because it is relatively easy to measure.

Every organism has an upper and a lower lethal temperature but these are not constant for each species; that is, organisms can adapt physiologically to different conditions (Hoar 1966, Chaps. 9 and 10). In fishes, for example, the lethal temperature depends on the temperature at which fish have been living. Brett (1956) illustrates this for two species of fish (Figure 18).

Temperature may act on any stage of the life cycle and can limit the distribution of a species through its effects on

1 Survival
2 Reproduction
3 Development of young organisms
4 Competition with other forms near the limits of temperature tolerance (or predation, parasitism, diseases)

If temperature acts to limit a distribution, what aspect of temperature is relevant—maximum temperatures, minimum temperatures, average tempera-

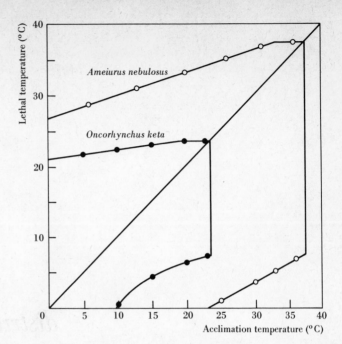

FIGURE 18

Lethal temperature relations for two species of fish. The bullhead, Ameiurus nebulosus, *is a highly tolerant species in contrast to the chum salmon,* Oncorhynchus keta. *The area enclosed by each trapezium is the zone of tolerance. (After Brett 1956.)*

tures? There is no overall rule that can be applied here, and the important measure will depend on the mechanism by which temperature acts and the species involved. Plants (and animals) respond differently to the same environmental variables during different phases of their life cycle (Figure 19). For this reason mean temperatures or other simple heat sums will not always be correlated with the limits of distributions, even if temperature is the critical variable.

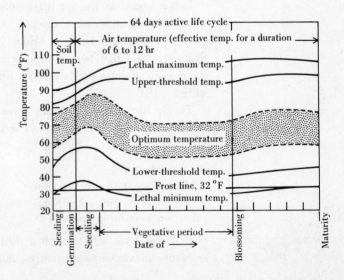

FIGURE 19

Thermal responses of canning peas (Pisum sativum). *(After Wang 1960.)*

There is an immense amount of work showing the effects of temperature on physiological processes such as the germination of seeds, flowering of plants, and speed of development in insects. I will not review this material here because the relevance of most of this work for the problem of distribution is not known. No one doubts that temperature affects the physiology of organisms—the ecological question to be answered is whether these temperature effects explain some part of the distributional limits of the species. Plants and animals that do not regulate their body temperature are strongly affected by environmental temperature. They operate not on a scale of time but on a scale of *time above a temperature threshold*. For this reason we would expect temperature to be one important environmental factor setting limits to distributions.

Hocker (1956) tried to describe the distribution range of the loblolly pine (*Pinus taeda*) from the meteorological data available from 207 weather stations in the southeastern United States. He included seasonal means for (1) average monthly temperature, (2) average monthly range of temperature, (3) number of days per month of measurable rainfall, (4) number of days per month with rainfall over 0.5 inch, (5) average monthly precipitation, and (6) average length of frost-free period. Weather stations were divided into two groups, one within the natural range of the pine and the other outside the range; from the difference between these two groups, Hocker mapped the climatic limits for loblolly pine (Figure 20). There is good agreement between observed limits of range and the limits mapped from meteorological data. The northern limit of this pine is probably set by winter temperature and rainfall. The rate of water uptake in

FIGURE 20

Natural distribution limits and calculated climatic limits of loblolly pine (Pinus taeda) *in the southeastern United States. (After Hocker 1956.)*

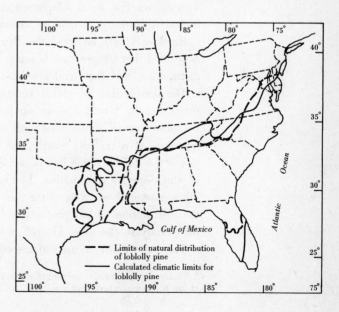

loblolly pine roots decreases rapidly at lower temperatures, and this would accentuate winter drought* in more northerly areas. Hocker predicted that a northern extension of the limits of loblolly pine was not feasible because of these basic climatic limitations.

Loblolly pine has been planted in many areas outside its natural range (Parker 1950). It has taken well in Australia, New Zealand, Uruguay, Japan, South Africa, and California. It has also been planted in Tennessee, southern Illinois, southern Indiana, and central New Jersey. Needles of trees in Ohio and southern Indiana are often winter-killed by frost. Seedlings planted in northern Idaho were all killed by low winter temperatures (Parker 1955). In contrast, loblolly pines planted near Stillwater, Oklahoma (230 miles northwest of its natural range), have grown well for 25 years and produced considerable numbers of seedlings 3 to 8 years old (Posey 1967). Allen (1961) showed that seed from different parts of the range of loblolly pine responded differently when planted in Virginia near the northeastern limits of its range:

Results after 6 years in Virginia

Seed source	Survival (%)	Average height (ft)
Virginia	90	7.8
Louisiana	88	7.4
Mississippi	81	7.4
Georgia	76	7.8
Florida	48	2.5

This shows that local adaptation can occur and that genetic and physiological uniformity cannot be assumed throughout the range of a species.

Hartley (1950) analyzed the distribution of the grasses of the world and concluded that temperature is much more important than rainfall in limiting distribution and that winter temperatures are especially critical.

The distribution of global vegetation units, such as the tundra and the tropical rain forest, are so obviously related to temperature that most botanists regard the question of whether temperature actually limits distribution as a trivially simple one. What is particularly interesting about this is the difficulty one has in trying to apply the global view to the details of single-species distribution. Livingston and Shreve (1921), for example, did a mammoth analysis of the role of temperature and moisture in limiting the distribution of vascular plants in the United States; the more detailed their analysis, the more blurred is the picture regarding temperature.

There are many records of the effects of late spring frosts on plants. For

---

* Winter drought occurs in plants when the roots are unable to take up water because of low soil temperatures but the leaves are losing water by transpiration.

example, a frost on May 31, 1919, in Utah caused severe damage to forest vegetation above 5000 ft (Korstian 1921). The question of cold hardiness in plants impinges on the problem of distribution and has been reviewed by Parker (1963) and Weiser (1970). Most temperate-zone plants are very resistant to midwinter cold. Red-osier dogwoods (*Cornus stolonifera*), a hardy shrub, collected from widespread areas in North America (Washington State to New York, Colorado to Alaska) were all able to survive a laboratory test at −196°C by midwinter when grown in Minnesota. In spite of this, dogwoods native to coastal areas with mild climates were often damaged by early fall frosts because they did not acclimate quickly enough (Figure 21). Similar differences occurred in the onset of spring growth. Cold hardiness is thus as much a matter of *timing* as of absolute resistance to cold.

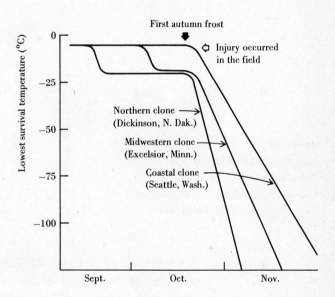

FIGURE 21

Typical seasonal patterns of cold resistance in the living bark of three climatic races of red-osier dogwood, Cornus stolonifera. *The acclimation curves shown are for clones from North Dakota, Minnesota, and Washington grown in the field in Minnesota. Over 24 clones which have been collected from widespread locations in North America became resistant to −196°C by midwinter in Minnesota. (After Weiser 1970.)*

Poikilothermic animals respond directly to temperature. Fishes, for example, can be readily separated into "cold-water" and "warm-water" species. Fry (1951) showed that the speckled trout (*Salvelinus fontinalis*) preferred to live at 14 to 19°C when given a choice, and that the upper lethal temperature was about 25°C, although slightly higher temperatures could be tolerated for short periods of time. These physiological facts are in accord with the field distribution of this species, which is absent from streams where the water temperature exceeds 24°C for any extended time (Ricker 1934).

The upper lethal temperature of fishes may vary seasonally, as Brett

(1944) has described for the bullhead (Figure 22), but this need not be a factor limiting distribution. The lethal temperatures of the freshwater fishes studied by Brett (1944) and Hart (1952) were well above the thermal extremes encountered in the fishes' environments, and the physiological characteristics of temperature tolerances seemed to have little ecological significance for distribution. Many of the fish species Hart studied possessed uniform temperature tolerances, including samples from populations in Ontario to Florida. Brett (1959), however, cautioned that upper lethal temperature limits may be ecologically meaningless if the fish become inactive at high temperatures. Inactive fish may be eaten by predators or subject to diseases, even though they are not dying from temperature stress. These studies on fish illustrate again the common problem that a clear general distinction (cold- vs. warm-water fishes) is often cloudy at the level of individual species.

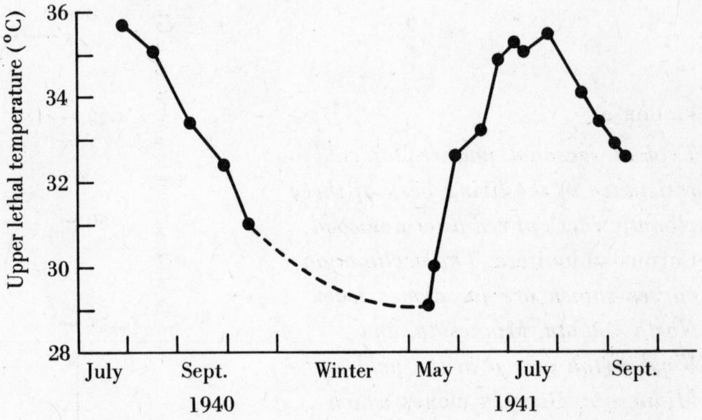

FIGURE 22

Seasonal variation in the upper lethal temperature of the bullhead (Ameiurus nebulosus) *in Algonquin Park, Ontario. (After Brett 1944.)*

Smallmouth black bass (*Micropterus dolomieu*) have been introduced into the lakes of Saskatchewan over a period of 40 years without becoming established. Rawson (1943) reported on an attempt to stock bass in Prince Albert National Park. Both adults and fry were planted. Adult bass survived in fair numbers and spawned in one lake. Success in rearing young was primarily a function of temperature. Fish will spawn when the temperature rises to 16°C (60°F), and continued water temperatures not less than 18°C (65°F) are necessary for rearing. Temperature conditions in these northern lakes are marginal for smallmouth bass because of reproductive requirements. In addition, none of the fry planted seemed to survive; a heavy population of predatory fishes may have been responsible.

The mosquito *Aedes aegypti* has a worldwide distribution within the tropical and subtropical zones and is a common vector of two important human diseases, yellow fever and dengue. In spite of its wide distribution, this mosquito is very strictly limited by latitude (Figure 23). The northern and southern limits of distribution appear to be related to temperature, but this relationship is not simple (Christophers, 1960, pp. 38–40). A temperature of 10°C (50°F) is just lethal to the larvae and adults, and winter temperatures in this zone would presumably eliminate this species. But the egg stage is much more temperature resistant, and in some areas *A. aegypti* overwinters in the egg stage. Apparently, the resistance of the egg to cold cannot be very important in allowing this mosquito to extend its area of distribution, since it has not colonized much of the temperate zone. Summer temperatures may be more important; however, low summer temperatures prevent pairing and oviposition, and most females may die before their eggs mature.

The northern limit of the intertidal barnacle *Balanus balanoides* is coincident with the boundary of the polar ice pack in late summer (Figure 24; Barnes 1957). Adult barnacles are not killed by winter freezing, and the limiting action of low temperatures seems to be on reproduction; nauplii must be released and the larvae must develop in the plankton, settle on rocks, and grow enough to withstand the winter period, all in a short, arctic summer. The southern limit of this barnacle seems to be set in exactly

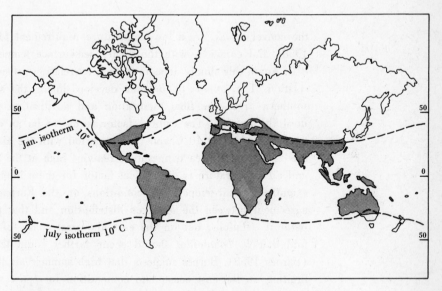

FIGURE 23

Northern and southern limits of the recorded distribution of the mosquito Aedes aegypti *and isotherms of 10°C. (After Christophers 1960.)*

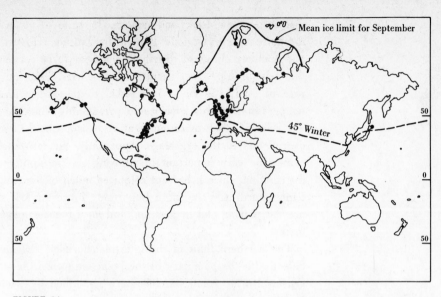

FIGURE 24

Distribution of the barnacle Balanus balanoides. *The southern limits are fitted by the minimum winter-surface water temperature of 45°F (8°C) and the northern limits by the mean annual polar ice limit for September. (After Hutchins 1947 and Barnes 1957.)*

the converse way, by a low-temperature requirement for breeding (Barnes 1958) and coincides with the winter sea-surface temperature minimum of 8°C. Again this simply appears to be a correlation rather than a cause–effect relation. The gonads of *Balanus* develop during the summer, but, in the southern areas, the final maturation and fertilization does not take place until the autumn. The critical factor seems to be an autumn drop in air temperature below 10°C and then a period with the air temperature below this critical level. Sea temperature remains high at the time of fertilization, and air temperature is the critical factor for these intertidal animals. If we examine the air-temperature conditions on the European coasts, we find agreement between the observed distribution and that predicted from temperature relations, but on the east and west coasts of North America we find that *B. balanoides* should occur farther south than it actually does (Barnes 1958). Barnes suggests that high summer air temperatures may be limiting on the east coast, and competition for space with other barnacles may be limiting further southern penetration on the west coast.

In addition to this geographic analysis, barnacles have been studied with respect to intertidal zonation. The upper and lower limits of dominant invertebrates and algae are often very sharp in the intertidal zone (Figure 25), and this zonation is a particularly graphic example of the problem of

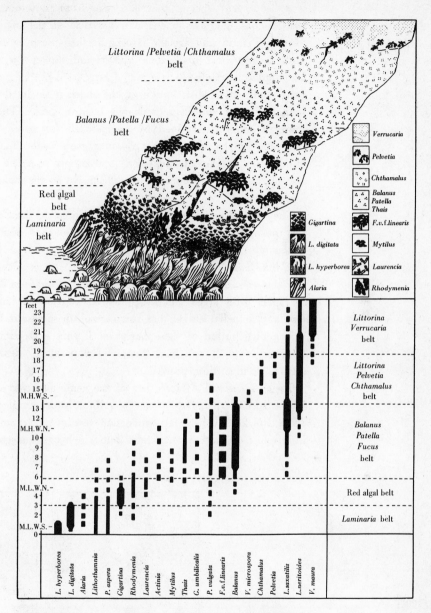

FIGURE 25

Type of barnacle-dominated slope that is very common on moderately exposed shores of northwestern Scotland and northwestern Ireland. (After Lewis 1964.) M.H.W.S., mean high water, spring; M.H.W.N., mean high water, neap; M.L.W.N., mean low water, neap; M.L.W.S., mean low water, spring.

distribution on a local scale. Two barnacles dominate the British coasts, and their British distributions are shown in Figure 26. *Chthamalus stellatus* is a "southern" species that is absent from the colder waters of the east British coast and is the common barnacle of the upper intertidal zone of western Britain and Ireland. Going farther north in the British Isles, one finds it restricted to a zone higher and higher on the intertidal rocks. *Chthamalus* is relatively tolerant of long periods of exposure to air, and the upper limit of its distribution on the shore is set by desiccation. This basic limitation does not seem to change over its range. The lower limit on the shore is often determined by competition for space with *B. balanoides*. Connell (1961b) showed that *Balanus* grew faster than *Chthamalus* in the middle part of the intertidal zone and simply squeezed *Chthamalus* out. He also showed that *Chthamalus* could survive in the *Balanus* zone if *Balanus* were removed.

The upper limit of *B. balanoides* is also set by weather factors, but since this barnacle is less tolerant to desiccation and high temperatures than *Chthamalus*, there is a zone high on the shore where *Chthamalus* can survive but *Balanus* cannot (Connell 1961a). The sensitivity of young barnacles sets this upper limit. The lower limit of *Balanus* is set by competition for space with algae and by predation, particularly by a gastropod *Thais lapillus*. Connell (1961b) has summarized these results in Figure 27.

The distribution of these barnacles is thus a striking example of limitations imposed by physical factors (temperature, desiccation) and biotic factors (competition, predation).

Tsetse are small African flies of the genus *Glossina* and comprise 22 different species distributed over 4 million square miles of Africa between 15°N and 28°S. Tsetse are important vectors for trypanosomes, which have little effect on native vertebrates but which cause *sleeping sickness* in man

FIGURE 26

Distribution of the two common British barnacles. Chthamalus stellatus *(a) is a southern species, and* Balanus balanoides *(b) is a northern species. (After Lewis 1964.)*

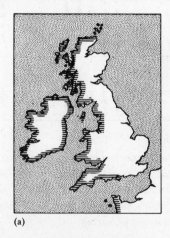

(a)

(b)

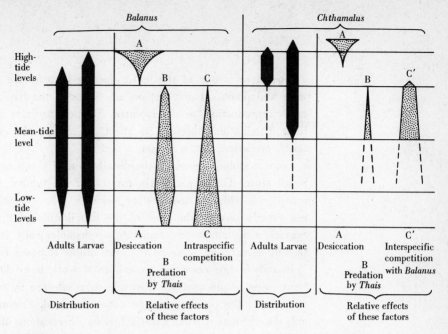

FIGURE 27

Intertidal distribution of adults and newly settled larvae of Balanus
balanoides *and* Chthamalus stellatus *at Millport, Scotland, with a
diagrammatic representation of the relative effects of the principal
limiting factors. (After Connell 1961a.)*

and *nagana* in domestic animals. Because of this, about one-fourth of Africa
was previously denied to all domestic animals except poultry. Tsetse are
woodland flies and are absent from grasslands and from highland areas
above 6000 ft. The northern limits of tsetse in Nigeria are set by high
temperatures in the dry season, and the altitudinal limits are set by low
temperatures. The most favorable temperature is about 24°C (Glasgow
1963), and the limits of tolerance are approximately 14 to 32°C. These
limits are related to fat metabolism (Bursell 1960). All the energy for pupal
development in tsetse comes from fat reserves, which cannot be replenished
until the first adult blood meal. At high temperatures the speed of fat
consumption is accelerated more than the speed of development, and beyond
32°C the fat reserves are exhausted before development is completed. Conversely, at low temperatures the speed of development is retarded more
than the speed of fat consumption, and emerging adults have very little fat
reserves. These two processes are in balance at 22 to 24°C, so adults emerging from that temperature have maximal fat reserves. Thus, in *Glossina*,
temperature acts through pupal development to limit distribution.

Temperature is one of the major factors limiting the distributions of animals and plants. It may act on any stage of the life cycle and affect survival, reproduction, or development. Temperature may also act indirectly to limit distributions through its effects on competitive ability, disease resistance, predation, or parasitism.

From a global viewpoint, the distribution of plants can be associated with temperature. The tropical rain forest and the tundra, for example, occupy areas with different temperature regimes. The effects of temperature are less clearly seen at the level of the distribution of the individual species. Species may adapt to temperature physiologically and genetically and thereby circumvent some of the restrictions imposed by temperature.

In only a few cases has experimental work been done on local populations—first to pinpoint the life-cycle stage affected by temperature and then to describe the physiological processes involved. For most species we have only an indication from natural history observations that temperature may limit distribution.

We began discussing the factors limiting distributions one by one, in isolation. But we have observed that temperature does not act alone but interacts with other limiting factors. For example, high temperatures may be lethal to some animals if water is in short supply but not lethal if there is abundant water; that is, *moisture and temperature may interact*. Low temperatures may reduce activity and increase predation rate in aquatic organisms; that is, *predation and temperature may interact*. Because of the interactions among different factors, the problem of what restricts distributions does not admit to simple answers involving only one environmental factor.

SELECTED
REFERENCES

ANDREWARTHA, H. G., and L. C. BIRCH. 1954. *The Distribution and Abundance of Animals*. Chap. 6, Weather: Temperature. University of Chicago Press, Chicago.

BRETT, J. R. 1956. Some principles in the thermal requirements of fishes. *Quart. Rev. Biol.* 31:75–87.

DAUBENMIRE, R. F. 1947. *Plants and Environment*. Chap. IV, The Temperature Factor. Wiley, New York.

GOOD, R. 1964. *The Geography of the Flowering Plants*. Chap. 17, The Factors of Distribution: II. Climatic Factors. Longmans, London.

MACAN, T. T. 1963. *Freshwater Ecology*. Chap. 8, Physical Factors (2): Temperature. Longmans, London.

PARKER, J. 1963. Cold resistance in woody plants. *Bot. Rev.* 29:123–201.

VERNBERG, F. J., and W. B. VERNBERG. 1970. *The Animal and the Environment.* Chap. 3, The Zone of Resistance. Holt, Rinehart & Winston, New York.

QUESTIONS AND PROBLEMS

1 Boyko (1947) states that for most species with wide distribution, the limits toward the pole are usually determined by temperature and the limits toward the equator by water balance. Discuss with respect to plants and animals.

2 Several schemes have been proposed to explain the distributions of animals and plants on the basis of single factors. One of the earliest of these was the *life-zone concept* of Merriam (1898), in which temperature played the key role. Merriam proposed two temperature laws:

a The northern limits of distribution for terrestrial animals and plants is governed by the sum of the positive temperatures for the entire season of growth and reproduction.

b The southward distribution is governed by the mean temperature of a brief period during the hottest part of the year.

Trace the subsequent history of the life zone scheme, and evaluate the criticisms that have been leveled against it.

3 "The frost line . . . is probably the most important of all climatic demarcations in plants" (Good 1964, p. 353). Locate the frost line from a climatological atlas, and compare the distributions of some tropical and temperate species of any particular taxonomic group with respect to this boundary.

4 With regard to plant distribution, Cain (1944, p. 11) presents two viewpoints:

a "the extremes of climatic factors are more important than the means."

b "It is not the extremes of environmental factors which are of importance, but the means."

Can you reconcile these two views with respect to the role of temperature in limiting distribution?

5 The British barnacle *Elminius modestus* extends higher on the shore in the intertidal zone than does the barnacle *Balanus balanoides*, when the two species occur together. These two species, however, have similar tolerances to desiccation, salinity, and temperature. The range of initial settlement of young barnacles is the same for the two species. Given these facts, can you suggest an explanation for the observation that *E. modestus* extends higher on the shore than *B. balanoides*? Consult Foster (1971, p. 47) and compare his explanation with yours.

6 In discussing the temperature tolerances of intertidal animals, Southward (1958, p. 65) states: "It is clear that the temperatures experienced on the shore are well within the tolerance limits of most of the animals, and even exceptional extremes of temperature may have little direct influence on the distribution of adult intertidal animals." The winter of 1962–1963 was very severe in Britain and much of Europe, and this provided an opportunity to study the effects of an unusual prolonged cold period on the distribution of intertidal animals. Review these effects (Crisp 1964, p. 165) and discuss the above quotation in the context of observations on the effects of the 1962–1963 winter.

6 Factors limiting distributions: moisture

Water, alone or in conjunction with temperature, is probably the most important physical factor affecting the ecology of terrestrial organisms. Aquatic organisms, of course, live in water and have different problems of water balance. Freshwater organisms have the physiological problem of keeping water *out*, since their body fluids have a higher osmotic pressure than the water. Marine organisms often have the opposite problem of retaining their body water in the presence of high-salinity seawater. We shall not go into these problems of the physiology of water balance, which are discussed by Hoar (1966, Chap. 11).

Since water is such a critical item in the life spans of animals and plants, it is not surprising that a variety of morphological and physiological adaptations are concerned with water retention. For example, plants may be divided into *hydrophytes* (plants living in wet habitats), *xerophytes* (plants living in dry areas), and *mesophytes* (everything else). Each type of plant has structural adaptations, such as a thick cuticle on the leaves of xerophytes to reduce water loss. Similarly, some desert rodents can get along without drinking free water.

For terrestrial organisms, moisture must be considered in terms of the humidity of the atmosphere, soil water for plants, and drinking water for animals. Some terrestrial animals—the active stages of the mollusks, amphibians, isopods, nematodes, and a few insects—usually live in situations where the atmosphere is saturated with water vapor. The vertebrates and the insects have been the most successful animal groups in colonizing dry habitats.

Just as with temperature, the limits of tolerance to water may determine the distribution of a species. The distribution of plants in particular can often be related to soil moisture. Figure 28 illustrates this for trees of the coastal redwood region of northern California.

The germination of seeds and the establishment of seedlings are critical phases in the life cycle of many plants. Moisture is an important variable affecting germination (Harper and Benton 1966). For example, various species of *Juncus* (rushes) are associated with water and waterlogged soils, and moisture has a strong effect on seed germination (Lazenby 1955):

Water table (inches below soil surface)	No. *Juncus effusus* seedlings germinated from 600 seeds
0	540
2	151
4	12
8	0

Seed germination can thus be a critical bottleneck in the limitation of distributions.

The vegetation of any site is usually considered a product of the climate of the area. This implies that climatic factors, temperature and moisture primarily, are the main factors controlling the distribution of vegetation. Geographers have often adopted this viewpoint and then turned it around to set up a classification of climate on the basis of vegetation. Native vegetation is assumed to be a meteorologic instrument capable of measuring all the integrated climatic elements.

Some geographers have tried to set climatic boundaries independently of vegetation. This has been done by Thornthwaite (1948). The basis of his climatic classification is *precipitation*, which is balanced against *potential evapotranspiration*. Potential evapotranspiration is the amount of water that would be lost from the ground by evaporation and from the vegetation by transpiration if an unlimited supply of water were available. There is no way of measuring potential evapotranspiration directly, and it is normally computed as a function of temperature. Diagrams can then be constructed; two extreme examples are shown in Figures 29 and 30 to illustrate the climatic regime at a desert station and a temperate deciduous forest station. Major vegetational types such as the grasslands, temperate deciduous

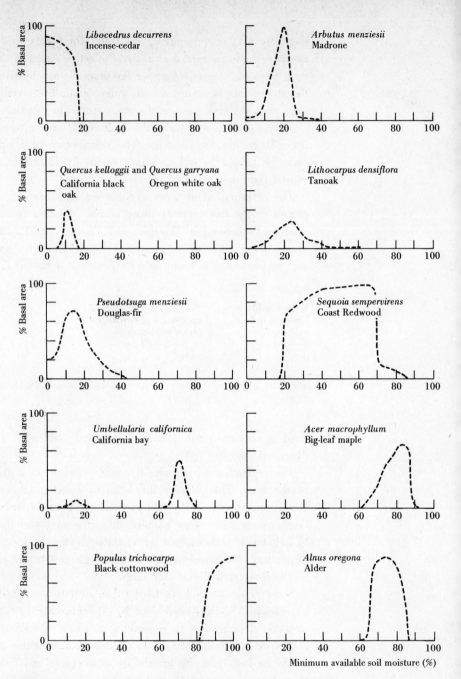

FIGURE 28

Distribution of trees in coastal redwood region of California in relation to minimum available soil moisture during the year. Each soil has a certain potential water-storage capacity, and the minimum available moisture is the lowest value to which soil moisture falls during the year, expressed as a percentage of storage capacity. (After Waring and Major 1964.)

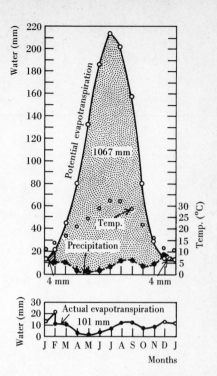

FIGURE 29

Climatic diagram for Blythe, California, a station in the hot, Sonoran desert. Available moisture limits plant activity. (After Major 1963.)

forest, and tundra are fairly well correlated with certain climatic types defined by Thornthwaite's system. However, when the details of local distributions are considered, the system breaks down. This is illustrated in the following example.

Daubenmire (1956) studied the relation between vegetation and climate in the northern Rocky Mountains. The pronounced vertical changes in climate are correlated with belts of vegetation up the mountains. Daubenmire could measure the climatic data at a series of stations up the mountains and could then test the relationship between climate and vegetation.

He described seven different vertical zones of vegetation (Figure 31). Daubenmire compared the climatic classification of stations within these vegetation zones to see (1) if the climatic classification within one zone was constant and (2) if the climatic classification between the zones differed. None of the climatic classifications he tried was successful in achieving these two goals, including Thornthwaite's most recent one, and Daubenmire concluded that while the climatic classifications may be well correlated with the very broad distribution of vegetation, they were of no use for detailed study. There is a close relationship between vegetation and climate, but the ordinary measures of climate that the meteorologists take are not the most important ones from the point of view of the plants.

Moisture and temperature interact to limit the geographical distribution of some of the larger woody plants. Parker (1969) has reviewed drought resistance in woody plants and concluded that *frost drought* and *soil drought*

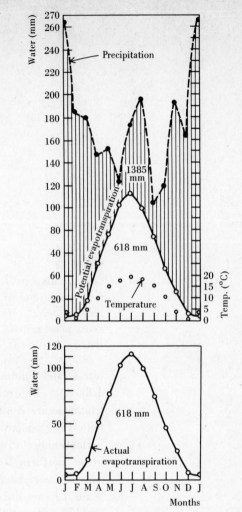

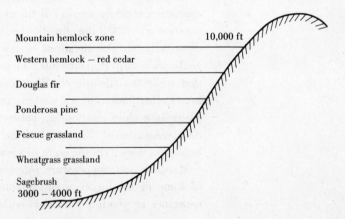

FIGURE 30

Climatic diagram for a station in the Great Smoky Mountains National Park, Tennessee, at 1160 m elevation, where available heat limits plant activity. The station is in a temperate, deciduous forest. (After Major 1963.)

Mountain hemlock zone   10,000 ft

Western hemlock — red cedar

Douglas fir

Ponderosa pine

Fescue grassland

Wheatgrass grassland

Sagebrush
3000 – 4000 ft

FIGURE 31

Vegetation zonation in the northern Rocky Mountains of the United States. (After Daubenmire 1956.)

are both critical in determining ranges of species. Soil drought is the usual "drought," in which soil moisture is deficient (e.g., the desert); it can usually be described as an *absolute* shortage of water in the soil. Frost drought is a situation in which water is present but not available to plants (e.g., tundra in winter); it can be described as a *relative* shortage of water for the plant. In both situations water loss from the plant's leaves and stems is greater than water intake through the roots. Thus low temperatures can produce symptoms of drought. This emphasizes that water availability is the critical variable, which has led to considerable research on how to measure "available" water in the soil. Many of the distributional effects attributed to temperature may operate through the water balance of plants.

Drought can lead to tree diseases, the entire etiology of which is still obscure. Diseases may be produced by direct injury, such as leaf injuries, stem cracking and blisters, or root injury from drought. Indirect effects may also be involved, the most puzzling category being the "dieback declines" which have occurred in the eastern deciduous forests of North America. The most striking diebacks have involved white ash (*Fraxinus americana*), sugar maple (*Acer saccharum*), paper birch (*Betula papyrifera*), red oak (*Quercus rubra*), black oak (*Quercus velutina*), and beech (*Fagus sylvatica*). These diebacks are usually initiated by a stress condition and probably have many different causes (Sinclair 1964).

During the early 1960s sugar maples (*Acer saccharum*) were dying in large numbers, particularly along roadsides in New England, Ontario, and Quebec. Westing (1966) attributes this dieback to the prolonged and severe drought in this area and notes that in the western and southern parts of the range, sugar maples had not been noticeably affected. Sugar maples are shallow rooted and thus especially subject to drought damage, particularly along roadsides. Diebacks also accompanied the drought of the 1930s. No pathogens have been found to account for these diebacks.

Sinclair (1964) compared the declines of white ash, scarlet oak (*Quercus coccinea*), and sugar maple in the northeastern United States and concluded that drought was the major causal factor. The first indications of these diebacks have been reductions in radial growth and terminal twig growth of the tree. Sinclair pointed out the relationship between radial growth and rainfall (Figure 32) in these hardwood trees, which suggests that drought is involved. Staley (1965), however, emphasized that drought was not sufficient to explain the dieback of oaks, and he implicated insect defoliation and root-rot diseases along with soil and climatic effects. How much these local diebacks affect tree distributions is not known. Waring and Major (1964) cautioned against interpreting range limits from isolated examples of climatic factors killing trees.

The "tree line" is a particularly graphical illustration of the limitation on plant distribution imposed by the physical environment. Not all tree

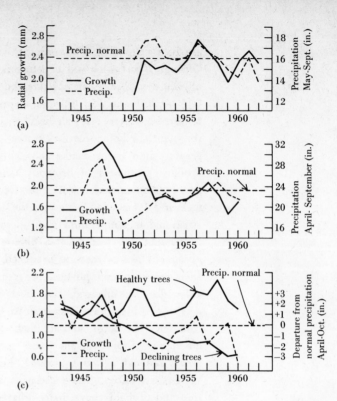

FIGURE 32

FIGURE 32

Relation of precipitation to radial growth of (a) white ash, (b) scarlet oak, and (c) sugar maple. (After Sinclair 1964.)

lines are controlled by the same factors, and Parker (1963) lists nine factors that have been suggested to affect timberlines:

1 Lack of soil
2 Desiccation of leaves in cold weather
3 Short growing season
4 Lack of snow, exposing plants to winter drying
5 Excessive snow lasting through the summer
6 Mechanical aspects of high winds
7 Rapid heat loss at night
8 Excessive soil temperatures in the day
9 Drought

These factors can be boiled down into three primary variables: temperature, moisture, and wind. As one proceeds up a mountain, temperature decreases, rainfall increases, and wind velocity increases. Because of freezing temperatures during much of the year, available soil moisture decreases. How can we separate the effects of temperature, moisture, and wind?

Timberlines in the northern Rocky Mountains are determined by wind, according to Griggs (1938). He observed that protected areas had large trees, whereas windswept areas had none. These protected areas had the same temperature regimes, have deeper snow drifts, and hence have a shortened growing season compared with exposed areas, yet they support large trees. Wind must therefore be the controlling factor.

Rydberg (1913) noted that in regions of large mountain masses the timberline was higher than on isolated mountains. This was first noticed in the Swiss Alps and Rydberg noted that it is also true in the Rocky Mountains. He could not explain this observation but suggested that wind velocity might be lower (or snowfall heavier) in large mountain masses, and hence more water would be available for summer growth of trees.

Daubenmire (1954) analyzed alpine timberlines in North America and reviewed the various factors that might affect them. Upper timberlines in North America decrease about 110 m in altitude for every degree of latitude one moves north, except between the equator and 30°N, where timberlines are approximately constant at 3500 to 4000 m.

In North America timberlines for any given latitide are lowest in the Appalachians and highest in the Rocky Mountains (Figure 33). This uniformity of timberline relations is surprising because many different tree species are involved.

Snow depth can affect the local distribution of trees near timberline but cannot explain the existence of timberline. In depressions where snow accumulates early and stays late, tree seedlings cannot become established. Only ridges will support trees in these circumstances, but these ridges also show a timberline, and consequently snow depth cannot be a primary factor.

Trees at upper timberline in the Northern Hemisphere are often wind blown and dwarfed, and this suggests wind as a major factor limiting trees on mountains. Climatic data show a very large increase in wind velocity as one goes up mountains (Table 3). Within the tropics and in the Southern Hemisphere wind effects seem to be absent. One difficulty with the wind hypothesis is that all the evidence is relevant to old trees, whereas it is the establishment of very young seedlings that is crucial to timberline formation. Daubenmire suggests that wind has secondary effects in altering tim-

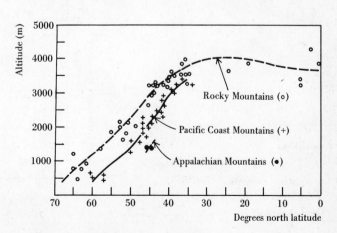

FIGURE 33

Timberlines in North America.
(After Daubenmire 1954.)

TABLE 3

Wind velocity in relation to mean timberline elevation in the United States

| Station | Elevation (m) | | Mean wind velocity (mph) of most windy month |
	Above sea level	In relation to timberline	
Pike's Peak, Colorado	4334	800 above	25.0
	3505	100 above	20.8
	3455	50 below	7.6
Boulder County, Colorado	3750	350 above	16.5
	3050	350 below	13.4
Mt. Washington, New Hampshire	1910	400 above	42.5

SOURCE: After Daubenmire (1954).

berlines in local situations; but, like snow depth, wind does not seem to be a primary cause of timberlines.

The climatic limits of timberlines coincide roughly with isotherms representing 10°C for the mean of the warmest month (Figure 34). Daily maximal temperatures may be more biologically relevant than daily means. Daubenmire suggests that heat is the critical factor for alpine timberlines and that a timberline is a point on the scale of diminishing heat supply where solar energy is adequate only for the annual requirements of respiration plus foliage renewal, with the result that no energy is left for maintenance and development of the roots and trunk of the tree. Although winter winds and deep snow may locally alter the elevation of timberlines, these

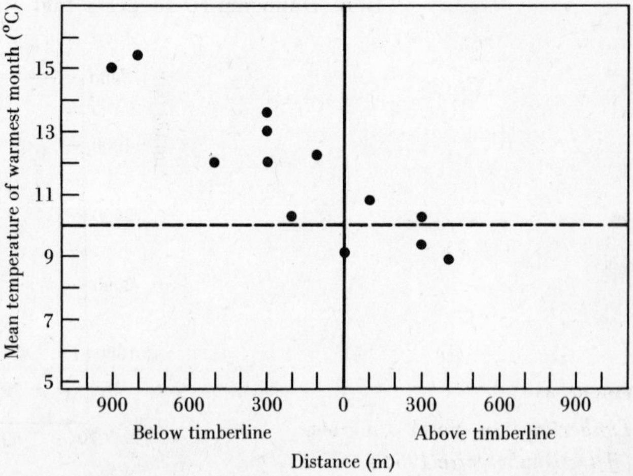

FIGURE 34

Mean temperature of warmest month at weather stations in North America near the timberline. (After Daubenmire 1954.)

influences do not disrupt the general conformity between timberlines and isotherms.

Almost no experimental work has been done to determine the causes for timberlines. In New Zealand the beech *Nothofagus* forms an evergreen forest that stops abruptly at timberline between 3000 and 5000 ft above sea level. Wardle (1965) showed that this timberline was produced by factors reducing seedling establishment. Good seed years near timberline are uncommon for *Nothofagus*, and timberline seed has poor germination (0 to 3%). Seedling survival is poor, and the death of seedlings is associated with drying out of the tops. Wardle transplanted small seedlings above the timberline. Seedlings planted in the open all died in their first year, but shaded seedlings survived well and became established 600 ft above timberline.

In many species at timberline the subalpine tree form is replaced by an alpine elfinwood, a low bush form (Figure 35). These elfinwood forms may

FIGURE 35

Growth forms of Pinus murrayana *on the eastern slope of the Sierra Nevada in California. (a) Single trunk tree ca. 30 m tall on south-facing slope at 10,200 ft. (b) Intermediate multitrunk tree 6 m tall with 6-m-wide elfinwood base on east-facing slope at 10,600 ft altitude. (c) Multitrunk elfinwood 2 m tall on south-facing slope at 10,800 feet. (After Clausen 1965.)*

extend several hundred meters farther upslope in some species and thus extend the distribution locally. Clausen (1965) suggested that elfinwood forms were inherited growth forms that were selectively favored at timberline. Griggs (1938) did not think that elfinwood forms of Rocky Mountain trees were genetically different from the normal growth types. The question remains unresolved.

Little work has been done to determine why alpine plants do not colonize areas downslope. In the Medicine Bow Mountains of southeastern Wyoming, alpine plants, which occur only above 3290 m, are temperature adapted to a much broader altitudinal range than they actually occupy (2700 to 3660 m). These plants must be limited in their lower altitudinal distribution by competition for light with subalpine plants and by drought, not by temperature (Godfrey and Billings 1968).

In addition to the alpine timberlines, there is another tree line set by the poleward extensions of forest in both the Northern and Southern Hemispheres (Figure 36). The explanation for the arctic and antarctic tree lines may not be the same as that for alpine timberlines.

Along the eastern side of Hudson Bay, the boreal forest gives way to arctic tundra over a broad transition zone, extending from 53 to 56°N. This transition zone is a patchwork of communities of tundra and spruce forest. Trees in this area grow on all areas of suitable soil, and areas unsuitable for trees because of insufficient soil are occupied by tundra (Marr 1948). Trees are invading the tundra as soil develops, and the growth rates of trees in this area are good. Thus the limit of spruce trees in this part of Quebec is not set by climatic factors but by insufficient soil on recent glacial sediments.

Griggs (1934) examined spruce trees at the forest–tundra edge in southwestern Alaska and found good growth rates and good reproduction. There were no indications of climatic suppression of trees, the forest was actively colonizing the tundra, and trees at the forest edge were small only because they were young. The forest edge in southwestern Alaska is not a climatic boundary, Griggs suggested, but a historical one remaining from the last glaciation and reflecting a lack of time for colonization.

The tree line in the central Canadian arctic has apparently not changed much in the last 50 years. Larsen (1965) noted that black spruce forest occupies most of the land at the southern end of Ennadai Lake but at the northern end of the lake, which is only 50 miles away, is confined to a few ravines. Topography and geology are similar over this area. Charred tree remnants indicate that approximately 1000 years ago spruce forest extended 175 miles farther north of Ennadai Lake. Drew and Shanks (1965) reported that the white spruce tree line in the Firth River Valley of the northern Yukon is stationary, neither advancing nor retreating.

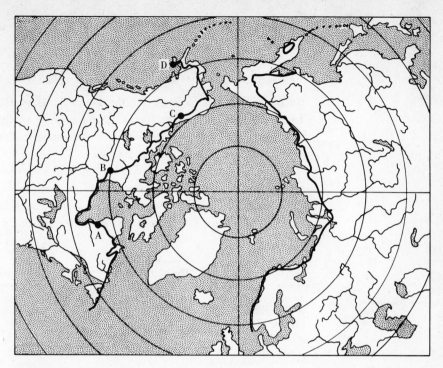

FIGURE 36

Polar limit of treelike conifers, irrespective of species. The area
studied by Marr (1948) is indicated by A, the area of Larsen (1965)
by B, and the area of Drew and Shanks (1965) by C. Grigg's
(1934) Alaskan studies are marked by D. (Map after Hustich 1953.)

The White Mountains of New Hampshire, by contrast, have a timberline
at 1740 m (5700 ft) or less, and the timberline seems to be receding
(Griggs 1946). Few seedlings can be found near the timberline, and old,
dead trees are much larger than current living ones.

The ranges of species are thus not static but dynamic, a point that we
shall see very clearly in subsequent chapters when we discuss community
ecology. If climate limits the distribution of a species, any changes in
climate should produce shifts in distributions. Unfortunately, species may
change their distribution for other reasons as well, and every distributional
shift should not automatically be attributed to climatic changes.

As well as having an upper timberline, trees in mountainous areas have
a lower limit of distribution, not usually as marked because it is a more
gradual transition. Soil moisture may be related to these lower limits of
range. Conifers from the Rocky Mountains differ in susceptibility to drought
in the seedling stage (Daubenmire 1943b):

higher altitude	Alpine fir	lower drought resistance
↑	Engelmann spruce	
	Douglas fir	
	Ponderosa pine	↓
lower altitude	Pinon pine	higher drought resistance

He concluded that moisture set the lower limits of altitudinal distribution. Temperature was not a major factor because all species could be grown at low elevations if they were watered. Atmospheric drought also had little effect. Soil drought was the critical factor.

Support for Daubenmire's conclusions has been obtained in several subsequent studies. In the San Bernardino Mountains of southern California three species of pines have different lower altitudinal limits, and Wright (1970) has shown that this is related to their drought resistance:

	Lower elevation limit (m)	Drought sensitivity
Knobcone pine (*Pinus attenuata*)	850	Least sensitive
Coulter pine (*P. coulteri*)	1200	Intermediate
Sugar pine (*P. lambertiana*)	1600	Most sensitive

These tolerances to drought are not necessarily constant over the range of a species. For example, Douglas fir, an important timber tree in western North America, has two forms, a coastal variety and an interior form called the blue Douglas fir (Anon. 1956). Seedlings from coastal and inland sites differ in their drought hardiness (Pharis and Ferrell 1966):

Source of seedlings	Average no. days to death under soil drought
Coastal	
Vancouver Island, British Columbia	*16.8*
Corvallis, Oregon	*17.3*
Valsetz, Oregon	*17.6*
Inland	
Montana	*19.4*
Utah	*19.6*
Arizona	*20.1*
Interior British Columbia	*21.0*
Northeastern Washington	*21.6*

These variations in resistance to drought are presumed to be genetic in origin.

Variations in drought tolerance can also be seen in slope effects. In the

Northern Hemisphere, south-facing slopes get more sunlight than north-facing slopes, and this difference is often expressed in different vegetation. In the Palouse Range of northern Idaho, the grand fir (*Abies grandis*) and the western red cedar (*Thuja plicata*) are common on north slopes; Ponderosa pine (*Pinus ponderosa*) and Douglas fir (*Pseudotsuga menziesii*) are common on south-facing slopes (Parker 1952). The main difference between these slopes is in soil moisture:

East Twin Mountain (4550 ft)	Percentage soil moisture in top soil layer	
	April 21	May 25
South slope (50 ft down from top)	37.9	11.7
North slope (50 ft down from top)	62.6	59.4

Moisture is lost more rapidly from the southern slopes in this area and soil temperatures are higher, so the wilting point for plants is reached more rapidly on the southern slopes. Southern-slope soils in this area are also more coarse textured and hold less water than the fine-textured northern-slope soils.

A recent analysis of the problem of distribution in a moss by Forman (1964) is a paradigm of careful analysis that should be applied to other species. The common moss *Tetraphis pellucida* grows on decaying wood in coniferous forests of the north temperate zone. Forman first determined in the laboratory the environmental conditions under which this moss would grow and survive. Neither pH nor light intensity were limiting over a wide range, and the major factors determining survival were temperature and humidity. Given the temperature and humidity conditions within which the moss can live, Forman predicted the range limits for North America from weather-station records of temperature and relative humidity (Figure 37). The agreement between observed and predicted distribution is reasonably close, if we consider that weather-station data are only roughly indicative of the actual microclimatic situations where the moss lives. This may explain the lack of fit in the Rocky Mountains and the river valleys of the Great Plains. There is a major anomaly in the Gulf Coast area from which the moss is absent, although climatic conditions are apparently suitable. Forman emphasized that the continental distribution of this moss could not be predicted from either temperature or humidity alone. Transplant experiments from alpine areas to warm deciduous forests were used to show that moss colonies would survive only in areas predicted to be suitable from temperature and humidity data.

Factors limiting distributions may vary with the scale of analysis. Forman pointed out that a hierarchy of distributional maps could be drawn

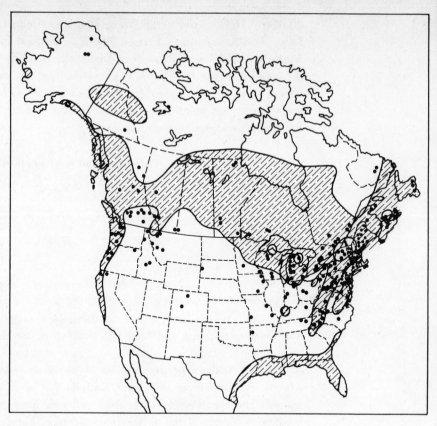

FIGURE 37

Predicted and actual distributions of the moss Tetraphis pellucida *in North America. The shaded area is the theoretical distribution based on temperature and relative humidity. The dots represent the actual distribution. (After Forman 1964.)*

for the moss *Tetraphis*, from the world distribution down to individual colonies and clumps (Figure 38). Thus temperature and humidity may restrict the regional distribution of *Tetraphis*, while instability of the soil substrate may prevent colonies of the moss from growing on soil litter between stumps. This emphasizes the importance of specifying *scale* when discussing distributional problems.

SUMMARY

Moisture is a major factor limiting the distributions of plants and animals. Geographers have recognized this by making climatic classifications based on vegetational distributions. The role of moisture is most clearly seen on a

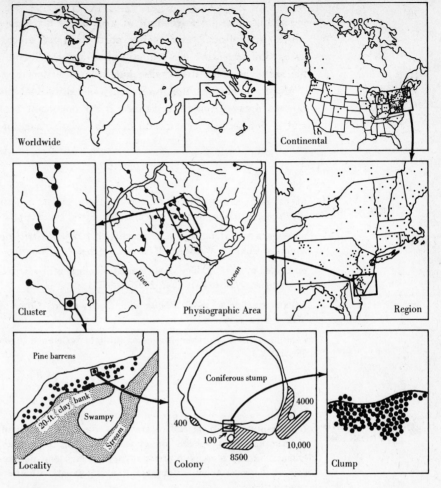

FIGURE 38

Example of the hierarchy of Tetraphis *distributions. Each map represents a magnification of the square in the preceding map. (After Forman 1964.)*

global scale, and the detailed way in which moisture acts on individual species in local situations is not always clear.

Water availability is the critical key to moisture effects on plants, and drought occurs when adequate amounts of water are not present and available to the plant. The soil may be saturated with water, but if it is all frozen, none may be taken up by plants, and they may suffer frost drought. Many of the distributional effects attributed to temperature may operate through the water balance of plants.

The tree line is a particularly graphic example of range limitations. Wind, temperature, and moisture are the primary determinants of timberlines on mountains. The poleward limit of trees in the arctic is a dynamic boundary, which is continually advancing north in some areas, stationary in other areas, and retreating south in still other areas. Climatic changes may explain the shifts in polar tree limits, but little experimental work has been done.

Moisture may set the lower limits of altitudinal distributions in mountainous areas. Drought resistance is an important ecological characteristic and is not necessarily constant over the whole range of a species.

SELECTED REFERENCES

ALLEE, W. C., A. E. EMERSON, O. PARK, T. PARK, and K. P. SCHMIDT. 1949. *Principles of Animal Ecology.* Chap. 12, Water. Saunders, Philadelphia.

ANDREWARTHA, H. G., and L. C. BIRCH. 1954. *The Distribution and Abundance of Animals.* Chap. 7, Weather: Moisture. University of Chicago Press, Chicago.

BILLINGS, W. D. 1952. The environmental complex in relation to plant growth and distribution. *Quart. Rev. Biol.* 27:251–265.

DAUBENMIRE, R. F. 1947. *Plants and Environment.* Chap. 3, The Water Factor. Wiley, New York.

PARKER, J. 1969. Further studies of drought resistance in woody plants. *Bot. Rev.* 35:317–371.

QUESTIONS AND PROBLEMS

1 Salisbury (1926, p. 323) states: "... the mere correspondence of the limits of distribution of a species or community with isothermal lines, or any other climatic limits, is at best presumptive evidence and no proof of any causal connection between them." Compare this statement with the following one by the same author:

Even though temperature be the master factor [in limiting plant distributions], we have seen that its influence may be modified by the reaction of the plant itself, by changes in topography, by differences in the character of the soil, by the effect of competition, etc. It is therefore not remarkable that the limits of species susceptible to temperature changes often show but little relation to isoclimatic lines; rather it is surprising that the correspondence is sometimes so close.

2 Cain (1944, p. 17) states:

Physiological processes are multi-conditioned, and an investigation of the effects of variation of a single factor, when all others are controlled, cannot be applied directly to an interpretation of the role of that factor in nature. It is impossible, then, to speak of a single condition of a factor as being the cause of an observed effect in an organism.

Discuss the implications of this principle that the factors of the environment act collectively and simultaneously, with regard to methods for studying distributional problems.

3 Jarvis (1963, p. 310), after studying the laboratory responses of some British plants to water stress, concluded: "It is therefore difficult to apply to field conditions the results of experiments revealing physiological differences between species in their response to soil or atmospheric drought." Why did she come to this conclusion? How could you avoid this problem?

4 Kangaroo rats (*Dipodomys* spp.) are desert rodents that can live without free water in the diet (Schmidt-Nielsen and Schmidt-Nielsen 1953). Consult a range map for one of the species of kangaroo rats in Hall and Kelson (1959, pp. 511ff.) and write a short essay on the natural history of the species. What limits the distribution of kangaroo rats?

7   *Factors limiting distributions: other physical and chemical factors*

I know of no cases in which light acts as a factor limiting the geographic distribution of plants or animals. Light does, however, play an important role in determining local distributions, especially in plants. Plants in general can be divided into two groups: shade-tolerant species and shade-intolerant ones. Shade-tolerant species have lower respiration rates (Table 4) and also lower growth rates (Table 5) than shade-intolerant species (Grime 1966). The metabolic rate of shade-tolerant seedlings is apparently lower than that of shade-intolerant seedlings. Plant species become adapted to live in a certain kind of habitat, and in this process evolve a series of characteristics which prevent them from occupying other habitats. Grime (1966) suggests that light may be one of the major components directing these adaptations (Table 6). Failure of seedlings in shaded situations is almost always associated with fungal attack, and part of adaptation to shade involves becoming resistant to fungal infections.

The ecological limitations of plants can often be attributed to adaptations to the light regime of their habitat. Grime (1965) has championed this

TABLE 4

Respiration[a] *of shade-tolerant and shade-intolerant trees in darkness at 25°C*

Shade-tolerant trees

Tsuga canadensis (eastern hemlock)	2.19	*Acer saccharum* (sugar maple)	1.80
Castanea mollissima (Chinese chestnut)	1.20	*Acer rubrum* (red maple)	2.12
Quercus rubra (northern red oak)	1.76	*Fagus grandifolia* (American beech)	2.58
Taxus brevifolia (Pacific yew)	1.17		

Shade-intolerant trees

Liriodendron tulipifera (tulip tree)	3.89	*Populus tremuloides* (quaking aspen)	4.17
Juglans nigra (black walnut)	2.70	*Betula lenta* (sweet birch)	3.62
Paulownia tomentosa	5.13	*Rhus copallina* (shining sumac)	6.62
Prunus serotina (black cherry)	4.80		

[a] Respiration was measured as the loss in dry weight of leaf discs for 12 hr (milligram dry weight lost per gram dry weight of leaf per hour).
SOURCE: After Grime (1966).

approach to plant ecology and illustrated it by several examples (Table 7). Not all ecological limitations in plants involve light, of course, and this approach can be generalized to cover nutrient limitations as well.

In dense stands of temperate forests, there is very little ground vegetation, whereas in open stands the ground vegetation is very well developed. These differences have usually been attributed to differences in the amount of light reaching the forest floor, but root competition for water or nutrients could also be involved. Trenching experiments can separate these effects, and Toumey and Kienholz (1931) describe such an experiment in the Yale Research Forest in New Hampshire. A plot 9 ft × 9 ft in a stand of white pine was surrounded by a trench 3 ft deep and 1 ft wide. All soil was removed from this trench and all roots cut in 1922; adjacent control plots were not disturbed. Trenching was repeated in 1924, 1926, and 1928. There was an immediate response to trenching and the consequent removal of root competition. The vegetation on the trenched plot became more luxuriant and new species appeared. Toumey and Kienholz reported the differences that had occurred by 1930:

	Trenched plot	Untrenched control
No. trees on plots		
White pine (*Pinus strobus*)	26	6
Eastern hemlock (*Tsuga canadensis*)	11	3
No. herbaceous plants on plots		
White violet (*Viola blanda*)	764	39
Blackberry (*Rubus hispidus*)	357	18
Five-finger (*Potentilla canadensis*)	279	12
Percent total vegetative cover	80.0	8.1
Average height of small trees (in.)		
Hemlock	37.7	2.6
White pine	14.2	2.6

TABLE 5

Relative growth rates of shade-tolerant and shade-intolerant tree seedlings grown in full sunlight[a]

	Relative growth rates (mg/g/hr)
Shade-tolerant tree seedlings	
Tsuga canadensis (eastern hemlock)	2.93
Castanea mollissima (Chinese chestnut)	1.78
Quercus rubra (northern red oak)	0.61
Acer saccharum (sugar maple)	0.55
Shade-intolerant tree seedlings	
Betula populifolia (gray birch)	4.36
Betula lenta (sweet birch)	4.54
Rhus glabra (smooth sumac)	2.78
Paulownia tomentosa	6.58

[a] Each estimate is the mean of five replicates, taken over a 5-day period in June 1964 at New Haven, Connecticut. Plants were grown on diluted Arnon solution in sand culture under long days in sunny weather.

SOURCE: After Grime (1966).

TABLE 6

Adaptations of seedlings in five types of habitat to show the source of possible conflicting selection pressures on seven seedling characteristics

Habitat type	Adaptative features of seedlings
1. Dry unproductive site	a. Numerous small seeds b. Low stature c. Compact shoot with heavy mutual shading d. Vertical laminae
2. Recently cleared moist productive site	a. Numerous small seeds b. Tall stature c. Large leaf area with minimal mutual shading d. Horizontal laminae e. Potential for high rates in photosynthesis and associated growth processes f. Rapid extension growth on shading
3. Grassland	a. Large seeds b. Tall stature c. Rapid extension growth on shading
4. Open woodland	a. Large leaf area with minimal mutual shading b. Potential for high rates in photosynthesis and associated growth processes c. Tall stature d. Horizontal laminae e. Rapid extension growth on shading
5. Dense woodland	a. Resistance to fungal attack b. Low respiration rate c. Horizontal laminae d. Limited extension growth in response to shading

SOURCE: After Grime (1966).

Thus root competition may have important consequences for the establishment of seedlings under forest stands.

These results on seedling establishment must not be extrapolated to the mature tree stage without further investigation. Lutz (1945) examined the trenched plot of Toumey and Kienholz 21 years after it had been established. By this time roots had grown back through the trench and into the study plot. Of the 26 white pine seedlings that had become established on the trenched plot, none were alive in 1943. All 11 hemlock seedlings had survived. Lutz suggests that radiation was too low for the shade-intolerant white pine and that only shade-tolerant hemlock seedlings could continue to grow with both root competition for water and reduced light levels.

Seedlings of pine often occur along the margins of forests in the Piedmont of North Carolina but do not occur within the woods. This failure of pine seedlings under the forest canopy was first attributed to shade intolerance, but trenched-plot experiments have suggested that root competition for water

TABLE 7

Examples of ecological limitations in plants and the suggested adaptive reasons

Species Geographical location Habitat	Ecological limitation	Probable basis	Suggested consequence in field	Causal adaptation	Suggested role of adaptation in field
Tsuga canadensis (eastern hemlock, seedling phase) N.E. United States Floor of closed forest	Slow growth rate under conditions of ample water, nutrients, and light	Low metabolic rate	Slow root penetration leading to drought failure in dry situations	Selection for low respiration losses over long periods of inadequate light	Allows persistence of seedling under dense forest shade
Ailanthus altissima (tree-of-heaven, seedling phase) N.E. United States Moist, productive, unshaded situations	Rapid failure in deep shade	Large respiration losses in shade	Failure in deep shade of closed forest	Selection for high growth rate on productive sites	Allows rapid exploitation of cleared ground and shade avoidance by rapid growth in height
Deschampsia flexuosa (common hair grass) Denmark Highly acidic grassland and heath	Iron chlorosis on nutrient solutions and soils of high pH	Insufficient iron reaching leaves	Failure on calcareous soils	Selection for low rate of absorption or translocation of iron and other toxic metals from acid soils	Prevents accumulation of heavy metals in toxic concentrations from acid soils

SOURCE: After Grime (1965).

might be involved. Korstian and Coile (1938) studied a set of seven trenched plots in North Carolina and showed that soil of trenched plots contained more moisture than did corresponding control plots. When soil moisture levels of control plots fell to critical lows during droughts, there was still adequate moisture in trenched plots. This caused a great change in the vegetation of these trenched sites.

Oosting and Kramer (1946) measured available soil water along the edges of forests and in the forest interior and found no differences. They attributed the successful pine reproduction at the forest edge to increased light intensity, and concluded that light was more significant than soil moisture in controlling the distribution of pine under forest stands. They criticized trenched-plot experiments because these experiments were not carried on for a sufficiently long time; the establishment of shade-intolerant tree seedlings does not mean that they will survive to maturity.

Why do pine seedlings not become established under forest stands where hardwood seedlings thrive? Kramer and Decker (1944) compared the rate of photosynthesis of seedlings under various light conditions. Oak seedlings showed higher rates of photosynthesis under all light conditions (Figure 39). Photosynthesis of loblolly pine increased with light intensity up to the highest light intensity (approximately full sun), whereas that of red oak reached a maximum at one-third full sunlight. Kozlowski (1949) repeated these observations and found that oak seedlings had larger and more rapidly growing root systems than pine and were able to absorb water better as the soil became dry. Thus a combined effect of low light intensity and low soil moisture under forest stands causes pine seedlings to die and oak seedlings to survive.

One experimental way of separating the effects of shade and low soil moisture is to supply additional water to shaded seedlings. Moore (1926) artificially supplied water to coniferous tree seedlings in Maine and found that in shaded plots the addition of water did not alleviate the adverse effects of heavy shade on the forest floor for shade-intolerant seedlings.

The same principles can be applied to rooted aquatic plants that grow at different water depths. The attenuation of light in a water column may limit the local distribution of aquatic plants in freshwater and marine situations.

In animals light is chiefly important in relation to behavior and also as a stimulus for those mechanisms which regulate life cycles and keep them in step with the seasons. There is an immense literature on *photoperiodism*— the way day length determines the breeding seasons of animals as well as plants. For example, one can bring some birds into breeding condition in

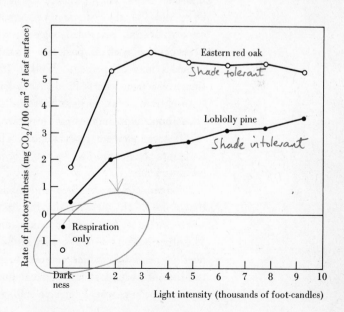

FIGURE 39

Photosynthesis of tree seedlings for 1-hr periods at various light intensities with temperature maintained at approximately 30°C. (After Kramer and Decker 1944.)

midwinter simply by increasing day length artificially (Wolfson 1964). Other examples of photoperiodism occur in plants. A *short-day plant* flowers when the day length is less than a certain critical length. A *long-day plant* flowers after a certain critical day length is exceeded. In both cases the critical day length differs from species to species. *Day-neutral plants* flower after a period of vegetative growth, regardless of photoperiod. Experimental work has shown that flowering in plants is a response to the *dark* period rather than to the *light* period (Devlin 1969, p. 375).

SOIL STRUCTURE AND NUTRIENTS

The structure and nutrient content of the soil is important, particularly for plants. There are intricate connections among climate, soil, and vegetation which make it difficult to separate cause and effect with regard to plant distribution. The soil is affected by the vegetation that grows on it, and it, in turn, can affect the nature of the vegetation. Most plant species are tolerant of a broad range of soil types, and consequently soil factors are not a major limitation to plant distribution.

Some of the best examples of soil effects on the distribution of plants are from soils that develop on unusual geological formations. One example is the *serpentine soils* which occur in scattered areas all over the world. These serpentine areas have many features in common (Whittaker 1954): (1) They are sterile and unproductive for farming or forestry; (2) they possess unusual floras, characterized by narrowly endemic species found nowhere else; and (3) they support vegetation that is strikingly different from that on normal soils. Serpentine vegetation is often stunted.

Serpentine rock is basically a magnesium iron silicate, but many other minerals may be present (Walker 1954). Plants that grow well on serpentine areas must, first of all, be tolerant of low calcium levels in the soil. In addition, some serpentine soils have high concentrations of nickel and chromium, high magnesium, low nitrogen and phosphorus, and low amounts of the trace element molybdenum. These soil characteristics are often lethal to plants, but some species have become adapted to this peculiar array of soil nutrients.

Emmenanthe penduliflora and *Emmenanthe rosea* are two California herbs that grow in chaparral areas, the first species being unknown on serpentine, whereas the second species occurs only on serpentine soils (Tadros 1957). The distributions of these two herbs thus present two questions: (1) Why does *E. penduliflora* not colonize serpentine areas? (2) Why does *E. rosea* not live in normal soils? Tadros showed that seedlings of *E. rosea*, the serpentine species, would survive and grow on sterilized garden soil but died on unsterilized soil, and he suggested that a soil microbe was responsible for keeping this herb confined to serpentine soils. *Emmenanthe penduliflora* presumably does not invade serpentine areas because of the chemistry of the soil. Wicklow (1966) questioned this interpretation; he notes that fire is necessary for these herbs to become established and indicates that *E. penduliflora* may occur in sparse numbers on serpentine areas.

Bogs are another example of nitrogen-deficient environments, and plants growing in these habitats must be adapted to low levels of nitrogen. Red maple (*Acer rubrum*) develops to maturity in the late stages of bog development in the northeastern United States but never develops beyond the seedling stage on open portions of the *Sphagnum* moss mat of the bog. Temperatures are lower on the *Sphagnum* mat compared with those in the nearby spruce–fir forest, and the frost-free season is very short in the open bog. Red maple does not seem to be affected by these temperature conditions, however. Germination is good on the open *Sphagnum* mat, but growth is poor because the bog is deficient in nitrogen and phosphorus (Moizuk and Livingston 1966). Most seedlings in the bog die after 1 or 2 years. Red maple seedlings will grow well on *Sphagnum* if supplemented with these limiting soil nutrients:

| Original weight (g) | Dry weight of 1-year-old seedlings after 2 months grown on *Sphagnum* in nutrient culture solutions containing: | | | | |
	H₂O only	P and K but no N	N and K but no P	N and P but no K	N and P and K
0.038	0.077	0.071	0.077	0.490	0.423

Potassium was not a limiting soil nutrient.

Roots of alder (*Alnus glutinosa*) have nodules containing bacteria that fix atmospheric nitrogen (Ferguson and Bond 1953). Thus alders can grow in nitrogen-deficient soils. The alder can tolerate much lower pH levels in the soil than can the nodule organisms; plants grew well at pH 4.2 if supplied with nitrate nitrogen, but nodules would not form at this highly acid pH.

The bog myrtle *Myrica gale* also has root nodules that are able to fix nitrogen. This plant occurs in Scotland on large areas of wet, acid, peat soils, over a soil pH range of 3.7 to 4.8. These bog and moorland soils are typically low in available nitrogen but are covered with plants containing nitrogen obtained from some source. Bond (1951) suggested that *M. gale* might fix nitrogen in bog soils and thereby serve as one source of this scarce nutrient for the other plants in the bog.

Patches of yellow pines (*Pinus ponderosa* and *Pinus jeffreyi*) occur in the western Great Basin of Nevada and California, scattered in the sagebrush and pinyon–juniper vegetation. These patches contain pines but almost no herbaceous vegetation or shrubs (Figure 40). Billings (1950) found that these unusual stands occurred on a yellow soil that contrasts sharply with the brownish soil of the surrounding desert. The yellow soils are derived from highly-weathered volcanic rocks and are strongly acid and deficient in phosphorus and nitrogen. Sagebrush and its associated plants will not grow on these yellow soils because of these mineral deficiencies and the low pH.

Bristlecone pines (*Pinus aristata*) are subalpine trees of the southwestern United States, and some of these trees are more than 4000 years old, the oldest living organisms. Wright and Mooney (1965) studied the distribution of this pine in the White Mountains of California and suggested that moisture balance was an important limiting factor which interacted with the soil type. Three types of soils occurred in this zone, with the following characteristics:

	Soils derived from:		
	Dolomite	**Sandstone**	**Granite**
Soil moisture	Highest	High	Lowest
pH	Alkaline	Slightly acidic	More acidic
Soil nutrients	Very low	Low	Low
Soil temperature	Low	Higher	Higher
Pinus aristata % cover	15.4	3.6	1.8
Artemisia tridentata (sagebrush) % cover	0.6	11.1	16.6

The distribution of bristlecone pine is complementary to that of sagebrush. Bristlecone pine is well developed on dolomitic soils and is favored by north-facing slopes. Sagebrush is best developed on granitic or sandstone soils, particularly on south-facing slopes, and is more drought resistant. Bristlecone pine does best on dolomitic soils because of the greater soil moisture, tolerance of very poor nutrient availability, and lack of competition by sagebrush and other plants. All the oldest bristlecone pines known have been found growing on dolomite under very adverse conditions.

Soil or substrate structure may be an important variable determining local distributions of aquatic invertebrates. This is particularly evident in marine habitats in the different fauna of rocky shores, sand flats, and mud flats (Ricketts and Calvin 1968). Often, however, marine species do not occur everywhere in a given habitat, and this raises the question of what restricts local distributions. Some cases are known in which the particle size of the substrate is critical.

FIGURE 40

*Stands of yellow pines on altered andesite (left) surrounded by
pinyon–juniper vegetation* (Pinus monophylla *and* Juniperus
utahensis *on unaltered andesite. Note the lack of shrubs and herbs
on the altered soils at the left compared with abundant ground
cover of low shrubs, grasses, and forbs on the unaltered soils at the
right. Altered soils are acid and deficient in phosphorus and nitrogen.
Geiger Grade area, Virginia Mountains, 12 miles southeast of
Reno, Nevada.* [*Photograph courtesy of W. D. Billings (1950),
with permission of* Ecology.]

The amphipod *Pectenogammarus planicrurus* has a very restricted distribution and inhabits shingle beaches around the British coast. Maximum
populations occur where the median diameter of beach particles is about
4 mm. In artificial substrates the amphipods show a marked preference for
particles retained by a 3.35-mm sieve, in comparison with larger or smaller
grain sizes. Morgan (1970) suggests that this crustacean is restricted to
habitats in which it can move rapidly from space to space between particles in the substrate; too small a space prevents movement and burrowing, and too large a space allows the animals to be washed out of the
substrate by tidal action. The largest diameter of adults averages 1.2 mm, of
juveniles 0.7 mm. The packing of substrate is such that the size of the
"throats" between the particles in the substrate is as follows:

| Sieve-mesh | Critical maximum diameter (mm) for animal passing through substrate voids | |
diameter (mm)	Tight packing of substrate	Loose packing of substrate
6.35	1.0	2.6
3.35	0.5	1.4
2.06	0.3	0.9
1.40	0.2	0.6

Adults can move in the voids between particles of substrate of the 6.35-mm and 3.35-mm grades, and juveniles should be able to move through all but the finest substrate tested (1.40 mm). Morgan (1970) noted a high mortality among adults that enter the 2.06-mm and 1.40-mm substrates, in which the space between substrate particles is too small.

The archiannelid *Protodrilus symbioticus* has a preference for a grain size from 200 to 300 μ. Although its substrate preference excludes this marine worm from certain sandy beaches, not all areas with this grain size are occupied. Gray (1966) showed that if one experimentally altered the sand from natural habitats by treating it with acid or alcohol, drying it, or heating it, the sand was no longer attractive to *P. symbioticus*. An innoculation of naturally-occurring sand bacteria restored the attractiveness of the substrate completely. Gray concluded that the distribution of *Protodrilus* within narrow zones of the beach is related to a surface film produced by certain bacteria and adsorbed on to the sand-grain surfaces.

Caddisfly larvae in freshwater streams construct cases of leaves, sticks, or sand grains and so can live only in those places where the necessary materials can be found. Cummins (1964) showed that two caddisflies in Michigan were habitat segregated in the late larval stages because one species (*Pycnopsyche lepida*) built its case of sand grains and lived on gravel substrates with an intermediate current velocity and the second species (*Pycnopsyche guttifer*) built its case of sticks and lived in silty areas along the stream margin. Substrate particle size may thus be an important environmental factor for bottom-dwelling forms.

WATER CHEMISTRY, pH, AND SALINITY

Marine and freshwater organisms may be affected in their distribution by the chemistry of the waters in which they live. Salinity in the open ocean is not variable and consequently does not limit the marine planktonic organisms, but near shores and in estuaries the dilution of seawater by freshwater runoff may reduce salinity to critical levels.

Many freshwater ecologists have studied water chemistry in the hope of explaining distributional problems and in most cases have been unsuccessful (Macan 1963, p. 254). Some associations can be described, but they cannot always be interpreted.

Sessile rotifers live attached to a solid substrate for most of their lives, and Edmondson (1944) studied the distribution of these rotifers in 194 localities of the northeastern United States and Wisconsin. Certain rotifers occurred in only some of the lakes Edmondson studied. Of the various factors of water chemistry studied, pH and bicarbonate seemed most important (Figure 41). Edmondson found eight species limited with reference to pH, not bicarbonate; six species limited with reference to bicarbonate, not pH; and three species limited with reference to both pH and bicarbonate. This relationship between water chemistry and distribution may be an indirect one: Water chemistry may limit substrate plant distribution, and sessile rotifers may be substrate specific. However, Edmondson found only three species of rotifers that were highly selective to substrate.

Calcium is probably the most variable ion in most freshwater lakes and streams. Soft waters may contain less than 1 mg/liter of calcium; hard waters may contain up to 100 mg/liter. Attempts have been made in many cases to relate distributions to calcium levels in fresh water.

Freshwater sponges are sensitive to water chemistry. Jewell (1939) showed that the calcium bicarbonate content of the water was a critical factor restricting distributions (Figure 42). Five of six species of sponges died when placed in waters whose calcium content was different from those where they normally occurred. One species (*Ephydatia everetti*) of the six

FIGURE 41

Distribution of the sessile rotifer Beauchampia crucigera *with reference to pH and bicarbonate concentration. Localities in which* Beauchampia *occurred are indicated by open circles and the area in which they lie is outlined by a solid line. For comparison, the lakes containing* Collotheca corynetis *are represented by triangles. The shaded area represents the range of values for all lakes studied and thus the potential range of occurrence. (After Edmondson 1944.)*

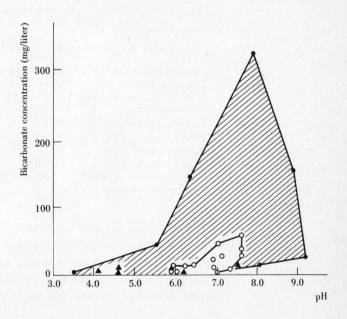

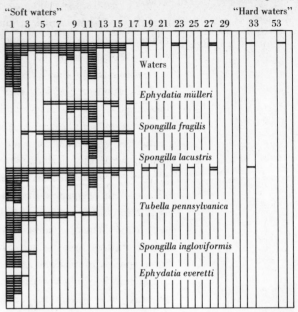

FIGURE 42

Occurrence of freshwater sponges in waters of various calcium concentrations in Wisconsin. Each horizontal line represents a lake or stream from which sponges were collected. The upper curve shows the frequency of sponge-bearing waters of the various concentrations of calcium. The remaining curves show the number of lakes or streams of each calcium content from which each of the species was collected. (After Jewell 1939.)

studied experimentally was able to grow over a much broader range of alkalinity (to pH 7.7) than that in which it occurred in nature (pH 5.0 to 6.6).

Reynoldson (1958) surveyed the distribution of planarians in British lakes and showed that the species composition could be related to the calcium content of the water, which in turn was correlated with the productivity of the lake:

Characteristic triclad flatworm species	Calcium range (mg/liter)	Lake productivity	No. exceptions
Phagocata vitta	≤2.4	Very low	0
Polycelis nigra alone	≤5.0	Low	4 of 31 lakes
Polycelis nigra, P. hepta, P. tenuis, and *P. felina*	>5.0	Intermediate	1 of 33 lakes
Polycelis spp. and *Dugesia polychroa* and/or *Dendrocoelum lacteum*	>10.0	High	1 of 44 lakes

Macan (1963, p. 250) emphasizes this point—that calcium may operate indirectly through its correlation with productivity and the amount of organic matter decomposing in a lake.

Rooted aquatic plants may be affected both by the substratum in which they grow and by the lake water in which they are immersed. Spence

(1967) suggests that the water chemistry of a lake controls whether or not aquatic plant species will grow there. In Sweden three species of water plants of the genus *Myriophyllum* inhabit waters of different ranges of chemical composition. *Myriophyllum spicatum* and *Myriophyllum verticillatum* both extend into waters having more calcium than one finds in waters with *Myriophyllum alterniflorum* (Figure 43). Hutchinson (1970) suggested that *M. spicatum* may be able to use the bicarbonate ion as a source of carbon in photosynthesis, whereas *M. verticillatum* cannot. In northern Sweden, where *M. verticillatum* does not occur, *M. spicatum* is found in soft-water lakes as well as hard-water lakes.

Soil pH was believed to be a primary factor influencing plant distribution in the early days of plant ecology. Less significance is now attached to it. Some plants have strict pH requirements; others are tolerant. For plants with strict pH requirements, the pH itself may not be important but a related soil nutrient. Stone (1944) could find no relationship between soil pH and the distribution of 10 herbaceous species in Ohio. Ten tree species were also distributed independently of soil pH; only hemlock (*Tsuga canadensis*) occurred in a restricted range of acid pH, and this is apparently caused by the acidity of its needles.

Earthworms are scarce in very acid soils, and it is not known whether this represents a fundamental pH limitation or is caused by a nutritional lack in acid soils. Satchell (1955) showed that some species of British earthworms were sensitive to pH and that extreme soil acidities were more

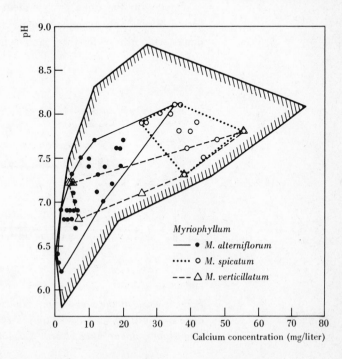

FIGURE 43

Occurrences of the three species of Myriophyllum *in the lakes of central Sweden in relation to calcium concentration and pH, with the shaded envelope enclosing the points for all the lakes studied in the region. (After Hutchinson 1970.)*

important in limiting the distribution of earthworms than deficiencies in calcium supply.

Larvae of many marine invertebrates will settle on a very restricted range of surfaces, and these settlement preferences may affect local distributions. One example is the larvae of the American oyster, *Crassostrea virginica*, which settle and attach gregariously, possibly influenced both by a chemical released by adult oysters in the vicinity and by the surface structure of old oyster shells on which they settle (Crisp 1967). Larvae would not settle on shells that had the outer protein layer destroyed by chemical treatment.

Wind-borne salt determines the distribution of dune plants on the North Carolina banks. Sea oats (*Uniola paniculata*) predominate on the exposed side of the foredune and at the crest of the rear dune, and *Andropogon littoralis*, another dune grass, is best developed in protected areas (Figure 44). The areas dominated by sea oats match the areas exposed to high atmospheric salt, and Oosting and Billings (1942) showed that *Andropogon* was seriously injured by daily spraying with seawater, while *Uniola* was only slightly affected. The distribution of these two species can therefore be explained partly by their tolerance to wind-borne salt.

Wagner (1964) transplanted sea oats (*Uniola*) to an area in the older, established dunes and showed that it did not survive there, possibly because of root competition with the established pine trees, shrubs, and other grasses. In contrast to *Uniola*, the loblolly pine is very sensitive to salt spray and will not grow near the coast in the spray zone (Wells and Shunk 1938).

Changes in the dune environment can affect these dune plants in unexpected ways. For example, Boyce (1954) fertilized four quadrats in the dunes with nitrate fertilizer and found that high nitrogen levels decreased

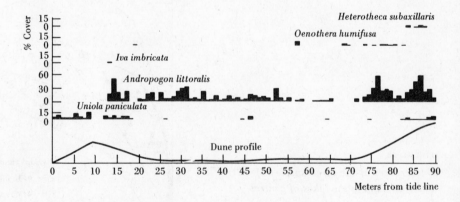

FIGURE 44

Percent cover of the major dune plants in a belt transect over the dune profile from spring tide line to the crest of the hind dune, New Dunes, Bogue Bank, North Carolina. (After Wagner 1964.)

tolerance to salt spray. All the plants that received nitrogen were killed or severely injured by salt spray, whereas control plots with very low nitrogen were not injured. Thus, if available nitrogen were increased in the sandy dune soils, a different pattern of plant distribution would occur.

Some attempts to relate distributions to chemical factors have not been very successful. Macan (1963, p. 256) studied the distribution of snails in small English lakes. The lakes were classified on the basis of total ion content and independently on the basis of snails found in them. An attempt was then made to correlate the distribution of the snails with the water chemistry. The analysis showed some correlation with calcium and total ionic content of the water, but there were so many exceptions that the effort was deemed a failure. Macan states that these poor correlations between water chemistry and snail distributions could be due to three things:

1 There is no correlation in reality, a possibility not to be admitted except as the last resort.

2 The chemist has supplied the wrong data. There are about 92 inorganic elements to study but usually concentrations of only 6 are measured; or it may be the organic compounds that are important.

3 The chemist has supplied the right data but the biologist does not know how to use them. Should we be looking for an excess of some substance or a deficiency of something else? Also there may be complicated interactions between these elements which would mask any simple relationships.

WATER CURRENTS, OXYGEN, AND FIRE

Many coastal marine invertebrates have a relatively sedentary adult phase and a planktonic larval phase. Such species are obviously dependent on ocean currents to bring the developed larval stages in the plankton back into coastal areas suitable for the adult. Efford (1970) discusses this problem for the sand crab (*Emerita analoga*) on the Pacific Coast of North America. Adult sand crabs live on exposed sandy beaches from Kodiak Island in Alaska to Magdalena Bay, Baja California; they also occur on the temperate coast of South America from Peru to the Strait of Magellan. From about southern Oregon to central Baja California, there is a countercurrent system in the ocean with the inshore Davidson Current flowing north and the offshore California Current moving south (Figure 45). Larvae released into the plankton in this area can drift from one current to another in side eddies and consequently remain relatively close to their point of origin for the approximately 4 months of larval life in the plankton. In this area *Emerita* is abundant. At the southern limits of its range in Baja California, the California Current turns sharply westward and all larvae present in this water are lost. Efford points out that this southern limit coincides

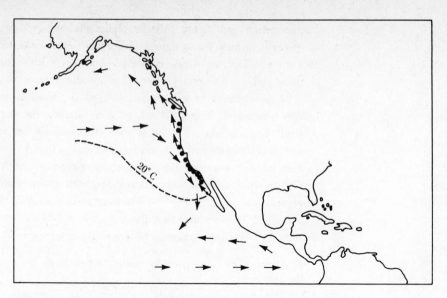

FIGURE 45

Distribution of the sand crab Emerita analoga *in North America and the surface currents of the North Pacific. Dashed line marks approximate position of average annual sea-surface temperature of 20°C. (After Efford 1969.)*

with the average sea-surface-temperature isotherm of 20°C, but this temperature correlation is spurious and current pattern is the important factor. From southern Oregon to northern Washington and Vancouver Island, *Emerita* populations are sustained only by immigration from the south, since all currents flow north. Some suitable beaches are not occupied, and populations become more and more isolated as one goes north into Alaska. Larvae produced from these northern populations can only drift farther north and then west in the Gulf of Alaska, and all these larvae must die.

Oxygen may restrict the local distribution of some species in freshwater lakes. During the summer some productive lakes develop stagnant basins of relatively cool bottom water low in oxygen. This oxygen-deficient environment can only be colonized by species that can survive anaerobically. Some midge larvae (chironomids) are abundant in these stagnant waters and show specialized adaptations for oxygen deficiency. For example, the larvae of chironomids living in streams consume more oxygen than do closely related chironomids living in lakes. Lake species of chironomids can withstand long periods of anaerobic conditions, while stream species die quickly without oxygen (Figure 46). Stream and lake chironomids have evolved along two independent adaptive lines and consequently cannot invade each other's habitat (Walshe 1948).

Fire has been the most important causative factor in the natural establishment of jack pine (*Pinus banksiana*). This pine has serotinous cones, which do not open spontaneously after maturation but remain sealed by resin on the cone scales. This resin is melted at cone temperatures above 140°F. Beaufait (1960) showed that jack pine cones could withstand temperatures up to 700°F for 60 seconds before burning and retain viable seeds. Forest fires thus open cones and are followed by large-scale establishment of jack pine seedlings.

The forest–prairie boundary in North America used to extend from Alberta to Texas in a most complex and interesting transition (Figure 47). This boundary was remarkably abrupt. When settlers began to colonize the Great Plains, one could pass from closed forest to grassland in a few yards. Numerous tongues of forest extended far out into the grassland along river valleys, and isolated patches of prairie existed as far east as Indiana and Ohio. What prevented deciduous trees from colonizing the prairies?

Two hypotheses can be used to explain why the prairies of North America are treeless: (1) The areas are deficient in precipitation; (2) fire has destroyed the trees and they are not able to return. Several points argue in favor of the fire hypothesis. Early explorers and settlers almost without exception commented on the extensive prairie fires. Woodlands occurred on escarpments and other topographic breaks throughout the grassland area in North America (Wells 1965). Early settlers did not build houses beyond the shelter of these wooded escarpments until plowing had stopped the autumn prairie fires (Sauer 1969). These fires may have been set by Indians, but some were caused by lightning.

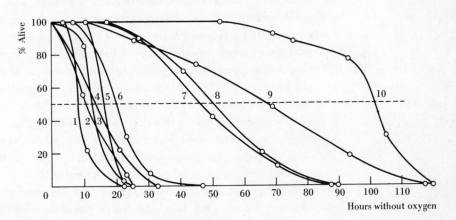

FIGURE 46

Duration of life under anaerobic conditions of various chironomid larvae. Species 1 to 6 are stream dwellers, and species 7 to 10 live in lakes and stagnant waters. (After Walshe 1948.)

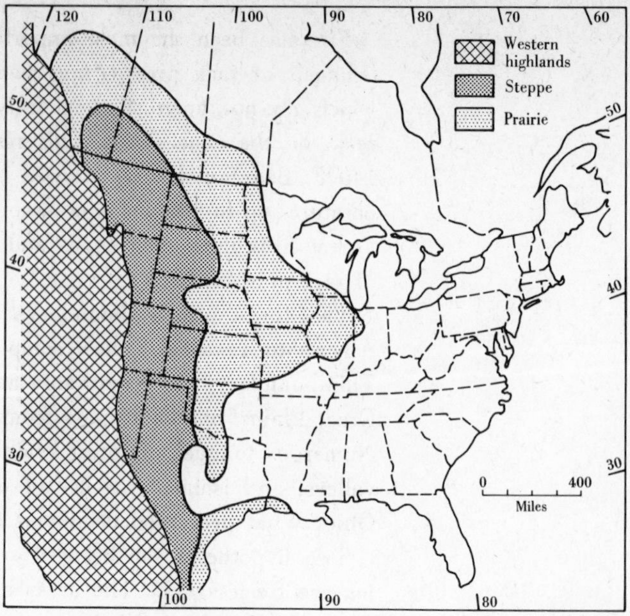

FIGURE 47

Grassland of North America east of the Rocky Mountains. Some investigators have defined a mixed tall grass–short grass prairie region in the gradient zone between the tall-grass prairie and the short-grass steppe. (After Borchert 1950.)

The northern and eastern parts of the Ozark Highlands in Missouri were largely grassland with open groves of trees, according to historical records from the seventeenth century (Beilmann and Brenner 1951). Areas that are now densely forested were open habitats of mixed forest and prairie as recently as 100 to 150 years ago. Beilmann and Brenner suggest that fire was the principal agent responsible for these conditions, but they also indicate a change toward a wetter climate in this area.

Grasslands in southern Texas have apparently decreased while woody vegetation has increased. Johnston (1963) emphasized that this involved a change in relative proportions of these plants and that mesquite (*Prosopis glandulosa*) was already present in small numbers in these grasslands over 100 years ago. The change has been from mesquite prairie to mesquite brush and not an invasion of mesquite from distant areas. Control of fires was suggested to explain this shift toward woody plants.

The alternative view, that climate set the prairie–forest boundary, is difficult to sustain for the eastern, moist edge of the prairie. Prairie areas in Illinois and Indiana by almost any criterion have a climate suitable for forest development (Eyre 1963, p. 113). Some workers have suggested that native grasses of the tall-grass prairie could successfully resist invasion by trees indefinitely. Tree-root systems cannot compete with grasses for soil moisture, and consequently the tree seedlings die (Pearson 1936). This suggests that once a prairie becomes established, it will maintain itself without fire. Some contrary evidence is available for Ponderosa pine in the western part of North Dakota. In this area Potter and Green (1964) showed that this pine is successfully invading grasslands that are protected from fire. Ponderosa pine is a western pine and consequently could not be an invader on the eastern side of the prairie.

Rather extensive areas (100 sq. km) of forest have been established in Nebraska by planting native trees, such as Ponderosa pine, that are drought adapted (Wells 1965). Unfortunately these observations are equivocal because the seedlings were planted by man, and the alternative view is that grasses prevent the *establishment* of trees from seed.

Weaver (1968, p. 112) interprets the prairie–forest boundary in climatic terms and suggests that trees survive well in the grasslands only in wet years and die back in years of drought. Weaver estimated that 50 to 60% of the trees in Nebraska and Kansas died during the drought of the 1930s.

The extension of the prairie into the midwestern United States, the "prairie peninsula," has been mapped and analyzed in detail by Transeau (1935). He points out that these eastern prairies existed in both upland and lowland sites on both poorly drained and well-drained soils and that all the same grasses dominated these prairies from Ohio west to Iowa. Transeau suggests that climatic differences explain the grassland–forest boundary, precipitation differences being critical. Tall prairie grasses, once established, exclude tree seedlings both by shadowing and by better water utilization in droughts. Fire as an ecological factor was not critical, according to Transeau. In forest climates fire retards tree development and may result in scrub forest, but it does not result in prairie. In a prairie climate fire will help to maintain the prairie and perhaps rarely to enlarge it.

The grassland climate is distinctive, principally because of its precipitation (Borchert 1950). The short-grass steppe receives much less summer rainfall than the eastern tall-grass prairie. Winter snow and rainfall are low. Summer rainfall is very variable in the prairie areas, and summer droughts are much more frequent than in adjacent forested regions (Figure 48). A hot dry airflow in summer from the eastern base of the Rocky Mountains accompanies severe drought years and accelerates the effects of lack of moisture. During most winters and the summers of drought years, the prairie peninsula thus has a climate more like that of the short-grass steppe than like that of the eastern deciduous forests. The observed boundaries of the grassland thus coincide with climatic gradients. As climate changes, the prairie boundary should also change. Borchert suggests that fire is overrated as a cause of the prairie boundary because "... the Grassland climates favor fire, just as they favor grass whether there are fires or not" (p. 39).

Curtis (1959, p. 302) reviewed all the evidence and concluded that climatic limitations associated with drought were the principal cause of the prairies of North America. Toward the wetter, eastern border of the prairies,

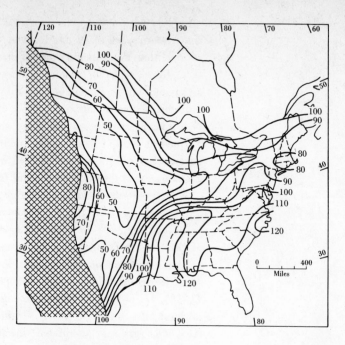

FIGURE 48

Percentage of normal rainfall in average July of major drought years. Note the wedge-shaped extension of the severe drought area into northern Illinois and Indiana. (After Borchert 1950.)

both grasses and trees could survive, and the presence or absence of fire was the main factor shifting the boundary, with fire favoring grasses and repressing trees.

SUMMARY

Many physical and chemical factors, in addition to temperature and moisture, can limit the distributions of plants and animals. Most of these cases involve details of local distributions rather than continental or worldwide distributions. Often they are concerned with the factors involved in habitat selection.

Light may determine the local distribution of shade-intolerant plants, but for animals light is primarily used as a behavioral stimulus. Soil or substrate structure can be important for plants growing on extreme soil types, and the nutrient content of the soil may also affect local distributions. Substrate structure is important for marine invertebrates that attach to solid substrates or burrow into soft sand or mud. Particle size of sediments may also affect freshwater bottom dwellers. Water chemistry is relatively constant in the sea but highly variable in fresh waters. Numerous attempts to relate freshwater distributions to water chemistry have led to relatively few successes, however. Wind-blown salt from the ocean may affect plants growing in coastal areas. Many coastal marine invertebrates have pelagic larval phases and are dependent on ocean currents to carry mature larvae into suitable coastal areas. Oxygen may be deficient in some local lake and pond environments, but this is unusual. Fire may affect plant distributions, and some species have special adaptations to withstand regular fires. The forest–prairie boundary in North America may have been influenced by fire, but soil drought was also a critical factor.

SELECTED REFERENCES

DAUBENMIRE, R. F. 1947. *Plants and Environment*. Chap. 5, The Light Factor; Chap. 8, The Fire Factor. Wiley, New York.

EYRE, S. R. 1963. *Vegetation and Soils: A World Picture*. Aldine, Chicago.

GRIME, J. P. 1965. Comparative experiments as a key to the ecology of flowering plants. *Ecology* 46:513–515.

GRIME, J. P. 1966. Shade avoidance and shade tolerance in flowering plants, pp. 187–207 in *Light as an Ecological Factor*, ed. by R. Bainbridge, G. C. Evans, and O. Rackham. Blackwell, Oxford.

MACAN, T. T. 1963. *Freshwater Ecology*. Chap. 9, Oxygen; Chap. 10, Salinity; Chap. 11, Calcium; Chap. 12, Other Chemical Factors. Longmans, London.

MOORE, H. B. 1958. *Marine Ecology*. Chap. 2, Physical Environmental Factors; Chap. 3, Chemical Environmental Factors. Wiley, New York.

QUESTIONS AND PROBLEMS

1 Ford (1967, p. 119) states: "Species can usually survive at the extreme edge of their range only by becoming stenoplastic and adapting themselves closely to some special type of habitat, one which may be very different from that which they normally occupy." Read this discussion in Ford (1967). Suggest a species that seems to fit this description, and try to determine the limiting factors.

2 Grime and Hodgson (1969, p. 68), in discussing why plants fail at the very edge of their distribution, state:

More typically however, fatalities are due to a complex of factors and in particular, the contribution of mineral nutritional factors remains obscure. Seedlings may persist for an indefinite period in a state of chronic nutrient deficiency and whilst it is often possible to recognize terminal phenomena, it is difficult to measure the extent to which plants may be predisposed to killing factors, by nutritional disorders.

Is this a serious problem in studying plant distributional problems?

3 Macan (1963, p. 243) points out that lakes which have a high concentration of salts but in proportions unlike those in the ocean contain a fauna that consists almost exclusively of animals of freshwater origin. Why should this be?

4 Many investigators attempt to identify the mechanisms controlling plant distributions and animal distributions by comparing the environments in which the species occurs with those from which it is excluded. Discuss this approach and its strengths and weaknesses.

5 Caves have very few species of animals and often the species have special adaptations for existence in the cave environment (Culver 1970, p. 463). What is the role of light in affecting the distributions of cave animals?

8 Complications: adaptation

From the theory of evolution, we know that species become adapted to their environments by a process of natural selection. This adaptation goes on within species as local populations adjust to local conditions. We have seen that some, and perhaps most, organisms cannot survive if they are transplanted outside their observed habitat range. This means that they have not become adapted to a biotic or abiotic limiting factor. On the face of it, this raises a curious problem: *Why has there not been more adaptation?* Two points may be kept in mind in considering this question: (1) We must distinguish adaptation toward biotic factors and abiotic factors. In the first case we have a variable approaching another variable; that is, evolution may occur in both biological systems in such a way that they neutralize each other. In the second case, we have a variable approaching a constant, a physical or chemical limitation. Some progress might be envisaged in this system. (2) Can species readily adapt to local environments, or are species genetically uniform over their geographic range? Perhaps genetic adaptation to local conditions is very difficult within a species. Only phenotypic adaptations may be possible because genetic adaptations lead to the formation of new species. We are led, then, to consider the genetic architecture of natural populations, and we wish to determine if species can extend their distribution by local adaptation to limiting environmental factors.

This problem in evolutionary ecology was recognized by Darwin, but the ecological implications of the theory of evolution were not evident until the early 1900s when a Swedish botanist, Göte Turesson, began looking at adaptations to local environmental conditions in plants. Turesson (1922) coined the word *ecotype* to describe genetic varieties within a single species. He recognized that much of ecology had been pursued as if hereditary diversity within species did not exist. In a series of publications he described some variation associated with climate and soil in a variety of plant species (Turesson 1925). The basic technique was to collect plants from a variety of areas and grow them together in field or laboratory plots in one site. The type of result he obtained in this early work can be illustrated with one example. *Plantago maritima* grows as a tall, robust plant in marshes along the coast of Sweden and also as a dwarf plant on exposed sea cliffs in the Faeroe Islands. When plants are grown side by side in an experimental garden this height difference is not as extreme but remains significant (Turesson 1930):

Plantago maritima from:	Mean height (cm) in experimental garden
Marsh population	*31.5*
Cliff population	*20.7*

Turesson described the study of ecotypes such as these as a new research field, *genecology*.

This transplant technique is an attempt to separate the *phenotypic* (environmental) and *genotypic* components of variation. Plants of the same species growing in such diverse environments as sea cliffs and marshes can be different in morphology and physiology in three ways: (1) All differences are phenotypic, and if seeds are transplanted from one situation to the other, they will respond exactly as the resident individuals; (2) all differences are genotypic, and if seeds are transplanted between areas, the mature plants will retain the form and the physiology typical of their original habitat; or (3) some combination of phenotypic and genotypic determination produces an intermediate result. In natural situations the third case is most usual. Many examples are now described, particularly in plants (Heslop-Harrison 1964).

One of the most intensively studied set of ecotypic races occurs in the perennial herb *Achillea* (yarrow), analyzed by Clausen, Keck, and Hiesey (1948) in a classical paper. Three very similar species of *Achillea* are

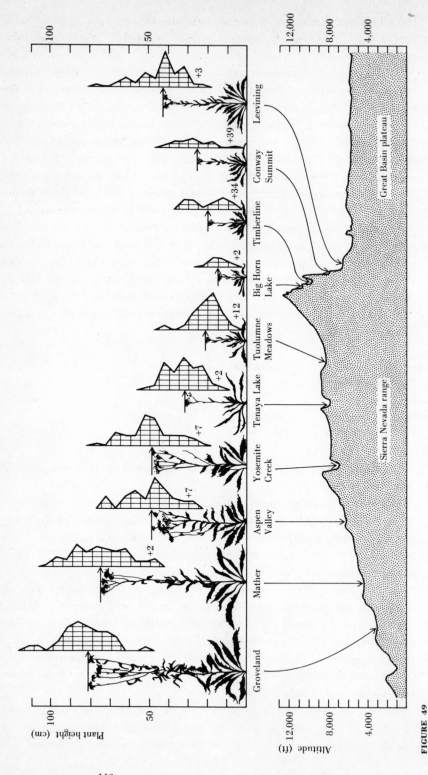

FIGURE 49

Representatives of populations of Achillea lanulosa as grown in a uniform garden at Stanford. These originated in the localities shown in the profile below of a transect across central California at approximately 38°N latitude. Altitudes are to the scale shown in feet. Horizontal distances are not to scale. The plants are herbarium specimens, each representing a population of approximately 60 individuals. The frequency diagrams show variation in height within each population; the horizontal lines separate class intervals of 5 cm according to the marginal scale, and the distance between vertical lines represents two individuals. The numbers to the right of some frequency diagrams indicate the nonflowering plants. The specimens represent plants of average height, and the arrows point to mean heights. (After Clausen, Keck, and Hiesey 1948.)

112

described, two from western North America and one from Europe. Clausen et al. (1948) studied the two North American species in detail. A maritime form of *Achillea borealis* lives in coastal areas of California as a low succulent evergreen plant that grows throughout the winter. Slightly farther inland there is an evergreen race that is similar but taller. A third race lives in the Pacific Coast Range, grows during the mild winter, and flowers quickly by April, becoming dormant during the hot, dry summer. In the Central Valley of California a giant race of *A. borealis* can be found which survives under high summer temperatures, a long growing season, and ample moisture.

In the Sierra Nevada, races of *Achillea lanulosa* occur. As one proceeds up in these mountains, winter temperature decreases below freezing, so winter dormancy is necessary and plants are smaller. On the eastern slope of the Sierra Nevada plants of *A. lanulosa* are late flowering and are adapted to the cold, arid climate. Clausen, Keck, and Hiesey collected seeds from a series of populations of *A. lanulosa* across California and raised plants in a greenhouse at Stanford, with the results shown in Figure 49. The major attributes of these races are maintained when grown under uniform conditions in the same place.

Clausen and his co-workers also raised *Achillea* in plots at Mather in the coniferous forest zone of the Sierra Nevada and at Timberline in the alpine zone. Table 8 gives some results of these transplant experiments for *A. lanu-*

TABLE 8

Growth and survival of ecotypes of A. lanulosa *grown in experimental plots at Stanford (100 ft elevation), Mather (4600 ft), and Timberline (10,000 ft) in California for 3 years*

Origin of plants[a]	Longest stems (cm)			Survival[b] (%)		
	Stanford	Mather	Timber-line	Stanford	Mather	Timber-line
Groveland	83.6	58.2	15.5	100	93	40
Mather	79.6	82.4	34.3	93	90	39
Aspen Valley	47.4	56.8	25.3	93	100	73
Yosemite Creek	42.6	56.2	30.1	97	97	90
Tenaya Lake	33.9	33.7	33.4	100	97	97
Tuolumne Meadows	24.5	32.7	28.4	90	97	93
Timberline	21.2	31.6	23.7	90	67	90
Big Horn Lake	15.4	19.5	23.6	83	67	91

[a] Origin of plants may be located in Figure 49.
[b] Based on samples of 30 plants (except Big Horn Lake, 12 plants).
SOURCE: After Clausen, Keck, and Hiesey (1948).

losa. Under the extreme conditions at Timberline, the Groveland and Mather ecotypes survived poorly. Transplants of *A. borealis* from the coastal region all died at Timberline.

Latitudinal races of *Achillea* also occur but have not been studied in detail. Figure 50 illustrates the magnitude of the difference that can occur between ecotypes of the same species and shows graphically how much the gene pool of a species can be altered by local adaptations to the environment.

Adaptations to climatic factors have been demonstrated in many species of plants. For example, orchard grass (*Dactylis glomerata*) grows in a variety of habitats. McKell, Perrier, and Stebbins (1960) compared the responses of two subspecies of this grass to increasing soil moisture stress. One subspecies (*lusitanica*), from coastal Portugal, lives in a mild climate; a second subspecies (*judaica*), from Israel, lives in a dry Mediterranean climate subject to summer drought. Transplanted grasses have variable survival, depending on the environment:

	Survival over first year (%)	
	lusitanica	*judaica*
Mild, coastal climate on fertile soil	75	45
Dry, inland climate on infertile soil	0	45

Soil moisture is used more rapidly by *lusitanica* than by *judaica* (Figure 51).

Cultivated varieties of orchard grass differ in their chances of survival when sown together. Charles (1961) showed that only 20% of seeds survived the first 2 months after sowing and only 10% survived the first year. This mortality fell unequally on different cultivated varieties, and one variety became dominant:

Time after sowing (months)	Composition of *D. glomerata* population in undisturbed stands (%)	
	Variety Danish	**Variety S 143**
March 0 (*start*)	50	50
August 5	73	27

The Danish variety is early flowering and tall growing; S 143 variety is late flowering and prostrate growing.

Some plant species occur on both serpentine and nonserpentine soils in California, and Kruckeberg (1951) showed that several of these species had serpentine and nonserpentine races. This ecotypic variation was found in *Gilia capitata*, an annual herb of the foothills of California:

(b)

Fresno, California

Seward, Alaska

Spread between average maximum
and minimum temperatures

Jan. Feb. Mar. Apr. May June July Aug. Sept. Oct. Nov. Dec.

(a)

(c)

FIGURE 50

Ecotypic variation between a northern (a) and a southern (b) race of Achillea borealis
*and (c) the approximate temperature ranges of their native habitats. A race from Selma,
California (a), and another from Seward, Alaska (b), growing in the Stanford garden
and reproduced to the same scale. (After Clausen, Keck, and Hiesey 1948.)*

| | Dry weight (g) at maturity | |
Source of seeds	In serpentine soil	In normal soil
Serpentine localities	*4.30*	*4.93*
Nonserpentine localities	*0.37*	*4.48*

This indicates the existence of edaphic races, or soil ecotypes, within a
plant species. These edaphic races may be produced in a short time period.
In the western United States two introduced weeds (*Prunella vulgaris* and

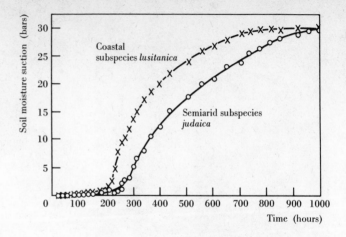

FIGURE 51

Rate of water use by orchard grass, Dactylis glomerata, *subspecies* judaica *and* lusitanica. *Soil was saturated at the start of the experiment and no additional water was added. (After McKell, Perrier, and Stebbins 1960.)*

Rumex acetosella) have evolved strains tolerant to serpentine soils, probably within the last 75 years (Kruckeberg 1967).

Arctic tundras and alpine tundras are rather different but severe environments, yet many plants live in both situations. The length of the photoperiod and the diurnal temperature range are quite different for a plant in the southern Rocky Mountains and another of the same species in northern Alaska. Mooney and Billings (1961) studied a small perennial herb, the alpine sorrel (*Oxyria digyna*), from arctic and alpine areas to look for evidence of ecotypic differentiation. Alpine sorrel has a broad distribution from 83°N latitude to 35°N in New Mexico (Figure 52). They found two types of *Oxyria*—a northern type with rhizomes and a southern alpine form

FIGURE 52

North American distribution of alpine sorrel, Oxyria digyna. *Numbers refer to areas from which populations were collected. (After Mooney and Billings 1961.)*

without rhizomes. Chromosome counts were the same for both types ($2n = 14$). Southern populations showed greater flower production and less leaf chlorophyll. Plants of northern populations had a higher rate of photosynthesis at lower temperatures (Figure 53); southern plants withstood higher temperatures and required more light for maximal photosynthesis. Thus *O. digyna* has achieved a wide distribution by ecotypic differentiation, by adaptation to local climatic conditions of arctic and alpine tundras.

The knotweed *Polygonum bistortoides* is a perennial herb found in the alpine and subalpine areas of western North America. Scattered populations also occur in coastal areas from California to Washington. Mooney (1963) showed that coastal and subalpine populations were physiologically and genetically different:

	California coastal population	Rocky Mountain subalpine population
Chromosome count	$2n = 48$	$2n = 24$
Reproduction	vegetatively by rhizomes	by seeds
Respiration rate	lower	higher

Thus the coastal population of *P. bistortoides* shows attributes usually associated with plants in severe environments, and this may indicate that the alpine races gave rise to polyploids that colonized some lowland habitats.

The boundary of forest and grassland (page 105) becomes more complex in the light of ecotypic studies. Simple considerations of grassland versus forest are not adequate because individual species of grasses (and trees) can adapt to local conditions (McMillan 1959). Climatic selection has produced northern populations of grasses that can grow and mature

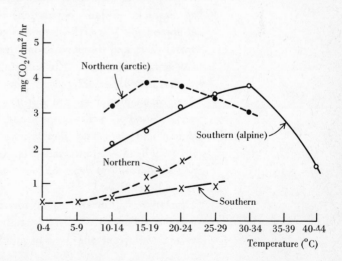

FIGURE 53

Average photosynthetic rates and average respiration rates for southern alpine races of Oxyria digyna *and northern arctic races. Photosynthetic rates (dots) are measured by uptake of* CO_2. *Respiration rates (crosses) are measured by release of* CO_2. *(After Mooney and Billings 1961.)*

under long day lengths and short growing seasons, and southern populations that mature under shorter day lengths and longer growing seasons. McMillan (1965) has described this ecotypic variation in several prairie grasses from the Great Plains.

Adaptations to light may involve not only differences in photoperiodic responses to day length in northern and southern populations, such as in the grasses on the Great Plains, but also adaptation to shaded and sunny habitats. *Solidago virgaurea* is a widespread Eurasian and North African weed that lives in a wide variety of habitats. Populations from shaded habitats differ in their photosynthetic apparatus from those obtained from exposed habitats. Strong light damaged chloroplasts of plants from shaded habitats. Weak light favored the shade plants over those from exposed habitats (Bjorkman and Holmgren 1963).

The breeding systems of plants may also vary in different ecological races of a single species. Lefebvre (1970) has described a case in *Armeria maritima* in Europe. Normal seaside populations of this plant do not contain individuals that are self-fertile, whereas populations living on zinc mine wastes contain individuals that have a high amount of self-fertility. This ability of self-fertilization is obviously advantageous to a plant colonizing a new waste area.

Several examples of local adaptation on a micro scale have indicated how tightly coupled plant populations may be to local environments. The common bent grass *Agrostis tenuis* has adapted to a wide variety of ecological environments in Wales, ranging from sandy soils in coastal habitats to old mine wastes to inland pastures to woodlands (Bradshaw 1959). The species is continuously distributed over an environmental patchwork, and distances of 50 m or less are sufficient to isolate populations from one another effectively. Bradshaw (1960) transplanted grasses from various areas into experimental plots in contrasting habitats and found large variations in tolerances. For example, lowland populations were damaged by winter conditions in an upland plot; growth of upland plants was affected by salt spray in the coastal plot; and the population from a normal pasture could not grow in a lead-contaminated soil. This physiological variation was not accompanied by morphological differences. Jowett (1959) indicated the considerable range of adaptation to soil mineral levels in this grass, which has populations tolerant of lead, copper, and nickel poisoning and of low levels of calcium and phosphate. Populations of *Agrostis* growing on old lead mines are often lead tolerant, and this genetic trait has evolved within a short span of 200 to 300 years or less, since none of the mines is older than 300 years (Jowett 1964).

Variation within species of forest trees has been studied for over 150 years (Callaham 1964). Such studies are important economically because moving seed from one area to another may not result in productive trees, if local populations are highly adapted to local conditions of climate and soil. Genetic variation in susceptibility to environmental changes must also be considered when introducing new tree species to foreign countries. In some cases these introductions have been successful, such as *Pinus radiata* into Australia and New Zealand, but in many cases introductions are not successful because of a failure to consider the geographical source of tree seed (Burley 1966).

The black cottonwood *Populus trichocarpa* is a Pacific Coast tree found from central Alaska south to Baja California. Pauley and Perry (1954) obtained trees from Alaska to California and established a plantation of this species in Massachusetts. They found marked variation in the time that annual height growth stopped in different trees, depending on the latitude of the original collection (Figure 54). Trees from higher altitudes in mountainous areas stopped growing approximately 1 month before trees from low altitudes. The length of the frost-free season varies greatly over the range of this cottonwood, and adaptation to specific climates is effected by a genetic mechanism that controls the duration of the seasonal growth period. The photoperiod functions as a timing device for this genetic mechanism. Experimental alteration of the photoperiod by lights at night increased the length of the growth period.

Sugar maple (*Acer saccharum*) is an important hardwood tree in eastern North America. A study of genetic variation in sugar maple by Kriebel (1957) in Ohio utilized seed from 37 localities from New Brunswick and Quebec south to Florida. He recognized three ecotypes in sugar maple:

1 A northern ecotype: low genetic resistance to drought, susceptibility to leaf damage from high solar radiation, and high resistance to winter injury.

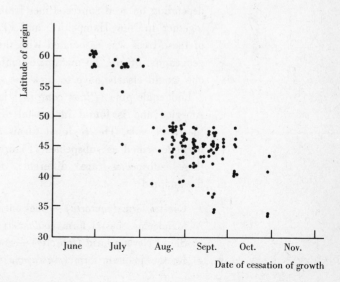

FIGURE 54

Date of cessation of height growth in black cottonwood trees (Populus trichocarpa) *in relation to original latitude of trees. All seedlings were grown in Massachusetts under uniform conditions. (After Pauley and Perry 1954.)*

2 A central ecotype: high resistance to drought, moderately high resistance to leaf scorch from high insolation, and high resistance to winter injury.

3 A southern ecotype: high drought resistance and high resistance to leaf injury by insolation, low resistance to winter injury, and poor growth form because of repeated forking of main and lateral shoots.

These genetic variations were ecologically important. For example, a severe summer drought in 1954 killed fewer seedlings of central and southern maples:

Source of seedlings	% Surviving 1954 summer drought
Northern	*22.6*
Central and southern	*38.9*

Growth patterns were also variable. Trees from northern sources stopped growing first; trees from the Gulf Coast continued growing until killed back by autumn frosts.

Most temperate tree species must be exposed to low temperatures for a minimum number of hours before they can break winter dormancy in a normal fashion. This requirement, for example, limits the cultivation of some fruit trees, such as peaches, in subtropical areas. The red maple (*Acer rubrum*) ranges from eastern Canada to southern Florida, and seedlings from different parts of its geographical range, when grown in Florida, showed different chilling requirements (Perry and Wu 1960). Plants from New York would not break dormancy without chilling, whereas plants from the Everglades of Florida had no chilling requirement. We have already seen another example of this limitation in red osier dogwood (see Figure 21).

Scotch pine (*Pinus sylvestris*) shows strong ecotypic variation in growth depending on seed source. Pines from Italy to northern Norway were grown together in New Hampshire, and Figure 55 shows that variation in height of these trees was associated with the length of the growing season at their geographic origin. To maximize lumber yield from a Scotch pine plantation, one would clearly have to pick the seed source carefully.

Lodgepole pine (*Pinus contorta*) is a widespread species of western North America and is found in coastal areas and in the Rocky Mountains and Sierra Nevada. The regional forms are sufficiently different that they have been described as subspecies (Figure 56). The ecological characteristics of these subspecies are different; for example, some populations are fire-adapted:

1 Coastal form (*contorta*)—cones open at maturity, not fire-adapted
2 Mendocino coastal form (*bolanderi*)—serotinous cones, opened by fire
3 Sierra Nevada form (*latifolia*)—cones open at maturity
4 Rocky Mountain form (*murrayana*)—serotinous cones

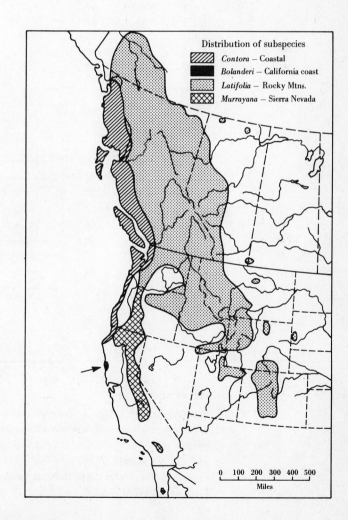

FIGURE 55

Average height of Scotch pine at 17 years of age in relation to length of growing season (days above 6°C) of seed-source area. All trees grown in New Hampshire. (After Langlet 1959.)

Average tree height (ft)

Length of growing season (days)

Distribution of subspecies

Contora – Coastal
Bolanderi – California coast
Latifolia – Rocky Mtns.
Murrayana – Sierra Nevada

0 100 200 300 400 500
Miles

FIGURE 56

Approximate geographical distribution of the four subspecies of lodgepole pine Pinus contorta. *(After Critchfield 1957.)*

When plants from various collections were grown in a greenhouse at Berkeley, there was considerable genetic variation in the seeding growth period (Figure 57), and this correlates well with the frost-free season at the point of seed origin (Critchfield 1957).

Tree species can also show ecotypic differences on a microgeographic scale. White cedar (*Thuja occidentalis*) forms dense stands in swamps in

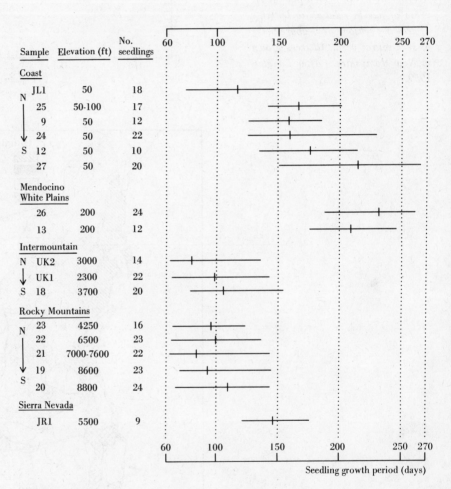

FIGURE 57

Seedling growth period in lodgepole pine from coastal and mountain areas all grown in uniform conditions at Berkeley, California. The growth period is the time between the appearance of the seedling and the maturation of the terminal bud. The vertical tick marks indicate values; thin lines indicate range of values observed. (After Critchfield 1957.)

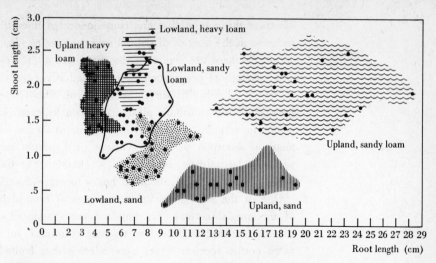

FIGURE 58

Graphic illustration of white cedar (Thuja occidentalis) *ecotypes.
The individual seedlings have been plotted on the basis of their
root and shoot development. Each dot represents one seedling. The
sand soil was well drained and relatively dry, the sandy-loam soil was
well drained and relatively moist, and the heavy loam soil was
poorly drained. (After Habeck 1958.)*

northern Wisconsin and is also common on upland, well-drained sites. These
habitats may exist only 100 ft apart, and adaptation to such soil conditions
is important if this adaptation allows a species to extend its range of distribution, for example to both uplands and lowlands. Habeck (1958) collected a total of 335 white cedar seedlings 2 to 3 years old from lowland,
wet areas and upland areas, and planted them in an upland site at Madison.
Survival of these seedlings during their first year was variable:

	Survival (%)
Upland seedlings	*72.8*
Lowland seedlings	*54.2*

Germination of upland cedar seeds was also higher. Growth of seedlings
showed variations associated with soil moisture levels (Figure 58). Lowland cedars showed constant root development but variable shoot length;
upland cedars were flexible in both root and shoot growth. This local scale
of adaptation shown by white cedar is important in forestry work when one
chooses seed sources for reforestation.

The question we raised earlier, Why has there not been more adaptation?,
is clarified somewhat by a consideration of cultivated plants. Crop plants

illustrate the maxim that one consequence of domestication is an enormous increase in the area of distribution of the species (Hutchinson 1965, p. 169). Although there are limits to the distribution of crop plants (e.g., tropical and subtropical crops such as corn and soybeans cannot be grown easily in damp, cloudy Britain), the range of climates occupied is remarkable because of the enormous plasticity shown by crop plants. All this plasticity is not necessarily genetic in origin. Figure 59 shows the seasonal development of Marquis wheat (a variety of *Triticum aestivum*), which ripens within a latitudinal range of 19°N (Mexico) to 64°N (Alaska) from an average day length of about 12 hours to more than 20 hours.

One of the most remarkable examples of crop-plant evolution is the case of the annual cottons. Six hundred years ago, all cottons were perennial shrubs, confined to frost-free tropical countries. In each of the four cultivated cotton species, forms were selected that fruited early enough to produce a sizable crop in the first growing season. These early-fruiting cottons were then planted in temperate climates with cold winters and hot summers, and the annual growth habit was imposed on them by winter frost. Selection for high productivity completed this cycle, and now almost all cultivated cottons are obligate annuals that can be grown in cold-winter areas and also in semiarid climates. Thus in a maximum of 600 generations the cotton plant has been selected to live in environmental conditions that were formerly lethal (Hutchinson 1965, p. 170).

We have concentrated so far on describing geographic variation in plants and have given examples to illustrate that local adaptation to environmental variables can occur, even on a microgeographic scale. Similar types of adaptation occur in animals, and I will mention only a few examples. Mayr (1963, Chap. 11) discusses additional cases.

The water temperature at which breeding occurs in marine invertebrates was often assumed to be a constant throughout the geographical range of a species. Korringa (1957) showed that this was not true for the European oyster (*Ostrea edulis*). The temperature at which swarming of larvae can be observed repeatedly was 17.5°C in a Dutch population but 25°C in a Norwegian population of oysters. Korringa noted that there were several different physiological varieties of the European oyster, varieties that breed at different water temperatures. This has clear implications for transplantation and introduction of oysters from one area to another.

FIGURE 59

Phenology (seasonal development) of a very adaptable variety of wheat, the Marquis variety, in several North American areas. (After Nuttonson 1955.)

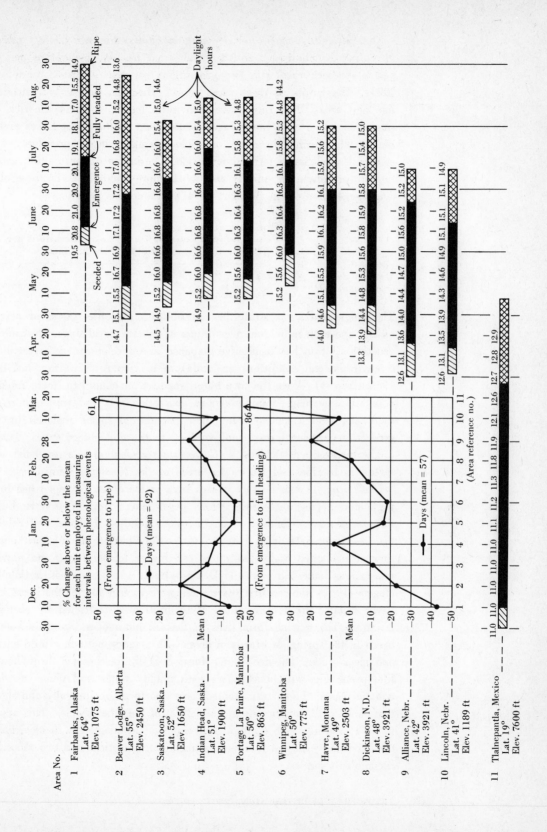

The European corn borer (*Pyrausta nubilalis*) has two distinct races in its native distribution, a northern race that has one generation per year and a southern race with two generations per year (Babcock and Vance 1929). The habits of these races persist when the insects are introduced into new areas. Both races have been introduced into North America. The single-generation corn borer race, predominant in the Great Lakes area, is biologically distinct from the multiple-generation insect prevalent in the eastern United States (Arbuthnot 1944). The larvae of the multiple-generation strain grow more quickly and pupate more rapidly than do those of the single-generation strain. Wishart (1947) showed this clearly:

	One generation per year, Prince Edward County, Ontario	Two generations per year, New England
Mean no. days to produce pupation	34.3	21.3

The single-generation strain has an obligate diapause (arrested development), and each individual overwinters in the late larval stage. The multiple-generation strain has facultative diapause, and development is arrested only if environmental conditions are unfavorable (see Andrewartha and Birch 1954, Chap. 4). When the corn borer was first introduced to North America, populations were predominantly one generation per year (univoltine). But there has been a tendency for these populations to be replaced by two-generation-per-year forms (multivoltine) in the midwestern states.

The three-spined stickleback (*Gasterosteus aculeatus*) is a small fish widespread in marine and freshwater areas of the Northern Hemisphere. Two "races" occur, a marine race, which lives in the ocean (except when breeding), and a freshwater race, which never leaves fresh waters. In Europe the marine race extends from arctic waters south to Holland and Belgium, the freshwater race from Belgium to the Mediterranean. Southern populations are adapted to low salinities and higher temperatures, and northern populations have converse adaptations (Heuts 1956). In British Columbia Hagen (1967) showed that these races were in fact species that were effectively isolated from each other. Hybridization is restricted by ecological isolation. The marine form lives in the sea but moves into freshwater to breed in the spring. It breeds in areas with a sandy bottom, a mild current, and clear water. The freshwater form lives in fresh water throughout its life, preferring quiet backwaters with muddy water and dense stands of aquatic plants. Hagen transplanted these two forms reciprocally and showed that each could not survive in the habitat of the other species. This appears to be a case in which ecological divergence and adaptation to local habitat conditions have passed the point of incipient speciation, and two races have become two species.

A species is usually thought of as being characterized by a particular geographical range and a particular ecological range of tolerance which does not change in time and is as characteristic of the species as its morphology. Many species have shown radical changes in their geographical range, often because of introductions by man or the colonization of new environments produced by agriculture. The ecological range of a species is the result of evolutionary processes, and consequently a real ecological expansion of a species must involve genetic adaptations to new environments. Thus, while geographic range expansion may occur in the absence of genetic changes in the species, ecological range extension involves genetic reorganization.

The problem of natural selection at the borderline of the geographic range of a species was considered by Mayr (1954), who recognized the puzzle that natural selection was so adept at producing populations with local adaptations just within the range limits but not slightly beyond them. Over evolutionary time, why are the tolerance levels to a limiting factor (such as temperature) not increased gradually, so that the species increases its geographic range? He suggested a genetic explanation for this: that the process of local adaptation in peripheral populations is annually disrupted by the infiltration of alien genes from the more central parts of the species' geographical range. This disruption prevents the selection of a stabilized gene complex adapted to the conditions of the border region. Species boundaries, then, can be interpreted genetically as the line of dynamic equilibrium between the two opposing forces of (1) selection for local adaptation to the environment, and (2) disruption of these selected gene groups by the immigration of individuals from central populations that were selected for other local conditions. This hypothesis is diagrammed in Figure 60.

Wallace (1960) examined Mayr's ideas, particularly the prediction that stopping gene flow from central to peripheral populations should allow a species to expand its geographical range. The most obvious way to cut off gene flow within a species is by self-fertilization. In plants some species have both cross-fertilization and self-fertilization breeding systems. Wallace cites one example of an annual herb *Gilia ochroleuca* in southern California. Within the main part of the distribution of this *Gilia* species, plants live in woodland and chaparral areas and cross-pollinate. On the edge of the species range a race of self-pollinating (autogamous) *G. ochroleuca* lives in the Mojave Desert (Figure 61). According to Mayr's hypothesis, the self-pollination breeding system allowed the peripheral populations to adapt to desert conditions and hold these adaptations against the influx of genes from cross-pollinating races. This allowed *G. ochroleuca* to expand its geographic range into the desert areas. Wallace points out that no experimental work has been attempted on this problem, and that case histories of this type can be interpreted in other ways as well.

We rarely catch a species in the process of an extension of its ecological range, yet this should be a focus of attention for ecologists interested in the problem of distribution. I know of a single case only. Lewontin and Birch

Original geographical range at   Prediction According to Mayr's hypothesis

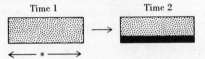

Time 1   Time 2

Mutation arises in center of distribution and is favorable, so it spreads throughout range. Range limits do not change.

(a)

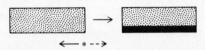

Mutation arises on edge of distribution and is favorable in present range but unfavorable beyond present limits. Range limits do not change.

(b)

> Any genetic change that possesses an adaptive advantage within the normal geographical range will be incorporated into the genotype of the species and will not allow the species to extend its distribution

Mutation arises on edge of distribution, is advantageous in present range, and could increase range limits if it were not swamped with genes from central part of distribution. Range limits do not change.

(c)

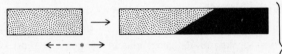

Mutation arises on edge of distribution, is disadvantageous in present range, and advantageous beyond present range limits. Species will extend range and new area will be occupied by new genotypes.

> Genetic changes at the range edge that are not adaptive in the normal range but are adaptive beyond it can allow range extension

(d)

FIGURE 60

Possible effects of genetic alterations on geographic ranges. Stars mark genetic alteration, and dashed arrows indicate that this alteration is eliminated, solid arrows that it is preserved. Predictions at time 2 are based on Mayr's hypothesis. The solid black area represents incorporation of new genetic material. (After Wallace 1960.)

FIGURE 61

Distribution of the annual herb Gilia
ochroleuca *in southern California.*
The Mojave Desert subspecies
G. o. ochroleuca is self-pollinating.
The dotted line marks the western
edge of the desert. (After Grant
and Grant 1956.)

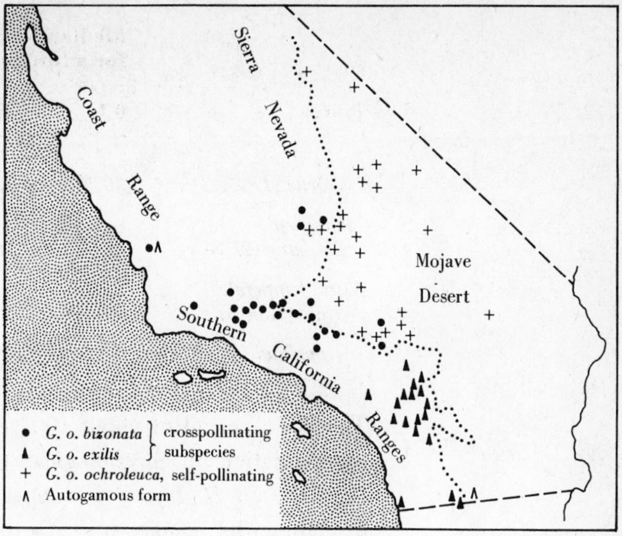

(1966) have described a case of a species of fruit fly (*Dacus tryoni*) which
has been rapidly expanding its ecological tolerance and geographical range
in Australia. *D. tryoni* lays its eggs in ripening fleshy fruits. It was originally
dependent on fruits in the tropical rain forest but has spread to cultivated
fruits since agriculture has made these available. At first glance this would
seem to be another instance of a native species moving into a new agricultural niche and becoming a pest. However, several facts argue that this is
not sufficient explanation for what has occurred:

1 The range of *D. tryoni* is not limited by transport. Local and sporadic outbreaks of this fruit fly have occurred in areas outside its present range, presumably because the species was carried on fruits to markets.

2 *Dacus tryoni* has expanded its range southward over the past 100 years and is
continuing to do so. It is endemic to tropical rain forests in northern Australia,
and its spread south is indicated very roughly in Figure 62.

3 The range of *D. tryoni* is not limited by host-plant availability. There is intensive cultivation of fruit in southeastern Australia beyond the limit of its present
distribution.

4 The distribution of *D. tryoni* was and is limited by climate. This is suggested
by its distribution. Also there was an altitudinal limit of about 1500 feet during
the 1930s such that orchards above this level suffered little damage from fruit
flies. Now orchards between 1500 and 2500 feet above sea level suffer severe
damage also. Thus the southward extension of range was paralleled by an altitudinal extension.

Flies from the southern part of the range of *Dacus* are genetically more
resistant to extremes of temperature:

Source	Median lethal dose (hr) for adult *Dacus*	
	0°C	37°C
Tropical Cairns (17°S)	*36.9*	*25.6*
Subtropical Brisbane (27°S)	*37.4*	*30.5*
Warm temperate Sydney (34°S)	*40.1*	*32.4*
Gippsland (38°S)	*40.4*	*40.3*

Thus in a period of about 100 years natural selection has built up a genetic differentiation in physiological tolerance to temperature extremes in this fruit fly. In *D. tryoni* we appear to have caught a species in the act of extending its range by a process of adaptation to new temperature environments.

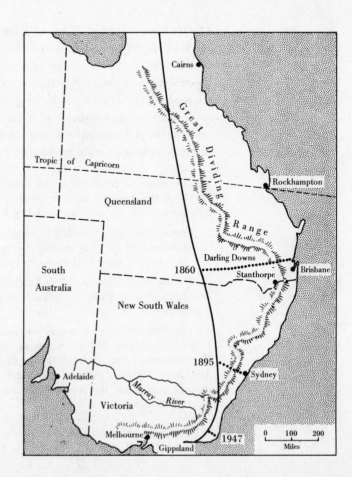

FIGURE 62

Present range of the fruit fly Dacus tryoni *in eastern Australia. The species is reliably found east of the solid line. The spread from north to south is roughly indicated. (After Lewontin and Birch 1966.)*

What was the source of the genetic variation for this rapid evolution? Two possibilities exist. Either it was always present in the gene pool of the species but unutilized, or new genetic variation was introduced into the population by hybridization and the introgression of genes from another species. Lewontin and Birch have attempted to show that the introgression of genes from a second species of *Dacus, Dacus neohumeralis,* into *D. tryoni* has taken place, and that this introgression can serve as a source of variation for selection to temperature extremes.

Dacus neohumeralis, a close relative of *D. tryoni,* occurs in tropical and subtropical Australia. Both species are found in the same habitats throughout the range of *neohumeralis* and appear to be virtually identical in their ecological requirements. The two species seem to hydridize in nature, because intermediates can be found in small numbers, but gene exchange has not been enough to merge them.

Lewontin and Birch raised *tryoni, neohumeralis,* and hybrid populations in large laboratory cages at three temperatures: 20, 25, and 31.5°C. They found that hybridization per se did not produce better adapted populations at all temperatures. That is, this is not a case of accidental heterosis. Hybrids between the two species seemed to be at a pronounced disadvantage in terms of the number of pupae produced per week. But at the high temperature of 31.5°C, the hybrid populations were clearly superior to the *tryoni* populations in larval viability and in fecundity and longevity of adults. For example:

	Larval viability (% eggs surviving to adults)		
	20°C	25°C	31.5°C
Dacus tryoni	67	63	26
Hybrids	63	61	37

Thus the introgression of genes from *neohumeralis* into *tryoni* by hybridization has accelerated the genetic adaptation of the population to a high temperature stress. These laboratory experiments tend to support the suggestion that the observed range extension in *D. tryoni* and increased toleration of higher temperatures resulted from the selection of new genetic material brought into the species by hybridization. This example fits the general model expressed in Figure 60.

Successful introduced species must become adapted to environmental conditions in their new location. Some species are able to adapt to new environments whereas others cannot, and this may explain some examples of introduced species that fail to colonize. A particularly graphic comparison can be made between two species of the starling family which were introduced to North America (Johnson 1971). The European starling was introduced to New York City in 1890 and spread rapidly across North America (Figure 1, page 18). About 1895 another species of the same genus, the crested mynah (*Sturnus cristatellus*), escaped from captivity in Vancouver, British Columbia. The mynah is an Asian species, brought from Hong Kong, and has maintained itself in the city of Vancouver since 1895 but has not spread. Why should the two starlings differ so much in colonizing ability?

The different incubation techniques of the two species may be a critical factor in determining success. Johnson (1971) found that both species laid the same number of eggs, but the crested mynah was less successful in producing young:

	European starling	Crested mynah
Eggs laid	*5.2*	*5.1*
Eggs hatched (%)	*82*	*58*
Young fledged (%)	*69*	*38*

For the crested mynah there is a great difference in air temperature at the time of nesting (April) between Vancouver and its native Hong Kong (Figure 63). Mynahs are tropical hole nesters and are irregular incubators

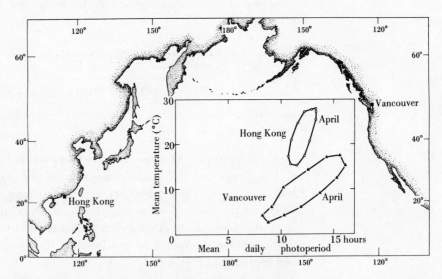

FIGURE 63

Comparison of native (Hong Kong) and introduced (Vancouver) home of the crested mynah, Sturnus cristatellus. *The climatograms are constructed by connecting means (air temperature and photoperiod) for succeeding calendar months. Egg laying starts in April at both localities. (After Johnson 1971.)*

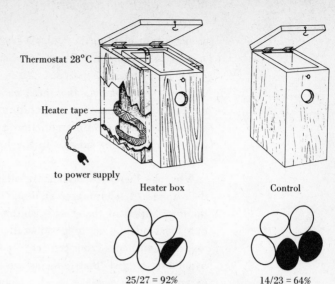

Experiment with altered nest microclimate in Vancouver; at five crested mynah nests a heater was installed and nest temperature maintained at Hong Kong levels (28°C). Hatching success at these nests is contrasted with the controls exposed to natural temperature fluctuations. (After Johnson 1971.)

Thermostat 28°C

Heater tape

to power supply

Heater box   Control

25/27 = 92%   14/23 = 64%

of their eggs. This behavior is adaptive in warm Hong Kong but not in cool Vancouver. By contrast, European starlings are much more constant incubators of their nests. Johnson (1971) cross-fostered eggs to illustrate this:

	Percentage hatching
European starling given eggs of mynah to incubate	90
Mynah given eggs of starling to incubate	62

The mynahs in Vancouver persisted in the incubation regime appropriate to their tropical home and failed to compensate for the low air temperatures of Vancouver. The critical experiment to test this suggestion was to heat the nests of mynahs in Vancouver. Figure 64 shows that when the nest microclimate was altered to Hong Kong levels (28°C), hatching success increased greatly. Thus the crested mynah has failed to adapt its incubation rhythm to temperate conditions and, partly because of this, has not been able to increase its geographic range.

SUMMARY

Species can adapt to new environments by a process of natural selection; but most of ecology has been pursued as if hereditary diversity within species did not exist. Turesson, a Swedish botanist, was one of the first to recognize the importance of *ecotypes*, genetic varieties within a single species. By transplanting individuals from a variety of habitats into a common garden or greenhouse, Turesson showed that many of the adaptations of plant forms were genotypic. Many ecotypes have now been described, particularly in plants, and these may involve adaptations to any environmental factor, including temperature, moisture, soil conditions, light, fire, or salinity. Ecotypic differentiation has often proceeded to the point where one ecotype cannot survive in the habitat of another ecotype of the same species.

Why has there not been more adaptation? Why do species not increase their range of tolerance to limiting factors over evolutionary time, so that the distribution of the species continually increases? One possible answer is that local adaptation in peripheral populations is suppressed by continual migration of genes from central to peripheral parts of the distribution. This hypothesis suggests that reducing gene flow to peripheral populations should permit them to achieve local adaptation to limiting factors and then to increase distribution.

Many species are known to have extended or reduced their geographical range in historical times, but few cases have been studied in detail. Consequently, we rarely know whether a species changed its distribution because the environment has changed or because the genetic makeup of the species has altered.

Adaptation is a universal biological fact. Therefore, genetic variation is an important component in the study of plant and animal distribution problems. The static view of distributions as changeless over time and of species as genetically homogeneous must be replaced by a dynamic view. When we conclude that factor x limits the distribution of a species at point y, we must enquire further to find why adaptation has not overcome this limitation. This meeting ground between ecology and genetics has been explored hardly at all.

SELECTED REFERENCES

CALLAHAM, R. Z. 1964. Provenance research: investigation of genetic diversity associated with geography. *Unasylva* 18(2–3):40–50.

HESLOP-HARRISON, J. 1964. Forty years of genecology. pp. 159–247 in *Advances in Ecological Research*, Vol. 2, ed. by J. B. Cragg. Academic, New York.

HIESEY, W. M., and H. W. MILNER. 1965. Physiology of ecological races and species. *Ann. Rev. Plant Physiol.* 16:203–216.

LEWONTIN, R. C., and L. C. BIRCH. 1966. Hybridization as a source of variation for adaptation to new environments. *Evolution* 20:315–336.

TURESSON, G. 1930. The selective effect of climate upon the plant species. *Hereditas* 14:99–152.

WALLACE, B. 1960. Influence of genetic systems on geographical distribution. *Cold Spring Harbor Symp. Quant. Biol.* 24:193–204.

1 "To become widespread a species must develop many ecological races" (Clausen, Keck, and Hiesey 1948, p. 121). Is this true in both animals and plants? Discuss with reference to colonizing species such as the starling.

2 The technique of transplanting together plants from a series of habitats into a uniform cultivated garden to study ecotypic variation can be criticized on several grounds. Discuss.

3 Good (1964, p. 418) states that the ecological tolerance range of a species is the sum of the tolerances of its constituent individuals. Evaluate this statement in the light of ecotypic studies.

4 Should a wide-ranging tropical species have as many ecotypes as a closely-related and equally-wide-ranging temperate or arctic species?

5 The common bent grass *Agrostis tenuis* is a wind-pollinated outbreeding plant. How is it possible for populations of this species to be isolated from one another genetically over a distance of 50 m or less (page 118)? Read Bradshaw (1959, p. 208) and discuss this problem.

6 Elfinwood growth forms of trees are found near timberline (Figure 35, page 79). How would you test the suggestion that elfinwood trees are genetically different from normal trees?

PART THREE

THE PROBLEM OF ABUNDANCE:
POPULATIONS

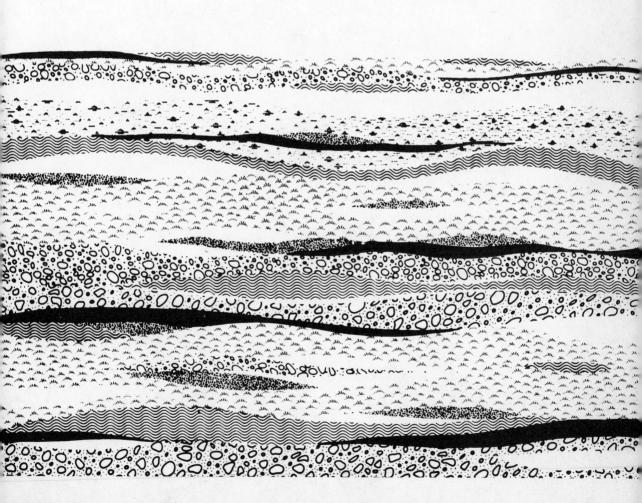

9 Population parameters

POPULATION AS A UNIT OF STUDY

A population may be defined as *a group of organisms of the same species occupying a particular space at a particular time.* Thus we may speak of the deer population of Brown County State Park, the deer population of Indiana, the human population of Kansas City, or the human population of the United States. The ultimate constituents of the population are *individual organisms* that are potentially interfertile. The population may be subdivided into *demes*, or local populations, which are groups of interbreeding organisms, the smallest collective unit of a plant or animal population. The boundaries of a population both in space and in time are vague and in practice are usually fixed by the investigator arbitrarily.

A good deal of interest has centered on populations as units of study, from both the field of ecology and the field of genetics. One of the fundamental principles of modern evolutionary theory is that the population is the unit that evolves in nature. Thus the fields of population ecology and population genetics have much in common.

The population has various group characteristics, which are statistical measures that cannot be applied to individuals. These group characteristics are of three general types. The basic characteristic of a population that we are interested in is its *size* or *density*. The primary population parameters that affect size are *natality* (births), *mortality* (deaths), *immigration,* and *emigration*. In addition to these attributes one can derive secondary characteristics of a population, such as its *age distribution, genetic composition,* and *dispersion* (distribution of individuals in space). Note that these population parameters result from a summation of individual characteristics.

ESTIMATION OF POPULATION PARAMETERS

The population attributes concerned with changes in abundance are interrelated as follows:

$$
\begin{array}{c}
\text{Immigration} \\
\Big\downarrow + \\
\text{Natality} \xrightarrow{\ +\ } \textit{Density} \xrightarrow{\ -\ } \text{Mortality} \\
\Big\downarrow - \\
\text{Emigration}
\end{array}
$$

Let us briefly look at the methods employed in estimating these vital statistics.

Density *Density* is defined as numbers per unit area or per unit volume. One can appreciate the problems involved in estimating density by considering some approximate densities of organisms in nature:

	Density	
	In conventional units	In no./sq. m (or cu. m)
Diatoms	5,000,000/cu. m	5,000,000
Soil arthropods	500,000/sq. m	500,000
Barnacles (adult)	20/100 sq. cm	2,000
Trees	200/acre	0.0494
Field mice	100/acre	0.0247
Woodland mice	5/acre	0.00124
Deer	10/sq. mile	0.0000039
Human beings		
Netherlands	375/sq. km	0.000375
Canada	2/sq. km	0.000002

This range of figures, covering more than a dozen orders of magnitude, gives you some idea of what we have to study. Techniques that work nicely with deer cannot be applied to protozoa. The two fundamental attributes that affect our choice of techniques are the *size* and *mobility* of the organism with respect to man.

In many cases it will be impractical to determine the *absolute density* of a population (e.g., in numbers per acre or per square meter), and we may find it adequate to know the *relative density* of the population (i.e., that area x has more organisms than area y). This division is reflected in the techniques developed for measuring density.

Measurement of absolute density (1) TOTAL COUNTS The most direct way to find out how many animals are living on an area is to count them. The best example of this is the human population census. Other good examples come mostly from the vertebrates. With territorial birds, for example, one can count all the singing males on an area. Or with bobwhite quail one can count the number of birds in each covey. Other animals, such as the northern fur seal, may be counted when they are all gathered in breeding colonies. Few invertebrates can be counted in total, the exceptions being the barnacles and other sessile invertebrates such as some rotifers. Large plants on small areas can sometimes be counted in total, but, in general, this is possible for very few organisms.

(2) SAMPLING METHODS Usually the investigator must be content to count only a small proportion of the population and use this sample to estimate the total. There are two general ways of sampling:

(*a*) *Use of quadrats* The general procedure here is to count all the individuals on several quadrats of known size and to extrapolate the average to the whole area. A quadrat is just a sampling area of any shape. Although the word strictly means a square, it has been used in ecology for all shapes of areas, including circles. An example will illustrate this: If you counted 19 individuals of a beetle species in a soil sample of 1/100 sq. m, you could extrapolate this to 1900 beetles per square meter of soil surface.

The reliability of the estimates obtained by this technique depends on three things: (1) The population of each quadrat must be known exactly; (2) the area of each quadrat must be known; and (3) the quadrats must be representative of the whole area. This last condition is usually achieved by random sampling procedures, and students acquainted with statistics will find a good discussion of this problem in Brown (1954, Chap. 2). The area of the quadrat can be measured exactly. The population of each quadrat may be counted without error in some organisms but only estimated in other species. Many special techniques have been developed for applying quadrat sampling techniques to different kinds of animals and plants in terrestrial and aquatic systems. I shall give just two examples of this method.

Lloyd (1967) sampled centipedes in 37 quadrats in central England and obtained the results shown in Figure 65. The mean density is

$$\frac{30 \text{ individuals}}{37 \text{ quadrats}} = 0.811 \text{ centipede per quadrat}$$

or, since each quadrat was 0.08 sq. m, the estimated density was 10.1 centipedes per square meter.

Wireworms are click beetle larvae that live in the soil and feed on seeds and damage the roots of agricultural crops. To estimate populations of wireworms, Salt and Hollick (1944) devised a technique of extracting all larvae from soil samples. This was done by breaking the lumps of soil, separating the very coarse and very fine material by sieves, and separating the wireworms from other organic material by benzene flotation (insects accumulate at the benzene–water interface, the plant matter stays in the water). Exhaustive tests were made at each step in this process to see if larvae were lost. They sampled soil by use of a corer that removed a cylinder of soil 4 in. in diameter and 6 in. deep. In one pasture near Cambridge, England, they obtained 240 samples with a total of 3742 larvae of the wireworm *Agriotes*, an average of 15.6 per 4-in. core, or an infestation of 7,800,000 per acre. Salt and Hollick were able to show by this careful work that wireworm populations were about three times as high in English pastureland as people had previously supposed.

Let us digress here briefly to consider two simple statistical concepts that continually recur in quantitative ecology. The first is the concept of central tendency, and the simplest illustration of this is the *mean*. When we make a series of repeated measurements, such as the number of centipedes in a quadrat, we are, first of all, interested in a descriptive measure that reduces all the measurements to a single "typical" value. Often this is the arithmetic average, or mean, but sometimes other measures, such as the median, are useful. The second concept is that of *variation*, or spread, and the simplest

FIGURE 65

Numbers of the centipede Lithobius crassipes *collected in 37 contiguous hexagonal quadrats of beech litter at Wytham Woods, near Oxford, England, on October 30, 1958. The quadrats are 1 ft (0.30 m) across, so the total area sampled is about 6 ft from side to side. Individual quadrats have an area of 0.866 sq. ft (0.08 sq. m). (After Lloyd 1967.)*

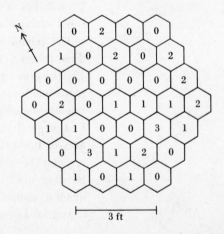

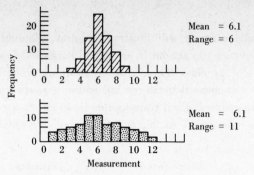

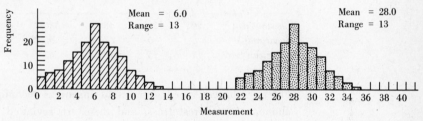

(a)

(b)

FIGURE 66

Statistical concepts of central tendency *and* variation. *In (a), two populations have equal means but different ranges of variability. In (b), two populations have equal variability but significantly different means.*

illustration of this is the *range* (maximum value minus minimum value). Two aspects of variation are to be noted. Biological systems all show a certain amount of real biological variability—not all students are the same height—and it is often important to describe variability. The other aspect is that differences between two populations must be judged to be "significant" or not, and this can be done only by considering central tendency and variation. This is one of the important areas of statistics: to work out methods for judging "significant" differences from a variety of experimental designs. Figure 66 illustrates these concepts and shows that distributions can have the same mean but different variabilities, or different means but the same variability. Simpson, Roe, and Lewontin (1960, Chaps. 4–6) discuss these concepts in detail.

Quadrats have been used extensively in plant ecology, and this is the most common method for sampling plants. There is an immense literature on the problems of sampling plants with quadrats, dealing for example with the relative efficiency of round, square, and rectangular quadrat shapes. We shall not go into these detailed problems of methodology; interested students should refer to Greig-Smith (1964, Chap. 2).

A single example will illustrate quadrat sampling of plant populations. A line transect was set out in an upland hardwood forest in southern Indiana by my ecology class. Three lines, each 106.7 m (350 ft) long, were used, and all trees more than 25 cm tall within a swath 1 m on each side of this line were counted. Each transect line is, in effect, a very long, thin quadrat, and comprises 213.4 sq. m, or 0.0527 acre. We obtained these results:

	No. counted			Estimated no./acre			
	Line A	Line B	Line C	Line A	Line B	Line C	Av.
Chestnut oak	20	28	18	380	531	342	417
Sugar maple	5	4	7	95	76	133	101
American beech	13	15	16	247	285	304	278

Foresters have devised a series of ingenious techniques for estimating the abundance of forest trees, and these are reviewed by Cottam and Curtis (1956) and by Phillips (1959).

Quadrats have been used extensively to sample plant populations and many invertebrates, and, if used properly, they provide an estimate of the mean population density and its variability on an area.

(b) Capture–recapture method The technique of capture, marking, release, and recapture is an important one in animal ecology because it allows one to obtain not only an estimate of density but also estimates of "birth rate" and "death rate" for the population being studied.

There are several models one can use for capture–recapture estimation. Basically they all depend on the following line of reasoning: If you capture animals and mark and release them on two or more occasions, the population at any particular time will consist of some *marked* and some *unmarked* animals. This is illustrated below for an arbitrary time period 7:

Time period 7

Total rectangle represents the entire population

M No. marked animals

U No. unmarked animals

The marked individuals (M) may have been caught and marked at the previous sampling time, or any prior time. Given this situation, we must know just two things to estimate the total population size: (1) *the number of marked animals alive* (M), and (2) *the proportion of the total population that is marked* (the ratio $M/M+U$). For example, if there were 500 marked animals and they made up one-third of the total population, the total population must have been 1500.

How can we get these two components? The second is easiest to determine. We can estimate the proportion of the total population that is marked by drawing a random sample. We assume that, if it is random, a sample will contain the same proportion of marked animals as that in the whole population:

$$\frac{\text{No. marked animals in sample}}{\text{Total caught in sample}} = \frac{\text{no. marked animals in total population}}{\text{total population size}}$$

We need then to estimate the size of the marked population, which decreases from one sampling period to the next because of death and emigration of marked individuals. This is more difficult but is done in the same general way as above. Consider now the marked population only (M). This segment contains two kinds of marked animals, as shown below:

Time period 7   Marked Population only

Total rectangle represents the entire marked population

M_c Marked animals actually caught at time 7

M_m Marked animals present but not caught at time 7

We need to know two things to estimate the size of this rectangle: (1) the number of marked animals actually caught (M_c), and (2) the proportion of marked animals actually caught (the ratio M_c/M_c+M_m). We already know the first because it is simply a count of marked animals in the catch. There are a number of ways in which the proportion (point 2) can be estimated, and this gives rise to several models of estimation, which are discussed in detail by Ricker (1958) and Cormack (1968). Appendix I gives details for one model of estimation.

Let us look at one situation to illustrate a simple type of population estimation known as the *Petersen method*. In this case there are only two sampling periods—time 1: capture, mark, release; and time 2: capture, check for marks. The time interval between the two samples must be short because this method assumes no recruitment of new animals into the population between times 1 and 2. Dahl (1919) marked trout (*Salmo fario*) in small Norwegian lakes to estimate the size of the population that was subject to fishing. He marked 109 trout and in a second sample a few days later caught 177 fish, of which 57 were marked. From these data we estimate:

$$\text{Proportion of population marked} = \frac{57}{177} = 0.322$$

The size of the marked population is known (109) in this simple case. Therefore,

$$\text{Population estimate} = \frac{\text{size of marked population}}{\text{proportion of population marked}}$$

$$= \frac{109}{0.322} = 338.5$$

This census procedure is simplified by the fact that the size of the marked population is known directly. In repeated censuses the number of marked animals decreases from deaths and emigrations and increases by the marking of new individuals from time to time. These changes complicate the estimation problem and are not treated in detail here.

The capture–recapture method makes three critical assumptions:

1   Marked and unmarked animals are captured randomly.
2   Marked animals are subject to the same mortality rate as unmarked animals.
3   Marks are not lost or overlooked.

All these assumptions have caused trouble at one time or another. For example, field mice may become trap-happy or trap-shy and thus violate assumption 1. Fish tagged on the high seas may be weakened by the nets and the tagging procedure (being held out of water) so that they suffer abnormal mortality just after release. In some cases fishermen have not returned tags from marked fish because they considered them good-luck charms. Leg rings may be lost from long-lived birds. There are numerous variations of the techniques of marking and recapture analysis, some of which may very cleverly circumvent some of these problems. The fisheries people in particular have been very active in this field (e.g., Ricker 1958).

Two additional points may be mentioned. First, under some conditions it is possible to test the crucial randomness of capture assumption from field data. Second, the reliability of these population estimates can be determined in standard statistical fashion. Both these points are reviewed and discussed by Cormack (1968) and Manly (1970).

Usually we are not interested in just a single population estimate, and we operate a mark-and-recapture scheme for several months or years, a *multiple census*. If we do this, we can begin to study the dynamics of a population. I have pointed out that it is possible to get an estimate of the "birth rate" and "death rate" of the population at the same time as we estimate its size. The gist of this procedure is as follows: Consider just two samples of the population, obtained by the general estimation technique outlined above. We have estimates of the marked population at the end of time 7 (M_7) and at the start of time 8 (M_8), and we also know the total population size at each of these times:

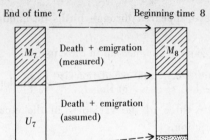

Between times 7 and 8, the marked population can only decrease, owing to deaths and emigrations. (The marked population can *increase* only during a sampling period when we are marking animals that were formerly unmarked.) We define the survival rate as the percentage of animals that survive the time interval:

$$\text{Survival rate } (\%) = \frac{M_8}{M_7} \times 100$$

Suppose, for example, that we have estimated 500 marked animals at the end of time 7 and 400 at the start of time 8. Then

$$\text{Survival rate} = \frac{400}{500} \times 100 = 80\%$$

The "death rate" (or, more properly, the *loss rate*, since it includes emigration) is defined simply as

$$\text{Loss rate} = 100\% - \text{survival rate}$$

These rates apply to the time interval between sample times 7 and 8; if this is 1 year, the estimated survival rate is 80% per year.

The "birth rate," which is more commonly called the *dilution rate* since it contains both immigration and births, is obtained indirectly. We assume that the survival rate estimated for the marked animals also applies to the unmarked animals. This is shown in the diagram, and a numerical example will illustrate how this operates:

	Time 7		Time 8
Marked animals	500	⟶ 400	*Therefore, survival rate* = 0.80
Unmarked animals	1000	⟶ (800)	*Estimated survival*
Total population estimate	1500	1400	*Therefore, dilution* = 200 new animals

If we project the observed survival rate, we find that we can account for 1200 animals at time 8 as survivors of those present at time 7. Clearly, 200 new animals have appeared through births or immigration, and this is the "dilution."

The principle here is summed up in the equation

$$\begin{array}{c}\text{total population size} \\ \text{at time } t + 1\end{array} = \begin{array}{c}\text{total population size} \\ \text{at time } t\end{array} + \text{dilution} - \text{deaths}$$

If we know any three of the variables in the equation, we can find the fourth by subtraction.

Developments in statistics have been very important for the study of ecology. It was not until 1936 that this technique of capture–recapture analysis was worked out in detail so that it could become an important ecological tool. In the last 10 years several important developments occurred in this field of analysis (Cormack 1968). Other statistical concepts, for example the problems of sampling, have been worked out only in the last 30 years. This is a good example of how developments in a science are dependent on progress in both pure and applied mathematics.

To summarize: The capture–recapture technique allows us to estimate the size of a population as well as its birth and death rates. It involves three critical assumptions and has been used mainly on larger forms such as butterflies, snails, beetles, and many vertebrates that can be readily marked.

Measurement of relative density The characteristic feature of all methods for measuring relative density is that they depend on the collection of samples that represent some relatively constant but unknown relationship to the total population size. Thus they provide no estimate of density but rather an index of abundance of more or less accuracy. There are a great many such techniques, and we shall list only a few:

1 Traps: These include mousetraps spread across a field, a light trap for night-flying insects, pitfall traps in the ground for beetles, suction traps for aerial insects, and plankton nets. The number of organisms trapped will depend not only on the population density but also on their activity, range of movement, and one's skill in placing traps, so one gets only a rough idea of abundance from these techniques.

2 Number of fecal pellets: This technique has been used for snowshoe hares, deer, field mice, and rabbits in Australia. If you know the number of fecal pellets in an area and the average rate of defecation, you can get an index of population size.

3 Vocalization frequency: The number of pheasant calls heard per 15 minutes in the early morning has been used as an index of the size of the pheasant population.

4 Pelt records: The number of animals caught by trappers has been used to estimate population changes in several mammals; some records extend back 150 years.

5 Catch per unit fishing effort: This measure can be used as an index of fish abundance, for example number of fish per 100 hours of trawling.

6 Number of artifacts: This count can be used for organisms that leave evidence of their activities, for example mud chimneys for burrowing crayfish, tree-squirrel nests, pupal cases from emerged insects.

7 Questionnaires: One can send questionnaires to sportsmen or trappers to get a subjective estimate of population changes. This is useful only when large changes in population size need to be detected among animals large enough to be noticed.

8 Cover: Botanists have used the percentage of the ground surface covered by a plant as a measure of relative density.

9 Frequency: The percentage of quadrats in which a particular species occurs has been used as a measure of relative abundance.

10 Feeding capacity: The amount of bait taken by rats and mice can be measured before and after poisoning to obtain an index of change in density.

These methods for measuring relative density all need to be viewed skeptically until they have been carefully studied and evaluated. They are most useful as a supplement to more direct census techniques and for picking up large changes in population density.

To conclude our discussion of techniques for measuring density, I should like to point out two things. First, detailed, accurate census information is obtainable from very few animals. In many cases we must be content with an order-of-magnitude estimate. Second, because of this, a disproportionate amount of work has been done on the more easily censused forms, particularly the birds and mammals. This introduces a possible bias into the discussions that follow.

Natality Populations increase because of natality. The natality rate is equivalent to the birth rate, natality simply being a broader word covering the production of new individuals by birth, hatching, germination, or fission.

Two aspects of reproduction must be distinguished. The fundamental notion of *fertility* is an actual level of performance in the population based on the numbers born. It must be distinguished from *fecundity*, which is the potential level of performance (or physical capacity) of the population. For example, the *fertility rate* for an actual human population may be only one birth per 8 years per female in the child-bearing ages, whereas the *fecundity rate* for humans is one birth per 9 to 11 months per female in the child-bearing ages.

Natality rate may be expressed as the number of organisms born per female per unit time. The measurement of natality or birth rate is highly dependent on the type of organism being studied. Some species breed once a year, some breed several times a year, and others breed continuously. Some produce many seeds or eggs, others few. For example, a single oyster can produce 55 to 114 million eggs. Fish commonly lay eggs numbered in the thousands, frogs in the hundreds. Birds usually lay between 1 and 20 eggs, and mammals rarely have litter sizes of more than 10 and often 1 or 2. Fecundity is inversely related to the amount of parental care given to the young. We shall not go into the details of natality measurements here, because we shall discuss them with examples later.

Mortality The biologist is interested not only in why organisms die but also why they die at a given age. Two types of longevity can be recognized: *physiological longevity* and *ecological longevity*. Physiological longevity may be defined as the average longevity of individuals of a population living under optimum conditions. In other words, the organisms die of "senescence" (Medawar 1957). Ecological longevity, on the other hand, is the empirical average longevity of the individuals of a population under given conditions. The distinction here is based on the fact that few organisms in nature actually die of senescence. Most of them are cut down by predators, disease, and other hazards long before they reach old age. Two examples will illustrate this. The European robin has an average expectation of life of 1 year in the wild, whereas it can live at least 11 years in captivity (Lack 1954). In ancient Rome the average expectation of life at birth for human females was about 21 years, and in England in the 1780s it was about 39 years (Pearl 1922). In the United States in 1960 females could expect to live 73 years on the average.

The measurement of mortality may be done directly or indirectly. The direct measure is achieved by marking a series of organisms and observing how many survive from time t to time $t + 1$. We have discussed this previously in the treatment of capture–recapture methods.

An indirect measure of survival may be gotten in several ways. For example, if one knows the abundance of successive age groups in the population, one can estimate the mortality between these ages. Data of this type are widely used in fisheries work, in the analysis of *catch curves*. Figure 67 illustrates a catch curve for bluegill sunfish in an Indiana lake. The survival rate can be estimated from the decline in relative abundance from age group to age group (except in the case of fish 1 year old, which are usually too small to be caught in the nets used). For example,

$$\text{Survival rate between II and III years} = \frac{\text{relative abundance of III fish}}{\text{relative abundance of II fish}}$$

$$= \frac{147}{292} = 0.50$$

Similarly, a drop of 147 to 54 between ages III and IV gives a survival estimate of 0.37 between these ages. In making these calculations we are assuming that the initial number of fish in each of the two age groups was

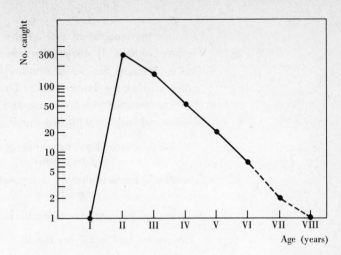

Catch curve for bluegill sunfish
(Lepomis macrochirus) *from*
Muskellunge Lake, Indiana, 1942.
(After Ricker 1958, p. 44.)

the same and that the survival rate has been constant over time for each age group. Ricker (1958, Chap. 2) discusses these problems in detail for fish populations. All indirect measures of survival involve some assumptions and should be used only after careful evaluation.

Immigration and emigration

Dispersal—immigration and emigration—is not often measured in a population study. In most cases one assumes either that it is negligible, that the two components are equal, or else it works in an island type of habitat, where it is presumably of reduced importance.

I have indicated in our discussion of the capture–recapture technique that one can measure the *loss rate* (deaths + emigration) and the *dilution rate* (births + immigration). If an area is sampled properly, it is possible to separate births from immigration and deaths from emigration in the following general manner (Jackson 1939). Lay out the sampling area as a large square divided into four smaller squares. The size of the small squares must be such that the dispersal rate is not too large, and this will of course depend on the type of organism being studied:

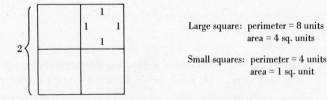

Large square: perimeter = 8 units
area = 4 sq. units

Small squares: perimeter = 4 units
area = 1 sq. unit

The death rate and the birth rate should be the same, subject to sampling errors, within the small squares and the large square. But the immigration rate and the emigration rate of the small squares should be twice those of the large square, if dispersal movements occur at random in all directions. This is because the small squares have twice as much perimeter relative to the area as the large square. Thus one applies the techniques described above to estimate the loss rate and the dilution rate for the two sizes of squares and ends up with two simultaneous equations:

Large square: death rate + emigration rate = 15% per month (for example)
   (of large square)

Small squares: death rate + 2(emigration rate) = 20% per month
   (of large square)

Subtracting, we obtain as estimates for the large square:

Emigration rate = 5% per month

Death rate = 10% per month

Using the same procedure, we can separate the birth rate from the immigration rate.

In a less formal way we can get an idea of the amount of emigration and immigration from observations on marked animals in two adjacent areas by noting how many move between the areas.

SUMMARY

We have looked briefly at methods of estimating population size for plants and animals. There is a crucial measurement problem here—every aspect of the problem of abundance comes down to this point: *How can we estimate population size?* Absolute density can be estimated by total counts or by sampling methods with quadrats or capture–recapture methods. Relative density can be estimated by many techniques which depend on the species studied. Once we obtain estimates of population size, we can investigate changes in numbers by analyzing the four primary demographic parameters of births, deaths, immigration, and emigration. The remaining chapters of Part Three will be an elaboration of this conceptually simple framework.

SELECTED REFERENCES

CHITTY, D. 1954. Methods of measuring rat populations. pp. 161–226 in *Control of Rats and Mice*, Vol. 1, ed. by D. Chitty, Oxford University Press, New York.

CORMACK, R. M. 1968. The statistics of capture–recapture methods. *Oceanogr. Mar. Biol. Ann. Rev.* 6:455–506.

MEDAWAR, P. B. 1957. Old age and natural death. Chap. 1, pp. 17–43, in *The Uniqueness of the Individual*, Methuen, London.

PHILLIPS, E. A. 1959. *Methods of Vegetation Study*. Chaps. 3–7. Holt, Rinehart & Winston, New York.

RICKER, W. E. 1958. *Handbook of Computations for Biological Statistics of Fish Populations*. Chaps. 1–3. Fisheries Research Board of Canada, Bull. 119.

SOUTHWOOD, T. R. E. 1966. *Ecological Methods with Particular Reference to the Study of Insect Populations*. Chaps. 3–9. Methuen, London.

QUESTIONS AND PROBLEMS

1 The catch (per 100 hours of trawling) for plaice (*Pleuronectes platessa*) in the southern North Sea is given below for three seasons. Plot catch curves from these data, and use the data to calculate survival rates for the various age classes.

Age of plaice	Catch 1950–1951	Catch 1951–1952	Catch 1952–1953
II	39	91	142
III	929	559	999
IV	2320	2576	1424
V	1722	2055	2828
VI	389	982	1309
VII	198	261	519
VIII	93	152	123
IX	95	71	106
X	81	57	61
XI	57	60	40
XII + older	94	87	99

SOURCE: After Gulland (1955).

2 An ecology class marking and releasing grasshoppers obtained the following data:

   Morning sample: 432 marked and released
   Afternoon sample: 567 caught, of which 47 were already marked

Apply the Peterson method of population estimation to these data, and discuss the necessary assumptions with particular reference to these animals. What are the implications of accidentally killing a grasshopper in the morning sample? In the afternoon sample?

3 Milne (1943) estimated the abundance of sheep ticks on farms in Scotland by dragging a wool blanket over the grass. Ticks will cling to anything brushing against them during the spring. Does this technique measure absolute density or relative density? How might you determine this?

4 Populations of some organisms, such as ground-dwelling carabid beetles, can be estimated either by quadrat methods or by capture–recapture techniques. List some of the advantages and disadvantages of each approach.

10 Demographic techniques

A life table is a convenient format for describing the mortality schedule of a population. Life tables were developed by human demographers, particularly those working for life insurance companies, which have a vested interest in knowing how long people can be expected to live. There is correspondingly an immense literature on human life tables, but there are not many data on other animals or on plants.

A life table is an age-specific summary of the mortality rates operating on a population; an example of a life table is given in Table 9. The columns of the life table are symbolized by letters, and these symbols are constantly used in ecology:

x = age interval
l_x = number of survivors at *start* of age interval x
d_x = number dying *during* the age interval x to $x + 1$
q_x = rate of mortality *during* the age interval x to $x + 1$
e_x = mean expectation of life for organisms alive at *start* of age x

To set up a life table, one must decide on age intervals to group the data. For humans the age interval may be 5 years, for deer 1 year, and for

TABLE 9

Life table for the barnacle Balanus glandula *at the upper shore level on Pile Point, San Juan Island, Washington*[a]

Age (yr) x	Observed no. barnacles alive each year	No. surviving at start of age interval x, l_x	No. dying within age interval x to $x + 1$, d_x	Rate of mortality, q_x	Mean expectation of further life for animals alive at start of age x, e_x
0	142	1000	563	0.563	1.58
1	62	437	198	0.453	1.96
2	34	239	98	0.410	2.17
3	20	141	32	0.227	2.34
4	(15.5)[b]	109	32	0.294	1.88
5	11	77	31	0.403	1.45
6	(6.5)[b]	46	32	0.696	1.11
7	2	14	0	0.000	1.50
8	2	14	14	1.000	0.50
9	0	0	—	—	—

[a] Data are from the 1959 year class, and begin 1 to 2 months after settlement. Individuals were counted each year until 1968, by which time all had died.
[b] Estimated number alive.
SOURCE: After Connell (1970).

field mice 1 month. By making the age interval shorter one increases the detail of the mortality picture shown by the life table.

The first important point to be made is that given any one of the columns of the life table, you can calculate the rest. To put this another way, there is nothing "new" in each of the four columns l_x, d_x, q_x, and e_x. They are just different ways of summarizing one set of data. The columns are related as follows:

$$l_{x+1} = l_x - d_x$$

$$q_x = \frac{d_x}{l_x}$$

For example, from Table 9,

$$l_3 = l_2 - d_2$$

$$= 239 - 98 = 141$$

$$q_2 = \frac{d_2}{l_2}$$

$$= \frac{98}{239} = 0.410$$

The calculation of expectation of further life (e_x) is somewhat more complicated. First, we must obtain the average number of individuals alive in each age interval, which we call the life-table age structure (L_x):

L_x = number of individuals alive on the average *during* the age interval x to $x + 1$

$$= \frac{l_x + l_{x+1}}{2}$$

For example, in the barnacle data above,

L_1 = average number alive in age interval 1 to 2 years

$$= \frac{l_1 + l_2}{2} = \frac{437 + 239}{2} = 338$$

We then sum these cumulatively from the bottom of the life table and obtain a set of values expressed in units of (individuals × time units), which we call T_x:

$$T_x = \sum_{x}^{\infty} L_x$$

For the barnacle data, for example,

$T_4 = L_4 + L_5 + L_6 + L_7 + L_8 + L_9$

= 205.5 barnacle-years

Finally, we can divide T_x by the number of individuals (l_x) to get the average expectation of life:

$$e_x = \frac{T_x}{l_x}$$

For example, from Table 9 data

$$e_4 = \frac{T_4}{l_4} = \frac{205.5}{109} = 1.88 \text{ years}$$

For all the barnacle data in Table 9, we thus obtain

x	l_x	L_x	T_x	e_x
0	1000	718.5	1577	1.58
1	437	338	858.5	1.96
2	239	190	520.5	2.17
3	141	125	330.5	2.34
4	109	93	205.5	1.88
5	77	61.5	112.5	1.45
6	46	30	51	1.11
7	14	14	21	1.50
8	14	7	7	0.50
9	0	—	—	—

This whole procedure, like most mathematical exercises in ecology, looks much more formidable than it really is.

The most frequently used part of the life table is the l_x column, the number of survivors at the start of age x. This is often expressed from a starting cohort of 1000, but human demographers prefer a starting cohort of 100,000 and other preferences include 100 (scale of percentage survival) or 1.00 (scale of proportion surviving, or probability of survival). The l_x data are plotted as a survivorship curve, and Figure 68 illustrates the survivorship

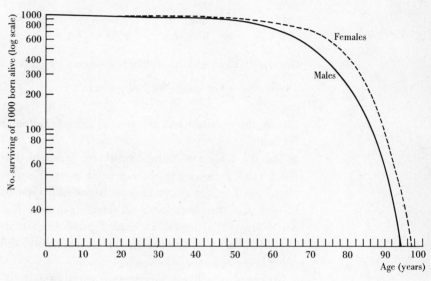

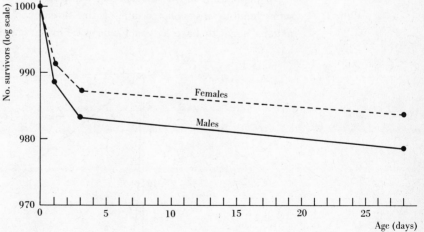

FIGURE 68

(a) Survivorship curve for all males and females, United States, 1959–1961. (b) Infant survival during first month. (National Center for Health Statistics 1968.)

curves for the human population of the United States in 1959–1961. Note that the l_x values are plotted on a logarithmic scale. Population data should be plotted this way when one is interested in *rates* of change rather than absolute numerical changes. A simple numerical example shows this: If half of a population dies, we obtain

Starting population size	No. dying	Final population size
1000	500	500
500	250	250
250	125	125

On a logarithmic scale, all these decreases are equal (base 10 logs):

$$\log(1000) - \log(500) = \log(500) - \log(250)$$
$$3.00 \quad - \quad 2.70 \quad = \quad 2.70 \quad - \quad 2.40$$

Clearly the *numbers* lost are greatly different, although the *rates of loss* are the same.

The life table was introduced to ecologists by Raymond Pearl in 1921. Pearl (1928) recognized three general types of survivorship curves (Figure 69). Type I curves are from populations with very little loss for most of the lifespan and then high losses of older organisms. The diagonal survivorship curve (type II) implies a constant rate of mortality independent of age. Type III curves indicate high loss early in life, followed by a period of much lower and relatively constant losses.

No population has a survivorship curve exactly like these ideal ones, but some tend to resemble certain of the three types. Man in the developed nations tends to have a type I survivorship curve. Many birds have a type

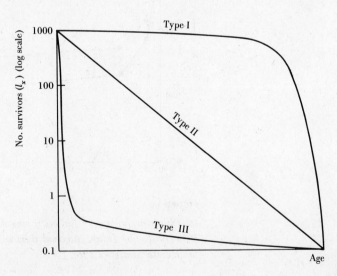

FIGURE 69

Hypothetical survivorship curves.
(After Pearl 1928.)

II survivorship curve, and many populations would fall in the intermediate area between types I and II. Often a period of high loss in the early juvenile stages alters these ideal type I and II curves. Type III curves occur in many fishes, marine invertebrates, and parasites.

Now that we have seen what a life table looks like, how do we get the data to construct a life table? This question brings up an important critical distinction: There are two different ways of gathering data for a life table and they produce two different types of life tables. These are the *static* life table (stationary, time-specific, current, or vertical life table) and the *cohort* life table (generation, horizontal life table). These two life tables are different in form, except under unusual circumstances, and are always quite different in meaning (Merrell 1947).

The *static* life table, calculated on the basis of a cross section of the population at a specific time, is illustrated in Table 10. In this example, the

TABLE 10

Static life-table data, human female population of Canada, 1966[a]

Age group (yr)	No. in each age group	Deaths in each age group	Mortality rate per 1000 population, $1000q_x$
0–1	189,208	3,822	20.2
1–4	879,408	775	0.88
5–9	1,128,036	480	0.43
10–14	1,022,258	318	0.31
15–19	908,767	467	0.51
20–24	734,183	403	0.55
25–29	622,332	384	0.62
30–34	611,199	564	0.92
35–39	636,375	845	1.33
40–44	632,319	1,293	2.04
45–49	547,163	1,823	3.33
50–54	489,981	2,434	4.97
55–59	402,911	3,115	7.73
60–64	333,404	4,064	12.19
65–69	276,771	5,393	19.49
70–74	228,399	7,063	30.92
75–79	161,398	8,695	53.87
80–84	96,655	9,048	93.61
85–over	59,769	10,964	183.44

[a] These data were obtained by tallying the number of females in each age group by 1966 birthdays, and tallying the number of deaths in 1966 for the same age groups.
SOURCE: Canada Year Book, 1969.

census data and mortality data are for human females in Canada in 1966. A cross section of the female population in 1966 provides a set of mortality rates (q_x) for each age group, and the q_x values can be used to calculate a complete life table in the way outlined above.

On the other hand, a *cohort* life table is calculated on the basis of a cohort of organisms followed throughout life. For example, you could, in principle, get all the birth records for New York City for 1921 and trace the history of all these people throughout their lives. This would involve following them when they move out of town and would be a very tedious task. You could then tabulate the number surviving at each age interval and get data similar to those in Table 11. Very few data like these are available for human populations.* This procedure would give you the survivorship

TABLE 11

Hypothetical cohort life-table data for humans[a]

Age group, x	No. survivors at start of age x
0–1	1850
1–4	1774
5–9	1728
10–14	1709
15–19	1699
20–24	1682
25–29	1669
30–34	1658
35–39	1641
40–44	1593
45–49	1547
50–54	1502
55–59	1459
60–64	1346
65–69	1243
70–74	1029
75–79	650
80–84	411
85 and over	131

[a] By following each individual through life one could observe the l_x function directly.

* For human populations, unlike those of other animals and plants, it is possible to construct cohort life tables indirectly from mortality rate (q_x) data. Thus, to construct a cohort life table for the 1921 year class of New York, we can obtain the mortality statistics for the 0- to 1-year-olds for 1921, the 1- to 5-year-olds for 1922–25, the 6- to 10-year-olds for 1926–1930, etc., and use these q_x rates to estimate the life-table functions. This approach was used to obtain Figure 70.

curve directly, and if you desired you could calculate the other life-table functions.

These two types of life table will be identical if and only if the environment does not change from year to year and the population is at equilibrium. But normally there will be good years and bad years, the birth and death rates will vary, and consequently there will be large differences between the two forms of life table. These differences can be illustrated very well for human populations. Figure 70 contrasts static and cohort life tables for the human male population of England and Wales in 1880. The static life table shows what the survivorship curve would have been like if the population had continued surviving at the rates observed in 1880. But the continual improvement in medicine and sanitation in the last 100 years has increased survival rates, and the people born in 1880 had a generation survivorship curve unlike that of any of the years through which they lived.

The insurance companies would like to have data from cohort life tables covering the future, but these are obviously impossible to get. They are definitely not interested in cohort life tables covering the past—the life table for the 1880 cohort would be of little use for predicting mortality patterns today with all the medical advances. So they use static life tables and correct them at each census. These predictions will never be completely accurate but will be close enough for their purposes.

Life tables from nonhuman populations are harder to come by. In general three types of data have been used to determine ecological life tables:

1 *Survivorship directly observed.* The survival (l_x) of a large cohort born at the same time is followed at close intervals throughout its existence. This is the best information to have since it does not involve the assumption that the population is stable in time. A good example of data of this type are those of Connell (1961a) on the barnacle *Chthamalus stellatus* in Scotland. This barnacle settles on rocks

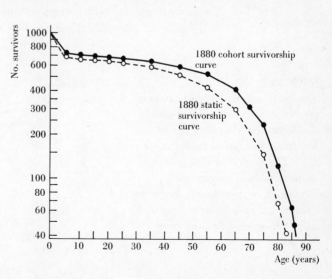

FIGURE 70

Comparison of cohort or generation survivorship of males born in 1880 in England and Wales with static or time-specific survivorship of males for 1880. (Data from Registrar General 1968.)

during the autumn. Connell did several experiments in which he removed a competing barnacle *Balanus balanoides* from some rocks but not from others, and then counted about once a month the *Chthamalus* surviving on these defined areas (Figure 71). Barnacles that disappeared had certainly died; they could not emigrate.

2 Age at death observed. If we use data on age at death to estimate the life-table functions, we must assume that the population is stable in time and that the birth and death rates of each age group remain constant. The best example of this type of data are those of Murie (1944) on the Dall mountain sheep (*Ovis dalli*) of Mount McKinley, Alaska. Murie collected all the skulls he could find in this area, animals that had died prior to his study. He got 608 skulls of sheep that had died before 1937 and classed them by age. The age at death was determined by the annular rings on the horns. There was no difficulty in sampling except for the very young animals, whose fragile skulls are probably underrepresented in the sample. Caughley (1966) estimated the first-year losses and provided the mortality estimates shown in Figure 72.

3 Age structure directly observed. There is much ecological information of this sort, particularly on birds and fish. In these cases one can often determine how many individuals of each age are living in the population. For example, if we fish a lake we can get a sample of fish and determine the age of each from annular rings on the scales. The same type of data can be obtained from tree rings. The difficulty is that to produce a life table from such data one must assume a constant age distribution, something that is rare for many populations. Therefore, data of this type are not always suitable for constructing a life table.

The age structure of a population of Himalayan thar (a goat-like ungulate) in New Zealand has been used by Caughley (1966) to construct a life table. The thar was introduced into New Zealand in 1904 and has since spread in the mountains of the South Island. Growth rings on the horns are laid down every winter after the first, and thus animals can be easily aged. The population sampled was believed to be stationary in numbers and the shooting sample appeared to be a random one. Figure 73 shows the survivorship curve with the raw data points and a smoothed l_x curve.

Attempts to gather together life-table data and to establish a general theory of mortality have all fallen short of their goal. Pearl and Miner

FIGURE 71

Survivorship curves of the barnacle Chthamalus stellatus, *which had settled naturally on the shore at Millport, Scotland, in the autumn of 1953. The survival of* Chthamalus *growing without contact with* Balanus *is compared with that in an undisturbed area.* Balanus *crowds out* Chthamalus *when the two species are together. (After Connell 1961a.)*

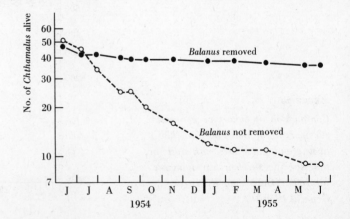

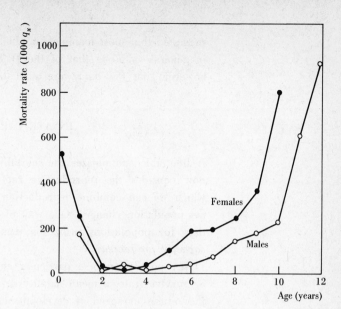

FIGURE 72

Dall sheep: mortality rate per 1000 for each age interval of 1 year ($1000q_x$), plotted against the start of the interval. Data from Murie (1944). (After Caughley 1966.)

(1935) concluded that insufficient data were available. Deevey (1947) recognized the difficulty of comparing life tables of different species because the basic data of the life table are sometimes of the "stationary" type, sometimes of the "cohort" type, and the point of origin of the life tables may be different—birth for mammals, egg laying for insects, or settling on rocks for barnacles. Caughley (1966) restricted his remarks to mammals and

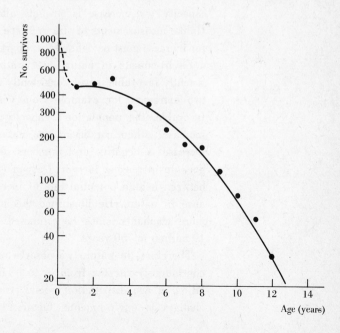

FIGURE 73

Survivorship curve constructed from a sample of female Himalayan thar (Hemitragus jemlahicus) shot in New Zealand in the summer of 1963–1964. (After Caughley 1966.)

suggested that most mammals might have U-shaped mortality curves similar in general shape to that of the Dall sheep (Figure 72). He pointed out, however, that few data were available for critical comparisons.

INNATE CAPACITY FOR INCREASE IN NUMBERS

A life table summarizes the mortality schedule of a population. We must now consider the reproductive rate of a population and techniques by which we can combine reproduction and mortality estimates to determine net population changes. One way of combining reproduction and mortality data for populations utilizes a demographic parameter called the *innate capacity for increase.*

Any population in a particular environment will have a mean longevity or survival rate, a mean natality or birth rate, and a mean growth rate of individuals or speed of development. The values of these means are determined in part by the environment and in part by a certain innate quality of the organisms themselves. This quality of an organism cannot be measured simply because it is not a constant, but we can measure its expression under specified conditions and thereby define for each population its innate capacity for increase (also called the intrinsic rate of natural increase, or Malthusian parameter).

The innate capacity for increase must be considered as a quality that is just as characteristic of a species as is its size or shape. It is, however, a character that is much more difficult to measure and define, since the innate capacity for increase is strongly affected by changes in the environment. Unlike measurements of size or shape, those of a population's innate capacity for increase must be defined for a particular environment.

Environments in nature are continuously varying. They are never consistently favorable, never consistently unfavorable, but fluctuate between these two extremes, for example from winter to summer. When conditions are favorable, the population's capacity for increase is positive and numbers increase; when conditions are unfavorable, the population's capacity for increase is negative and numbers decrease. It is clear that no population goes on increasing forever. Darwin (1859, Chap. 3) recognized the contrast between a high potential rate of increase and an observed approximate balance in nature. He illustrated this problem by asking why there were not more elephants, since he estimated that two elephants could give rise to 19 million in 750 years.

Therefore, in nature we observe an actual rate of increase (r) which is continuously varying from $+$ to $-$ in response to changes within the population in age distribution, social structure, and genetic composition and to changes in environmental factors. In the laboratory, on the other hand, we can eliminate unfavorable changes in weather, provide ideal food, and eliminate predators and diseases. In this artificial situation we can observe the *innate capacity for increase* (r_m). We define r_m, the innate capacity for increase, as the *maximal rate of increase attained at any particular combination of temperature, humidity, quality of food, etc., when the quantity of food, space, and other animals of the same species are kept to an optimum and other species are entirely excluded from the experiment* (Andrewartha and Birch, 1954, p. 33). Environmental factors are thus separated into two kinds when we determine r_m for any organism:

1 Optimal
   a Quantity of food or nutrients
   b Space
   c Density

2 Not necessarily optimal but controlled and specified
   a Quality of food or nutrients
   b Temperature
   c Humidity
   d Light, etc.

Thus the innate capacity for increase is arbitrarily defined with regard to a specific laboratory situation. This does not make r_m useless from the point of view of understanding nature; the importance of this measure is that it gives us a model with which we can compare the actual observed rates of increase in nature.

An organism's innate capacity for increase depends on its fertility, longevity, and speed of development. For any population these are measured by the birth rate and the death rate. Now, when the birth rate exceeds the death rate, the population will increase. If we wish to estimate quantitatively the rate at which the population increases or decreases, we run into troubles because *both the birth rate and the death rate vary with age.*

Students of human populations were the first to appreciate these problems. Alfred Lotka, in particular, stands out for his mathematical analysis of population growth. In 1925 Lotka derived a function, which he called the "natural rate of increase," to take account of changes in birth and death rates with age.

How can we express the variations of birth and death rates with age? We have just discussed the method of expressing survival rates as a function of age. The life table includes a table of age-specific survival rates. The portion of the life table that we need to compute r_m is the l_x column, the survivorship curve, expressed on the basis of 1.00 as the starting point. Similarly, the birth rate of a population is best expressed as an age schedule of births. This is a table which gives the number of offspring produced per unit of time per female aged x and is called a *fertility table*, or m_x function. Usually only the females are counted, and the demographer typically views populations as females giving rise to more females. Table 12 gives the survivorship table and the fertility table for females in the United States in 1967. The l_x schedule we are familiar with, except that now it is expressed on the basis of 1.00 so that we have the probability of surviving to a given age. In this case the great majority of women live through the child-bearing ages. The fertility table gives the expected number of *female* offspring for each female living through the 5 years of each age group. For example, slightly more than 4 in 10 women between the ages of 20 and 25 will, on the average, have a female baby.

Given these data, we can obtain a useful statistic, the *net reproductive rate* (R_0). If a cohort of females lives its entire reproductive life at the survival and fertility rates given in Table 12, what will this cohort or generation leave as its female offspring? We define as the net reproductive rate:

$$\text{Net reproductive rate} = R_0 = \frac{\text{no. daughters born in generation } t + 1}{\text{no. daughters born in generation } t}$$

R_0 is thus the multiplication rate per generation* and is obtained by multi-

---

* A generation is defined as the mean period elapsing between the birth of parents and the birth of offspring. See page 170 and Figure 77.

TABLE 12

Survivorship table (l_x) and fertility table (m_x) for women in United States, 1967

Age group, x	Pivotal age	Probability of surviving to pivotal age, l_x	No. female off-spring per female aged x per time unit (5 years), m_x	Product of $l_x m_x$, V_x
0–9	5.0	0.9775	0.0	0.0
10–14	12.5	0.9752	0.0022	0.0021
15–19	17.5	0.9730	0.1656	0.1611
20–24	22.5	0.9698	0.4244	0.4116
25–29	27.5	0.9661	0.3478	0.3360
30–34	32.5	0.9613	0.1934	0.1859
35–39	37.5	0.9541	0.0939	0.0896
40–44	42.5	0.9434	0.0259	0.0244
45–49	47.5	0.9275	0.0017	0.0016
50–Over	—	—	0.0	0.0

$$R_0 = \sum_0^\infty l_x m_x = 1.212$$

SOURCE: National Center for Health Statistics, 1969.

plying together the l_x and m_x schedules and summing over all age groups, as shown in Table 12:

$$R_0 = \sum_0^\infty l_x m_x = \sum_0^\infty V_x$$

We thus temper the birth rate by the fraction of expected survivors to each age. If survival were complete, R_0 would just be the sum of the m_x column. In this example (Table 12), the human population of the United States, if it continued at these 1967 rates, would multiply 1.212 times in each generation. The net reproductive rate is illustrated in Figure 74.

Given these two tables expressing the age-specific rates of survival and fertility, we may enquire at what rate a population subject to these rates would increase, assuming (1) that these rates remain constant and (2) that no limit is placed on the population growth. Since these survival and fertility rates vary with age, the actual birth and death rates of the population will depend on the existing age distribution. Obviously if the whole population was over 50 years of age, there would be no increase. Similarly, if all females were between 20 and 25, the rate of increase would be much higher than if they were all between 30 and 35. Before we can calculate the population's rate of increase, it would seem that we must specify (1) age-specific survival rates (l_x), (2) age-specific birth rates (m_x), and (3) age distribution.

This conclusion is not correct. Lotka (1922) has shown that a population which is subject to a constant schedule of age rates will gradually approach a fixed or *stable age distribution*, whatever the initial age distribution may have been, and will then maintain this age distribution indefinitely. When the population has reached this stable age distribution, it will increase in numbers according to the differential equation

$$\frac{dN}{dt} = r_m N \qquad r_m = b_{rate} - d_{rate}$$

$$\begin{pmatrix} \text{rate of change in} \\ \text{numbers per unit time} \end{pmatrix} = \begin{pmatrix} \text{innate capacity} \\ \text{for increase} \end{pmatrix} \times \begin{pmatrix} \text{population} \\ \text{size} \end{pmatrix}$$

This same equation may be rewritten in integral form:

$$N_t = N_0 e^{r_m t}$$

where

N_0 = number of individuals at time 0
N_t = number of individuals at time t
e = 2.71828 (a constant)
r_m = innate capacity for increase for the particular environmental conditions
t = time

This is the equation describing the curve of geometric increase in an expand-

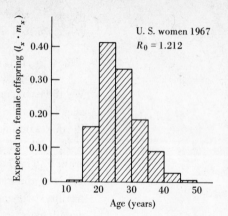

FIGURE 74

Expected number of female offspring for each female born in the United States, 1967. Data in Table 12. The area under the curve is the net reproductive rate (R_0). $R_0 = 1.212$.

ing population (or geometric decrease to zero if r_m is negative). A simple example illustrates this equation. Let the starting population (N_0) be 100 and let $r_m = 0.5$ per female per year. The successive populations would be

Year	Population size
0	100
1	$(100)(e^{0.5}) = 165$
2	$(100)(e^{1.0}) = 272$
3	$(100)(e^{1.5}) = 448$
4	$(100)(e^{2.0}) = 739$
5	$(100)(e^{2.5}) = 1218$

This hypothetical population growth is plotted in Figure 75. Note that on a logarithmic scale the increase follows a straight line, and hence geometric population growth is sometimes erroneously called "logarithmic growth."

To summarize to this point: (1) Any population subject to a fixed age schedule of births and deaths will increase in a geometric way; and (2) this

FIGURE 75

Geometric growth of a hypothetical population when $N_0 = 100$ and $r_m = 0.5$. (a) Logarithmic scale, (b) arithmetic scale.

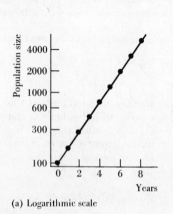

(a) Logarithmic scale

(b) Arithmetic scale

geometric increase will dictate a fixed and unchanging age distribution called the stable age distribution.

Let us invent a simple model organism to illustrate these points. Suppose we have a parthenogenetic animal that lives 3 years and then dies. It produces two young at exactly 1 year of age, one young at exactly 2 years of age, and no young at year 3. The life table and fertility table for this hypothetical animal are thus extremely simple:

x	l_x	m_x	$V_x (= l_x m_x)$	$(x)(l_x)(m_x)$
0	1.00	0.0	0.0	0.0
1	1.00	2.0	2.0	2.0
2	1.00	1.0	1.0	2.0
3	1.00	0.0	0.0	0.0
4	0.00	—	—	—

$$R_0 = \sum_0^4 l_x m_x = 3.0 \qquad 4.0$$

If a population of this organism starts with one individual aged zero, the population growth will be as shown in Figure 76, or, in tabular form, as follows:

Year	Number at ages 0	1	2	3	Total population size	% Age zero in total population
0	1	0	0	0	1	100.00
1	2	1	0	0	3	66.67
2	5	2	1	0	8	62.50
3	12	5	2	1	20	60.00
4	29	12	5	2	48	60.42
5	70	29	12	5	116	60.34
6	169	70	29	12	280	60.36
7	408	169	70	29	676	60.36
8	985	408	169	70	1632	60.36

Note that the age distribution quickly becomes fixed or stable with about 60% age 0, 25% age 1, 10% age 2, and 4% age 3. This demonstrates the conclusion of Lotka (1922) that a population growing geometrically develops a stable age distribution.

We may also use our model animal to illustrate how r_m can be calculated from biological data. The data of the l_x and m_x tables are sufficient to allow one to calculate r_m, the innate capacity for increase in numbers. To do this we first need to calculate the net reproductive rate (R_0), which we have explained above. For our model animal, $R_0 = 3.0$, which means that

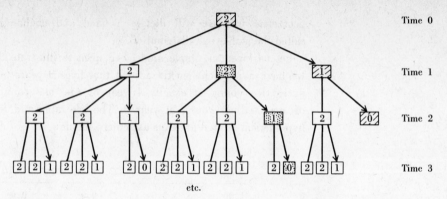

etc.

FIGURE 76

Population growth of a simple model animal that is parthenogenetic.
Each box represents one live individual, and the numbers within each
box indicate the number of young to be produced at the next time
interval. Arrows indicate aging of individuals from one year to the next.

the population can triple its size each generation. But how long is a generation? The *mean length of a generation* (G) is the mean period elapsing
between the birth of parents and the birth of offspring. Obviously this is
only an approximate definition, since offspring are born over a period of
time and not all at once. The mean length of a generation is defined approximately as follows (Dublin and Lotka 1925):

$$G = \frac{\sum l_x m_x x}{\sum l_x m_x} = \frac{\sum l_x m_x x}{R_0}$$

For our model organism, $G = 4.0/3.0 = 1.33$ years. Figure 77 illustrates
the approximate meaning of generation time for a human population. Leslie
(1966) has discussed some of the difficulties of applying the concept of
generation time to a continuously breeding population with overlapping
generations. For organisms such as annual plants and many insects with a

FIGURE 77

Mechanical interpretation of mean
length of one generation. Histogram
of daughters from cohort of 100,000
mothers starting life together is
balanced by sum of total daughters
(116,760) at 28.46 years from
fulcrum. $R_0 = 1.168.$ *Data from*
U.S. population, 1920. (After Dublin
and Lotka 1925.)

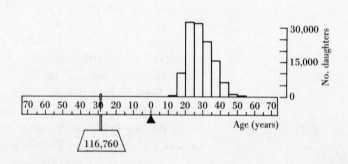

fixed length of life cycle, the mean length of a generation is simple to measure and to understand.

Knowing the multiplication rate per generation (R_0) and the length of a generation (G), we can now determine r_m directly as an instantaneous rate:

$$r_m = \frac{\log_e(R_0)}{G}$$

For our model organism,

$$r_m = \frac{\log_e(3.0)}{1.33} = 0.824 \text{ per individual per year}$$

Because the generation time G is an approximate estimate, this value of r_m is only an approximate estimate when generations overlap.

The innate capacity for increase can be determined more accurately by solving the formula derived by Lotka (1907, 1913):

$$\sum_{x=0}^{\infty} e^{-r_m x} l_x m_x = 1$$

By substituting trial values of r_m, we can solve this equation. Our model animal can again be used as an example. For our estimate of $r_m = 0.824$, we get

x	$l_x m_x$	$e^{-0.824x}$	$e^{-0.824x} l_x m_x$
0	0.0	1.00	0.000
1	2.0	0.44	0.877
2	1.0	0.19	0.192
3	0.0	0.08	0.000
4	0.0	0.04	0.000

$$\sum e^{-r_m x} l_x m_x = 1.070$$

Clearly the estimate $r_m = 0.824$ is slightly low. We repeat, with $r_m = 0.85$, and after several trials we find that, for this model organism, $r_m = 0.881$ provides

$$\sum e^{-r_m x} l_x m_x = 1.0004$$

which is a close enough approximation. Birch (1948) works out another example in detail. Mertz (1970) has provided a lucid derivation and discussion of these formulas.

The innate capacity for increase is an instantaneous rate and can be converted to a finite rate* by the formula

Finite rate of increase $= \lambda = e^{r_m}$

For example, if $r_m = 0.881$, $\lambda = 2.413$ per individual per year in our model

* Appendix II gives a general discussion of instantaneous and finite rates.

organism. Thus, for every individual present this year, there will be 2.413 present next year.

It should now be clear why the innate capacity for increase in numbers cannot be expressed quantitatively except for a particular environment. Any component of the environment such as temperature, humidity, or rainfall might affect the birth and death rates and hence r_m.

One example of the effect of the environment on the innate capacity for increase was shown by Birch (1953a) in his work on *Calandra oryzae*, a beetle pest that lives in stored grain. The innate capacity for increase in this species varied with the temperature and with the moisture content of the wheat, as shown in Figure 78. The practical implications of these results are that wheat should be stored where it is cool and/or dry to prevent losses from *C. oryzae*.

Grain beetles live in an almost ideal habitat, surrounded by food, protected from most enemies, and with relatively constant physical conditions. They are also easy to deal with in the laboratory, so they have been used extensively in ecology lab experiments. Birch (1953a) studied two species, *C. oryzae* (a temperate species) and *Rhizopertha dominica* (a tropical species). He found that in both species r_m varied with temperature and moisture (Figure 79). The line $r_m = 0$ marks the limit of the possible ecological range for each species with respect to temperature and moisture. *Calandra* is more cold resistant; *Rhizopertha* can increase at higher temperatures and lower humidities. The distribution of the two species in Australia agrees with these results: *Rhizopertha* is a pest only in the warmer parts of the country and is absent from Tasmania, where *Calandra* occurs as a pest.

In general r_m is not correlated with rareness and commonness of species. Species with a high r_m are not always common and species with a low r_m

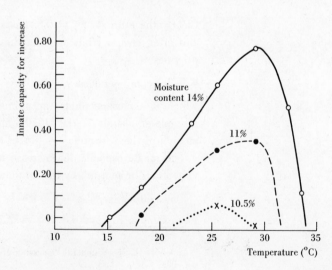

FIGURE 78

Innate capacity for increase (r_m) of the grain beetle Calandra oryzae *living in wheat of different moisture contents and at different temperatures. (After Birch 1953a.)*

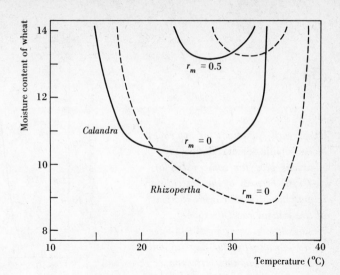

FIGURE 79

Approximate contours of the innate capacity for increase (r_m) for the two grain beetles Calandra oryzae *and* Rhizopertha dominica *living in wheat of different moisture contents and at different temperatures. (After Birch 1953a.)*

are not always rare (Slobodkin 1961, p. 53). Thus some species, such as the buffalo in North America, the elephant in central Africa, and the periodical cicadas, are (or were) quite common and yet have a low r_m value. Many parasites and other invertebrates with a high r_m are nevertheless quite rare. Darwin pointed this out in *The Origin of Species*.

We can calculate how certain changes in the life history of a species would affect the innate capacity for increase in numbers. In general, three things will increase r_m: (1) reduction in age at first reproduction, (2) increase in litter size, and (3) increase in number of litters (increased longevity). In many cases the most profound effects are achieved by changing the age at first reproduction. For example, Birch (1948) calculated for the grain beetle *C. oryzae* the number of eggs needed to obtain $r_m = 0.76$ according to the age at first reproduction:

Age at which breeding begins (weeks)	Total no. eggs that must be laid to produce $r_m = 0.76$	
1	15	
2	32	
3	67	
4	141	(actual life history)
5	297	
6	564	

The earlier the peak in reproductive output, the larger the r_m value for a species usually. Lewontin (1965a) provides an excellent example to illustrate this in *Drosophila serrata* (Figure 80). The Rabaul race of this fruit fly survives poorly and lays fewer eggs than the Brisbane race, but because it begins to reproduce at an earlier age (11.7 compared with 16.0 days), its

FIGURE 80

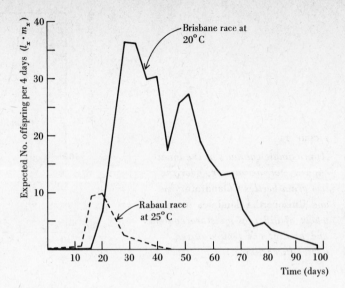

Observed V_x functions for two races of Drosophila serrata. *Both V_x functions give the same value of r_m (0.16) because of the overriding importance of earlier reproduction of the Rabaul race. Brisbane females lay an average of 546 eggs at 20°C, while Rabaul flies lay only 151 eggs during their lifespan. (After Lewontin 1965a.)*

innate capacity for increase is equal to that of the longer-living, more fertile Brisbane race.

These principles also apply to human populations. We can use these formulas to investigate how changes in the age at first reproduction and family size could affect the innate capacity for increase in humans. Cole (1954) was one of the first to make these calculations (Figure 81), and he gives some illustrations. If all women were 20 at the time of their first reproduction, 3.0 children would provide an $r_m = 0.02$; if the first birth is delayed until age 30, 3.5 children are required to provide $r_m = 0.02$. To obtain an $r_m = 0.04$ women could start at 13 and produce 3.5 children, or start at 25 years and have 6.0 children. The age at first reproduction is obviously important in determining the growth of human populations, and it is a mistake to view the whole problem in terms of family size.

To conclude: The concept of an innate capacity for increase in numbers which we have just discussed is an abstraction from nature. In nature we do not find populations with stable age distributions or with constant age-specific rates of mortality and fertility. For these reasons the actual rate of increase we observe in natural populations is much more complex than the theoretical r_m. The importance of r_m lies mostly in its use as a model to compare with the actual rates of increase we see in nature.

AGE DISTRIBUTIONS

We have already discussed the idea of age distribution in connection with the innate capacity for increase. We have noted that a population growing geometrically with constant age-specific mortality and fertility rates would assume and maintain a stable age distribution. The stable age distribution can be calculated for any set of life tables and fertility tables. We define the stable age distribution as follows:

C_x = proportion of organisms in the age category x to $x + 1$ in a population increasing geometrically

Mertz (1970) has shown that

$$C_x = \frac{\lambda^{-x} l_x}{\sum_{i=0}^{\infty} \lambda^{-i} l_i}$$

where
  $\lambda = e^{rm}$ = finite rate of increase
  l_x = survivorship function from life table
  x, i = subscripts indicating age

Let us go through these calculations with our model organism.

$\lambda = e^{rm} = e^{0.881} = 2.413$

Age (x)	l_x	λ^{-x}	$\lambda^{-x} l_x$
0	1.0	1.0000	1.0000
1	1.0	0.4144	0.4144
2	1.0	0.1717	0.1717
3	1.0	0.0711	0.0711
4	0.0	0.0295	0.0000

$$\sum_{x=0}^{4} \lambda^{-x} l_x = 1.6572$$

FIGURE 81

Average reproductive performances required to give specified values of r_m, the innate capacity for increase, in human populations. This graph shows the extent to which total progeny number would have to be altered to maintain a specified innate capacity for increase while shifting the age at which reproduction begins. Sex ratio at birth is assumed to be 50% males. Births are assumed to follow one another at 12-month intervals until completed family size is achieved. (After Cole 1954.)

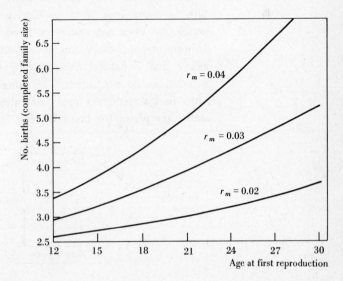

Thus, to calculate C_0, the proportion of organisms in the age category 0 to 1 in the stable age distribution, we have

$$C_0 = \frac{\lambda^{-0} l_0}{\sum_{i=0}^{4} \lambda^{-i} l_i} = \frac{(1.0)(1.0)}{1.6572} = 0.6035$$

For C_1 we have

$$C_1 = \frac{(0.4144)\,(1.0)}{1.6572} = 0.250$$

In a similar way,

$$C_2 = 0.104$$
$$C_3 = 0.043$$

Compare these calculated values to those obtained empirically above (page 169). Birch (1953a) illustrates another method of calculating the stable egg distribution for a set of l_x and m_x schedules.

Populations that have reached a constant size, in which the birth rate equals the death rate, will also assume a fixed age distribution, called a *stationary age distribution* (or life-table age distribution), and will maintain this distribution, termed L_x in the life-table section above. The stationary age distribution is a hypothetical one, and it illustrates what the age composition of the population would be at a particular set of mortality rates (q_x) if the birth rate were set to be exactly equal to the death rate. Figure 82 contrasts the stable and stationary age distributions for the short-tailed vole in a laboratory colony.

These are the only two conditions in which a fixed, constant age structure is maintained in a population. Under any other circumstances the population does not assume a fixed age structure but changes over time. In natural populations the age structure is almost constantly changing. We rarely find a natural population that has a stable age structure, because populations do not increase for long in an unlimited fashion. Nor do we often find a stationary age distribution, because populations are rarely in a stationary phase for long. We can illustrate these relationships as follows:

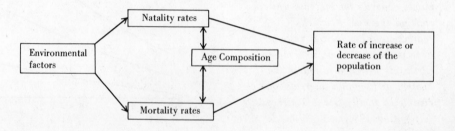

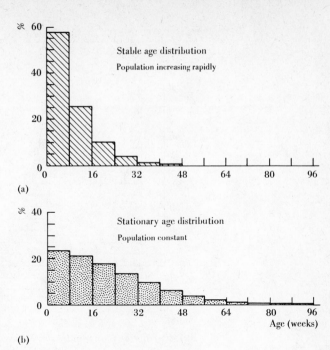

FIGURE 82

(a) Stable age distribution and (b) stationary age distribution of the vole, Microtus agrestis. *(After Leslie and Ranson 1940.)*

With proper care, information on age composition can be used to judge the status of the population. Increasing populations typically have a predominance of the younger age groups, while stable or declining populations tend to have fewer young organisms (Figure 82). Figure 83 illustrates this idea with the human population of Algeria, which was increasing at 3.3% per year in 1967 and had an average expectation of life at birth between 35 and 40 years, and of the United States, which was increasing at 0.8% per year in 1968 and had an average expectation of life of approximately 70 years. The age structure of human populations has been analyzed in detail because of its economic and sociological implications (Coale 1958; Bogue 1969, Chap. 7). A population with a large fraction of children, such as Algeria (47% under age 15), has a much greater demand for schools and other child services than another population like the United States (30% under age 15).

In natural populations even more variation is apparent. In long-lived species such as trees and fishes one may find *dominant year classes.* Figure 84 illustrates this for a commercial whitefish (*Coregonus clupeaformis*) population in which some year classes may be 10 times as strong as others. In these situations the age composition can change greatly from one year to the next. Alexander (1958) has discussed the use of age composition information in the management of wildlife populations, and Ricker (1958, Chap. 2) discussed this problem in exploited fish populations.

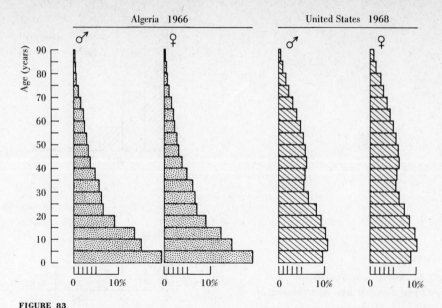

FIGURE 83

*Age distributions for rapidly increasing human population in Algeria and slowly increasing population in United States. (*Demographic Yearbook *1968.)*

SUMMARY

Population changes can be analyzed with a set of quantitative techniques first developed for human population analysis. A life table is an age-specific summary of the mortality rates operating on a population. Life tables are necessary because mortality does not fall equally on all ages, and often the very young and the old suffer high mortality.

The reproductive rate of a population can be described by a fertility table that summarizes reproduction with respect to age. The innate capacity for increase of a population is obtained by combining the life table and the fertility table for specified environmental conditions. This concept leads to an important demographic principle: *A population that is subject to a constant schedule of death and birth rates (1) will increase in numbers geometrically at a rate equal to the innate capacity for increase, (2) will assume a fixed or stable age distribution, and (3) will maintain this age distribution indefinitely.* A hypothetical organism is invented to illustrate these conclusions empirically.

The age distribution of a population is fixed and unchanging only during geometric increase (the stable age distribution) and during a period of

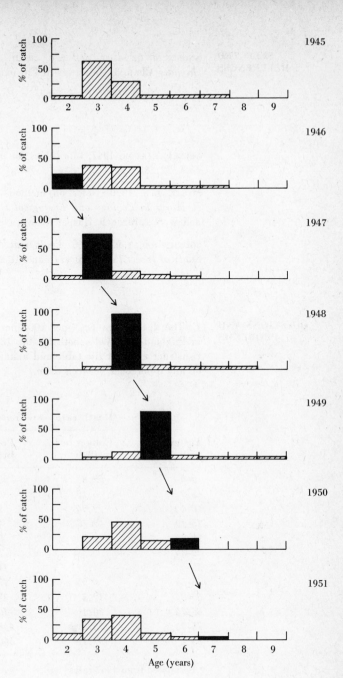

FIGURE 84

Age composition of samples from Lake Erie commercial whitefish catch for 1945–1951. Note the strong 1944 year class (solid bars) and the large changes in age composition from year to year. (After Lawler 1965.)

constant population size (the stationary age distribution). Under other circumstances the age distribution will shift over time, which is the usual condition in natural populations.

SELECTED
REFERENCES

ANDREWARTHA, H. G., and L. C. BIRCH. 1954. *The Distribution and Abundance of Animals*. Chap. 3. University of Chicago Press, Chicago.

BARCLAY, G. W. 1958. *Techniques of Population Analysis*. Chaps. 4–7. Wiley, New York.

DEEVEY, E. S., JR. 1947. Life tables for natural populations of animals. *Quart. Rev. Biol.* 22:283–314.

MERTZ, D. B. 1970. Notes on methods used in life-history studies. pp. 4–17 in *Readings in Ecology and Ecological Genetics*, ed. by J. H. Connell, D. B. Mertz, and W. W. Murdoch. Harper & Row, New York.

SOUTHWOOD, T. R. E. 1966. *Ecological Methods with Particular Reference to the Study of Insect Populations*. Chaps. 10 and 11. Methuen, London.

QUESTIONS AND
PROBLEMS

1 The death rates (q_x) per 1000 per year are given below for human females in England and Wales both for the 1891 cohort and for the population in 1891. Construct a cohort life table and a static life table from these data and comment on any differences between them.

	Death rates experienced by:	
Age group (yr)	Cohort born in 1891	Population in 1891
0–4	*52.8*	*53.7*
5–9	*4.15*	*4.7*
10–14	*2.24*	*2.9*
15–19	*2.76*	*4.3*
20–24	*3.25*	*5.2*
25–34	*4.53*	*7.1*
35–44	*4.51*	*11.1*
45–54	*6.95*	*17.1*
55–64	*12.3*	*33.4*
65–74	*30.1*	*70.6*
75–84	*(75.3)*[a]	*148.1*
85 and above	*(192.1)*[a]	*300.7*

[a] Estimated from 1967 rates.

SOURCE: *The Registrar General's Statistical Review of England and Wales for the Year 1967.*

2 In human populations differences in mortality rates have very little effect on age composition, while changes in birth rates have a large effect on age structure (Barclay 1958, p. 229). Why should this be? Would the same principle hold for plant and animal populations?

3 Connell (1970) gives the following data for the barnacle *Balanus glandula*:

Age (yr)	1959 Settlement		1960 Settlement	
	l_x	m_x	l_x	m_x
0	1.0	0	1.0	0
1	0.0000620	4,600	0.0000640	4,600
2	0.0000340	8,700	0.0000290	8,700
3	0.0000200	11,600	0.0000190	11,600
4	0.0000155	12,700	0.0000090	12,700
5	0.0000110	12,700	0.0000045	12,700
6	0.0000065	12,700	0.0	—
7	0.0000020	12,700	—	—
8	0.0000020	12,700	—	—

Calculate the net reproductive rate (R_0) for these two year classes. What does this tell you about these populations? Estimate the innate capacity for increase from these data, and calculate the stable age distribution (C_x) and the stationary age distribution (L_x). Explain any difficulties and interpret the results in biological terms.

4 Slobodkin (1961, p. 55) states that "the geographical distribution of each species is controlled, at the limit, by the range of physical conditions that permit a positive value of $[r_m]$." Discuss with particular reference to the ideas contained in Chapter 8.

5 What additional data, if any, are required to determine the stable age distribution for the human population described in Table 12?

6 "A woman who gives birth to a set of twins at the age of 19, and subsequently gives birth to one other child, contributes as much to the future population of America as does a woman who produces five children, but whose age at birth of the initial child was 30" (Slobodkin 1961, p. 54). Under what conditions is this not true? Estimate the r_m value for populations with these two types of reproductive schedules. In making these estimates, assume for simplicity that the female survivorship is constant at $l_x = 0.965$ for the reproductive ages (approximately true for U.S. females, 1960).

7 Calculate a complete life table for the data in Table 10.

11   *Population growth*

A population that has been released into a favorable environment will begin to increase in numbers. What form will this increase take, and how can we describe it mathematically? Let us start by considering a simple case in which generations are separate, as in annual plants.

Discrete generations

Consider a species with a single annual breeding season and a lifespan of one year. Let each female produce R_0 female offspring, on the average, which survive to breed in the following year. Then

$$N_{t+1} = R_0 N_t$$

where

N_t = population size at generation t
N_{t+1} = population size at generation $t + 1$
R_0 = net reproductive rate, or number of female offspring produced per female per generation

Clearly, what happens to this population will very much depend on what R_0 is. Consider two cases:

1. *Reproductive rate constant* Let R_0 be a constant. If $R_0 > 1$, the population increases geometrically without limit, and if $R_0 < 1$, the population decreases to extinction. For example, let $R_0 = 1.5$, $N_0 = 10$:

$$N_{t+1} = 1.5N_t$$

Generation	Population size
0	10
1	15 = (1.5)(10)
2	22.5 = (1.5)(15)
3	33.75 = (1.5)(22.5)

Figure 85 shows some examples of geometric population growth with different R_0 values.

2. *Reproductive rate dependent on population size* Clearly populations do not, in fact, grow with a constant reproductive rate. At high densities reproductive rates decline in some manner, and we need to express the way in which reproductive rate slows down as density increases. How is reproductive rate related to density? The simplest mathematical model is a linear one—assume that there is a straight-line relationship between density and reproduction so that the higher the density, the lower the reproductive rate (Figure 86). The point where the line crosses $R_0 = 1.0$ is a point of

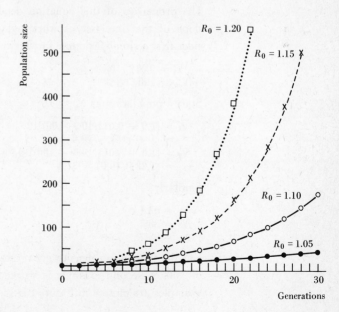

FIGURE 85

Geometric population growth, discrete generations, reproductive rate constant. $N_0 = 10$.

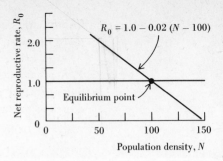

FIGURE 86

Reproductive rate as a linear function of population density. In this hypothetical example, equilibrium density is 100.

$$R_0 = 1.0 - 0.02(N - 100)$$

Net reproductive rate, R_0

Equilibrium point

Population density, N

equilibrium in population density. It is convenient to measure population density in terms of *deviations* from this equilibrium density:

$$x = N - N_{eq}$$

where

x = deviation from equilibrium density
N = observed population size
N_{eq} = equilibrium population size (i.e., where $R_0 = 1.0$)

The equation of the straight line shown in Figure 86 is thus

$$R_0 = 1.0 - B(N - N_{eq})$$
$$= 1.0 - Bx$$

where $(-)B$ = slope of line
R_0 = net reproductive rate

In Figure 86, $B = 0.02$. Our basic equation can now be written

$$N_{t+1} = R_0 N_t$$
$$= (1.0 - Bx_t)N_t$$

The properties of this equation depend on the equilibrium density and the slope of the line. Let us work out a few examples to illustrate this. Consider first a simple example in which

$B = 0.011$
$N_{eq} = 100$

Start a population at $N_0 = 10$:

$$N_1 = [1.0 - 0.011(10 - 100)]10$$
$$= (1.99)(10) = 19.9$$
$$N_2 = [1.0 - 0.011(19.9 - 100)]19.9$$
$$= (1.881)(19.9) = 37.4$$

Similarly,

$N_3 = 63.1$
$N_4 = 88.7$
$N_5 = 99.7$

and the population density converges smoothly toward the equilibrium point of 100. A second example is worked out in Table 13, and three additional examples are plotted in Figure 87.

TABLE 13

Hypothetical population growth, discrete generations, reproductive rate a linear function of density[a]

General formula: $N_{t+1} = [1.0 - 0.025(N_t - 100)]N_t$

$N_1 = [1.0 - 0.025(50 - 100)]50$
$= (2.25)(50) = 112.5$

$N_2 = [1.0 - 0.025(112.5 - 100)]112.5$
$= (0.6875)(112.5) = 77.34$

$N_3 = [1.0 - 0.025(77.34 - 100)]77.34$
$= (1.5665)(77.34) = 121.15$

$N_4 = [1.0 - 0.025(121.15 - 100)]121.15$
$= (0.4712)(121.15) = 57.09$

Similarly,

$N_5 = 118.33$

$N_6 = 64.09$

$N_7 = 121.63$

$N_8 = 55.80$

The population oscillates in a stable pattern.

[a] Assume that $B = 0.025$, $N_{eq} = 100$, and the starting density is 50.

FIGURE 87

Examples of population growth with discrete generations and reproductive rate a linear function of population density. Starting density is 10, equilibrium density is 100. Three examples are shown with different slopes of reproduction curve. When B = 0.013 the population grows smoothly to asymptotic density. When B = 0.023 the population oscillates continuously in a two-generation cycle. When B = 0.033 the population shows divergent oscillations, until it becomes extinct in the eighth generation.

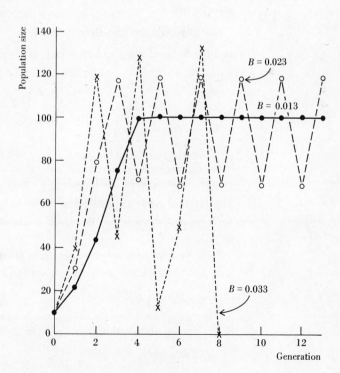

Maynard Smith (1968) has shown that, if we define $L = BN_{eq}$, then

1 If L is between 0 and 1, the population approaches the equilibrium without oscillations.

2 If L is between 1 and 2, there are oscillations of decreasing amplitude to the equilibrium point (convergent oscillations).

3 If L is above 2, there are oscillations of increasing magnitude (divergent oscillations).

This model, in which reproductive rate decreases in a linear way with density, is the discrete-generation version of the "logistic equation" described below.

Overlapping generations In populations that have overlapping generations and a prolonged or continuous breeding season, we can describe population growth more easily by the use of differential equations. As above, we shall assume for the moment that the growth of the population at time t depends only on conditions at that time and not upon past events of any kind.

1. *Reproductive rate constant* Assume that, in any short time interval dt, an individual has the probability $b\ dt$ of giving rise to another individual. In the same time interval it has the probability $d\ dt$ of dying. If these are instantaneous rates of birth and death, the instantaneous rate of population growth will be

$$\text{rate of population growth} = r_m = b - d$$

and the form of the population increase is given by

$$\frac{dN}{dt} = r_m N = (b - d)N$$

where

  N = population size
  t = time
  r_m = innate capacity for increase
  b = instantaneous birth rate
  d = instantaneous death rate

This is the curve of geometric increase in an unlimited environment that we have just discussed with regard to the innate capacity for increase (Chapter 10).

Note that we can use the geometric growth model to estimate the doubling time for a population growing at a certain rate:

$$\frac{N_t}{N_0} = e^{r_m t}$$

But if the population doubles, $N_t/N_0 = 2$. Thus

$$2.0 = e^{r_m t}$$

or

$$\log_e(2.0) = r_m t$$

$$\frac{0.69315}{r_m} = t$$

where

t = time for population to double its size
r_m = innate capacity for increase

A few values for this relationship are given below for illustration:

r_m	t
0.01	69.3
0.02	34.7
0.03	23.1
0.04	17.3
0.05	13.9
0.06	11.6

Thus if a human population is increasing at an instantaneous rate of 0.0300 per year (finite rate = 1.0305), its doubling time would be about 23 years, if geometric increase prevailed.

2. *Reproductive rate dependent on population size* But populations do not show continuous geometric increase. When a population is growing in a limited space, the density gradually rises until eventually the presence of other organisms reduces the fertility and longevity of the population. This reduces the rate of increase of the population until eventually the population ceases to grow. The growth curve defined by such a population is *sigmoid,* or S-shaped (Figure 88). The S-shaped curve differs from the geometric curve in two ways: (1) It has an upper asymptote (i.e., the

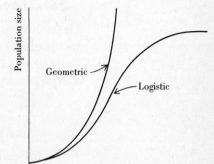

FIGURE 88

Population growth. Geometric growth in an unlimited environment and logistic growth in a limited environment.

curve does not exceed a certain maximal level), and (2) it approaches this asymptote smoothly, not abruptly.

The simplest way to produce an S-shaped curve is to introduce into our geometric equation a term that will reduce the rate of increase as the population builds up. We also want to reduce the rate of increase in a smooth manner. We can do this by making each individual added to the population reduce the rate of increase an equal amount, as in Figure 86. This produces the equation

$$\frac{dN}{dt} = r_m N \left(\frac{K - N}{K} \right)$$

where

N = population size
t = time
r_m = innate capacity for increase
K = upper asymptote or maximal value of N

This equation states that

$$\begin{pmatrix} \text{rate of increase} \\ \text{of population} \\ \text{per unit time} \end{pmatrix} = \begin{pmatrix} \text{innate} \\ \text{capacity} \\ \text{for increase} \end{pmatrix} \times \begin{pmatrix} \text{population} \\ \text{size} \end{pmatrix} \times \begin{pmatrix} \text{unutilized oppor-} \\ \text{tunity for} \\ \text{population growth} \end{pmatrix}$$

This is the differential form of the equation for the *logistic curve*. This curve was first suggested to describe the growth of human populations by Verhulst in 1838. The same equation was independently derived by Pearl and Reed (1920) as a description of the growth of the population of the United States.

The integral form of the logistic equation can be written as follows:

$$N_t = \frac{K}{1 + e^{a - r_m t}}$$

where

N_t = population size at time t
e = 2.71828 (base of natural logarithms)
a = a constant of integration defining the position
    of the curve relative to the origin
r_m, K, t as defined above

Let us look for a minute at the factor $(K - N)/K$, which has been called the unutilized opportunity for population growth. To demonstrate that this factor does put the brakes on the basic geometric growth pattern, consider a situation like this:

$K = 100$
$r_m = 1.0$
$N_0 = 1$ (starting density)

Very early in population growth there is little difference between the curves for the logistic and the geometric equations (Figure 88). As we approach the middle segment of the curve, they begin to diverge more. As we approach the upper limit, the curves diverge much farther, and when we reach the upper limit the population stops growing because $(K - N)/K$ becomes zero. The following calculations demonstrate this:

r_m	Population size, N	Unutilized opportunity for population growth, $(K - N)/K$	Rate of population growth, dN/dt
1.0	1	99/100	0.99
1.0	50	50/100	25.00
1.0	75	25/100	18.75
1.0	95	5/100	4.75
1.0	99	1/100	0.99
1.0	100	0/100	0.00

Note that the addition of one animal has the same effect on the rate of population growth at the low and at the high end of the curve (in this example, 1/100).

The logistic equation can be written in yet another way by rearranging terms:

$$\log_e \frac{K - N}{N} = a - r_m t$$

This is the equation of a straight line in which the coordinates are

y coordinate: $\log_e \dfrac{K - N}{N}$

x coordinate: time

and the slope of the line is r_m. This relationship can be used to fit a logistic equation to actual biological data (Pearl 1930).

Two attributes of the logistic curve make it attractive: (1) its mathematical simplicity and (2) its apparent reality. The differential form of the logistic curve contains only two constants: r_m is the innate capacity for increase which we have already discussed. It seems reasonable to attribute to K a biological meaning, the density at which the space being studied becomes "saturated" with organisms.

There are two ways of viewing the logistic curve. One is to view it as an empirical description of how populations tend to grow in numbers when conditions are favorable. This is the more general, more flexible viewpoint. The other way is to view the logistic as an implicit strict theory of population growth, as a "law" of population growth. The logistic curve was proposed as a strict theory of population growth, and we shall now examine this theory.

Does the logistic curve fit the facts? There are two ways to test this: (1) A colony of organisms may be reared in a constant space with a constant supply of food. From this information a logistic curve can be calculated and we can look to see if the data fit the curve. (2) The several assumptions on which the logistic theory rests may be examined separately and studied by experimental methods. We shall now look into both of these approaches.

LABORATORY TESTS OF THE LOGISTIC THEORY

Many populations have been followed in the laboratory as they increase in size. Let us consider relatively simple organisms first. Gause (1934) studied the growth of populations of *Paramecium aurelia* and *Paramecium caudatum*. He used 20 *Paramecium* to begin his experiments in a tube with 5 cc of a salt solution buffered to pH 8. Each day Gause added a constant quantity of bacteria, which served as food. The bacteria could not multiply in the salt solution. The cultures were incubated at 26°C and every second day they were washed with fresh salt solution to remove any waste products. Thus Gause had a *constant environment* in *limited space*; the temperature, volume, and chemical composition of the medium were constant, waste products were removed frequently, and a uniform amount of food was added each day. The growth of some of Gause's *Paramecium* populations is shown in Figure 89. In general the fit of these data to the logistic curve was quite good. The asymptotic density (*K*) was approximately 448/cc in *P. aurelia* and 128/cc for *P. caudatum* under these conditions.

Carlson (1913) grew yeast in laboratory cultures and Pearl (1927) calculated logistic curves for his data. These yeast data give a very good fit

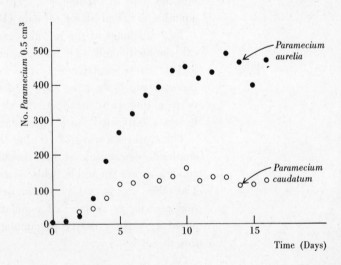

FIGURE 89

Population growth in the protozoans Paramecium aurelia *and* P. caudatum *at 26°C in buffered Osterhout's medium, pH 8.0, "one-loop" concentration of bacterial food. (After Gause 1934.)*

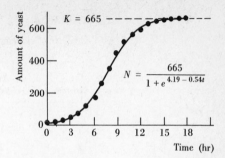

FIGURE 90

Growth of a population of yeast cells. (Data from Carlson 1913, after Pearl 1927.)

to the logistic equation (Figure 90), and we can use them to investigate one alternative form of the logistic:

$$\log_e \frac{K - N}{N} = a - r_m t$$

An approximate estimate of the parameters r_m and a of the logistic can be obtained from this equation as follows. The asymptotic density is estimated by eye or by taking the mean of some of the data points that appear to be at the equilibrium density. Once you have estimated K, you can obtain the $K - N/N$ term of the above equation. Table 14 gives the raw data for Carlson's yeast, and Figure 91 plots these in the linear form. The slope of this line is an approximate estimate of the innate capacity for increase (r_m), and the y intercept is an estimate of a. More detailed information on the methods of fitting the logistic curve to actual data are given in Pearl (1930).

Bacterial population growth has been studied in detail under laboratory conditions (Meadow and Pirt 1969; Novick 1955), and we will give just one illustration here. Jordan and Jacobs (1947) grew *Escherichia coli* aerobically at constant temperature with constant pH and continuously renewed food supply. They counted both viable bacteria and total cells; Figure 92 gives the resulting population growth curves for two temperatures.

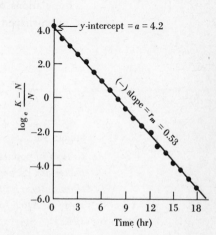

FIGURE 91

Logistic growth of a yeast population. Data plotted in the linear form of the logistic: $\log_e [(K - N)/N] = a - r_m t$. *See Table 14.*

TABLE 14

Growth of a yeast population[a]

Hours, t	Amount of yeast, N	$\dfrac{K-N}{N}$	$\log_e \dfrac{K-N}{N}$
0	9.6	68.27	4.223
1	18.3	35.34	3.565
2	29.0	21.93	3.088
3	47.2	13.09	2.572
4	71.1	8.353	2.123
5	119.1	4.584	1.522
6	174.6	2.809	1.033
7	257.3	1.585	0.460
8	350.7	0.896	−0.110
9	441.0	0.508	−0.677
10	513.3	0.296	−1.219
11	559.7	0.188	−1.671
12	594.8	0.118	−2.137
13	629.4	0.056	−2.872
14	640.8	0.038	−3.276
15	651.1	0.021	−3.847
16	655.9	0.014	−4.278
17	659.6	0.008	−4.805
18	661.8	0.005	−5.332

[a] These data are plotted in Figures 90 and 91. K is 665.
SOURCE: Data of Carlson (1913), after Pearl (1927).

At 35°C growth was logistic, but at 25°C these bacteria increased rapidly but not in a sigmoid manner.

Populations of organisms with more complex life cycles may also increase in an S-shaped curve. Pearl (1927) fitted a logistic curve to the growth

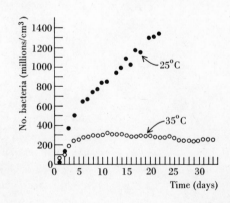

FIGURE 92

Growth of populations of the bacterium Escherichia coli *at two temperatures with a constant food supply. (After Jordan and Jacobs 1947.)*

of *Drosophila melanogaster* laboratory populations which he maintained in bottles with yeast as food. The fit of the data was fairly good (Figure 93), and Pearl ushered in the "logistic era," in which he proclaimed the logistic curve to be the universal law of population growth. But Sang (1950) criticized the application of the logistic to *Drosophila* populations and pointed out that there were some complexities in the *Drosophila* cultures which Pearl did not recognize. First, the yeast that was the source of food was not constant but was itself a growing population. Hence the flies did not receive a constant amount of food. Also the composition of the yeasts varied as the cultures aged. Second, the fruit fly has several stages in its life cycle, and it is not clear just what we should use to measure "population size." Pearl counted only the adult flies, but the adults and larvae to some extent feed on the same thing.

Beetles that live in flour (*Tribolium*) and wheat (*Calandra*) have been used very much for experimental population studies. These beetles are preferable to *Drosophila* because, even though they have as complex a life cycle (involving eggs–larvae–pupae–adults), they live in a dead food medium which can be precisely controlled, and also because the adults and the larvae eat much the same thing. Chapman (1928), one of the first to use *Tribolium* for laboratory studies in ecology, found that colonies of these beetles grew in a logistic fashion (Figure 94). Most workers stopped their cultures as soon as they reached the upper asymptote. Thomas Park, however, reared populations of *Tribolium* for several years and obtained the results shown in Figure 95. The upper asymptote of the logistic is imaginary—the density does not stabilize after the initial sigmoid increase but rather shows a long-term decline. Similar studies have been done by Birch (1953b) on *Calandra oryzae*, and he found logistic growth initially followed by large fluctuations in density with no indication of stabilization around an asymptote.

FIGURE 93

Growth of an experimental population of the fruit fly Drosophila melanogaster. *The circles are observed census counts, and the smooth curve is the fitted logistic. (After Pearl 1927.)*

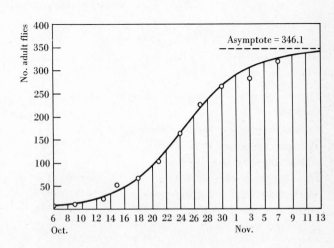

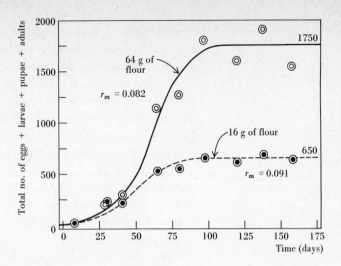

FIGURE 94

Trends in the numbers of the flour beetle Tribolium confusum *in 16 g and 64 g of flour at 27°C. The smooth curves are calculated logistic curves. The observed points represent the combined numbers of eggs, larvae, pupae, and adults. (After Gause 1931.)*

One important point to note here is that these populations of a single species living in a constant climate with constant food supply show wide fluctuations in numbers. These fluctuations are brought about by the influence of the animals on each other completely independently of any fluctuation in temperature, food, predators, or disease. There have been as yet no cases demonstrated where the population of any organism with a complex life history comes to a steady state at the upper asymptote of the logistic curve.

What assumptions are inherent in the logistic equation? When we say that the growth of a population may be represented by a logistic curve, we imply the following five things about that population:

1 The population has a stable age distribution initially. The logistic model assumes that a population beginning growth [when $((K - N)/K)$ is very nearly 1.0] increases at a rate approximately equal to $r_m N$. But r_m is only realized as a

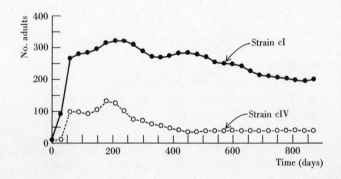

FIGURE 95

Population growth of the flour beetle Tribolium castaneum *at 29°C, 70% relative humidity, in 8 g of flour. There is considerable variation in population growth among different genetic strains. (After Park, Leslie, and Mertz 1964.)*

rate of population increase when there is a stable age distribution. Thus all experiments on logistic growth should be started with the population in an approximate stable age structure. Few studies have taken this problem into account.

2 The density has been measured in appropriate units. We have already noted the difficulty of deciding whether to include only *Drosophila* adults in the population, or to include eggs, larvae, and pupae as well. An additional problem arises here: Many plants and animals are smaller in size when they are raised in crowded situations. For example, with flies we may be adding large flies at the start of population growth and small flies near the end. In these situations it may be more accurate to measure *biomass*.

3 There is a real attribute of the population corresponding to r_m, the innate capacity for increase. Some workers have objected that r_m may be a rate of increase that is never realized in experimental populations, even though it is incorporated into the logistic equation. This problem can be attacked by calculating r_m for the same species in two ways: (a) as we have noted previously from life tables and fertility tables, and (b) by fitting a logistic equation to actual population growth data and thus obtaining an independent estimate of r_m. This has been done by Andrewartha and Birch (1954, pp. 365–368) for flour beetles, and the agreement between the two estimates of r_m was quite good, which suggests that this assumption is probably satisfactory.

4 The relationship between density and the rate of increase is linear. This can be seen by rewriting the logistic equation:

$$\frac{dN}{dt}\frac{1}{N} = r_m - \frac{r_m}{K}N$$

which says that the rate of population increase per individual is a linear function of population density. Morisita (1965) has shown that this instantaneous equation is algebraically equivalent to the finite difference equation

$$\frac{N_{t+1} - N_t}{N_t} = A - BN_{t+1}$$

where

N = population density
t = time
A = a constant = $e^{r_m t} - 1.0$
B = another constant = A/K (where K is asymptotic density)

Few direct experiments have been done to test this assumption, which is probably violated in many growing populations. Smith (1963) forced *Daphnia magna* populations to grow at certain predetermined rates and then measured the density they achieved. The relation between rate of population growth and density was not linear in this case (Figure 96) either when he used numbers as a measure of density or when he used biomass (dry weight) as a measure.

5 The depressive influence of density on the rate of increase operates instantaneously, without any time lags. It is highly unlikely that in organisms with complex life cycles the rate of population increase could respond instantaneously to changes in density. This is because of the time lags built into every life history. For example, it may take from a week to several months for an insect larva to become an adult (or even more, e.g., the 17-year periodical cicadas). With simple forms like *Paramecium* or bacteria this assumption should be approximately true.

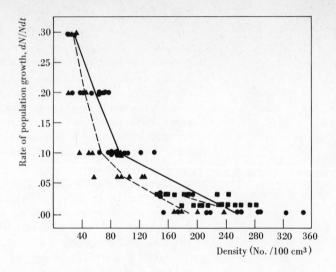

FIGURE 96

Observed densities of the water flea Daphnia magna *at various specific rates of growth, with number of individuals as the measure of density. Three separate series of experiments were run. (After Smith 1963.)*

FIELD DATA ON POPULATION GROWTH

Population growth does not occur continuously in field populations. Many species in seasonal environments show population growth during the favorable season each year. Long-lived organisms may show population growth only rarely. In all but a few cases the population is rarely filling up a vacant habitat in a manner analogous to the laboratory studies we have just discussed. Some examples we have are from situations where animals were introduced onto islands or other new habitats and then studied as they built up.

Reindeer have been introduced into many parts of Alaska since 1891 to replace the dwindling caribou herds in the economy of the Eskimo. In 1911 reindeer were introduced onto two of the Pribilof Islands in the Bering Sea off Alaska. Four males and 21 females were released on St. Paul Island (41 sq. miles), and 3 males and 12 females on St. George Island (35 sq. miles). The stockings were an immediate success. The subsequent history of these herds is of interest because the islands were completely undisturbed environments, there has been little hunting pressure, and there are no predators. The two herds have had quite different histories on the two islands (Figure 97). The St. George herd reached a low ceiling of 222 reindeer in 1922 and then subsided to a small herd of 40 to 60 animals. The St. Paul herd grew continuously to about 2000 reindeer in 1938, overgrazed the habitat, and then abruptly declined to only 8 animals in 1950. The ecological differences between these two islands appear to have been very slight (they had the same type of vegetation and same climate), and no one understands why the two populations behaved so differently (Scheffer 1951).

Reindeer were introduced to St. Matthew Island (128 sq. miles) in the

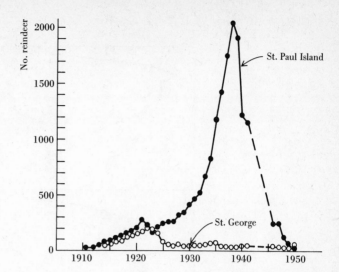

FIGURE 97

Reindeer population growth on the Pribilof Islands, Bering Sea, from 1911, when they were introduced, until 1950. (After Scheffer 1951.)

Bering Sea in 1944. They increased from an initial 29 animals (24 females, 5 males) in 1944 to 1350 in 1957, to 6000 in 1963, and then crashed to 42 animals in 1966 (Klein 1968), thus repeating the St. Paul Island sequence in a slightly shorter time span.

Populations of some seabirds have been increasing rapidly in recent decades. Fisher and Vevers (1944) traced the increase in colonies of the North Atlantic gannet (*Sula bassana*) off southwestern Britain (Figure 98). This increase has coincided with reduced exploitation of gannet colonies by man, who formerly used the birds for fish bait.

Many organisms show strong annual fluctuations in density, and thus one can observe the pattern of population growth once a year. The diatom *Asterionella formosa* shows a spring maximum in numbers in lakes of northwestern England (Lund 1950). These populations increase in a general sigmoid manner (Figure 99) but then decline rapidly, possibly because of silica depletion in the lake waters.

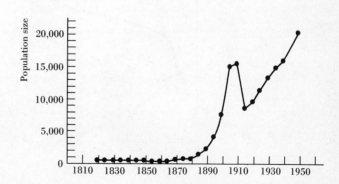

FIGURE 98

*Population growth in colonies of the North Atlantic gannet (*Sula bassana*) off southwestern Britain. (After Fisher and Vevers 1944 and Fisher and Lockley 1954.)*

197 POPULATION GROWTH

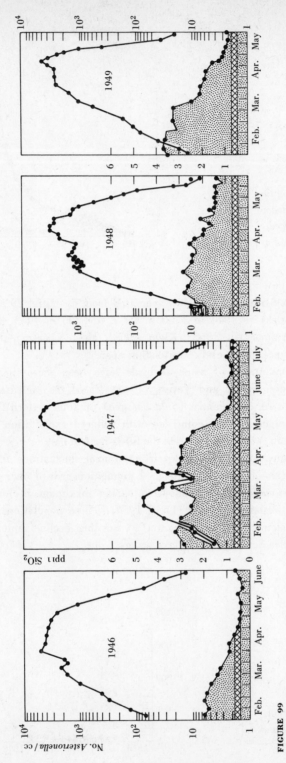

FIGURE 99

Population growth of the diatom Asterionella formosa in the spring, Blelham Tarn, English Lake District, 1946–1949. The top line represents the number of live Asterionella cells per cubic centimeter in water from 0 to 5 m depth. The solid area at the bottom represents dissolved silica (mg/liter) content of the water. Silica may be a factor limiting population growth. (After Lund 1950.)

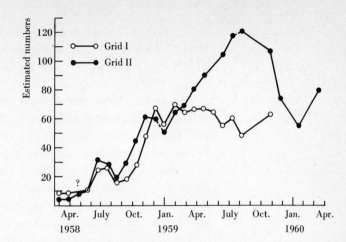

*Population growth in a small mammal (*Clethrionomys glareolus*) on two areas 0.5 mile apart in central England. (After Newson 1963.)*

Field mice and other small mammals fluctuate in abundance from year to year, and population growth can occur rapidly. Newson (1963) studied two populations of bank voles (*Clethrionomys glareolus*) 0.5 mile apart near Oxford, England, and found them to increase about ten fold in a single year (Figure 100).

Many field data on population growth are too rough to show definitely whether the logistic curve is a good representation of the data or not. The cases we have illustrated here suggest that the logistic is only an approximate model to describe field population increases.

The logistic curve was used by Pearl and Reed (1920) to predict the future growth of the U.S. population. They fitted the logistic curve to the census data from 1790 to 1910 and projected it to asymptotic density, a value of 197 million to be reached in approximately 2060 (Figure 101). The census data for 1920 to 1940 fit the curve very well (Pearl, Reed, and Kish 1940), but subsequent census data show a nearly geometric increase

Census counts of the population of the United States from 1790 to 1970. The smooth curve is the logistic equation fitted to the census counts from 1790 to 1910 inclusive. The broken lines show the extrapolation of the curve beyond the data to which it was fitted. (After Pearl, Reed, and Kish 1940, with census data for 1950–1970 added.)

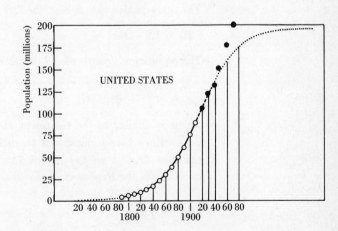

199 POPULATION GROWTH

rather than a logistic one. The predicted asymptote of 197 million was, in fact, reached in 1968, and current estimates for the U.S. population in 2020 range from 300 to 440 million (Statistical Abstract of the United States 1970).

We conclude from this analysis that population growth may be sigmoid in natural populations and thus fit the logistic model but that often it is not. The asymptotic stable density of the logistic is almost never achieved by natural populations, and thus the logistic model has serious drawbacks as a general model of population growth. What can be done about this? There are two lines along which work has proceeded on population growth models. One line has been to analyze the effect of time lags on the logistic model, since this is the assumption most clearly out of touch with the biological realities of complex organisms. The other line has been to construct probabilistic (*stochastic*) models of population growth. Let us look briefly at these two approaches.

TIME-LAG MODELS OF POPULATION GROWTH

Consider a simple model with discrete generations, and assume that the reproductive rate at generation t depends on density in a linear manner but that, instead of depending on density at generation t (as in Figure 86), it depends on density at generation $(t - 1)$. Measure density as a deviation from the equilibrium point:

$$x = N - N_{eq}$$

where

$\quad x$ = deviation from equilibrium density
$\quad N$ = observed population size
$\quad N_{eq}$ = equilibrium population size (i.e., where $R_0 = 1.0$)

The reproductive rate is described by Figure 86 as a straight line:

$$R_0 = 1.0 - Bx$$

The population growth model can thus be written

$$N_{t+1} = R_0 N_t$$
$$= (1 - Bx_{t-1})N_t$$

which is similar to the treatment above except that the reproductive rate is now defined by the density of the previous generation. The properties of this equation depend on the equilibrium density and the slope of the line. Let us work out the hypothetical case discussed above without any time lag:

$$B = 0.011$$
$$N_{eq} = 100$$

Start a population at $N_0 = 10$ (and use $N = 10$ for first-generation calculation of the time-lag term):

$$N_1 = [1.0 - 0.011(10 - 100)]10$$
$$= 19.9$$
$$N_2 = [1.0 - 0.011(10 - 100)]19.9$$
$$= 39.6$$
$$N_3 = [1.0 - 0.011(19.9 - 100)]39.6$$
$$= 74.4$$

Similarly,

$$N_4 = 123.9$$
$$N_5 = 158.7$$

This population oscillates more or less regularly with a period of six to seven generations between peaks in numbers, in contrast to the smooth approach to equilibrium density which occurred when there was no time lag in regulation. This contrast is shown in Figure 102 for a hypothetical example. A delay in feedback by one generation can change a stable population growth pattern into an unstable one. Maynard Smith (1968, p. 25) has shown that, if $L = BN_{eq}$, then

If $0 < L < 0.25$ stable equilibrium, no oscillation
If $0.25 < L < 1.0$ convergent oscillation
If $L > 1.0$ divergent oscillation

Compare the results of this time-lag model with those obtained without any time lags.

The logistic equation can be readily modified to incorporate time lags (Wangersky and Cunningham 1956). The simplest case involves a *reaction time lag*, a lag between a change in the environment and the corresponding change in the rate of population growth. This time lag in the logistic can be incorporated into the regulation term $(K - N)/K$ as follows:

$$\frac{dN}{dt} = r_m N \left(\frac{K - N_{(t-r)}}{K} \right)$$

FIGURE 102

Hypothetical population growth with and without a time lag, discrete generations, reproductive rate a linear function of density. Starting density = 10, slope of reproductive curve = 0.011, equilibrium density = 100.

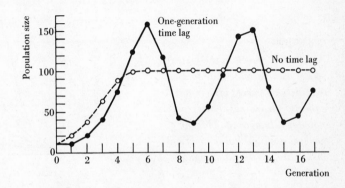

where r is the reaction time lag. A great variety of growth curves can be produced by the introduction of time lags into the logistic equation. Figure 103 illustrates some examples. The mathematics of time-lag equations becomes somewhat complex, however, and solutions are most readily obtained by analog-computer techniques (Cunningham 1954).

A second time lag is also involved in complex organisms, a *reproductive time lag*, which may be measured by the gestation time or its equivalent. This can also be incorporated into the logistic equation:

$$\frac{dN}{dt} = r_m N_{(t-g)} \left(\frac{K - N_{(t-r)}}{K} \right)$$

where

    g = reproductive time lag
    r = reaction time lag

In the early phases of population growth this reproductive time lag may be important in slowing the rate of population increase.

Laboratory populations of *Daphnia* are a good example of the effect of time lags on population growth. Pratt (1943) followed the development of *Daphnia* populations in the laboratory at two temperatures. The populations, in 50 cc of filtered pond water, were started with two parthenogenetic females each. *Daphnia* were counted every 2 days and transferred to a fresh culture. The only food used was a green alga *Chlorella*. Populations at 25°C showed oscillations in numbers (Figure 104), whereas those at 18°C were approximately stable. Oscillations occurred at 25°C because there was a delay in the depressing effect of population density on birth rates and death rates. At 25°C the birth rate is affected first by rising density, and only later is the death rate increased. This causes the *Daphnia* population to continuously "overshoot" and then "undershoot" its equilibrium density. Note that these oscillations are intrinsic to the biological system and not caused by external environmental changes.

FIGURE 103

Population growth in the logistic model with variable time lags. Numbers on curves are (innate capacity for increase) × (reaction time lag). Longer time lags in general produce more numerical instability. (After Cunningham 1954.)

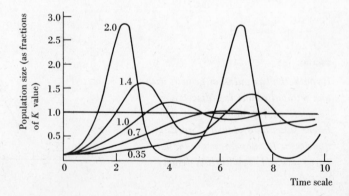

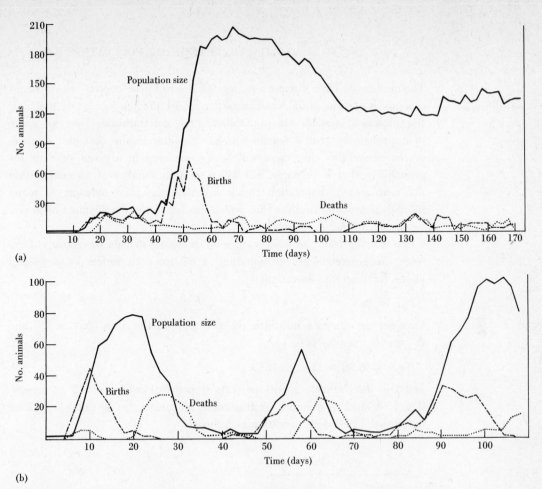

FIGURE 104

Population growth in the water flea Daphnia magna *at (a) 18° C
and (b) 25° C in 50 cc of pond water. The numbers of births and
deaths have been doubled to make them visible. (After Pratt 1943.)*

Thus the introduction of time lags into simple models of population
growth causes the stable asymptote of the logistic curve to be replaced by
one of three possible alternatives: (1) a converging oscillation toward equilibrium, (2) a stable oscillation about the equilibrium level, or (3) a
smooth approach to equilibrium density. In addition, some configurations
of time lags will produce a divergent oscillation that is unstable and leads
to extinction of the population. These outcomes are clearly more realistic
models of what seems to occur in natural populations.

The models we have discussed so far are *deterministic* models, which means that given certain initial conditions the model predicts one exact outcome. But biological systems are probabilistic, not deterministic. Thus we speak of a probability that a female will have a litter in the next unit of time, or the probability that there will be a cone crop in a given year, or the probability that a predator will kill a certain number of animals within the next month. Population trends are thus the joint outcome of many individual probabilities like this, which has led to the development of probabilistic or *stochastic* models.

We can illustrate the basic nature of stochastic models very simply. Consider the geometric growth equation, a deterministic model we developed above for discrete generations:

$$N_{t+1} = R_0 N_t$$

Consider an example in which the net reproductive rate (R_0) is 2.0 and the starting density is 6,

$$N_1 = (2.0)(6) = 12$$

and the deterministic model predicts a population size of 12 at generation 1. A stochastic model for this could be constructed as follows: Assume the probabilities of reproduction as follows:

	Probability
One offspring	0.50
Three offspring	0.50

Clearly, on the average two parents will leave four offspring, so $R_0 = 2.0$. But now use a coin to construct some numerical examples. If the coin flips heads, one offspring is produced; if tails, three offspring.

Parent	Outcome of trial:			
	1	2	3	4
1	(h) 1	(t) 3	(h) 1	(t) 3
2	(t) 3	(h) 1	(t) 3	(h) 1
3	(h) 1	(t) 3	(h) 1	(h) 1
4	(t) 3	(t) 3	(t) 3	(t) 3
5	(t) 3	(t) 3	(t) 3	(h) 1
6	(t) 3	(t) 3	(h) 1	(h) 1
Total population in next generation	14	16	12	10

Some of the outcomes are above the expected value of 12 and some are below it. If we continued doing this very many times, we could generate a frequency distribution of population sizes for this simple problem; an example is shown in Figure 105. Note that populations starting from exactly the same point with exactly the same biological parameters could, in fact, finish one generation later with either 6 or 18 members.

The population growth of species with overlapping generations can also be described by stochastic models. Geometric growth in this case follows the differential equation:

$$\frac{dN}{dt} = r_m N$$
$$= (b - d)N$$

where

b = instantaneous birth rate
d = instantaneous death rate

In the simplest case (the pure birth process) assume that $d = 0$ so that no organisms can die. If we assume a simple binary fission type of reproduction, the probability that an organism will reproduce in the next short time interval dt is $b\ dt$, where b is the instantaneous birth rate. Consider an example where $b = 0.5$ and $N_0 = 5$ (starting population). In one time interval, according to the deterministic model,

$$N_t = N_0 e^{r_m t}$$
$$N_1 = (5)e^{(0.5)(1)} = 8.244$$

For the stochastic equivalent of this simple model, we must determine from the instantaneous rate of births:

Probability of not reproducing in one time interval = $e^{-b} = 0.6065$
Probability of reproducing at least once in one time unit = $1.0 - e^{-b} = 0.3935$

Thus for five organisms, the chance that none of the five will reproduce in the next unit of time is

$(0.6065)(0.6065)\ (0.6065)(0.6065)(0.6065) = 0.082$

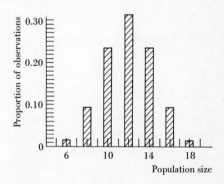

FIGURE 105

Frequency distribution for size of a population after one generation for the example discussed in the text. $N_0 = 6$, $R_0 = 2.0$, probability of having one offspring = 0.5, probability of having three offspring = 0.5.

so that in approximately 1 trial out of 12 there will be no population change in the unit of time ($N_1 = 5$). We could laboriously count up all the other possibilities, remembering that each individual may undergo fission more than once in each unit of time. Or we may follow a mathematician into an application of probability theory to this problem (Pielou 1969, p. 9) to reach the conclusions shown in Figure 106. Note again the possible variation from initial to final population size when births are considered in a probabilistic manner. Figure 107 illustrates these principles about stochastic models of population growth.

If we use probabilistic models and allow both births and deaths to occur in a random manner, there is a chance of a population becoming extinct. What is the chance of extinction for a population starting with N_0 organisms and undergoing stochastic changes in size with instantaneous birth rate (b) and death rate (d), as in Figure 107? Pielou (1969, p. 17) has discussed two cases:

(1) *Birth rate > death rate* These populations should increase geometrically, but may by chance drift to extinction, particularly during the first few time periods. The probability of extinction at some time is given by

$$\text{Probability of extinction} = \left(\frac{d}{b}\right)^{N_0} \qquad \text{as time becomes very large}$$

For example, if $b = 0.75$ and $d = 0.25$, for $N_0 = 5$ we have

$$\text{Probability of extinction} = \left(\frac{0.25}{0.75}\right)^5 = 0.0041$$

But if $b = 0.55$, $d = 0.45$, and $N_0 = 5$,

$$\text{Probability of extinction} = 0.367$$

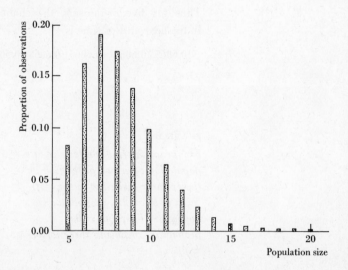

FIGURE 106

Frequency distribution of the size at time 1 of a population undergoing a pure birth process. $b = 0.5$, $N_0 = 5$. (After Pielou 1969.)

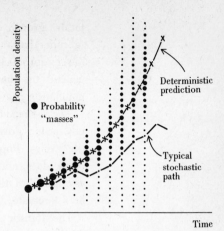

FIGURE 107

Stochastic model of geometric population growth for continuous, overlapping generations. (After Skellam 1955.)

Thus the larger the initial population size and the greater the difference between birth and death rates, the more chance a population has of staying in existence.

(2) *Birth rate = death rate*   These populations are stationary in numbers, as is typical of the real world on the average, and by the formula above,

$$\text{Probability of extinction} = \left(\frac{d}{b}\right)^{N_0} = (1.0)^{N_0} = 1.0 \qquad \text{as time} \to \infty$$

Thus extinction is a certainty for any stationary population subject to stochastic variations in births and deaths, if we allow a long enough time span.

Stochastic models of population growth thus introduce an important idea of biological variation into the consideration of population changes. The probability approach to these ecological problems thus is more realistic. The price we must pay for the greater realism of stochastic models is the greater difficulty of the mathematics, but part of this difficulty can be resolved by the use of computers. The variation inherent in stochastic models becomes more important as population size becomes smaller, which is pointed out clearly in human populations. Predictions about what change in size an individual family will show from one year to the next are much less certain than predictions about what change in size the world population will show. If all populations were in the millions, stochastic models could be eliminated and deterministic models would be adequate.

SUMMARY

The growth of a population can be described with simple mathematical models for organisms with discrete generations and for those with overlapping generations. If the reproductive rate is constant, geometric population growth occurs. Populations stabilize at a finite size only if the reproductive rate depends on population size and large populations have lower reproductive rates than small populations. For species with overlapping generations the logistic equation is a simple mathematical description of population growth to an asymptotic limit.

The S-shaped logistic curve is an adequate description for the laboratory population growth of *Paramecium*, yeast, and other organisms with simple life cycles. Population growth in organisms with more complex life cycles often does not follow the logistic very closely. In particular the stable asymptote of the logistic is not achieved in natural populations, but numbers fluctuate.

The logistic equation contains five assumptions which are discussed in detail for possible violations in natural populations. Two general modifications of the logistic have been used. *Time-lag models* have been used to analyze the effects of different time lags on the curve of population growth. The introduction of time lags into the simple models of population growth can produce oscillations in population size instead of a stable asymptotic density. *Stochastic models* of population growth introduce the effects of chance events on populations. Populations starting from the same density with the same average birth and death rates may increase at different rates because of chance events. Chance events can lead to extinction as well and are particularly important in small populations.

SELECTED REFERENCES

ANDREWARTHA, H. G., and L. C. BIRCH. 1954. *The Distribution and Abundance of Animals*. Chap. 9, pp. 347–398. University of Chicago Press, Chicago.

BARTLETT, M. S. 1960. *Stochastic Population Models in Ecology and Epidemiology*. Chaps. III and IV. Wiley, New York.

MAYNARD SMITH, J. 1968. *Mathematical Ideas in Biology*. Chaps. 2 and 3. Cambridge University Press, New York.

PEARL, R. 1927. The growth of populations. *Quart. Rev. Biol.* 2:532–548.

PIELOU, E. C. 1969. *An Introduction to Mathematical Ecology*. Chaps. 1 and 2. Wiley-Interscience, New York.

SMITH, F. E. 1963. Population dynamics in *Daphnia magna* and a new model for population growth. *Ecology* 44:651–663.

QUESTIONS AND PROBLEMS

1 Plot the logistic data of Table 14 on semilog paper (logarithmic scale for population density, arithmetic scale for time). What shape of curve does this give and why?

2 Determine the population growth curve for 10 generations for an annual plant with net reproductive rate of 25, starting density of 2. Assume a constant reproductive rate.

3 Determine the population growth curve for this same annual plant if reproductive rate is a linear function of density of the form $R_0 = 1.0 - 0.01x$ ($x =$ deviation from equilibrium density), equilibrium density is 1000, and starting density is 2. Repeat under the assumption that there is a one-generation time lag in changing reproductive rate.

4 Determine the doubling times for the following human populations:

Country	Instantaneous rate of growth, r_m
Algeria	0.033
South Africa	0.024
Canada	0.019
Argentina	0.015
United Kingdom	0.006
Ireland	0.004
East Germany	−0.002

What assumptions must one make to predict these doubling times?

5 Chapman (1928) gives the following population growth data for the flour beetle *Tribolium confusum* (eggs + larvae + pupae + adults):

Days	Number in 32 g of flour
0	2
8	47
28	192
41	256
63	768
79	896
97	1120
117	896
135	1184
154	1024

Determine the parameters of the logistic equation for these data. Use the mean value of the last five censuses for an estimate of K. Use the logistic formula to determine the estimated density for each of the census days, and compare these estimated densities to the observed values.

6 Construct a stochastic model of a geometrically increasing population with continuous generations. Assume a finite probability of surviving of 0.667 per unit of time (instantaneous death rate = $\log_e (0.667) = -0.405$). Assume a probability of undergoing binary fission ($1 \rightarrow 2$) of 0.5 for each unit of time (which corresponds to an instantaneous birth rate of 0.693 if we arbitrarily allow only one possible fission per time unit). Begin with a population of five organisms, and use a coin or die to determine the fates of each individual over each time period for at least 5 time units. [For example, for the first individual toss a die and let an odd number (1, 3, 5) on the die be a "birth" fission and an even number be no fission; let 1 or 2 be death and 3, 4, 5, or 6 be survival.] What is the deterministic prediction for population size at the end of five time units? What is the chance of extinction of this population at some point in time?

7   Clarke (1954, pp. 339–340) states: "Populations of a wide variety of organisms, ranging from bacteria to whales, have been found to follow the logistic curve in their growth form . . . The growth of man's population follows a similar pattern." Discuss, and contrast this view with the conclusion drawn by Watt (1968, pp. 8–12) about the human population.

12   Species interactions:
competition

Organisms do not exist alone in nature but in a matrix of other organisms of many species. Many species in an area will be unaffected by the presence or absence of one another, but in some cases two or more species will interact. The evidence for this interaction is quite direct: Populations of one species are different in the absence and in the presence of a second species. Illustrations of interactions can be found all too easily in the relationships between man and exploited species such as the passenger pigeon and the buffalo.

For the present we shall consider only the *negative* forms of interactions between two species. Two possible forms may be distinguished: *competition* and *predation. Competition occurs when a number of organisms (of the same or of different species) utilize common resources that are in short supply; or, if the resources are not in short supply, competition occurs when the organisms seeking that resource nevertheless harm one or other in the process* (Birch 1957). Competition may be *interspecific* (between two or more different species) or *intraspecific* (between members of the same species). In this chapter we shall deal mostly with interspecific competition. Competition occurs for food and for space and may take several forms. An "exploitation" component can be recognized when a resource such as food is in short supply and the food eaten by one species is thus not available to the second species. An "interference" component can also arise when organisms harm one another in attempting to gain a needed resource. When there is interference the resource is not necessarily in short supply. Several consequences of the process of competition must be kept clear. First, there is no need for animals to see or hear their competitors. A species that feeds by day on a plant may compete with a species that feeds at night on the same plant if the plant is in short supply. Second, many or most of the organisms that an animal does see or hear will not be competitors. This is true even if there are resources shared by the organisms. Oxygen, for example, is a resource shared by most terrestrial organisms, yet there is no competition for oxygen among these organisms because the resource is superabundant. Third, competition in plants usually occurs among individuals rooted in position and thus differs from competition among mobile animals. The spacing of individuals is thus more important in plant competition.

Predation occurs when members of one species eat those of another species. Often this involves the killing of the prey but not always. Four types of predation may be distinguished. *Herbivores* are animals that prey on green plants or their seeds and fruits; often the plants eaten are not killed but may be damaged. Typical predation occurs when *carnivores* prey on herbivores or on other carnivores. *Insect parasitism* is another form of predation, in which the insect parasite lays eggs on or near the host insect, which is subsequently killed and eaten. Finally, *cannibalism* is a special form of predation, in which the predator and the prey are the same species.

Mathematical models have been used extensively to build up hypotheses about what happens when two species live together either sharing the same food, occupying the same space, or one preying on or parasitizing the other. The best-known models of these phenomena are the *Lotka–Volterra equations*, which were derived independently by Lotka (1925) in the United States and Volterra (1926) in Italy.

Lotka and Volterra derived two different sets of equations: One set applies to the *predator–prey* situation, the other set to *nonpredatory* situations involving competition for food or space.

COMPETITION FOR FOOD OR SPACE

Mathematical model

The Lotka–Volterra equations, which describe the competition between organisms for food or space, are based on the logistic curve. We have seen that the logistic curve is described by

$$\frac{dN_1}{dt} = r_1 N_1 \left(\frac{K_1 - N_1}{K_1} \right) \qquad \text{simple logistic for species 1}$$

$$\frac{dN_2}{dt} = r_2 N_2 \left(\frac{K_2 - N_2}{K_2}\right) \qquad \text{simple logistic for species 2}$$

where

N_1 = population size of species 1
t = time
r_1 = innate capacity for increase of species 1 (r_m for species 1)
K_1 = asymptotic density for species 1

and similarly for species 2.

If these two species are interacting, that is, affecting the population growth of each other, another term must be introduced into each equation. We may visualize this with the following simple analogy: Consider the environment with regard to species 1 as a box that will hold K_1 number of blocks of this species. But some of this space can also be occupied by the competitor species 2:

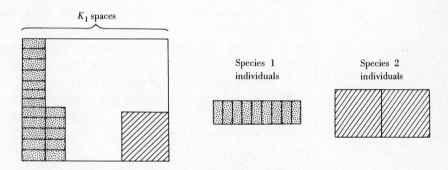

Now in most cases the "space" occupied by one species 2 individual is not exactly the same as that occupied by one individual of species 1. For example, species 2 may be larger and require more of the critical food that is contained in K_1. For this reason we need a conversion factor to convert species 2 individuals into an equivalent number of species 1 individuals. We define, for this competitive situation,

$$N_1 = \alpha N_2$$

where α is the conversion factor for expressing species 2 in units of species 1. This is of course a very simple assumption, which states that under all conditions of density there is a constant conversion factor between the competitors. We can now write the competition equation for species 1:

$$\frac{dN_1}{dt} = r_1 N_1 \left(\frac{K_1 - N_1 - \alpha N_2}{K_1}\right) \qquad \begin{array}{l}\text{population growth of species 1} \\ \text{in competition}\end{array}$$

This is mathematically equivalent to the simple analogy we have just developed. Figure 108 shows this graphically. There are two extreme cases shown: All the "space" for species 1 is used (1) when there are K_1 individuals of species 1 or (2) when there are K_1/α individuals of species 2.

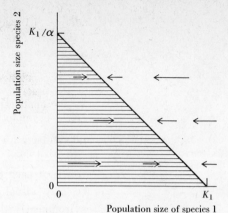

FIGURE 108

*Changes in population size of species
1 when competing with species 2.
Populations in the shaded area will
increase in size and come to
equilibrium at some point on the
diagonal line.*

The two extreme cases are shown at the ends of the diagonal line in Figure
108. Populations of species 1 inside this line will increase in size until they
reach the diagonal line, which represents all points of equilibrium. Note
that we do not yet know *where* along this diagonal we will finish, but it
must be somewhere at or between the points $N_1 = K_1$ and $N_1 = 0$.

Now we can retrace our steps and apply the same line of argument to
species 2. We now have a volume of K_2 spaces to be filled by N_2 individuals
but also by N_1 individuals. Again we must convert N_1 into equivalent numbers of N_2, and we define

$$N_2 = \beta N_1$$

where β is the conversion factor for expressing species 1 in units of species 2. We can now write the competition equations for the second species:

$$\frac{dN_2}{dt} = r_2 N_2 \left(\frac{K_2 - N_2 - \beta N_1}{K_2} \right) \qquad \begin{array}{l}\text{population growth of species 2} \\ \text{in competition}\end{array}$$

Figure 109 shows this equation graphically.

Let us now try to put these two species together. What might be the outcome of this competition? Only three outcomes are possible: (1) Both
species coexist, (2) species 1 becomes extinct, or (3) species 2 becomes
extinct. Intuitively, we would expect that species 1, if it had a very strong
depressing effect on species 2, would win out and force species 2 to become
extinct. The converse would apply for the situation where species 2 strongly
affected species 1. In a situation where neither species has a very strong
effect on the other, we might expect them to coexist. These intuitive ideas
can be evaluated mathematically in the following way.

Solve these simultaneous equations at equilibrium:

$$\frac{dN_1}{dt} = 0 = \frac{dN_2}{dt}$$

This can be done by superimposing figures (like Figures 108 and 109) and adding the arrows by vector addition. Figure 110 shows the four possible geometric configurations. In each of these I have abstracted the vector arrows, and the results can be traced by following the horizontal and vertical hatching. Species 1 will increase in areas of horizontal hatching, and species 2 will increase in areas of vertical hatching. There are a number of principles to keep in mind in viewing these kinds of curves. First, there can be no equilibrium of the two species unless the diagonal curves cross each other. Thus in cases 1 and 2 there can be no equilibrium, and one species is able to increase in a zone in which the second species must decrease. This leads to extinction of one competitor. Second, if the diagonal lines cross, the equilibrium point represented by their crossing may be either a *stable* point or an *unstable* point. It is stable if the vectors about the point are directed toward the point and unstable if the vectors are directed away from the point. In case 4 the point where the two lines cross is unstable because if by some small disturbance the populations move slightly downward they reach a zone of horizontal hatching in which N_1 can increase but N_2 can only decrease, which results in species 1 coming to an equilibrium by itself at K_1. Similarly, slight movement upward will lead to an equilibrium of only species 2 at K_2.

Plant ecologists have developed models of competition to describe interactions between annual plants. These models, which seem to differ so much in form from the Lotka–Volterra equations above, are basically the same (de Wit 1961) and can be used to provide an alternative view of competition theory. In annual plants the central variable is *seed number*, and we are interested in the relationship between seeds planted and seeds harvested at the end of the annual growing season. Competition in such organisms is an input–output problem.

FIGURE 109

Changes in population size of species 2 when competing with species 1. Populations in the shaded area will increase in size and come to equilibrium at some point on the diagonal line.

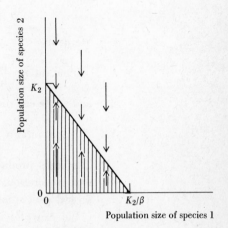

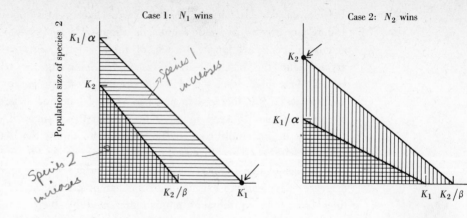

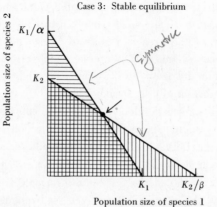

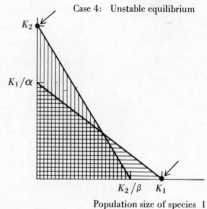

Population size of species 1

FIGURE 110

*Four possible outcomes of competition between two species. Arrows
indicate equilibrium points.*

We define

$$\text{Input ratio} = \frac{\text{no. seeds planted of species 1}}{\text{no. seeds planted of species 2}}$$

and at the end of the growing season we obtain

$$\text{Output ratio} = \frac{\text{no. seeds produced by species 1}}{\text{no. seeds produced by species 2}}$$

The seeds produced can be sown, and this becomes the input ratio for the
next generation. Consequently the experiment can be carried on through
several generations.

We can plot these ratios on graphs as shown in Figure 111. When the

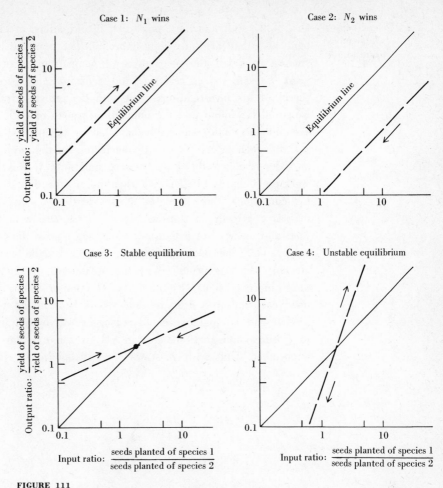

FIGURE 111

Input–output diagrams to illustrate possible outcomes of competition in annual plants. (After de Wit 1960.)

input ratio equals the output ratio, obviously there is an equilibrium point, and again this may be stable or unstable. In the two simplest cases there is no equilibrium and the output ratio always exceeds the input ratio, so species 1 wins; or vice versa, and species 2 wins. In the two cases in which an equilibrium point is obtained, the stability of the equilibrium depends on the slope of the line at this point. These input–output diagrams thus illustrate the same conclusions we obtained from the Lotka–Volterra equations.

Given these mathematical formulations, we must now see if these are an adequate representation of what happens in biological systems.

Experimental laboratory populations

One of the first and most important investigations of these competitive systems was that of a Russian microbiologist named Gause. Gause (1932) studied in detail the mechanism of competition between two species of yeast, *Saccharomyces cervisiae* and *Schizosaccharomyces kephir*. The first aspect of his investigations dealt with the growth of these two species in isolation. He found that the population growth of both species of yeast was sigmoid and could reasonably be fitted by the logistic curve.

Gause then asked: What are the factors in the environment that depress and stop the growth of the yeast population? It was known from earlier work by Richards (1928) that when the growth of yeast stops under anaerobic conditions, there remains a considerable amount of sugar and other necessary growth substances. Since growth ceases before the reserves of food and energy are exhausted, something else in the environment must be responsible. The decisive factor seems to be the accumulation of ethyl alcohol, which is produced by the breakdown of sugar for energy under anaerobic conditions (Figure 112). The action of the alcohol is to kill the new yeast buds just after the bud separates from the mother cell. Richards (1928) showed that one could reduce growth by artificially adding alcohol to cultures and that changes in pH of the medium were of secondary importance. Thus with yeast we have an apparently quite simple relation-

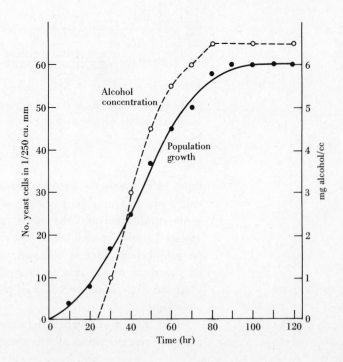

FIGURE 112

Population growth and ethyl alcohol accumulation in a yeast (Saccharomyces). (After Richards 1928.)

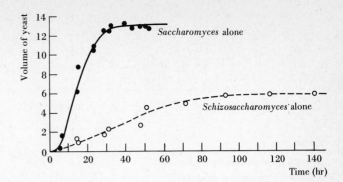

FIGURE 113

*Population growth of pure cultures
of two yeasts* Saccharomyces *and*
Schizosaccharomyces. *(After Gause
1932.)*

ship with the population being limited principally by one factor—ethyl alcohol concentration.

Gause then investigated what would happen when the two yeast species were grown together. When grown separately they reacted as shown in Figure 113. From these curves he calculated logistic curves (calculated in units of volume):

	Saccharomyces	*Schizosaccharomyces*
K	13.0	5.8
r_m	0.22	0.06

He then grew them together and got the results shown in Figures 114 and 115. Gause assumed that these data fit the Lotka–Volterra equations, and using the equations on his data from these mixed cultures he obtained (species 1, *Saccharomyces*; species 2, *Schizosaccharomyces*)

Age of culture (hr)	α	β
20	*4.79*	*0.501*
30	*2.81*	*0.349*
40	*1.85*	*0.467*
Mean value	*3.15*	*0.439*

FIGURE 114

Growth of populations of the yeast
Saccharomyces *in pure cultures and
in mixed cultures with*
Schizosaccharomyces. *(After Gause
1932.)*

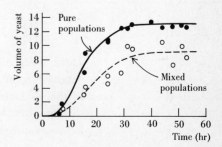

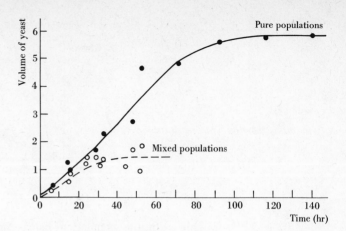

FIGURE 115

Growth of populations of the yeast Schizosaccharomyces *in pure cultures and in mixed cultures with* Saccharomyces. *(After Gause 1932.)*

The influence of *Schizosaccharomyces* on *Saccharomyces* is measured by α, and this means that, in terms of competition, *Saccharomyces* finds that its K_1 spaces can be filled according to the equivalence

1 volume of *Schizosaccharomyces* = 3.15 volumes of *Saccharomyces*

Note that the α values tend to decrease with the age of the culture, but as a first approximation we can assume α to be a constant.

If alcohol concentration is the critical limiting factor in these anaerobic yeast populations, Gause argued that we should be able to determine the competition coefficients α and β by finding the alcohol production rate of the two yeasts. He found

	Alcohol production (% EtOH per cc yeast)
Saccharomyces	0.113
Schizosaccharomyces	0.247

Gause then argued that the competition coefficients, α and β, should be determined by a direct ratio of these alcohol production figures, since alcohol was the limiting factor of population growth:

$$\alpha = \frac{0.247}{0.113} = 2.18$$

$$\beta = \frac{0.113}{0.247} = 0.46$$

These independent physiological measurements agree in general with those obtained from the population data above. Gause attributes the differences in the α's to the presence of other waste products affecting *Saccharomyces*.

Gause (1934) also studied competition between *Paramecium aurelia* and *Paramecium caudatum*. Each species would grow well separately, but when raised in the same tube *P. caudatum* always became extinct (Figure 116). This competitive situation was not as simple as the yeast one. Gause found with these paramecia that the values of α and β varied with the age of the culture. The two species competed for the same food in these cultures; in addition, the bacteria which were the food source produced a toxin that was more deleterious to *P. caudatum* than *P. aurelia*.

In experiments of a similar type, Birch (1953b) raised the grain beetles *Calandra oryzae* and *Rhizopertha dominica* at several different temperatures. He found that *Calandra* would invariably eliminate *Rhizopertha* at 29°C but that *Rhizopertha* would always eliminate *Calandra* at 32°C (Figures 117 and 118). Birch could predict these results from the innate capacity for increase; for example,

	r_m	Temperature	Winner
Calandra	0.77	29.1°C	*Calandra*
Rhizopertha	0.58		
Rhizopertha	0.69	32.3°C	*Rhizopertha*
Calandra	0.50		

Thus one could change the outcome of competition by changing only one component of the environment—temperature—and that by only 3°C.

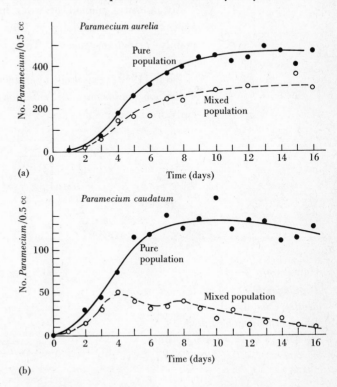

FIGURE 116

Population growth of the protozoans (a) Paramecium aurelia *and (b)* P. caudatum *in pure and mixed cultures. (After Gause 1934.)*

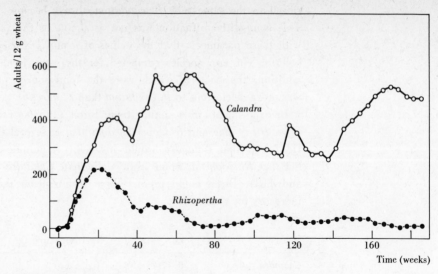

FIGURE 117

Population trends of adult grain beetles, Calandra oryzae *and*
Rhizopertha dominica, *living together in wheat of 14% moisture
content at 29.1°C. (After Birch 1953b.)*

An immense amount of work has been done by Thomas Park and his
students at the University of Chicago on competition among flour beetles,
mainly *Tribolium* species. This research has proceeded through several
stages.

Park (1948) explored interspecies competition using two flour beetles,
Tribolium confusum and *Tribolium castaneum.* The variables studied in this
early work were

FIGURE 118

*Population trends of adult grain
beetles,* Calandra oryzae *and*
Rhizopertha dominica, *living
together in wheat of 14% moisture
content at 32.3°C. (After Birch
1953b.)*

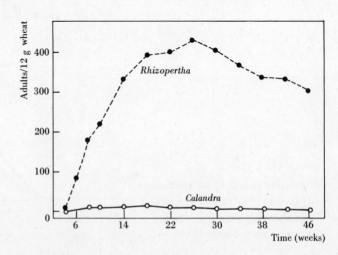

1 Constant
  a Climate
  b Initial density
  c Food
2 Varied
  a Volume of flour
  b Presence or absence of *Adelina*, a sporozoan parasite

Park found that the amount of space (volume of "universe") did not greatly affect the pattern of population growth or the outcome of competition between these two species. When the two beetle species were cultivated together, *T. confusum* usually won over *T. castaneum* (66 of 74 cases) regardless of the amount of space in the culture. All these cultures were infested with *Adelina*, a sporozoan parasite that may kill the beetles. *Adelina* was found to have an important effect on *T. castaneum* but not on *T. confusum* (Figure 119). The mean densities of larvae, pupae, and adults were (number per gram of flour)

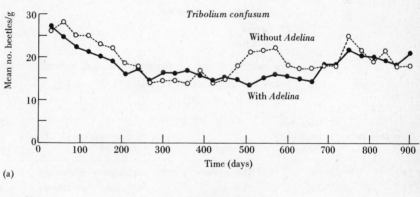

(a)

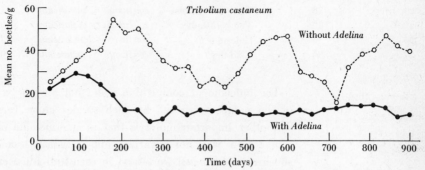

(b)

FIGURE 119

Population changes in Tribolium *flour beetles in sterile cultures and in cultures infected with the sporozoan parasite* Adelina*: (a)* T. confusum, *(b)* T. castaneum. *(After Park 1948.)*

	T. confusum	T. castaneum
With *Adelina*	19.2	13.3
Without *Adelina*	18.9	33.5

What happens to the competitive ability of these species if we remove *Adelina* from the cultures? The outcome of competition was completely reversed when *Adelina* was removed from the mixed species cultures. *Tribolium castaneum* won in 12 of 18 replicates. One important point to note here is that the outcome of these experiments was not absolute; one species did not always win. Rather, one outcome was more probable than another.

Park (1954) continued to study *T. confusum* and *T. castaneum* but he concentrated on different variables:

1 Constant
   a Volume of "universe"
   b Initial density
   c Food
   d Absence of *Adelina*
2 Varied
   Climate

Six combinations of temperature and humidity were investigated, with the following generalized results:

Temperature (°C)	Relative humidity (%)	Climate	Single species numbers	Mixed species (% wins) confusum	Mixed species (% wins) castaneum
34	70	Hot-moist	*confusum = castaneum*	0	100
34	30	Hot-dry	*confusum > castaneum*	90	10
29	70	Temperate-moist	*confusum < castaneum*	14	86
29	30	Temperate-dry	*confusum > castaneum*	87	13
24	70	Cold-moist	*confusum < castaneum*	71	29
24	30	Cold-dry	*confusum > castaneum*	100	0

The outcome of competition could not always be predicted on the basis of the numbers reached by each species alone (e.g., cold-moist climate). The other important point is that in intermediate climates the outcome of competition was not invariate but statistical—sometimes *confusum* won, sometimes *castaneum* won—and in each individual culture the outcome was unpredictable. This idea is illustrated in Figure 120.

The results of these competition experiments in *Tribolium* have always been that one species is eliminated from mixed cultures. What is the mechanism of this competition? Adult and larval *Tribolium* cannibalize their own eggs and pupae. This cannibalistic predation is a complex process and is

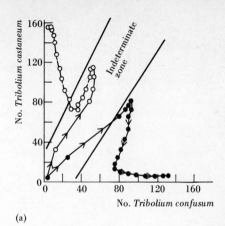

(a)

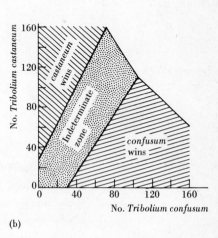

(b)

FIGURE 120

Probabilistic nature of interspecific competition between Tribolium confusum *and* T. castaneum. *Part (a) shows two case studies from cultures raised at 24°C and 70% relative humidity in which* T. confusum *wins 71% of the time. Each point represents a census 30 days apart. Part (b) shows a generalized diagram for this climatic regime. (After Neyman, Park, and Scott 1956.)*

responsible for most of the mortality of these flour beetles (Park et al. 1965). *Tribolium castaneum* is more cannibalistic than *T. confusum* in general. The "competition" between these beetles, then, is not competition over food, but a special form of mutual predation.

The *Tribolium* work was then turned to an investigation of variations within species. What relation do natality and mortality characteristics have to the outcome of competition? Park et al. (1964) used eight genetic strains of *Tribolium*, which differed greatly in their biological attributes (Table 15). In the competition experiments between these strains, the following design was used:

1 Constant
   a Volume of "universe"
   b Initial density
   c Food
   d Climate
   e Absence of *Adelina*

TABLE 15

Population attributes of the genetic strains of T. castaneum *and* T. confusum *developed by Thomas Park at Chicago*

Species	Strain	Mean population size	Fecundity (eggs per female per 3 days)	Adult death rate (per 30 days)	r_m	Relative cannibalistic tendency
T. castaneum	cI	388	46	0.15	0.67	Highest
	cII	177	21	0.13	0.46	Lower
	cIII	184	30	0.18	0.43	Lower
	cIV	179	37	0.20	0.56	High
T. confusum	bI	774	29	0.12	0.52	Lowest
	bII	601	27	0.26	0.49	Low
	bIII	247	24	0.26	0.50	High
	bIV	117	31	0.17	0.52	High

SOURCE: Data of Park et al. (1961, 1965).

2 Varied
Genetics of populations

Park found that these different strains varied greatly in their competitive ability. Table 16 gives the outcomes of these competition experiments. In these genetic experiments it was the strain of *T. castaneum* that characteristically determined the outcome. For example, strain cI of *T. castaneum* always wins and strain cIII always loses. Thus Park demonstrated that under constant conditions one could completely reverse the outcome of competition by changing the genetics of the population.

Competition experiments on laboratory populations of *Tribolium* flour beetles have thus demonstrated that the outcome of competition is not invariant but rather is affected both by extrinsic agencies like weather and parasites and by intrinsic properties like the genetic composition of the competing populations.

In all the experiments discussed so far one species has died out completely. These all fall under cases 1, 2, and 4 in our treatment of the Lotka–Volterra equations. What about case 3, where the species coexist?

Under the conditions of extreme crowding in the laboratory experiments it is possible for two species to live together indefinitely if they differ slightly in their requirements. For example, Crombie (1945) reared the grain beetles *Rhizopertha* and *Oryzaephilus* in wheat and found that they would coexist indefinitely. The larvae of *Rhizopertha* live and feed inside the grain of wheat; the larvae of *Oryzaephilus* live and feed from outside the wheat. The adults of both species are the same, feeding outside the grain. Apparently these larval differences were sufficient to allow coexistence.

The green hydra (*Chlorohydra viridissima*), which has green algae in its endoderm, wins in competition with the brown *Hydra littoralis* in the light and in the absence of predation (Slobodkin 1964). Either darkness or very intense predation permits the two species to coexist in laboratory cultures.

Gause (1935) found that *Paramecium aurelia* and *Paramecium bursaria* would coexist in a tube containing yeast. *Paramecium aurelia* would feed on the yeast suspension in the upper layers of the fluid, whereas *P. bursaria* would feed on the bottom layers. This difference in feeding behavior between these species allowed them to coexist.

Thus, by introducing only a very slight difference in the species habits or in the environment, one can get coexistence between competing animal species under laboratory conditions.

Competition between two species of plants can be studied very readily in greenhouse plots. Let us look first at a simple system of barley and oats (Table 17). Plots are seeded with a range of proportions of barley to oat seeds, from a pure culture of oats to a pure culture of barley. The series of plots are then harvested at the end of the growing season (Table 17)

TABLE 16

Results of competition experiments between the flour beetles
T. castaneum *and* T. confusum[a]

T. castaneum strain	T. confusum strain	Number of cultures in which:	
		castaneum wins	confusum wins
cI	bI	10	0
	bII	10	0
	bIII	10	0
	bIV	10	0
cII	bI	1	8
	bII	0	10
	bIII	0	10
	bIV	4	6
cIII	bI	0	10
	bII	0	9
	bIII	0	10
	bIV	0	10
cIV	bI	9	1
	bII	9	0
	bIII	9	1
	bIV	8	2

[a] The eight genetic strains described in Table 15 were used in these experiments.
SOURCE: After Park, Leslie, and Mertz (1964).

TABLE 17

Results of a competition experiment between barley (Hordeum vulgare) *and oats* (Avena sativa)

Seeds planted			Seeds harvested (millions per hectare)		
Proportion of barley	Proportion of oats	Input ratio (barley/oats)	Barley	Oats	Output ratio (barley/oats)
0.0	1.0	—	0	162	—
0.2	0.8	0.25	42	113	0.37
0.4	0.6	0.67	81	56	1.45
0.6	0.4	1.50	98	32	3.06
0.8	0.2	4.00	105	13	8.08
1.0	0.0	—	123	0	—

SOURCE: After de Wit (1960).

and the input–output seed ratios are plotted as in Figure 121. This graph shows that whatever the seed input ratio (barley/oats), the seed output ratio is greater, so barley increases in frequency and would ultimately replace the oats entirely if these greenhouse conditions obtained.

In perennial grasses competition may be measured by shoot counts or some measure of biomass. Figure 122 illustrates an input–output experiment on competition between the grasses *Phleum pratense* (timothy) and *Anthoxanthum odoratum* (sweet vernal grass). The data points fall almost exactly on the equilibrium line, which indicates that any mixture of these two grasses would be stable over time and would remain near the starting ratio. A contrasting situation occurs in competition between perennial rye-

FIGURE 121

Input–output diagram for a competition experiment between barley and oats. Since the seed output ratio is always greater than the seed input ratio, barley will displace oats when they are in competition. Original data in Table 17. (After de Wit 1960.)

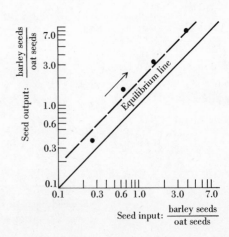

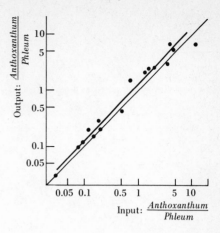

FIGURE 122

Input–output ratios for the perennial grasses Anthoxanthum odoratum *and* Phleum pratense *grown in the laboratory. Input and output were measured by the number of tillers at the start and end of a growing season. (After de Wit 1961.)*

grass (*Lolium perenne*) and clover (*Trifolium repens*). Figure 123 shows that mixtures of these two species should stabilize at some point where clover is approximately 10 to 50 times as abundant as ryegrass.

Two annual species of wild oats inhabit the annual grasslands of central California. Marshall and Jain (1969) studied the competitive relationships between these two annuals in 6-in. pots under six different densities from 8 to 256 plants per pot. Figure 124 shows their results. In each case the ratio line crosses the equilibrium line, so mixtures of these two plants should form stable populations. We can calculate the theoretical composition of these stable populations. For example, at a density of 8 plants per pot, the equilibrium ratio point is 2.68 (from Figure 124), and thus the proportion of *Avena fatua* should be

$$\text{Proportion of } A.\ fatua = \frac{A.\ fatua \text{ output at equilibrium}}{\text{total } Avena \text{ output at equilibrium}}$$

$$= \frac{2.68}{3.68} = 0.729$$

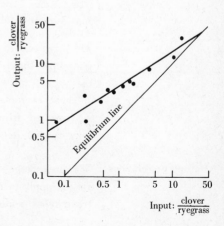

FIGURE 123

*Input–output ratios for perennial ryegrass (*Lolium perenne*) and clover (*Trifolium repens*). Ratios are the length of stolons of clover and number of tillers of ryegrass at the start and end of a growing season. (After de Wit 1961.)*

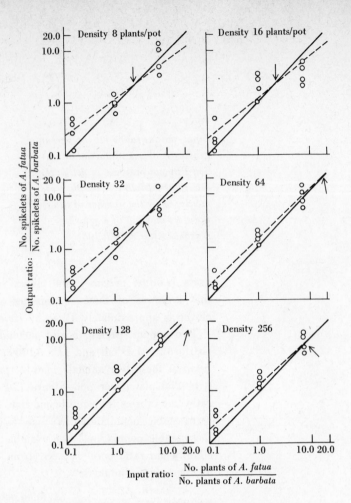

FIGURE 124

*Input–output ratios for two species of wild oats (*Avena*) grown in pots at six densities. Arrows indicate equilibrium ratios. (After Marshall and Jain 1969.)*

and hence the proportion of *A. barbata* is 0.271. We obtain

Density (no. per pot)	8	16	32	64	128	256
% *A. barbata* of total *Avena*	27	29	22	5	0.01	9

This suggests that for densities up to 32 plants per pot (equivalent to 128 plants per square foot) about 20 to 30% *A. barbata* should be maintained in the population.

These examples of plant studies of competition illustrate the conclusions we reached from the Lotka–Volterra model of competition: Two species may coexist in some manner or one may be eliminated from the mixture.

Natural populations   We now come to the question of how these theoretical and laboratory results apply to nature. In asking this question we come up against one controversy of modern ecology, the problem of Gause's hypothesis.

Gause (1934) wrote: "...as a result of competition two similar species scarcely ever occupy similar niches, but displace each other in such a manner that each takes possession of certain peculiar kinds of food and modes of life in which it has an advantage over its competitor" (p. 19). Gause referred to Elton (1927), who had defined *niche* as follows: "...the niche of an animal means its place in the biotic environment, its relations to food and enemies" (p. 64). Elton thus used the term *niche* to describe the role of an animal in its community, so one could speak (for example) of a broad herbivore niche, which could be further subdivided.

Gause went on to say that the Lotka–Volterra equations do "not permit of any equilibrium between the competing species occupying the same 'niche,' and (lead) to the entire displacing of one of them by another" (p. 48). He continued, "both species survive indefinitely only when they occupy different niches in the microcosm in which they have an advantage over their competitors" (p. 48). Gause obviously identifies case 3 (coexistence) with the situation of "different niches" and cases 1, 2, and 4 with the situation of "same niche."

Gause himself never formally defined what is now called Gause's hypothesis, and who was the first to identify this idea with Gause is not known. In 1944 the British Ecological Society held a symposium on the ecology of closely-related species. An anonymous reporter wrote that year in the *Journal of Animal Ecology* that "The Symposium centred about Gause's contention (1934) that two species with similar ecology cannot live together in the same place . . . ."

As is usual, several workers immediately searched out and found earlier statements of "Gause's hypothesis." Monard, a French freshwater biologist, had expressed the same idea in 1920. Grinnell, a California biologist, wrote much the same thing in 1904. The same idea was apparently in Darwin's mind but was never expressed clearly by him. It has been suggested that we drop the use of names and call this idea the *competitive exclusion principle*. Hardin (1960) states this principle succinctly: "Complete competitors cannot coexist."

There is a wide range of opinion on the importance of Gause's hypothesis, or the competitive exclusion principle. Hutchinson and Deevey (1949) believed that it is "the most important development in theoretical ecology" and "one of the chief foundations of modern ecology." Cole (1960), on the other hand, dismissed Gause's hypothesis as a "trite maxim." What is the basis of this controversy?

The niche concept is intimately involved with the competitive exclusion principle, and we must first clarify this concept. The term *niche* was almost simultaneously defined to mean two different things. Joseph Grinnell in 1917 was one of the first to use the term *niche* and viewed it as a subdivision of the habitat (Udvardy 1959). Each niche was occupied by only one species. Elton in 1927 independently defined the niche as the "role" of the species in the community. These vague concepts were incorporated into Hutchinson's redefinition of the niche in 1958. Consider just two environmental variables, such as temperature and humidity, and determine for each species the range of values that allows the species to survive and multiply. This is illustrated in Figure 125. This area in which the species can survive is part of its niche. Now introduce other environmental variables, such as pH or size of food, until all the ecological factors relative to the species have been measured. The addition of the third variable produces a volume, and ultimately we arrive at an *n*-dimensional hypervolume which we call the *fundamental niche* of the species.

This idea of a fundamental niche has some practical difficulties. First, it has an infinite number of dimensions, and we cannot completely determine the niche of any organism. Second, we assume that all environmental variables can be linearly ordered and measured. This is particularly difficult for the biotic dimensions of the niche. Third, the model refers to a single instant in time, and yet competition is a dynamic process. MacArthur (1968) suggests one way to escape these problems: Restrict discussion to statements about differences between niches in one or two dimensions only. Thus we can discuss the differences in the *feeding niches* of two closely-related birds, and can avoid discussing the attributes of unmeasurable entities such as the entire fundamental niches of the two species.

Every hypothesis has its limits, and we should be careful to set down at the start some situations in which competitive exclusion would *not* be expected to occur. These are (1) in colonizing species which live in unstable environments that never reach equilibrium, (2) in species that do not compete for resources, and (3) in fluctuating environments that reverse the direction of competition before extinction is possible (Hutchinson 1958).

FIGURE 125

Hypothetical diagram of part of the niche space of two species S_1 and S_2. Only two environmental variables are used for illustration, but this could be extended to three or more variables to define a hypervolume which Hutchinson (1958) called the fundamental niche *of a species. Note that the niche space of organisms may overlap to a greater or lesser extent.*

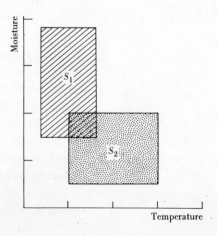

Field naturalists began the first assaults on Gause's hypothesis. They pointed out that one may see in the field many examples of closely-related species living together and apparently in the same habitat. Anyone who has made field collections of plants or insects will attest to the great number of species living in close association. This observation is the ecological paradox of competition: How can we reconcile the frequent extinction of closely-related species in laboratory cultures and the apparent coexistence of large numbers of species in field communities?

Two simple views have developed in attempting to answer this question. One holds that competition is rare in nature, and since species are not competing for limited resources, there is no need to expect evidence of competitive exclusion in natural communities. The other view holds that competition is common enough in nature to be a major factor guiding the evolution and development of species in a community.

How common is competition in nature? Much investigation has centered on closely-related species on the assumption that taxonomic similarity should promote possible competition. Lack (1944, 1945), for example, studied the ecology of closely-related species of birds in an attempt to test Gause's hypothesis. One example of his work was that on the cormorant (*Phalacrocorax carbo*) and the shag (*Phalacrocorax aristotelis*). These species are very similar in habits and appeared to overlap widely in their ecological requirements; they are both cliff nesters and feed on fish. Lack showed that the cormorant nests chiefly on flat broad cliff ledges and feeds chiefly in shallow estuaries and harbors; the shag nests on narrow cliff ledges and feeds mainly out at sea. Thus there were significant ecological differences between these closely-related species.

Lack (1944) analyzed all the pairs of closely-related species of British passerine birds. He obtained the following results:

	Cases (pairs)
Geographical separation	*3*
Separation by habitat	*18 or more*
Separated by feeding habits	*4*
Separated by size differences	*5*
Separated by different winter ranges	*2*
Apparent ecological overlap	*5–7*

Lack believed that further study would reveal differences between these 5 to 7 pairs, which apparently overlap.

The boreal forests of New England are inhabited by five warbler species of the genus *Dendroica*. All these birds are insect eaters and about the same size. Why does one species not exterminate the others by competitive exclusion? MacArthur (1958) showed that these warblers feed in different positions in the canopy (Figure 126), feed in different manners, move in different directions through the trees, and have slightly different nesting dates. The feeding-zone differences seem sufficiently large to explain the coexistence of the blackburnian, black-throated green, and bay-breasted warblers. The myrtle warbler is uncommon and less specialized than the other species. The Cape May warbler is different from these other species

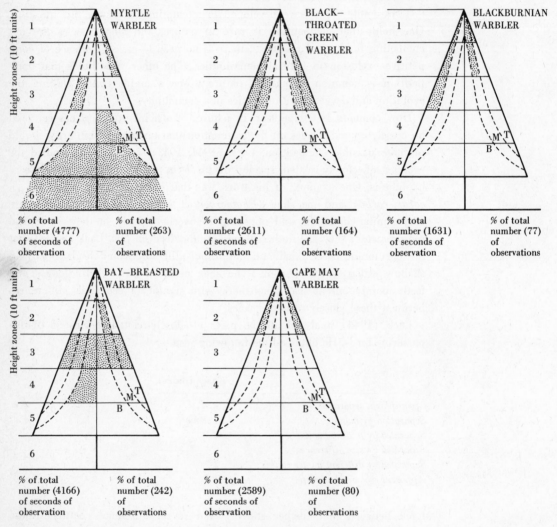

FIGURE 126

Feeding positions of five species of warblers in the coniferous forest of northeastern United States. The zones of most concentrated feeding activity are shaded. B, base of branches; M, middle; T, terminal. (After MacArthur 1958.)

because it depends on occasional outbreaks of forest insects to provide superabundant food for its continued existence. During outbreaks of insects the Cape May warbler increases rapidly in numbers and obtains a temporary advantage over the others. During years between outbreaks they are reduced in numbers to low levels.

Thus closely-related species of birds either live in different sorts of places or else use different sorts of foods. Lack suggested that these differences arose because of competition in the past between these closely-related species. Thus, because of Gause's hypothesis and its associated selection pressure, species either "moved" to different places and so avoided competition or changed their feeding ecology to avoid competition.

Ross (1957) worked on leafhopper populations in Illinois and claimed that there were numerous instances in nature among insects where more than one species was occupying the same niche. He studied six species of leafhoppers of the *lawsoni* complex* of the genus *Erythoneura*. All six species breed on sycamore trees and are the only leafhoppers to breed there. All these species appear to have identical habits; they all mature at the same time, feed in the same manner, often side by side on the same leaf, hibernate at the same time, and so on. Ross could find no evidence that these six species occupied different niches and no evidence that they harmed each other. He concluded that Gause's hypothesis was false.

Fryer (1959) studied the ecology of *Cichlidae* fish in Lake Nyasa. He was particularly interested in the species group that lives in the rocky littoral zone. Off these rocky shores there are 12 species, very closely related, which feed almost entirely on attached algae. Of these 12, 7 feed only on one type of algae. Of these 7,

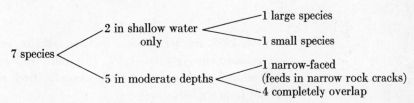

Fryer believed that the 4 overlapping species could live in the same place because there was no competition for food; he thought their numbers were kept down by predators and thus that competitive exclusion would not occur.

The paradox of the plankton has been aptly described by Hutchinson (1961) as a possible exception to the competitive exclusion principle. The phytoplankton of marine and freshwater environments consists of a large number of plant species which utilize a common pool of nutrients and undergo photosynthesis in a relatively unstructured environment. How can

---

*A species complex is a group of closely-related species which look very much alike in most morphological features.

all these species coexist, especially since natural waters are often deficient in nutrients and hence competition should be strong? Hutchinson suggested that these species could coexist because of environmental instability; before competitive displacement could have time to occur, seasonal changes in the lake or the sea would occur. The phytoplankton may thus be viewed as a nonequilibrium community of competing species and may not be an exception to the principle of competitive exclusion.

There are very few cases in which species have been studied during an episode of competitive exclusion. The best example is an agricultural one. Three parasitic wasps of the genus *Aphytis* have been introduced into southern California to help control the California red scale (*Aonidiella aurantii*), an insect pest of orange trees (DeBach and Sundby 1963). *Aphytis chrysomphali* was accidentally introduced from the Mediterranean area around 1900 and became widely distributed in southern California and very common in some areas (Figure 127a). In 1948 a second species, *Aphytis lingnanensis*, was introduced from south China and began to displace *A. chrysomphali* from orchards. This displacement was very rapid in some regions, covering a 4000 sq.-miles area in about 10 years. For example:

	Individuals (%)	
	A. chrysomphali	*A. lingnanensis*
Santa Barbara County		
1958	*85*	*15*
1959	*0*	*100*
Orange County		
1958	*96*	*4*
1959	*7*	*93*

In 1956–1957 another species, *Aphytis melinus*, was imported from India and released during 1957–1959. This third species immediately began to displace the second species, *A. lingnanensis*, from the interior, hotter areas but not from coastal areas:

	Individuals (%)	
	A. lingnanensis	*A. melinus*
Coastal, Santa Barbara County		
1959	*100*	*0*
1960	*95*	*5*
1961	*100*	*0*
Interior, San Fernando County		
1959	*50*	*50*
1960	*6*	*94*
1961	*4*	*96*

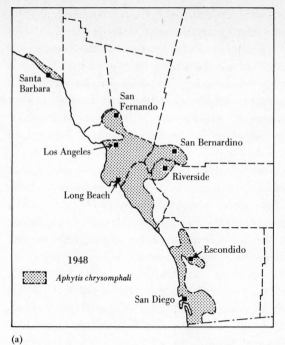

(a)

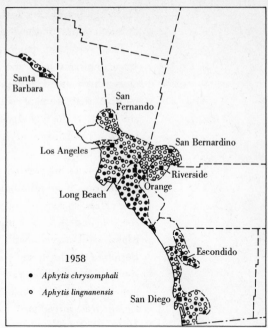

(b)

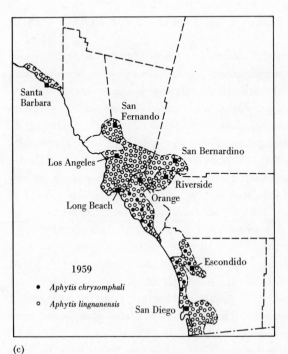

(c)

FIGURE 127

Distribution of the introduced parasitic wasps Aphytis chrysomphali *and* A. lingnanensis *in citrus-growing areas of southern California in (a) 1948, (b) 1958, and (c) 1959. (After DeBach and Sundby 1963.)*

Thus competitive exclusion may result in these two species living in two different parts of the orange-growing area, coastal versus interior.

This series of competitive displacements occurred in the presence of superabundant food and without any disturbance to two other insect parasites which attack the same red scale host. The mechanism by which competitive displacement occurred is not clear. DeBach and Sundby (1963) showed that no two *Aphytis* species could coexist in laboratory populations, but the mechanism of interference in the presence of superabundant food was not obvious.

Some ants have extended their distributions with the help of man and in the process have eliminated the native ant fauna through competition. Relatively few species of ants have shown a striking ability to displace resident species, and two such highly aggressive colonizers have invaded the oceanic island of Bermuda within the last century. *Pheidole megacephala* invaded Bermuda in the latter part of the nineteenth century and apparently drove some of the native ants to extinction (Haskins and Haskins 1965). This ant is now being replaced by the Argentine ant (*Iridomyrmex humilis*), which was introduced into Bermuda around 1949 (Crowell 1968). From 1953–1959 *Iridomyrmex* increased its distribution in Bermuda at the rate of 394 hectares/year, replacing *Pheidole* in all habitats. Since 1959 the rate of displacement has slowed markedly, and whether or not some equilibrium will be established short of extinction of *Pheidole* is not yet known. The nature of the competition between the ants is not known; it could involve direct aggressive fighting, a shortage of suitable food, or chemical repellants.

Two ant species of the genus *Lasius* may occur together in British grasslands. *Lasius flavus* is a mound builder and does not require special nesting structures. It forages mainly beneath the surface and is a subordinate species. *Lasius niger* depends on stumps and stones or bare soil in which to nest, forages above ground on plants, preys on other ants (including *L. flavus*), and is a dominant species. These two ants have been observed to coexist for periods exceeding 14 years in British grasslands, and Pontin (1961) suggests that they can coexist indefinitely because each species interferes more with itself than it does with its competitor species (case 3 of Lotka and Volterra, page 216. He demonstrated this experimentally by transplanting colonies of the subordinate *L. flavus*. The transplanted colonies reduced alate queen production (a measure of colony success) to a greater extent in neighboring *L. flavus* than in the other species *L. niger*. Conversely, the removal of *L. flavus* colonies from an area stimulated more production from the remaining *L. flavus* colonies than from the neighboring *L. niger* colonies (Pontin 1969). The net result is stable interspecific competition and continued coexistence.

Three species of whirligig beetles (Gyrinidae) can be collected in lakes and ponds in Michigan. A transition occurs between a northern species *Dineutes nigrior* and a southern species *Dineutes horni* in this region (Figure 128). A third species of *Dineutes* is also found but is rare in Michigan lakes. These beetles are often found segregated in different habitats but some definite cases of stable coexistence are also evident. Istock (1967) recorded one instance of transient competitive exclusion in these beetles from a northern Michigan pond. In one pond the frequency of the southern species *D. horni* increased greatly during one generation in competition with the northern species *D. nigrior*:

	Proportion of *D. horni* in pond
Spring 1966, adults	0.21
Summer 1966, pupae	0.79

This large competitive displacement was erased in late summer when the new adults emerged and mixed with neighboring populations containing large numbers of *D. nigrior*. In laboratory experiments Istock showed that *D. horni* always replaced *D. nigrior* because the larvae of *D. horni* are more cannibalistic and more aggressive than the larvae of *D. nigrior* as food shortage begins to develop. In the field complete competitive exclusion of *D. horni* over *D. nigrior* does not occur because the environment does not remain constant and because the competitively inferior *D. nigrior* has a "refuge" since it is able to live in small ponds in northern Michigan which will not support *D. horni*. Thus competitive exclusion and competitive coex-

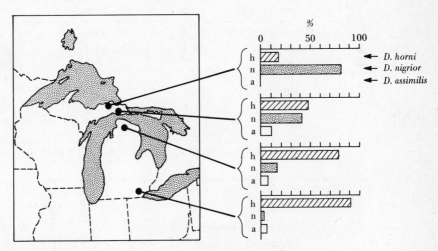

FIGURE 128

Relative abundance of three species of whirligig beetles in Michigan lakes. Dineutes horni *is a southern species and* D. nigrior *a northern species. (After Istock 1966.)*

istence are both possible in natural populations and depend on the rate of displacement of one species by another.

In cases of competitive coexistence, the presence of one species should depress the average population size of the second species. This suggests experimental removal as a technique for studying competition, but few experiments of this kind have been done on animals. House mouse (*Mus musculus*) populations do not reach high densities in the presence of meadow mice (*Microtus californicus*) in California, and DeLong (1966) was able to show experimentally in the field that the rate of population growth of *Mus* was cut in half by the presence of *Microtus*. He was able to trace this interaction to the effect of *Microtus* on the recruitment of juvenile *Mus* (Figure 129) and found in laboratory experiments that adult meadow mice would disturb nesting house mice females and cause them to desert their litters.

Plant ecologists have repeatedly demonstrated the effect of one plant on another for agricultural crops; one example will illustrate this. Wild oats (*Avena fatua*) is a serious weed in the Northern Great Plains of North America, where it competes with the crop flax (*Linum usitatissimum*) as well as wheat and barley. Wild oats persists in flax fields because its seeds ripen earlier than the flax and drop to the ground. There is a serious reduction in yields of flax at increasing oats densities (Bell and Nalewaja 1968):

Wild oats density (no./sq. yd)	Flaxseed yield (bushels/acre) at Fargo in 1966		
	Fertilized plots	Unfertilized plots	Average reduction %
0	19.5	17.9	—
10	13.4	14.3	26
40	6.7	8.0	60
70	4.3	6.3	72
100	3.5	4.2	80
130	3.4	3.4	82
160	2.9	2.3	86

Hence the concern of agriculturalists with weeds.

FIGURE 129

*Interference between field mice (*Microtus*) and house mice (*Mus*) in central California grasslands. The presence of* Microtus *reduces the juvenile production of* Mus. *(After DeLong 1966.)*

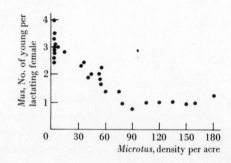

These effects of competition among plants are not confined to agricultural situations. Cable (1969) showed that annual grass production in the semidesert area of central Arizona was reduced by competition for water with burroweed (*Aplopappus tenuisectus*) and with perennial grasses:

	Production (lb dry wt/acre) of annual grass (mostly *Bouteloua aristidoides*)	
	Wet year (1961)	Dry year (1962)
Annual grass alone	663	50
Annual grass + burroweed	451	35
Annual grass + burroweed + perennial grass	240	30

There is great variation in production from year to year because of rainfall, but the effects of competition could usually be seen in reduced yields.

Two annual plants dominate the grasslands of the Great Central Valley of California, *Bromus mollis* and *Erodium botrys*. They are important grazing species, and unfertilized land is dominated by grasses like *Bromus*. *Erodium* has a low growth form but rapid root penetration in the seedling stage, so it is favored in competition for soil nutrients. *Bromus* grows taller and if adequate nutrients are available, it becomes the superior competitor for light and shades out *Erodium*. A balanced competition thus seems to exist in which *Erodium* is favored in poor soils and in drought years, and *Bromus* is favored in better soils when adequate moisture is available (McCown and Williams 1968).

Some of the difficulties of applying laboratory results to field populations are illustrated by Marshall and Jain's work on wild oats. Laboratory studies discussed above indicated that *Avena barbata* should reach equilibrium with *A. fatua* at some mixture between 10 and 30% *A. barbata* (see page 230 and Figure 124). But in field populations in central California many more pure stands are found than mixed stands (Marshall and Jain 1969):

	No. stands in:	
% *A. barbata* of total *Avena*	Region I (Mediterranean warm summer)	Region II (Mediterranean cool summer)
0	35	7
1–9	1	3
10–29	3	0
30–49	3	6
50–69	5	13
70–89	5	14
90–99	6	9
100	10	31
Total no. stands	68	83

Thus about half or more of grasslands are pure stands of one *Avena* species or the other, and the explanation for this is not known.

The effects of competition may be very different in different taxonomic groups. Opportunities for specialization may be relatively poor for plants, which all require light, nutrients, and space, in comparison with birds, which inhabit complex structured plant associations. Freshwater fish in general are not specialized but have a wide tolerance of habitat conditions and feeding conditions (Larkin 1956). Fish also have a very plastic growth rate and can thus live through long periods of unfavorable conditions. This plasticity or flexibility is also found in many aquatic invertebrates and in many plants, and contrasts with the specialized and often fixed patterns of growth and reproduction in birds and mammals. Thus poor environmental conditions, which might cause a mammal population to die out, might cause a fish population to stop growing or an invertebrate population to enter a dormant phase.

SUMMARY

Theoretical models of competition indicate that, in cases of competition between two similar species, one species may be displaced or both may reach a stable equilibrium mixture. The possibility of displacement has given rise to the *competitive exclusion principle,* which states that complete competitors cannot coexist. In simple laboratory populations one species often becomes extinct but sometimes coexists with another species. Natural communities show many examples of similar species which are coexisting, and this must be reconciled with the principle of competitive exclusion. One approach to solving this paradox is to suggest that competition is rare in nature, and hence displacement is not to be expected. Another approach is to suggest that competition has occurred and the interrelations we now see are the outcome of competition, displacement, and subsequent evolution in the past. Both views agree that competition is not common in present-day populations, but this may not be true. Experimental work with agricultural crops and range plants suggests that competitive interactions are very great in field populations, but little work of this kind has been done with animal populations. Transferring the results of laboratory work on competition to field populations has proved difficult.

SELECTED
REFERENCES

AYALA, F. J. 1969. Experimental invalidation of the principle of competitive exclusion. *Nature* 224:1076–1079.

BIRCH, L. C. 1957. The meanings of competition. *Amer. Naturalist* 91:5–18.

HARDIN, G. 1960. The competitive exclusion principle. *Science* 131:1292–1297.

HARPER, J. L. 1961. The evolution and ecology of closely related species living in the same area. *Evolution* 15:209–227.

LACK, D. 1971. *Ecological Isolation in Birds*. Blackwell, Oxford.

MACARTHUR, R. 1969. Species packing, and what interspecies competition minimizes. *Proc. Nat. Acad. Sci. U.S.* 64: 1369–1371.

MILLER, R. S. 1967. Pattern and process in competition. *Advances Ecol. Res.* 4:1–74.

PARK, T. 1962. Beetles, competition, and populations. *Science* 138:1369–1375.

DE WIT, C. T. 1961. Space relationships within populations of one or more species. pp. 314–329 in *Mechanisms in Biological Competition* (Symp. Soc. Exp. Biol. 15), ed. by F. L. Milthorpe. Cambridge University Press, New York.

QUESTIONS AND PROBLEMS

1 Narise (1965) studied competition between *Drosophila simulans* and *Drosophila melanogaster* in the laboratory. He obtained these results at medium population density:

Frequency of D. simulans	Input ratio (D. simulans/D. melanogaster)	Output ratio
0.0	—	—
0.1	0.111	0.035
0.2	0.250	0.124
0.3	0.429	0.212
0.4	0.667	0.321
0.5	1.000	0.462
0.6	1.500	0.750
0.7	2.333	1.237
0.8	4.000	2.398
0.9	9.000	4.965
1.0	—	—

He concluded that an indigenous species like *D. simulans* could successfully compete with and eliminate occasional migrants of a dominant alien species like *D. melanogaster*. Analyze this conclusion with the ratio diagrams developed by de Wit (1961).

2 MacArthur (1958, p. 600) states that "differences in food and space requirements are neither always necessary nor always sufficient to prevent competition and permit coexistence." This suggests (1) that there are cases of coexisting species in which food and space requirements are nearly identical; (2) that there are cases of species with different food and space requirements that do compete and cannot coexist. Discuss the implications of this with regard to studies of closely-related species.

3 Analyze the yeast results of Gause (1932) by the use of Lotka–Volterra plots (as in Figure 110), and predict the outcome of this competition from the estimates of α, β, K_1, and K_2.

4 Ennik (1960) grew clover (*Trifolium repens*) and ryegrass (*Lolium perenne*) under low light conditions and obtained these results over one growing season (clover—length of stolons in centimeters per pot; grass—number of tillers per pot):

Input		Output	
Clover	Grass	Clover	Grass
13.5	84	40	84
22.5	86	49	84
29.5	73	71	71
38	76	108	73
53	67	110	66
52	45	87	44
91	43	81	43
93	32	84	40
80	24	76	51
79.5	24	61	52
80.5	14	53	40
125	5	70	20

Construct a ratio diagram for these data and interpret the results.

5 Review the work of Connell (1961a) discussed in Chapter 5 and discuss the role of competitive exclusion in affecting distributions of organisms.

6 In the Lotka–Volterra competition model, what is the meaning of a situation in which $\alpha = \beta$? In which $\alpha = \beta = 1$? What outcome is predicted when $\alpha = \beta = 1$ and $K_1 = K_2$? What is implied if $\alpha = 1/\beta$ and if $\alpha \neq 1/\beta$?

7 Charles Darwin (1859) in *The Origin of Species*, Chapter 3, states:

As the species of the same genus usually have, though by no means invariably, much similarity in habits and constitution, and always in structure, the struggle will generally be more severe between them, if they come into competition with each other, than between the species of distinct genera.

Discuss.

13   *Species interactions:*

predation

In addition to competing for food or space, species may interact directly by predation. The word *predation* is used here in a general sense to describe the eating of one species by another, and includes herbivory, carnivory, insect parasitism, and cannibalism (see page 212). All these processes can be described with the same kind of mathematical models, and consequently we shall begin by considering them together as "predation." The effect of predation on populations has been studied theoretically and practically because it has great economic implications for man.

MATHEMATICAL MODELS

Discrete generations   Let us explore first a simple model of predator–prey interactions using a discrete generation system. Assume that the prey population in the absence of predation can be described by the logistic equation (Chapter 11)

$$N_{t+1} = (1.0 - Bx_t)N_t$$

where

N = population size
t = generation number
B = slope of reproductive curve (of Figure 86)
$x_t = (N_t - N_{eq})$ = deviation of present population size from equilibrium population size

In the presence of a predator we must modify this equation by a term allowing for the individuals eaten by predators, and this could be done in a number of ways. All the prey above a certain number (the number of "safe sites") might be killed by predators. Or each predator might eat a constant number of prey. If, however, the abundance of the predator is determined by the abundance of the prey, the whole predator population must eat proportionately more prey when prey are abundant and proportionately less prey when prey are scarce. They could do this by becoming more abundant when prey are abundant, or by being very flexible in their food requirements. We introduce a term into the prey's logistic equation:

$$N_{t+1} = (1.0 - Bx_t)N_t - CN_tP_t$$

where

P_t = population size of predators in generation t
C = a constant measuring the efficiency of the predator

What about the predator population? We assume that the reproductive rate of the predators depends on the number of prey available. We can write this simply:

$$P_{t+1} = QN_tP_t$$

where

P = population size of predator
N = population size of prey
t = generation number
Q = a constant measuring the efficiency of utilization of prey for reproduction by predators

Note that if the prey population (N) were constant, this equation would describe geometric population growth (Chapter 11) for the predator.

To put these two equations together and interpret them, we must first obtain the maximum reproductive rates of the predator and the prey. When predators are absent and prey are scarce, the net reproductive rate of the prey will be, approximately,

$$N_{t+1} = (1.0 - BN_{eq})N_t$$

or

$$R = \frac{N_{t+1}}{N_t} = 1.0 - BN_{eq}$$

where R is the maximum reproductive rate of prey. For the predator, when the prey population is at equilibrium, a few predators will increase at

$$P_{t+1} = QN_{eq}P_t$$

or

$$S = \frac{P_{t+1}}{P_t} = QN_{eq}$$

where S is the maximum reproductive rate of the predator.

Let us now work out an example. Let $R = 1.5$ and $N_{eq} = 100$ so that the slope of the reproductive curve $B = 0.005$. Assume that the constant C measuring the efficiency of the predator is 0.5. Thus

$$N_{t+1} = (1.0 - 0.005x_t)N_t - 0.5N_tP_t$$

Assume that under the best conditions the predators can double their numbers each generation $(S = 2.0)$, so the constant Q is

$$S = QN_{eq}$$
$$2.0 = Q(100)$$
or
$$Q = 0.02$$

Consequently, the second equation is

$$P_{t+1} = 0.02N_tP_t$$

Start a population at $N_0 = 50$ and $P_0 = 0.2$:

$$N_1 = ([1.0 - 0.005(50 - 100)]50) - [(0.5)(50)(0.2)]$$
$$= 62.5 - 5.0 = 57.5$$
$$P_1 = (0.02)(50)(0.2)$$
$$= 0.2$$

For the second generation,

$$N_2 = ([1.0 - 0.005(57.5 - 100)]57.5) - [(0.5)(57.5)(0.2)]$$
$$= 69.72 - 5.75 = 63.97$$
$$P_2 = (0.02)(57.5)(0.2)$$
$$= 0.23$$

These calculations, more tedious than difficult, can be carried over many generations to produce the results shown in Figure 130.

A stable oscillation in the numbers of predators and prey is only one of four possible outcomes: (1) stable equilibrium with no oscillation, (2) stable oscillation, (3) convergent oscillation, and (4) divergent oscillation leading to the extinction of either predator or prey. Maynard Smith (1968) has shown that the range of variables for a stable equilibrium without oscillation is very restricted. One example will illustrate this solution. Let

FIGURE 130

Population changes in a hypothetical predator–prey system with discrete generations. For the prey population, $N_{eq} = 100$, $B = 0.005$, and $C = 0.5$. For the predator, $Q = 0.02$.

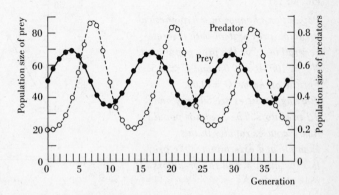

$N_{eq} = 100$, $B = 0.005$, and $C = 0.5$ for the prey, while $Q = 0.0105$ ($S = 1.05$) for the predator. For the first generation,

$$N_1 = ([1.0 - 0.005(50 - 100)]50) - [(0.5)(50)(0.2)]$$
$$= 57.50$$
$$P_1 = (0.0105)(50)(0.2)$$
$$= 0.105$$

Similarly,

	N	P
Second generation	66.7	0.063
Third generation	75.7	0.044
Fourth generation	83.2	0.035
Fifth generation	88.7	0.031

The populations gradually stabilize around a level of 95.2 for the prey and 0.025 for the predator.

Figure 131 shows one additional example of a hypothetical predator–prey interaction which leads to extinction.

Continuous generations Lotka (1925) and Volterra (1926) independently derived a set of equations to describe the interaction between populations of predators and prey. For the prey, assume a state of geometric increase in the absence of predation:

$$\frac{dN}{dt} = r_1 N \qquad \text{geometric increase of prey alone } (r_1 \text{ is positive})$$

where

N = density of prey
t = time
r_1 = innate capacity for increase of prey (r_m for prey)

FIGURE 131

Population changes in a hypothetical predator–prey system with discrete generations. For the prey population, $N_{eq} = 100$, $B = 0.03$, and $C = 0.5$. For the predator, $Q = 0.04$. Starting densities are 50 prey and 0.2 predators. The predator population increases rapidly in this example and exterminates the prey in generation 5, and the predators then starve.

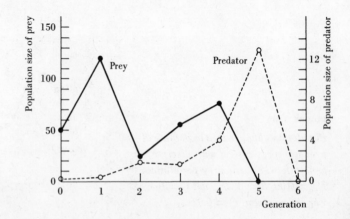

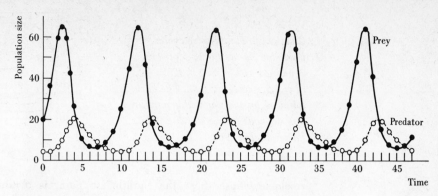

FIGURE 132

*Classical predator–prey cycles predicted by the Lotka–Volterra
equations with $r_1 = 1.0$, $K_1 = 0.1$, $r_2 = 0.5$, and $K_2 = 0.02$. Starting
population size of prey is 20, of predator 4. The equilibrium point is
25 prey and 10 predators. These data are also illustrated in Figure
133 as the middle curve.*

For the predator, assume that the population will decrease geometrically
in the absence of the prey:

$$\frac{dP}{dt} = -r_2 P$$

where

P = density of predators

r_2 = instantaneous death rate of the predators in the absence of prey

If the predator and prey are put together in a limited space, the rate of
increase of the prey is slowed by a factor depending on the density of the
predators:

$$\frac{dN}{dt} = (r_1 - K_1 P)N \qquad \text{equation for prey population}$$

where K_1 = a constant measuring the ability of the prey to escape predators.

Similarly, the predator population will be increased at a rate that depends
on the density of the prey population:

$$\frac{dP}{dt} = (-r_2 + K_2 N)P \qquad \text{equation for predator population}$$

where K_2 is a measure of the skill of the predator in catching prey.

These predator–prey equations are characterized by a *periodic solution*—
the populations oscillate in numbers in a systematic way (Figure 132).
The amplitude of the oscillation depends on the starting densities of predator
and prey. Figure 133 illustrates this by abstracting time and plotting the
subsequent prey density against predator density. A family of curves that

FIGURE 133

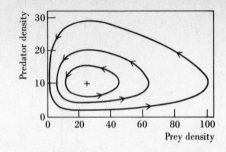

Classical predator–prey cycles predicted by the Lotka–Volterra equations with $r_1 = 1.0$, $K_1 = 0.1$, $r_2 = 0.5$, and $K_2 = 0.02$. The curve followed by any particular population depends on the starting point. (After Pielou 1969.)

resemble ellipses near the equilibrium point is obtained. Any population will continue indefinitely to follow the cyclical path on which it starts, in a counterclockwise direction. The equilibrium point is defined by the densities:

$$N = \frac{r_2}{K_2} \quad \text{and} \quad P = \frac{r_1}{K_1}$$

There are no conditions under which the oscillations become divergent in this simple model.

A generalization of the predator–prey model has been made in a graphical analysis by Rosenzweig and MacArthur (1963). We must assume that the predator is limited in numbers by the amount of food available in the form of prey organisms. Figure 134 indicates three possible situations. In each graph the zone of predator and prey densities for which the prey population can increase is shaded. This zone is determined by predator densities in part but also by other environmental variables, such as food supply. The predator population, since by assumption it is limited by prey numbers, can start increasing only when prey densities have reached a certain threshold, and the point of intersection is an equilibrium point. The behavior of the predator–prey oscillations depends on the position of this equilibrium point. If it is exactly at the peak of the prey zone of increase, the oscillations are stable (classical oscillations). If it is on the descending part, the oscillations are damped, and if it is on the ascending part, the oscillations are divergent and lead to extinction. The generalized results of this graphical analysis are similar to those found previously with the discrete generation model, and the question of what occurs in laboratory and field populations of predators and their prey can now be raised.

LABORATORY STUDIES

Gause (1934) was the first to make an empirical test of the Lotka–Volterra model for predator–prey relations. He reared the protozoans *Paramecium caudatum* (prey) and *Didinium nasutum* (predator) together in an oat medium. In these initial experiments *Didinium* always exterminated

Paramecium and then died of starvation; that is, instead of the classical oscillations Gause got divergent oscillations and extinction. This result occurred under all the circumstances Gause used for this system—making the culture vessel very large, introducing only a few *Didinium*, and so on. The conclusion was that the *Paramecium–Didinium* system did not show the periodic oscillations predicted by Lotka and Volterra. Gause believed that the theoretical oscillations were not achieved because of a biological peculiarity of *Didinium:* It was able to multiply very rapidly even when prey were scarce, with individuals becoming smaller and smaller in the process.

Gause then introduced a complication into the system: He used an oat medium with a sediment. *Paramecium* in the sediment were safe from *Didinium*, which never entered it. Consequently, Gause had added a *refuge* for the prey to his simple system. In this type of system the *Didinium* again eliminated the *Paramecium*, but only from the clear-fluid medium; *Didinium* then starved to death, and the *Paramecium* hiding in the sediment emerged to increase in numbers (Figure 135). The experiment ended with many prey and no predators. Again Gause failed to get the classical oscillations predicted by the mathematical model.

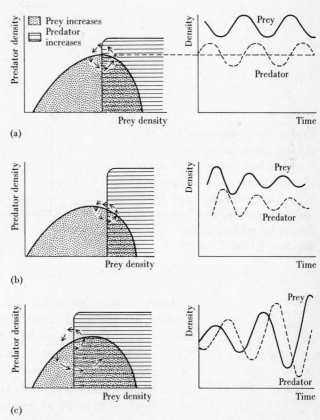

FIGURE 134

Graphical analysis of predator–prey interaction with a simple food-limited predator: (a) stable oscillations, (b) damped oscillations, and (c) divergent oscillations. Predator and prey zones of increase are shown at the left and the corresponding population trends at the right. (After MacArthur and Connell 1966.)

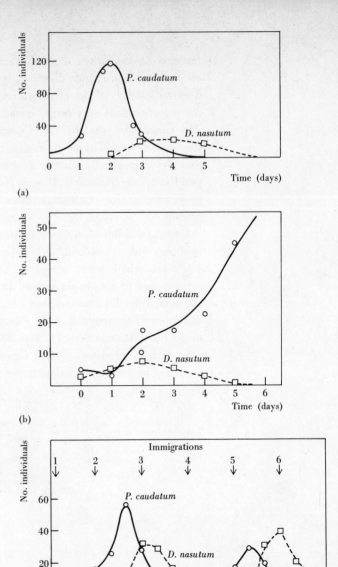

Predator–prey interaction between the protozoans Paramecium caudatum *and* Didinium nasutum *in three microcosms: (a) oat medium without sediment; (b) oat medium with sediment; (c) with immigrations in oat medium without sediment. (After Gause 1934.)*

Gause, being a determined soul, tried another system, introducing *immigrations* into the experimental setup. Every third day he added one *Paramecium* and one *Didinium*, and he got the results shown in Figure 135. Gause concluded that in *Paramecium* and *Didinium* the periodic oscillations in numbers of the predators and the prey are not a property of the predator–prey interaction itself, as Lotka and Volterra thought, but apparently occur as a result of constant interference from outside the system.

Gause's experiments, then, do not support the conclusions of Lotka and Volterra on the predator–prey system.

Huffaker (1958) questioned these conclusions of Gause that the predator–prey system was inherently self-annihilating without some outside interference such as immigration. He claimed that Gause had used too simple a microcosm. Huffaker studied a laboratory system of a phytophagous mite *Eotetranychus sexmaculatus* as prey and a predatory mite *Typhlodromus occidentalis* as predator. The prey mite infests oranges, and Huffaker used these for his experiments. When the predator was introduced onto a single prey-infested orange, it completely eliminated the prey and died of starvation (like Gause's *Didinium*). Huffaker gradually introduced more and more spatial heterogeneity into his experiments. He placed 40 oranges on rectangular trays like egg cartons and partly covered some oranges with paraffin or paper to limit the available feeding area; in other cases he used rubber balls as "substitute" oranges. Huffaker could then disperse the oranges among the rubber balls or place all the oranges together. Finally, he could add whole new trays and set up artificial barriers of Vaseline, which the mites could not cross.

In all Huffaker's simple systems the results were extermination of the populations. Figure 136 illustrates a population that became extinct in a moderately complex environment of 40 oranges. Finally, Huffaker produced the desired oscillation in a 252-orange universe with a complex series of Vaseline barriers; in this system the prey were able to colonize oranges in a hop-skip-and-jump fashion and keep one step ahead of the predator, which

FIGURE 136

Densities per orange area of the prey mite, Eotetranychus sexmaculatus, *and the predator mite,* Typhlodromus occidentalis, *with 20 small areas of food for the prey (orange surface) alternating with 20 foodless positions. (After Huffaker 1958.)*

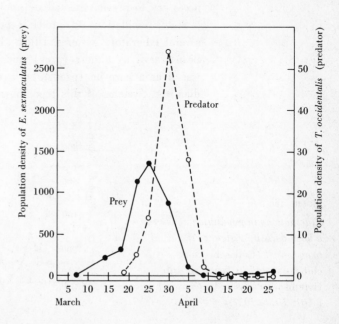

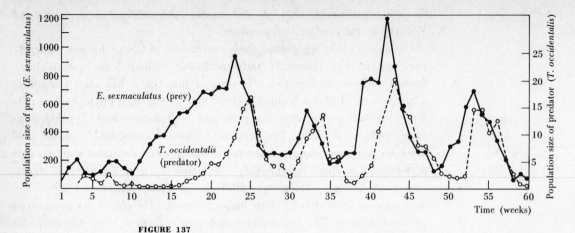

FIGURE 137

Predator–prey interaction between two mites in a complex laboratory environment with a 252-orange system with one-twentieth of each orange exposed for possible feeding by the prey. (After Huffaker, Shea, and Herman 1963.)

exterminated each little colony of the prey it found (Figure 137). The predators died out after 70 weeks and the experiment was terminated.

Huffaker concluded that he could establish an experimental system in which the predator–prey relationship would not be inherently self-destructive. He admits, however, that his system is dependent on local emigration and immigration and that a great deal of environmental heterogeneity is necessary to prevent immediate annihilation of the system.

Stable oscillations of predator–prey interactions have been obtained in several laboratory systems. Utida (1957) maintained a system of the azuki bean weevil as a host (prey) and a wasp parasitic on the larvae of the weevil as a parasite (predator) in a Petri dish 1.8 cm high by 8.5 cm in diameter. Systems of this type show oscillations (Figure 138) which Utida

FIGURE 138

*Fluctuations in population density in a host–parasite system of the azuki bean weevil (*Callosobruchus chinensis*) and its larval parasite* Heterospilus prosopidis *(a wasp). (After Utida 1957.)*

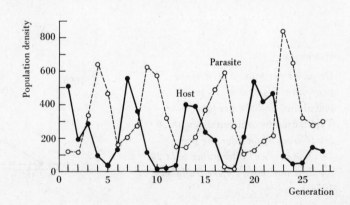

followed for a maximum of 112 generations (14 complete oscillations). The oscillations were gradually damped in amplitude (convergent oscillations), and Utida noted that a long-term trend was imposed on the cycle; the host population gradually increased in density and the parasite population gradually declined. This raised an interesting question: Can there be evolutionary changes in laboratory predator–prey systems during short experiments? Lotka and Volterra of course assumed a constant and unchanging prey species and a constant and unchanging predator species, and other ecologists have often followed their lead in assuming that evolution cannot occur on an ecological time scale.

Evolutionary changes in predator–prey systems in the laboratory have been studied most thoroughly by Pimentel and his co-workers at Cornell. In one study, a population system of the house fly (*Musca domestica*) and a wasp parasite (*Nasonia vitripennis*) maintained for 20 generations showed significant evolutionary changes (Pimentel, Nagel, and Madden 1963). These changes occurred in both the host flies and the parasite wasps: The host became more resistant to the parasite, and the parasite became less virulent to the host. This is indicated in the population parameters given in Table 18. Selection had produced evolutionary changes in a short time to reduce the intensity of interaction between the host and the parasite. Thus the genetic properties of both host and parasite were not constant.

TABLE 18

Evolutionary changes in a host–parasite system of the house fly (M. domestica) *and a wasp parasite* (N. vitripennis) *after 20 generations of interaction in the laboratory*

	Reproductive rate (average no. progeny per female wasp)	Parasitism rate (percentage of fly pupae parasitized)	Longevity of female wasps (days)	Longevity of male wasps (days)
Control wasps on control flies	140	51.7	7.0	1.6
Experimental wasps on experimental flies[a]	46	39.6	4.6	1.4
Control wasps on experimental flies[b]	68	46.0	5.2	1.4
Experimental wasps on control flies[c]	123	52.6	6.6	1.7

[a] Measures evolutionary changes in both hosts and parasites.
[b] Measures evolutionary changes in host resistance.
[c] Measures evolutionary changes in parasite virulence.
SOURCE: After Pimental et al. (1963).

Laboratory studies of predator–prey systems have thus carried us a long way from our starting point. What might we look for in field populations of predator–prey systems? We have assumed so far that predators determine the abundance of their prey and vice versa, and we should consider first whether this generalization holds for field situations. If it does, we might expect to see evidence of predator–prey oscillations in some natural systems and also some evidence of divergent oscillations. Stable associations of predator and prey might be expected from evolutionary changes, and these evolutionary changes could be looked for in species that have recently come into contact in the field.

FIELD STUDIES

How can we find out whether predators determine the abundance of their prey? The suggested experiment is to remove predators from the system and observe its response. Few direct experiments like this have been done properly, but let us examine some case studies.

Atlantic salmon (*Salmo salar*) are important in both commercial and sport fishing along the east coast of Canada, and declining stocks have been a serious problem. One attempt to increase production came from the observation that bird predators, particularly kingfishers and mergansers, were eating a large fraction of the young salmon population. Atlantic salmon lay their eggs in fresh water, and the young salmon live 2 or 3 years in fresh water before they emigrate to sea as smolts. White (1939) removed 154 kingfishers and 56 mergansers from the Margaree River in Nova Scotia in 1937–1938 and obtained increased numbers of young salmon:

	No. salmon smolts going to sea
1937, before bird control	*1834*
1938, after bird control	*4065*

Two objections can be raised to this experiment: (1) Salmon smolt production varies greatly from year to year normally and no control data are available to counter the possibility that 1938 was just a "good" salmon year; (2) even if more young salmon are produced, we do not know whether this will mean more adult salmon returning 1 or 2 years later.

Elson (1962) repeated this experiment on a longer time scale by removing for 6 years an average of 54 mergansers and 164 kingfishers a year from a 10-mile stretch of the Pollett River in New Brunswick. He obtained these results:

	Year	No. salmon fry planted	Surviving to smolts (2 yr) (%)
No bird control			
	1942	16,000	12
	1943	16,000	6
	1945	249,000	2
Bird control program			
	1947	273,000	8
	1948	235,000	6
	1949	243,000	8
	1950	246,000	10

Other side effects were found. Most species of coarse fish in the river approximately doubled their numbers as a result of the bird control. Elson concluded that intensive bird control could increase Atlantic salmon production from streams.

Young sockeye salmon (*Oncorhynchus nerka*) are attacked by a variety of predatory fishes in Cultus Lake, British Columbia, from the time they leave the gravel until a year later when they move to sea. From 1935 to 1938 predatory fishes were removed from Cultus Lake by gill netting (Foerster and Ricker 1941). Over 10,000 squawfish and 2300 trout were removed, so the number of predators was seriously reduced. The survival rate of young sockeye salmon increased concurrently with this predator control and fell off again after it was stopped:

	Survival rate to smolt stage (1 yr)	
	Natural from spawning	**Planted from fry**
Before predator control	1.78	4.16
After predator control	7.81	13.05

Survival rate was approximately three times as high after predator removal. Moreover, the smolts were larger than usual at migration time. This is important indirect evidence, because Foerster (1954) has shown that the larger the smolts at the time of seaward migration, the higher the percentage return of adult fish. Later counts of returning adults confirmed this (Figure 139): The higher survival and growth of juvenile salmon carried through to produce even more adults than expected in the returning spawning run.

Ruffed grouse (*Bonasa umbellus*) populations fluctuate greatly in numbers, and the importance of this species in hunting has led to several predator control experiments. A total of 557 predatory birds and mammals were removed from about 2000 acres in New York, and an adjacent area was

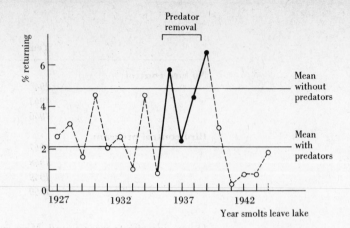

FIGURE 139

Effect of predator removal on the percentage of sockeye salmon smolts that survive to return as breeding adults, Cultus Lake, British Columbia. Predator control increased the survival of salmon in the lake and also produced better than average return of adults. (After Foerster 1954.)

left as a control. The results of this experiment were as follows (Edminster 1939):

	1931		1932	
	Predators removed	No removal	Predators removed	No removal
Nest loss (%)	24	51	39	72
Chick mortality (%)	57	67	54	55
Adult loss (%)	11	15	32	21
Grouse population density in fall (birds per 100 acres)	13.0	9.8	18.7	18.0

Thus predator removal greatly improved nesting success, but there was no carryover to higher population densities of adults in the fall.

After a year to recover, this experiment was repeated with the control and experimental areas reversed. The same results were obtained; predator control reduced nest losses but did not alter chick mortality, and the population density on the two areas in September was 17.7 grouse per 100 acres on the predator-removal area and 18.1 grouse per 100 acres on the area with no removal. Edminster (1939) concluded that predator control was not an effective means of increasing grouse densities.

There were two objections to these grouse experiments: (1) Grouse could move onto and off the experimental and control areas; (2) predators could colonize the removal area, and hence the experiment might alter predator numbers over a greater area than desired. Both objections were answered by repeating the experiment on an island population of grouse (Crissey and Darrow 1949). From 1940 to 1945 predators were removed from 1050-acre Valcour Island in Lake Champlain, New York. The results were again the same: Predator removal increased nest success but had little effect on chick losses or adult losses. A substantial decline in population density of grouse occurred over the winter of 1943–1944 on Valcour Island, yet predator removal was almost complete by this time.

Paul Errington studied muskrats (*Ondatra zibethicus*) in the marshes of Iowa for 25 years and tried to determine the effects of predation on muskrat populations. He questioned the common assumption that if a predator kills a prey animal, the prey population must then be lower by one animal than it would have been without predation. You cannot study the effects of predation, Errington argued, by counting the numbers of prey killed; you have to determine the factors that condition predation, the factors that make certain individuals vulnerable to predation whereas others are protected. Mink predation on muskrats was a primary cause of death in Iowa marshes, but Errington considered that mink were only removing surplus muskrats that were doomed to die for other reasons. The numbers of muskrats were determined by the territorial hostility of muskrats toward one another, and the muskrats driven out by this hostility over space were doomed to die—if not from predators, then from disease or exposure. Predators were merely acting as the executioners for animals excluded by the social system (Errington 1963).

The California vole (*Microtus californicus*) is a small field mouse that inhabits annual grasslands in California. Populations of these voles are subjected to intensive predation by birds and mammals, including house cats, raccoons, gray foxes, skunks, owls, and hawks. Pearson (1966) measured the impact of the mammalian predators on high vole populations before and during an episode of predator control and obtained these results on a 35-acre study plot:

	1961, before predator control	1963, during predator control
Population decline of voles (July–Jan.)	*4400 → 100*	*7600 → 200*
No. voles killed by carnivores during this decline	*3870*	*1916*
Destroyed by carnivores (%)	*88*	*25*

Approximately one-half the carnivores were removed during the predator control operation in 1963, and carnivore predation was not necessary to account for the severe 1963 population decline in the California vole. Carnivores thus appear to be feeding on a doomed surplus of prey, and the explanation for the vole decline must be sought in a factor other than predation.

Spectacular examples of the influence of predators on prey have occurred where man has accidentally introduced a new predator. A striking example is the virtual elimination of the lake trout fishery in the Great Lakes by the sea lamprey (*Petromyzon marinus*). The marine lamprey lives on the Atlantic Coast of North America and migrates into fresh water to spawn. The adult lampreys have a sucking, rasping mouth by which they attach themselves to the sides of fish, rasp a hole, and suck out body fluids. The passage of the lamprey to the upper Great Lakes was presumably blocked by Niagara Falls before the Welland Canal was built in 1829. In 1921 the first sea lamprey was found in Lake Erie, in 1936 in Lake Michigan, in 1937 in Lake Huron, and in 1945 in Lake Superior (Applegate 1950). Lake trout catches decreased to virtually zero within about 20 years of the lamprey invasion (Figure 140). Control efforts have been applied to reduce the lamprey population since 1951, and attempts are now being made to rebuild the Great Lakes fishery (Baldwin 1964).

We conclude that in some but not all cases the abundance of predators does influence the abundance of their prey in field populations. This raises an important question: *What is it about certain predators that makes them effective in controlling their prey?* Can we find some type of system by which we can classify predators? This question has great economic implications both in the management of fish and wildlife populations and in agricultural pest control. It is of course possible to proceed in a case-by-case manner and to investigate each individual predator—prey system on its own, but this is clearly inefficient, and we would rather attempt to reach some generalizations that applied to many individual cases.

Let us begin by asking how predators can respond to an increase in prey population density. Two possible responses are (1) a *numerical* response, in which the density of the predators increases; and (2) a *functional* response, in which the consumption of prey by individual predators changes. Holling (1959) demonstrated these two responses for the small mammals that prey on cocoons of the European pine sawfly (*Neodiprion sertifer*) in Ontario. Figure 141 shows the numerical responses of three small mammals to changes in sawfly abundance over 4 years. The functional responses of these predators are measured by the number of cocoons opened per day per individual predator, and these are shown in Figure 142. Each predator species has a characteristic numerical and functional response to the increase in prey density. Note that there need be no direct relationship between the numerical and the functional response of a predator. In a simple system where predator numbers are limited by the abundance of the prey, the numerical response will be closely tied to the functional response. But if a predator's abundance is determined by other factors, it may show a functional response with no numerical response.

If the predators do not interfere with one another when searching for

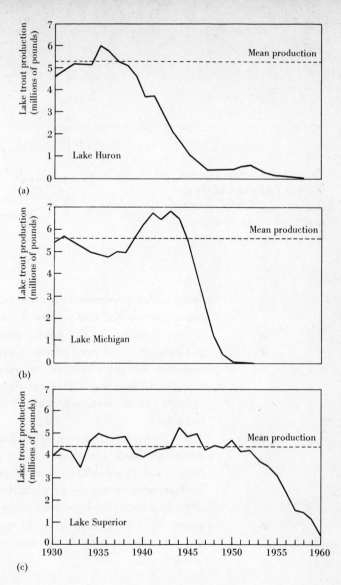

FIGURE 140

*Effect of sea lamprey introduction
on the lake trout fishery of the upper
Great Lakes. Lampreys were first
seen in (a) Lake Huron and (b)
Lake Michigan in the 1930s and in
(c) Lake Superior in the 1940s.
(After Baldwin 1964.)*

prey, the functional and numerical responses may be combined by simple multiplication. For example, if each masked shrew (*Sorex*) eats about 100 cocoons per day at a sawfly density of 600,000 cocoons per acre, and the shrew population has increased to 18 shrews per acre, the total shrew predation over the 100 days that the cocoons are in the soil will be approximately

$$100 \times 18 \times 100 = 180,000 \text{ of } 600,000 \text{ cocoons}$$

or approximately 30% predation loss of sawfly cocoons to *Sorex* shrews. Figure 143 shows the combined functional and numerical responses for the small mammals preying on the cocoons of the pine sawfly. Note that these combined curves have a rising sector and a falling sector. In the

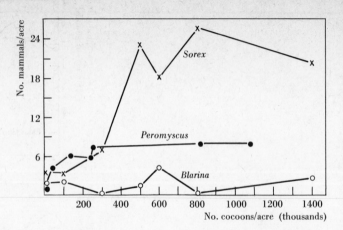

FIGURE 141

Numerical responses of the shrews
Sorex *and* Blarina *and the deer*
mouse Peromyscus *to changes in*
abundance of the European pine
sawfly. (After Holling 1959.)

rising sector predation losses are increasing as prey density increases, and this predation loss acts to slow down and possibly stop the prey population from increasing. In the falling sector, the predators are actually causing less damage as the prey become more abundant, and if the prey reach these densities, they have *escaped* any possible control by the predators. For the pine sawfly once the number of cocoons per acre exceeds about 600,000 to 800,000, small mammals will be ineffective in preventing further prey increase.

The functional response of predators can be affected by the quality of alternative foods available, by such characteristics of the prey as "vulnerability" and "palatability," and by such characteristics of the predators as food preferences and sensory abilities. Three basic types of functional and numerical responses have been suggested by Holling (1959, 1965) and are shown in Figure 144. Type 2 functional responses occur among many invertebrates and type 3 responses among vertebrate predators.

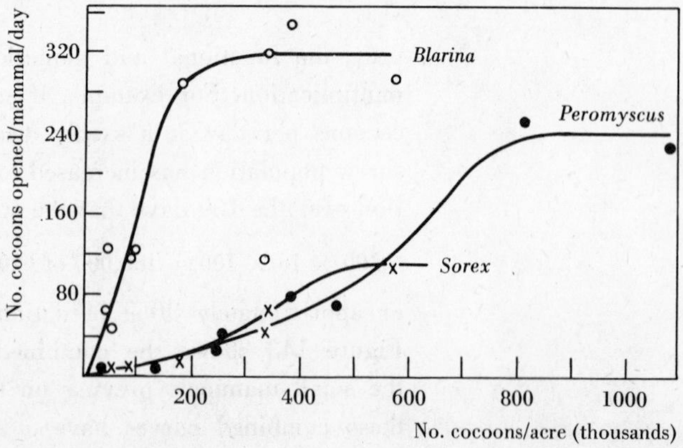

FIGURE 142

Functional responses of the shrews
Sorex *and* Blarina *and the deer*
mouse Peromyscus *to changes in*
abundance of the European pine
sawfly. (After Holling 1959.)

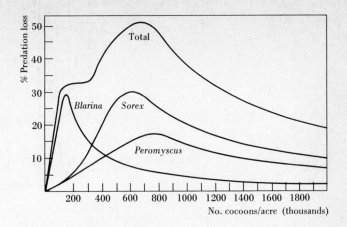

Combined functional and numerical responses for the small mammal–sawfly system to show the relation between percent predation losses to small mammals and the density of cocoons of the European pine sawfly. (After Holling 1959.)

Numerical responses of predators may occur without the predator exerting any controlling influence on the numbers of prey. For example, the bay-breasted warbler (*Dendroica castanea*) increased 12-fold during an outbreak of the spruce budworm (*Choristoneura fumiferana*) in eastern Canada. Both a numerical and functional response occurred in this warbler (Figure 145), but an 8000-fold increase in the budworm reduced this predator to an insignificant agent of loss (Morris et al. 1958).

Other predators seem to maintain stable population densities by living on alternative foods when their main prey is scarce. A tawny owl (*Strix aluco*) population near Oxford, England, was remarkably stable in spite of great fluctuations in the abundance of the small rodents that served as the

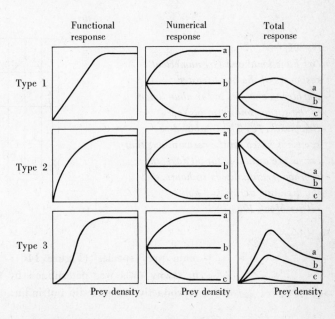

Three major types of functional and numerical responses of predators to changes in the abundance of their prey. (After Holling 1959.)

(a)

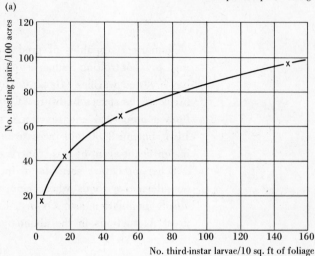

(b)

FIGURE 145

(a) Functional and (b) numerical responses of the bay-breasted warbler to changes in the abundance of the spruce budworm in New Brunswick. (c) The combined response is based on the assumptions that larvae are available for 30 days, the average feeding day is 16 hours, and the digestive period is 2 hours. (After Mook 1963.)

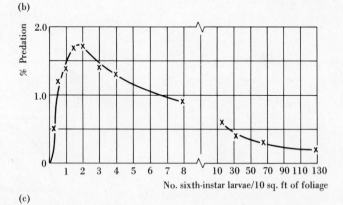

(c)

main prey species (Figure 146). The amount of successful reproduction in tawny owls was determined by the abundance of the prey rodents, but reproductive success did not influence subsequent population size of the owls.

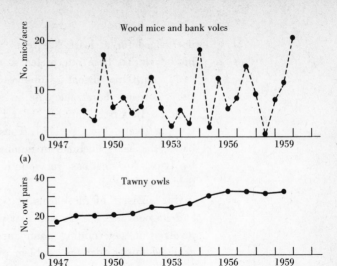

(a)

(b)

FIGURE 146

Abundance of (b) tawny owls near Oxford, England, in relation to changes in abundance of their principal prey species, (a) the wood mouse and bank vole. Changes in prey abundance are not reflected in the avian predator's population size. (After Southern 1970.)

The mathematical demonstration by Lotka and Volterra that predator–prey interactions could produce oscillations seems strikingly applicable to some biological systems. The Canada lynx (*Lynx canadensis*) eats snowshoe hares (*Lepus americanus*) and shows dramatic cyclic oscillations in density with peaks every 9 to 10 years (Figure 147). Charles Elton analyzed the records of furs traded by the Hudson's Bay Company in Canada for over 200 years and showed that the cycle is a real one that has persisted

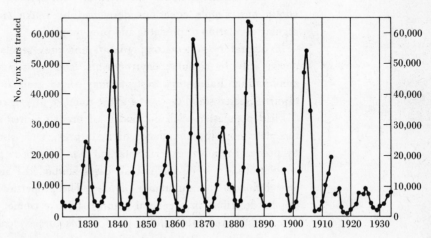

FIGURE 147

Canada lynx fur returns of the Northern Department, Hudson's Bay Company, 1821–1913, and of equivalent area 1915–1934. (After Elton and Nicholson 1942.)

unchanged for at least 200 years (Elton and Nicholson 1942). This lynx–
hare cycle has been interpreted as an example of an intrinsic predator–prey
oscillation. One dissenting observation unfortunately destroys this hypothesis: Snowshoe hares fluctuate in a 10-year cycle in the absence of lynx,
both on lynx-free Anticosti Island and in the plains area of south-central
Canada (Keith 1963, p. 115). Thus, although the lynx depend on snowshoe
hares, the hares fluctuate in numbers for some reason other than predation
by lynx. No one has yet found a classical predator–prey oscillation in
field populations.

Our analysis of the effects of predators on the abundance of their prey
and its converse has showed that predation is only one factor that may be
involved in determining abundance in field situations. Our focus is thus
changed to consider the problem of abundance in general and the role that
predation, disease, weather, and other factors play in determining abundance
in different organisms. We shall consider this general question now and
then return to discuss two of the practical applications of predator–prey
theory—the role of man as a predator and the biological control of pests.

SUMMARY

Species may interact directly by predation. Simple mathematical models can
be used to describe this interaction. When generations are discrete, simple
models can produce stable equilibria of predator and prey but usually
produce oscillations in the numbers of both species. When generations are
continuous, simple equations developed by Lotka and Volterra lead to a
regular oscillation of predator and prey numbers.

In laboratory systems of predators and prey regular oscillations are produced only in complex environments, and most simple systems are self-
annihilating. Laboratory systems may show gradual evolutionary changes
toward greater stability over a short number of generations.

Field populations will be models of predator–prey systems only if predators determine the abundance of their prey. This assumption can be tested
by predator-removal experiments, but few have been properly done on field
populations. In some but not all cases studied the abundance of predators
does influence the abundance of prey. The properties of effective predators
can be described in a general manner, but we cannot predict at the present
time which predators will be good agents of prey control without actually
doing field tests. Both the predator and the prey species are affected by
many other factors in the environment, and consequently the population
trends shown with simple predator–prey models are not obtained in field
populations.

SELECTED
REFERENCES

ERRINGTON, P. L. 1956. Factors limiting higher vertebrate populations. *Science* 124:304–307.

HOLLING, C. S. 1965. The functional response of predators to prey density and its role in mimicry and population regulation. *Mem. Ent. Soc. Canada* No. 45: 1–60.

HUFFAKER, C. B. 1958. Experimental studies on predation: dispersion factors and predator-prey oscillations. *Hilgardia* 27:343–383.

LESLIE, P. H., and J. C. GOWER. 1960. The properties of a stochastic model for the predator-prey type of interaction between two species. *Biometrika* 47:219–234.

PIMENTEL, D., W. P. NAGEL, and J. L. MADDEN. 1963. Space-time structure of the environment and the survival of parasite-host systems. *Amer. Naturalist* 97:141–167.

ROSENZWEIG, M. L., and R. H. MACARTHUR. 1963. Graphical representation and stability conditions of predator-prey interactions. *Amer. Naturalist* 97:209–223.

ROYAMA, T. 1970. Factors governing the hunting behaviour and selection of food by the great tit (*Parus major* L.). *J. Anim. Ecol.* 39: 619–668.

QUESTIONS AND
PROBLEMS

1 Calculate the population changes for 10 generations in a hypothetical predator–prey system with discrete generations in which the parameters for the prey are $B = 0.03$, $N_{eq} = 100$, $C = 0.5$, and starting density is 50 prey; and for the predators: $Q = 0.02$ (or $S = 2.0$) and starting density is 0.2 predator. How would the prey population change in the absence of the predators?

2 Assume that in the ruffed grouse predator-control experiments nest losses were reduced but chick and adult survival were unchanged and population density changes were unaffected by predator removal. Discuss the demographic mechanics of how this is possible.

3 Buckner and Turnock (1965) studied bird predation on the larch sawfly in Manitoba. They obtained the following data for the chipping sparrow (*Spizella passerina*):

	Plot I		Plot II	
	Sparrows per acre	Sawfly larvae per acre	Sparrows per acre	Sawfly larvae per acre
1954	—	—	3.2	235,000
1956	—	—	2.9	33,400
1957	1.4	2,138,700	2.3	40,000
1958	0.5	879,400	2.5	41,200
1959	0.4	437,800	2.2	27,300
1960	0.2	354,300	2.2	54,600
1961	0.5	199,900	2.3	15,000
1962	1.1	191,800	5.0	3,200
1963	0.2	366,800	0.3	3,900

Plot the numerical response of chipping sparrows to changes in sawfly larval abundance, and discuss the differences between plots I and II for this predator–prey system.

4 How does the "predation" by herbivores on green plants differ from the "predation" of insect parasites on their hosts and the predation of carnivores on herbivores? Make a list of similarities and differences, and discuss how these affect the simple modes of predation that we have discussed.

5 Gause (1934, p. 116) states that ". . . a population consisting of homogeneous prey and homogeneous predators in a limited microcosm, all the external factors being constant, must according to the predictions of the mathematical theory possess periodic oscillations in the numbers of both species." Discuss.

6 Introduce a time lag into the simple predator–prey model for discrete generations by making the predator density change in relation to prey density at generation $t - 1$ rather than generation t. Repeat the calculations for one of the examples discussed in the text and determine what effect this time lag has on the system's behavior.

7 One of the "textbook" examples of the effects of predator control is the Kaibab deer herd. According to several textbooks, the removal of predators from the Kaibab mule deer population allowed the deer to increase dramatically in numbers, overgraze their food supply, and starve. Trace the history of this example from Rasmussen (1941) to the critique by Caughley (1970).

14   Natural regulation of
population size

One can make two fundamental observations about populations of any plant or animal. The first is that abundance varies from place to place. There are some "good" habitats where the species is common on the average and some "poor" habitats where it is on the average rare. The second observation is that no population goes on increasing without limit, and the problem is to find out what prevents unlimited increase in low- and high-density populations. This is the problem of explaining fluctuations in numbers. Figure 148 illustrates these two problems, which are often confused.

FIGURE 148

Hypothetical annual census of four populations occupying different types of habitat. Two questions may be asked about these populations: (1) Why do all fail to go on increasing indefinitely? (2) Why are there more organisms on the average in the good habitats B and C compared with the poor habitats A and D? (After Chitty 1960.)

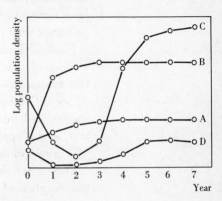

The controversies that have arisen over the problems of natural regulation of populations are probably best treated in a chronological fashion. Before 1900 many authors, Malthus and Darwin included, had noted that no population goes on increasing without limit, that there were many agents of destruction that reduced the population. It was not, however, until the twentieth century that an attempt was made to analyze these facts more formally. The stimulus for this came primarily from economic entomologists, who had to deal with both introduced and native pests. Most of the ideas we have on natural regulation can be traced to entomologists.

BIOTIC SCHOOL, CLIMATE SCHOOL, AND COMPREHENSIVE SCHOOL

A considerable amount of activity around the turn of the century centered around attempts to control insect pests by the introduction of parasites. Howard and Fiske (1911), two economic entomologists with the U.S. Department of Agriculture, studied the parasites of two introduced moths, the gypsy moth and the brown-tail moth, in an attempt to control the damage these defoliators were doing to New England trees. Howard and Fiske believed that each insect species was in a state of balance so that it maintained a constant density if averaged over many years. For this balance to exist, they argued, there must be, among all the factors that restrict the insect's multiplication, at least one or more *facultative* agents which exert a relatively more severe restraint when the population increases. They argued that only a very few factors, such as insect parasitism, were truly facultative.

Furthermore, Howard and Fiske said, a large proportion of the controlling factors, such as destruction by storms, high temperatures, and other climatic conditions, should be classed as *catastrophic*, since they are wholly independent in their action upon whether the insect is rare or abundant. For example, a storm that kills 10 out of 50 caterpillars on a tree would undoubtedly have destroyed 20 if 100 had been there or 100 if 500 had been there. Thus the average percentage of destruction remains the same no matter what the abundance of the insect.

Finally, Howard and Fiske noted that other agencies such as birds and other predators work in a radically different manner. These agents maintain constant populations from year to year and destroy a constant number of prey. Consequently when the prey species increases, they will destroy a smaller and smaller percentage of the prey (i.e., they work in a manner that is the opposite of "facultative" agents). Howard and Fiske did not give factors of this type a distinct name.

They concluded that a natural balance can be maintained only through the operation of facultative agencies which effect the destruction of a greater proportion of individuals as the insect in question increases in abundance. Howard and Fiske believed that *insect parasitism* was the most effective of the facultative agencies; *disease* operated only rarely, when densities got very high, and *starvation* was the ultimate facultative agency, which almost never operated.

Thompson (1929), another entomologist, suggested that the natural control of organisms is primarily due to the intrinsic limitations of the organisms themselves. Thus the attempt to find limiting factors or regulating factors responsible for the control of a species throughout its range is unlikely to be successful. The environments in which the species cannot survive are multiple, and hence the limiting factor one year may be predators, the next year weather, and so on. The "factors of control" in nature form an indissoluble complex. Thompson studied the natural control of the European corn borer and concluded that control was produced by a complex of agricultural, meteorological, and parasitic factors that were not constant over the whole range of the species. No one factor was capable of controlling the corn borer in the absence of the others. He concluded that there were no such things as specific limiting factors for a species. Thompson said that there was no general underlying cause of insect outbreaks and that all one could say was that outbreaks arise because the environment has for a time approached the optimum for the species concerned. Thompson was thus the first to espouse a *comprehensive theory of natural control*; that is, he included all factors in his scheme, from climate to parasites, and suggested that control was due to a complex of factors varying in space and in time.

Meanwhile another school of thought, the *climate school*, was in the process of formation. Bodenheimer (1928) was one of the first to hold that the population density of insects is regulated primarily by the effects of weather both on development and on survival. Bodenheimer was impressed by all the work done in the 1920s on the environmental physiology of insects, showing, for example, how low temperatures affect the rate of egg laying and speed of development. He was also impressed by the fact that weather was responsible for the largest part of the mortality of insects, often 85 to 90% of the insects in their early stages being killed by weather factors.

Uvarov (1931) published a large paper, "Insects and Climate," in which he reviewed the effects of climatic factors on growth, fertility, and mortality of insects. He emphasized the correlation between population fluctuations of insects and the weather, and he regarded these weather factors as the prime agents controlling populations. Uvarov questioned the idea that all populations are in a stable equilibrium in nature and emphasized the instability of field populations.

Three important ideas were expressed by the early climate school: (1) Weather has strong effects on insect population parameters, (2) weather could be correlated with insect outbreaks, and (3) emphasis was placed on fluctuations in populations, not on stability.

It is important to realize here that all this controversy was over *insect* populations and their regulation; work on vertebrate populations had hardly begun by 1930, and there had been no work on the populations of other invertebrates or of plants.

In 1933 the *Journal of Animal Ecology* published a supplement entitled "The Balance of Animal Populations" by A. J. Nicholson, an Australian economic entomologist. This paper is probably the most controversial paper ever published in population ecology. Nicholson was interested in the parasite–host system of insects, and he teamed up with a mathematician V. Bailey to construct a model of this system. Nicholson disliked the predator–prey models of Lotka and Volterra and criticized them because they did not allow for time lags in the system, because they ignored age groups (assuming that all individuals are equivalent), and because Lotka and Volterra used calculus rather than finite methods of mathematical analysis. Nicholson expanded his ideas on the host–parasite system to cover all interactions between animals.

The first idea Nicholson discussed was the concept of *balance* in nature. He pointed out that there is a relation between population size and environmental conditions, and the existence of this relationship must mean that populations are in a *state of balance* with their environments. Without balance the population densities would be indeterminate. As evidence for this balance he pointed to the logistic curves Pearl published on *Drosophila:* The flies reach a stable asymptote, a state of balance.

Nicholson went on to dispute the contention of Bodenheimer and Uvarov that, because changes in climate are reflected by changes in population density, climate determines the densities of animals. He drew an analogy between the ocean and the population. We observe that the surface of the ocean rises and falls with the position of the moon. From this we do not conclude that the position of the moon determines the *depth* of the oceans but rather that it determines only the *change in depth* of the ocean. Thus climate is like the moon; it may vary the density but can never determine how these densities are limited and held in a state of balance.

Nicholson then made an important definition:

For the production of balance, it is essential that a controlling factor should act more severely against an average individual when the density of animals is high, and less severely when the density is low. In other words, the action of the controlling factor must be governed by the density of the population controlled.

He then pointed out that obviously no variation in the density of a population will modify the intensity of the sun or the severity of frost. Consequently, climate cannot control population density. The only factor that can control populations in this way is *competition* of some kind.

Nicholson went on to attack another tenet of the climate school. The belief that climate determines the density of a population is based on the confusion of two distinct processes, destruction and control. He gives an example: Suppose that an insect can increase 100-fold each generation, so that a 99% mortality is required for an equilibrium population. Suppose that climate destroys 98% of these insects. In this situation the insect population will double each generation. Climate could never check this increase since its action is not affected by density. However, if some other factor, such as a parasite, were present whose action was affected by density, the destruction of the necessary 1% would soon be accomplished. In this situation the parasite is wholly responsible for control, since the effect of climate alone would have allowed the population to increase forever. Thus climate *destroys* 98% but does not *control*; parasites destroy 1% and do control the population. He says then that if we wish to evaluate the relative importance of various factors affecting a population, we can place no reliance whatever on the proportion of animals destroyed by any given factor. Instead we must find out what factors are influenced by changes in the density of the population.

Nicholson and Bailey constructed a mathematical model based on the idea of competition between parasites and their hosts. They were concerned in particular with internal parasites of insects, but they included a consideration of the predator–prey system and competition for food or space. They assumed three things: (1) that the hosts were distributed uniformly over the area, (2) that the environment was constant, and (3) that the parasites searched at random with respect to other parasites. Nicholson produced a string of 76 conclusions based on his mathematical model. He showed, for example, that the interaction of a *specific host* (which has only one parasite) and a *specific parasite* (which has only one host) would produce increasing oscillations under his assumptions.

The controlling factor was always *competition*, according to Nicholson— competition for food, competition for a place to live, or the competition of predators or parasites. Nicholson's theory was predominately a biotic one, and he is usually considered as the cornerstone of the *biotic school*.

Nicholson's main ideas were essentially the same as those of Howard and Fiske. To these he added a mathematical model and the notion of competition as the controlling factor. Nicholson's points were given much stronger emphasis by Smith (1935). Smith considered the problem of population regulation in some detail. He pointed out first of all that populations are characterized both by stability and by continual change. Population densities are continually changing but their values tend to vary about a characteristic density. This characteristic density itself may vary. Smith compared a population to the sea, the surface of which is paradoxically a universal point for altitude measurements but which is continuously being changed by tides and waves. Smith thus reaffirmed Nicholson's ideas on balance.

Different species of animals tend to have different average densities, and the same species will have different average densities in different environments. The variations about the average density are stable because there is always a tendency to return to the average density (i.e., populations do not usually become extinct or increase to infinity). This is what is loosely termed the "balance of nature."

The equilibrium position, or average density, may itself change with time. This is what causes the economic entomologists so much trouble. The equilibrium position of an introduced pest may be so high that constant damage occurs to crop plants. Smith then set out to analyze the factors that determine the equilibrium position or average density. He pointed out that the number of injurious insects is very small relative to the total number of insects and that we must study both *common* and *rare* species if we hope to understand the reasons for the abundance of species.

Smith analyzed this problem using the logistic curve, and although the assumptions of the logistic are not realistic for most populations, the analysis illustrates a principle. For the logistic curve we know that the rate of increase of the population is a linear function of density. If we assume that, in a closed system, the birth rate is constant (and equal to r_m), the death rate must be a linear function of density also, since

Rate of population increase = birth rate — death rate

As the population increases according to the logistic curve, the death rate increases until an equilibrium is reached where the instantaneous birth rate equals the instantaneous death rate (Figure 149). This approach allows us to see graphically why a species is abundant in some habitats and rare in others. If we increase the slope of the death-rate line, we reduce equilibrium density (Figure 149).

Note that the conditions at equilibrium are the same no matter what the density:

Death rate = birth rate

FIGURE 149

Determination of equilibrium population density according to the simple logistic model. An equilibrium is reached when the birth rate equals the death rate, and the position of this equilibrium depends on the slope of the death-rate line. (After Smith 1935.)

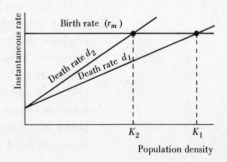

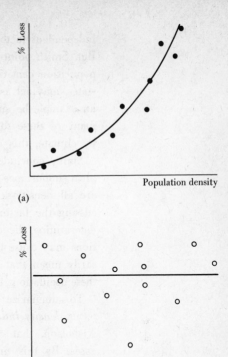

FIGURE 150

Hypothetical relationship between percentage loss and population density for (a) a density-dependent process and (b) a density-independent process.

The equation for the straight line representing the death rate is, in general,

$$d = cN + A$$

where

d = instantaneous death rate
c = slope of line
N = population density
A = y intercept

Note that the death-rate equation is composed of two parts: (1) cN, which is a function of density, and (2) A, which is a constant. This distinction corresponds to that recognized by Howard and Fiske between *facultative* and *catastrophic* agencies, and Smith renamed these *density-dependent* mortality factors and *density-independent* mortality factors (Figure 150).

The average density of a population, Smith concluded, can never be determined by density-independent factors. Only if the death-rate line has a slope (i.e., a density-dependent component) can the population reach equilibrium. Thus only density-dependent mortality factors can determine the equilibrium density of a population.

He went on to point out that the density-dependent factors are mainly *biotic* in nature—parasitism, disease, predation—and that the density-independent factors are mainly physical or *abiotic* factors, mainly climate. But, Smith pointed out, we should not conclude from this that the average population densities of species are *never* determined by climate. Climate, he states, may act as a density-dependent factor under some circumstances. For an example he suggests the case of *protective refuges:* If there are only so many of these to go around and all the unprotected individuals are killed by climate, this climatic mortality would be density-dependent.

Smith concluded that insect parasites, predators, and diseases were of great importance in determining average population densities, since these are all density-dependent factors. Finally, he emphasized that he was discussing the factors determining *average population density*, not the factors determining the oscillations in density about the average. Weather conditions may cause the numbers of insects to oscillate, but this does not necessarily mean that weather also determines the average density about which these oscillations take place.

To summarize: Smith restated the main points of Nicholson, adding the terms *density independent* and *density dependent*, and stated, in contrast to Nicholson, that climate might act as a density-dependent factor in some cases. By this time, then, the main tenets of the *biotic school* had been crystallized: the idea of balance in nature, that this balance was produced by density-dependent factors, and that these factors were usually biotic agents, such as parasites, predators, and diseases.

Schwerdtfeger (1941), a German forest entomologist, considered the problem of explaining *gradations* (outbreaks) in forest insects. He had data on the population fluctuations of four moths that feed as larvae on the needles of Scotch pine (*Pinus sylvestris*) in Germany. These species fluctuated irregularly (Figure 151), and each of these fluctuations is termed a *gradation*.

Schwerdtfeger rejected the parasite–predator theories such as Nicholson's because he thought that they ignored other important factors such as

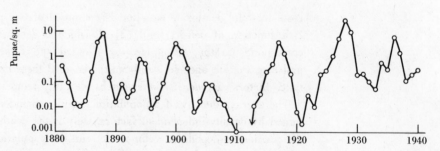

FIGURE 151

Winter population estimates of the pupae of the defoliating moth Bupalus piniarius *per square meter of forest floor at Letzlingen, Germany. (Data of Schwerdtfeger, after Varley 1949.)*

climate; similarly, he rejected the climatic theories because they ignored the biotic factors. He concluded that these gradations are the result of the joint action of many factors. Schwerdtfeger emphasized the indirect effects involved in population changes. Thus climate may affect food, which in turn may affect the insect pest. He emphasized not only the connection between factors but also between *species*. He illustrated this in a diagram:

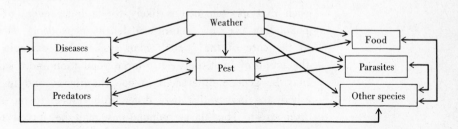

The particular species we are interested in is hemmed in by a network of abiotic and biotic factors. The whole network is in constant ferment. Schwerdtfeger termed this network the *gradocoen,* which he defined as the totality of all the factors that affect the population changes of the species. This gradocoen varies from place to place and from time to time and differs for different species. Thus Schwerdtfeger falls into the same group as Thompson, in espousing a *comprehensive theory* in which all physical and biotic factors play a role. Schwerdtfeger emphasizes the *network* of interrelations involved in population control.

In general most ecologists in the 1930s and 1940s were adherents of the Nicholsonian system of density-dependent, biotic control of population size. The comprehensive theories of Thompson and Schwerdtfeger were usually labeled obscurantist or philosophical and dismissed. The climate school had more or less fallen into disrepute. But there was considerable stirring on the empirical level. More and more work was accumulating on vertebrate populations as well as insect populations, and it was not long before the roof began to fall.

In 1954 two important books appeared on the problem of population regulation. These were (1) Andrewartha and Birch's *The Distribution and Abundance of Animals* and (2) David Lack's *The Natural Regulation of Animal Numbers.*

Andrewartha and Birch are two Australian zoologists who completely disagree with Nicholson's ideas. They revived in their book a highly modified version of the climatic school's ideas and have been the center of a rather violent controversy ever since. Andrewartha and Birch concentrate on the individual organism and base their whole approach on this question: *What are the factors that influence the animal's chance to survive and multiply?* Given this question they proceed to classify environmental factors.

First, they reject the distinction Howard and Fiske and others made between the physical (abiotic) and biotic factors. For example, food and shelter may sometimes be biotic, sometimes abiotic. Hence this distinction does not help us much to classify the environment.

Second, they reject the classification of the environment based on density-dependent factors and density-independent factors. They reject this distinction because they believe that there is no component of the environment such that its influence is likely to be independent of the density of the population (i.e., all factors are density dependent). Here they are striking at the core of the Nicholsonian system. For example, they say, consider the action of frost. Between a large population and a small population there may be genetic differences in cold hardiness, and in addition the places where the insects live may differ with respect to the degree of protection from frost. Thus large populations may be forced to occupy marginal habitats and so suffer more from frost. They conclude then that density-independent factors do not exist, and hence there is no need to attach any special importance to density-dependent factors in classifying the effects of the environment on a population. They continually refer to the dogma of density dependence and point out again and again that Nicholson's ideas have never been tested empirically.

How, then, can one classify environmental factors? Andrewartha and Birch suggest that the environment may be divided into four components: (1) *weather,* (2) *food,* (3) *other animals and pathogens,* and (4) *a place in which to live.* These components of the environment are nonoverlapping and they may be subdivided if necessary, for example into other animals of the same species, other animals of different species. Together these four components and the interactions between them completely describe the environment of any animal.

Consequently, say Andrewartha and Birch, for any given species we must ask which of the four components of environment affect the animal's chances to survive and multiply. Once we can answer this question we will be able to determine the reasons for the animal's distribution and abundance in nature. Andrewartha and Birch present a general theory of the numbers of animals in natural populations. First, they say that one cannot use expressions like "balance," "steady states," "equilibrium densities," or "ultimate limits," because there is no empirical way of giving a meaning to these words. Second, they say that one must take account of the fact that all animals are distributed patchily in nature, never uniformly. These "patches" or *local populations* are the basic component with which they deal.

According to Andrewartha and Birch, the numbers of animals in a natural population may be limited in three ways: (1) by shortage of material resources, such as food, places in which to make nests, and so on; (2) by inaccessibility of these material resources relative to the animal's capacities for dispersal and searching; and (3) by shortage of time when the rate of increase (r) is positive. Of these three ways they believe that the last is probably the most important in nature, and the first is probably the least important. Regarding the third case, the fluctuations in the rate of increase may be caused by weather, predators, or any of the components of the environment.

Andrewartha and Birch point out that in any population an animal's chances to survive and multiply depend on all four components of the environment—weather, food, other animals, and a place to live—yet in most cases one or two of these factors will be of overwhelming importance. Thus we may speak of cases in which population size is largely determined by weather, and other cases in which population size is largely determined by other animals.

Andrewartha and Birch were principally concerned with insect populations and their field experience was with insects occupying the very severe desert and semidesert areas of Australia. Their main contribution to ecology has been to reemphasize the importance of *empirical data* to the problems of population regulation. They continually raise the ever-bothersome question: How can this idea be *tested* in real populations?

Another book to appear in 1954 was by an English ornithologist, David Lack, entitled *The Natural Regulation of Animal Numbers.* In spite of its title the book is very largely concerned with bird populations. Lack begins his book with a consideration of the stability of bird populations, which fluctuate in size but only between very restricted limits. He accepts the view of Nicholson that this stability or balance must be brought about by density-dependent factors. The density-dependent changes might involve *reproduction* or *mortality* and so he set out to analyze these.

Are reproductive rates in birds affected by changes in population density? In general there is a slight depression of reproduction in birds at high densities, but Lack points out that this is too small to have an important effect on subsequent population size. The conclusion from this is clear: If reproduction changes little with density, mortality must be the density-dependent process regulating the population size of birds.

Lack then investigates the mortality of birds. He finds that the death rate is always higher in juvenile birds than in the adults. For example, in passerines 45% of the eggs laid give rise to flying young and only 8 to 18% of the eggs laid give rise to adult birds. Thus in passerines there is an 82 to 92% death rate in the first year of life. The annual adult death rate is 40 to 60% in passerines, and this death rate is constant and independent of age. Wild birds live only a small fraction of their potential life span, and none die of old age.

What then causes density-dependent mortality to control the population size of birds? Only three factors can be involved says Lack: *food shortage, predation,* or *disease.* He decides it must be food and gives four reasons: (1) In many birds few adults die of predation or disease; (2) birds are usually more numerous where their food is abundant; (3) each species eats different foods and if food were not limiting it is difficult to see why this differentiation in food habits should have evolved (c.f. Gause's hypothesis); and (4) birds fight over food, especially in the winter. But one rarely finds a starving bird in nature; how can this be reconciled to Lack's hypothesis? This, states Lack, is because only a few individuals starve at any one time and these are never found (and may be eaten by predators).

Lack considers food shortage to be the factor limiting most vertebrate populations. The numbers of plant-eating insects, however, are not limited by food, since they rarely destroy their food supply; these are limited by parasites and predators.

Climatic factors cannot control bird populations, says Lack, because they are density independent in action. Unusual weather may cause heavy losses of birds, but the population usually recovers quickly. Climate does, however, affect the distribution of birds; many species are increasing their ranges as a result of changing climate.

Lack thus applies Nicholsonian concepts to bird populations and concludes that food shortage is the most important factor regulating bird populations and that it operates through density-dependent changes in mortality operating chiefly on juvenile birds.

Recent attempts to fuse a comprehensive view recognize that the biotic and climate schools are both valid but for different types of environments (Figure 152). In environments that are typically favorable to the species, numbers will change because of density-dependent processes. This may occur near the central part of a species' range or in permanent habitats that remain stable. At the other extreme, in environments that fluctuate

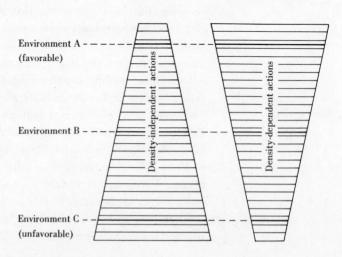

FIGURE 152

Relative role of density-dependent and density-independent processes in causing changes in population density under different types of environments. (After Huffaker and Messenger 1964.)

Environment A - - - - - -
(favorable)

Density-independent actions

Density-dependent actions

Environment B - - - -

Environment C - - - - -
(unfavorable)

greatly and are often unsuitable for the species, numbers will change because of density-independent processes. These environments may occur at the edge of a species' distribution or in temporary habitats that are unstable. The stability of the environment can be defined only with regard to a particular species, and consequently the details of this scheme cannot be specified for any general case. A habitat stable for a fish population may be unstable for a zooplankton population. Winter weather may be a critical factor determining environmental favorability for a forest insect but unimportant for a hibernating mammal in the same area.

SELF-REGULATION SCHOOL

Most of the previous theories of natural control have concentrated on the role of the *extrinsic* factors in control: food supply, natural enemies, weather, diseases, and shelter. Many of these theories tend to assume that the individuals making up the population are all identical, like atoms or marbles. This neglect of the importance of individual differences in population regulation has been challenged by a group of workers in diverse fields. Their rallying point has been a search for *intrinsic* changes in populations, changes that might be important in natural control.

Two basic types of changes can occur in individuals, *phenotypic* and *genotypic*, and the proponents of self-regulatory mechanisms differ in what importance they attach to each of these basic types. Of course, no matter what the mechanism operating, it must have been evolved by the species concerned, and consequently these theories of self-regulation all become concerned with evolutionary arguments, which there was no need to consider in the previous theories emphasizing extrinsic control.

Chitty (1955) has presented the fundamental premise underlying all ideas on self-regulatory mechanisms. Suppose, Chitty argues, that we observe a population at two times, i and n, and that at time n there is a death rate (D_n) higher than the death rate at time i (D_i). This death rate is the result of the interaction of the organisms (O) with their mortality factors (M). Our problem now is to determine why D_n is greater than D_i. The first hypothesis to be explored is that on both occasions we are dealing with organisms whose biological properties are identical. In this case we must look for a difference between the mortality factors at the two times. In other words, we might expect to find at time n that there are more predators or parasites or that the weather is less favorable. Some population changes can certainly be explained in this manner, but in other cases this method has failed to turn up the right clues. We must look at the matter from another angle.

Consider, Chitty continues, the possibility that the environmental conditions are much the same at all times, that there is no real difference between the mortality factors at times i and n. In this case any change in the death rate must be due to a change in the nature of the organisms, a change such that they become less resistant to their normal mortality factors. For example, the animals might die in cold weather at time n, weather they might have survived at time i. These ideas can be summarized as follows:

	First hypothesis		Second hypothesis	
Time	i	n	i	n
Death rate	$D_i < D_n$		$D_i < D_n$	
Organisms	$O_i = O_n$		$O_i \neq O_n$	
Environment	$M_i \neq M_n$		$M_i = M_n$	

The first hypothesis describes the classical approach to population regulation used, for example, by Lotka and Volterra, Nicholson, Thompson, Uvarov, and many others. The second hypothesis describes an ideal self-regulatory approach to population regulation. It is unlikely in nature that this second situation would occur in such an ideal form, but more likely that some mixture of these two situations would be found in self-regulatory populations. Note that the concept of density dependence becomes ambiguous under the second hypothesis. The idea that the environment can be subdivided into density-dependent and density-independent factors has meaning only insofar as the properties of the individuals in the population are constant. Self-regulatory systems have added an additional degree of freedom to the system, the individual with variable properties.

Variation among individuals in a population may be either genetically based or environmentally induced. The British geneticist E. B. Ford (1931) was one of the first to point out the possible importance of genetic changes in population regulation. He suggested that natural selection is relaxed during population increases, with the result that variability increases within the population and many inferior genotypes survive. When conditions return to normal these inferior individuals are eliminated through increased natural selection, causing the population to decline and at the same time reducing variability within the population. Thus, Ford argued, population increase inevitably paves the way for population decline.

From a study of population fluctuations in small rodents, Chitty (1960) set up the general hypothesis that *all species are capable of regulating their own population densities without destroying the renewable resources of their environment or requiring enemies or bad weather to keep them from doing so.* All populations of a given species will not necessarily be self-regulated, and the mechanisms evolved will be adapted only to a restricted range of environments. The species may well live in poor habitats where this mechanism seldom if ever comes into effect. The self-regulatory hypothesis proposed by Chitty states that under appropriate circumstances indefinite increase in population density is prevented through a deterioration in the quality of the population. If this theory is true, it is improbable that the action of weather is independent of population density, as the biotic school often claims. Chitty postulates that the effects of independent events, such as weather, become more severe as numbers rise and quality falls.

The actual mechanisms by which self-regulation can be achieved in natural populations involve some form of mutual interference between individuals, or intraspecific hostility in general. The most important environmental factor for such populations is *other organisms of the same species*, and the resulting competition for food or space controls changes in population size.

The problem of self-regulation has been approached from another angle by V. C. Wynne-Edwards, a British ecologist whose major work has been on birds. Wynne-Edwards (1962) begins his analysis with the observation that most animals have highly effective mechanisms of dispersal. If we look in nature we will usually find that organisms concentrate at places of abundant resources and avoid unfavorable areas. This is the first point to note—that animals are dispersed in close relation to their essential resources.

The "essential resource" most critical to animals is clearly *food*, Wynne-Edwards observes. Of course, many other requirements must be met before a species can survive in an area, but food is almost always the critical factor that ultimately limits population density in a given habitat. We must then study the food resource as the key to understanding population control.

Wynne-Edwards suggests that some artificial and harmless type of competition has been evolved as a buffer mechanism in many species to stop population growth at a level below that imposed by food exhaustion. The best example of this kind of buffer mechanism is the territorial systems of birds. The territories that birds defend so fiercely are just a parcel of ground, but the possession of a territory eliminates competition for food, since the owner and his dependents enjoy undisputed feeding rights on that area. Provided that the size of the territory varies with the productivity of the habitat, we get a perfect illustration of this model: Population density is controlled by territoriality, which ensures that the food supply will not be exhausted.

Population densities, then, are limited below the starvation level by the device of substituting conventional goals of competition—territorial rights and social status—in place of any direct contest for food itself. This type of regulation requires that the species have some type of social organization. These conventions for which animals compete vary greatly from one group to another, depending on the social structure of the species, and Wynne-Edwards (1962) discusses many examples of these conventions. Populations are self-regulated, or homeostatic, and many types of social displays can be viewed as functioning to feed back information on population size and its relations to available food resources.

The operation of the homeostatic machine can be best visualized by means of the following equation (Wynne-Edwards 1962, p. 486):

Recruitment + immigration
$$= \text{uncontrollable losses} + \text{emigration} + \text{social mortality}$$

Of these five factors that influence the rise and fall of density, only one, the uncontrollable losses (involving parasites, predators, weather, and disease), is not directly under the control of the population itself. Wynne-Edwards believes that the classical density-dependent factors—parasites, predators, diseases—are on the whole hopelessly undependable and fickle in their action, and often not density dependent, as most people have thought. Many, if not all, of the higher animals can limit their densities by intrinsic means, through mechanisms involving recruitment, immigration, emigration, and social mortality.

The margins of a species' range will probably not show this self-regulation, Wynne-Edwards states. Physical factors will predominate in these harsh environments (see Figure 152, p. 280, and hence we should concentrate our attention on the more typical parts of the range, where self-regulation is the usual situation. Also a few species will ultimately fail to be limited by food, and these will not fit into the scheme of Wynne-Edwards.

Many changes in abundance can be attributed to changes in extrinsic factors, such as weather, disease, or predation. But some changes in abundance are the result of changes in the genetic properties of the organisms in a population. Such evolutionary changes are produced by the *genetic feedback mechanism*, described by Pimentel (1961), a Cornell entomologist. Pimentel believes that natural population regulation has its foundation in the process of evolution. One process of evolution, called the genetic feedback mechanism, integrates herbivore and plant, parasite and host, and predator and prey in the community. This feedback system can be illustrated very simply as follows:

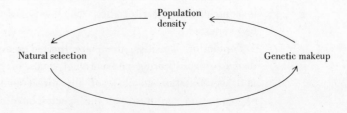

Pimentel (1961) catalogs some spectacular examples of genetic changes of this type playing a role in population regulation. For example, the Hessian fly population was reduced drastically in Kansas after 1942 when resistant varieties of wheat were introduced. By changing the genetic makeup of the wheat plant, the herbivore population of Hessian flies was significantly reduced. Another example is the myxomatosis–rabbit interaction in Australia. The high rabbit populations of the 1940s were decimated by the introduced myxomatosis virus during the early 1950s. Now the virus has evolved so that attenuated strains have replaced the virulent strains, and in addition the rabbits are intrinsically more resistant to this disease. The rabbit population in Australia is now much smaller than it was before myxomatosis.

A simple model will illustrate the type of systemic changes that could be involved in the genetic feedback mechanism. Consider a two-species system of one plant and one herbivore, and, to make the model simple, let us focus on only one gene on one chromosome in the plant. The hypothetical gene has a major effect on (1) the ability of the plant to survive in its environment and (2) the palatability of the plant to the herbivore. Two different alleles (A and a) occur at the hypothetical gene locus, and the properties of the genotypes are

	Genotype of plant		
	AA	**Aa**	**aa**
Ability of plant to survive	Good	Poor	Very poor
Palatability to herbivores	High	Low	Very low

Thus plants of genotype AA are able to survive very well but attract many herbivores because they are desirable food. Each plant genotype can support only a limited number of herbivores before it is killed by overgrazing. Finally, we assume that the reproductive rate of the herbivore will be affected by the genotype of plant on which it lives, so highly palatable plants are best for herbivore reproduction.

This simple model is a variant of the discrete generation predator–prey model we discussed earlier, in which the plant is the "prey" and the herbivore is the "predator." The major change in the model is that we allow genetic variation within the plant population. Figure 153 illustrates one pattern of equilibrium for a hypothetical system starting with 150 herbivores and a plant population with genotype frequencies of 0.36 AA, 0.50 Aa, and 0.14 aa. The system stabilizes under some initial conditions (as in this example) but with other assumptions may be unstable with divergent oscillations (compare Figure 131, page 248).

Pimentel's concept of a genetic feedback mechanism involves interspecific

FIGURE 153

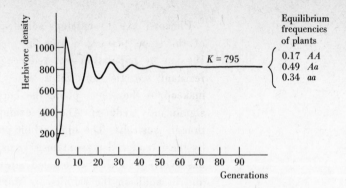

*Determination of average herbivore
density resulting from the interaction of a plant and a herbivore
through the genetic feedback
mechanism. Starting conditions
given in the text. (After Pimentel
1961.)*

interactions and suggests some possible implications of these interactions to the determination of average abundance. This concept emphasizes the role of evolution in questions of average abundance, and in doing this it serves as a warning to the continual introduction of new species into ecological communities of distant areas.

The self-regulation school thus emphasizes the importance of quality (behavioral, physiological, and genetic) of individuals to the problems of abundance. Average abundance may be altered by genetic changes in the populations of interacting species. Unlimited increase may be prevented by intraspecific hostility, leading to a deterioration in the quality of individuals as density rises. Both *quantity* and *quality* must be considered in the problems of abundance.

In Chapter 15 we shall look at some examples of populations in nature and see some of the successes and the difficulties of applying these theories to the real world.

SUMMARY

Populations of plants and animals do not increase without limits but show more-or-less restricted fluctuations. Two questions may be raised: (1) What stops population growth? (2) What determines average abundance?

Three general theories answer these two questions by focusing on the interactions between the population and the environmental factors of weather, food, shelter, and enemies (predators, parasites, diseases). The biotic school suggests that density-dependent factors are critical in preventing population increase and in determining average abundance. Natural enemies are postulated to be the main density-dependent factors in many populations. The climate school emphasizes the role of weather factors affecting population size and suggests that weather may act as a density-dependent control. The comprehensive school stresses that all factors are important, both density-dependent and density-independent ones, and that population changes are controlled by a complex of biotic and physical factors varying in space and in time.

By contrast, the self-regulation school focuses on events going on within a population, on individual differences in behavior and physiology. The general premise of this school is that abundance may change because the quality of individuals changes. Population increase may be stopped by a deterioration in the quality of individuals as density rises rather than by a change in environmental factors. Average abundance may be altered by genetic changes in populations. Quality and quantity are both important aspects of populations.

The theories of natural regulation of numbers are not mutually exclusive but overlap, and a synthesis of several approaches may be most useful in attempts to answer practical problems. The natural regulation of populations is a critical area of theoretical ecology because it is central to many questions of community ecology and because it has enormous practical consequences, which we shall explore in the next three chapters.

SELECTED REFERENCES

ANDREWARTHA, H. G., and L. C. BIRCH. 1954. *The Distribution and Abundance of Animals.* Chap. 14, pp. 648–665. University of Chicago Press, Chicago.

CHITTY, D. 1960. Population processes in the vole and their relevance to general theory. *Can. J. Zool.* 38:99–113.

HARPER, J. L. 1968. The regulation of numbers and mass in plant populations. pp. 139–158 in *Population Biology and Evolution*, ed. by R. C. Lewontin. Syracuse University Press, Syracuse, N.Y.

HUFFAKER, C. B., and P. S. MESSENGER. 1964. The concept and significance of natural control. pp. 74–117 in *Biological Control of Insect Pests and Weeds*, ed. by P. DeBach. Chapman & Hall, London.

KLOMP, H. 1962. The influence of climate and weather on the mean density level, the fluctuations and the regulation of animal populations. *Arch. Neerl. Zool.* 15:68–109.

MURDOCH, W. W. 1970. Population regulation and population inertia. *Ecology* 51:497–502.

NICHOLSON, A. J. 1954. An outline of the dynamics of animal populations. *Aust. J. Zool.* 2:9–65.

WATSON, A., and R. MOSS. 1970. Dominance, spacing behaviour and aggression in relation to population limitation in vertebrates. pp. 167–218 in *Animal Populations in Relation to Their Food Resources*, ed. by A. Watson. Blackwell, Oxford.

QUESTIONS AND PROBLEMS

1 Morris (1957, p. 49), in discussing the interpretation of mortality data in population studies, states:

We tend to overlook the fact that these mortality estimates do not represent an ultimate objective in population work. Long columns of percentages, which are sometimes presented only with the conclusion that high percentages indicate important mortality factors and low percentages indicate unimportant ones, contribute little to our understanding of population dynamics.

Discuss this claim.

2   Milne (1962, p. 29) criticizes Pimentel's hypothesis about population regulation through a genetic feedback mechanism, and one objection he states is the following:

There seems to be no need for the mechanism. Vast numbers of animal species—the scavengers of carrion, dung, and detritus, and all plant species, have to be, and are, controlled without such a mechanism. It is noteworthy that Pimentel's model denies to parasites, predators and herbivores precisely those factors which control scavengers and plants, namely intraspecific competition and the variability of weather and enemy action.

Discuss this criticism.

3   Milne (1958, p. 254) states:

Theories of natural control in mammal and bird populations are not likely to be very useful for insects. Mammals and birds, being "warm-blooded" and having more efficient water-conserving mechanisms, are far less affected by the irregular vagaries of weather, and they may also exhibit "territorial" behavior which is important in limiting density.

Discuss whether different theories of population regulation should be developed for different taxonomic groups.

4   Almost all the discussion of population regulation has been carried on by zoologists (and entomologists in particular). Review the various theories presented in this chapter with *plants* in mind, and discuss the application of these ideas to plant populations.

5   Darwin (1859) wrote in Chapter II of *The Origin of Species*: "Rarity is the attribute of a vast number of species of all classes, in all countries." Discuss the possible effects of rarity and commonness on population-regulation mechanisms.

6   Review the population growth models discussed in Chapter 11 for discrete generations, and relate these models to the theories discussed in this chapter. One of the principles of the biotic school is that density-independent processes cannot prevent a population from becoming extinct or from increasing to excessive numbers (starvation). Try to demonstrate this axiom with the discrete-generation growth model given on page 204.

15   Some examples of
population studies

LOCUST POPULATIONS

Locusts are pests of long standing, and in view of the great economic damage they do it is not surprising that a good deal of work has been done on them. A plague of desert locusts in Somaliland in 1957 was estimated to comprise 1.6×10^{10} locusts and weigh about 50,000 tons; and since locusts eat about their own weight in green food per day it is easy to see why they are so destructive (Gunn 1960). Figure 154 shows a swarm of desert locusts.

Locusts are distinguished from *grasshoppers* in that locusts exhibit *swarming* (mass migration of large bands), whereas grasshoppers do not exhibit definitely developed swarming habits, although they may multiply rapidly and become pests of local importance. We shall discuss locusts only, but many aspects of grasshopper population problems may be identical. There is no sharp taxonomic difference between locusts and grasshoppers.

There are relatively few species of locusts in the world; a list of 8 to 10 species will cover almost all the swarming species known. Three species in particular have been studied more than the others: desert locust (*Schistocerca gregaria*), African migratory locust (*Locusta migratoria migratorioides*), and red locust (*Nomadacris septemfasciata*). The distributions of these species are shown in Figures 155 to 157.

FIGURE 154

*Swarm of desert locusts (*Schistocerca gregaria*) in Morocco, 1954. (Photograph courtesy of FAO and the Anti-Locust Research Centre.)*

All locusts undergo gradual metamorphosis: egg, nymph (hoppers), adult. In general there is only one generation per year, but there are some exceptions. Let us look briefly at the life history of one of these locusts in order to provide a background for the population problem. The red locust produces one generation per year and is capable of a 100-fold increase in 1 year. Copulation begins in November and December, at the time of the year when the first rains come. Oviposition follows shortly. Each female lays 2 to 3 egg pods at 2-week intervals during the breeding season, and the eggs hatch in the soil about 1 month later. The hoppers pass through 6 or 7 instars and become adults 65 to 70 days after hatching. Most of the year is spent in the adult stage:

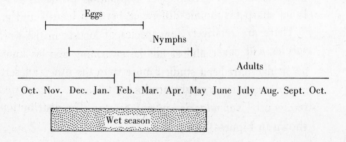

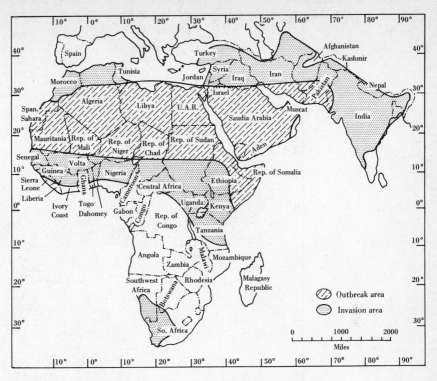

FIGURE 155

*Outbreak area and invasion area of the desert locust (*Schistocerca gregaria*). (After Waloff 1966.)*

The red locust is distributed in two important types of area: *outbreak areas* and *invasion areas*. Outbreak areas of the red locust cover 1500 square miles in northern Zambia and southern Tanzania (Figure 157); these are areas of permanent inhabitation, high survival, and high reproduction, and the ecological conditions of these areas sometimes lead to swarm formation. Outbreak areas of the red locust are hot grass plains without trees, with bare ground between the grass plants, with a mosaic of patches of short and tall grass and subject to seasonal flooding and to seasonal burning. No one knows why these areas produce swarms (Gunn 1952). The swarms migrate out of the outbreak areas and then occupy the *invasion areas*, which for the red locust may cover 3 million square miles of southern Africa; this is a ratio of 1500 : 1 of invasion area : outbreak area. Swarms cannot form in the invasion areas.

Three times in the past century Africa has suffered from widespread and prolonged plagues of the red locust. The last outbreak lasted from 1929 to 1944 and affected most of Africa south of the equator. Earlier plagues of the red locust started in 1847 and 1892, and between these outbreaks there

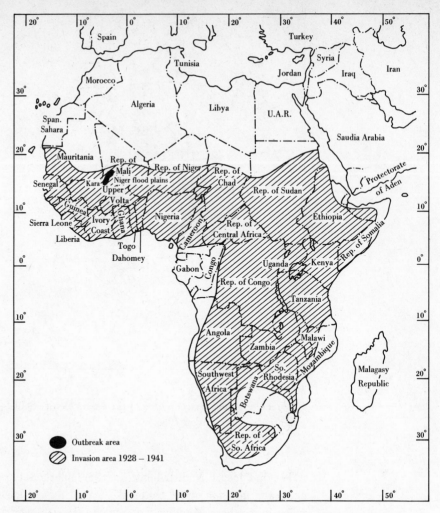

FIGURE 156

Outbreak area and invasion area of the African migratory locust
(Locusta migratoria migratorioides) *during the last plague from*
1928 to 1941. (After Albrecht 1967.)

were recession periods with no swarms for 40 years and 20 years. Since
there are few outbreak areas for the red locust in Africa, control efforts can
be concentrated in these areas. An attempt is being made to stop swarm
formation before it gets going; spraying of chemical poisons has been the
chief technique used (Gunn 1952).

A second locust species, the African migratory locust, had two major
outbreaks between 1871 and 1960. Each of these plagues lasted about 15
years and occupied most of Africa south of the Sahara. Between these two

plagues there was a population low that lasted 23 years (Figure 158), and since 1942 there has been no outbreak of this locust (Betts 1961). The 1928–1941 plague seemed to originate in the Niger Flood Plains in western Africa (Figure 156).

The desert locust has been known as an important crop pest for over 3000 years, since swarms of this locust constituted one of the plagues of Egypt described in the Old Testament. Since 1908 there have been four major plagues (Figure 159), ranging in duration from 7 to 13 years and alternating with short periods of population recession lasting up to 6 years.

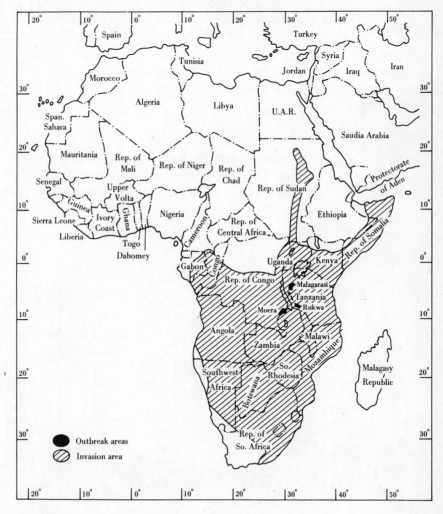

FIGURE 157

*Outbreak and invasion areas of the red locust (*Nomadacris septemfasciata*) from the 1927–1944 outbreak. (After Albrecht 1967.)*

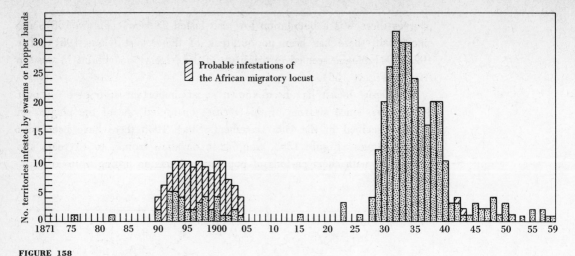

FIGURE 158

*Yearly fluctuations in the number of territories infested by the
African migratory locust (*Locusta migratoria migratorioides*),
1871–1959. (After Betts 1961.)*

The desert locust has been in a state of plague for 37 of the last 56 years,
about two-thirds of the time. This contrasts with the red locust and the
African migratory locust, which have both gone through only one plague
since 1910. The differences among the three species in the number of

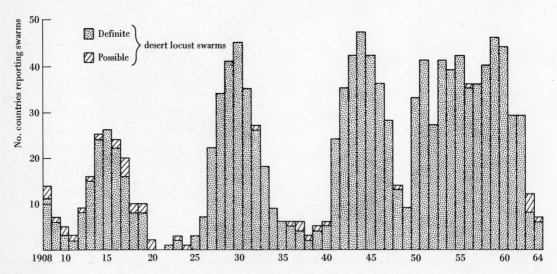

FIGURE 159

*Fluctuations of the desert locust plague, 1908–1964. (After Waloff
1966.)*

plague years may be due to the relationship between the outbreak and invasion areas.

The outbreak area of the desert locust occupies about 5,700,000 sq. miles (Figure 155), and in this area locusts have been found during population recessions. Outbreaks of the desert locust seem to arise from a much more diffuse area than they do in the other two African locusts; there is no single, stable, and small area to serve as a focus for control efforts. The invasion area occupies about 11,400,000 sq. miles, approximately twice the land area of the outbreak area (excluding the separate South African populations).

Outbreaks of the desert locust do not necessarily arise from preexisting mobile swarms. Waloff (1966) estimated the population changes in the desert locust during a period of low numbers from 1934 to 1941 (Figure 160). There was no indication that the plague upsurge that began in 1940–1941 was preceded by an uninterrupted succession of swarming populations left over from the previous plague.

In spite of all the destruction caused by locusts, it was not until 60 years ago that any attempt was made to understand their biology. By 1911 taxonomists had named most of the different forms of locusts as distinct species,

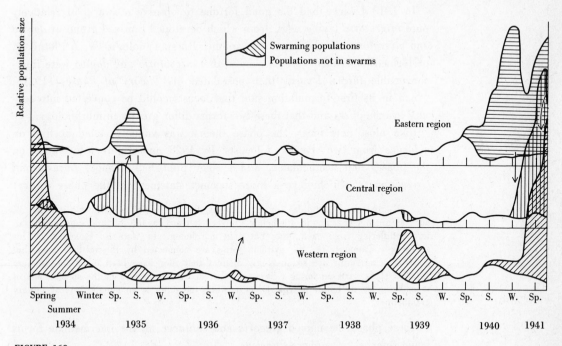

FIGURE 160

Changes in swarming and nonswarming populations during a long recession (1934–1941) of the desert locust. Arrows indicate movement of swarms from one region to another. (After Waloff 1966.)

and ecologists had not yet arrived to unscramble the resulting confusion. From an ecological point of view the situation was an enigma; swarms of locusts seemed to appear and disappear into thin air.

In one particular case there were two closely-related locusts, *Locusta migratoria* and *Locusta danica,* which a Russian entomologist, B. P. Uvarov, began studying in 1911 to find out what characters would separate the two, which he assumed to be distinct specifically. In addition to differences in pronotum shape and habitat, there were a number of other differences between the two locusts:

Locusta migratoria	*Locusta danica*
Elytra long	*Elytra short*
Hind femora short	*Hind femora long*
Males 4% smaller than females	*Males 20% smaller than females*
Coloration dark	*Coloration pale*
Gregarious	*Solitary*

Uvarov found that neither these nor any other characters would enable him to separate these two species (i.e., overlap was very common).

In 1913 Uvarov had the good fortune to observe a swarm of relatively pure *migratoria* laying eggs, from which developed a mixed group of *danica* and *migratoria*. In the same year another Russian biologist, V. I. Plotnikov, performed experiments which showed that *migratoria* and *danica* were inter-convertible forms. Uvarov then postulated his *Theory of Phases* (1921), which in its first formulation said that locusts could be converted into solitary grasshoppers and that these two forms differ greatly in morphology.

Like most new ideas, the phase theory was vaguely stated at first on evidence from two species of locusts. By 1928 much more information on the phases had accumulated, and Uvarov published a book, *Locusts and Grasshoppers,* which gave a more succinct statement of the phase theory:

> ...all gregarious Acrididae, or true locusts, belong to *polymorphic species,* that is, such as are not constant in all their characters, but are capable of producing a series of forms, differing from each other not only morphologically but also biologically. This series is continuous, i.e. the extreme forms are connected by intermediate ones, but these extreme forms are so strikingly distinct that they have been taken for different species. These extreme forms I have proposed to call the *phases* of the species, one of them being by its habits a typical locust, while the other is an equally typical solitary grasshopper.

These phases he named *gregaria* and *solitaria,* all the intermediate forms being referred to as phase *transiens.*

The phase theory was very quickly accepted as a spectacular step forward in locust biology. It solved the very baffling problem of what became of the dense swarms of locusts that appeared periodically. But the phase theory was put forward not only as the solution of a taxonomic puzzle but also as the solution of the larger problem of the intermittency of locust plagues.

Uvarov reasoned the following scheme to account for the development of a plague:

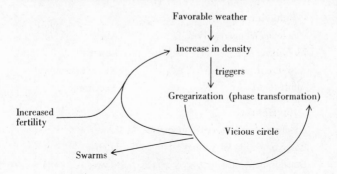

Uvarov believed that the first impulse to the increase in numbers of locusts is given by favorable weather in one or several successive seasons.

The development of the phase theory since 1928 may be broken apart and followed along three lines: (1) the characterization of the phases, (2) the mechanism of phase transformation, and (3) the relation of phases to population dynamics.

Characterization of phases

Four main types of characteristics have been used to distinguish phases in locusts: color, morphology, behavior, and physiology. Some idea of what sort of differences we are dealing with can be gathered from Table 19.

The solitary and swarming phases of the same species of locusts can be distinguished most easily by coloration and biometrical characters. Dirsh (1951) showed that one good morphological index of phase was the ratio of the length of the posterior femur (F) and the maximum head width (C), which changed significantly in all species. For example, in the desert locust:

Phase	Mean F/C ratio	Observed range
Male		
Solitaria	3.86	3.5–4.3
Gregaria	3.11	2.7–3.4
Female		
Solitaria	3.93	3.5–4.4
Gregaria	3.18	2.9–3.4

It was originally thought that the phase characteristics for *gregaria* and *solitaria* were constant, that all phase *solitaria* locusts of a given species

TABLE 19

Some features of phase polymorphism in locusts

	Solitaria	*Gregaria*
Behavior		
Tendency to aggregation	Absent	Present
Mobility	Lower	Higher
Activity rhythm	Not synchronized	Synchronized
Adult flight	Nocturnal	Diurnal
Physiology		
Food and water reserves at birth	Lower	Higher
Early mortality of young	Higher	Lower
Development rate	Slower	Faster
Instar number	Greater	Less
Hopper coloration	Uniform (green)	Yellow-black pattern (no green)
Adult coloration	No changes	Changes with maturation and age
Fecundity	More, but smaller, eggs	Fewer, but larger, eggs
Morphology		
Head	Smaller	Larger
Tegmen	Shorter	Longer
Hind femur	Longer	Shorter
Sexual-size dimorphism	Pronounced	Slight

SOURCE: After Uvarov (1961).

would have identical color, morphology, behavior, and physiology. If this were so, it would not matter what character one used to define the phases, since there would be perfect correlation between characters. Obviously this would be very convenient, as it would allow prediction of future and present behavior from morphology.

However, it soon became evident that, although there was a general, overall correlation between the phases and these characters, in any one particular instance the correlation between these characters might be poor. For example, a nymph showing *solitaria* coloration might be showing *gregaria* behavior patterns; morphometrically *gregaria* swarms might not migrate; migrating swarms might be completely *solitaria* in morphology.

These observations seem to be explained in part by the fact that there is a sequential development of these characters as the degree of gregariousness increases:

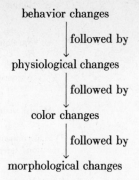

behavior changes

|
followed by
↓

physiological changes

|
followed by
↓

color changes

|
followed by
↓

morphological changes

These different rates of change have been the source of endless confusion in locust work, since some workers define the phases as morphological types, others as behavioral types.

Mechanism of phase transformation

How do locusts transform from one phase to the other? No one knows, in spite of a great deal of work. The process of phase transformation and outbreak development may be broken down into several components (Figure 161). First, there must be *multiplication* of the locusts. This must be followed by *concentration*, the absolute increase in population density in an area. Concentration may be produced in two ways: (1) by active centripetal movements into an area, or (2) by localized breeding without immigration. Concentration alone cannot produce an outbreak, because of the dense vegetation, since even dense populations of *solitaria* could not meet sufficiently closely and frequently in the field to cause the change of phase. That is, concentration is necessary for an outbreak but is not by itself sufficient.

Next comes *aggregation*, the grouping of concentrated individuals in contact with each other so that other locusts assume an important role in the sensory experience of each individual. This leads to a behavioral change of *mutual habituation*, as the locusts become more and more addicted to being together, which then leads into the vicious circle of swarm formation.

The first important thing to note about this scheme is that it is mainly a *behavioral* phenomenon. The essential characteristic of locusts is their ability to develop gregarious behavior. This is, of course, the reason locusts are so important economically. The differences in mean density between the solitary and the gregarious locust populations are not as great as one might expect (Uvarov 1961). If the respective populations could be scattered out evenly over the whole area, densities would be similar. But the main feature distinguishing solitary from gregarious locusts is the clumped distribution of the gregarious phase.

What ecological factors are important in causing phase transformation and the development of outbreaks? Weather factors are usually considered

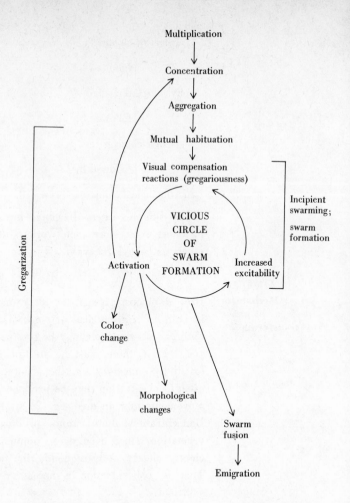

Multiplication

↓

Concentration

↓

Aggregation

↓

Mutual habituation

↓

Visual compensation
reactions (gregariousness)

VICIOUS
CIRCLE
OF
SWARM
FORMATION

Activation   Increased
excitability

Gregarization

Incipient
swarming;
swarm
formation

Color
change

Morphological
changes

Swarm
fusion

↓

Emigration

FIGURE 161

Major component processes of the
outbreak process and phase
transformation in locusts. (After
Key 1950.)

the most important component. Moisture is required for egg development of locusts and also for the green food needed by the nymphs and adults, but wet weather is detrimental to both nymph and adult survival. These opposing requirements make locust populations extremely sensitive to variations in weather. Moisture thus seems to be the most important factor affecting population size. Shortage of water often limits species in arid areas, especially tropical species (such as the desert locust), which have several generations a year. Conversely, temperate species and those in marshy habitats are favored by drought. When weather conditions are favorable, population size may be controlled by emigration and by phase changes. Parasites, predators, and diseases seem to be unimportant in determining changes in locust populations (Dempster 1963).

The importance of wind in the concentration of locusts has been emphasized by Rainey (1963). In the desert locust in particular, winds carry swarms to places where rainfall may be expected. The eggs of locusts must be laid in moist soil, and a soil moisture equivalent to about 20 mm of rain is a necessary condition for oviposition. The main breeding areas of the desert locust are characterized by scanty and erratic rainfall, and some mechanism is needed to enable adult locusts to reach areas with suitable soil moisture. The behavior of individual locusts flying in a swarm is often oriented with respect to other locusts, but the movement of the whole swarm is downwind even if individuals are oriented upwind or crosswind. This behavior brings the swarms together in zones of air convergence, where rainfall is concentrated (Rainey 1963).

Increases of the red locust in the outbreak area can be forecast from the rainfall of the previous year (Figure 162): the higher the rainfall, the lower the subsequent locust population. Three tentative explanations have been suggested (Symmons 1959): (1) Heavy rains may produce a high water table the following year, so the soil during the next rainy season is too wet for the eggs; (2) heavy rains may increase grass growth and reduce oviposition sites; and (3) parental losses may be high in the dry season after heavy rains. An alternative suggestion by Stortenbeker (1967) is that high rainfall favors the development of dragonflies, which prey on the locust nymphs of the following year. Whatever the mechanism involved, this ability to forecast has been used in planning control operations for the red locust.

Unfortunately we have few detailed data on population parameters of locusts. Although we do have a general idea of the processes involved in phase transformation and outbreak development, we do not yet understand the details. Part of the difficulty in getting these details is due to the remoteness of many of the areas in which locusts are common, and difficulties of studying mobile swarms, which cross political boundaries without stopping for official immigration clearance. Also, a large-scale chemical control pro-

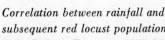

FIGURE 162

Correlation between rainfall and subsequent red locust populations at Lake Rukwa, Tanzania, 1942–1957. Rainfall over the Rukwa Valley in a given wet season is plotted against the level of adult locust infestation in the dry season 18 months later. (After Symmons 1959.)

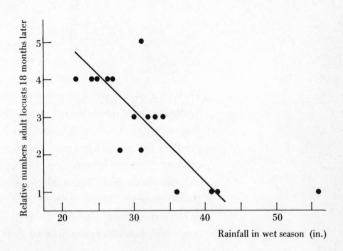

gram has been operating, so every time a population does begin to increase, it is hit with an insecticide before anyone gets a chance to study it.

Let us look at the allied problem of the expression of phase characters—how it is determined what characters an individual will show. Early experiments showed that phaselike effects, such as changes in coloration, could be produced by crowding in the laboratory. Gunn and Hunter-Jones (1952) showed that one could reproduce the full range of color types of *Locusta migratoria* by crowding the nymphs in cages in the laboratory:

No. nymphs per cage	Hopper color—% classed as:		
	Pale (*solitaria*-like)	Intermediate	Dark (*gregaria*-like)
1	100	—	—
2	61	39	—
4	36	64	—
16	18	77	5
64	1	59	40
256	—	12	88

But laboratory crowding did not reproduce the full range of morphological differences seen in field populations: for example, the elytron/femur ratios (E/F) of female *Locusta migratoria*:

No. hoppers per cage	Mean E/F ratio	Mean E/F ratio in field
1	1.86	*solitaria* = 1.81
2	1.89	
4	1.86	
16	1.92	
64	1.94	
256	2.00	*gregaria* = 2.19

This type of experiment suggests that locusts cannot be transformed experimentally from *solitaria* to *gregaria* in one generation, which must mean that something inherited is passed on from generation to generation to produce the phase changes. Two forms of inheritance have been suggested: ordinary genic inheritance through the chromosomal DNA; or extra-chromosomal inheritance through the cytoplasm of the egg. Gunn and Hunter-Jones (1952) showed that one could select for E/F ratio in the African migratory locust. In four generations they selected from a common stock two divergent lines of E/F ratio:

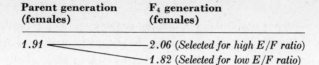

Parent generation (females)	F₄ generation (females)

1.91 ———————— 2.06 (*Selected for high E/F ratio*)
     ———————— 1.82 (*Selected for low E/F ratio*)

Thus it is possible that some of the phase transformation could operate through natural selection.

There are thus three factors involved in the expression of phase characters: density effects, nongenic inheritance, and genic inheritance.

The current conception of the relative importance of these three factors is as follows:

1 There is no genetic change involved in phase transformation; that is, the genotypes of *gregaria* and *solitaria* are identical.

2 Phase characters are transmitted from generation to generation by nongenic inheritance through the cytoplasm of the egg.

3 Within each generation there are strong phenotypic effects caused by crowding, which is the principal factor accounting for the phase characteristics observed.

A good deal of research is now going on in regard to these three factors. Current research on nongenic inheritance is focused on maternal influences on progeny quality. Crowded female locusts produce progeny that differ from progeny of isolated locusts in reproductive rate and growth rate (Albrecht, Verdier, and Blackith 1959). These maternal influences might be passed on for several generations. Other workers are questioning whether phase changes in nature are primarily a crowding effect caused by increased density. Lea (1968) suggests that natural selection alternatively favors one of two types of locusts:

1 Density-sensitive type—high viability, undergoes phase transformation at lower densities.

2 Density-insensitive type—lower viability, undergoes phase transformation at higher densities.

At the beginning of an outbreak the population might consist mainly of density-sensitive locusts; at the end of an outbreak the population might consist mainly of density-insensitive types. Lea suggests that weather conditions may retard or accelerate an outbreak, but only when the composition of the population is right will favorable weather trigger an outbreak. Unfortunately there is as yet no information to determine if Lea's ideas are correct. Nolte (1967) has made a start in this direction by analyzing the chromosomes of *solitaria* and *gregaria*. It is evident that even after 30 years of intensive work in locusts there are many unanswered questions regarding phase transformation.

Can we study the population ecology of locusts without studying phase changes? The answer to this is no—phase transformation in locusts is an integral part of the problem. Let us look at some of the phase differences in *Locusta migratoria* that must affect its population ecology:

Relation of phases to population dynamics

	Solitaria	*Gregaria*
Longevity	*Shorter*	*Longer*
Time required to mature	*Shorter*	*Longer*
Fecundity	*Higher*	*Lower*
Rate of oviposition	*Higher*	*Lower*
Crowding in adults as affecting reproduction	*No effect*	*Considerable effect*

So, the locusts are a good example in which changes in quality of individuals profoundly affect the population dynamics of a species. As such, their population outbreaks may fit in with self-regulation theories.

Why have locusts evolved an elaborate system of phase transformation while many grasshoppers remain solitary? The key to this problem seems to lie in the habitat requirements of grasshoppers and locusts. Grasshoppers live in more continuous habitats than locusts. Kennedy (1956) suggested that locusts are species with two ways of life, two habitats, and that they alternate between them by the process of phase transformation. Dempster (1963) views the *gregaria* phase as the dispersal form of the species and suggests that locust outbreaks are part of a strategy of colonization for species with a patchy, discontinuous habitat.

We may note here, parenthetically, that phenomena closely resembling this phase polymorphism of locusts also occur in other groups of insects (Uvarov 1961). Coloration changes occur in army worms (*Leucania unipuncta*), which are gregarious Lepidoptera larvae. Crickets (family Gryllidae) show changes in color and morphology as population density varies. A similar system of changes in the western tent caterpillar is described later (page 321).

To summarize: The most important factor involved in locust population changes seems to be *weather* (particularly moisture) operating in and through the process of *phase transformation*. But the relationship between the triangle of weather–phase transformation–density is far from being understood.

PRAIRIE GRASSES AND DROUGHT

Grassland areas are periodically subjected to severe summer drought, and two of these droughts have been studied on the Great Plains of the United States by J. E. Weaver and F. W. Albertson. The great drought of 1933–

1939 coincided with the Great Depression in the United States, and the dust storms that accompanied it carried as far east as the Atlantic coast.

Figure 163 shows the response of two perennial grasses of the short-grass prairie—buffalo grass and blue grama—to drought conditions. During the great drought of 1933–1939 buffalo grass entirely disappeared from some ranges and in others was reduced to a few small patches. As the drought ended in 1940–1942, buffalo grass responded rapidly to the increased moisture and reached high levels of abundance. By contrast, blue grama is much more drought resistant than buffalo grass and was never killed so uniformly or completely over a wide area. In nearly every range some bunches of blue grama persisted during the drought years. However, the rate of recovery of blue grama was very slow on all ranges, compared with that of buffalo grass. The reason for this slow recovery is not known; perhaps it was due to shading from weeds.

The abundance of these two perennial grasses thus depends on the amount of moisture available for growth, and the recurrence of drought seems to

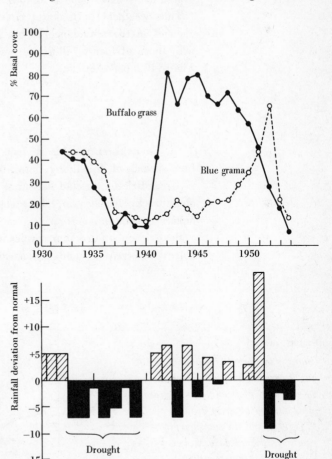

FIGURE 163

*Changes in the relative abundance of buffalo grass (*Buchloe dactyloides*) and blue grama (*Bouteloua gracilis*) on a short-grass prairie area ungrazed by cattle since 1932 in central Kansas. Deviation of total annual rainfall from the normal amount of 22.9 inches at Hays, Kansas, shows the two drought periods of 1933–1939 and 1952–1955. (After Weaver and Albertson 1956.)*

thwart other biological interactions. Drought affected buffalo grass, for example, on ungrazed, moderately grazed, and overgrazed sites in much the same way (Figure 164). Buffalo grass is an example of a species that is highly resistant to grazing pressure, and it may increase in relative frequency under the impact of heavy cattle grazing (Tomanek and Albertson 1957):

	Site (Atwood, Kansas)		
	Upland	Hillside	Lowland
Buffalo grass (*% of all plant cover*)			
No grazing	16	10	1
Heavy grazing	91	70	37

Other grasses are not resistant to grazing and decrease in abundance when grazed heavily by domestic animals.

Thus weather (particularly moisture) plays a dominant role in causing changes in the abundance of prairie grasses, and these populations, along with those of locusts, illustrate systems in unfavorable environments (C in Figure 152, page 280).

PLANARIA POPULATIONS

T. B. Reynoldson and his students have studied the population ecology of four species of free-living flatworms (class Turbellaria, order Tricladida) in Great Britain. Triclad flatworms are very abundant in the shallow waters along rocky beaches in lakes. They cling to the underside of rocks and aquatic vegetation.

Reynoldson studied four species in detail: *Polycelis nigra, Polycelis tenuis, Dugesia polychroa,* and *Dendrocoelum lacteum* (Figure 165). *Polycelis*

FIGURE 164

*Changes in the relative abundance of buffalo grass (*Buchloe dactyloides*) on ungrazed plots and on overgrazed plots during the great drought of 1933–1939 and the subsequent recovery, Hays, Kansas. (After Weaver and Albertson 1956.)*

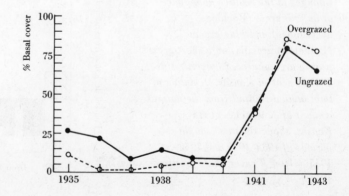

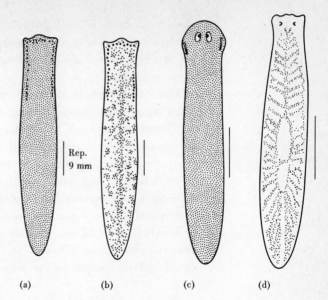

FIGURE 165

Four lake species of triclad studied by Reynoldson: (a) Polycelis nigra, *(b)* P. tenuis, *(c)* Dugesia polychroa, *and (d)* Dendrocoelum lacteum. *Vertical lines show the relative, average size of adults. (After Reynoldson 1966.)*

Rep.
9 mm

(a)   (b)   (c)   (d)

nigra is the most common species, occurring in 63% of the lakes in northern Britain and also in streams. The other three species occur in lakes and in streams only in still-water areas. *Polycelis tenuis* occupies 54% of the lakes in northern Britain and *Dugesia polychroa* and *D. lacteum* only 30%. Triclads do not feed on plants or decaying organisms. Reynoldson found that the four species fed on small oligochaetes, small arthropods, and mollusks (mainly snails). *Polycelis nigra* and *P. tenuis* overlap broadly in their food requirements, feeding mainly on oligochaetes but taking some arthropods and mollusks (Table 20). *Dugesia polychroa* feeds mainly on gastropod mollusks but also eats to a lesser degree small arthropods and oligochaetes. These three planarians are not efficient hunters but feed

TABLE 20

Percentage composition of the diet in four species of triclad flatworms in Britain

	Food items				Sample size
	Asellus	*Gammarus*	Oligochaeta	Gastropoda	
Polycelis tenuis	25	8	57	10	156
Polycelis nigra	8	7	68	17	155
Dugesia polychroa	16	4	22	57	176
Dendrocoelum lacteum	63	23	14	0	157

SOURCE: After Reynoldson and Davies (1970).

mainly on damaged or immobilized prey. *Dendrocoelum* by contrast is an efficient hunter and feeds on both intact and living organisms. There was no evidence of one triclad species preying on another or of them eating their own young.

These four triclads all breed in the spring and early summer mainly, but *P. nigra* also has a breeding peak in late summer. Young triclads do not breed during their first year. All three species have a marked ability to become smaller during starvation and to recover when food is available. They do this by digesting their own internal organs bit by bit. Life span is at least 3 years, and triclads are potentially immortal, no signs of senescence ever having been noted. They have few enemies; only a few insects and fish have been found to feed on them.

Reynoldson could not estimate absolute population size in most of his studies. Instead, he obtained an index of population size by placing a freshly-slit earthworm in the water and counting the planarians attracted to it.

The annual cycle of events seemed to be the same in the three triclad species belonging to the family Planariidae. *Polycelis tenuis* may be used as an example. The size structure of the population changes seasonally (Figure 166). There are three main features of this annual cycle: (1) the gradual disappearance of adults after the March peak, (2) the small number of young produced, and (3) the change in size structure of the population in summer. Let us analyze these three features.

The percentage of adults declines from about 40% in March to as low

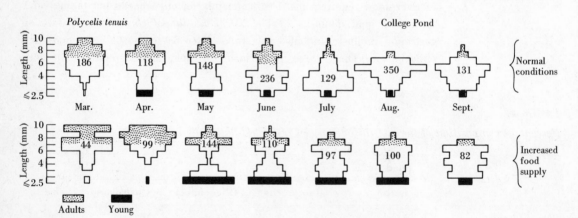

FIGURE 166

Changes in size structure of a population of the triclad flatworm Polycelis tenuis *in College Pond; upper row in a normal season, lower row under conditions of increased food supply. (After Taylor and Reynoldson 1962.)*

as 7% in September. Three explanations seem most likely, according to Reynoldson. This decrease in adults may be due to *mortality*, to *dilution* by new young animals, or to *shrinkage* in size. The first explanation, mortality, was eliminated because adults brought into the lab in July lived for several months even in complete starvation. The second explanation, dilution, was eliminated because the number of young was too small to change the percentage of adults very much. Hence the most likely explanation seemed to be shrinkage, and the most likely cause of shrinkage seemed to be food shortage.

Only a small number of young seem to result from breeding. Recruitment over the whole season was only 50% of the initial population, whereas laboratory populations, fed weekly, increased as much as 1800 to 2700%. Thus actual fertility was far less than potential fecundity.

The change in size structure of the population from April to September was gradual, from a maximum percentage of triclads in the largest sizes in March and April to a maximum percentage in the smallest sizes in July. In part this change was caused by recruitment of young, but the main effect seems to be caused by shrinkage of the older triclads into the smaller size classes. There was a sudden change in size structure between July and August, when there was little breeding, and a large fraction of the two smallest size classes disappeared. This sudden change can only be explained by mortality and the subsequent growth of individuals.

Thus all three features of the population biology of these planarians suggest that shortage of food is the dominant factor affecting population changes. This hypothesis Reynoldson tested by increasing the amount of food in two ways: (1) by adding food to the pond, and (2) by removing animals from the pond.

From February until August 1959 Reynoldson added chopped earthworms to a small pond containing *Dugesia*. He got a spectacular increase in the percentage of breeding adults and in the recruitment of young to this population (Table 21). Other experiments with *P. tenuis* produced the same response (Figure 166).

In a second experiment Taylor and Reynoldson (1962) removed all the *P. nigra* from a small pond during one winter. Then they reintroduced one-third of the individuals into this underpopulated habitat and followed their population changes. About 85% of the population was breeding in April, and tremendous numbers of young were produced in May and June. By August there were signs of food shortage, with 1207 *Polycelis* in the pool, roughly twice as many as the pool had held the previous year. About 36% of these died between August and October, and the smallest sizes suffered the highest mortality. Thus Reynoldson showed that the fall shift in size structure of the population was accompanied by mortality, as postulated.

Reynoldson, then, demonstrated experimentally that food shortage was

TABLE 21

Effect of increasing the food supply of triclad flatworms upon the total recruitment and proportion of breeding adults in late summer or early fall

Species	Total recruitment (%)		Percentage adults	
	Normal	Increased food	Normal	Increased food
Polycelis tenuis (College Pond)	50	350	4.3	55.2
Dugesia polychroa	38	137	2.2	32.9
Polycelis nigra	90	500	—	—

SOURCE: After Reynoldson (1964).

responsible for population regulation in these three planarians. By adding food to the system he could alleviate the three main effects characteristic of natural populations of triclads.

Reynoldson suggested that three features of triclad biology result in their populations existing at the upper limit of their food supply: (1) ability to postpone death from starvation by shrinkage, (2) scarcity of natural predators, and (3) relative stability of their physical–chemical habitat.

If these planarians are existing almost continuously at the limit of their food supply and if the food habits of the species overlap, there should be evidence of interspecific competition. Several lines of evidence support this conclusion (Reynoldson 1966). First, the size of *P. nigra* populations is apparently reduced when *P. tenuis* occurs in the same lake. If we compare the number of *Polycelis* collected per hour in two types of lakes, we obtain

	Productivity of lake	
	Intermediate	Very high
Polycelis nigra alone	140	179
Polycelis nigra in presence of *P. tenuis*	76	38

Second, the breeding season is curtailed by the presence of other species. When *P. nigra* was in a habitat containing no other triclads, it had two peaks of breeding, spring and late summer, but while in a habitat also containing *P. tenuis* and *Dugesia*, it had no second peak of breeding (Taylor and Reynoldson 1962). Third, two introductions of *Polycelis* into natural habitats containing the other *Polycelis* species have failed. This negative evidence is not conclusive because introductions may fail for a variety of reasons other than interspecific competition for food.

Triclads thus seem to be a simple case in which the distribution and abundance of the individual species are determined primarily by competition for food. The three genera that Reynoldson has studied all have a "food refuge" and in this way avoid complete competitive exclusion (Reynoldson and Davies 1970). *Dugesia* alone feeds mainly on snails, and only *Dendrocoelum* feeds extensively on the isopod *Asellus* (Reynoldson and Young 1966) and can capture intact prey items. An explanation for the coexistence of *P. nigra* and *P. tenuis* is more difficult, and Reynoldson suggests possible feeding differences within the oligochaetes, but no data are available.

Lakes of low productivity support smaller triclad populations and fewer species than do lakes of higher productivity (Figure 167). This suggests that competition for a limited food resource may become more severe as lake productivity declines. Triclad species that can compete successfully in productive lakes may thus be absent from unproductive waters because of this severe competition.

Population studies on planarians have been limited by two basic problems. First, census information on population density is very difficult to obtain, and we must rely on indirect methods of sampling to decipher population levels and possible variations from year to year or lake to lake. The accuracy of these indirect methods is insufficient to provide detailed population parameters. Second, the *available* food supply is very difficult to

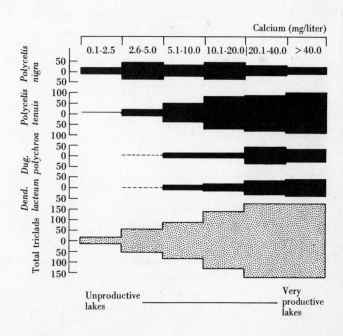

FIGURE 167

Average abundance of individual triclad flatworm species in British lakes as related to calcium content of the water. (After Reynoldson 1966.)

measure since three of the four species feed on damaged prey items. Ideally we should measure the size of the available food supply and show how this relates to population levels or changes from year to year, and if Reynoldson is correct we should find that the triclad populations track the available food supply very closely. Young and Reynoldson (1966) have been able to show this tracking in one instance for *Dendrocoelum* (Figure 168) feeding on *Asellus*. If this close tracking can be observed repeatedly in field populations, the next step would be to manipulate *Asellus* experimentally. This is necessary because many aquatic invertebrates increase in numbers in the spring and decrease in the fall (Figure 168), and thus many species show correlated changes that are not cause and effect.

To sum up: Reynoldson's triclads are a good example of species whose populations are regulated by a severe food shortage which occurs each year as a result of breeding. Triclad populations apparently press against the limits of their food supply continually.

CHEATGRASS ABUNDANCE

Cheatgrass (*Bromus tectorum*) is an annual grass introduced from Europe about 1900. It has spread widely in western North America and become a major part of some grasslands. In every location where cheatgrass thrives, its successful establishment can be associated with a disturbance of some kind (Klemmedson and Smith 1964). It was first found in Idaho in 1900, since then has become a dominant species on 4,000,000 acres, and is colonizing other areas subjected to fire or overgrazing. Cheatgrass is an undesirable species of rangeland grass for several reasons. First, it is a

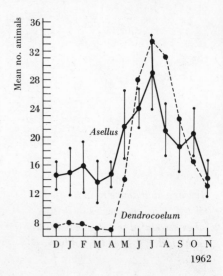

FIGURE 168

Changes in the population density of the triclad Dendrocoelum lacteum *and the isopod* Asellus meridianus *estimated by quadrat samples from a small pond in Wales. (After Young and Reynoldson 1966.)*

winter annual, and typically starts growth in the fall and drops seed and dies by early summer. This reduces herbage yield to grazing cattle, particularly in the summer. Second, cheatgrass is not a preferred grass for grazing animals, which select the native perennial grasses. Third, cheatgrass burns more readily than native grasses, and this fire hazard carries over to adjacent plant communities.

Because of these undesirable features, many attempts have been made to convert cheatgrass areas back to native perennial grasses. These have been largely unsuccessful. Wheatgrass (*Agropyron*), when sown into areas occupied by *Bromus*, germinates well, but the seedlings die within the first few weeks, apparently from a lack of soil moisture. Once established, however, wheatgrass proceeds to crowd out cheatgrass over several years by establishing an extentive root system (Stewart and Hull 1949).

Stands of *B. tectorum* may thus be very resistant to displacement by native perennials like *Agropyron*. In Washington *Agropyron* has not been able to invade cheatgrass stands even after 30 to 40 years of protection from fire and grazing (Harris 1967). Seedling survival of *Agropyron* depends on the density of *Bromus*:

	Agropyron spicatum (wheatgrass)	
Bromus density	Average survival of seedlings over first summer (%)	Average height of seedlings in June (cm)
Sparse	86	38.2
Moderate	69	31.1
Dense	39	17.5

Once germination has occurred, the roots of *Bromus* grow much more rapidly than the roots of *Agropyron*, part of this growth occurring over the winter. This may result in *Bromus* using all the available water in the upper soil before *Agropyron* can use it. The greater the competition from *Bromus*, the shallower the *Agropyron* roots (Figure 169). Thus *Bromus* outcompetes *Agropyron* by rapid root growth and then by maturing 4 to 6 weeks earlier in the summer. Most of the soil moisture is thereby exhausted by *Bromus* before *Agropyron* can utilize it.

In addition to rapid root growth, cheatgrass is a successful species for three other reasons: (1) large numbers of viable seeds are produced and carried from one year to the next in the litter and soil, (2) reductions in density of the cheatgrass may result in an *increased* total seed production, and (3) seed germination in the field is not immediate, but some seeds delay germination for several weeks or even for several years (Young, Evans, and Eckert 1969). Thus treatments with chemicals to destroy seedlings are not successful unless applied several years in a row.

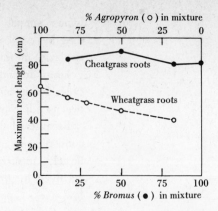

FIGURE 169

*Maximum root lengths of wheat-grass (*Agropyron spicatum*) grown in competition with cheatgrass (*Bromus tectorum*) under field conditions. The deeper roots of* Bromus *make it a superior competitor under conditions of water shortage. (After Harris 1967.)*

The production of cheatgrass stands changes greatly from year to year and is presumably related to variations in available soil moisture. Because the production of cheatgrass is much more variable than the production of crested wheatgrass, it is difficult for ranchers to adjust grazing pressures. For example, in southern Idaho from 1940 to 1946 the production varied as follows (Hull and Pechanec 1947):

	Production (lb/acre)	
	Mean	**Minimum—maximum**
Cheatgrass (*Bromus*)	1705	361–3461
Crested wheatgrass (*Agropyron*)	1803	1285–2472

Another important aspect of production is that of seeds for next year's generation, but the relative role of weather and other plant competitors in changing seed production has yet to be investigated in field populations.

EUROPEAN TITMICE

Studies on the European titmice (Passeriformes: Paridae) are among the most comprehensive population studies yet made on birds. This work was begun in the Netherlands in 1912 and is still in progress under the guidance of H. N. Kluyver; in England the work was begun in 1947 by D. Lack, under whose guidance it, too, is still in progress. There are six species of *Parus* breeding in Britain and western Europe, but only three are important to note here: the great tit (*Parus major*), the blue tit (*Parus caeruleus*), and the coal tit (*Parus ater*).

Tits, and other birds, can be censused accurately during the breeding

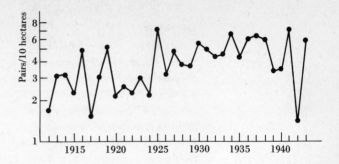

*Changes in the breeding population density of the great tit (*Parus major*) on a forest plantation in the Netherlands, 1912–1943. (After Kluyver 1951.)*

season, but because of their mobility they are more difficult to census at other times of the year. Breeding populations of the great tit fluctuate from one year to the next, unlike birds that maintain stable populations (e.g., tawny owl, Figure 146). Yearly counts of the great tit during the breeding season are available for three English areas and for several areas in the Netherlands as far back as 1912. These data provide a basis for the following discussion.

Two points are evident in these data. First, breeding densities are far from constant from one year to the next (Figure 170). Second, there is a tendency for areas to show synchronous population changes. Very high population levels were reached in 1957 and 1961 on three separate British areas and one Dutch area. In Marley Wood near Oxford, England, the great and blue tit populations rose and fell in tandem (Figure 171). This synchrony in population changes over a wide area in two species both living in very different types of woods suggests a link with climatic factors (Lack 1964).

Kluyver (1951) found in Holland that the annual fluctuations of the great tit population are correlated with the population changes in the blue tit (Figure 172). Within the great tit population, changes in different localities in Holland were often synchronous, but a few fluctuations, some of which were quite large, were not synchronous in different localities. Kluyver felt

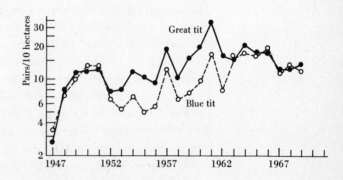

FIGURE 171

Changes in the breeding population density of the great tit and the blue tit in Marley Wood near Oxford, England, 1947–1969. (After Lack 1966 and J. Krebs, personal communication.)

FIGURE 172

*Relationship between population
density changes in the great tit and
the blue tit in the O.N.O. forest
plantation in the Netherlands,
1912–1943. The rate of population
increase is measured by the change
in breeding density from one year to
the next by* $\log_e (N_{t+1}/N_t)$. *When
this rate is positive, numbers are
rising; when negative, numbers are
falling. (After Kluyver 1951.)*

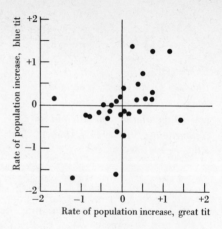

that this synchrony was brought about by general factors, such as severe
winters, which had a similar effect on all species and all localities, but he
did not believe that these catastrophes were the main factor regulating
population size.

Tits are hole-nesting birds under natural conditions, but the tits in all
these studies nested in artificial nest boxes. What effect does the provision of
nest boxes have on the population? Perrins (1965) suggests that nest
boxes were always superabundant in Marley during his studies. About 3
nest boxes per acre (7.5 per hectare) were available in Marley (66 acres,
about 200 boxes). This density of boxes, though superabundant, is still
well below the number of holes that would be found naturally in primaeval
woodland, according to Perrins (1965). Hence, while the erection of nest
boxes in a modern British woodland *may* lead to higher breeding densities
of tits, the Marley population during 1947–1971 must have been limited
by something other than nest sites. The same conclusion seems to apply to
the other woodlands studied.

The reproductive rate in birds is determined by clutch size and the number of clutches. Kluyver (1951) has shown that several factors affect clutch
size in great tits, and Perrins (1965) substantiated this in Marley Wood.
The size of the clutch, which varies between 5 and 12 eggs, becomes progressively smaller as the breeding season progresses. Kluyver (1951) found
that average clutch size declined from 10.3 in the first half of April to 6.0
in July. Clutch size also decreases as the population increases. In Marley
an increase in density from 30 to 60 pairs reduced clutch size from about
10 eggs to 8 (Figure 173). Clutch size is also smaller in birds breeding for
the first time, and finally some individuals consistently have larger clutches
than others. Habitat differences can also strongly affect clutch size. Clutches
were consistently lower in Oxford gardens than in Marley Wood, and, even
within Marley Wood, areas with many large oaks had higher clutch sizes

than did areas with fewer large trees (Perrins 1965). Clutch size of Marley great tits showed no relationship with food abundance before eggs were layed (number of caterpillars per square meter) (Perrins 1965).

Second broods are rare in English oak woodland, and less than 5% of the pairs raise second broods (Gibb 1950). In similar habitats in Holland about 35% of the pairs renest (Kluyver 1951). Also, in pinewoods there is a higher percentage of second broods: 76% in Holland as opposed to 28% in England. The difference between these rates in the two countries is not understood. The difference between pinewoods and broad-leaved woods is related to food supply, which is better later in the summer in pinewoods than in oak woodland (Gibb and Betts 1963). Kluyver (1951) found in Holland that second broods were most frequent (1) in years of low density, (2) among older birds, and (3) in pinewoods.

Total losses of eggs or young due to predation vary greatly from year to year and from place to place. In most years only a few losses occurred, mostly due to squirrels (*Sciurus vulgaris* and *Sciurus carolinensis*) and weasels (*Mustela nivalis*). Heavy losses of whole broods were sporadically caused by weasels. In Marley between 3 and 15% of the nests of great, blue, and coal tits were destroyed from 1947 to 1956, while 57% of the nests were destroyed in 1957, mainly by weasels (Lack 1958). Predation on eggs is a density-dependent mortality factor (Krebs 1970).

Beyond these predation losses, hardly any young great tits died in the nest in Marley. About 90 to 95% of the young left the nest successfully, regardless of their weight. Most of the young of the year die between leaving the nest and the start of winter. Much of this mortality seems to fall disproportionately on young that are light in weight at fledging. Perrins (1965) has documented this extensively for the great tit in Marley Wood near Oxford (Figure 174).

Young in larger broods are usually lighter in weight at fledging and

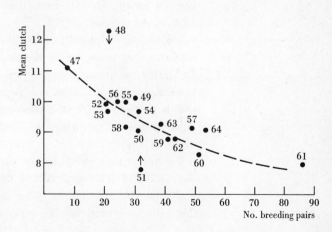

FIGURE 173

Relation between mean clutch size and number of breeding pairs each year of great tit in Marley Wood (arrows indicate abnormally early or late seasons). (After Lack 1966.)

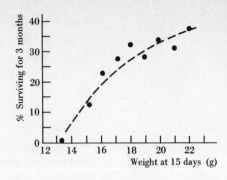

FIGURE 174

Survival of young great tits during their first summer after leaving the nest in relation to nestling weight at 15 days of age, Wytham Woods, Oxford, England, 1960. Data are shown for 1 year only, but the trend is the same in all years studied. (After Perrins 1965.)

these thus suffer more mortality. For example, the great tit in Marley during 1959:

Brood size	No. broods	No. young	% Recovered in autumn	No. recovered/ brood
1-5	28	120	15.8	0.63
6-8	42	286	13.8	0.90
9-11	31	308	13.6	1.36
12-14	21	264	7.5	0.95

In most years broods of 9 to 10 gave rise to the largest number of survivors per brood, and these brood sizes are also the most common (see page 566 for further discussion of this relationship).

The caterpillars fed to the young tits are abundant for only 2 to 3 weeks in the spring in Marley (Gibb 1950); hence late broods may suffer from poor feeding conditions. Survival of young great tits also decreases as the season progresses. The weight of the chicks at fledging thus becomes more crucial to survival for broods later in the season. Underweight young survive poorly early in the season, but later they have virtually no chance of survival at all. Thus it seems likely that food availability affects the survival of the young.

The changes in density from year to year must be explained either by the *production of young* or by the subsequent *mortality* or *movement* of birds. In Marley the annual variations in production rate of young are not closely correlated with the observed population changes (Lack 1964). This is shown in Figure 175. One must conclude, therefore, that changes in population density of great tits in Marley are produced by mortality or movements of young.

The proportion of young tits surviving during the first 3 months of life was estimated from the ratio of juveniles to older birds caught in the fall. Since the mortality rate of older birds is constant and independent of age, this ratio measures juvenile survival rate to the fall (Kluyver 1951). The

FIGURE 175

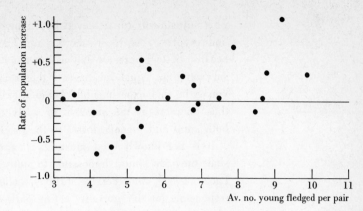

*Number of young great tits raised
per adult pair in Marley Wood in
relation to the rate of population
increase or decline in the subsequent
year. Data from 1947–1969. (After
Lack 1966 and J. Krebs, personal
communication.)*

ratio of juveniles to older birds varies markedly from year to year (Figure 176) and is correlated with the observed population changes in Marley (Perrins 1965).

A recent experiment by Kluyver (1966) has shed some light on the mechanism of regulation in great tit populations. Kluyver removed eggs and young birds from nests on an isolated island in the North Sea. This "birth control" reduced the average number fledged per pair and the juvenile/adult ratio in fall to very low levels. However, this did not cause the population to decline, as would be predicted from Figures 175 and 176. The population remained at the same density even though there was no possible immigration:

	Av. no. breeding birds	Av. no. fledglings produced	Annual survival rate	
			Adults	Juveniles
Control years (1956–1960)	*52*	*274*	*0.26*	*0.11*
Experimental "birth control" years (1960–1964)	*55*	*110*	*0.54*	*0.20*

FIGURE 176

*Ratio of juvenile to adult great tits
in the autumn in Marley Wood in
relation to the rate of population
increase or decline in the subsequent
year. The juvenile/adult ratio is a
measure of juvenile survival from
fledging to autumn. The rate of
population increase is $\log_e$
(N_{t+1}/N_t). Data from 1947–1969.
(After Lack 1966 and J. Krebs,
personal communication.)*

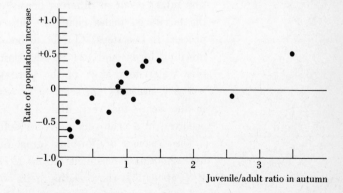

This adjustment was achieved by an increase in adult and juvenile survival and occurred before winter set in. The adult survival did not improve because of less parental exhaustion from feeding large families; chances of survival were equal for parents that raised 1 to 4, 6 to 10, and 11 to 15 young in this experimental period. Some mortality or emigration process thus operates in the summer or early autumn in a way that can adjust both adult and juvenile losses to the production of young that has occurred.

It is not known what mortality factors affect birds during this period, since they are almost impossible to study or observe until the fall leaf drop. Lack (1964) and Perrins (1965) believe that food shortage is mainly responsible for the mortality acting particularly during June, the first month after the juveniles have left the nest, and eliminating primarily birds underweight at fledging. Kluyver (1951), on the other hand, suggests that the main factor is not direct mortality, but that territorial aggressiveness in September may lead to a large number of young birds emigrating. Perrins (1965), however, believed that few great tits left Wytham Woods and that it was essentially a closed system. This assumption has been questioned by Chitty (1967).

Let us summarize to this point: (1) Breeding densities of the great tit fluctuate greatly from year to year; (2) the critical factor causing these population changes is juvenile survival between June and November; and (3) two hypotheses are proposed to explain juvenile mortality—elimination by food shortage or by territorial behavior.

Lack (1964) suggests that territorial behavior could not be limiting density in Marley because the population fluctuated greatly from year to year. The assumption here is that all populations regulated by territorial behavior will show relative stability from year to year, the territories being comparable to rubber discs that can be compressed over restricted limits only. This assumption may not be valid. The critical fact to be determined is whether in any given area there are birds capable of breeding which are prevented from doing so by territorial males. These "surplus" birds may be around for only a short time in the spring (and possibly fall). Such limitation might occur at different densities in different years if the "hostility" of the territorial males changes. Thus a study of territorial limitation must proceed in two steps: (1) the demonstration of the existence of surplus nonbreeding birds, and (2) the determination of what factors affect the "hostility" (territory size) of the territorial males. In the great tit in Marley, territory size does not seem to be regulated by the abundance of food later in the year—the very high 1961 population with very small territories occurred in a year very poor for defoliating caterpillars (Lack 1964).

The existence of "surplus" great tits in the spring has been demonstrated by a shooting experiment (Krebs 1971). In March 1968 and again in March 1969 about half the breeding pairs were shot from Bean Wood near Oxford in England. These shot birds were rapidly replaced: 13 birds replaced the 14 removed in 1968, and 14 replaced the 14 removed in 1969. Replacement started within a few hours of the removals. This demonstrated that some pairs are prevented from settling on an area by the territorial behavior of the residents.

Where do these replacement birds come from? Krebs found that they were mostly first-year birds that had been living in hedgerows in the surrounding farmland. Hedgerows are marginal habitat for the great tit; hedgerow birds raise fewer young than woodland birds. Spring territorial behavior thus limits the breeding density in the optimal woodland habitat, and birds excluded from the woodland settle in marginal hedgerows.

The next step in this analysis must be to find out what sets the level of aggressiveness in spring territorial behavior. Male great tits do not adopt a territory of constant size but one that varies greatly from year to year. What causes these variations is not known. Winter food supply does not seem to affect the subsequent level of territorial strife, and some other factor must be critical (Krebs 1971).

The disagreement over what regulates great tit populations raises an important issue: *Is it necessary to assume that the same factors or processes control population changes in all parts of a species' distribution?* How much heterogeneity are we to allow in our explanations? Can we argue that one mechanism is operating in the British woodlands and yet another is operating in the Dutch areas? The answer to these questions is unknown at the present time.

At least five major problems remain unsolved in these titmice studies: (1) What factors are associated with the production of underweight young at fledging? Is this a matter of available food supply? (2) When in the first 5 months of life does the heavy juvenile mortality fall? Is food shortage sufficient to explain this mortality? (3) What role is emigration and immigration playing in these population changes? (4) Does spring territorial behavior limit numbers every year, and does it play any role in causing the populations to fluctuate in density from year to year? (5) How do females adjust their clutch size in relation to population density?

WESTERN TENT CATERPILLARS

Wellington (1957, 1960) has studied the population ecology of western tent caterpillars (*Malacosoma pluviale*) on Vancouver Island, British Columbia. Tent caterpillars are widespread over North America and fluctuate widely in numbers, reaching high densities roughly every 8 years. In 1956 an outbreak reached a peak on southern Vancouver Island, and Wellington has studied its subsequent decline.

Individuals of the western tent caterpillar overwinter as fully developed embryos in egg masses attached to twigs of their food trees, usually alders, willows, and orchard trees (mainly apple). Each egg mass contains 100 to 300 first instar larvae, which hatch in April or May. Once they emerge the larvae are colonial, moving in groups along the twigs to begin feeding on leaves. They lay silk trails as they travel, and soon begin to construct a communal tent, which serves as a resting and moulting shelter from which they emerge to feed. Individuals leave the colony to pupate alone in June or July, in cocoons spun in rolled leaves, on twigs, and so on, after having moved considerable distances from their tent. The winged moths emerge in July and lay their eggs in masses on twigs to start the life cycle over again. Only one generation occurs per year.

Wellington became interested in this population problem while studying the behavioral reactions of larval tent caterpillars to light. He observed that when newly hatched larvae were exposed to light from a fluorescent tube, individuals differed in their reactions; some would move directly into the light in a straight line, some would move only slightly, others would not move at all.

He removed the first group and called them *type I* larvae; these are capable of independent, direct movements when isolated from other larvae. These are the most active individuals.

The inactive larvae he called *type II*, and he broke these down into three groups: (1) *Type II-a* larvae are relatively active but cannot orient themselves independently when isolated from their neighbors; when in a group they can orient and they are good at following silk trails set down by other larvae; (2) *Type II-b* larvae are less active and they cannot orient either individually or in groups; they can follow silk trails left by other larvae, but otherwise they are completely unable to fend for themselves in moving about; (3) *Type II-c* larvae are the weakest members of the colony; some fail to emerge from their eggs, and many die soon after hatching; they are extremely sluggish and few survive in the field.

In nature no colony can consist of all one type of larvae. There are advantages and disadvantages of each type. Type I larvae are very active independently and search out new sources of food by moving along twigs; their disadvantage is that they spin poor tents, which makes them susceptible to death by desiccation. Type II-a individuals supplement type I's by increasing the activity level of the colony. Type II-b larvae are very important to the colony because they spin the best silk tents, which protect the colony from predation and desiccation; their disadvantage is that they may starve to death in the midst of plenty because they are so inactive. Type II-c larvae are not only prone to starvation but they spread disease readily because of their sluggish habits. It is unlikely that any such individuals in nature ever contribute to the next generation.

Wellington found that the different types of larvae had different rates of development:

Type of larvae	Duration of larval stages (21°C, 80% relative humidity)	No. instars
I	36 days	5
II-a	39 days	6
II-b and II-c	43 days	6

The shape of the tent constructed by the larvae depends on the percentage composition of the colony. Active colonies, those which contain many type I and II-a larvae, construct several *elongate* tents during their first instar. Sluggish colonies, those which contain few type I and II-a larvae and many type II-c larvae, construct only one or two *compact* tents in the same time.

In the field Wellington found that newly-established infestations contained a high percentage of active colonies making elongate tents. In contrast, heavy old infestations consisted largely of sluggish colonies making compact tents:

Age of infestation (yr)	Active colonies (%)	Sluggish colonies (%)
2	61	39
3–4	42	58
5	26	74

The outbreak Wellington studied decreased abruptly from 1956 to 1959, and associated with this numerical change were several qualitative changes in this population:

	1956	1957	1958	1959
No. colonies	74,000	3,164	390	251
Av. no. larvae per colony	81	61	41	68
Mean no. eggs per egg mass	216	201	155	170
Type I larvae (%)	13	11	10	13
Type II-c larvae (%)	20	25	32	18

As the population declined from 1956 to 1958 there was an increase in the percentage of sluggish individuals and a decrease in the percentage of active individuals. The population began an upswing in 1959.

The adults produced by type I larvae are more active than adults produced by any other larval type. This has important ecological effects, because the more active adults tend to disperse farther and consequently lay their eggs in new areas, whereas the sluggish adults lay their eggs in the immediate vicinity of where they pupated.

The picture obtained by Wellington was this: An infestation begins with a predominance of active colonies. As it builds up in size it accumulates more and more sluggish colonies. These sluggish colonies are more susceptible to weather changes, to starvation, to virus diseases, and to predation; and sooner or later one of these factors destroys the tent caterpillars in large numbers, bringing about the end of the outbreak.

Deterioration of a local population is thus caused by differential dispersal. There is a steady increase in the proportion of sluggish individuals in a given locality as time passes. These sluggish colonies die out, primarily by starvation because they are too sluggish to leave their tents. They die in the absence of enemies, in favorable climate, and surrounded by superabundant food and at low or high density. It requires about 4 to 5 years (generations) for this deterioration to occur. Once the population has died out, the whole process begins again by recolonization by active moths. The population increase occurs in years of warm dry weather (Wellington 1964).

What determines the different types of individuals among the progeny? Wellington (1965) has shown that all types of individuals may appear in the progeny of a single female. The different larval types are concentrated in different parts of the egg mass:

	First half of egg mass	Second half of egg mass
Active larvae (%)	39	13
Very sluggish larvae (%)	4	18

The most active, type I, progeny come from the first eggs laid, and the least viable, type II-c, progeny from the last eggs laid. The reason for this seems to be an unequal partitioning of the maternal food reserves among the eggs. These effects are cumulative. The less active larvae have a lower feeding rate and lower food capacity than the active larvae. Less active larvae produce adults with less food reserves for egg production. With less food reserves moths produce fewer active progeny and more inactive ones. The whole scheme repeats in a vicious circle, and ultimately leads to extinction.

Note that these maternal influences are not hereditary in the usual genetic sense; nonetheless they are transmitted from generation to generation. Exactly how the depleted egg food reserves act to determine the type of the individual is not yet known.

The importance of Wellington's work is that it pointed to *individual differences* as a factor in population regulation. A fluctuating population of tent caterpillars might regulate its own density by a built-in mechanism of deterioration in the quality of individuals. He has suggested that *intrinsic* factors are involved in the population control of tent caterpillars.

There are many unanswered questions in Wellington's work. What is happening during the period of low population density? How does an extrinsic factor such as weather initiate the outbreaks? What role does dispersal of active moths play when high densities are widespread? How widespread might a system like this be in other forest insect pests? What effect would spraying with an insecticide have on the population?

RANGE DETERIORATION IN THE SOUTHWESTERN UNITED STATES

It is almost an axiom that the most widespread and significant ecological changes in populations are the ones least documented and least studied. The ecologist in this case becomes something like a detective in trying to unravel possible causes. A good example of this dilemma is the recent deterioration of vegetation in the southwestern United States.

During the last 90 years the range in Arizona and the adjacent Sonora region of Mexico has shown a steady deterioration of the grasses and several other groups of plants. Accompanying this degeneration of the grasslands has been an alarming spread of mesquite and several other range weeds unpalatable to livestock. Hastings and Turner (1965) have documented this change by analyzing historical records for this area and by assembling a set of "before–after" pictures showing areas photographed from 1883 to 1935 and the same areas rephotographed from 1960 to 1965.

In this area the zonation of the vegetation in order of increasing elevation is desert, desert grassland, oak woodland, pine forest, Douglas fir, and spruce–fir forests. Only the first three zones, collectively comprising the first mile above sea level, are dealt with by Hastings and Turner. Of these three the desert occupies the largest expanse.

The oak woodland is an open community of trees set in a matrix of grasses and some succulents between about 4000 and 5500 ft elevation. Over the last 75 years three trends could be detected in the oak woodland. At all stations below about 4500 feet the oaks have died faster than they have become established (Figure 177). This mortality has been most severe at the lower edge of the woodland and has resulted in an upward migration of the boundary separating the woodland from the desert grassland. Finally, the woodland has become less open at all elevations because of shrub invasion.

Desert grassland typically lies between 3000 and 4000 ft elevation. The grass flora of this zone is exceedingly rich, comprising at least 48 species of grasses. The changes in the desert grassland of the Sonoran Desert in the past 80 years have been principally a decline in the dominance of grasses and an increase and takeover by the woody species. At the present time the grasses are so scarce that they hardly give any indication of their former dominance. Mesquite, acacias, burroweed, and other woody species now dominate the landscape.

The desert, which typically occupies the area below 3000 ft elevation, has shown changes in vegetation that are neither as striking nor as con-

(a)

(b)

sistent as the changes that have occurred over the last 80 years in the desert grassland and oak woodland. In some localities shrubs have increased, in others decreased. The saguaro is less abundant on some areas but more abundant on others. The problem here is this: Should one expect random and unsystematic fluctuations in the vegetation of an arid region as a necessary concomitant of high spatial variation in rainfall? Whatever the answer to this question may be, only a few desert species show clear trends. The paloverdes have increased in the upper parts of their range and decreased in the lower parts. Mesquite seems to have done the same.

To summarize: The most common pattern of change has been an upward displacement of species' ranges along the xeric–mesic gradient. What caused these vegetational changes? Four agents have commonly been suggested.

(1) *The effect of cattle* There is a close association in time between the rapid expansion of the cattle industry in southeastern Arizona in the 1880s and the onset of arroyo cutting and vegetation change in that area. We know that livestock scatter viable seeds of some shrubs in their droppings. Severe grazing of grasslands contributes to the establishment of shrubs such as mesquite which cannot get established in an undisturbed grassland.

FIGURE 177

*(a) 1890. From a station 7 miles southwest of Patagonia, Arizona, looking west toward what George Roskruge, the photographer, calls the Hill of San Cayetano. The Grosvenor Hills are at right; the San Cayetano Mountains, left. At this time the area evidently lay on the lower edge of the oak woodland. The trees are widely spaced and confined to ravines and north-facing slopes. A few junipers may be scattered among the oaks. The small, round tussocks are probably sotol (*Dasylirion wheeleri). Elevation 4200 ft. (b) 1962. Not a single living oak can be seen in the picture, although some relict Mexican blue oak can be found in sheltered spots nearby. Death has occurred recently enough so that an impressive number of carcasses still remain. None of them bears axe or fire marks, and as isolated as the area still is, any overt interference by man can be ruled out. Mesquite, the new dominant, shows much the same habitat preference as oak, the old; its greatest density occurs along ravines and on north-facing slopes. Another recent invader is ocotillo (right midground and scattered over the hill). Also present are desert broom, wait-a-minute, beargrass, Santa Rita cactus, kidneywood, gray thorn, netleaf hackberry, a few one-seed junipers, and a species of yucca. The hummocks are composed mainly of fairy-duster and mimosa. Sotol has markedly declined but is still common. (After Hastings and Turner 1965.)*

Trampling by cattle also greatly affects the soil structure. The most serious objection to the cattle hypothesis is historical. Large-scale cattle raising began in Sonora around 1700, but no significant vegetational changes accompanied it. Other localities (a crater, an island group) show significant vegetational changes even though they have never been visited by livestock (Figure 178). This evidence suggests that cattle have not been the primary agent of change, although they may have had a considerable secondary influence, particularly in the desert grassland areas (see the next section, on saguaro).

(2) *The effect of rodents and rabbits* There is no obvious evidence of an increase in rodent and rabbit populations following predator-control operations that occurred after settlement. The effects of these natural herbivores are most strongly felt on ranges that have already deteriorated for other reasons. The available evidence suggests that these mammals did not play any significant part in initiating these vegetational changes.

(3) *The effect of fire* Burning kills many shrubby seedlings, but there is no good historical evidence of extensive burnings before 1880, and extensive and frequent burnings would be required to keep the desert grassland relatively free of shrubs. The available evidence suggests rather that fires (or reports of fires) increased in frequency after 1880. Fire suppression, then, does not seem to be a primary cause of the observed changes.

(4) *The effect of climate* The only hypothesis that cannot be rejected is that of climate. The 20-year period from 1875 to 1895 saw the inauguration of arroyo cutting in Arizona, New Mexico, Utah, and Sonora. White settlement in these areas took place at various times from 1598 to the 1870s. Grazing commenced at equally diverse times. The uniform onset of erosion points to the operation of a broad regional factor such as climate.

The vegetation changes are toward more arid vegetation. At the lower edge of their range, where moisture is probably the controlling factor, several species such as mesquite have retreated away from hot, dry habitats. At the upper edge of their ranges, where temperature is probably the controlling factor, they have advanced.

There is then a loose temporal association between climatic variation and vegetative changes. Since 1898 winter rainfall has dropped and winter temperatures have risen. Summer rainfall has remained about the same, but summer temperatures have increased sharply. Unfortunately the critical period from 1870 to 1898 remains vague; no weather data are available and few detailed vegetative data were taken. Another difficulty with the climate hypothesis is that little is known of the detailed effects of higher temperatures and lower precipitation on desert plants.

(a)

(b)

FIGURE 178

(a) One of the Islas Melisas in the bay at Guaymas, Sonora, Mexico, in 1903. The desert reaches all the way to sea level at this point on the Gulf of California. The tall cactus in this picture is cardón, Pachycereus pringlei. *Elevation is about mean sea level. (b) 1961. The Islas Melisas represent a partially controlled situation, and grazing can be dismissed as an ecological factor. The islands are near enough to the shore to be reached by swimmers and near enough to Guaymas to ensure that they are, in fact, frequently visited. Nevertheless, they should be among the more stable desert habitats: The temperature and humidity are controlled within unaccustomedly narrow limits by the water; animal interference with the plant life is minimal. A major fluctuation in the population of a long-lived perennial is difficult to account for. (After Hastings and Turner 1965.)*

Hastings and Turner conclude that climatic variation was probably the most important single agent producing these changes in the vegetation, but that climatic variation is not a sufficient explanation for all the changes.

If the climate would revert to the pre-1870 condition, would the vegetation return to its former state? Probably not, Hastings and Turner suggest. If the woody invasions represent the combined result of overgrazing and climatic stress, the vegetation may never return to its former condition. Once established, these woody species may become a permanent part of a new vegetation type, one evolved by a unique combination of cultural and climatic stress imposed over the last 80 years.

SAGUARO POPULATIONS

The saguaro, or giant cactus (*Carnegiea gigantea*), is one of a large group of tropical and subtropical cacti which grow in a massive columnar form. Its range is confined to the Sonoran Desert of the southwest, including Arizona and the state of Sonora in Mexico. Within this desert the saguaro often forms dense forests that dominate the landscape. The giant cactus extends only to about 4500 ft elevation in Arizona, and this distributional limit seems to be imposed by freezing temperatures. Shreve (1911) showed that young saguaro plants were not affected by freezing for up to 15 hours but were killed by freezing for more than 20 hours.

The saguaro may live for 175 years or more, and populations turn over slowly. Since 1900 many observers of the desert southwest have commented on the failure of saguaro to reproduce itself in some places. Not all saguaro populations are declining, but in some areas decreases have been spectacular. The Saguaro National Monument was established in 1933 near Tucson, Arizona, and the population decline was noticed in this area as well. The saguaro decline has accompanied the general deterioration in woody perennial survival in some parts of the southwest (see the previous section; Hastings and Turner 1965), and this effect is assumed to have a common cause in either (1) changing climate or (2) grazing by cattle and rodents.

Obviously, successful reproduction in a long-lived plant need occur only occasionally, and saguaro stands may go for 50 years without any successful reproduction and the population would not disappear. Shreve (1910) estimated the age of saguaro from their height and calculated the age structure of a stand of 240 cacti on Tumamoc Hill in central Arizona. The age structure was greatly biased in favor of older cacti (Figure 179), and Shreve concluded in 1910 that this species was not maintaining itself and was dying out. The same area, fenced from cattle in 1907, was sampled by Niering, Whittaker, and Lowe (1963) and found to have abundant reproduction (Figure 179). Thus current trends may be reversed over a number of years. What might cause this reversal?

Two obvious factors might be sufficient to explain the presence or absence of successful saguaro reproduction: moisture and grazing. Small saguaros

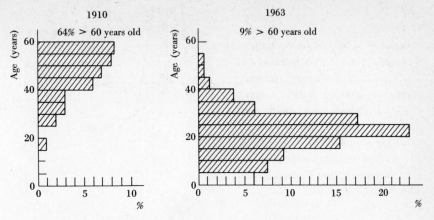

FIGURE 179

Age structure of the saguaro (giant cactus) at Tumamoc Hill near Tucson, Arizona, when first studied by Shreve (1910) and later by Niering, Whittaker, and Lowe (1963). Note the complete absence of seedlings in the 1910 sample in which 64% of the total population was over 60 years of age. This area was fenced from cattle in 1907 and seedlings have since become established. Age estimates are only approximate.

are often found beneath desert trees and shrubs but not in the intervening spaces. Apparently the woody perennials produce local patches in the desert where saguaro seedlings can survive. During the later years of a saguaro's lifespan the "nurse plant" often dies. The age at which a saguaro becomes independent of the nurse plant is not known; Turner et al. (1966) estimate 5 to 10 years of age (3 to 6 inches tall). During the early growth stages a saguaro has small water-storage capacity and thus may become dehydrated more easily. Water loss is presumably less in the shade of the nurse plant.

Shade thus seems essential to small-seedling survival. In plots screened from rodents 1200 unshaded seedlings all died within 1 year (Turner et al. 1966). An equal number of shaded seedlings had a 65% mortality. This result suggests that the fate of saguaro populations is closely tied to that of the other perennials (nurse plants) of the desert.

If shade is necessary for successful reproduction, grazing pressure may be a critical additional factor. The decline in successful saguaro reproduction in the 1870–1880s was associated with the rapid growth of the cattle industry. Later efforts to control predators such as coyotes were suggested to have reduced predation losses on rodents and rabbits so that these grazers could also destroy saguaro seedlings.

An experimental transplant of 1600 saguaro seedlings was made in 1957 at the Saguaro National Monument to test the effect of rodent and rabbit

FIGURE 180

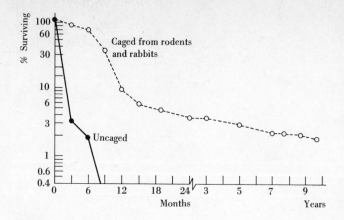

*Survival of 1600 saguaro seedlings
5 cm tall (2 yr old) transplanted on
level terrain at the Saguaro National
Monument, Arizona, in 1957. Cages
to exclude rodents were placed over
half of the plots. All 800 uncaged
seedlings were dead by 1 year; 1.9%
of the caged seedlings were alive
after 10 years. (After Turner,
Alcorn, and Olin 1969.)*

grazing on seedling survival. Figure 180 shows that caged seedlings suffered much less loss than uncaged seedlings.

Under normal conditions only about 1 in 1000 saguaro seeds ever germinates. Steenbergh and Lowe (1969) broadcast 64,000 seeds and obtained 185 seedlings (0.29% establishment). Many of the seeds are eaten by birds, mammals, and insects, and many others have insufficient moisture to germinate. Seedlings become established more easily in flat terrain than in rocky hillsides, but the subsequent survival of seedlings is higher in rocky habitats (Figure 181). Biotic agents (rodents, insects) killed 26% of the saguaro seedlings in the rocky area but killed 55% in the flat area. About half of the biotic deaths were caused by insects; rodents ate only 2 plants; 30 seedlings were killed by ground squirrel digging activity.

If grazing pressure, expanded now to include cattle, rodents, rabbits, and insects, restricts saguaro establishment, we must explain the fluctuations

FIGURE 181

*Survival of 85 naturally germinated
saguaro seedlings in rocky habitats
and in flat areas at the Saguaro
National Monument, Arizona.
Survival beyond 1 year of age was
restricted to seedlings growing in
rocky areas. (After Steenbergh and
Lowe 1969.)*

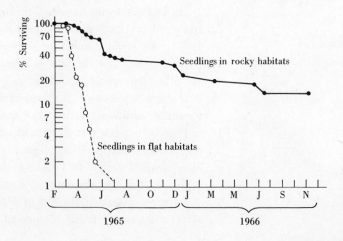

in grazing pressure that have allowed some stands to reproduce and others not to reproduce. Niering et al. (1963) show that areas now protected from cattle grazing have good seedling establishment and also that rocky slopes inaccessible to cattle also have better saguaro reproduction. This circumstantial evidence favors the view that grazing pressure is the critical limiting factor that has determined saguaro population changes (compare Figure 178). Experimental confirmation of this view is lacking, however, and the alternative view is that grazing losses merely speed up the destruction of seedlings doomed to die from shortage of moisture anyway. This view can be tested only by experiments of even longer term than that reported in Figure 180. Finally, the separate roles of cattle, insects, rodents, and rabbits must be experimentally disentangled in order to make the grazing hypothesis more precise and thus more amenable to test.

SPRUCE BUDWORM POPULATIONS

The spruce budworm (*Choristoneura fumiferana*) is another forest insect pest. Its caterpillars are probably the most destructive defoliators in the Canadian coniferous forests. They eat the buds, flowers, and needles of spruce and fir trees, causing the greatest amount of damage to adult balsam fir trees. Records of the spruce budworm in eastern Canada go back to 1770. Normally the species is rare and remains at low densities, but periodically it erupts to epidemic proportions for 5 to 10 years, causing heavy timber losses. These outbreaks have occurred every 35 to 40 years (e.g., in 1878, 1912, and 1945 in eastern Canada).

In 1945 R. F. Morris, a forest entomologist with the Canadian Department of Agriculture, instigated a long-term study of spruce budworm populations, just as a major outbreak was starting. An immense amount of manpower and money has gone into this work, partly because of its tremendous economic importance to the lumbering industry. The results of this study are summarized in Morris (1963).

The spruce budworm is native to North America and does not occur elsewhere. In eastern Canada it has a 1-year life cycle, with the second instar larva overwintering in diapause. Female moths lay about 200 eggs in late July or early August on the needles of conifer trees. The larvae hatch in mid-August and immediately spin a hibernaculum in which they spend the winter. The second instar larvae emerge in May and begin feeding. By late June the larval stages are over, and they pupate on the same branches they had previously been feeding on. Adults emerge in 8 to 12 days (mid-July) and live about 2 weeks.

The spruce budworm population in northern New Brunswick began increasing between 1945 and 1947 when this study was begun. By 1949 defoliation was severe in some small areas. By 1953 over 6 million acres were severely infested. Populations began declining in 1956–1957 and reached low levels again by 1960 (Figure 182). Morris distinguished this high-density epidemic phase of the population from the normal low-density endemic phase and suggested that different factors may regulate the population in these different phases.

The idea behind the investigations of the spruce budworm was to measure all the factors that affect *survival* for all the life-history stages of the budworm. The procedure used was to calculate life tables for the different ages and to partition the life table mortality into factors such as parasitism and disease. A typical life table for the budworm is given in Table 22, and a typical survivorship curve is shown in Figure 183. Morris and his co-workers constructed more than 70 different life tables for the different years and for different places.

The next step was to analyze the losses operating in each phase of the life cycle. There is a large but relatively constant loss of larvae in the instar I stage and this is caused by dispersal. These larvae often spin a silk thread and launch themselves into the wind to be carried for long distances. There is a second period of even heavier loss in the large larval stages (instars III to VI) during June, and variation in the total survival rate for a particular generation depends largely on variations in this loss of large larvae.

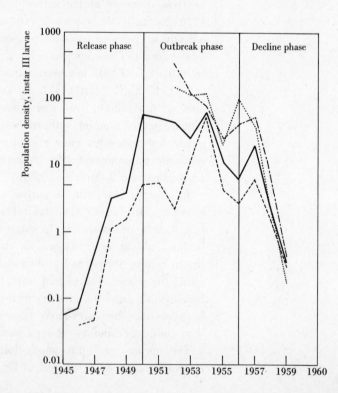

FIGURE 182

Population trends in the spruce budworm in four forest stands of northern New Brunswick. (After Morris 1963.)

TABLE 22

Life table for the 1952–1953 generation of the spruce budworm on plot G4 in the Green River watershed of New Brunswick

Age interval, x	No.[a] alive at start of age interval, l_x	Factor responsible for mortality	No.[a] dying during age interval, d_x	Mortality rate (%), $100q_x$
Eggs	174	Parasites	3	2
		Predators	15	9
		Other	1	1
		Total	19	11
Instar I	155	Dispersal	74.4	48
Hibernacula	80.6	Winter	13.7	17
Instar II	66.9	Dispersal	42.2	63
Instars III–VI	24.7	Parasites	8.92	36
		Disease	0.54	2
		Birds	3.39	14
		Other	10.57	43
		Total	23.42	95
Pupae	1.28	Parasites	0.10	8
		Predators	0.13	10
		Other	0.23	18
		Total	0.46	36
Moths	0.82		0.82	100
Total for generation (egg to adult)			173.18	99.53

[a] All numbers expressed per 10 sq. ft of branch surface.
SOURCE: After Morris and Miller (1954).

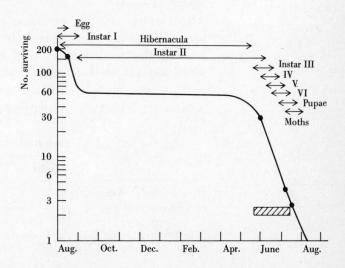

FIGURE 183

Average survivorship curve for the spruce budworm during the 1945–1960 outbreak in New Brunswick. This insect has one generation per year, and females can lay 200 eggs. Regular census points on curve are indicated by dots, and the critical large larval stage in early summer is indicated by crosshatching. (After Miller 1963.)

Once we have located this key* stage in the life cycle we can try to find out what determines the losses of that stage. Seven factors that might affect the survival of these large larvae were studied by Morris and his co-workers: weather, parasites, predators, diseases, starvation, insecticides, and soil factors associated with the nature of the forest stand. Let us consider each of these factors briefly.

Insect parasites did not seem to play a necessary part in stopping this spruce budworm outbreak. The amount of parasitism on the large larval stages actually decreased as the density of the budworm increased. This was a surprising result to many entomologists, who assumed with Nicholson that most insect populations were held in check by insect parasites (see page 273).

Some predators were strongly affected by the outbreak of spruce budworm. Red squirrels, for example, eat considerable numbers of budworm when they are abundant. Spiders also prey on budworms. Nevertheless, only a minute fraction of the budworms could be eaten by all these predators during the outbreak; they are swamped by too many prey (see Figure 145). Consequently, predators did not stop the budworm epidemic.

Many diseases affect the spruce budworm, but all of them are of low virulence. There was no evidence of any widespread mortality due to disease in this outbreak; hence disease was dismissed as an adequate explanation for the decline of the budworm outbreak.

About 6 million acres of forest in New Brunswick were sprayed with DDT one or more times between 1952 and 1958 to protect the forest from the spruce budworm. After the immediate high mortality due to the insecticide, there was an *increase* in survival rates of the budworms for the next two generations, and the budworm thus compensated for this heavy mortality. The outbreak declined at the same time on the sprayed and on the unsprayed areas.

The spruce budworm can cause heavy tree mortality over large forest areas because the larvae completely defoliate the trees. This led many to postulate that the outbreak ended because of larval starvation, the budworm having eaten itself out of food. Survival of the large larvae was measured on moderately-infested and severely-infested stands, with results that were the opposite of what one might have expected:

| | Infestation | |
	Moderate	Severe
Mean survival of instar II–VI larvae (%)	*6.1*	*34.4*

*The key stage in the life cycle is usually the stage suffering the highest and also the most variable losses. See Morris (1957) for further discussion.

This large larval stage is the most critical one from the point of view of competition for food. The critical life-cycle stage, then, survived relatively *better* in severe infestations where much defoliation occurred and many trees were killed. The reason for this seems to be that there is an advantage over predators and parasites when large numbers of larvae are present, and total survival improves as density rises. There was no evidence that direct mortality through larval starvation was an important factor causing the outbreak to stop.

Two factors seemed to be most important for the development of an outbreak: *weather* and *forest-stand factors*. Periodic outbreaks of the spruce budworm appear to be part of a natural cycle of events associated with the maturing of extensive and continuous areas of balsam fir and with climatic variation. The survival of the late larval stages is favored by dry, sunny summer weather. Larvae do not feed well in wet weather and they also become more susceptible to diseases. Four of the five summers from 1954 to 1958 were wet and cold and hence unfavorable to larval survival; during these summers the outbreak collapsed (Figure 184). This correlation between weather pattern and the population outbreak has led to the postulation of *climatic release*—the budworm is released from its low-level endemic phase by a series of years with favorable summer weather.

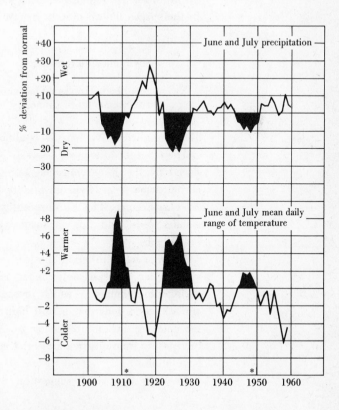

FIGURE 184

Percentage deviation from normal summer rainfall and temperature for meteorological stations in New Brunswick. Spruce budworm outbreaks began in 1912 and 1949. (After Morris 1963.)

The action of forest-stand factors on the development of outbreaks is not clear. Mature continuous stands of balsam fir forests are known to be most vulnerable to attack; exactly why this is so remains unknown. During the outbreak, populations increased at a more rapid rate in mature fir stands than in immature stands. It was first thought that staminate flower production, which is higher in mature forests and is a favored larval food, might be the explanation; but no relationship could be found between larval survival and staminate flower production.

Maturity of the forest leads to more crown exposure of the trees, and some workers have suggested that this is the key factor. More crown exposure to sunlight favors large larval development and survival through microclimatic changes in evaporation. This ties in with the postulated weather effect of dry summers. Immature stands of balsam fir or stands shaded by heavy growth of birch and poplars never develop high budworm populations. Another factor involved is that female moths prefer to lay their eggs in the most dominant and exposed trees.

Possible qualitative differences among individuals were not studied in this investigation, and this represents a major gap. One reason for thinking this is some recent work by Campbell (1962) on the genetics of the spruce budworm. Campbell has suggested a possible genetic basis for explaining the outbreak. He found that there were two different types of X chromosomes in the spruce budworm (sex determination is XX = male, X– = female):

X_H large body size, slow larval development, small eggs, high fecundity, low environmental resistance

X_L small body size, rapid larval development, large eggs, low fecundity, high environmental resistance

The fecundity of X_H females is almost double that of X_L females.

These large differences between X_H and X_L individuals seem to be produced by the X chromosome acting on the rate of cell division. The X_H chromosome seems to cause a more rapid rate of cell division than does the X_L chromosome. The X_H chromosome produces individuals with more, and smaller cells, and this in turn causes a higher metabolic rate in these individuals.

Weather has a differential selective effect on these two genotypes. X_H individuals can increase only under ideal weather—cold winters, dry, warm springs and summers—which presage the spruce budworm outbreaks. Thus climatic conditions that permit high survival also elicit a genetic response—the increase in the frequency of X_H individuals—which leads to a vast increase in reproductive potential and other physiological changes in the population.

There is also some suggestion that the X_H females are nonmigratory, whereas the X_L females do disperse. This self-regulatory hypothesis could be diagrammed as follows:

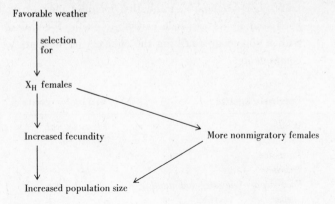

The converse would apply in conditions of unfavorable weather. Unfortunately this hypothesis was suggested after the budworm outbreak had dissipated, and there is no information on its possible role in the field.

To summarize: Outbreaks of the spruce budworm are associated with mature, continuous balsam fir forests and a series of warm dry summers. The exact mechanism of how this occurs remains obscure. Parasites, predators, disease, and food shortage did not appear to cause the outbreak to collapse. Weather seemed most important, and possible genetic changes over the outbreak were not studied.

SUMMARY

Let us try to abstract from these cases a series of steps that define a population study. The first step must be to define the problem under study: What exactly do you want to explain? This is necessary because there is not only *one* question that we can ask but *many* different questions. The object of many studies is to understand why numbers change from year to year, but other questions can be asked, such as: Why are numbers higher in one area than in another area? Or, why are numbers stable in one population and highly variable in another population of the same species? These questions can be broadly classified along the lines suggested by physics; some are questions of *dynamics*, of changes in numbers; others are questions of *statics*, of equilibrium conditions and average values.

In questions of dynamics, which seek to explain changes in numbers, we begin by finding if there is a critical stage of the life cycle or a critical time of the year. Often the very young stages of development are the key to understanding why numbers change from year to year, and other stages of the life cycle need not be studied in detail. If we can pinpoint a stage as critical, we can then determine what factors operate to determine losses at that stage, keeping in mind that changes may occur both in the organism itself and in its extrinsic causes of death. We thus finish our investigation with a statement ascribing the changes in numbers to one or more of these components:

Extrinsic agents	Intrinsic agents
Weather	*Physiological*
Predators	*Behavioral*
Parasites	
Diseases	
Food supply (quantity and quality)	
Shelter	

In the simplest cases we do not have to worry about intrinsic changes in individual quality, but this is not always true.

We are a long way from being able to answer questions of dynamics in a comprehensive way, and we are unable to generalize about population changes. How individualistic are populations? If we can understand spruce budworm outbreaks in New Brunswick, will we also understand them in Ontario? Will we be able to generalize to all defoliating forest insects?

Questions of statics, which seek to explain equilibrium conditions, should be more easily tested because at equilibrium the birth rate must equal the death rate and none of the details of dynamics need be considered. We shall discuss some examples of this in Chapter 17. If we wish to know why one area supports more animals than another area, we can experimentally manipulate variables to see if, for example, areas with more predators have lower average densities.

Perhaps the principal message these case studies should leave is that natural populations are very complex systems that we do not fully understand in a single case, and that all encompassing theories and simple generalizations are impossible without a great deal more experimental work on field populations.

SELECTED REFERENCES

1 Locusts

DEMPSTER, J. P. 1963. The population dynamics of grasshoppers and locusts. *Biol. Rev.* 38:490–529.

KENNEDY, J. S. 1956. Phase transformation in locust biology. *Biol. Rev.* 31:349–370.

LEA, A. 1968. Natural regulation and artificial control of brown locust numbers. *J. Entomol. Soc. S. Africa* 31:97–112.

2 Prairie Grasses

WEAVER, J. E., and F. W. ALBERTSON. 1956. *Grasslands of the Great Plains*. Johnsen Publishing Co., Lincoln, Nebr.

3 Planaria

REYNOLDSON, T. B. 1966. The distribution and abundance of lake-dwelling triclads —towards a hypothesis. *Advances Ecol. Res.* 3:1–71.

4 Cheatgrass

HARRIS, G. A. 1967. Some competitive relationships between *Agropyron spicatum* and *Bromus tectorum*. *Ecol. Monogr.* 37:89–111.

5 Great Tit

KLUYVER, H. N. 1966. Regulation of a bird population. *Ostrich* 6:389–396.

KREBS, J. R. 1971. Territory and breeding density in the great tit, *Parus major* L. *Ecology* 52:2–22.

LACK, D. 1966. *Population Studies of Birds*. Oxford University Press, New York.

6 Western Tent Caterpillar

WELLINGTON, W. G. 1964. Qualitative changes in populations in unstable environments. *Can. Entomol.* 96:436–451.

7 Range Deterioration

HASTINGS, J. R., and R. M. TURNER. 1965. *The Changing Mile*. University of Arizona Press, Tucson.

8 Saguaro

NIERING, W. A., R. H. WHITTAKER, and C. H. LOWE. 1963. The saguaro: a population in relation to environment. *Science* 142:15–23.

9 Spruce Budworm

MORRIS, R. F. (ed.). 1963. The dynamics of epidemic spruce budworm populations. *Mem. Entomol. Soc. Can. No. 31.* 332 pp.

QUESTIONS AND PROBLEMS

1 Shreve (1910) states that saguaro less than 60 years old formed 36% of the population on one site and hence average life expectancy for the giant cactus was 175 years. How could he make this calculation? What assumptions must be made to do this?

2 Apply the theory of Nicholson and Smith on population regulation by biotic factors to the locust example and the saguaro example and suggest experiments to test any hypotheses arising from your analysis. Do the same with the ideas of Andrewartha and Birch on climatic control.

3 Hairston, Smith, and Slobodkin (1960) argued that in general plants are abundant and largely intact and are rarely killed by meteorological catastrophes. Thus green plants must not be limited by herbivores or by catastrophes but must be limited by exhaustion of a resource, usually light or water. Herbivores in general do not destroy all their food plants and are not limited by weather factors, so they must in general be limited by predation and parasitism. Discuss the relevance of these conclusions to the example of the western tent caterpillar and that of the spruce budworm.

4 Key (1950, p. 403) states that "the whole field of locust ecology and epidemiology can be studied without reference to phases." Discuss.

5 Devise a comprehensive plan to determine the causes for population outbreaks in one of the African locusts. Include in your plan a list of specific questions to be asked and the priority assigned to each, and a list of suggested experiments with possible outcomes and their interpretation.

6 Is it necessary to know the causes of death to understand the natural regulation of populations? Chitty (1960, p. 106), in the following statement, argues that it is not:

In contrast to hypotheses according to which the animals die a violent death from epidemics, predators, parasites, climatic catastrophes, or shock disease, no specific causes of death are postulated. Nor for the following reasons is it thought to be profitable to try to discover them. At various times in its life an animal has a number of experiences, the last of which, naturally enough, is followed by death. If death comes through a pure accident, such as drowning, most of the animal's previous experiences will be irrelevant to its chances of survival. In other cases, however, many circumstances in its earlier life are likely to affect its probability of dying later on. . . . In order to understand a particular death rate it may be more important to examine early events of this sort than those immediately associated with death.

Discuss this problem with reference to some of the examples discussed in this chapter.

7 In Chapter 14 (page 273) the biotic school argued that the percentage destruction caused by a mortality factor was *not* necessarily important in determining whether it was an important cause of population control. Yet in our discussion of the spruce budworm (page 336) we dismissed diseases as unimportant because none caused extensive mortality. Discuss this apparent contradiction.

8 Analyze critically the theory of climatic release for the spruce budworm outbreak. Utilize the data given in Figures 182 and 184, and discuss methods of testing the general hypothesis of climatic release as an explanation of outbreaks.

16   *Applied problems I*

THE OPTIMUM-YIELD PROBLEM

To manage a population effectively we must have some understanding of its dynamics. Almost all of human history might be said to illustrate this idea in graphic detail, and a list of populations destroyed by inadequate management should be both a warning and a stimulus for us to achieve some understanding of harvesting principles. The central problem of economically-oriented fields such as forestry, agriculture, fisheries, and wildlife management is how to produce the greatest crop without endangering the resource being harvested. The problem may be illustrated with a simple example from forestry. If you were managing a forest woodlot that was growing to maturity, you would obviously not cut the trees when they are saplings because this would give little wood production and less profit. At the other extreme, you would prevent the trees from growing too old and starting to rot, since again you would get little timber to sell. Somewhere between these two extremes will be some optimum point to harvest the trees, and the problem is how to locate it.

Next to forestry and agriculture, the greatest amount of work on the problem of optimum yield has been done in fishery biology. This is because of the tremendous economic importance of marine fisheries in particular.

Many marine fisheries have dwindled in size during the last 60 years because of overfishing, and this has stimulated a great deal of research on "the overfishing problem."

For any harvested population the important unit of measure is the crop or *yield*. The yield may be expressed in *numbers* or *weight* of organisms and always involves some unit of time (often a year). We are interested in obtaining from any harvested population the optimum yield, and we shall leave the concept of optimum yield purposely vague in order to require a definition of "optimum." In a simple situation the optimum yield will be the *maximum* yield in biomass, but in more complex situations it may be the maximum yield of fish over 4 pounds, or maximum number of deer with antlers of certain sizes, or maximum weight of edible protein. The definition of optimum yield may thus include economic variables, esthetic judgments, and social considerations; and it becomes involved with questions of harvesting strategy, which are critical to large industries such as fishing and forestry. In our discussion we shall consider only the simple situation of maximum yield in biomass as the optimum yield. Implicit in the optimum-yield concept is the idea of a sustained yield over a long time period.

Russell (1931) was one of the first to deal in detail with the optimum-yield problem. In any exploited population there will usually be a portion of the population that cannot be caught by the type of gear used or that are purposely not harvested. In the case of a fishery, we can show this as

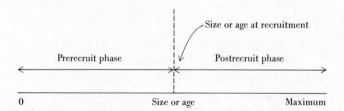

For a fishery, interest normally centers on yield in weight. Russell pointed out that two factors decrease the weight of the catchable stock during a year: natural mortality and fishing mortality. Similarly, two factors increase the weight of the stock: growth and recruitment. Consequently, one can write a simple equation to describe this relationship:

$$S_2 = S_1 + R + G - M - F$$

where

S_2 = weight of the catchable stock at the end of the year
S_1 = weight of the catchable stock at the start of the year
R = weight of new recruits
G = growth in weight of fish remaining alive
M = weight of fish removed by natural deaths
F = yield to fishery

If we wish to balance the fish population, $S_1 = S_2$, and hence

$$R + G = M + F$$

This means that in an unexploited stage, in which the stock remains approximately constant from one year to the next, all growth and recruitment is on the average balanced by natural mortality. When exploitation begins, the size of the exploited population is usually reduced, and the loss to the fishery is made up by (1) greater recruitment rate, or (2) greater growth rate, or (3) reduced natural mortality. In some populations none of these three occurs, and the population is exploited to extinction.

Note that stability at *any* level of population density is described by the equation

Recruitment + growth = natural losses + fishing yield

The crucial question thus arises: What level of population stabilization safely permits the greatest weight of catch to the fishery? One of the early attempts to solve this problem was made by Graham (1935), who proposed the *sigmoid-curve theory*.

Start by considering a very small stock of fish in an empty area of the sea, said Graham. At what rate will such a stock increase its weight? Graham suggested that the growth of this population would follow a sigmoid curve like the one described by the logistic equation (Figure 185). Initially the population grows slowly in absolute size, reaches a maximum rate of increase near the middle of the curve, and grows slowly again as it approaches the asymptote of maximal density. We can use the terminology of the logistic equation to show that two factors interact to determine the amount of increase per year. Let $K = 200$ units and $r_m = 1.0$ for simplicity:

Point on curve	Population size (N)	$\dfrac{K - N}{K}$	$r_m N$	Amount of increase (dN/dt)
S_1	20	0.90	20	18
S_2	50	0.75	50	38
S_3	100	0.50	100	50
S_4	150	0.25	150	38
S_5	180	0.10	180	18

According to the logistic, the amount of population increase is

$$\frac{dN}{dt} = r_m N \left(\frac{K - N}{K} \right)$$

and this is maximal at the midpoint of the curve (S_3).

If you wish to maintain the maximal yield from such a population, Graham pointed out, you should keep the stock around point S_3 of the curve.

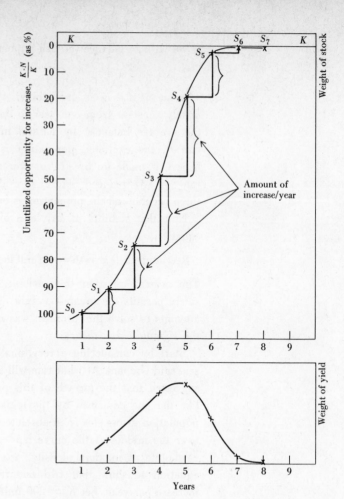

FIGURE 185

Sigmoid curve to describe the growth of a population that could be exploited. The amount of increase per year is the yield that could be taken by the fishery. (After Graham 1939.)

The important point here is that the highest production from such a population is not near the top of the curve where the fish population is relatively dense, but at a lower density. This can be expressed as a rule of exploitation: *Maximum yield is obtained from populations at less than maximum density.*

As we have already mentioned, the logistic growth model is not very realistic for complex animal populations in nature. For this reason the sigmoid-curve theory has been replaced by more comprehensive models.

All the vital statistics of an exploited population—recruitment, growth, and natural mortality—may be a function of population density and also of age composition. Since in most fisheries we do not know how these vital statistics relate to density or age, we employ some simplifying assumptions. Two alternative approaches have been developed for determining optimum yield; these are called *logistic-type models* and *dynamic pool models* (Schaefer 1968).

In logistic-type models we do not distinguish growth, recruitment, and natural mortality but combine these into a single measure, rate of population increase, which is a function of population size. The "sigmoid-curve theory" of Graham is a classic example of this type of model. The general case can be written:

rate of population increase = f(population size) − amount of fishing losses

If we specify that the function of population size in the above equation is a simple linear function,

$$f(\text{population size}) = \frac{r_m}{K}(K - N)$$

we obtain the logistic equation modified for fishing losses:

$$\frac{dN}{dt} = r_m N \left(\frac{K - N}{K}\right) - qXN$$

where
    N = population size
    t = time
    r_m = innate capacity for increase
    K = asymptotic density (in absence of fishing)
    q = constant
    X = amount of fishing effort (so qX = fishing mortality rate)

This model, although crude, may be useful in populations that are in approximately steady states and not changing greatly from year to year.

DYNAMIC POOL MODELS

In these models various simplifying assumptions are made. Natural mortality rate is assumed constant, independent of density, and the same for all ages. Growth rates are assumed to be age specific but not related to population density. Fishing mortality (effort) is assumed to act just like natural mortality, to be independent of density, and constant for all ages of fish. The object is to determine what yield a given level of fishing mortality will produce. In this simple model, the population size of R recruits after t years in the fished population is given by the formula for geometric decrease:

$$N_t = Re^{-(F+M)t}$$

where
    N_t = number of recruits alive at t years after entering fishery
    t = time in years since recruits entered fishery
    R = number of original recruits
    F = instantaneous fishing mortality rate
    M = instantaneous natural mortality rate

This is the familiar curve of geometric increase (or decrease). If $R = 1$, this formula gives the fraction of recruits alive at any time since entering the fishery. The yield to the fishery in this simple model is defined as

Yield = (number in age class) $\times$ (average weight) $\times$ (fishing mortality rate)

summed over all age classes caught in the fishery. This can be written

$$Y = \sum_{t=t_c}^{\infty} F N_t W_t$$

where

Y = yield in weight for a year
F = instantaneous fishing mortality rate per year
N_t = population size of age t fish
W_t = average weight of age t fish
t_c = age at which fish enter the fishery

Let us illustrate this simple dynamic pool model with an example from the European fishery for plaice (*Pleuronectes platessa*) in the North Sea. The plaice is a shallow-water flatfish which is an important commercial species in the North Sea. The females spawn in midwinter when they are 5 to 7 years old and the males are 4 to 6 years old. Females can lay up to 350,000 fertile eggs, and this enormous reproductive rate is balanced by very high mortality. On the average all but 10 animals out of every 1 million eggs must die before reaching maturity, and the actual range observed by Beverton (1962) during 26 years was only between 999,970 and 999,995 dying of every 1 million laid. Much of this loss occurs during the pelagic phase, when the eggs float in the plankton until hatching, and the larval plaice are carried about by water currents in the North Sea. After about 2 months the larval plaice settle out on nursery areas off the sandy coasts of Holland, Denmark, and Germany. There the young plaice remain until between 2 and 3 years of age, when they begin to move off the coast and toward the middle of the North Sea. They enter the commercial fishery between 3 and 5 years of age, at a length of 20 to 30 cm.

The plaice population has remained fairly stable, with the exception of the periods during World Wars I and II, when fishing was reduced and stocks increased. We can illustrate a dynamic pool model most easily in this type of near-equilibrium condition. First, we must determine growth rate with respect to age in the plaice, and we can do that with samples from the fishery (Figure 186). We assume in this simple model that growth does not depend on the population density. Second, we need to specify recruitment, and we assume a constant number of recruits each year. For the plaice this is not an unreasonable first approximation (Figure 186). Third, we must determine the natural mortality rate. We can do this by mark-and-recapture techniques (Chapter 9) or by indirect means. We assume in the

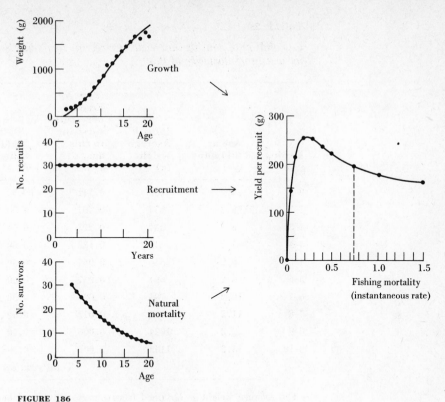

FIGURE 186

*Simple model of equilibrium yield for plaice in the North Sea. The
fishing intensity before World War II is indicated by the dashed line.
(After Beverton and Holt 1957.)*

simple case that natural mortality is constant at all ages and at all population densities. For the plaice Beverton and Holt (1957) estimate $M = 0.10$,
and in Figure 186 it is shown how a cohort of recruits would decline according to predictions of natural mortality *only*.

Since recruitment is assumed constant, we can express the yield as yield
per recruit, and by summing the three factors we obtain the yield curve
shown in Figure 186. One example of how this yield for plaice was calculated for a fishing mortality of 0.5 is given in Table 23. This is only an
approximate calculation because we should use calculus instead of finite
summation to find the yield (details in Beverton and Holt 1957). Figure 186
also shows the pre-World War II fishing intensity ($F = 0.73$), which was
clearly not at the point of optimum yield.

This approach can give the annual equilibrium yield of the fishery, but it
has hidden in it one flaw: It assumes that a constant number of recruits
enter the usable stock every year. But does any fishery in fact have a con-

TABLE 23

Calculation of equilibrium yield per recruit for North Sea plaice for a fishing mortality of 0.5[a]

Fishing year	Age at midpoint (yr)	$(1) = W_t$ Average weight (g)	$(2) = N_t$ Fraction of recruits surviving to this age, $e^{-(F+M)t}$	(3) Yield to fishery, F	Product $(1) \times (2) \times (3)$
0–1	4.2	158	0.741	0.50	58.54
1–2	5.2	237	0.407	0.50	48.23
2–3	6.2	331	0.223	0.50	36.91
3–4	7.2	435	0.122	0.50	26.54
4–5	8.2	546	0.067	0.50	18.29
5–6	9.2	664	0.037	0.50	12.28
6–7	10.2	784	0.020	0.50	7.84
7–8	11.2	904	0.011	0.50	4.97
8–9	12.2	1024	0.006	0.50	3.07
9–10	13.2	1143	0.003	0.50	1.71

Total yield per recruit 218.38 g

[a] The average weight is obtained from the growth curve shown in Figure 186. The fraction of recruits is calculated by applying a constant loss per year of $(F + M)$, which in this example is $(0.5 + 0.1)$. The yield per recruit is obtained from the formula

$$Y = \sum_{t_c}^{\infty} FN_tW_t$$

The age at recruitment is 3.7 years.

stant recruitment? A constant recruitment implies that the number of recruits does not depend on population size; to put it another way, it assumes that two adult fish could produce the same number of progeny as 10,000 adults. This is on the face of it quite impossible, and we are thus led to inquire into the relationship between population size (stock) and recruitment. The remarkable result is that in no case of a major fishery is there any detectable relationship between density and recruitment! Figure 187 illustrates this for North Sea plaice and Figure 188 for sockeye salmon of Karluk River, Alaska.

Why should this be? Recruitment in fish populations is often variable from one year to the next, and this variation is presumed to be caused by weather effects on the survival of young fish. The variation seems to swamp out any density effects that might occur, with results like those in Figure 188. The variability in recruitment may be quite different in different

FIGURE 187

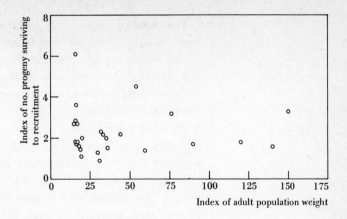

FIGURE 187

Stock and recruitment relationship in the plaice of the North Sea. The number of progeny surviving to recruitment bears no relation to the biomass of adult fish. (After Beverton 1962.)

species. For example, in the North Sea haddock, the abundance at recruitment has varied 500-fold in 30 years of study, whereas the variation in recruitment of the North Sea plaice has been only sixfold in 26 years of study (Beverton 1962). Recruitment is independent of stock density both in the plaice and in the haddock.

This dilemma, the absence of any detectable relation between stock and recruitment, can easily be resolved on the theoretical level because it involves the question of population regulation. Some component of the vital statistics—births, deaths, and dispersal—must be related to population density in order to prevent unlimited population growth. As we saw in Chapter 11, population growth cannot be curtailed unless the net reproduction curve is depressed below 1.0 at high population densities (Figure 86). This can occur by adult mortality increasing with density, but fishery ecologists think that natural mortality of adult fish is not related to density. Consequently, density-dependent regulation can occur only in the early-life-cycle stages.

FIGURE 188

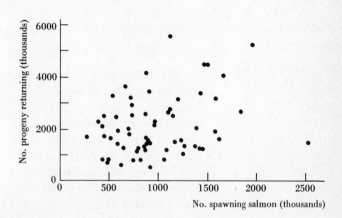

FIGURE 188

Stock and recruitment relationship of sockeye salmon of Karluk River, Alaska, 1887–1948. There is no clear indication that allowing more spawners past the fishery will produce a larger return. (After Rounsefell 1958.)

The essential requirement for stock-recruitment relations is that recruitment falls off at high population densities. Three possible models are shown in Figure 189. Because there is so much environmental "noise" in this relationship, there seems at the moment to be no way of deciding the shape of these stock-recruitment curves. Ricker (1958, Chap. 11) discusses this problem in detail.

We have treated fishing mortality in the same way that we treated natural mortality, using man as just another "predator" of the system. This fishing mortality rate must be converted into fishing effort before the results of a yield analysis, such as that in Figure 186, can be applied to an operating fishery. This application is a complex problem that revolves about the types of gear used, efficiency of gear, the interactions between different units of gear, and the spatial and seasonal patterns of exploitation. Beverton and Holt (1957, Secs. 12–14) discuss these problems in some detail, and the analysis depends on the type of fishery operation.

Once we have built a dynamic pool model of a fishery we can test it by regulating the fishery accordingly. Thus in the North Sea plaice we would predict from Figure 186 that an increased yield would result from lowering fishing mortality to one-third or one-half the pre-war level of 0.73. This is the critical test of any model: Does it predict accurately? And this important step has yet to be taken with any model. Alternatively, we can use the model (assuming it is accurate) to investigate the effect of various changes in the vital statistics on the yield to the fishery. One example will illustrate this. Suppose the natural mortality of plaice in the North Sea changes. What effect will this have on the yield curve shown in Figure 186, where natural mortality (M) is assumed to be 0.10? Figure 190 shows the results of changing natural mortality rates over a range from $M = 0.05$ to 0.50. Note that the maximum in the yield curve is reduced as natural mortality increases, so maximum yield when $M = 0.50$ could be achieved only at very high fishing intensities. This emphasizes the importance of estimating natural mortality accurately.

FIGURE 189

Possible relations between stock and recruitment. Curve a represents constant recruitment and curve b recruitment directly proportional to stock size. Curve c with a descending upper section is the Ricker model, and curve d, which tends to plateau, is the Beverton and Holt model. (After Gulland 1962.)

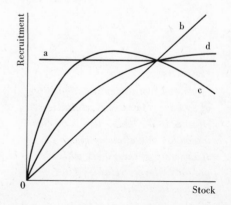

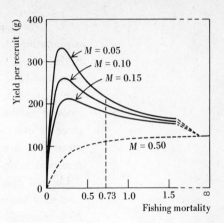

FIGURE 190

Yield curves for plaice in the North Sea. The effect of varying natural mortality from M = 0.05 to 0.50 is to flatten and finally eliminate the peak in the yield curve at low fishing intensities. (After Beverton and Holt 1957.)

LABORATORY STUDIES

Populations vary greatly in their ability to withstand sustained losses. This ability is shown in striking fashion by some insect populations. Nicholson (1954a) maintained sheep blowfly populations in laboratory cultures and destroyed a percentage of the newly-emergent adults. The result of this induced "predation" is summarized in Table 24. The population compensated for the losses in two ways: (1) Adult lifespan increased, and (2) birth rate increased. These compensations produced an increase in the number of new adults emerging per day, so even with 90% destruction, the average adult population was reduced only to one-third that of the control. These laboratory populations were limited by the amount of food supplied to the adults, and the destruction of adults thus alleviated competition for food.

TABLE 24

Compensatory reaction of laboratory populations of the Australian sheep blowfly (Lucilia cuprina) *to the destruction of adult flies*

Emerging adults destroyed (%)	Adults emerging per day	Mean adult population	Mean adult lifespan (days)	Mean no. viable eggs laid per adult per day
0	573	2520	4.4	0.25
50	712	2335	6.6	0.33
75	878	1588	7.2	0.60
90	1260	878	7.0	1.55

SOURCE: After Nicholson (1954a).

A particularly clear demonstration of the relationship among rate of exploitation, population size, and yield is shown in the experimental work of Silliman and Gutsell (1958) on guppies (*Lebistes reticulatus*) in laboratory aquaria. They maintained two populations as unmanipulated controls and two populations as experimental fisheries subjected to a sequence of four rates of fishing (Figure 191). Populations were counted once each week and cropped every third week, so (for example) a 25% cropping rate would mean that every fourth fish was removed from this population during the census at weeks 3, 6, 9, and so on.

Control guppy populations reached a stationary plateau by week 60 and remained there until the end of the experiment in week 174. Cropping at 25% triweekly reduced the experimental populations to about 15 g biomass compared with 32 g for the controls. Reduction of the cropping to 10% increased both experimental populations to about 23 g biomass, and the imposition of 50% cropping in week 121 caused a decline in population size to about 7 g. A cropping intensity of 75% every third week was too

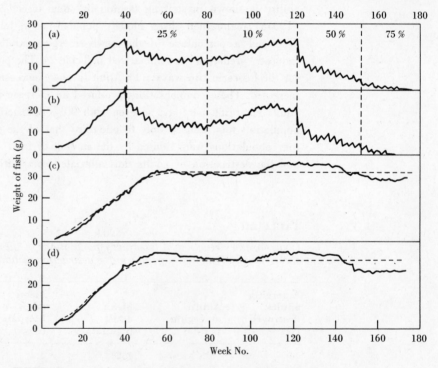

FIGURE 191

Population biomass changes in guppies maintained in the laboratory. (c) and (d) are control populations that are not exploited. (a) and (b) are experimental populations subjected to harvesting after week 40 at the indicated rates. (After Silliman and Gutsell 1958.)

great for these fish to withstand, and both experimental populations were driven extinct by this severe "overfishing."

We can use these data to construct a yield curve directly. We weigh the fish removed at each cropping and obtain these results:

Exploitation rate (%)	Weeks	Experimental population (av. wt. in g/cropping)	
		A	B
25	61–76	3.35	3.58
10	100–118	2.20	2.51
50	136–148	3.88	3.58
75	163–172	0.82	0.40

Only data for the last half of each exploitation period are used, to approximate an equilibrium fishery condition.

These are the yields to the "fishery." We now need to express the fishing intensity as an instantaneous mortality rate (F):

$$\frac{\text{percentage exploitation}}{100} = 1 - e^{-F}$$

and consequently we obtain (rates per 3 weeks)

Percentage exploitation	Instantaneous fishing mortality
25	0.29
10	0.11
50	0.69
75	1.39

We plot fishing mortality against yield to obtain the yield curve for guppies shown in Figure 192. There is a maximum yield to be obtained at exploitation rates between 30 and 40%, with a population biomass of 8 to 12 grams compared with 32 g in unexploited controls.

The experiments on guppies by Silliman and Gutsell (1958) illustrate well four principles of exploitation:

1 Any exploitation of a population reduces its abundance, and the greater the exploitation, the smaller the population becomes.

2 Below a certain level of exploitation populations are resilient and increase survival or growth to compensate for removals.

3 Exploitation rates may be raised to a point where they cause extinction of the resource.

FIGURE 192

Equilibrium yield in relation to fishing intensity for the laboratory populations of guppies studied by Silliman and Gutsell (1958). Maximum yield could be obtained at a fishing mortality of approximately F = 0.5 (an exploitation rate of 40% removal triweekly). Closed circles, population A; open circles, population B. (After Silliman and Gutsell 1958.)

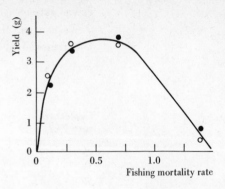

4 Somewhere between no exploitation and excessive exploitation there is a level of maximum sustained yield.

Two case studies of populations that were overexploited will now be presented to illustrate principle 3.

PACIFIC SARDINE FISHERY

The Pacific sardine was not commercially exploited in any amount until World War I, when the demand for food increased. The catch rose to a peak in 1936 and has since fallen to almost nothing (Figure 193). The demand for sardines has always been high, and this decline in the catch is not a result of economic changes. Many of the sardinelike fishes are impor-

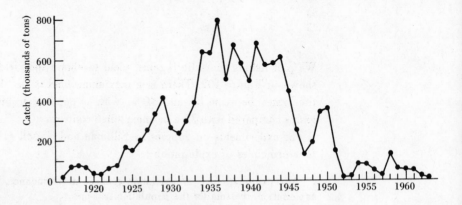

FIGURE 193

Annual catch of sardines (Sardinops caerulea) along the Pacific Coast of North America. (After Murphy 1966.)

tant in other world fisheries, and all seem subject to great variations in yield from year to year.

Adequate fishery statistics are available for the Pacific sardine from 1932 on, and Murphy (1966) has analyzed these. The fishery operates on two distinct "races" or stocks of sardine—a northern race, which is larger and dominated the fishery until 1949, and a southern race, which is smaller and has dominated the fishery since 1949. Coincident with this shift in dominance the natural mortality rate increased:

	Estimated annual mortality rate from natural causes
1932–1949 (*northern race*)	*0.33*
1950–1960 (*southern race*)	*0.55*

The reason the southern race has a higher mortality rate is not known. Only about half of age II fish are spawners in the area of the northern race, but all age II fish spawn in the area of the southern race.

The size of the sardine population has declined greatly since 1932 (Figure 194). There is no relationship between the breeding stocks of sardines and the subsequent number of progeny recruited. The variation in the amount of recruitment from year to year (Figure 195) is great and is presumably due to some environmental effect, but simple variables such as temperature seem not to be the cause of this variation (Murphy 1966).

The age structure of the sardine population has been shifted toward the younger age classes by heavy fishing pressure. This shift may explain the

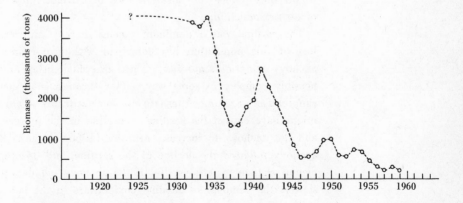

FIGURE 194

Estimated abundance of Pacific sardines along the Pacific Coast of North America. All fish 2 years or older included. Compare with Figure 193. (After Murphy 1966.)

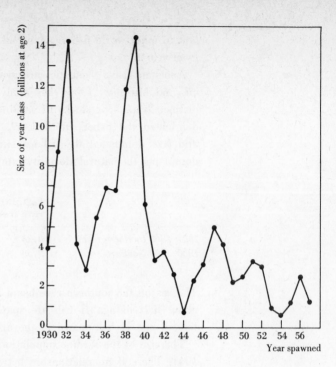

FIGURE 195

Variations in year-class strength in the Pacific sardine. (After Murphy 1966.)

decline of the northern race after 1949. From 1945 to 1950 the population size was small (Figure 196), and over 85% of the sardines were ages II and III. If we assume a failure of reproduction in the northern race for 1949 and 1950 (for an unknown environmental catastrophe), all the 1949 and 1950 year classes would be southern-race fish. The annual loss of about one-third of the adult fish from natural causes plus some fishing mortality would thus reduce the northern race to extremely low levels in two years of no reproduction.

The sardine was a dominant species in the California Current, and the loss of this population has coincided with a rise in the density of the anchovy (*Engraulis mordax*). These two small fishes are similar and might possibly compete in some way, either through food competition or direct cannibalism of young. Alternatively, some sequence of environmental changes might have caused the sardine to decline in the presence of heavy fishing and the anchovy to increase. Murphy (1966) suggests that the rise of the anchovy *followed* the decline of the sardine, and this supports the environmental change hypothesis. But if the anchovy population can increase only slowly, the removal of sardine competitors might not have had instantaneous effects.

The important conclusion from this is that we must treat an exploited species in a definite framework with other species, since the result of harvesting one species may change the environment for its competitors. The maximum sustained yield to a sardine fishery might be different if anchovies were present or absent. In this case the relationship between sardines and anchovies could be tested by shifting the fishery to the anchovy and reducing the remaining pressure on the sardine.

ALASKA SALMON FISHERY

The decline of the Alaska salmon fishery is a good example of overfishing applied to an "inexhaustible resource"; Cooley (1963) has documented how greed, scientific ignorance, politics, and federal mismanagement all collaborated to deplete this fishery resource. Five species of salmon are part of the Pacific salmon fishery, although red (sockeye) salmon and pink salmon are the major commercial species. Adult salmon are caught by the fishery along the Pacific Coast as they return to spawn in freshwater streams. Many Indian tribes along the coast were dependent on salmon as a staple food before the white man began fishing salmon commercially.

Commercial exploitation in Alaska began about 1880 and increased at a slow rate (Figure 197). Most of the salmon taken commercially have been used for canned salmon. The peak year of commercial exploitation was 1936, when 8,500,000 cases of canned salmon were packed (one case is 48 pounds net weight). Since then, the packs have declined to the point that the 1959 pack was at the same level as the 1900 pack. This increase and subsequent decline in the commercial catch did not occur in neighboring British Colum-

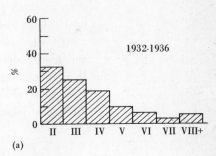
(a)

FIGURE 196

Age composition of the Pacific sardine population (a) in 1932–1936 when the population was large and the fishery was just starting, and (b) in 1955–1959 when the population was severely reduced. Note the shift toward more fish in the younger age groups. (After Murphy 1966.)

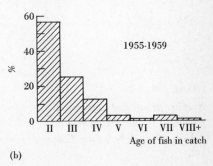
(b)

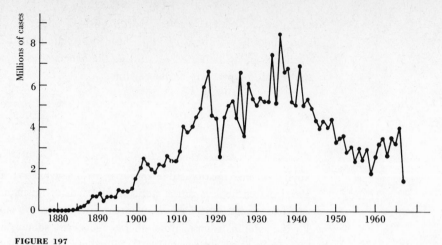

FIGURE 197

Total pack of canned salmon in Alaska, 1878–1967. Each case is 48 pounds net. (Data from Fishery Statistics of the United States.)

bia, and consequently the demise of the Alaska salmon fishery cannot be blamed on global ecological changes.

Throughout this time, the amount of fishing gear used in the Alaska salmon fishery has steadily increased (Figure 198). Thus there were about 200 seine boats operating in 1910 and over 1000 in the 1950s. There were about 1000 gillnet boats operating in 1909 and about 9000 in 1955. This increase in gear (and hence in fishermen) was accompanied by a striking drop in catch per unit of gear. Figure 199 shows that the average gillnet boat caught about 15,000 salmon in 1908 but only 1500 salmon in 1954, a 90% decrease. Thus more and more fishermen have been catching fewer and fewer salmon. This violation of common sense is understandable only in economic terms. The real price of a can of salmon has about tripled from 1910 to 1955, and this permitted the average fisherman to increase his income, at least until 1945, when it began to decline slightly.

FIGURE 198

Number of units of gillnet boat gear used in the Alaska salmon fishery, 1906–1959. (After Cooley 1963.)

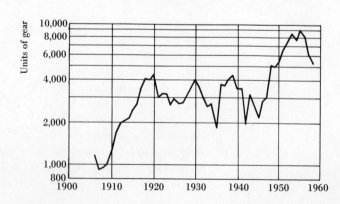

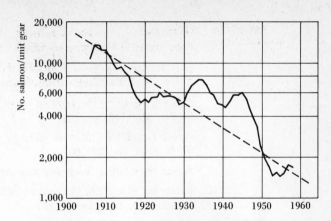

FIGURE 199

*Average number of salmon caught
per unit of gillnet gear in the
Alaska salmon fishery, 1906–1959.
(After Cooley 1963.)*

The core of this overfishing problem and many others lies in the peculiar common-property status of the fishing resource. Salmon fishing is open to everyone who has the equipment needed, and the only way to limit the catch is to limit the efficiency of men and gear. This situation reached the point in the salmon fishery where 4 or 5 days a week would be closed to fishing. Complex regulations have put a great premium on law enforcement and no premium at all on voluntary restraint of the fisherman or the cannery owners.

Part of the reason for the overfishing of the Alaska salmon can be found in ecological ignorance. There was almost no information on the spawning population sizes for most of the major rivers of Alaska until the late 1940s. Population changes in salmon are still not understood. Consequently, there is no way to know how many spawners are needed to produce an adequate return. There has been a tendency to fix on numerical rules, such as allowing 50% of the returning adults to be caught by the fishery and 50% to reach the spawning streams, without the biological basis to know if these are good rules or not.

SUMMARY

To harvest a population in an optimal way we must understand the factors regulating the abundance of that population. That man so frequently mismanages exploited populations like the Pacific sardine is partly a measure of his ignorance of population dynamics. Management of forestry, fishery, and wildlife resources is presently based more on rules of thumb and empirical results than on scientific knowledge and forecasting, and one of the great challenges of modern ecology is to place resource management on a scientific basis. We can all be very good at managing yesterday's populations. When will we be equally adept at managing tomorrow's?

SELECTED REFERENCES

BEVERTON, F. J. H., and S. J. HOLT. 1957. *On the Dynamics of Exploited Fish Populations.* H.M. Stationary Office, London.

CRUTCHFIELD, J. A. (ed.). 1965. *The Fisheries: Problems in Resource Management.* University of Washington Press, Seattle.

GRAHAM, M. 1939. The sigmoid curve and the overfishing problem. *Rapp. Conseil Explor. Mer* 110:15–20.

GROSS, J. E. 1969. Optimum yield in deer and elk populations. *Trans. N. Amer. Wildl. Conf.* 34:372–386.

RICKER, W. E. 1954. Stock and recruitment. *J. Fish. Res. Bd. Can.* 11:559–623.

SCHAEFER, M. B. 1968. Methods of estimating effects of fishing on fish populations. *Trans. Amer. Fish. Soc.* 97:231–241.

SILLIMAN, R. P., and J. S. GUTSELL. 1958. Experimental exploitation of fish populations. *Fish. Bull. (U.S.)* 58(133):215–252.

WATT, K. E. F. 1968. *Ecology and Resource Management.* McGraw-Hill, New York.

QUESTIONS AND PROBLEMS

1 Murphy (1967, p. 733) gives the following estimates* for the vital statistics of the Pacific sardine living under optimal conditions:

Age, x (yr)	l_x	m_x
2	1.000	0.5147
3	0.6703	1.3618
4	0.4493	1.6819
5	0.3012	1.8816
6	0.2019	2.0257
7	0.1353	2.1358
8	0.0907	2.2357
9	0.0608	2.2686
10	0.0408	2.2686
11	0.0273	2.2686
12	0.0183	2.2686
13	0.0123	2.2686

Calculate the net reproductive rate and the innate capacity for increase of this sardine population. Use this value of r_m to calculate a logistic curve for an unexploited sardine population (assume that $K = 2,400,000$ tons and $a = 7.785$). How many years would it take for this unexploited sardine population to recover from a starting point of 10,000 tons to a level of 2,000,000 tons if it followed this logistic curve?

2 What would be the yield per recruit in the North Sea plaice fishery if the fishing mortality were infinitely large? (Data in Table 23.)

*This is a relative life table and fertility table (starting at age 2), and it can be converted to the usual format by dividing the l_x values by 71,000 and multiplying the m_x values by this amount. It is given in this way to avoid cumbersome numbers.

3 Suppose that, in fact, there is no relationship between stock and recruitment in the sockeye salmon (Figure 188). Discuss the implications of this with respect to the various theories of population control (Chapter 14).

4 Construct an equilibrium yield curve showing the relationship between yield (biomass) and hunting mortality rate for a hypothetical deer population with constant recruitment of 1000 fawns per year and an instantaneous natural mortality rate of 0.7 per year for age 0 to 1 and 0.4 per year for older deer. Assume for simplicity that all growth, recruitment, and losses occur at a single point each year and that hunting operates only on animals age 2 and over. The growth curve is as follows:

Age (yr)	Weight (lb)	No. survivors (natural mortality only)
0	10	1000
1	50	497
2	80	333
3	90	223
4	100	150
5	110	100
6	120	67
7	130	45
8	140	30
9	150	20
10	160	14
11	170	9

Calculate the equilibrium yield in numbers for this population at a harvest rate of 20% per year.

5 Plot the following hypothetical reproduction curves (like Figure 189) for a species that reproduces only once (numbers are arbitrary "egg units"):

Population A		**Population B**	
Adult egg production	Progeny egg production	Adult egg production	Progeny egg production
2	4	1	5
4	6	2	8
6	7.5	4	11
8	8	5	12
10	7.5	6	11
12	6	8	8
14	3	10	5
		12	2
		14	1

Use these plots to determine graphically population changes for 20 generations from starting adult stocks of 14, 6, and 2. Introduce random environmental variations to this simple model by flipping a coin each generation and multiplying progeny egg production by 0.5 for heads and 1.5 for tails. What effect does this random factor have on the population curves?

6 Examine the catch statistics for a fishery in your area. Sources of data might be the *Fisheries Statistics of the United States, Fisheries Statistics of Canada,* or the Food and Agricultural Organization's *Yearbook of Fishery Statistics* published by the United Nations. If the fishery you choose has been managed, is there any evidence of overfishing?

7 List criteria by which you might recognize that a population was being over-exploited, and discuss the relative value of different criteria.

8 One of the assumptions of optimum-yield models is that birth, death, and growth responses to population density are repeatable, so that a given population density will always be characterized by the same vital statistics. What mechanisms may make this assumption false?

17   *Applied problems II*

BIOLOGICAL CONTROL

Some species interfere with man's activities, in which case they are assigned the label "pests." One's first idea about pests is to *control* them. Control used in this context means to *control damage*. One of the obvious ways of controlling damage is to reduce the average abundance of the pest species, but there are other ways of reducing damage by pests (such as using insect repellants) which do not affect abundance.

A species is defined as being controlled when it is not causing excessive economic damage, and being uncontrolled when it is. The boundary between these two states will depend on the particular pest. An insect that destroys 4 to 5% of an apple crop may be insignificant biologically but may destroy the grower's margin of profit. Conversely, forest insect pests may defoliate whole areas of forest without bankrupting the lumbering industry.

Biological control is a special type of control in which the damage caused by a pest is reduced or eliminated by a biological agent. This contrasts with *chemical control* and *mechanical control* as one possible way of dealing with pest species. Biological control is an attempt to reduce the average density of a pest population by the introduction of diseases, parasites, or predators. It is thus one aspect of the problem of the natural regulation of population size and may be viewed as a practical application of the problem of what determines average abundance (Chapter 14).

The general procedure dealt with in biological control is this: A pest, often an introduced species, is causing heavy damage. Efforts are then made to find insect predators and parasites in the pest's home country that can be introduced to its new country. If the efforts are successful the pest population is reduced to a level at which no economic damage occurs. Let us look at a couple of examples of biological control.

COTTONY-CUSHION SCALE *(Icerya purchasi)*

One of the most striking and critical successes of biological control concerned the cottony-cushion scale, a small coccid insect that sucks sap from leaves and twigs of citrus trees. This scale insect was first discovered in California in 1872, and by 1887 the whole citrus industry of southern California was threatened with destruction. Because of the size of the infested area, chemical control by cyanide and other sprays was a failure. In 1888 Albert Koebele of the Division of Entomology was sent to Australia by the U.S. government to represent the State Department at an international exposition in Melbourne. As all foreign travel had been restricted for the Division of Entomology, this was the only subterfuge by which an entomologist could travel to Australia to search for parasites of the cottony-cushion scale, a native of Australia. Koebele sent two insects back to California, a small dipteran parasite *Cryptochaetum iceryae* and a predaceous ladybird beetle called the vedalia, *Rodolia cardinalis*. The dipteran parasite was thought to be an important possible agent for control, but Koebele sent the ladybird beetles along apparently without thinking that they could be very useful. In late 1888 the first ladybird beetles were received in California, and by January 1889 a total of 129 individuals had been released near Los Angeles under an infested orange tree covered by a large tent. By April 1889 all the cottony-cushion scales on this tree had been destroyed; the tent was then opened. By June 1889 over 10,000 beetles had been sent to other citrus orchards from this first release point. By October 1889, scarcely 1 year since *Rodolia* was found in Australia by Koebele, the cottony-cushion scale was virtually eliminated from large areas of citrus orchards in southern California. Within 2 years it was difficult to find a single individual of the scale *Icerya*, and this control continued so that the pest was effectively eliminated. The cost: about $1500; the saving: millions of dollars every year. The California Legislature was impressed, and California became a center of activism in promoting the value of biological control (Doutt 1964).

The cottony-cushion scale reappeared with the advent of DDT. Infestations of the scale that had not been seen in over 50 years were found after DDT had eliminated the vedalia beetle from some local areas. Under these circumstances the beetle has to be continuously reintroduced.

Some of the host plants of the cottony-cushion scale are not suitable for the vedalia. For example, the scale infests scotch broom (*Cytisus scoparius*) and maples in central California, but the vedalia will not become established on these plants, for unknown reasons (Clausen 1956). Such host plants serve as a reservoir for the scale, which can recolonize citrus trees.

The great success in controlling the cottony-cushion scale ushered in an era in which biological control was viewed as a panacea for all pest problems. Large numbers of insects were collected from all over the world and released in North America without any testing or quarantine procedures. Fortunately only time and money were wasted with all these importations, and a sequence of repeated failures in control stopped this dangerous policy (Turnbull and Chant 1961).

PRICKLY PEAR *(Opuntia* spp.*)*

Prickly pear is a cactus native to North and South America. There are several hundred species of prickly pear, about 26 of which have been introduced to Australia for garden plants. One species, *Opuntia stricta,* has become a serious weed in Australia. In 1839 *O. stricta* was brought to Australia as a plant in a pot from the southern United States and was planted as a hedge plant in eastern Australia. It gradually got out of control and was recognized as a pest by 1880. By 1900 it occupied some 10,000,000 acres and spread rapidly in Queensland and New South Wales:

	Area (acres) infested with *Opuntia*
1900	10,000,000
1920	58,000,000
1925	60,000,000

About one-half of this area was dense growth completely covering the ground, rising 3 to 6 feet in height, and too dense for anyone to walk through (Figure 200).

Prickly pear is propagated by seeds and by segments. The cactus pads, when detached from the parent plant by wind or by man, can root and begin a new plant. Seeds are viable for at least 15 years. The problem of eradicating this weed was largely one of cost. The grazing land it occupied in eastern Australia was worth only a few dollars an acre, and poisoning the cactus cost about $25 to $100 an acre. Consequently, homesteads had to be abandoned to this invasion.

(a)

(b)

FIGURE 200

(a) Dense stand of prickly pear prior to the release of Cactoblastis, *October 1926, Chinchilla, Queensland, Australia. (b) The same stand is shown 3 years later after attack by* Cactoblastis, *October 1929. (After Dodd 1940; photographs courtesy of A. P. Dodd and Commonwealth Prickly Pear Board.)*

In 1912 two entomologists were sent from Australia to visit the native habitats of *Opuntia* and to suggest possible biological control agents that could be introduced. They sent back from Ceylon a mealy bug, *Dactylopius indicus*, which was released, and in a few years had destroyed a minor pest, *Opuntia vulgaris*. But the major pest, *O. stricta*, continued to spread, and after World War I it was subjected to a more intensive effort of biological control. Beginning in 1920, investigations in the United States, Mexico, and Argentina resulted in 50 species being sent back to Australia for possible control. Of these only 12 species were released; three were of some help in controlling *O. stricta*, but only one, the moth *Cactoblastis cactorum*, was capable of eradicating *O. stricta*.

Cactoblastis cactorum is a moth native to northern Argentina. Two generations occur each year. Females lay about 100 eggs on the average, and the adults live about 2 weeks. The larvae damage the cacti by burrowing and feeding inside the pads and by introducing bacterial and fungal infections by their burrows. Only one introduction of *Cactoblastis* was made. Approximately 2750 eggs were shipped from Argentina in 1925, and two generations were raised in cages until March 1926, when 2 million eggs were set out at 19 localities in eastern Australia. The moth was immediately successful, and further efforts were expended from 1927 to 1930 in spreading eggs and pupae from one field area to another.

By 1928 it was obvious that *Cactoblastis* would control *O. stricta*, so further parasite introductions were curtailed. *Cactoblastis* multiplied rapidly up to 1930, and between 1930 and 1931 the *Opuntia* stands were decimated by an enormous *Cactoblastis* population (Figure 200). This collapse of the prickly pear caused the moth population to fall steeply in 1932–1933, and the cactus then began to recover on some areas. Between 1935 and 1940 *Cactoblastis* recovered and completely controlled the cactus. Prickly pear survived after 1940 only as a scattered plant in the community (Dodd 1940, 1959). The present picture is that of a hop-skip-jump interaction between small local colonies of *Opuntia* and *Cactoblastis*. The cactus begins a new colony, which is eventually found and destroyed by *Cactoblastis*, and in the meantime the cactus has started another colony elsewhere. Larval *Cactoblastis* cannot move from one plant to another if cacti are 2 m or more apart. Thus the spatial distribution of moth and cactus shifts continually but the average densities of both species remain low.

KLAMATH WEED *(Hypericum perforatum)*

Klamath weed, or St. John's wort, is a noxious weed that has become widely distributed in the temperate zone throughout the world. It was introduced into North America about 1900 along the Klamath River in northern California. It is a native of Eurasia and northern Africa and is an aggressive perennial that gets established on overgrazed pasture land and then eliminates desirable grasses and herbs. It is particularly noxious because it is poisonous if eaten in quantity, and even when taken in small doses may irritate the mouth and reduce the appetite of cattle and sheep.

By 1944 Klamath weed occupied over 2 million acres in California, Oregon, Washington, Idaho, and Montana and, although it could be killed by chemical weed killers, cost on ordinary rangeland was too great. Since this same weed had become a pest earlier in Australia, a background of work on possible biological control agents was available. Over 600 species

(a)

(b)

of insects feed on Klamath weed in its native habitats, but only three of these were considered useful for biological control. In 1945–1946 two leaf-eating beetles, *Chrysolina quadrigemina* and *Chrysolina hyperici*, were introduced into California from France and England. Both species became established, but *Chrysolina quadrigemina* was clearly the more successful species.

The critical action of these leaf-feeding beetles seems to be the larval feeding. The larvae eat the basal leaves of Klamath weed in winter and keep the plants defoliated in the spring, which prevents the roots from building up food reserves. After about 3 years of such defoliation, the plants die in the summer dry season.

These beetles, mainly *C. quadrigemina*, have reduced Klamath weed from an extremely important pest of rangeland to a roadside weed (Figure 201). It is now less than 0.5% of its former abundance, and this control has persisted for 20 years (Figure 202).

One interesting development occurred in the habitat distribution of the weed during this reduction by the beetles. Klamath weed grows best on open, sunny, well-drained slopes, and grows poorly in the shade. The beetles prefer to lay their eggs in sunny areas, and consequently the weed is eliminated best from sunny, open areas. The result of this is that now the Klamath weed occurs more frequently in shady areas ("preferred habitat") than in sunny areas. Huffaker (1957) also points out that if one studied the weed–beetle relationship now, when both species are "rare," one would conclude that the abundance of the weed was not greatly affected by the presence of the beetle, and that temperature and rainfall are the main factors responsible for controlling the weed at its present low density.

An attempt was made to control Klamath weed in British Columbia with the same *Chrysolina* species that were successful in California. Both *Chrysolina* beetles became established but, for reasons unknown, the control of the weed has not been satisfactory (Holloway 1964).

FIGURE 201

Klamath weed control by the beetle Chrysolina
quadrigemina *at Blocksburg, California. (a)
Klamath weed in heavy flower in foreground;
remainder of the field has just been killed by the
beetle (1948). (b) Same location after a heavy
grass cover had replaced the Klamath weed
(1950). (c) Control of Klamath weed has persisted
since 1950 (1966). (After Huffaker and Kennett
1969; photographs courtesy of C. B. Huffaker.)*

(c)

EUROPEAN CORN BORER *(Ostrinia nubilalis)*

Not all biological control projects are successful. Let us look at a failure.

The European corn borer was first recorded in North America in 1917.
By 1925 it had become such a serious pest that, hard as it may be to
believe this today, many farmers considered abandoning corn as a major
crop. Biological-control studies were started as early as 1920, and between
1923 and 1940 24 species of insect parasites from Europe were imported
into the United States. Only 6 have become established. Many of the unsuccessful importations were propagated on a massive scale. For example,
Bracon brevicornis, a small parasitic wasp, was colonized with almost 3 million adults in 11 states. Not one recovery has ever been made (Clausen
1956). In Canada 20 species of parasites were released, and 3 became established, but the percentage of parasitism was so low that it did not control
the corn borer (Turnbull and Chant 1961).

About 1940 the corn borer in the midwestern United States began to
switch from the one-generation-a-year race to the two-generation-a-year race
(see page 126). This has made it more of a pest but has also increased the
percentage parasitism. Unfortunately the borer is still not adequately controlled by the introduced parasites.

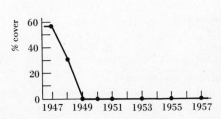

FIGURE 202

*Changes in the abundance of Klamath
weed at the Blocksburg, California,
study site shown in Figure 201. The
leaf-eating beetle* Chrysolina quadrigemina *was first released in 1946
and control was complete by 1949.
(After Huffaker and Kennett 1959.)*

Biological control is something akin to gambling—it works, sometimes. But how often? Table 25 summarizes data from the United States and Canada which suggest that biological control works about one-fourth of the time. Turnbull and Chant (1961) concluded that well over half of Canadian biological-control projects were failures. Why is this? What makes some biological control agents like the vedalia work so well, while others completely fail? A number of empirical generalizations have been suggested.

Most successful biological control programs have operated quickly. Clausen (1951) suggests that three generations (or a maximum of 3 years) is the outside limit, and that if definite control is not achieved in the vicinity of the colonization point within this time, the control agent will not be a success. This rule of thumb suggests that colonization projects should be discontinued after 3 years if no success is achieved and that prolonged efforts at establishment are wasting money. Most of the successful biological control examples to date support this rule, which would suggest that major evolutionary changes in the host–parasite system seldom occur in introduced pests (see Table 18). If a parasite is not already adapted to control the host, it will not evolve quickly into a successful control agent.

TABLE 25

Summary of biological control efforts in the United States and Canada against insect pests

	United States	Canada Forest insect pests	Agricultural pests
No. pest species	91	36	27
No. pest species effectively controlled[a]	18	6	10 (?)
Percentage controlled	20	17	37
No. species of parasites and predators released	485	104	85
No. species of parasites and predators established[b]	95	36	28
Percentage established	20	35	33

[a] Not including partial or local successes.
[b] Including species that became established but exerted no significant control.
SOURCE: Data from Clausen (1956) and McLeod, McGugan, and Coppel (1962).

Five principal attributes of a biological control agent are important for success: (1) general adaptation to the environment and the host, (2) high searching capacity, (3) high rate of increase relative to its host, (4) general mobility adequate for dispersal, and (5) minimal lag effects in responding to host changes in numbers (Huffaker and Kennett 1969). These attributes seem *necessary* for a good control agent, but they are clearly not *sufficient*. The unfortunate truth is that we can evaluate a biological control agent only in retrospect, and biological-control programs are part gambling; we release a parasite and hope for the best. A vital historical lesson is the frequency with which a critical species like the vedalia was released more on faith than on any evidence that it could control the pest. There is at the moment no evidence that biological control would not be just as successful if one released a random sample of the enemies of the pest species.

Most successful biological-control programs have resulted from a single species of parasite or predator, which raises the question: If one parasite species is good, are two species better? Turnbull and Chant (1961) argued that only one species should be released at a time for pest control, because two parasites might interfere with each other when the pest is reduced to low numbers. This argument follows from the observation that native insect pests have a great number of predators and parasites. The spruce budworm, for example, has over 35 species of parasites and many predators, yet it is a serious forest pest. Is the spruce budworm a pest because it has many parasites? Or does it have many parasites because it is moderately abundant?

What can we conclude regarding the problem of natural regulation from these examples on biological control? This is a difficult question. Belief in the success of biological control is based on a thoroughly biased sample. Economic pressures run high in this field, since crops worth millions of dollars may be destroyed by a single pest. Consequently, states like California have full-time bureaus devoted solely to searching the world for insects to control current agricultural pests. Candidates for control are carefully screened before they are released, to make sure that they will not destroy the native fauna rather than the pest. However, once these control agents are introduced, little further work is usually done. Either they work and the pest decreases, or they do not work and the entomologists go looking for another parasite or predator. Consequently, the literature is full of all sorts of spurious correlations that are seldom checked out.

In general two opposing camps have arisen over the problem of biological control. The supporters of biological control believe that predators and parasites are the factors regulating most animal and plant populations. They support their claim with the dozen or so spectacular examples of pests being decimated to a low level by introduced predators or parasites. In general, supporters of biological control seem to have a Nicholsonian outlook.

The opposition points to the greater number of failures. Many insect pests have plenty of predators and parasites, yet remain pests. The addition of any lethal factor to a population will reduce the average density, and this is what is occuring in biological control.

The two main difficulties associated with the problem of biological control are these:

1 The species considered are always introduced pests, which makes one ask if studies on introduced pests have any relevance to the *natural* regulation of animal numbers. Are they instances of natural control writ large, as some believe, or are they atypical problems associated with man's disturbance of natural systems?

2 Biological control has become an applied science in itself, attached more to agriculture than to ecology, and dictated mainly by economic problems. Attention is seldom paid to proper experimentation or testing of ecological principles. The only good insect pest seems to be a dead one.

The problem of biological control leads into the whole problem of pest control by biological and chemical agents. We shall not attempt to discuss these applied problems of pest control in this book, and interested students should refer to Rabb and Guthrie (1970).

SUMMARY

There are several dozen cases of introduced pests being reduced in numbers by predators or insect parasites that are specially introduced for purposes of control. Many other attempts have failed and left the pest to be controlled by chemical means. We cannot adequately account for even one of the successes, nor can we explain why failure is so common. Biological control will remain an art until we can do this.

SELECTED REFERENCES

DeBACH, P. (ed.). 1964. *Biological Control of Insect Pests and Weeds*. Chaps. 2, 5, and 24. Chapman & Hall, London.

HUFFAKER, C. B. 1959. Biological control of weeds with insects. *Ann. Rev. Entomol.* 4:251–276.

HUFFAKER, C. B., and C. E. KENNETT. 1969. Some aspects of assessing efficiency of natural enemies. *Can. Entomol.* 101:425–447.

LeROUX, E. J. 1971. Biological control attempts on pome fruit (apple and pear) in North America, 1860–1970. *Can. Entomol.* 103: 963–974.

RABB, R. L. and F. E. GUTHRIE (eds.) 1970. *Concepts of Pest Management*. North Carolina State Univ., Raleigh.

SIMMONDS, F. J. 1956. The present status of biological control. *Can. Entomol.* 88:553–563.

TAYLOR, T. H. C. 1955. Biological control of insect pests. *Ann. Appl. Biol.* 42:190–196.

TURNBULL, A. L., and D. A. CHANT. 1961. The practice and theory of biological control of insects in Canada. *Can. J. Zool.* 39:697–753.

QUESTIONS AND PROBLEMS

1 In discussing the control of the Klamath weed, Huffaker (1957, p. 128) states:

It is believed that in the absence of detailed knowledge of the history of this weed and unless he made specific detailed studies, a trained entomologist or ecologist would conclude, even after close observations of ranges cleared of the weed now for seven consecutive years, that the dominant insect species, *Chrysolina gemellata*, is not a significant influent on the stand of vegetation and that the few plants of Klamath weed seen here and there are not primarily limited by this insect. He might also erroneously conclude that this plant is a shade-loving species, since the beetle checks it much less effectively under shade.

Discuss these claims.

2 Review the evidence for and against the idea that biological control is much more successful on islands like Hawaii than on continental areas (see DeBach 1964, p. 136).

3 One of the outstanding successes of biological control of forest insect pests is that of the spruce sawfly (*Diprion hercyniae*) in Canada (references in Turnbull and Chant 1961, pp. 720–721). Review this example and design in retrospect a program of study that would have reduced to a minimum the number of mistakes and waste of money.

4 Elton (1958) showed that introduced species often increase enormously and then subside to a more static, lower density level. How might this occur in a species that was not the subject of introductions for biological control? How could you distinguish this case from a decline that followed the introduction of some parasites for biological control?

5 Count in a recent volume of the *Journal of Economic Entomology* the papers dealing with pest control and classify these according to the principal means utilized, chemical or biological. Discuss your findings.

6 It is customary to obtain insect parasites from the home country of an introduced pest and to use only these parasites for possible biological control. Pimentel (1963) suggests another strategy of introducing the parasites of other species closely related to the pest you want to control. Review Pimentel's ideas on population regulation (Chapter 14) and discuss the rationale for this recommendation.

PART FOUR

DISTRIBUTION AND ABUNDANCE
AT THE COMMUNITY LEVEL

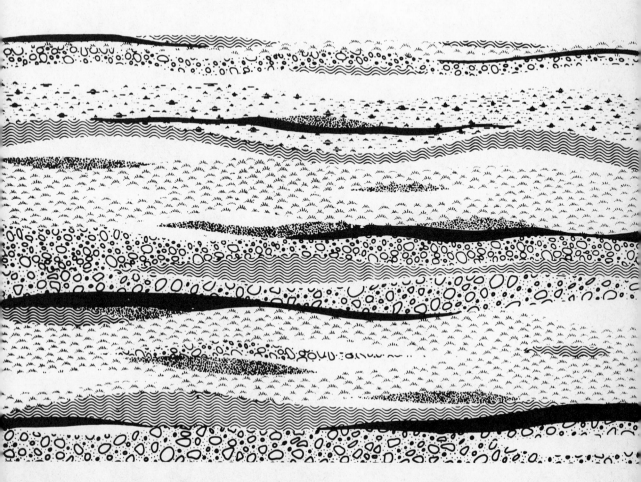

DISTRIBUTION AND ABUNDANCE
AT THE COMMUNITY LEVEL

18   *Community parameters*

COMMUNITY AS A UNIT OF STUDY

Neither organisms nor species populations exist by themselves in nature but are always part of an assemblage of species populations living together in the same area. We have already discussed the interactions of two or more of these species populations in predation and competition for food, but this has always been with the focus on the individual species populations. Now we shall focus on the assemblage of populations in an area, the *community*. A community is *any assemblage of populations of living organisms in a prescribed area or habitat.* This is the most general definition one can give. We can thus speak of the community of animals in a rotting log or the community of plants in the beech–maple deciduous forest. A community may be of any size.

Much of plant ecology has been concerned with community studies or plant sociology; consequently, a whole series of terms has been specially devised. The fundamental unit of plant sociology is the *association*—an association is a plant community of definite floristic composition. To plant sociologists, an association is like a species. An association is composed of a number of *stands*, which are the concrete units of vegetation observed in the field. Plant ecologists use the term *community* in a very general sense, whereas the term *association* has a very specific meaning. Zoologists, on the other hand, use the word *community* both in the general sense and in the specific sense of the botanical *association*. No end of confusion arises from this.

Various botanists and zoologists have defined the community in widely different ways, usually attempting to include in their definition a particular idea of how a community operates. Three main ideas are involved in community definitions. First, the minimum property of a community is the presence together of several species in an area. Second, some authors claim that collections of virtually the same groups of species recur in space and in time. This means that one can recognize a "community type" which has a relatively constant composition. Third, some authors claim that communities have a tendency toward dynamic stability, that this balance or steady state tends to be restored once it has been upset; that is, the community shows self-regulation or *homeostasis*. The extreme proponents of this third idea look on the community as a type of superorganism. Both the second and the third ideas are disputed, and we shall discuss them presently.

In general the approach of zoologists and botanists to community studies has been quite different. Zoologists have been more concerned with functional relationships such as food webs and energy flow through the community; botanists have been more concerned with taxonomic or structural relationships in the community and the way these change in time and space. The more comprehensive studies have come from zoologists because they have to deal with the plants as animal food; botanists have tended to ignore the animals.

COMMUNITY CHARACTERISTICS

Like a population, a community has a series of attributes that do not reside in its individual species components and have meaning only with reference to the community level of integration. There are five characteristics of communities that we can measure and study:

1 Species diversity: The first question we can ask is what species of animals and plants live in a particular community. This is a simple measure of species richness, or species diversity.

2 Growth form and structure: We can describe the type of community by major categories of growth forms: trees, shrubs, herbs, and mosses. We can further detail the growth forms into categories such as broad-leaved trees and needle-leaved trees. These different growth forms determine the stratification, or vertical layering, of the community.

3 Dominance: This refers to the fact that not all species in the community are equally important in determining the nature of the community. Out of the hundreds of species present in the community, relatively few exert a major controlling influence by virtue of their size, numbers, or activities. Dominant species are those which are highly successful ecologically and which determine to a considerable extent the conditions under which the associated species must grow.

4 *Relative abundance:* This idea is closely related to the idea of dominance but emphasizes the relative proportions of different species in the community.

5 *Trophic structure:* Who eats whom? The feeding relations of the species in the community will determine the flow of energy and materials from plants to herbivores to carnivores.

These attributes can all be studied in communities that are in equilibrium or in communities that are changing. The changes may be temporal ones, which are called *succession* and which lead to a stable *climax community.* Or the changes may be spatial, along environmental gradients, and we may study, for example, how the characteristics of a community are altered as we move along a gradient of moisture or temperature.

Techniques of measuring the five characteristics of communities will be discussed in subsequent chapters because these characteristics are difficult to quantify, although they are intuitively clear. Let us now look at the sort of questions one can ask about a community.

MEASUREMENTS OF SPECIES GROUPINGS

How do we recognize a community? If we are to study an item, whether it be ferric oxide or the beech–maple forest association, we have to have some way of recognizing it. One answer to this is the subjective one—the beech–maple association is what I, the community ecologist, recognize to be this association—but this authoritarian view has been superseded by more objective methods.

A great deal of work in community ecology has been aimed at the measurement of association between species. The basic idea behind this is to avoid the subjective problems of deciding (1) what species should be grouped together as a community, and (2) where community boundaries should occur. The hope is to formalize in an objective quantitative manner the basic idea of community organization: that species tend to be associated in a nonrandom manner. Put another way, the idea is to search for recurrent groups of species.

The simplest matter to determine is the association between two species. This can be done by the use of a 2×2 *contingency table:*

	Species x	
Species y	**Present**	**Absent**
Present	type a	type b
Absent	type c	type d

Four types of observations are possible. A sample in which both species x and species y were present would be a type a observation. If there is a positive association between the species, we expect most of the quadrats we sample to fall in types a and d; if a negative correlation, types b and c. If there is no association between them, we expect all four situations to be found proportionally. There are simple statistical tests for tables of this type to determine whether the species are associated.

Let us look at one example to illustrate this technique. The presence or absence of two grasses, *Ammophila breviligulata* and *Andropogon scoparius*, were recorded by an ecology class in 1-m square quadrats in the sand dunes bordering southern Lake Michigan. These were the results:

Andropogon	*Ammophila* Present	Absent	Total
Present	8	47	55
Absent	75	20	95
Total	83	67	150

The probability of obtaining *Andropogon* in a quadrat is 55/150 or 0.367, and the probability of obtaining *Ammophila* in a quadrat is 0.553. Now if these two species are not associated (independent), the probability of getting them both in one quadrat should be

$$\text{Joint probability} = (0.367)(0.553) = 0.203$$

or in 150 quadrats we would expect 30.4 joint occurrences. We actually observe only 8, and so we might expect that these two species are negatively associated.

A simple statistical test with a 2×2 contingency table can be used to test the hypothesis that species are not associated. For the generalized table

Species y	Species x +	−
+	a	b
−	c	d

the statistic is a chi-squared value calculated as follows (n = total samples = $a + b + c + d$):

$$\chi^2 = \frac{n(ad - bc)^2}{(a + b)(c + d)(a + c)(b + d)}$$

This value can then be referred to the χ^2 table with one degree of freedom (Simpson et al. 1960). The decision rule for this simple test can be stated as follows: If the observed χ^2 value is greater than 3.84, the probability of getting this great a value of χ^2 is less than 5% if the species are independent; if the observed χ^2 is greater than 6.64, the probability is less than 1%.

If we apply this test to our previous data, we obtain

$$\chi^2 = \frac{150[(8)(20) - (47)(75)]^2}{(55)(95)(83)(67)} = 58.45$$

so there seems to be a strong negative association between these two grasses.

The strength of the association between the two species in a contingency table can be estimated from a coefficient of association defined by

$$V = \frac{ad - bc}{\sqrt{(a + b)(c + d)(a + c)(b + d)}}$$

This coefficient varies from −1 to +1 and is zero when there is no association. For our grass example

$$V = \frac{160 - 3525}{\sqrt{29,056,225}} = -0.62$$

which shows strong but not perfect negative association.

This method seems simple and straightforward, but unfortunately for a statistical reason there is a serious problem of interpretation: *The results of association analyses from quadrat data depend on the size of quadrat used.* This can be illustrated by a hypothetical example. Consider the plants distributed in an area shown by Figure 203. Clearly in this community species A and B are positively associated, and species (A and C) and (B and C) are negatively associated. Now if we sample this community with quadrat size 1 (Figure 203), which is roughly equal in size to the individuals, most quadrats will contain only A, or B, or C, or none of them. The χ^2 test above would show a strong negative association between all species. If we sample

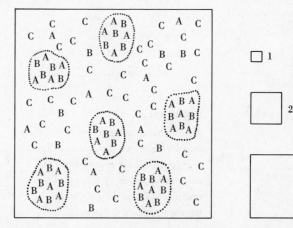

FIGURE 203

Relationship between quadrat size and trend of association among three species, A, B, and C (see the text). (After Kershaw 1964.)

with quadrat size 2, species A and B would be found together and species C alone, so the obvious trends of association would be confirmed by the χ^2 test. If we sample with quadrat size 3, nearly all quadrats would contain all three species, and we would conclude that there was a strong positive association between all the species.

Thus when we do a test of association we are testing both a *species effect* and a *quadrat effect*. Species effects are what interest us. Quadrat effects that may arise because of quadrat spacing or quadrat size can be analyzed by the use of a variety of sizes and spacings (Pielou 1969, Chap. 14). The importance of tests of association must be assessed carefully to make sure that significant effects are caused by biological phenomena and not sampling phenomena.

Are there other possible techniques by which we can avoid quadrat effects? One way is to use "plotless" sampling methods, which measure only distances between individuals. In this way we can study the pattern of distribution of two species relative to each other. We do this by looking at "nearest neighbors" and ask for any individual of species x: Is the nearest neighbor of this individual a species x or a species y individual? If species x is relatively clumped (as in Figure 204), it is more likely that a species x individual will be the nearest neighbor, and the two species are segregated (negatively associated).

This technique is similar to the one we have just discussed. We obtain for each individual in a population the species of its nearest neighbor and set out the results in a table:

Species of base plant	Species of nearest neighbor	
	x	y
x	a	b
y	c	d

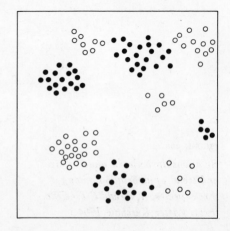

FIGURE 204

Hypothetical two-species population in which the two species are highly segregated. This means that the nearest neighbor of a species x individual is most likely to be another species x individual.

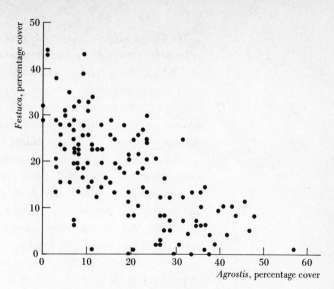

FIGURE 205

Negative association between the grasses Agrostis tenuis *and* Festuca rubra *in grasslands in the North Downs of England. (After Kershaw 1964.)*

We can use the χ^2 test described above to test these data for the hypothesis that the species are randomly mingled. An example from the two beach grasses discussed above will illustrate this idea.

Species of base plant	Species of nearest neighbor		Total
	Ammophila	*Andropogon*	
Ammophila	85	8	93
Andropogon	21	54	75
Total	106	62	168

$$\chi^2 = \frac{n(ad - bc)^2}{(a + b)(c + d)(a + c)(b + d)}$$

$$= \frac{168(4590 - 168)^2}{(93)(75)(106)(62)} = 71.66$$

We conclude that the hypothesis of random mingling of these two grasses is highly unlikely and that the two species are segregated in beach sites.

These measures of association are *qualitative* and involve presence–absence criteria. We may also estimate association by quantitative means. The simplest technique involves sampling quadrats to measure the cover or density of two species and plotting these against each other for the two species. Figure 205 shows one example from a British grassland area in which there is a negative association between the grasses *Agrostis tenuis* and *Festuca rubra*. Correlation or regression analysis, which are discussed in standard statistical textbooks, can be used to describe the associations inherent in quantitative data of this sort. Quadrat size and spacing will also affect the magnitude and direction of associations measured with quantitative data.

We can analyze all the pairs of species in the community in this way and determine which are positively associated, which are negatively associated, and which show random association. Can we use this information from the field to set the boundaries of consistent groupings of species? If so, we can call these groups of species a community or an *association*. This will enable us to quantify a common observation of naturalists that discrete species groupings can be recognized in the field.

One of the first systems proposed for the detection of associations was a qualitative one suggested by Braun-Blanquet (1932), a European plant ecologist who founded the Zürich–Montpellier school of phytosociology. Braun-Blanquet set out to describe and classify all the plant communities of the world in much the same way that a taxonomist sets out to describe and classify a group of species. The system Braun-Blanquet proposed is quite subjective in nature and is based on the idea of *fidelity*. Basically four steps are involved:

1 Choosing uniform areas of vegetation
2 Describing the species in these areas with the measures of frequency, abundance, and dominance
3 Segregating species lists from areas that are alike (belong to the same vegetational unit)
4 Grouping the units according to their affinities

Braun-Blanquet recognized five degrees of fidelity. *Characteristic species* have high fidelity and are rigidly limited to definite plant communities. The best characteristic species are the exclusive species, which are completely confined to one community. At the other extreme of fidelity are *indifferent species*, which occur in many communities, and *accidental species*, which are intruders from other communities. The important species ecologically are the characteristic species. This system has been applied widely and successfully in Europe to describe and classify the vegetation. The main objection to the system is that it is too subjective and consequently cannot be used to investigate important community problems. For example, by choosing only homogeneous stands for analysis, one cannot answer the ecological question of whether communities have sharply defined boundaries. Braun-Blanquet's system may be most useful in the preliminary stages of describing the vegetation before any detailed ecological questions are asked (Poore 1956).

Many attempts have been made to establish community groupings by objective methods. The basic approach is to measure the degree of association between every two species in the samples. Stands are chosen at random from a given area, and using objective mathematical techniques, usually with the aid of a computer, one searches for recurrent species groups. One example will illustrate this approach.

Juncus effusus is an important weed in upland pasture in Wales, and Agnew (1961) studied 99 quadrats spread through all community types that contained this weed. Species that were found less than 5 times in the ninety-nine 1-sq.-m quadrats were eliminated, and 53 plant species remained. χ^2 tests of association were run on all species pairs (Table 26). These results can be shown graphically in a species constellation as in Figure 206. This constellation shows only the positive associations, and the position of any species in the figure is largely a matter of trial and error. Three "groups" of species can be recognized (shaded in Figure 206), and these might be

TABLE 26

Complete chi-square matrix for 99 J. effusus *stands in North Wales*[a]

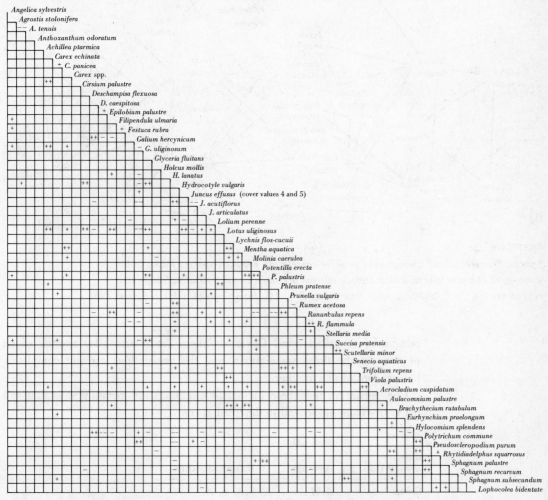

[a] The table shows the significant positive and negative species relationships among the 53 plant species.

SOURCE: After Agnew (1961).

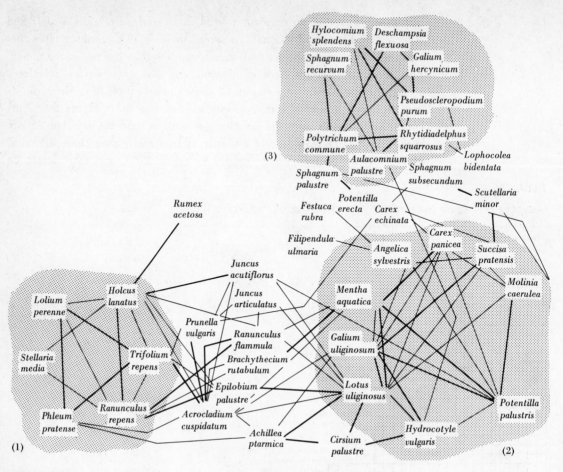

FIGURE 206

Species "constellation," showing the positive correlation between species found in 99 samples of communities in which Juncus effusus *occurred in north Wales. Single line represents* 5% > P > 1%, *double line shows* P < 1% *for* χ^2 *values. (After Agnew 1961.)*

recognized as associations. Obviously there are intermediate species which fit none of the three associations, and the associations are not completely independent of one another.

One indication that these biological groupings are meaningful is that soil pH varies from the second to the third group:

Juncus association	Soil pH	
	Average	Range of values
Group 1	5.41	4.83–6.20
Group 2	5.29	4.40–6.37
Group 3	4.78	3.93–5.23

Group 1 also contained more species that grew in clumps, and Agnew (1961) argued that group 1 was an artificial community maintained by man's disturbances, and that without disturbance group 1 would tend toward group 2.

Obviously a great deal of work is necessary to get the data for a community analysis, since one must often deal with 100 or more species of plants. The result obtained in several cases in which this work has been done is illustrated in general by Figure 206; groups of species occur but they are not distinct and isolated. What, then, is a community? This is the important question to which we are led, and we must now inquire into the nature of the community.

SUMMARY

A community is an assemblage of populations living in a prescribed area. A community is claimed to have one or more of the following attributes: (1) co-occurrence of species, (2) recurrence of groups of the same species, and (3) homeostasis or self-regulation. A number of parameters such as species diversity can be measured in a community, but the interpretation of these community parameters depends on the nature of the community. Species associations can be measured with simple statistical tests, although there are some possible difficulties of interpretation from sampling with quadrats. We can use these species associations to construct groups of species, and these techniques raise the general question about the recurrence of groups of species in natural communities.

SELECTED REFERENCES

FAGER, E. W. 1957. Determination and analysis of recurrent groups. *Ecology* 38: 586–595.

GREIG-SMITH, P. 1964. *Quantitative Plant Ecology*, 2nd ed. Chap. 4. Butterworth, London.

HURLBERT, S. H. 1969. A coefficient of interspecific association. *Ecology* 50:1–9.

KERSHAW, K. A. 1964. *Quantitative and Dynamic Ecology*. Chaps. 2, 5, and 8. Edward Arnold, London.

PHILLIPS, E. A. 1959. *Methods of Vegetation Study*. Holt, Rinehart & Winston, New York.

PIELOU, E. C. 1969. *An Introduction to Mathematical Ecology*. Chaps. 13–15. Wiley-Interscience, New York.

1 Ritchie (1959) obtained the following data from a series of 77 quadrats, each 10-m square, on an esker (sandy ridge) in northern Manitoba:

Empetrum hermaphroditum	*Vaccinium vitis-idaea*	
	Present	**Absent**
Present	44	12
Absent	7	14

Cladonia rangiferina	*Cladonia pleurota*	
	Present	**Absent**
Present	13	27
Absent	12	25

Use a χ^2 test to determine if there is significant association between these species pairs.

2 La Roi (1967, p. 236) provides the following data for the relative abundance of white spruce and balsam fir in 34 quadrats in the northern boreal forest:

Quadrat	White spruce	Balsam fir	Quadrat	White spruce	Balsam fir
1	6	0	18	5	2
2	6	0	19	2	6
3	6	0	20	6	2
4	6	0	21	2	5
5	5	0	22	4	2
6	4	0	23	4	5
7	3	0	24	5	5
8	6	0	25	4	5
9	6	0	26	1	6
10	6	0	27	3	5
11	6	0	28	4	5
12	6	0	29	1	6
13	5	0	30	1	2
14	6	2	31	1	6
15	6	1	32	2	6
16	5	3	33	2	6
17	6	3	34	0	6

Plot the relative abundance of these two trees, determine if they are related in some way, and try to determine why by referring to literature on these two species.

19 The nature of the community

The study of community ecology is pervaded by an important controversy over the nature of the community. Most of the discussion on this question has centered on plant communities, but the issue is equally important for animal communities. The question is this: *Is the community anything more than an abstraction made by ecologists from continuously varying vegetation?* Or, to put the question another way, is the community an organized system of recurrent species or a haphazard collection of populations with minimal integration? Two extreme schools have developed over this question. On the one extreme are the views of F. E. Clements and A. G. Tansley that the community is a superorganism or a quasi-organism. At the other extreme is the individualistic view of H. A. Gleason that the community is a collection of populations with the same environmental requirements. What are the consequences of these views and how can we distinguish between them empirically?

A major assumption of many community ecologists is that some "fundamental unit" of natural communities does really exist and that this unit is natural in the sense that it is present in nature and is not a product of human classification. This assumption led some ecologists to draw the analogy between the "species" concept and the "community" concept. If fundamental units exist in nature, we ought to be able to discover these units and classify them, perhaps in the way we classify species. This view has been held by a majority of ecologists in Europe and North America, and the famous plant ecologists Braun-Blanquet (France), Clements (United States), and Tansley (United Kingdom) all strongly supported this assumption.

The fundamental-unit assumption of community ecology was attacked almost simultaneously by Ramensky in Russia, Gleason in the United States, and Lenoble in France (Whittaker 1962). These workers emphasized the principle of vegetational continuity and the principle of species individuality. Each species has its own specific range. An association can be regarded as an assemblage of wandering populations and is an arbitrary unit, unlike a species. The individualistic school argues that communities can be recognized and classified, but any classification is for the convenience of the human observer and is not a description of the fundamental structure of nature.

RELEVANT EVIDENCE

Most of the argument about the nature of the community can be centered on two statements:

1 Stands and associations (are, are not) discontinuous with one another.
2 Species (are, are not) organized into discrete groups corresponding to associations.

Four types of evidence may be considered as bearing on these two questions (Whittaker 1962), and we shall discuss each in turn.

Similarity and dissimilarity of stands

If associations are natural units, they should consist of groups of stands that are very similar to one another but clearly different from other stands of a second association. The suggestion is to sample the vegetation without any selection of stands, but this is what virtually no one does. Usually samples of stands are taken to represent certain associations, and this subjective selection obviously assumes beforehand the truth of the fundamental-unit assumption.

When samples are taken by unprejudiced means, many of them are "atypical," "mixed," or "transitional." For example, more than three-fourths of the weed stands studied in the Ulm district of Germany were "intermediate" to two or three associations (Ellenberg 1954, cited in Whittaker 1962). "Mixtures" predominated in 1029 grassland samples selected at random by Klapp et al. (1954, cited in Whittaker 1962), and only 25% of the samples represented community types. Brown and Curtis (1952) studied 55 stands of upland forest in northern Wisconsin and found that every stand differed to some degree from every other stand. The *Juncus effusus* stands sampled in North Wales and discussed in Chapter 18 did not fall into discrete groups (Figure 206).

Continuity and discontinuity of stands

If associations are natural units, contacts between stands of two different associations should be sharp and discontinuous. Three types of boundaries between communities might occur: sharp, diffuse, or mosaic. All three have been found in nature. The boundary between the prairie and the deciduous forest in the eastern United States was apparently very sharp. Clements would interpret this to show that associations were discrete natural units, whereas Gleason would interpret it as an artificial boundary maintained by fire disturbance. One difficulty of interpreting boundaries is that the human observer fixes on a few dominant species, often trees for example, and more analytical assessment of shrubs, herbs, or grasses might give a different view of how sharp the boundary is.

We should try to eliminate from this discussion all boundaries caused by sharp environmental discontinuities and by disturbance, but this is difficult to do. Striking breaks in soil type (Figure 40) will produce discontinuity, but all the competing schools of thought agree about this type of discontinuity. Other sharp boundaries are possibly due to environmental discontinuities but need more study. For example, the boreal forest in northern Canada gives way to the tundra over a broad zone of overlap, which is a mosaic of sharp community boundaries (Figure 207). This sharp boundary may mark a sharp break between areas that have soil and are well drained and areas that have little soil and are poorly drained (Marr 1948). Should we interpret forest–tundra boundaries as evidence for discrete associations á la Clements?

A number of plant ecologists almost simultaneously began to question the discontinuity of stands and to emphasize that vegetation was a complex *continuum* of populations rather than a mosaic of discontinuous units. This group has developed a series of techniques, called *gradient analysis*, to study the continuous variation of vegetation in relation to environmental factors (Whittaker 1967). R. H. Whittaker and the Wisconsin school under J. T. Curtis have been the leading North American proponents of gradient analysis.

The simplest application of gradient analysis is to take samples at intervals along an environmental gradient, such as elevation on a mountain slope. Figure 208 shows the relative abundance of three species of *Pinus* along an altitudinal gradient from 1400 to 4700 ft on south-facing slopes in the Great Smoky Mountains of Tennessee. There is no discontinuity evident

FIGURE 207

Mosaic of communities at the zone between the tundra and the boreal forest in southwestern Alaska. The forest, dominated by white spruce, is sharply separated from the tundra. (Photograph by the author.)

in Figure 208, and Whittaker (1956) presents data from 24 other tree species to illustrate that there is a continual gradation from the Virginia pine forest at low elevations, to the pitch pine heath at middle elevations, to the table mountain pine heath at higher elevations.

A second example of an altitudinal gradient is shown in Figure 209 from the Siskiyou Mountains of Oregon and California. The transition here is from a mixed evergreen forest at lower elevations, through montane forests dominated by Douglas fir (*Pseudotsuga menziesii*), to subalpine forests with mountain hemlock (*Tsuga mertensiana*). Figure 209 shows only three species but illustrates the lack of discontinuity along this gradient.

Elevation is a complex environmental gradient, since it includes gradients of temperature, rainfall, wind, and snow cover. Other gradients can be used as well to show the continuity of vegetation. For example, Whittaker (1960) grouped stands along a moisture gradient at a fixed elevation in the Siskiyou Mountains (Figure 210). Some species, such as Port Orford cedar (*Chamaecyparis lawsoniana*), are found only in moist sites; others, such as Pacific madrone (*Arbutus menziesii*), are most common on dry sites.

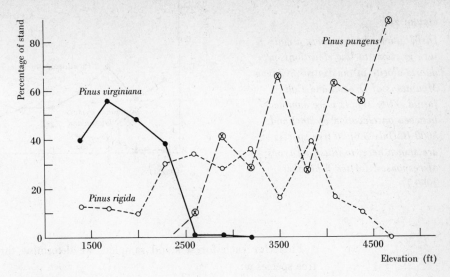

FIGURE 208

Transect of the elevation gradient along dry, south-facing slopes in the Great Smoky Mountains of Tennessee. No boundaries separate the three community types an ecologist is likely to distinguish along this gradient: Pinus virginiana *forest at low elevations,* Pinus rigida *heath at middle elevations, and* Pinus pungens *heath at high elevations (see Figure 223). (After Whittaker 1956.)*

Elevation gives us an easily obtained environmental gradient, but in many areas we cannot find a simple gradient to measure. In this situation we can use techniques of *ordination* by which we rank the samples in relation to one another. Let us consider a simple example of ordination applied to the conifer–hardwood forests of northern Wisconsin (Brown and Curtis 1952).

FIGURE 209

Distribution of trees along an elevation gradient on quartz diorite in the central Siskiyou Mountains of Oregon and California. Samples grouped in 1000-ft classes. Only 3 of the 25 species studied are shown to illustrate trends. (After Whittaker 1960.)

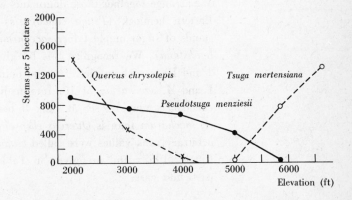

FIGURE 210

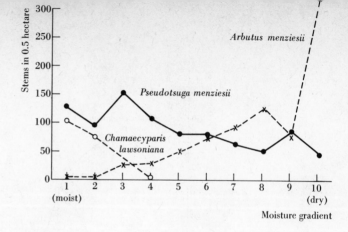

Distribution of trees along a moisture gradient at low elevations on quartz diorite in the central Siskiyou Mountains of Oregon and California. Fifty stands were sampled between an elevation of 2000 and 3000 ft. Only 3 of 20 tree species are shown here, to illustrate types of responses. (After Whittaker 1960.)

First, for each forest stand sampled, we determine three values for each tree species x:

$$\text{Relative density} = \frac{\text{no. individuals of species } x}{\text{total individuals of all species}} \times 100$$

$$\text{Relative frequency} = \frac{\text{frequency of species } x}{\text{sum of frequency values for all species}} \times 100$$

$$\text{Relative dominance} = \frac{\text{basal area of species } x}{\text{total basal area of all species}} \times 100$$

Frequency is defined as the probability of finding the species in any one quadrat. Basal area is the cross-sectional area of the tree at a point 4.5 ft above ground. The three values are summed to obtain for each species its *importance value:*

$$\begin{matrix} \text{Importance value} \\ \text{of species } x \end{matrix} = \begin{matrix} \text{relative} \\ \text{density} \end{matrix} + \begin{matrix} \text{relative} \\ \text{frequency} \end{matrix} + \begin{matrix} \text{relative dominance} \\ \text{of species } x \end{matrix}$$

Since each of the three is a percentage ranging from 0 to 100, the scale of importance values ranges from 0 to 300.

We then average together all stands with the same leading species (with the highest importance value) to determine the results given in Table 27. We arrange together those dominants which seem most similar. For example, Eastern hemlock (*Tsuga canadensis*) stands are clearly more similar to stands of sugar maple (*Acer saccharum*) than to stands of jack pine (*Pinus banksiana*). We recognize this by giving an arbitrary rank value between 1 and 10 to each species. The end points are clear: Set *P. banksiana* at rank 1 and *A. saccharum* at 10. Intermediate ranks are more arbitrary. *Tsuga canadensis* may be set at rank 8 because it is somewhat less similar to *A. saccharum* than is *Quercus ellipsoidalis* (rank 2) to *P. banksiana*. These arbitrary rank values were called *climax adaptation numbers* by Brown and Curtis (1952) and are given in Table 28 for all species of trees for this particular case.

TABLE 27

Average importance value of trees in stands with given species as leading dominant—104 stands from upland forests of northern Wisconsin

No. stands	Leading dominant	Acer saccharum	Tsuga canadensis	Betula lutea	Acer rubrum	Quercus rubra	Betula papyrifera	Pinus strobus	Pinus resinosa	Populus tremuloides	Quercus ellipsoidalis	Pinus banksiana
23	Acer saccharum	145	25	21	7	22	6	1	—	1	—	—
23	Tsuga canadensis	40	152	47	11	3	5	4	3	—	—	—
6	Quercus rubra	27	1	3	29	138	23	10	8	5	3	—
6	Betula papyrifera	48	8	7	27	16	108	19	1	29	1	—
19	Pinus strobus	12	6	2	24	12	12	150	39	9	5	—
9	Pinus resinosa	3	—	1	12	15	14	56	156	24	4	2
4	Populus tremuloides	11	—	—	10	29	34	14	19	140	—	—
4	Quercus ellipsoidalis	—	—	—	5	7	1	11	9	9	103	56
10	Pinus banksiana	—	—	—	3	3	3	13	12	14	36	213

SOURCE: After Brown and Curtis (1952).

TABLE 28

Climax adaptation numbers of tree species found in stands of upland forests in Northern Wisconsin

Tree species	Climax adaptation no.
Pinus banksiana (jack pine)	1
Quercus ellipsoidalis	2
Quercus macrocarpa	2
ª*Populus balsamifera*	2
Populus tremuloides	2
Populus grandidentata	2
Pinus resinosa	3
Pinus pennsylvanica	3
Quercus alba	4
Prunus serotina	4
Prunus virginiana	4
Pinus strobus	5
Betula papyrifera	5
ª*Juglans cinerea*	5
Acer rubrum	6
ª*Acer spicatum*	6
ª*Fraxinus nigra*	6
ª*Picea glauca*	6
Quercus rubra	6
Abies balsamea	7
ª*Thuja occidentalis*	7
ª*Carpinus caroliniana*	7
Tsuga canadensis	8
Betula lutea	8
ª*Carya cordiformis*	8
Fraxinus americana	8
Tilia americana	8
Ulmus americana	8
Ostrya virginiana	9
Fagus grandifolia	10
Acer saccharum (sugar maple)	10

ª Climax adaptation number is tentative only, because of the low abundance of these species in the stands studied.
SOURCE: After Brown and Curtis (1952).

Finally, we determine the continuum index for each stand from the formula

$$\text{Continuum index} = \sum[(\text{importance value}) \times (\text{climax adaptation no.})]$$

where the sum is taken over all species. For example, in stand 084, Brown and Curtis obtained

	Importance value	Climax adaptation no.	Product
Pinus banksiana	272	1	272
Quercus ellipsoidalis	4	2	8
Populus tremuloides	9	2	18
Pinus resinosa	12	3	36
Acer rubrum	4	6	24
		Continuum index = total =	358

At the other extreme, in stand 114 they obtained

	Importance value	Climax adaptation no.	Product
Acer saccharum	268	10	2680
Ostrya virginiana	7	9	63
Tilia americana	8	8	64
Betula lutea	6	8	48
Quercus rubra	3	6	18
		Continuum index = total =	2873

The continuum index is assumed to measure a complex environmental gradient in much the same way as elevation up a mountainside. We can thus plot the importance values for all the tree species against the continuum index. Typical results for the northern Wisconsin forests are shown in Figure 211. The continuum analysis may be viewed as a simple way of quantifying the subjective feeling one can obtain from looking at many stands of vegetation—discrete units with sharp boundaries are uncommon in nature.

The environmental variables responsible for the vegetation gradient can

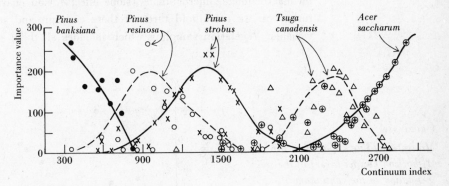

FIGURE 211

Gradient analysis of a continuum for the upland conifer–hardwood forests of northern Wisconsin. Only the dominant trees species are shown here. (After Brown and Curtis 1952.)

be studied in relation to the continuum index in the same way that one can measure changes in temperature and rainfall up a mountainside. Figure 212 shows that the moisture-holding capacity of the upper soil layer (A_1 horizon) varies with the continuum index. Jack pine stands tend to occur on soils that dry out easily whereas sugar maple stands occur on soils that hold more moisture, but this relationship is not very tight.

At this point you may well wonder how anyone could possibly question the continuity of vegetation and the fact that discrete stands do not occur. The advocates of the fundamental-unit view, that associations do occur as discrete units, question the whole approach of gradient analysis. They make two fundamental criticisms: (1) The stands that have been studied by gradient analysis are all disturbed stands, or stands not in equilibrium with the environment; and (2) the techniques of gradient analysis are such as to force the data into looking like a continuum. Langford and Buell (1969) and Daubenmire (1966) summarize these objections.

The first objection to the gradient-analysis school is that to evaluate the hypothesis that discrete associations occur in nature one must study stands in equilibrium; but Curtis and his co-workers have studied stands of trees that were clear cut only 26 years before and others that have been selectively logged. Langford and Buell (1969) suggest that all the Wisconsin stands would develop to a common end point if they were undisturbed for a few hundred years. We shall discuss the ideas of vegetation change in Chapter 20; here we note that all schools agree that stages of vegetation that change toward a stable end point will always show a continuum of species.

The second objection is that the techniques of gradient analysis are insufficient to solve the question at issue. Daubenmire (1966) points out that one must sample stands that differ in only one environmental variable and are otherwise homogeneous. Thus, if we know that vegetation is affected by macroclimate, microclimate (slope effects), soil characteristics, and disturbances, we must hold three of these constant and study the remaining variable. Vegetation sampling which includes all these sources of variation

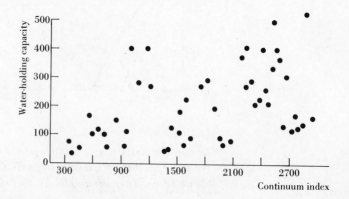

FIGURE 212

Moisture-holding capacity of the A_1 horizon (upper layer) of the soil in relation to the continuum of upland conifer–hardwood forests of northern Wisconsin illustrated in Figure 211. (After Brown and Curtis 1952.)

all mixed together must produce results in which everything overlaps with everything else.

Gradient analysis assumes that all species are equal, and only the species names and their relative abundances are used for analysis. Daubenmire (1966) suggests that this produces erroneous conclusions because some species are dominant to others, and thus all species are not of equal value in determining the community. Community boundaries may be fixed by one or two species only, and there is no need to postulate a complete boundary of all species at the same geographical position.

There is certainly a continuum in the distribution of coniferous trees with respect to altitude in eastern Washington and northern Idaho, Daubenmire (1966) points out, but this is a floristic continuum and not an ecological continuum. If you examine the stands closely, you find that within certain zones one tree species is competitively dominant over the others (Figure 213). This ecological fact is the basis for recognizing discrete communities in an altitudinal transect.

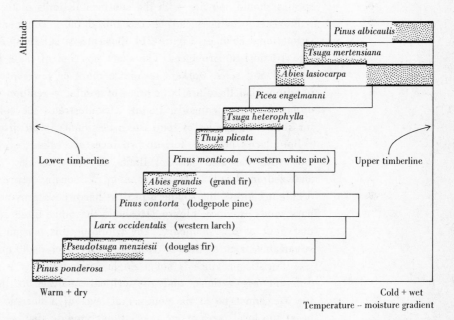

FIGURE 213

Coniferous trees in the area centered in eastern Washington and northern Idaho, arranged vertically to show the usual order in which the species are encountered with increasing altitude. The horizontal bars designate upper and lower limits of the species relative to the climatic gradient. The shaded area indicates that portion of the altitudinal range of a species in which it can maintain a self-reproducing population in the face of intense competition. (After Daubenmire 1962.)

The advocates of the individualistic school reply that we must study vegetation as it exists now over large areas. We cannot select from a vast area only a few stands of "homogeneous" nature to group into an association. This is too subjective, and we must employ objective quantitative techniques to eliminate human subjectivity if we are to achieve a science of community ecology. Community boundaries should not be fixed by only one or two species; we must use all the species present to look for boundaries of "natural units" if the community concept is to be meaningful (Cottam and McIntosh 1966).

Distributional relations of species

If the separate stands that make up a community are similar, all or many of the species must have similar geographic distributions. This should ideally operate both on a micro scale and on a macro scale over the continent. Plant species that comprise an association should have distributional maps that closely coincide on a local level, and the geographic limits of the species should coincide with the continental limits of the association.

Floristic provinces can be recognized on a continental scale by major vegetational changes. Figure 214 illustrates a subdivision of North America into 10 floristic provinces. The exact position of these boundaries is often debated and some workers recognize more or fewer provinces, but no one questions that there are large areas of similar vegetation in which the ranges of many species coincide. Figure 215 illustrates the coincidence of ranges for some tree species of the eastern deciduous forest province.

Boundaries between floristic provinces are called *tension zones* and coincide with the distributional limits of many species. Curtis (1959) has analyzed in detail a tension zone in Wisconsin between two parts of the deciduous forest, the southern prairie–hardwoods province and the northern hardwoods province. Figure 216 shows the range limits for 182 plant species that abut at this boundary. The width of this tension zone in Wisconsin is variable, from as little as 10 miles to as much as 30 miles.

A floristic province is not a single community but is composed of many different associations, and the critical analysis of the distributions of species cannot be at the continental level of a floristic province but must be at the local level of an association. Suppose that we study a number of stands of a particular association in Wisconsin and another group of stands in Michigan. How can we compare the similarity of these two samples? Several measures of community similarity are available (Greig-Smith 1964, Chap. 6); we shall discuss one simple measure based on species presence only. In two communities, one with a number of species and another with b number of species, and c species occurring in both communities, we define

$$\text{Index of similarity} = \frac{2c}{a + b}$$

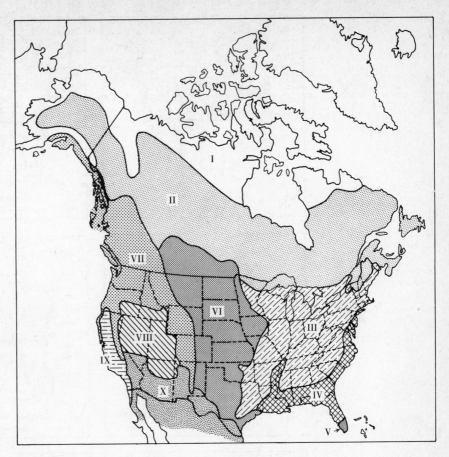

FIGURE 214

*Floristic provinces of the continental United States and Canada.
I, tundra province; II, northern conifer province; III, eastern
deciduous forest province; IV, coastal plain province; V, West
Indian Province; VI, grassland province; VII, cordilleran forest
province; VIII, Great Basin province; IX, California province; X,
Sonoran province. For this map the lines between the provinces have
been drawn boldly, to show the general outlines rather than the
ultimate details. The actual boundaries are in general not sharp;
they overlap and interfinger extensively, and small enclaves of one
province may be wholly surrounded by another. (After Gleason and
Cronquist 1964.)*

This index ranges from 0 to 1.0 to quantify the range from no similarity
to complete similarity. For example, the southern mesic forests of Wisconsin
contain 26 tree species (dominated by sugar maple, basswood, beech, and
red oak), and the northern mesic forests of Wisconsin contain 27 tree

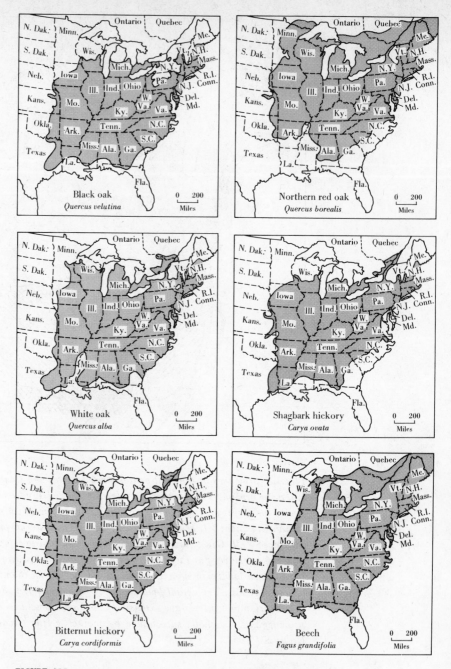

FIGURE 215

Ranges of certain forest trees of the eastern deciduous forest of North America. (After Gleason and Cronquist 1964.)

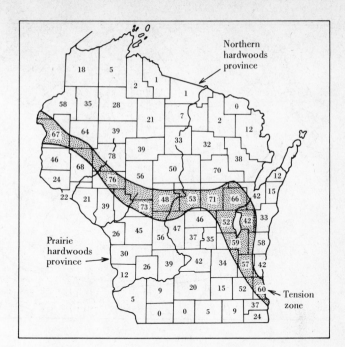

FIGURE 216

Tension zone between two floristic provinces in Wisconsin. Summary of range limits for 182 species of plants. The figures in each county indicate the number of species attaining a range boundary there. The shaded band is the tension zone. (After Curtis 1959.)

species (dominated by sugar maple, eastern hemlock, beech, yellow birch, and basswood). Seventeen species occur in both communities, and the index of similarity for tree species is calculated as

$$\text{Index of similarity} = \frac{(2)(17)}{26 + 27} = 0.64$$

We can illustrate the use of the index of similarity for the northern conifer province shown in Figure 214.

The boreal forest extends in a broad crescent across North America from Alaska to Newfoundland and is the dominant plant community in the northern conifer province. In the boreal forest on undisturbed sites the forest is dominated either by white spruce (*Picea glauca*), black spruce (*Picea mariana*), balsam fir (*Abies balsamea*), or a mixture of these. La Roi (1967) sampled 34 stands dominated by white spruce and balsam fir from Alaska to Newfoundland (Figure 217); we can use these data to inquire about the similarity of stands within the boreal forest.

Trees that dominate the white spruce and fir stands in the boreal forest do not have a uniform geographical distribution. In Alaska and the Yukon there was no balsam fir associated with white spruce. Conversely, in Newfoundland there was no white spruce associated with balsam fir. Trembling aspen and balsam poplar were present from Ontario westward; white pine occurred only to the east of Ontario. Figure 218 shows these ranges

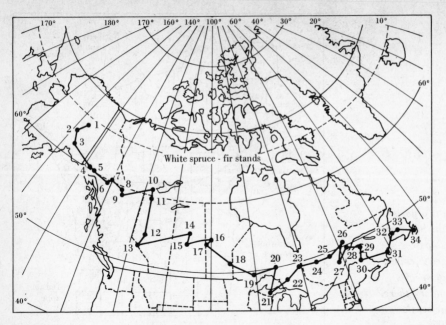

FIGURE 217

Locations of white spruce–balsam fir stands sampled by La Roi (1967) across the boreal forest of North America. (After La Roi 1967.)

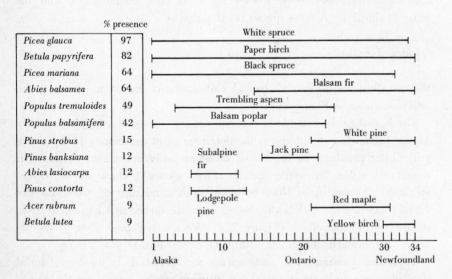

	% presence
Picea glauca	97
Betula papyrifera	82
Picea mariana	64
Abies balsamea	64
Populus tremuloides	49
Populus balsamifera	42
Pinus strobus	15
Pinus banksiana	12
Abies lasiocarpa	12
Pinus contorta	12
Acer rubrum	9
Betula lutea	9

FIGURE 218

Geographic distribution of tree species in the 34 stands of white spruce and fir of the North American boreal forest. Map locations of stands are shown in Figure 217. Percentage of the 34 stands in which the species occurred is also given. (After La Roi 1967.)

and indicates that stands in the eastern part of the boreal forest must differ from stands in the western part.

We can quantify these shifts by the use of the index of similarity. In this case we choose an intermediate site (stand 17) and compare the other 33 stands to this central stand. We can do this for trees, shrubs, and herbs, with the results shown in Figure 219. There is a gradual change from stand 17 in Manitoba both east and west, so the community represented by the white spruce–fir stands gradually changes in composition. There are no sharp breakpoints.

If we repeat this kind of analysis for many different associations we find that some are more homogeneous over large areas than others. Curtis (1959), for example, pointed out the great floristic homogeneity of the deciduous forests of eastern North America. On mesic sites sugar maple is dominant over most of this area, and beech, basswood, and buckeye are leading dominants over large areas. By contrast, the conifer swamp community, originally thought to be very uniform, changes completely in floristic composition from west to east. Only two trees, tamarack and black spruce, remain constant; it is they alone that produce an appearance of a similar community type to the casual observer.

Another way of viewing the distributional problem of species in a community is to look at the geographical ranges of species that make up a community. In the Great Basin area of Nevada and California, large expanses of small-leaved shrubby vegetation, called the *sagebrush formation,* occupy the semiarid valleys. Two associations can be generally recognized within the sagebrush formation—a shadscale zone, characterized by the universal presence of *Atriplex confertifolia,* and a sagebrush zone dominated by *Artemesia tridentata.* Billings (1949) analyzed the shadscale zone (Figure 220) and showed that the sites it occupied were drier than those in the

FIGURE 219

Index of similarity for 34 white spruce–fir stands of the North American boreal forest. Stand 17 in Manitoba was chosen as a central location and all stands were compared to it. Trend line fitted by eye. (After La Roi 1967.)

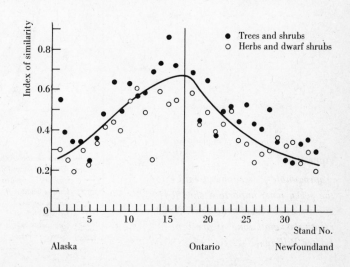

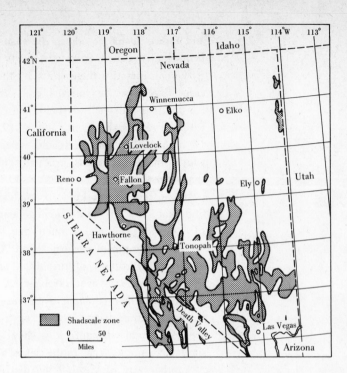

FIGURE 220

*Areal extent of the shadscale zone
in Nevada and eastern California.
(After Billings 1949.)*

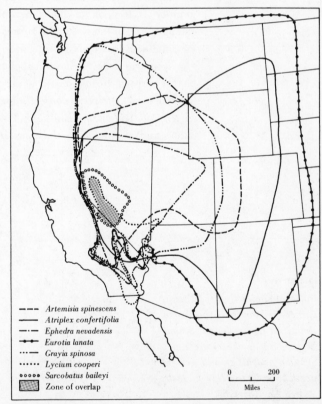

FIGURE 221

*Approximate geographical ranges of
the seven most important shrubby
species of the shadscale zone. Note
relatively small zone of overlap.
(After Billings 1949.)*

sagebrush zone and that it occurred on gray desert soils of variable salinity. Each stand in the shadscale zone was different from every other stand in species composition and density of vegetation, even though one could recognize shadscale vegetation as a natural unit. The ties between the members of this community would seem to be weak. The geographical distributions of the seven most important shrub species of this community, shown in Figure 221, are all independent and extend far beyond the range of the shadscale community, which occurs only in Nevada and eastern California. The shadscale zone seems to grade into adjacent plant associations, particularly to the south and east, and no sharp boundaries may be recognized.

Dynamic relations between species populations

If the association is a natural unit, species populations should be bound together in a network, organized by obligate interrelations. This is the basic idea of the "web of life." In order to evaluate how strong the network of interrelations is, we must go back to a discussion of the factors that limit the distribution and abundance of species populations.

We can recognize a sequence of relationships between two species of organisms on a schematic scale:

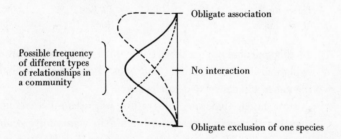

Possible frequency of different types of relationships in a community

Obligate association

No interaction

Obligate exclusion of one species

We must now ask where on this scale most of the species in a community would fall. Another way of stating this question is to ask how frequently the distribution and abundance of one species is determined by interactions with other species. No one knows the answer to this at present, but we can make a few general statements.

Obligate associations may occur in certain parasites that have a single host species, or certain animals that feed on only one species of plant. Very few plants and only a small number of animals seem to have life cycles so tightly coupled to one other species. Most species have only a partial dependence on others. An insect may feed on one of several plant species, and predators may eat a variety of prey species. Partial dependency of this type seems most common in nature and grades off into a state of indifference in which species do not interact (Whittaker 1962). For example, Table 26 (page 387) shows that a majority of the species pairs in *Juncus effusus* stands show no evidence of interaction.

At the other limit, species distributions may be limited by competitive exclusion, a mechanism that could generate sharp boundaries of communities. We have already discussed competitive exclusion and shown that the results of competition rarely lead to such a clear conclusion (Chap. 12). If we assume that only closely-related species should show evidences of competition, there is no reason to suppose that this would affect all the members of a community in the same way. Competition operates between a few species only and does not involve the whole community.

An attempt to measure the relative importance of competitive interactions in limiting distribution was made by Terborgh (1971) using the bird fauna along an elevation gradient in the eastern Andes of Peru. The upper and lower elevational limits of bird species were examined and the limits classified as being caused by (1) competitive exclusion, (2) discontinuities between zones of vegetation, or (3) environmental gradients. Terborgh classified the limits of 261 species of birds, as follows:

Cause of distributional limit

	Competition	Vegetation discontinuity	Environmental gradients
Lower limits	*36%*	*21%*	*43%*
Upper limits	*28%*	*16%*	*56%*

In this particular case about one-third of the distributional limits could be explained by competition, and most limits were probably set by environmental gradients related to elevation.

How much dynamic integration is present in a community is a critical question that arises again and again in community ecology, and cannot yet be answered. Whittaker (1962) suggests that, if all species interactions were known, the distribution would be bell shaped, with most species hovering around the middle (no interaction) and a few species at each extreme of obligate association and dissociation. If this is true, the relationships between species populations will not be strong enough to organize all species into a well-defined community.

Hidden in much of this discussion is an unavoidable bias. Most of the work on communities has been done in the north temperate zone, and when tropical communities are studied in more detail we may have to revise our generalizations (Langford and Buell 1969).

The present view of the nature of the community lies closer to Gleason's individualistic view than to Clements' superorganismic interpretation. Species are distributed individualistically according to their own genetic characteristics. Populations of most species tend to change gradually along environmental gradients. Most species are not in obligatory association with other species, and this suggests that associations will be formed with many combinations of species and will vary continuously in space and in time. To classify such associations into discrete units is a highly artificial undertaking.

A historical footnote serves to emphasize the conclusion of the individualistic nature of the community. Historical changes in vegetation can be interpreted in some detail by the use of fossil pollen grains in lake sediments. If one reconstructs the forest history of an area such as Minnesota (Wright 1968), one finds a continuous series of species coming and going. Some modern forest communities have no analog in the past, and conversely some associations found in the past do not exist anywhere at the present time. Historical evidence supports the view that we reached from an analysis of modern communities.

Almost all of the discussion about the nature of the community has been based on plant communities; relatively few animal ecologists have gotten involved in this dispute. A few studies on bird-species communities have supported the individualistic view of Gleason (Bond 1957, Beals 1960). But a more telling commentary is that the most recent book on animal community ecology (Elton 1966) does not even refer to Gleason or Clements.

CLASSIFICATION OF COMMUNITIES

The problems of classifying communities are interwoven with the question of the nature of the community. If communities were discrete entities like species, we should be able to construct a taxonomy of communities. But if they vary continuously and are not discrete units, we can still classify them, but we can use a variety of different classification systems, since no single scheme is the "natural" classification. Classification is more for human convenience than for delimiting nature's true structure.

Goodall (1963) has proposed a geometrical model to conceptualize the problem we face: First, construct a geometric system in which each species in the community is one axis, and then measure the abundance of the species in some manner, such as percentage cover. If we have two species in the community, we have a two-dimensional model, and this oversimplified version is shown in Figure 222. If we have 200 species, we have a 200-dimensional community hyperspace, which is impossible to picture (so we think of this space in terms of two or three dimensions to get the illustration). Every stand we sample will now be a point in this community space, and the question we need to consider is how these points are arranged. Do they form clouds of points separated by mostly empty space? Or are the points continuously distributed throughout the space? Regardless of how the points are scattered in space, we can divide the space up into little boxes. One's view of the nature of the community affects the way one interprets these little boxes.

There are many different kinds of classification one can use to classify

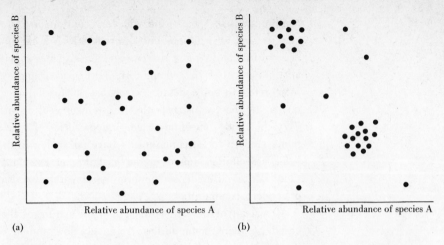

(a)   (b)

FIGURE 222

"Vegetation space" to illustrate two different conceptions of vege-
tation, one (a) with no clustering and the other (b) with clear
clustering into compact clouds of points ("nodes") representing
discrete communities.

communities. Three choices immediately confront a student who is attempting to classify a series of items (Pielou 1969, Chap. 19) :

1 Should the classification be *hierarchical* or *reticulate?* The hierarchical classification is the familiar one of taxonomy in which there are levels that are sub-
classes of higher levels. In a reticulate classification the groups are defined
separately and linked in a network:

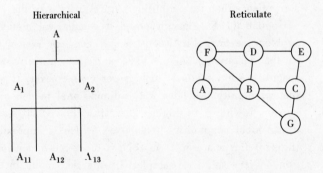

2 Should the classification be *divisive* or *agglomerative?* In a divisive classification we begin with the whole and divide it up into parts. In an agglomerative
classification we begin with the parts and add them together into classes, combining and recombining them into more inclusive groups.

3 Should the classification be *monothetic* or *polythetic?* In a monothetic classification two closely-related groups are distinguished by a single attribute. In a
polythetic classification, two groups are distinguished on the basis of a number
of attributes.

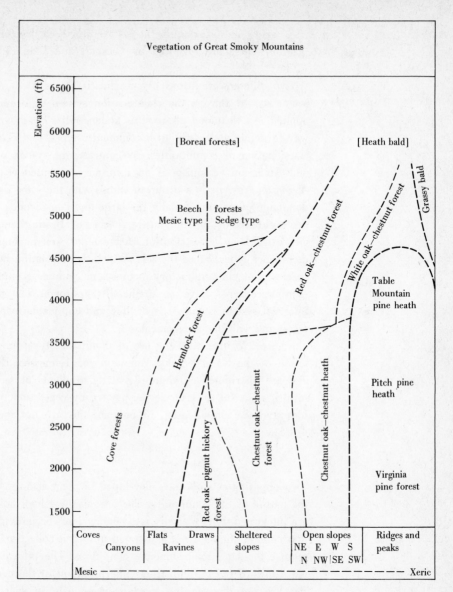

FIGURE 223

Chart of vegetation types in relation to elevation and topography in the Great Smoky Mountains, Tennessee. The vertical axis is the complex gradient of temperature and other factors related to elevation; the horizontal axis is the complex gradient of moisture relations and other factors from moist or mesic situations on the left to dry or xeric on the right, as affected by topographic position. (After Whittaker 1956.)

A variety of statistical methods have now been developed for use in classification. These are reviewed by Lambert and Dale (1964) and by Pielou (1969).

Two different traditions of classification have predominated among plant ecologists. In Europe the classification system of Braun-Blanquet has been applied. As we noted above, this system relies on diagnostic species as the way to define and distinguish community types, and produces a hierarchical classification of communities. By contrast, the system used by most British and American ecologists is an informal one based on "dominance types." A *dominance type* is a group of stands with the same dominant species. The dominant species are usually the large and conspicuous ones and are almost the antithesis of the diagnostic species of Braun-Blanquet. Dominant species often have a distribution that extends well beyond the limits of their dominance types. Since there is often little association between the dominant species and the understory plants and animals, communities defined by dominance types have an artificiality to them. The major value of this informal system is that it is flexible and applicable to practical problems in forest and wildlife management.

Figure 223 illustrates the use of dominance types in describing the vegetation of the Great Smoky Mountains of Tennessee. Even though the species are distributed continuously along gradients of moisture and temperature, it is useful to describe the pattern by vegetation types. The continuum idea and the classification of communities are not incompatible concepts.

SUMMARY

Two opposing schools have developed in plant ecology over the question of the nature of the community. The organismic school holds that communities are integrated units with discrete boundaries. The individualistic school holds that communities are not integrated units but collections of populations that require the same environmental conditions. The information available leans more toward the individualistic interpretation of the community. Communities are not discrete but grade continuously in space and in time, and species groups are not consistent from place to place. In spite of this continuous variation, communities can be classified, but this classification is for the convenience of man and not a description of the fundamental structure of nature.

SELECTED REFERENCES

DAUBENMIRE, R. 1966. Vegetation: identification of typal communities. *Science* 151:291–298.

GOODALL, D. W. 1963. The continuum and the individualistic association. *Vegetatio* 11:297–316.

LANGFORD, A. N., and M. F. BUELL. 1969. Integration, identity and stability in the plant association. *Advances Ecol. Res.* 6:83–135.

MCINTOSH, R. P. 1967. The continuum concept of vegetation. *Bot. Rev.* 33:130–187.

WEBB, D. A. 1954. Is the classification of plant communities either possible or desirable? *Bot. Tidsskr.* 51:362–370.

WHITTAKER, R. H. 1962. Classification of natural communities. *Bot. Rev.* 28:1–239.

QUESTIONS AND PROBLEMS

1 Whittaker (1967, p. 207) states that "Gradient analysis and classification are alternative approaches to the vegetation of a landscape." Discuss your agreement or disagreement with this view.

2 Discuss the significance of ecotypes to the problem of community description and classification, and suggest possible ways of alleviating any difficulties that you uncover in your analysis.

3 In discussing the classification of plant communities Ashby (1948, p. 223) states:

When the ecologist stops his car and decides that he has reached a "suitable place" for throwing quadrats on a community, he has already performed the major act of classification and he has performed it subjectively. Any subsequent quantitative analysis only elaborates, and possibly obscures, the original subjective decision.

Discuss this claim.

4 Discuss the role that allelopathic agents might play in determining the integrity and stability of the association.

5 Morey (1936, p. 54) studied two stands of virgin forest in northwestern Pennsylvania and found 93 species of plants common to both stands, 91 species found only in Heart's Content stand, and 57 species found only in Cook Forest stand. Calculate the index of similarity for these two virgin stands.

6 Construct an ordination of the following hypothetical data. Assign climax adaptation numbers to the 8 species and plot the resulting gradient analysis as in Figure 211.

Importance value of species

Stand	A	B	C	D	E	F	G	H
1	150	20	50	10	5	5	30	30
2	10	70	10	—	60	20	30	100
3	20	40	20	—	10	—	200	10
4	—	10	—	90	70	120	—	10
5	20	110	20	10	30	10	60	40
6	260	—	30	—	—	—	10	—
7	—	10	—	20	200	30	—	40
8	—	60	—	—	50	—	—	190
9	—	10	—	130	60	80	—	20
10	70	10	160	—	—	—	50	10
11	—	30	10	20	100	80	—	60
12	—	—	10	—	270	10	—	10

7 Compare and contrast the controversy over the nature of the community with the controversy between classical and numerical taxonomy (see Sokal and Sneath, 1963, Chap. 2, for references). How have these controversies helped to clarify important theoretical issues?

20 Community change

One of the most important features of vegetation is change, and since animals are directly dependent on plants, any change in vegetation causes changes in the animal community. There are two main types of temporal changes in communities: directional changes in time, called *succession*; and nondirectional changes in time, which are *cyclic* (fluctuate about a mean). We shall discuss each of these in turn, and focus on two questions: (1) How predictable are community changes? (2) What factors cause community changes?

SUCCESSION

An area of bare ground when stripped of its original vegetation by fire, flood, or glaciation does not remain devoid of plants and animals. The area is rapidly colonized by a variety of species which subsequently modify one or more environmental factors. This modification of the environment in turn allows additional species to become established. This development of the community by the action of vegetation on the environment leading to the development of new species is termed *succession*. Succession is the universal process of directional change in vegetation. It can be recognized by the progressive change in the species composition of the community.

The concept of succession was largely developed by the botanists Warming (1896) and Cowles (1901), who studied the stages of sand-dune development. The ideas of succession were elaborated in great detail by F. E. Clements, who developed a complete theory of plant succession and community development called the *monoclimax hypothesis*. The biotic community, according to Clements, was a highly integrated superorganism. It showed development through a process of succession to a single end point in any given area—the *climatic climax*. The development of the community was gradual and progressive, from simple pioneer communities to the ultimate or climax stage. This succession was due to biotic reactions only; the plants and animals of the pioneer stages alter the environment so as to favor a new set of species, and this cycle recurs until the climax is reached. Development through succession in a community is thus analogous to development in an individual organism, according to Clements' view (Clements 1936, Phillips 1934–1935). Thus retrogression was not possible unless some disturbance such as fire, grazing, or erosion intervened.

The climax community in any region is determined by climate in Clements' view. Other communities may result from particular soil types, or fire, or grazing, but these are understandable only with reference to the end point of the climatic climax. The natural classification of communities must therefore be based on the climatic climax, which represents the state of equilibrium for the area.

How well do natural communities fit the ideas of Clements? Does succession in a region converge to a single end point? Let us look at a few examples of succession. Numerous examples of succession have been described in detail, but there are relatively few cases in which the succession can be related to a time scale. Some examples have been investigated in detail where time scale is known and I should like to describe these briefly.

Glacial moraine succession in southeastern Alaska During the past 200 years there has been a generalized retreat of glaciers in the Northern Hemisphere. As the glaciers retreat they leave moraines whose age can be determined by the age of the new trees growing on them or, in the case of the last 70 years, by direct observation. The most intensive work on this problem of moraine succession has been done at Glacier Bay in southeastern Alaska. Since about 1750 the glaciers there have retreated about 61 miles, an extraordinary rate of retreat (Figure 224).

The pattern of succession in this area proceeds as follows (Cooper 1939, Lawrence 1958). The exposed glacial till is colonized first by mosses, fireweed, *Dryas*, willows, and cottonwood. The willows begin as prostrate plants

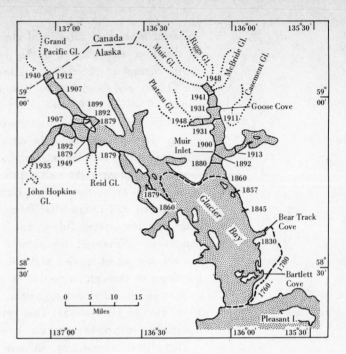

FIGURE 224

Glacier Bay fiord complex of south-eastern Alaska showing the rate of ice recession since 1760. (After Crocker and Major 1955.)

but later grow into erect shrubs. Very quickly the area is invaded by alder (*Alnus*), which eventually forms dense pure thickets up to 30 ft tall. This requires about 50 years. These alder stands are invaded by Sitka spruce, which, after another 120 years, forms a dense forest. Western hemlock and mountain hemlock invade the spruce stands, and after another 80 years the situation has stabilized with a climax spruce–hemlock forest. This forest, however, only remains on well-drained slopes. In areas of poor drainage the forest floor of this spruce–hemlock forest is invaded by *Sphagnum* mosses, which hold large amounts of water and acidify the soil greatly. With the spread of conditions associated with *Sphagnum*, the trees die out because the soil is waterlogged and too oxygen deficient for tree roots, and the area becomes a *Sphagnum* bog, or *muskeg*. The climax vegetation then seems to be muskeg on the poorly drained areas and spruce–hemlock forest on the well-drained areas.

The bare soil exposed as the glacier retreated was quite basic, with a pH of 8.0 to 8.4 because of the carbonates contained in the parent rocks. The soil pH falls rapidly with the advent of vegetation, and the rate of change depends on the vegetation type (Figure 225). There is almost no change in the pH due to leaching in bare soil. The most striking change is caused by alder, which reduces the pH from 8.0 to 5.0 in 30 to 50 years. The leaves of alder are slightly acid, and as they decompose they become more acid. As the spruce begins to take over from the alder the pH stabilizes at about 5.0, and it does not change in the next 150 years.

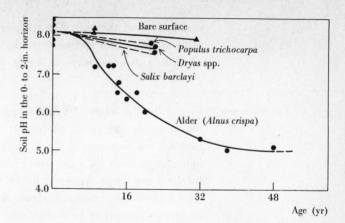

FIGURE 225

Soil pH change at Glacier Bay, Alaska, under different types of pioneer vegetation. The soil becomes acid very rapidly under alder. (After Crocker and Major 1955.)

The organic carbon and total nitrogen concentrations in the soil also show marked changes with time. Figure 226 shows the changes in nitrogen levels. One of the characteristic features of the bare soil is its low nitrogen content. Almost all the pioneer species begin the succession with very poor growth and yellow leaves because of the inadequate nitrogen supply. The exceptions to this are *Dryas* and alder; these species have some way of fixing atmospheric nitrogen (Lawrence et al. 1967). The rapid increase in soil nitrogen in the alder stage is caused by the presence of nodules on the alder roots which contain microorganisms that actively fix nitrogen from the air. Spruce trees have no such adaptations; consequently, the soil nitrogen level falls when alders are eliminated. The spruce forest develops by using the capital of nitrogen accumulated by the alder.

The important point to notice here is the reciprocal interrelations of the

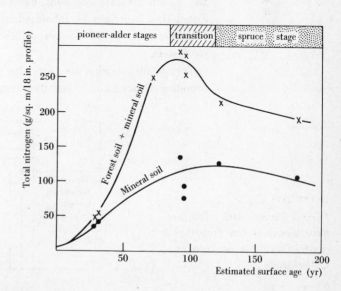

FIGURE 226

Total nitrogen content of soils recently uncovered by glacial retreat at Glacier Bay, Alaska. Plant succession is shown along top. (After Crocker and Major 1955.)

vegetation and the soil. The pioneer plants alter the soil properties, which in turn permit new species to grow, and these species in turn alter the environment in different ways, bringing about succession.

Insects in cow droppings

In a delightful essay, "Cattle droppings as ecological units," Mohr (1943) illustrates the ideas of succession for a microhabitat that changes very rapidly. The sequence of insect species attacking cow dung varies seasonally and also among habitats. Dung deposited in the shade attracts different species from dung deposited in the sun. Dung deposited in the woods contains a different community from dung in open pasture. Let us describe a sequence appropriate to midsummer in Illinois in an open pasture.

A new cow pat is immediately attacked by the ubiquitous horn fly, *Haematobia irritans*. This fly lands instantly on new dung, moving over the surface quickly and depositing eggs. Most of these flies return to sit on the cow after 30 seconds. A series of other species of dung flies colonize the dropping in a sequence shown in Figure 227. For about a week the populations of these flies in the larval stages increase and then decrease as the dung begins to dry out.

Predatory beetles such as *Sphaeridium scarabaeoides* may arrive at the cow pat very quickly and burrow through the dung, laying eggs. The larvae of this beetle are predatory on the fly larvae inside the dropping. A parasitic wasp *Xyalophora quinquelineata* arrives very quickly at a new dropping and deposits its eggs in maggots of *Sarcophaga* spp. flies during the first few days.

As the cow dung ages it becomes more acceptable to a variety of soil invertebrates, and a great many species may then be found in the dropping. But within 30 days the dung has been broken down and dried out to the extent that it cannot be inhabited by insects. During the total sequence of breakdown 40 to 60 species of insects may be collected from this simple system.

The details of why the particular sequence of species occurs in the cow dropping is not known, and the system would repay further work.

FIGURE 227

Periods during which adult flies were present on cow droppings in central Illinois during summer. (After Mohr 1943.)

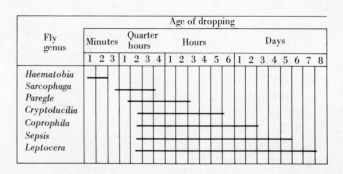

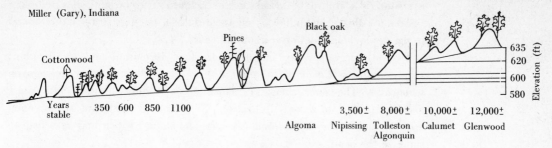

Miller (Gary), Indiana

Cottonwood Pines Black oak

Years stable 350 600 850 1100 3,500± 8,000± 10,000± 12,000±

Algoma Nipissing Tolleston Calumet Glenwood
Algonquin

Elevation (ft): 635 620 600 580

FIGURE 228

*Diagrammatic profiles across Indiana sand dunes at the southern
end of Lake Michigan. Successively older dune systems originated
along earlier and higher beaches. (After Olson 1958.)*

Lake Michigan
sand-dune
succession

Cowles (1899) from the University of Chicago worked on the sand-dune
vegetation of Lake Michigan and made a classic contribution to the ideas of
plant succession. Olson (1958) has reexamined the successional stages in
this area in relation to an absolute time scale.

During and after the retreat of the glaciers from the Great Lakes area
the resulting fall in lake level left several distinct "raised beaches" and their
associated dune systems. These systems, which run roughly parallel to the
present shoreline of Lake Michigan, are about 25, 40, and 55 ft above the
present lake level (Figure 228). Olson dated the older dunes by radiocarbon
techniques and the younger areas by tree-ring counts and recorded historical
changes since 1893.

The dunes offer a near-ideal system for studying plant succession because
many of the complicating variables are absent. The initial substrate for all
the area is dune sand, the climate for the whole area is similar, the relief
is similar, and the available flora and fauna are the same. Hence the differences between the different dunes should be due only to *time,* the *biological processes of succession,* and *chance events* associated with dispersal and
colonization.

Two processes produce bare sand surfaces ready for colonization. One is
the slow process of a fall in lake level; the other is a rapid process, the
blowout of an established dune. These blowouts result from the strong
winds that come off the lake. This wind erosion sets up a moving dune
which is gradually stabilized after migrating inland. The dunes are stabilized
only by vegetation.

The bare sand surface is colonized first by dune-building grasses, of
which the most important is Marram grass (*Ammophila breviligulata*).
Marram grass usually propagates by rhizome migration, only rarely by
seed. It spreads very quickly and can stabilize a bare area in 6 years. After

the sand is stabilized Marram grass declines in vigor and dies out. The reason for this is not known, but the result is that this grass is not found in the stable dune areas after about 20 years.

Two other grasses are important in dune formation and stabilization: sand reed grass (*Calamovilfa longifolia*) and the little bluestem (*Andropogon scoparius*). The sand cherry (*Prunus pumila*) and willows (*Salix* spp.) also play a role in dune stabilization. The first tree to appear in the young dune is usually the cottonwood (*Populus deltoides*), which may also help to stabilize the sand.

Once the dune is stabilized it may be invaded very quickly by jack pine and white pine if seed is available; normally pines are found after 50 to 100 years of development. Under normal conditions black oak replaces the pines, entering the succession at about 100 to 150 years. A whole group of shrubs that require considerable light invade the early pine and oak stands; they are replaced by more shade-tolerant shrubs as the forest of black oak becomes denser.

Cowles believed that this succession to black oak might be part of the succession sequence, which would then proceed to a white oak–red oak–hickory forest, and finally to the "climatic climax," beech–maple forest. But Olson questioned whether this could ever occur. The oldest dunes Olson studied still had black oak associations (12,000 years), and he could see no tendency for any further succession. Moreover, the black oak community was very heterogeneous and Olson recognized four different types of understory communities that could occur under black oak. Figure 229 summarizes the successional patterns on the dunes.

Olson also studied the changes in the soil in relation to this time sequence. The pH of the soil decreased with dune age, from high values of 7.6 at the start of succession to 4.0 after 10,000 years. The initial drop in pH is caused by carbonates being leached from the soil very quickly. Soil nitrogen increases rapidly in the first 1000 years of development, from very low values initially to approximately 0.1%, and then remains unchanged in older dunes. Organic carbon in the soil develops similarly.

Thus most of the soil improvements of the original barren dune sand occur within about 1000 years after stabilization. As a result of these trends in the soil, Olson pointed out that the nutritional conditions for succession toward beech and maple probably become *less* favorable with time. (These trees require more calcium, near neutral pH, and larger amounts of water.) It appears improbable that this succession will move beyond the black oak stage, contrary to what Cowles had suggested. Beech and maple associations in this area are found only in favorable situations such as moist lowlands, where the soil characteristics differ from those of the dry dunes. The low fertility of the dune soils favors vegetation, such as the black oak, that has limited nutrient and water requirements. But this sort of vegeta-

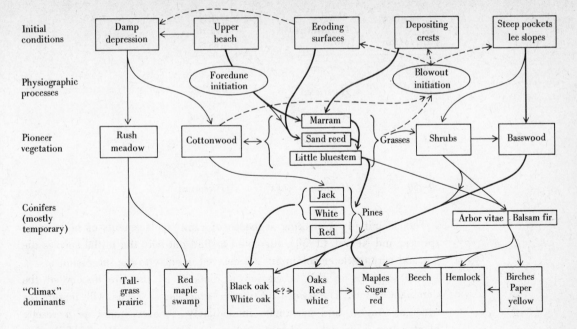

Initial conditions · Physiographic processes · Pioneer vegetation · Conifers (mostly temporary) · "Climax" dominants

FIGURE 229

*Alternative dune successions in Lake Michigan sand dunes. Beaches,
foredunes, and blowout dunes provide diverse sites that undergo
different successions. The center of the diagram gives oversimplified
outline of "normal" succession, from dune builders to jack or white
pine to black oak–white oak with several undercover types. (After
Olson 1958.)*

tion is ineffective in returning nutrients to the dune surface in its litter,
which continues the cycle of low fertility.

As far as the dunes are concerned, probably the most striking vegetational changes occur in the first hundred years, and the system seems to
become stabilized with the black oak association by about 1000 years.
Olson pointed out that it was a mistake to distort the different dune successions into a single linear sequence leading from pine to black oak to
oak–hickory to beech–maple. Successions in the dunes go off in different
directions with different destinations, depending on the various soil, water,
and biotic factors involved at a particular site. Instead of *convergence* to a
single climax, Olson suggested, we may get *divergence* of different communities on different sites.

**Abandoned
farmland in
North Carolina**

When upland farm fields are abandoned in the Piedmont area of North Carolina, a succession of plant species colonizes the area. The sequence is as
follows:

Years after last cultivation	Dominant plant	Other common species
0 (fall)	Crabgrass ↓	
1	Horseweed ↓	Ragweed
2	Aster ↓	Ragweed
3	Broomsedge ↓	
5–15	Shortleaf pine ↓	(Loblolly pine)
50–150	Hardwoods (oaks)	(Hickories)

This is initially a striking sequence of rapid replacements of herbaceous species, and Keever (1950) attempted to find out why the initial species die out and why the later colonizers are delayed in entry to the succession.

The sequence of this succession is dictated by the life history of the dominant plants. Horseweed (*Erigeron canadensis*) seeds will mature as early as August and germinate immediately. It overwinters as a rosette plant which is drought resistant, and grows, blooms, and dies the following summer (an annual). The second generation of horseweed plants is stunted and does not grow well in the second year of the succession. Decaying horseweed roots inhibit the growth of horseweed seedlings. The density of horseweed individuals is much greater in second-year fields, but these individuals do not do well with increased competition from aster and other horseweed. The result is a great reduction of horseweed in second-year fields.

Aster (*Aster pilosus*) seeds mature in the fall too late to germinate in the year that plowing ceases. Seeds germinate the following spring, and seedlings grow slowly during their first year to 2 to 3 inches by autumn. This slow growth is partly caused by shading by horseweed, and decaying horseweed roots stunt aster growth. Horseweeds therefore do not pave the way for asters; if anything, they have a detrimental effect on them. Asters enter the succession in spite of horseweeds, not because of them.

Aster (a perennial) blooms in its second year, after horseweed declines, but is not drought resistant. Seedlings of aster are present in large numbers in third-year fields, but these succumb to competition for moisture with the drought-resistant broomsedge (*Andropogon virginicus*). In fields with more available water, aster is able to last into the third year, but eventually broomsedge overwhelms it.

Broomsedge seeds will not germinate without a period of cold dormancy. A few broomsedge plants are found in 1-year fields but do not drop seed until fall of the second year. Broomsedge is a very drought-resistant perennial and competes very well for soil moisture. There are few broomsedge

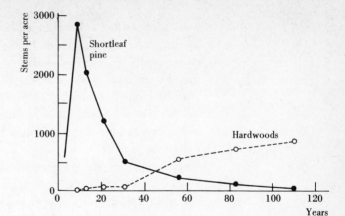

FIGURE 230

Decline in the abundance of short-
leaf pine and increase in the density
of hardwood tree seedlings during
succession on abandoned farmland
in the Piedmont area of North
Carolina. (After Billings 1938.)

plants in 1- and 2-year fields because few seeds are present. Once some plants begin seeding, broomsedge rapidly increases in numbers (third year). Broomsedge grows better in soil with organic matter, especially in soil with aster roots. It grows very poorly in the shade.

Early succession in Piedmont old fields is thus governed more by competition than by cooperation between plants. The early pioneers do *not* make the environment more suitable for later species, and the later species achieve dominance in spite of the changes caused by the early species rather than because of them. If seeds were available, broomsedge could colonize an abandoned field immediately rather than following after horseweed and aster.

After this succession by herbs and grasses, abandoned farmland of the Piedmont of North Carolina is invaded in great numbers by shortleaf pine (*Pinus echinata*). Pine seeds can germinate only on mineral soil and are able to become established only when there is little root competition. The density of pines is very high but falls rapidly as the pines lose their dominance to hardwoods (Figure 230). After approximately 50 years several species of oaks become important trees in the understory, and the hardwoods gradually fill in the community. Reproduction of shortleaf pine is almost completely lacking after about 20 years (Figure 231) because there

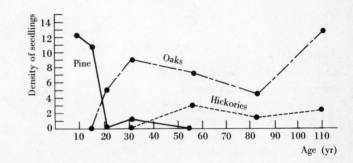

FIGURE 231

Density of reproduction of pines,
oaks, and hickories during the
shortleaf pine succession in the
Piedmont area of North Carolina.
(After Billings 1938.)

is no bare soil for seed germination and pine seedlings cannot live in shade. The networks of pine roots in the soil become closed very quickly, and the accumulation of litter under the pines causes the old-field herbs to die out (Figure 232). Oak seedlings first appear after 20 years, when enough litter has been accumulated to protect the acorns from desiccation and the soil is able to retain more moisture. Hardwood seedlings persist in the understory because they develop a root system deep enough to exploit soil water (see page 93).

Soil properties change dramatically along with this plant succession on Piedmont soils. Organic matter accumulates in the surface layers of the soil, and increases in the deeper soil layers (Figure 233). Since the moisture-holding capacity of the soil increases with organic content, the soil becomes more able to hold colloidal water for use by the plants.

Shortleaf pine is thus independent of the early succession in that it requires only bare soil for germination. If all herbaceous species could be eliminated from the early succession, this would not affect colonization by pines. Oaks and other hardwoods, by contrast, depend on the soil changes caused by pine litter, so oak seedlings could not become established without the environmental changes produced by pines.

Abandoned farmland in Oklahoma

Abandoned cropland in Oklahoma goes through a sequence of plant succession that can be shown as follows (Booth 1941):

Stage	Duration of stage
Weeds	2 years
↓	
Annual grass (*Aristida oligantha*)	9–13 years
↓	
Bunch grass (*Andropogon scoparius*)	25 + ? years
↓	
Tall-grass prairie	climax vegetation

FIGURE 232

Decline in the number of herbaceous species and increase in the soil organic matter during the succession from old-field to shortleaf pine in the Piedmont area of North Carolina. (After Billings 1938.)

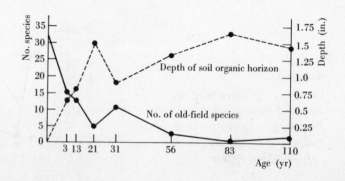

FIGURE 233

*Increase in organic-matter content
of the soil during old-field succession
in the Piedmont area of North
Carolina. Soil moisture-holding capacity is closely related to organic-
matter content. The A₂ layer is the
zone of maximum leaching in the
upper mineral soil. (After Billings
1938.)*

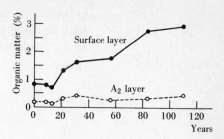

The order in which grasses invade abandoned farmland in Oklahoma is apparently controlled both by dispersal rate of seeds and by nutrient requirements (Rice et al. 1960). The sequence of the three grasses is

Successional stage	Early $\longrightarrow$		Late
Grass	*Aristida oligantha* →	*Andropogon scoparius* →	*Panicum virgatum*
Seed dispersal distance	Long	Short (6 ft)	?
Nitrogen requirement	Low	Moderate	High
Phosphorus requirement	Low	Moderate	High
Potassium requirement	Low	Low	Low

[handwritten: 9–13 years]

[handwritten: strongly clonal by long rhizomes]

[handwritten: Clonal]

Since soils in the early stages after crop abandonment have a low nitrogen and phosphorus content, the succession of these grasses fits their nutrient requirements.

Nitrogen is fixed in soils by nitrogen-fixing bacteria and blue-green algae, and the pioneer plant species in Oklahoma old fields produce chemicals that inhibit nitrogen-fixing bacteria and algae (Rice 1968). This slows the rate of addition of nitrogen to the soil and thereby increases the length of the succession. Plants that require low amounts of nitrogen, and produce the inhibitory chemicals, would thus be at a selective advantage over plants with high nitrogen requirements. Rice and his colleagues have been able to identify some of the chemicals involved in the growth inhibition.

The usual explanation for successional changes in old fields is that each stage increases the organic matter of the soil and improves soil structure and water capacity so that a new set of species can take hold. This has not been an adequate explanation for the early stages of old-field succession in Oklahoma and Kansas (Parenti and Rice 1969). The weed stage is replaced very rapidly by the grass *Aristida oligantha,* but this grass can live in worse soil and water conditions than the pioneer species it replaces. Rice postulated that the weed species produced chemical inhibitors which affected themselves but not *A. oligantha,* and this explained the rapid succession.

Crabgrass (*Digitaria sanguinalis*) is prominent in the weed stage but is lost almost immediately. An extract of whole crabgrass plants inhibited the growth of its own seedlings as well as other annuals and *A. oligantha.* Two-week-old seedlings were grown with and without crabgrass extract for 10 to 12 days with the following results (Parenti and Rice 1969) :

	Dry weight of seedlings (mg)	
	Without crabgrass extract	With crabgrass extract
Amaranthus retroflexus	53	4
Aristida oligantha	35	10
Digitaria sanguinalis	100	18
Helianthus annuus	153	108

Crabgrass extracts reduced seed germination in three of the four species but not in *A. oligantha:*

	Seeds germinated (%)	
	Without crabgrass extract	With crabgrass extract
Amaranthus retroflexus	57	24
Aristida oligantha	97	96
Digitaria sanguinalis	34	17
Helianthus annuus	23	11

The significant release of the inhibitory chemicals was from the roots of crabgrass. Decaying crabgrass did not affect other plants. Crabgrass is the only species of the weed stage that inhibits the annual grass *A. oligantha*, and this may explain the absence of *Aristida* from the earliest succession stage.

The sunflower *Helianthus annuus* is another important component of the weed stage of succession in Oklahoma old fields, and it also produces chemicals that inhibit itself and other weeds. But sunflower does not affect the grass *A. oligantha*, which comes in to replace the weed stage (Wilson and Rice 1968).

To summarize: The suggestion is that the pioneer weeds inhibit each other chemically and thereby pave the way for the invasion of the grass *A. oligantha*, which is not affected by the weed toxins. This grass improves the soil slowly, but it secretes chemicals that retard nitrogen-fixing bacteria, thereby slowing the rate of succession to the bunchgrass *Andropogon scoparius.* This bunchgrass invades very slowly because of a low rate of seed dispersal and because it requires more soil nitrogen and phosphorus. Finally, the tall-grass prairie species become established as the soil becomes improved, but this may require 50 years or longer, and less is known of the final changes to a climax prairie.

THE CLIMAX STATE

In the examples of succession just described the vegetation has developed to a certain stage of equilibrium. This final stage of succession is called the *climax.* Numerous definitions of the climax have been made (Phillips 1934–1935). *A climax is the final or stable community in a successional series. It is self-perpetuating and in equilibrium with the physical and biotic environment.* There are three schools of thought about the climax state—the monoclimax school, the polyclimax school, and the climax-pattern view.

The *monoclimax* theory was an American invention of F. E. Clements (1916, 1936). According to the monoclimax theory every region has only one climax community, toward which all communities are developing. This is the fundamental assumption of Clements—that given time and freedom from interference a climax vegetation of the same general type will be produced and stabilized irrespective of earlier site conditions. Climate, Clements believed, was the determining factor for vegetation, and the climax of any area was solely a function of its climate.

But it was clear in the field that in any given area there were communities that were not climax communities. For example, tongues of tall-grass prairie extended into Indiana from the west, and isolated stands of hemlock occurred in what is supposed to be deciduous forest. In other words, we observe communities in nature that are nonclimax according to Clements but apparently in equilibrium. These communities are determined by topographic, edaphic (soil), or biotic factors.

These stable communities controlled by topographic and edaphic factors are not denied by the supporters of Clements' monoclimax view, but are regarded as exceptions and categorized by the introduction of special terms:

1 *Subclimax*: The subclimax is the next-to-last stage of a succession that may last a long time but is eventually replaced by the true climax.
2 *Disclimax*: The disclimax is the community replacing the climax after a disturbance of the climax community. For example, overgrazing by livestock may cause desert grasslands to become desert dominated by shrubs and cacti instead of the climax grassland.
3 *Postclimax*: Communities reflecting colder or wetter conditions than the average are termed postclimax. Thus hemlock stands in Indiana would be a postclimax community, because hemlock forests are climax vegetation in northern Michigan and places farther north.

4 Preclimax: Communities reflecting warmer and/or drier conditions than the average are termed preclimax. They are supposed to occur farther south or in drier climates.

Unfortunately Clements' followers got so involved in classifying climaxes that they worked themselves into a terminological jungle. Now we have the paraclimax, conclimax, anticlimax, peniclimax, metaclimax, pseudoclimax, quasi-climax, coclimax, and superclimax. There were so many exceptions found to this ideal of the single climax controlled by climate that some workers began to question the fundamentals of the Clementian system (Whittaker 1953).

The *polyclimax* theory arose as the obvious reaction to Clements' monolithic system. Tansley (1939) was one of the early proponents of the polyclimax idea—that many different climax communities may be recognized in a given area, climaxes controlled by soil moisture, soil nutrients, activity of animals, and other factors. Daubenmire (1966) is also a proponent of the idea that there may be several stable communities in a given area.

The real difference between these two schools of thought lies in the time factor of measuring relative stability. Given enough time, say the monoclimax students, a single climax community would develop, eventually overcoming the edaphic climaxes. The problem is: Should we consider time on a geological scale or on an ecological scale? If we view the problem on a geological time scale we would classify communities such as the coniferous forest as a seral stage to the establishment of deciduous forest. The important point here is that climate fluctuates and is never constant. We see this vividly in the Pleistocene glaciations and more recently in the advances and retreats of mountain glaciers in the last 1000 years (Figure 224). *Thus the condition of equilibrium can never be reached because the vegetation is not approaching a constant climate but a variable one.* Climate varies on an ecological time scale as well as on a geological time scale. Succession in a sense, then, is continuous because we have a variable vegetation approaching a variable climate.

Whittaker (1953) proposed a variation of the polyclimax idea, the *climax-pattern hypothesis*. He emphasized that a natural community is adapted to the whole pattern of environmental factors in which it exists—climate, soil, fire, biotic factors, wind. Whereas the monoclimax theory allows for only one climatic climax in a region and the polyclimax theory allows several climaxes, the climax-pattern hypothesis allows a continuity of climax types, varying gradually along environmental gradients and not neatly separable into discrete climax types. The climax-pattern hypothesis is thus an extension of the continuum idea and the approach of gradient analysis to vegetation (Whittaker 1953). The climax is recognized as a steady-state community with its constituent populations in dynamic balance with environmental gradients. We do not speak of a climatic climax but of prevailing climaxes that are the end result of climate, soil, topography, and biotic factors, as well as fire, wind, salt spray, and other influences, including "chance." The utility of the climax as an operational concept is that similar sites in a region should produce similar climax stands. This stand-to-stand regularity thus should allow prediction for new sites of known environment, and we can say (for example) that this particular site should develop in 100 years a stand of sugar maple and beech of specified density.

How can we recognize climax communities? The operational criterion is the attainment of a steady state over time. Since the time scale involved is very long, observations are lacking for most presumed successional sequences. We assume, for example, that we can determine the time course of succession from a spatial study of younger and older dune systems around Lake Michigan (Figure 228), but this translation of space and time may not be valid. In forests we can use the understory of young trees to look for changes in species composition, because the large trees must reproduce themselves on a one-for-one basis if a steady state has been achieved. Forest changes may be very slow. Figure 234 shows the composition of the dominant trees and the understory trees for a site near Washington, D.C. This site was undisturbed for almost 70 years and still was not in equilibrium because the dominant oaks were not reproducing themselves while beech and sugar maple were invading the understory in large numbers.

Some communities may appear to be stable in time and yet may not be in

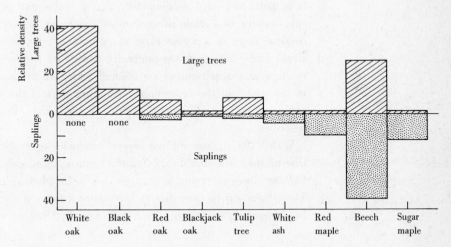

FIGURE 234

Composition of a forest stand near Washington, D.C. This stand has been protected from disturbance for 67 years. The absence of oak saplings (3 to 12 inches in circumference) and the predominance of beech and sugar maple among the younger trees indicates a slow successional change. (After Dix 1957.)

equilibrium with climatic and soil factors. A striking example of this occurred after the outbreak of the disease myxomatosis in the European rabbit in Britain. Before 1954 rabbits were common in many grassland areas. Myxomatosis decimated the rabbit population in 1954, and the consequent release of grazing pressure caused dramatic changes in grassland communities (Thomas 1960, 1963). The most obvious change was a dramatic increase in the abundance of flowers. Species that had not been seen for many years suddenly appeared in large numbers. There was also an increase in woody plants, including tree seedlings that were commonly grazed by rabbits. No one anticipated these effects, which followed the removal of rabbits. Botanists have tended to neglect the influence of animal grazing on plant community composition.

We conclude from this discussion that climax vegetation is an abstract concept that is, in fact, seldom realized, owing to the continuous fluctuations of climate. The climate of an area has clear overall control of the vegetation, but within each of the broad climatic zones there are many modifications, caused by soil, topography, and animals, which lead to many climax situations. The rate of change in a community is rapid in early succession but becomes very slow as one approaches the climax.

CYCLIC CHANGES IN COMMUNITIES

It is usual to regard a community that is stable and in equilibrium with its environment as a static thing that will no longer change. This is misleading because there is a whole class of community changes that are nonsuccessional and cyclic, and are internally caused by species interrelations. These cyclic events usually occur on a small scale and are repeated over and over in the whole of the community. They are part of the internal dynamics of the community rather than a part of succession. Four examples will be described.

Watt (1947b) has studied several examples of cyclic vegetation changes. One of these was the dwarf *Calluna* heath in Scotland. The dominant plant, *Calluna*, loses its vigor as it ages and is invaded by the lichens *Cladonia*. The lichen mat in time dies to leave bare ground. This bare area is invaded by *Arctostaphylos*, which in turn is invaded by *Calluna*.

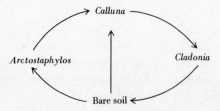

FIGURE 235

Profile of the four phases in the Calluna *cycle in Britain. Like many perennial plants heather loses vigor with age. (After Watt 1955.)*

The heath plant *Calluna* is dominant, and *Arctostaphylos* and *Cladonia* are allowed to occupy the area that is temporarily vacated by *Calluna*.

The cycle of change can be divided into four phases (Figure 235):

1 Pioneer: establishment and early growth in *Calluna*, open patches, with many plant species. Years: 6 to 10.

2 Building: maximum cover of *Calluna* with vigorous flowering, few associated plants. Years: 7 to 15.

3 Mature: gap begins in *Calluna* canopy and more species invade the area. Years: 14 to 25.

4 Degenerate: central branches of *Calluna* die, lichens and bryophytes very common. Years: 20 to 30.

Barclay-Estrup and Gimingham (1969) describe this sequence in detail from maps of permanent quadrats in Scotland. The life history of the dominant plant *Calluna* controls the sequence.

Watt also studied cyclic changes associated with microtopography in a grassland: the *hummock-and-hollow cycle*. The vegetation of the grassland Watt studied was very patchy, and he could recognize four stages (Figure 236). The whole scheme centers around the grass *Festuca ovina*. The seedlings of this grass get established in the bare soil of the hollow stage. It builds a "tussock" by trapping windborne soil particles and by its own

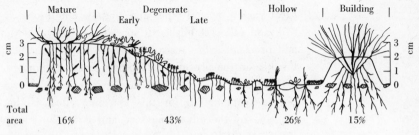

FIGURE 236

Phases of the hummock-and-hollow cycle showing change in flora and habitat and indicating the "fossil" shoot bases and detached roots of Festuca ovina *in the soil. (After Watt 1947b.)*

growth. The vigor of this grass declines with age so that it begins to degenerate in the mature phase and is invaded by lichens in the early degenerate phase. These lichens use the organic matter and in turn die, and the hummock is eroded down to base level, only to begin the process again.

At any given time all four stages can be found in a *Festuca* grassland. Seedlings cannot usually get established except in the hollow and building phases. Fescue seems to be the dominant plant (Figure 237). Lichens dominate the degenerating phase when they can use the organic remains now accumulated. Bryophytes seem to suffer competition from fescue and cannot get established except in the degenerate or hollow phase.

In Iceland, raised beaches have a vegetation mosaic made up of four phases of dwarf heath plants. A small mat plant *Dryas octopetala* is common in all phases, but the most abundant species changes with time (Figure 238). The vegetation cover changes with phase, as does the performance of *Dryas* (Anderson 1967):

	Phase			
	I	II	III	IV
Most abundant species	Dryas octopetala	Kobriesia myosuroides	Betula nana	Betula pubescens
Mean cover of all vegetation (%)	17	49	85	96
Mean cover of Dryas only (%)	12	22	22	~1
Mean no. Dryas flowers per clone	9.0	1.9	0.9	—
Mean dry weight (mg) of Dryas leaves per clone	10.2	7.6	5.3	—

There is a clear drop in the vigor of *Dryas* with time, but the reasons for this are not known.

Bracken fern (*Pteridium aquilinum*) is a cosmopolitan species living in a great variety of soil types and climatic conditions. It forms rhizomes in the soil, and once established it spreads vegetatively. Almost nothing eats ferns, and bracken is fire resistant because of its rhizomes. Watt (1947a) studied bracken in the process of invading grassland, and found a vigorous "front" of invading bracken but reduced vigor in older fronds (Figure 239). The obvious explanation for this marginal effect is that some soil nutrient is depleted by the advancing fern and is in short supply in the older stands. But Watt (1940) could find no soil change to account for the reduced vigor, and the addition of fertilizers to sample plots in the older stands produced no effect. The significant variable seems to be rhizome age. Younger rhizomes produce more vigorous fronds. The explanation for this is not known.

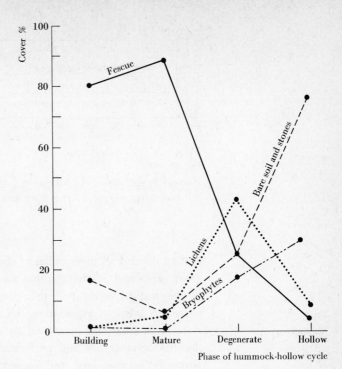

FIGURE 237

Relative abundance of the dominant grass Festuca ovina *in the different phases of the hummock-and-hollow cycle and the changes in lichens, bryophytes, and bare soil. (After Watt 1947b.)*

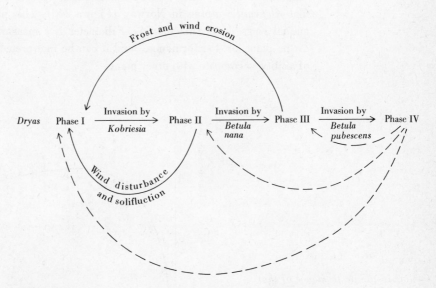

FIGURE 238

Representation of possible routes of succession in vegetation mosaic at Melgraseyri, Iceland. Solid lines indicate the existence of circumstantial evidence, dashed lines an absence of unequivocal field evidence. (After Anderson 1967.)

435 COMMUNITY CHANGE

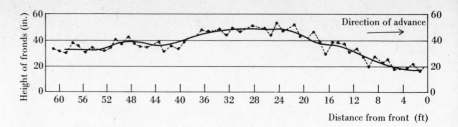

FIGURE 239

*Average height above the soil surface of bracken fern fronds across
the advancing margin. (After Watt 1940.)*

Watt divided all these cycles of change into an *upgrade* series and a *down-grade* series and pointed out that the total productivity of the series increases to the mature phase and then decreases. What initiates the downgrade phase? A possible explanation lies in the relationship between the general vigor of a perennial plant and its age. There seems to be a general relationship between age and performance in most perennial plants, and consequently between age and competitive ability (Kershaw 1964). Several studies on the relation of leaf diameter to age also support this idea.

Kershaw (1960) showed that leaf diameter varied with age in the perennial *Alchemilla alpina* in Norway (Figure 240). This plant can be aged by annual rings in its rhizomes. Leaf diameter is a measure of general vitality of the plant, or "performance," and it can be interpreted as a crude measure of ability to compete with other plants.

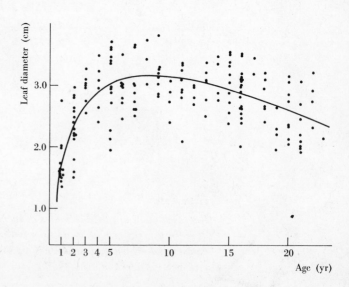

FIGURE 240

*Decline in the performance of the
perennial plant* Alchemilla alpina
*(Roseaceae) with age. Each point
represents the leaf diameter of an
individual plant. (After Kershaw
1960.)*

For this reason a stable community will be in a constant state of phasic fluctuation, one species becoming locally more abundant as another species reaches its degenerate phase. These dynamic interrelationships in natural communities may not be conspicuous without detailed measurement.

The underlying mechanism for this change in performance with age is not yet known. One suggestion is that it may be caused by the relationship between photosynthesis and respiration interacting with competition for light. In young plants in relatively open situations there is a large leaf area available for photosynthesis and a small volume of plant undergoing respiration. As the plant grows older, the vegetation becomes more dense, and light is available for photosynthesis only on the peripheral exposed leaves. At the same time the bulk of stems and rhizomes is growing, so more material is undergoing respiration. The suggestion is that perennial plants may reach a compensation point where respiration begins to exceed assimilation by photosynthesis, and consequently the plant enters the degenerate phase.

Thus climax communities are dynamic and may change in cyclic patterns because of the life cycle of dominant species. Four phases can often be recognized: pioneer, building, mature, and degenerate. A "stable" community may be a mosaic of these four phases of cyclic change operating at a local level.

SUMMARY

Communities may change with time either in a directional way (succession) or in a nondirectional way (cyclic). Most of the work on community changes has been done on plants, but the same principles apply to animal communities.

Succession proceeds through a series of stages from the pioneer stage to the climax stage. The *monoclimax hypothesis* suggested that there was only a single predictable end point for whole regions, and that given time all communities would converge to the climatic climax. This hypothesis has been superseded by the *polyclimax hypothesis*, which suggests that many different climaxes could occur in an area, climaxes controlled by soil moisture, nutrients, fires, or other factors.

Succession does not always involve progressive changes from simple to complex communities. The causes of succession have been worked out for few sequences and may involve physical limitations (tolerances to moisture levels, nutrients, etc.) or biological interrelations (competition for water, allelopathic effects, etc.).

Cyclic changes are repeated over and over again as part of the internal dynamics of the community. The life cycle of the dominant organisms dictates the cyclic changes, many of which are caused by the decline in vigor of perennial plants with age.

Communities are not stable for long periods in nature because of short-term changes in climate (or other environmental factors) and the cyclic changes of growth and decay within the community. For most communities we observe changes over time but do not know the factors causing the changes, which makes it impossible to suggest manipulations to alleviate undesirable trends. This problem is particularly critical in communities influenced by man's technology.

SELECTED REFERENCES

CLEMENTS, F. E. 1949. *Dynamics of Vegetation*. Hafner, New York.

HORN, H. 1971. *The Adaptive Geometry of Trees*. Princeton Univ. Press, Princeton, N.J.

KEEVER, C. 1950. Causes of succession on old fields of the Piedmont, North Carolina. *Ecol. Monogr.* 20:229–250.

PARENTI, R. L., and E. L. RICE. 1969. Inhibitional effects of *Digitaria sanguinalis* and possible role in old-field succession. *Bull. Torrey Bot. Club* 96:70–78.

PHILLIPS, J. 1934–1935. Succession, development, the climax, and the complex organism: an analysis of concepts. *J. Ecol.* 22:554–571; 23:210–246, and 488–508.

WATT, A. S. 1947. Pattern and process in the plant community. *J. Ecol.* 35:1–22.

WATT, A. S. 1964. The community and the individual. *J. Ecol.* 52 (Suppl.):203–211.

WHITTAKER, R. H. 1953. A consideration of climax theory: the climax as a population and pattern. *Ecol. Monogr.* 23:41–78.

QUESTIONS AND PROBLEMS

1 Rowe (1966, p. 23) states:

To map climates on the basis of vegetation is illogical; vegetation zones are vegetation zones, not bioclimatic zones. Just as illogical is the attempt to define "natural" regional boundaries on the basis of former vegetational patterns, traced out with painstaking labor through study of old surveys and other historical records. To reconstruct the vegetation as it used to be 100, 200 or 1000 years ago may have various values, but a better understanding of the potential of the land, or of presumed "natural" climatic or soil boundaries, is not among them. To go back in time is not necessarily to find greater stability, a more perfect fit of vegetation to climate and soils, but perhaps less. Instability in nature is a fact that must be recognized ... it is a tragedy that such an untidy fact should have dispatched the neat theory of "climax."

Discuss.

2 Abundance (%) within size classes in an undisturbed hemlock–beech association at Heart's Content, Pa., was measured by Lutz (1930, p. 27):

Tree species	Size class				
	0–0.9 ft[a]	1.0 ft[a] to 0.9 in. DBH[b]	1–3.5 in. DBH[b]	3.6–9.5 in. DBH[b]	≥10 in. DBH[b]
Hemlock	23.4	44.0	19.2	13.5	36.1
White pine	0.2	0.1	0	0	11.1
Beech	4.9	22.7	59.9	50.3	24.0
Red maple	66.5	17.0	6.6	9.2	10.6
Chestnut	0.2	1.5	0.4	9.2	8.8
White oak	0	0	0	0	1.6
Red oak	0.1	0.2	0	0.7	1.8
Black birch	0.8	1.4	4.8	10.4	2.7
Black cherry	0.3	1.0	1.7	0.9	0.8
Yellow birch	0.5	0.1	0.6	1.7	0.1
Sugar maple	0.4	1.2	1.1	0.7	0.3
White ash	0.1	0	0	0.1	0
Miscellaneous others	2.6	10.8	5.7	3.3	2.1
Total	100.0	100.0	100.0	100.0	100.0

[a] Height of tree.

[b] DBH, diameter at breast height.

Lutz stated that "the hemlock–beech association is believed to represent a stage in forest succession somewhat less advanced than the climatic climax of the region. Probably in the climax forest the amount of white pine entering into the stand is considerably smaller." Do these data support this conclusion? If so, how? If not, what additional data could support it?

3 Langford and Buell (1969, p. 130) state:

Whereas biotic influences play an outstanding role in determining the nature of climax vegetation in moist temperate areas, abiotic factors are outstandingly pre-eminent in controlling vegetation in arid or very cold regions. In such regions succession, which is essentially due to modification of the environment by organisms, with its direction of course somewhat variable according to the availability of various propagules, may be almost absent.

Search for data on succession and the climax for either desert or arctic plant communities, and discuss them with reference to this statement.

4 Discuss the application of the succession concept to communities in the sea.

21   Community metabolism I

PRIMARY PRODUCTION

Animal ecologists in general have approached community studies from a functional point of view—*how does it work?* In contrast to the botanists they have not been overly interested in naming or classifying communities.

One of the main focal points of research for zoologists in the functional organization of communities has been the study of community metabolism, which is basically a study of the food relationships in the community.

FOOD CHAINS AND FOOD WEBS

The transfer of food energy from the source in plants through herbivores to carnivores is referred to as the *food chain*. Elton (1927) was one of the first to apply this idea to ecology and analyze its consequences. He pointed out the great importance of food to organisms, and he recognized that the length of these food chains was limited to four or five links. Thus we may have a *pine tree–aphids–spiders–warblers–hawks* food chain. Elton recognized that these food chains were not isolated units but were hooked together into food webs. Let us look at a few examples of food chains.

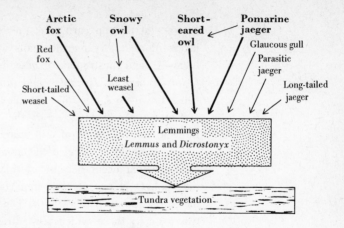

Food relations among lemmings and their predators in the Barrow region of northern Alaska. Names of the more important species among the various bird and mammal predators are shown in boldface letters. (After Pitelka et al. 1955.)

In northern Alaska the vertebrate food chain of the tundra is centered on lemmings (Figure 241). Lemmings graze the grasses and sedges, and in turn are hunted by a variety of bird and mammal predators. This vertebrate food chain ignores the insects and some of the birds, which are also components of the tundra community.

In the rocky intertidal zone of the Gulf of California Paine (1966) described a food web that contained four links of carnivores. Figure 242

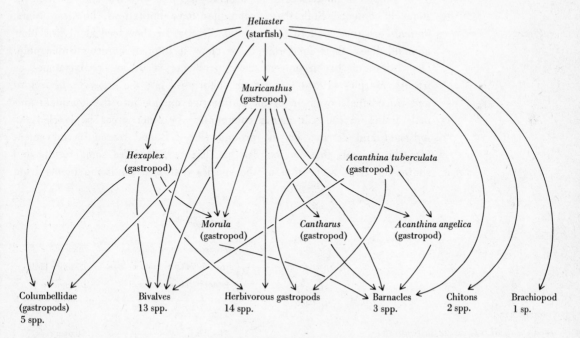

FIGURE 242

Feeding relationships of the Heliaster *dominated food web in the northern Gulf of California. (After Paine 1966.)*

shows that the top carnivore, the starfish *Heliaster kubiniji*, preys on two layers of predatory marine snails in addition to the herbivorous barnacles, bivalves, and gastropods. These feeding relationships are not constant. *Heliaster* can eat *Hexaplex* and *Muricanthus* only to a certain size, above which these two species also become top carnivores.

Along the eastern coast of the United States from North Carolina to Florida runs a band of salt marsh. This community consists of a few species adapted to survive the great changes in salinity, temperature, and exposure that occur because of tidal variations and surface drainage from the land. Only one plant is important in this relatively simple community, the grass *Spartina alterniflora*. The herbivorous fauna can be divided into two groups: those which feed directly on living plants, and those which feed on plants that have died and fallen to the ground (detritus feeders). Bacterial decomposition is an important part of the detritus breakdown, and the bacteria, algae, and associated detritus are all food for the detritus feeders. Different carnivores feed on the two groups of herbivores (Figure 243).

Since the salt marsh community has been studied in some detail, we can use it to illustrate one way of studying food chains. The general problem is this: How can we determine who eats what in a complex community? Two simple techniques are to observe feeding directly and to look at stomach contents. Both these techniques have limitations, however. Some animals are too small to be observed directly, or they feed at night. Other animals digest their food rapidly or chew it into an unrecognizable pulp. One technique to circumvent these problems is to use radioisotopes as tracers. Marples (1966) injected phosphorus-32 into the grass *S. alterniflora* and traced the movement of the radioactive nuclide into the dominant animals living in the salt marsh community. In other areas he labeled the sediment and detritus on the ground with ^{32}P and traced its movement into the animals that fed on detritus. Figure 244 gives some results and shows the clear separation of the species that feed on living plants from

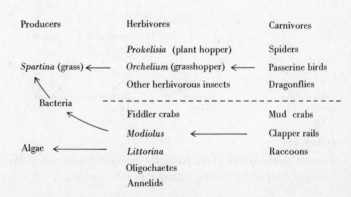

FIGURE 243

Food web of a Georgia salt marsh with groups listed in their approximate order of importance. (After Teal 1962.)

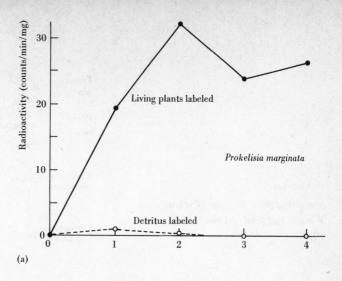

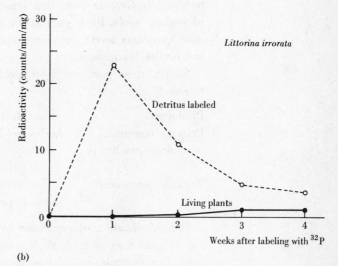

FIGURE 244

Uptake of radioactive phosphorus in a Georgia salt marsh in two experiments in which either the living grasses or the detritus were labeled. (a) Prokelisia marginata, a plant hopper that feeds on the living plants. (b) Littorina irrorata, a snail that feeds on detritus. (After Marples 1966.)

those that feed on detritus. Predatory species such as spiders pick up the radionuclide from the herbivores after a time lag. Using this technique, Marples was able to substantiate the conclusions about food webs reached earlier with natural history observations.

Wytham Woods near Oxford in England has been studied very intensively as a community by Elton (1966). A simplified food chain for this woodland is shown in Figure 245. Oaks (*Quercus robur*) are one dominant tree in Wytham Woods and throughout the deciduous forests of western Europe, and are fed on by more than 200 species of Lepidoptera. The winter moth (*Operophtera brumata*) is the most common oak defoliator in Wytham and it serves as food for shrews, voles, mice, titmice, and predatory ground beetles (*Philonthus, Feronia,* and *Abax*) and is parasitized by a

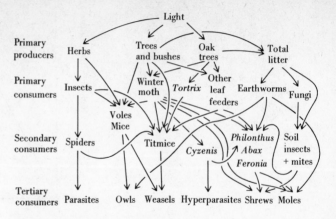

FIGURE 245

Simplified food web for Wytham Woods, England. (After Varley 1970.)

tachinid fly *Cyzenis*. Note that small mammals and birds occupy a variety of feeding levels. Birds such as the great tit and the blue tit feed on beech mast (producer level), on winter moth females (herbivores), and on spiders and beetles (carnivores).

Within these complex food webs we can recognize several different trophic levels:

Producers	green plants	first trophic level
Primary consumers	herbivores	second trophic level
Secondary consumers	carnivores, insect parasites	third trophic level
Tertiary consumers	higher carnivores, insect hyperparasites	fourth trophic level

The classification of organisms by trophic levels is one of *function* and not of species as such. A given species may occupy more than one trophic level. For example, male horse flies feed on nectar and plant juices while the females are blood-sucking ectoparasites. Great tits in Wytham Woods feed on three trophic levels (Figure 245).

Size has a great effect on the organization of food chains, as Elton (1927) recognized. Animals of successive trophic levels in a food chain tend to be larger. There are, of course, definite upper and lower limits to the size of food which a carnivorous animal can eat. The structure of an animal puts some limit on the size of food that it can take into its mouth. Except in a few cases, large carnivores cannot live on very small food items because they cannot catch enough of them in a given time to provide for their metabolic needs. The one obvious exception to this is man, and part of the reason for his biological success is that he can prey upon almost any level of the food chain and eat any size of prey.

A very complex pattern of feeding relationships is obvious if we look at the food web of a community. How can we evaluate the relative importance of the different species in the food web? There may be 5000 species of animals on the 2 sq. miles of Wytham Woods in Britain (Elton 1966). We feel intuitively that all these 5000 species are not equally important and that many or most of them could be removed without affecting the woodland.

Three measurements might be used to define relative importance in a community:

1 *Biomass*: We could use the weight or standing crop of each species as a measure of importance. This is useful in some circumstances such as the lumbering industry, but it cannot be used for dynamic comparisons for some of the reasons given when we discussed optimum yield. In a dynamic situation in which *yield* is important we need to know how rapidly a community produces new biomass. When metabolic rate and reproductive rates are high, production may be very rapid, even from a low standing crop. Figure 246 illustrates the idea that yield need not be related to biomass.

2 *Flow of chemical materials*: We can view the community as a superorganism taking in food materials, using them, and passing them out. Note that all chemical materials can be recycled many times through the community. A molecule of phosphorus may be taken up by a plant root, used in a leaf, eaten by a grasshopper which dies, and released by bacterial decomposition to reenter the soil.

3 *Flow of energy*: We can view the community as an energy transformer that takes solar energy, fixes some of it in photosynthesis, and transfers this energy from green plants through herbivores to carnivores. Note that energy flows through a community only once and is not recycled but is transformed to heat and ultimately lost to the system. Only the continual input of new solar energy keeps the community operating. Again we may draw the analogy between a community and an organism that processes food energy.

To study the dynamics of community metabolism we must decide whether to use chemical materials or energy as the base variable. Most ecologists have decided to use *energy* for two reasons. First, chemicals are tied up in biological peculiarities of organisms. Vertebrates or mollusks contain much more calcium than most freshwater invertebrates because of the presence

FIGURE 246

Hypothetical illustration of two equilibrium communities (input = output): (a) low input, low output, slow turnover; (b) high input, high output, rapid turnover. Standing crop is not related to production or yield because turnover time for all systems is not a constant.

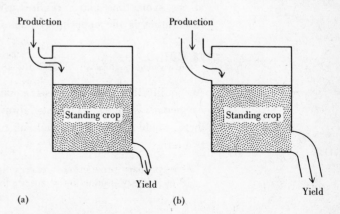

of bone or shell. Some marine invertebrates concentrate certain chemical elements. Even within an individual there are variations. Calcium in the teeth and bones of a mammal may be stable for long periods while calcium in the blood serum may be turning over rapidly because of ingestion and excretion. This makes the description of the calcium flow through a community very difficult. Second, energy is not recirculated and is therefore easier to measure than are chemical materials.

Note that we must make some critical assumptions about community processes when we decide to use energy or materials to analyze food webs. In each case we assume that the abundance of each species in the community is determined by its food supply. If we use energy, we are assuming that it is the energy content of the food that is critical. If we use chemical materials, we are assuming that it is the chemical composition or quality of the diet that is critical.

Energy enters the community as radiant energy from the sun, and we turn now to consider the fixation of solar energy by photosynthesis.

PRIMARY PRODUCTION

The process of photosynthesis is the cornerstone of all life and the starting point for studies of community metabolism. The bulk of the earth's living mantle is green plants (99.9% by weight); only a small fraction of life consists of animals.

Photosynthesis is the process of transforming solar energy into chemical energy, and can be simplified as

$$12H_2O + \underset{\text{(from air)}}{6CO_2} + \text{solar energy} \xrightarrow[\text{enzymes}]{\text{chlorophyll +}} \underset{\text{(carbohydrate)}}{C_6H_{12}O_6} + \underset{\text{(to air)}}{6O_2} + 6H_2O$$

If photosynthesis were the only process occurring in plants we could measure production by the accumulation of carbohydrate. But, unfortunately, at the same time plants respire, using energy for maintenance activities. Respiration is the opposite of photosynthesis, in an overall view:

$$\underset{\text{(carbohydrate)}}{C_6H_{12}O_6} + \underset{\text{(from air)}}{O_2} \xrightarrow[\text{enzymes}]{\text{metabolic}} \underset{\text{(to air)}}{CO_2 + H_2O} + \text{energy for work and maintenance}$$

At equilibrium photosynthesis equals respiration, and this is called the *compensation point*. If plants always existed at the compensation point there would be no production of food materials for animals. We define two terms:

Gross primary production = energy fixed in photosynthesis
Net primary production = energy fixed in photosynthesis
— energy lost by respiration

How can we measure these two aspects of primary production in natural systems?

For terrestrial plants the direct way is to measure the change in CO_2 or O_2 concentrations in the air around plants. Most studies measure CO_2 uptake by an enclosed branch or a whole plant. During daylight conditions CO_2 uptake measures net production because both photosynthesis and respiration are operating simultaneously. At night only respiration occurs and the amount of CO_2 released can be used to estimate the respiration component.

Photosynthesis and respiration are both affected by temperature; photosynthesis is also affected by light intensity. Figure 247 illustrates this for a single tree species for one day in spring and one day in summer. The daily changes in leaf temperature and light intensity determine the net production for each day.

We can determine the energetic equivalents of photosynthesis measurements from the chemical thermodynamics of the reaction:

$$12H_2O + 6CO_2 + 709 \text{ kcal} \underset{\substack{\text{solar} \\ \text{energy}}}{\rightarrow} C_6H_{12}O_6 + 6O_2 + 6H_2O$$

Thus the absorption of 6 moles (134.4 liters at standard temperature and pressure) of CO_2 indicates that 709 kcal has been absorbed.

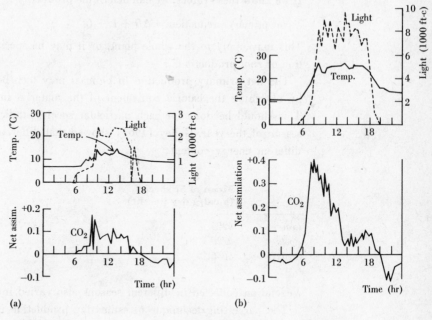

(a)

(b)

FIGURE 247

Typical daily patterns of net CO_2 assimilation in Douglas fir during (a) spring and (b) summer. There is an uptake of CO_2 in the daylight which is the net outcome of photosynthesis and respiration. At night CO_2 is released by respiration. (After Helms 1965.)

The measure of gas exchange around plants in the field has been used relatively little because it requires sophisticated and expensive electric instrumentation. A slightly different approach to measuring CO_2 uptake is to introduce radioactive $^{14}CO_2$ in the air surrounding a plant (covered by a transparent chamber) and after a time to harvest the whole plant and count the quantity of radioactive ^{14}C taken up by photosynthesis. This technique can be used in sites where electricity is not available.

The simplest method of measuring primary production is the harvest method. The amount of plant material produced in a unit of time can be determined from the difference between the amount present at the two times:

$$\Delta B = B_2 - B_1$$

where

ΔB = biomass change in the community between time 1 (t_1) and time 2 (t_2)
B_1 = biomass at t_1
B_2 = biomass at t_2

Two possible losses must be recognized:

L = biomass losses by death of plants or plant parts
G = biomass losses to consumer organisms

If we know these values, we can determine production:

Net primary production = $\Delta B + L + G$

This may apply to the whole plant, or it may be specified as *aerial* production or *root* production.

The net primary production in biomass may then be converted to energy by obtaining the caloric equivalent of the material in a bomb calorimeter. This should be done for each particular species studied as well as for each season of the year. Golley (1961) showed that different parts of plants have different energy content:

	Mean of 57 species (g cal/g dry weight)
Leaves	4229
Roots	4720
Seeds	5065

Vegetation collected in different seasons also varied in caloric content.

The harvesting technique of estimating production is used in a variety of situations. Foresters have used a modified version of it for timber estimation, and agricultural research workers use it to determine yield of crops. The application of harvesting techniques to natural vegetation involves some specialized problems and techniques that we shall not describe here; Milner and Hughes (1968) and Newbould (1967) give details of techniques.

In aquatic systems primary production can be measured in the same general way as in terrestrial systems. Gas-exchange techniques can be applied to water volumes, and usually oxygen release is measured instead of carbon dioxide uptake. This procedure is usually repeated with a dark bottle (respiration only) and a light bottle (photosynthesis and respiration) so that both gross and net production can be measured. Vollenweider (1969) discusses details of techniques for measuring production in aquatic habitats.

How does primary production vary over the different types of vegetation on the earth? This is the first general question we can ask about community metabolism. Table 29 gives some average values for net pri-

TABLE 29

Net primary productivity of the main types of vegetation of the world and the standing crop of plant matter in each

Vegetation	Net primary production[a] (dry g/sq. m/yr)	Standing crop (g/sq. m)	Green parts of total biomass (%)
Arctic tundras	100	500	15
Dwarf-shrub tundras	250	2,800	11
Fir forests			
North taiga	450	10,000	8
Middle taiga	700	26,000	6
South taiga	850	33,000	6
Beech forests	1,300	37,000	1
Oak forests	900	40,000	1
Steppes			
Temperate	1,120	2,500	18
Dry	420	1,000	15
Deserts			
Dwarf, semishrub	122	430	3
Subtropical	250	600	3
Subtropical forests	2,450	41,000	3
Dry savannahs	730	2,680	11
Savannahs	1,200	6,660	12
Tropical rain forests	3,250	50,000	8
Sphagnum bogs with forest	340	3,700	41
Mangroves	930	12,730	6
Open ocean	125	3	—
Continental shelf	350	10	—
Agricultural land	650	1,000	—

[a] Including roots, leaves, stems, and flowers.
SOURCE: After Rodin and Basilevich (1968) and Whittaker (1970).

mary production in biomass for different vegetation types. In general primary production is highest in the tropical rain forest and decreases progressively toward the poles. Productivity of the open ocean is very low, approximately the same as that of the arctic tundra, and oceans occupy about 71% of the total surface of the earth. Grassland and tundra areas are less productive than forests in the same general region. The standing crop of forests is very large and green parts are a relatively small fraction of the total biomass of a forest.

How efficient is the vegetation of different communities as an energy converter? We can determine the efficiency of utilization of sunlight by the ratio:

Efficiency of gross primary production
$$= \frac{\text{energy fixed by gross primary production}}{\text{energy in incident sunlight}}$$

For example, Kozlovsky (1968) calculated the efficiency of the aquatic community of Lake Mendota, Wisconsin:

Efficiency of gross primary production
$$= \frac{5017 \text{ kcal/sq. m/yr gross primary production}}{1,188,720 \text{ kcal incident solar radiation}}$$
$$= 0.42\%$$

Less than one-half of one percent of the incident solar energy is converted into gross production. This low value is not unusual. Golley (1965) measured the efficiency of primary production in an old-field broomsedge community in South Carolina for 3 years and obtained values ranging from 0.22 to 0.36%. In an oak–pine forest on Long Island, New York, about 2% efficiency was achieved (Woodwell and Whittaker 1968). In general, the efficiency of gross primary production is 2% or less in most communities.

How much of the energy fixed by photosynthesis is subsequently lost by respiration of the plants themselves? A great deal of energy is lost in converting solar radiation to gross primary production. Net primary production, which is what interests animals and man, must therefore be even less efficient. Westlake (1963) suggested that 40 to 60% of the gross primary production will be used in respiration, so the net production will be approximately half of gross. Nielsen and Jensen (1957) estimated that net productivity is about 75% of gross in the oceans. Few measurements have been made on natural communities, however. Vallentyne (1965) calculated that the overall efficiency of net primary production for the globe is about 0.4% for land and about 0.2% for the oceans.

Factors limiting primary productivity The most important question about primary production is this: *What controls the rate of primary production in natural communities?* What factors could we change to increase the rate of primary production for a given community? Note that this question could be broken down into many questions of the same type for each plant-species population. The control of primary production has been studied in greater detail for aquatic systems than for terrestrial systems. Let us look first at some details of production in aquatic communities.

Marine communities *Light* is the first variable one might expect to control primary production, and the depth to which light will penetrate in a lake or ocean will be critical in defining the zone of primary production. Water absorbs solar radiation very readily. More than half of the solar radiation is absorbed in the first meter of water, including almost all the infrared energy. Even in "clear" water only about 5 to 10% of the radiation may be present at a depth of 20 m. This decrease can be described reasonably well by a geometric curve of decrease in radiation:

$$\frac{dI}{dt} = -kI$$

where

  I = amount of solar radiation
  t = depth
  k = extinction coefficient (a constant)

This relationship is illustrated in Figure 248 for several values of k, the extinction coefficient. Large k values indicate less transparent waters. Figure 249 illustrates the decrease in photosynthesis with depth in three California lakes. Clear Lake is a *eutrophic* lake with high production and little light penetration. Castle Lake is a lake of intermediate productivity, in which the zone of photosynthesis extends below a depth of 20 m. Lake Tahoe is an alpine lake of remarkably clear water in which the zone of photosynthesis extends to a depth of 100 m (Goldman 1968).

  Too much light inhibits photosynthesis of green plants, and this inhibi-

FIGURE 248

Theoretical attenuation of solar radiation (I) with depth in a water column. Light intensity falls geometrically with depth, and the larger the extinction coefficient (k), the faster the loss of light. An extinction coefficient of 0.02 would occur in pure water; one of 0.10 would occur in oceanic seawater. Coastal seawater would have higher extinction coefficients (approx. 0.30).

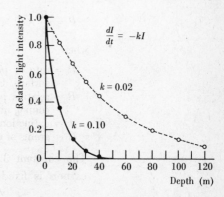

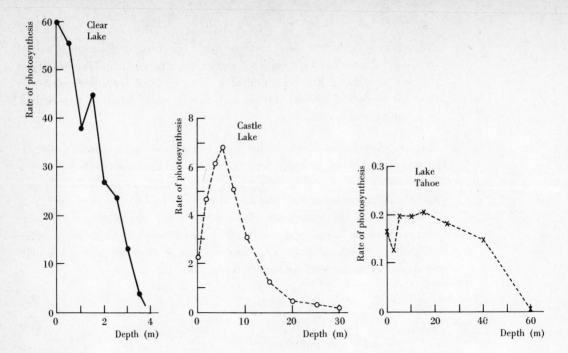

FIGURE 249

*Change in photosynthesis with depth in three California lakes during summer. Note
changes in scale of depth and rate of photosynthesis (measured as milligrams of carbon
assimilated per cubic meter of water per hour). (After Goldman 1968.)*

tion can be found in tropical and subtropical surface waters throughout
the year. When surface radiation is excessive, the maximum in primary
production will occur several meters beneath the surface of the sea. Figure
250 illustrates this for tropical oceans.

Light is an important factor limiting primary production in the ocean
(Ryther 1956). If you know the rate at which light decreases with depth
(extinction coefficient), the amount of solar radiation, and the amount of
plant chlorophyll in the water, you can calculate the net production of the
phytoplankton by the formula

$$P = \frac{R}{k} \times C \times 3.7$$

where

P = rate of photosynthesis of phytoplankton (g of carbon fixed/sq. m ocean
surface/day)

R = relative photosynthesis rate (from Figure 251) for the amount of light
coming in

k = extinction coefficient (defined above, Figure 248) per meter

C = grams of chlorophyll per cubic meter of water in the water column

The constant 3.7 is determined experimentally and indicates that 3.7 g of
carbon is fixed in photosynthesis by each gram of chlorophyll in 1 hour

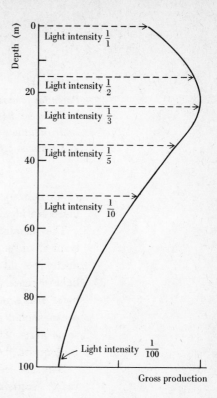

FIGURE 250

Light intensity and rate of gross production at different depths in the ocean. This curve represents average values for a tropical station on a clear day. (After Nielsen and Jensen 1957.)

under light-saturation conditions. For example, in the Gulf of Alaska the following values were measured (Ryther and Yentsch 1957):

$$\text{Solar radiation} = 229 \text{ g cal/sq. cm/day}$$
$$\text{Extinction coefficient} = 0.10 \text{ per meter}$$
$$\text{Chlorophyll} = 0.0025 \text{ g/cu. m of water}$$

Thus from Figure 251 R is approximately 14.5, and thus

$$P = \frac{14.5}{0.10} \times 0.0025 \times 3.7 = 1.34 \text{ g carbon/sq. m/day}$$

which compares to the actually measured primary production rate of 1.50 g

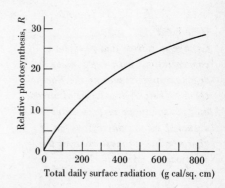

FIGURE 251

Relation between solar radiation and relative photosynthesis rate (R) beneath 1 sq. m of ocean surface. (10 g cal/sq. cm = 1 k cal/sq. m.) (After Ryther and Yentsch 1957.)

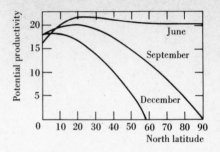

FIGURE 252

Potential photosynthetic productivity in the ocean based on amount of solar radiation at different latitudes and seasons. (After Ryther 1963.)

of carbon/sq. m/day. This formula gives relatively accurate predictions under a wide range of conditions.

The amount of incoming solar radiation varies greatly from polar to tropical areas in the ocean. Figure 252 illustrates how much primary production could be supported at various latitudes with winter and summer light regimes. Clearly, light is limiting primary production in winter in the polar seas, and we would predict that tropical and subtropical parts of the ocean should show maximal productivities. Unfortunately, this is not true; some parts of the tropics, such as the Sargasso Sea, are very unproductive. In contrast, the Antarctic Ocean is the most productive oceanic region.

Why are tropical oceans unproductive when the light regime is good all year? *Nutrients* appear to limit primary production in tropical and subtropical seas. We have just seen that primary productivity can be predicted from a knowledge of light and biomass of chlorophyll, and the action of limiting nutrients is on the biomass of chlorophyll in the phytoplankton. Two elements, nitrogen and phosphorus, often limit primary production in the oceans. One of the striking generalities of the oceans is the very low concentrations of nitrogen and phosphorus in the surface layers where the phytoplankton live (Figure 253), whereas the deep water contains much higher concentrations of nutrients.

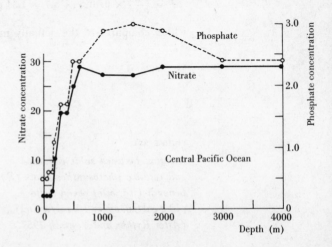

FIGURE 253

Change in nitrate and phosphate concentrations with depth at an oceanographic station in the Pacific Ocean. The very low levels of nitrate and phosphate in surface waters occupied by the phytoplankton is characteristic of most areas of the open ocean. (After Nielsen and Jensen 1957.)

Nitrogen may be a limiting factor for phytoplankton in many parts of the ocean (Ryther and Dunstan 1971). Figure 254 illustrates this for a coastal area of New York. Pollution from duck farms along the bays of Long Island adds both nitrogen and phosphorus to the coastal water, but,

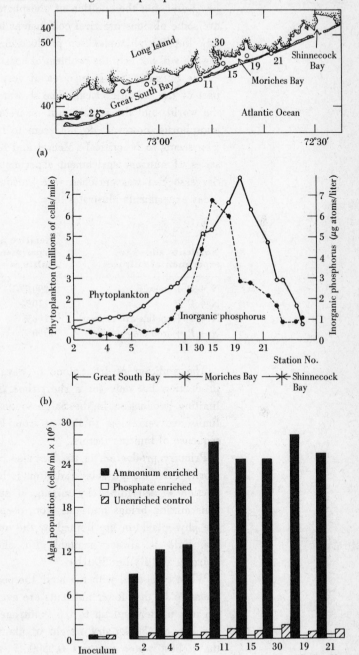

FIGURE 254

Experiments on nutrient limitations to phytoplankton production in coastal waters of Long Island: (a) coast of Long Island, New York; (b) abundance of phytoplankton and distribution of phosphorus arising from duck farms in Moriches Bay; (c) nutrient-enrichment experiments with the alga Nannochloris atomus *in water from the bays. Phosphorus is superabundant and the availability of nitrogen seems to limit algal growth. (After Ryther and Dunstan 1971.)*

unlike phosphorus, the nitrogen added is immediately taken up by algae, so no trace of nitrogen can be measured in the coastal waters. This was confirmed by nutrient-addition experiments (Figure 254). The addition of nitrogen (in the form of ammonium) caused a heavy algal growth in bay water, but the addition of phosphate did not induce algal growth. There are some obvious practical conclusions to this work. If nitrogen is the factor now limiting phytoplankton production, the elimination of phosphates from sewage will not help the problem of coastal pollution.

The Sargasso Sea is an area of very low productivity in the subtropical part of the Atlantic Ocean. The seawater is among the most transparent in the world, and the surface waters are very low in nutrients. Nitrogen and phosphorus, however, do not seem to be limiting primary production, and iron seems to be critical (Menzel and Ryther 1961a). This was shown by a series of nutrient enrichment experiments in which surface water from the Sargasso Sea was enriched with various nutrients. The following series of 3-day experiments illustrates this:

Nutrients added to experimental cultures	Relative uptake of ^{14}C for experimental cultures (control cultures = 100%)
N + P + metals	1290%
N + P	110%
N + P + metals except iron	108%
N + P + iron only	1200%

The addition of iron alone to Sargasso Sea water stimulated primary production but only for a short time. This suggests that iron is the factor limiting production in the Sargasso Sea but that nitrogen and phosphorus limits are very close to that of iron. Figure 255 illustrates this idea of a sequence of limiting factors.

Primary production in the Sargasso Sea is highest in winter (November–April) even though solar radiation is highest in summer. High winter production is determined by mixing of surface waters by winds and storms. This mixing brings nutrients from deeper water back to the surface, where the phytoplankton are limited by the nutrients available. In this subtropical sea, light is always available for photosynthesis but nutrients are not (Menzel and Ryther 1961b).

When compared with the land, the ocean is very unproductive; the reason seems to be that fewer nutrients are available. Rich, fertile soil contains 5% organic matter and up to 0.5% nitrogen. One square meter of soil surface can support 50 kg dry weight of plant matter. In the ocean, by contrast, the richest water contains 0.00005% nitrogen, four orders of magnitude less than that of fertile farmland soil. One square meter of rich seawater

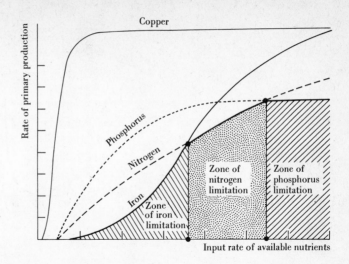

FIGURE 255

Hypothetical illustration of a sequence of nutrient factors limiting primary productivity. Such a sequence may be operating in the Sargasso Sea. The rate of primary production will follow the heavy line and be limited first by iron, then (as more iron becomes available) by nitrogen, and finally by phosphorus. Some nutrients, such as copper, may always be present in superabundant amounts.

could support no more than 5 g dry weight of phytoplankton (Ryther 1963). Thus, in terms of standing crops, the sea is a desert compared with the land. And although the maximal rate of primary production in the sea may be the same as the maximal rate obtained on land, these high rates in the sea can be maintained for a few days only unless the water is enriched by upwelling.

Areas of upwelling in the ocean are exceptions to the general rule of nutrient limitation. The largest area of upwelling occurs in the Antarctic Ocean, where cold, nutrient-rich, deep water comes to the surface along a broad zone near the Antarctic Continent. Other areas of upwelling occur off the coast of Peru, California, and in many coastal areas where a combination of wind and currents moves the surface water away and allows the cold, deep water to move up to the surface. In these areas of upwelling fishing is especially good, and in general there is a superabundance of nutrients for the phytoplankton.

Thus primary production in the ocean is limited by light in some areas but also by the shortage of nutrients such as nitrogen and phosphorus, which are critical for plant growth.

Freshwater communities In freshwater communities, much the same conclusion seems to hold. Solar radiation limits primary production on a day-to-day basis in lakes (Figure 256) and Goldman (1968) has shown that within a given lake you can predict the daily primary productivity from the solar radiation. Temperature is closely linked with light intensity in aquatic systems and is difficult to evaluate as a separate factor. Nutrient limitations also operate in freshwater lakes, and the great variety of lakes is associated with a great variety of limiting nutrients.

For growth, plants require nitrogen, calcium, phosphorus, potassium,

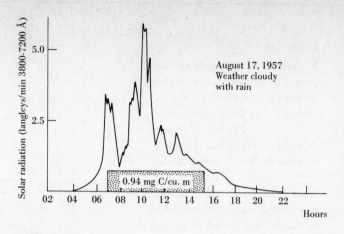

FIGURE 256

Average photosynthetic carbon assimilation with variation in solar radiation at Brooks Lake, Alaska. The primary productivity on a cloudy day is compared with that occurring on a bright day. (After Goldman 1960b.)

sulfur, chlorine, sodium, magnesium, iron, manganese, copper, iodine, cobalt, zinc, boron, vanadium, and molybdenum. These nutrients do not all act independently, which has made the tracing of causal influences very difficult (Lund 1965). It was commonly thought that nitrogen and phosphorus were the major limiting factors in freshwater lakes. This conclusion was a practical one reached by the fertilization of small farm ponds to increase fish production.

Primary production in small fishponds can be increased by fertilization. Hepher (1962) showed that small ponds fertilized with phosphate and ammonium sulfate increased primary production four to five times above that of unfertilized ponds (Figure 257). However, a double addition of fertilizers did not increase primary production in the fishponds any more than a single application.

Many Canadian lakes are poor in dissolved minerals and low in productivity, and by artificial fertilization one might hope to increase the fish yield of these lakes. Four lakes in Algonquin Park, Ontario, were fertilized with a nitrogen–phosphorus–potassium fertilizer during 2 years, and one lake was studied as a control (Langford 1948). There was a rapid increase in phytoplankton about 3 to 4 weeks after fertilization in the spring. Later fertilizations in the summer seemed to have no effect. The average numbers of large phytoplankton per liter in the lakes from July to September were as follows:

Lake	Year	
	Before fertilization (1946)	After fertilization (1947)
Brewer	*7,000*	*135,400*
Kearney	*47,000*	*74,600*
McCauley	*19,100*	*31,100*

The response of the zooplankton population was less striking and in some lakes was not detectable.

In spite of 40 years' work on aquatic fertilization for fish culture, we know very little about the details of this aquatic food chain. The results of studies to date make it safe to predict that fertilization with inorganic or organic compounds will lead to an increase in aquatic productivity of one kind or another, but we have progressed little beyond this primitive stage of

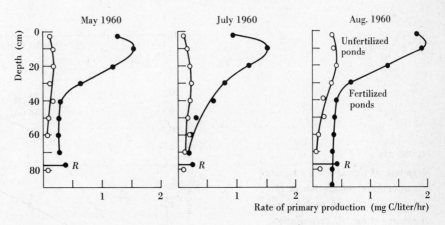

FIGURE 257

Variations in primary production with depth, in fertilized (filled circles) and unfertilized (open circles) fishponds between 1000 and 1200 hr on cloudless days. R, respiration in black bottles. (After Hepher 1962.)

prediction (Gooch 1967). The results of these studies may even be contradictory. Gooch (1967) points out that in some cases fish production in ponds decreases with nitrogen content of water, whereas in other cases it increases with the nitrogen content.

Recent work has indicated that some of the trace elements may be limiting primary production in fresh waters. When the trace element molybdenum was added to Castle Lake in California, the primary productivity increased substantially (Figure 258). Wetzel (1965) has shown that primary productivity in alkaline lakes in Indiana could be increased by adding a variety of inorganic and organic agents. For example, vitamin B_{12} increased production when added to cultures of lake water (Figure 259).

Part of the difficulty of studying nutrient limitations of phytoplankton production is that nutrients may occur in several chemical states in aquatic systems. In some conditions nutrients are present but not available to the organisms because they are bound up in organic complexes in the water or mud (Wetzel and Allen 1971). This has been shown in a striking manner by acid bog lakes, which contain large amounts of phosphorus in forms not available to the phytoplankton. Waters (1957) showed that fertilizing acid bog lakes in Michigan with lime ($CaCO_3$) increased the pH, allowed phosphorus to be released from sediments, and greatly increased the phytoplankton abundance.

Two factors are important if a community is limited in productivity by nutrients. First, the rate of nutrient cycling must be studied. We can visualize this problem with a simple model of an aquatic community containing water, plants, and herbivores (Figure 260). We call these the three *com-*

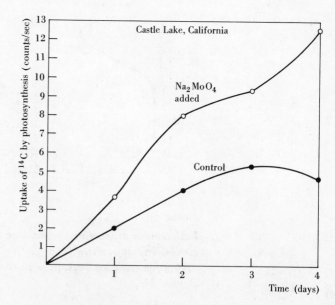

FIGURE 258

Response of Castle Lake's natural phytoplankton population to the addition of 100 ppb molybdenum as measured by ^{14}C assimilation. The hard-glass culture containers were maintained in the lake under natural conditions of light and temperature in midsummer. (After Goldman 1960a.)

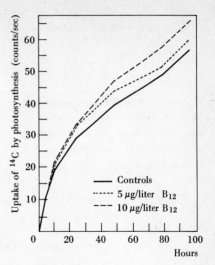

FIGURE 259

*Growth responses of natural phyto-
plankton populations to vitamin B_{12}
in Crooked Lake, Indiana, August
14–18, 1964. Growth was further
enhanced by higher concentrations,
to 20 μg of B_{12}/liter, in Crooked Lake.
(After Wetzel 1965.)*

partments of the system, and we can describe the nutrient cycle by knowing the standing crop of nutrients in each compartment and the rate of
flow of nutrients between compartments. We could by measurements describe
these flow rates and standing crops for the system; Figure 261 gives some
hypothetical data. The critical question now is this: *What would happen
if the nutrient inflow was doubled, or halved?* To answer this question we
have to know what environmental variables determine the flow rates from
one compartment to the next, and at the present time there is not a single

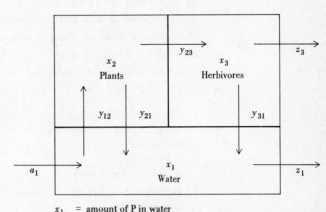

FIGURE 260

*Flow diagram for phosphorus in a
very simple ecosystem composed of
three compartments. (After Smith
1970.)*

x_1 = amount of P in water
x_2 = amount of P in plants
x_3 = amount of P in herbivores
a_1 = rate of inflow of P in water
z_1 = rate of outflow of P in water
z_3 = rate of outflow of P in herbivores
y_{12} = rate of uptake of P from water by plants
y_{21} = rate of loss of P from plants to water
y_{23} = rate of uptake of P from plants by herbivores
y_{31} = rate of loss of P from herbivores to water

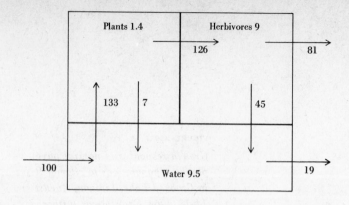

FIGURE 261

Hypothetical distribution (mg) and
rates of movements (mg/day) of
phosphorus in the three-compartment
ecosystem after equilibration to a
constant input rate of 100 mg/day.
(After Smith 1970.)

community for which this knowledge exists. Hence comes part of the problem with pollution.

Second, the rate of nutrient recycling must be determined. All nutrients must be regenerated in order to reenter food chains, and this is done by decomposers. In terms of the simple model in Figure 260, there must ultimately be a connection from z_1 and z_3 to the inflow a_1. The recycling problem may be geological in its time reference or much more rapid. An experiment in artificial circulation of a lake illustrates this point.

Hooper, Ball, and Tanner (1953) pumped bottom water from a small Michigan trout lake to the surface during a 10-day period in midsummer. This artificial mixing increased the phosphorus content of the surface water and caused a 8- to 10-fold increase in the volume of phytoplankton. Thus by increasing the rate of recycling they increased the primary production of the lake without any nutrient additions. Rigler (1964) discusses the phosphorus cycle in some Ontario lakes and points out how little is really understood about this nutrient cycle in aquatic systems.

To summarize, in freshwater communities primary production is limited by the following array of factors:

1 Major controlling factors
   a Light (and temperature)
   b Nitrogen
   c Phosphorus
   d [Silicon for diatoms]

2 Occasionally controlling factors
   a Manganese
   b Iron
   c Molybdenum

3 Rarely controlling factors
   a Cobalt
   b Sulfur
   c Carbon

d Potassium
e Calcium
f Chlorine
g Sodium
h Zinc
i Copper
j Iodine
k Boron
l Vanadium

Terrestrial communities In terrestrial habitats temperature ranges are much greater than in aquatic habitats, and the great variation in temperature from coastal to alpine or continental areas makes it possible to uncouple the solar radiation–temperature variable, which is so closely linked in aquatic systems. What limits primary production in terrestrial communities? Rosenzweig (1968) showed that actual evapotranspiration could predict the above-ground production with good accuracy (Figure 262). Actual evapotranspiration is a measure of solar radiation, temperature, and rainfall; it is the amount of water pumped into the atmosphere by evaporation from the ground and by transpiration from the vegetation. Rosenzweig used only climax vegetation in his analysis.

Net production of forests in the Great Smoky Mountains of Tennessee decreases with altitude (Figure 263). Pine forests, which inhabit dry sites, have lower productivity than deciduous forests or other conifer forests in moist areas.

Root production is an important part of primary productivity. Bray

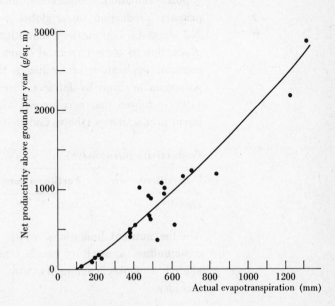

FIGURE 262

Prediction of net primary production of terrestrial communities from climatological data on solar radiation, temperature, and moisture (measured by actual evapotranspiration; see Figure 29). (After Rosenzweig 1968.)

FIGURE 263

Relation of forest net production to the elevation gradient in the Great Smoky Mountains, Tennessee, for broad-leaf deciduous forests of moist environments, evergreen coniferous forests (hemlock, spruce, and fir) of moist environments, and pine forests of dry environments. (After Whittaker 1970.)

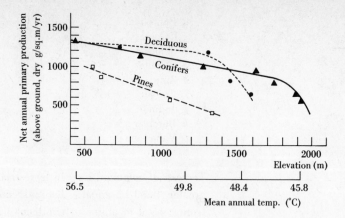

(1963) showed that herbaceous species tended to produce more roots relative to aerial parts, when compared with trees. The ratios he obtained were

	Below ground parts / Total above and below	Percentage below ground
Temperate herbs (28 species)	$\dfrac{3.9}{9.8}$	40
Temperate trees (4 species)	$\dfrac{1.9}{10.8}$	18

Thus comparisons of production based only on aerial plant parts may be misleading and may introduce some error into the comparisons in Figure 262.

Solar radiation, temperature, and moisture are sufficient predictors of primary production on a global scale in terrestrial situations, as Figure 262 suggests, but nutrient limitations on a local scale may determine the production of some terrestrial communities. This conclusion agrees with the common application of fertilizers that contain nitrogen, phosphorus, and potassium to crops by farmers. For example, Bray, Lawrence, and Pearson (1959) showed that corn grown with and without fertilizers had very different productivities (shoots and roots):

Productivity (g/sq. m/yr)

Unfertilized corn	Fertilized corn
410	1050

Are the nutrient limitations, which are now common in agricultural plant communities, a result of man's interference with vegetation? No one has altered a climax community with a large addition of nutrients to test this idea.

In unexploited virgin forest all nutrients which the plants take up from the soil and hold in various plant parts are ultimately returned to the soil as litter to decompose. The net flow of nutrients must be stabilized (input = output) or the site would deteriorate over time. But in a timber forest the situation is fundamentally different because nutrients are being continuously removed from the site by timber cutting, just as with agricultural crops. This makes it necessary to study the nutrient demands of forests so that the forest soils will not be progressively exhausted of their nutrient capital. Rennie (1957) showed, for example, that pines removed fewer nutrients from the soil than other conifers; hardwoods removed the greatest amount of nutrients when they were harvested for timber. If forests are to be cropped like farmland, we must adopt a policy of replenishing from outside sources all the nutrients removed in the crop of trees.

Fertilizers are now being used on a broad scale in forestry. Swan (1965) suggests that more than one nutrient often has to be added to a forest soil to improve yields. Nitrogen, phosphorus, and potassium are usually implicated as most important. Two examples will illustrate the use of fertilizers to increase primary production in forests.

Single applications of fertilizer can have long-lasting effects on forest stands. Gentle, Humphreys, and Lambert (1965) reported on a forest site in Australia that was fertilized with phosphate 8 years after a fire. The fertilized pines (*Pinus radiata*) grew to more than twice the size of the unfertilized trees:

	Basal area (sq. ft/acre) of pines	
Time period	Unfertilized plots	Fertilized plots
15 years after fertilizer added	*52*	*117*

Fertilization of a 20-year stand of Douglas fir with nitrogen fertilizer increased radial growth by approximately 60%. Trees treated with 200 pounds of nitrogen per acre responded the same way as those treated with 400 pounds per acre. The effect of nitrogen was to increase the amount of foliage on the trees; rate of photosynthesis per area of leaf surface was the same in fertilized and unfertilized trees (Brix and Ebell 1969).

If nutrients are critical factors limiting primary production in forests, one should be able to find a relationship between soil nutrient content and productive capacity. In most studies, however, no relationship has been found between soil nutrients and forest growth (Gessel 1962). This can be interpreted to mean that soil nutrients may be present but not available to plants.

Terrestrial communities, especially forests, have large nutrient stores tied up in the standing crop of plants. In this way they differ from communities in the sea and in fresh water. This concentration of nutrients in the standing vegetation has important implications for nutrient cycles in forest communities. Figure 264 illustrates the general relationships of nutrient cycling in a forest ecosystem. If the community is stable, the input of nutrients should equal the output, and a considerable amount of research effort is now being directed at a study of nutrient cycles in terrestrial communities. One example will illustrate this type of work.

Figure 265 shows the potassium cycle in two adjacent woodlands in Great Britain. In the oak woodland the potassium flow is largely through the oak trees and is returned to the soil as litter every year. In the pine woodland the bulk of the potassium flows through the ground flora (particularly bracken fern), and the pines take up relatively little potassium. Details of the nutrient cycles in forests must be studied if we are to utilize forest products without destroying the soil's fertility.

In summary, terrestrial communities are limited in their primary productivity by temperature, light, and moisture. Nutrient limitations are well documented for agricultural systems and forests harvested by man, but whether nutrients limit primary production in climax communities is not known.

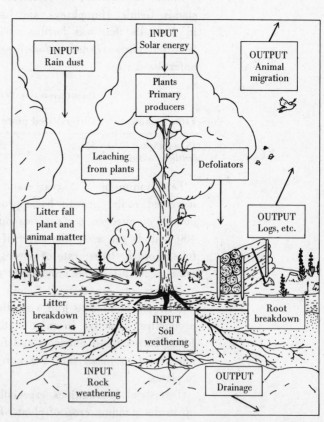

FIGURE 264

Forest ecosystem dynamics. Arrows indicate the flows of matter and energy. (After Ovington 1962.)

Quercus robur aged 47 years

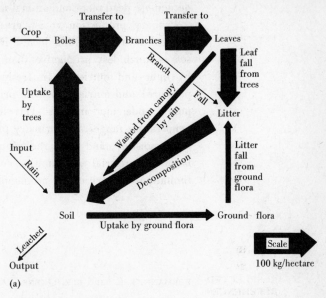

(a)

Pinus sylvestris aged 47 yr

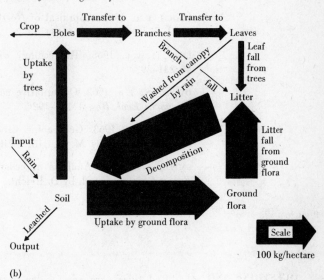

(b)

FIGURE 265

Potassium circulation in adjacent (a) oak and (b) pine woodlands growing under similar conditions. The thickness of the arrow indicates the magnitude of flow. Note the relatively large amount of potassium circulating through the bracken ground flora of the pine plantation and the greater uptake of potassium by the oak trees. (After Ovington 1965.)

SUMMARY

Community metabolism has its source in green plants, which convert solar energy to carbohydrates with an energetic efficiency of approximately 1%. Plants are thus the primary producers and form the first trophic level.

Herbivores form the second trophic level, and carnivores the next. In addition to this food chain, there is a separate chain of detritus feeders which decompose dead plant and animal material.

Primary production varies greatly over the globe; it is highest in the tropical rain forests and lowest in arctic, alpine, and desert habitats. The sea is much less productive than the land because of limitations imposed by light and nutrients. In freshwater communities light (including temperature) and nutrients restrict primary productivity, but nutrient cycles are poorly understood in lakes. Terrestrial communities are subjected to greater temperature ranges, and primary production seems to be limited by temperature, moisture, and solar radiation. The standing crop of nutrients is very large in terrestrial communities, compared with that in the sea, and nutrient limitations are critical in cropland and forests harvested by man.

SELECTED REFERENCES

BORMANN, F. H., and G. E. LIKENS. 1967. Nutrient cycling. *Science* 155:424–429.

GOLDMAN, C. R. 1968. Aquatic primary production. *Amer. Zool.* 8:31–42.

GOOCH, B. C. 1967. Appraisal of North American fish culture fertilization studies. *FAO Fisheries Repts.* 44(3):13–26.

LUND, J. W. G. 1965. The ecology of the freshwater phytoplankton. *Biol. Rev.* 40:231–293.

OVINGTON, J. D. 1962. Quantitative ecology and the woodland ecosystem concept. *Advances Ecol. Res.* 1:103–192.

RYTHER, J. H. 1963. Geographic variation in productivity. pp. 347–380 in *The Sea*, Vol. 2, ed. by M. N. Hill. Wiley-Interscience, New York.

SMITH, F. E. 1970. Analysis of ecosystems. pp. 7–18 in *Analysis of Temperate Forest Ecosystems*, ed. by D. Reichle. Springer, Berlin.

QUESTIONS AND PROBLEMS

1 "Red tides" are spectacular algal blooms that occur in the sea and often lead to mass mortality of marine fishes and invertebrates. Review the evidence available about the origin of red tides and discuss the implications for general ideas about what controls primary production in the sea. Brongersma-Sanders (1957) reviews this problem, and Seliger et al. (1970) give some recent data.

2 Calculate the attenuation of solar radiation through a water column (and the depth at which radiation falls to 1% of its surface value) for the following extinction coefficients:

	Extinction coefficient (per meter)
Pure water	*0.03*
Coastal water, minimum	*0.20*
Coastal water, maximum	*0.40*
Eutrophic lake	*1.50*

3 In discussing the effect of light on primary productivity in the ocean, Nielsen and Jensen (1957, p. 108) state: "It is thus quite likely that a permanent reduction of the light intensity at the surface (to e.g. 50 per cent of its normal value without the other factors being affected—a rather improbable condition in Nature) in the long run would have very little influence on the organic productivity as measured per surface area." How could this possibly be true?

4 The concentration of inorganic phosphate in the water of the North Atlantic Ocean is only about 50% of that found in the other oceans. Yet the North Atlantic is more productive than most of the other oceans. How can you reconcile these observations if nutrients limit primary productivity?

5 In discussing the cycle of nutrients in lakes, Rigler (1964, p. 4) states:

In any system involving living things the flow of energy and the cycle of an element, regardless whether the element is Mo, Co, N, or P, are inseparable. Before we can increase and direct the productivity of lakes as we do that of the land we will have to know much about the cycle of phosphorus as well as the cycles of many other trace elements.

Discuss.

6 Westlake (1963, p. 386) states:

The ecologist who is interested in the dynamics of communities, rather than their description, is deeply concerned with the magnitude of this primary photosynthetic production, and the factors influencing it, for the rate of primary production is ultimately one of the main factors controlling the rates of multiplication and growth of the organisms in a community.

Discuss.

22 Community metabolism II

SECONDARY PRODUCTION

MEASUREMENT OF SECONDARY PRODUCTION

The biomass of plants which accumulates in a community as a result of photosynthesis can go in one of two directions eventually: to herbivores or to detritus feeders. The fate of the energy and materials captured in primary productivity can be shown most simply by looking at the metabolism of an individual herbivore.

The partitioning of food materials and energy for an individual animal can be seen as a series of dichotomies. Using energy, we have

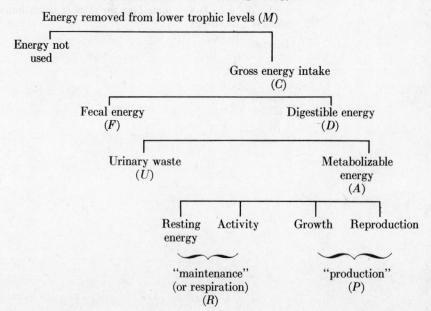

This scheme could be presented for calcium intake, or any essential nutrient, and again we have the choice of using chemical materials or energy to study the system.

Let us look at this scheme in detail. Every animal will remove some energy or material from the lower trophic level for his food. Some of this energy will not be used. For example, a beaver fells a whole tree and eats only some of the bark. In this case most of the energy removed from the plant trophic level is not used by the beaver but is left to decompose. Of the material consumed, some energy passes through the digestive tract and is lost in the feces. Of the energy digested, some is lost as urinary output and the rest is available for metabolic energy. It is usually convenient to lump the energy losses of urine and feces when actually determining the metabolizable energy. We have now reached the level of assimilation, or metabolizable energy, and this energy can be subdivided into two general pathways: production or maintenance. All animals must expend energy just to subsist through the process of respiration. Production occurs by using metabolizable energy for growth and for reproduction.

How can we measure the components of secondary productivity in an animal community? Several techniques are available (Petrusewicz and Macfadyen 1970), but the general procedure is as follows. Each species of animal is considered separately. To determine the gross energy intake of the population we must know the feeding rate. This can be measured by confining an animal to a feeding plot and measuring herbage biomass before and after feeding. In some species, such as birds of prey, the number of food items being consumed can be counted by direct observation. Indirect techniques such as weight of stomach contents can also be used but require knowledge of the rate of digestion and rate of feeding.

Assimilation, or metabolizable energy, can be measured very simply in the laboratory where the gross intake can be regulated and feces and urine can be collected, but in the field it is most difficult to estimate assimilation directly. The usual approach is to measure it indirectly by use of the relation

Assimilation = respiration + net production

If we can measure respiration and production we can get assimilation by addition.

Respiration can be measured very easily in laboratory situations by confining an animal to a small cage and measuring oxygen consumption, CO_2 output, or heat production directly. There is a minimum rate of metabolism, called *basal metabolic rate*, which is a simple function of body size in warm-blooded animals:

Basal metabolism (kcal/day) = $70 \times$ (weight)$^{3/4}$

when weight is expressed in kilograms. This relationship is shown in Figure 266. Basal metabolism is measured under resting conditions with no food

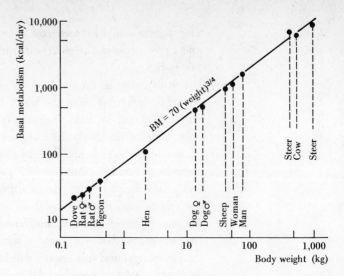

FIGURE 266

Relationship between weight and metabolic rate over a range of homeothermic vertebrates. (After Kleiber 1961.)

in the stomach at a temperature where the animal is not required to expend energy for extra heat production. Measured in such an abstract way, basal metabolism is not closely related to respiration losses in field situations, where activity is necessary, temperature varies, and digestion is occurring. Average metabolic cost for maintenance was estimated by Brody (1945) to be approximately twice the basal metabolic rate. Grodzinski and Gorecki (1967) showed that average daily metabolic rate in the field mouse *Microtus agrestis* was approximately 1.5 times basal metabolism.

Respiration losses are affected by a variety of environmental factors. Temperature is particularly important, both in homeotherms and in poikilotherms. For example, Smalley (1960) showed that respiration in the salt marsh grasshopper *Orchelimum fidicinium* was a function of the size of the individual and the environmental temperature (Figure 267).

Net production can be measured by the growth of individuals in the population and the reproduction of new animals. We have discussed techniques for measuring the changes in numbers in Chapter 9, and growth can be measured by weighing individuals at successive times. The only admonition we must make here is that sampling must be frequent enough that individuals are not born and then die in the interval between samples. Net production is usually measured as biomass and converted to energy measures by determination of the caloric value of a unit weight of the species.

Figure 268 gives a schematic representation of how production can be determined from information on population changes and growth. In this hypothetical population, production is the sum of growth and natality additions:

Production = growth + natality
= 20 + 10 + 10 + 10 + 10 + 30 − 10 − 10 = 70 units of biomass

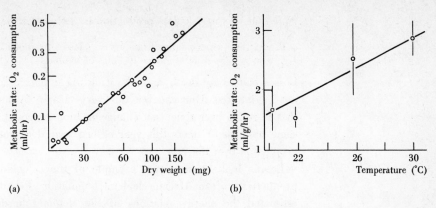

(a)   (b)

FIGURE 267

Respiration of the salt-marsh grasshopper Orchelimum *as a function of (a) body weight and (b) environmental temperature. (After Smalley 1960.)*

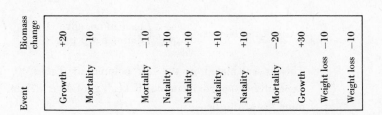

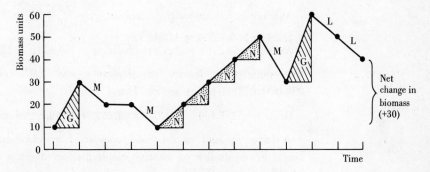

FIGURE 268

Changes in biomass of a hypothetical population to illustrate the factors contributing to secondary production. The net change in biomass over a given time period is the outcome of gains from growth and reproduction and losses from death and emigration.

Note that we can calculate production in a second way:

Production = net change in biomass + losses by mortality
= + 30 + 40 = 70 units of biomass

Losses caused by death or emigration are a part of production and should not be ignored. One can see this very clearly by looking at a population that is stable over time (net change in biomass zero): A ranch that has the same biomass of steers this year as last year does not necessarily have zero production over the year.

Let us look at an actual example of the calculations of the secondary productivity of an African elephant population. Petrides and Swank (1966) estimated the energy relations of the elephant herds in Queen Elizabeth National Park, Uganda. In order to do these calculations, we must assume a stable population of elephants. The population was counted and the age structure estimated in order to construct a life table (see page 162). The maximum age was estimated at 67 years, and the survivorship schedule is given in Table 30. Weight growth was estimated from some records of zoo animals and a limited amount of field data on weights. The average weight at each age is also given in Table 30, and the average increase in weight from one year to the next. If the age structure is stationary, the growth in biomass of the elephant population will be approximately equal to

$$\text{Growth in biomass} \cong \sum_{\text{all ages}} \begin{pmatrix} \text{median no. alive} \\ \text{during age } x \text{ to } x+1 \end{pmatrix} \times \begin{pmatrix} \text{average weight} \\ \text{growth for ages} \\ x \text{ to } x+1 \end{pmatrix}$$

This is calculated in the last column of Table 30. The caloric value of elephants is approximately 1.5 kcal/g of live weight. Therefore, we determine growth to be

1000 elephants lived 10,487.5 elephant-years and produced 2,552,875 lb of growth

Average growth (in weight)/elephant/yr $= \dfrac{2,552,875}{10,487.5} = 243.4$ lb

243.4 lb $\times$ 0.45359 = 110.40 kg
Average growth (in energy)/elephant/yr = 110,400 g $\times$ 1.5 kcal/g = 165,600 kcal

The population density of elephants was 2.077 elephants/sq. km. or 0.000002077 elephant/sq. m. Thus

Growth = 165,600 kcal $\times$ 0.000002077 = 0.34 kcal/sq. m/yr

A large amount of the food consumed by elephants passes through as feces. From studies on captive elephants, an average 5000-pound elephant would consume 23.59 kg dry weight of forage per day and produce from this 13.25 kg dry weight of feces. The food plants are worth approximately 4 kcal/g dry weight, and so we can calculate

Average consumption = 23,590 $\times$ 4 = 94,360 kcal/day/elephant
Average fecal production = 13,250 $\times$ 4 = 53,000 kcal/day/elephant

TABLE 30

Elephant life table and production data, Queen Elizabeth National Park, Uganda, November 1956 to June 1957

(1) Age, x	(2) No. alive at beginning of age x	(3) Mortality rate	(4) Median no. alive	(5) Weight average (lb)	(6) Weight increment (lb)	(7) Population weight increment (lb) (4) × (6)
1	1,000	0.30	850.0	200	200	170,000
2	700	0.20	630.0	450	250	157,500
3	560	0.10	532.0	700	250	133,000
4	504		478.5	1,000	300	143,550
5	453		430.5	1,350	350	150,675
6	408		387.5	1,750	400	155,000
7	367		348.5	2,200	450	156,825
8	330		313.5	2,650	450	141,075
9	297		282.0	3,100	450	126,900
10	267	0.05	260.5	3,550	450	117,225
11	254		247.5	4,000	450	111,375
12	241		235.0	4,450	450	105,750
13	229		223.5	4,850	400	89,400
14	218		212.5	5,250	400	85,000
15	207	0.02	205.0	5,700	450	92,250
16	203		201.0	6,150	450	90,450
17	199		197.0	6,600	450	88,650
18	195		193.0	7,000	400	77,200
19	191		189.0	7,450	450	85,050
20	187		185.0	7,900	450	83,250
21	183		181.0	8,250	350	63,350
22	179		177.0	8,500	250	44,250
23	175		173.0	8,700	200	34,600
24	171		169.5	8,900	200	33,900
25	168		166.5	9,000	100	16,650
26–67	3,107[b]	0.02–0.20	3,026.5[b]	9,000	0	0
Total	10,933		10,487.5	(5,041)[a]	9,000	2,552,875

[a] Average body weight.

[b] Sum of the numbers of animals in each year class for ages 26 to 67.

SOURCE: After Petrides and Swank (1966).

Counting these for a whole year and multiplying by the number of elephants per square meter, we obtain

Food consumed = (94,360 kcal/day/elephant)

$\times$ (365 days) $\times$ (0.000002077 elephant/sq. m)

= 71.5 kcal/sq. m/yr

Feces produced = (53,000 kcal/day/elephant)

$\times$ (365 days) $\times$ (0.000002077 elephant/sq. m)

= 40.2 kcal/sq. m/yr

We know that

Food energy consumed = feces + growth + maintenance

71.5 = 40.2 + 0.34 + maintenance

and consequently, maintenance must be 31.0 kcal/sq. m/yr if we ignore the losses due to urine production and the production due to newborn animals.

We can also estimate maintenance from Figure 266 for basal metabolic rate of a standard 5000-pound elephant:

$BM = 70W^{3/4}$

$= (70)(2268 \text{ kg})^{3/4} = 23,005 \text{ kcal/day/elephant}$

If active metabolism is approximately twice basal metabolism, we can estimate the maintenance energy used:

Maintenance = (2) $\times$ (23,005 kcal/day/elephant)

$\times$ (365 days) $\times$ (0.000002077 elephant/sq. m)

= 34.9 kcal/sq. m/yr

This compares reasonably well with our estimate of 31.0 obtained above by subtraction; consequently, we are encouraged to think that our calculations may not be too inaccurate.

Finally, we can determine the standing crop of elephants in energetic terms:

Standing crop = (0.000002077 elephant/sq. m) $\times$ (2,268,000 g) $\times$ (1.5 kcal/g)

= 7.1 kcal/sq. m

A rough estimate of primary productivity by the harvest method produced an estimate of net primary productivity of 747 kcal/sq. m/yr for the foraging area of the elephants.

We can summarize these estimates for the African elephant population of Queen Elizabeth Park:

	Energy (kcal/sq. m/yr)
Net primary production	747[a]
Secondary production	
Food consumed	71.5
Fecal energy lost	40.2
Maintenance metabolism	31.0
Growth	0.34
Standing crop of elephants	7.1

[a] Probably a low estimate; compare Table 29, page 449.

Clearly the greatest part of the energy intake of these elephants is used in maintenance or lost in fecal production.

The details of estimating secondary production will obviously vary from species to species, and the number of assumptions one must make will depend on how well studied the species is. The procedure is to repeat these calculations for all dominant species in the community and by addition to obtain the secondary production of the community. This procedure is more tedious than conceptually difficult, and we can turn to consider the results of this kind of analysis.

ECOLOGICAL EFFICIENCIES

If we view the community as an energy transformer, we can ask questions about its relative efficiency. A large number of ecological efficiencies can be defined (Kozlovsky 1968) and we shall be concerned here with four. First, we can measure efficiency *within* a trophic level. Two measures can be used for this purpose*:

$$\text{Respiration loss} = \frac{\text{respiration at trophic level } n}{\text{assimilation at trophic level } n}$$

$$\text{Growth efficiency} = \frac{\text{net productivity at trophic level } n}{\text{assimilation at trophic level } n}$$

There are very few measurements of these efficiencies for whole communities. Figure 269 summarizes the available estimates, and two conclusions are evident:

1 Respiration consumes a larger fraction of the assimilated energy in higher trophic levels. While plants used about 40% of their photosynthesis energy for respiration, carnivores used about 65%.

2 Net productivity is reduced at higher trophic levels, in relation to assimilation. This is implicit in conclusion 1 and means that the efficiency of plant growth is usually greater than the efficiency of animal growth.

Few workers have been able to measure the efficiency of whole communities, but data on individual species are readily obtained. We can thus estimate these efficiencies for individual species to see if they obey the same trends suggested by Figure 269. Table 31 summarizes data on herbivores. In general, respiration seems to utilize 97 to 99% of the energy assimilated in mammals, and consequently only 1 to 3% of the energy is net production. For insects the loss is less, approximately 63 to 84% of the energy assimilated being used for respiration. This difference between insects and

* These two efficiencies are just different ways of viewing the same data and are not independent, since (as percentages) respiration loss + growth efficiency = 100%.

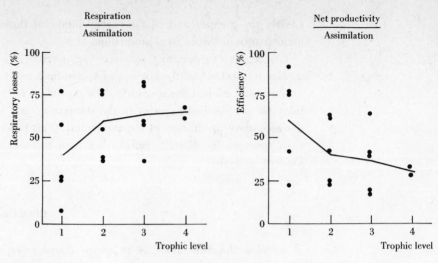

FIGURE 269

Two measures of ecological efficiencies within *whole trophic levels.*
Data from the study of five communities: Lake Mendota, Wisconsin;
Cedar Bog Lake, Minnesota; a Georgia salt marsh; Silver Springs,
Florida; and a temperate cold spring in Massachusetts. Trophic levels
1 to 4 are green plants, herbivores, primary carnivores, and
secondary carnivores. (After Kozlovsky 1968.)

mammals may be a reflection of the cost of homeothermy. But both groups of
herbivores show more respiration losses than those which Figure 269 suggests
as a mean value for trophic level 2 (herbivores). Mann's (1965) data on five
species of fish from the River Thames also show a high respiration loss of 91
to 94% of the energy assimilated.

Studies on the energetics of individual species populations do not suggest
constant ecological efficiencies. The amount of energy available for growth
and reproduction, the converse of the amount used for respiration, can vary
with the type of diet and with the amount of food consumed. Figure 270
gives one example from a laboratory study of fish metabolism, in which the
proportion of the food consumed which is used for respiration declines at
high feeding rates. This type of complication makes it difficult to estimate
energy flow through a population.

We can also measure efficiencies *between* trophic levels, using either of
two measures:

$$\text{Lindeman's efficiency} = \frac{\text{assimilation at trophic level } n}{\text{assimilation at trophic level } n-1}$$

$$\text{Consumption efficiency} = \frac{\text{intake at trophic level } n}{\text{net productivity at trophic level } n-1}$$

TABLE 31

Proportion of energy assimilated that is lost by respiration in herbivores[a]

Community	Species	Respiration, R	Assimilation, A	Proportion, R/A
Old fields (South Carolina)	Savannah sparrow	3.56	3.6	0.99
	Old-field mouse	6.6	6.7	0.98
	Grasshoppers	21.6	25.6	0.84
Old field (Michigan)	Spittlebugs	0.80	0.88	0.91
	Grasshoppers	0.86	1.37	0.63
	Deer mice	0.62	0.63	0.98
	Sparrows	2.29	2.34	0.98
	Ground squirrels	3.69	3.80	0.97
Coastal salt marsh (Georgia)	Grasshopper	19	30	0.63
	Plant hopper	205	275	0.75
African grasslands	Large grazing mammals	155.0	158.1	0.98
African savannah	Elephants	31.0	31.3	0.99
Grassland (Michigan)	Meadow vole	17.0	17.4	0.98

[a] Dominant species populations studied separately. All values of energy as kilocalories per square meter per year.
SOURCE: After Wiegert and Evans (1967).

Many other efficiency measures can be defined (see Kozlovsky 1968). Consumption efficiency measures the relative pressure of one trophic level on the one beneath it. Figure 271 gives these efficiencies for the five communities presented in Figure 269. Lindeman's efficiency appears to be a constant around 10% for each set of trophic levels, and this was suggested to be a

FIGURE 270

*Proportion of energy used in respiration in yearling sculpins (*Cottus perplexus*) held separately in aquaria and fed measured amounts of midge larvae in the fall. (After Warren and Davis 1967.)*

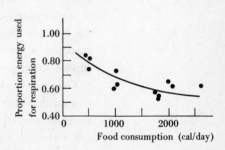

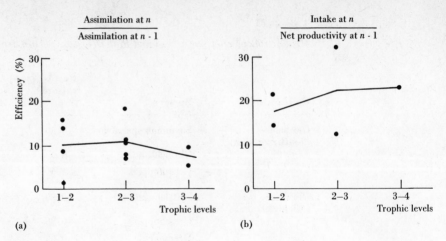

FIGURE 271

Two measures of ecological efficiencies between *trophic levels: (a) Lindeman's efficiency, (b) consumption efficiency. Data from the study of five communities: Lake Mendota, Wisconsin; Cedar Bog Lake, Minnesota; a Georgia salt marsh; Silver Springs, Florida; and a temperate cold spring in Massachusetts. (After Kozlovsky 1968.)*

significant ecological generalization (Slobodkin 1961). Recent data on marine food chains suggest that this may be wrong and that Lindeman's efficiency may reach about 70% in some cases (Petipa, Paulova, and Mironov 1970).

Consumption efficiency may rise slightly from the first trophic levels but in general seems to fall in the 20 to 25% range. This means that 75 to 80% of the net production of each trophic level goes into the decomposer chain, is lost to the system, or is used to increase population biomass. Most goes to the decomposers. Figure 272 shows the complete energy flow for the Georgia salt marsh whose food web was given in Figure 243. Note that the producers are also the most important consumers; much of the energy fixed in photosynthesis is used for plant respiration. The bacteria are second in importance in degrading energy, and as decomposers they use about one-seventh the energy the plants used. The animal consumers are a poor third in importance, since they degrade about one-seventh the amount of energy the bacteria use. In the salt marsh a substantial amount of production is exported as plant debris into the estuaries, where it is available as detritus for further decomposition.

The large role that bacteria can play in energy-flow networks might suggest that animals are not an important part of the community. If animals were eliminated from the Georgia salt marshes, for example, would this affect the community of plants and microbes? The answer seems to be yes.

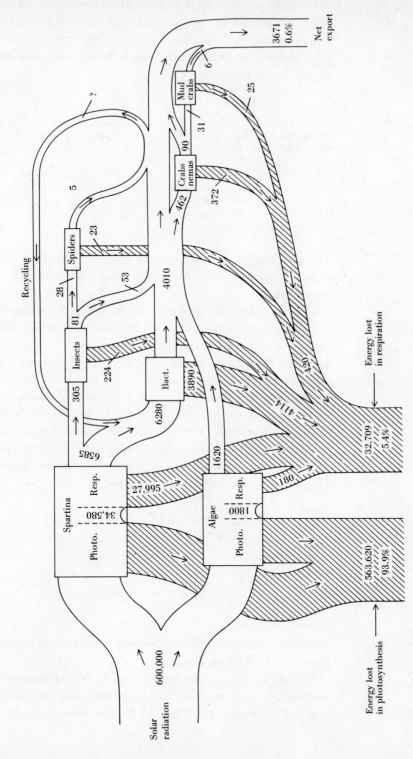

FIGURE 272

Energy-flow diagram for a Georgia salt marsh. (After Teal 1962.)

The activity of soil animals is essential for decomposition, even though their energetic contribution is small. Edwards and Heath (1963) demonstrated this by putting oak and beech leaves in nylon mesh bags in the soil. By using different mesh bags, they could exclude larger invertebrates from the leaves. They obtained these results:

Bag mesh size (mm)	Fauna that could enter bags	Oak leaves disappearing within 9 months (%)
7.0	All	93
0.5	Small invertebrates, microorganisms	38
0.003	Microorganisms only	0

The activities of the soil animals promote the action of microbes in a symbiotic manner, and earthworms were most important in starting leaf breakdown.

Efficiencies between trophic levels could also be estimated for individual species populations, but relatively little of this has been done. The African elephant population we discussed earlier had a consumption efficiency of 71.5/747 kcal/sq. m = 9.6%. Golley (1960) estimated the consumption efficiency of a meadow mouse (*Microtus*) population feeding on grass to be 250,000/15,800,000 kcal/hectare = 1.6%, and Lindeman's efficiency for the grass–*Microtus* trophic link to be 0.3%, a very low value. Most of the species we as humans tend to think "important" turn out to have little role in energy transfers. For example, Varley (1970) estimated the consumption efficiencies for many of the vertebrates in Wytham Woods (food web in Figure 245) which depend on the oak tree:

Species	Consumption efficiency (%)
Great tit	0.33
Pigmy shrew	0.10
Wood mouse	0.75

Even the dominant forms consume only a fraction of 1% of the net primary production in Wytham Woods.

Nutrient cycles have not been studied in relation to secondary production, even though work on individual populations has suggested that it is nutrients and not energy which may be limiting animal populations (Klein 1970,

Dixon 1970). Gerking (1962) has approached fish production from the viewpoint of nitrogen (protein) metabolism and shown that the bluegill population of Indiana lakes had a growth efficiency of 15 to 26% in terms of protein. The protein consumption efficiency of bluegills in relation to the bottom fauna of midges was about 50% during the summer months, when the fish population was severely cropping the bottom fauna. Gerking's work is one of the few attempts to apply the principles of nutrition of domestic animals (Maynard and Loosli 1956) to field populations.

One consequence of low ecological efficiencies is that organisms at the base of the food web are much more abundant than those at higher trophic levels. Elton recognized this in 1927, and the resulting pyramids of numbers have been called *Eltonian pyramids* in his honor. Figure 273 illustrates a pyramid of numbers for an annual grassland in California. Note that pyramids can be constructed on the basis of numbers, biomass, or energy of standing crop. They illustrate graphically the rapid loss of energy as one moves from plants to herbivores to carnivores, a biological illustration of the second law of thermodynamics.

WHAT LIMITS SECONDARY PRODUCTION?

This is one of the critical questions we need to answer. As a first approximation, we could state that secondary production is limited by primary production and the second law of thermodynamics. The second law of thermodynamics states that no process of energy conversion is 100% efficient. This answer is partly satisfying but not entirely so. Why do trophic levels take in only about 20% of the energy produced by the previous level? Why not 30%, or 40%? Few workers have attempted to answer this question for a whole community. Let us consider four case histories.

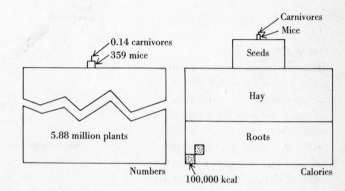

FIGURE 273

Pyramids of numbers and caloric content on 1 acre of annual grassland in California at the time of peak plant and animal standing crops. (After Pearson 1964.)

Marion Lake is a small shallow lake in the Coast Mountains of southern British Columbia. It contains a relatively simple community whose trophic relationships are shown in Figure 274. The sources of energy to the Marion Lake system are five:

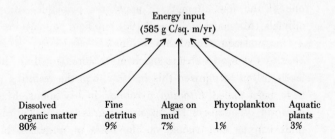

The lake is somewhat unusual in that most of the energy input comes from the surrounding forest and watershed in the form of organic detritus.

Phytoplankton production in Marion Lake is very low and about equal to that of an arctic lake. The efficiency of conversion of solar radiation to phytoplankton is only 0.0009%. Three factors seem to limit phytoplankton production: low water temperature in winter, very low nutrient levels, and high flushing rate. After a heavy rain the runoff may be so great as to

FIGURE 274

Main energy pathways in Marion Lake, British Columbia. Broad arrows indicate the routes considered to be most important. Heavy rainfall in the vicinity of the lake results in regular flushing of the lake and loss of much of the pelagic material through the outflow. (After Efford 1969.)

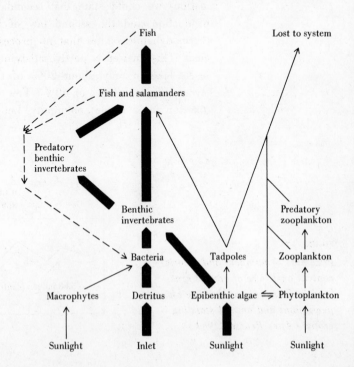

replace all the water in the lake in less than 2 days. Dickman (1969) showed that the high flushing rate was the principal factor restricting phytoplankton production. Wooden enclosures in the lake, which prevented water from leaving, had primary productivity two to four times that of the open lake. The rapid movement of water into and out of Marion Lake acts as a cropping agent, removing phytoplankton before they are able to build up in biomass. The same general effect might be achieved by heavy grazing pressure in other systems.

Zooplankton are very scarce in Marion Lake and do not form an important part of the food of carnivores in the lake.

Large aquatic plants around the edges of the lake fix some energy which enters the lake as detritus. This forms a small fraction of the energy input, and the factors limiting the production of aquatic plants are not known.

Algae growing on the mud surface are next in importance in energy production. The productivity of these algae is largely determined by temperature, but in shallow water (where temperatures are higher) algal standing crop and production is relatively low (Figure 275). This reduction in algal production in shallow water is not due to excessive light; samples moved to shallow areas showed increased photosynthetic production, as long as

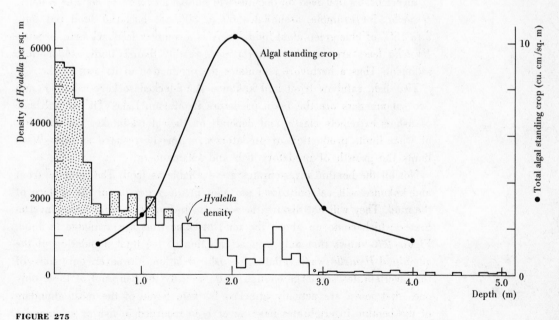

FIGURE 275

Depth distribution of the amphipod Hyalella azteca *in Marion Lake in relation to the standing crop of bottom algae. The shaded part of the* Hyalella *distribution shows densities above which one can expect a reduction in the algae by grazing. (After Efford 1971.)*

herbivores were excluded. The grazing of herbivores, such as the amphipod *Hyalella azteca*, on the algae growing on the bottom mud seems to reduce shallow-water algal populations. This grazing effect is concentrated in shallow water because the invertebrates are concentrated there (Figure 275).

Detritus is the main energy source to Marion Lake, and bacteria are important agents of breakdown of detritus. At least 60 different types of bacteria are found on the mud surface, and one of the large unsolved problems is whether we can treat all these bacteria together or whether we must consider the action of several types of bacteria independently. Temperature is the principal factor limiting bacterial activity. In addition, the bottom-dwelling invertebrates ingest the sediment and may hold bacterial populations down by their grazing pressure.

Herbivores in Marion Lake are held in check by three processes: predation, temperature, and food. The frog *Rana aurora* lays about 300,000 eggs in Marion Lake each spring, but only 20,000 tadpoles survive after 2 months, probably because of predation by two salamanders, *Ambystoma gracile* and *Taricha granulosa*, and some invertebrates.

Temperature seems to restrict the benthic invertebrates of Marion Lake to a single generation a year, and this restricts the annual production of the lake.

Invertebrates that feed on detritus will not eat all forms of detritus equally. *Hyalella*, for example, assimilates 60 to 80% of bacterial food but only 5 to 15% of blue-green algal food. There is a complex feedback here, because *Hyalella* feces are used by bacteria more readily than is undigested bottom sediment. Thus a herbivore stimulates the production of its own food.

Two fish, rainbow trout and kokanee (land-locked sockeye salmon), and two salamanders are the main predators in Marion Lake. The growth rate of fish is extremely elastic and depends on their food intake. The question of what limits production of predators can thus be restated as this: What limits the growth of predatory fish and salamanders?

Not all the benthic invertebrates are available as food. The rainbow trout and kokanee will eat only food particles in the water or on the surface of the mud. They will not disturb the sediment to find food. Only those invertebrates which come up above the mud at some time are available as food. Figure 276 shows that only a small fraction of the total population of the amphipod *Hyalella* was available for fish predation. Moreover, only some of the invertebrates are large enough to be seen by the fish, and of these only ones that move are actually attacked by fish. Some of the most abundant of the benthic invertebrates have never been recorded in fish or salamander stomachs. This great contrast between food organisms present and those available is one reason that energy flow to predators is restricted.

Competition over food may possibly limit secondary production. The kokanee specializes on food in the water column, while the rainbow trout

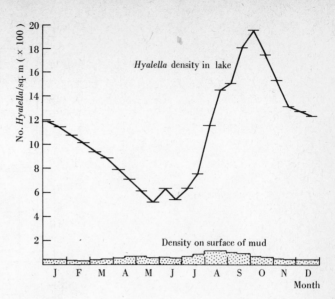

FIGURE 276

Density of Hyalella azteca *in Marion Lake during the year compared to number of individuals on the sediment surface, where they could be seen by the fish. (After Efford 1971.)*

and salamanders remove the same kinds of food from the bottom (Figure 277). The salamander *Taricha* is relatively uncommon in the lake, and the main possible competition would be between the rainbow trout and the salamander *Ambystoma*. Of all the food eaten by predators the proportions consumed are rainbow trout, 56%; kokanee, 25%; *Ambystoma*, 19%; and *Taricha*, 1%. There is as yet no critical evidence that competition for food does limit growth in the four predators, but it remains a possibility.

The next step in the Marion Lake project is to build a mathematical model of the processes we have described verbally. This should lead to perturbation experiments of the community. What would happen to benthic invertebrate populations if rainbow trout were removed from the lake? Or what would be affected if the flushing rate of the lake were greatly reduced? We are still a long way from being able to predict the outcome of manipulations like these on the whole community.

Trout production in a sucrose-enriched stream

Excessive additions of nutrients and organic materials to streams and lakes by man can have undesirable effects on secondary production. But up to some point the addition of small amounts of nutrients to aquatic systems can stimulate desirable secondary production. Warren et al. (1964) showed this by the experimental addition of sucrose to Berry Creek in Oregon. The flow in a 1500-ft section of Berry Creek was controlled and diverted so that four sections of the creek could be studied. Each experimental section contained a riffle and a pool. The water in two sections was enriched by the continuous flow of a few milligrams of sucrose per liter of water.

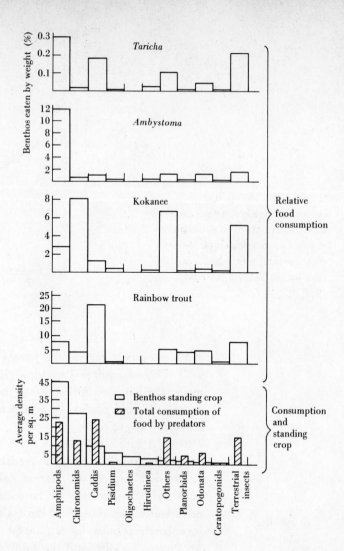

FIGURE 277

*Food of the two fish and two sala-
manders in Marion Lake presented
as a percentage of the total food
all four species eat. In the bottom
graph the total food eaten by all
four vertebrate predators (inner
bars) is compared with the average
annual density of the same organisms in the sediment. (After
Efford 1971.)*

Cutthroat trout production was very high on the sucrose-enriched sections:

Cutthroat trout	Unenriched		Enriched	
	Section I	Section II	Section I	Section II
Growth production (kcal/sq. m/yr)	0.79	−0.30	5.92	5.40
Total annual food consumption (kcal/sq. m/yr)	25	20	47	34

This experiment was repeated three times, and the growth of trout was usually increased sevenfold on the enriched stream sections. Food consumption by trout was also increased on the enriched areas, but only about twofold. On the enriched sections the trout used proportionately much less of their energy intake for maintenance metabolism and consequently had more energy available for growth.

The benthic insects that live in the riffles all increased in abundance in the sucrose-enriched sections. The chironomid midges were particularly important as a food source for the trout and were particularly abundant in the enriched sections:

	Unenriched		Enriched	
	Section I	Section II	Section I	Section II
Biomass of midge larvae and pupae in stream (kcal/sq. m)	0.04	0.10	4.21	2.75
Percent of midges in trout diet	12	9	37	34

The increased biomass of the benthic insects in the enriched sections was caused by the increased availability of bacterial food in the form of a slime bacterium, *Sphaerotilus natans*.

Warren et al. (1964) point out that not all energy pathways through this stream community lead to trout production. Trout feed on only a restricted set of the invertebrates present. These invertebrates, which were stimulated to higher production by a small amount of sucrose, would be eliminated if sucrose addition were increased greatly, because slime bacteria would then smother the bottom. Thus experimental changes in the energy income of a community can be done only to some ill-defined point before the system breaks down and is altered to a new type of community.

A marine food chain

In the oceans there is a relatively simple food chain from nutrients in the water, to phytoplankton (the producers), to zooplankton (herbivores), and then to a series of carnivores. If we understand what controls primary and secondary production in the sea, we ought to be able to build a model of this food chain. Riley (1946, 1963) has shown that simple models can give us some insight into the phytoplankton and zooplankton sectors of this food chain.

Consider first the phytoplankton in the ocean. The change in biomass of these small plants is the net outcome of gross production gains and respiration and grazing losses. The rate of change in the phytoplankton community can thus be described by a simple equation:

$$\frac{dx}{dt} = x(P - R - G)$$

where

x = phytoplankton population size
t = time
P = rate of photosynthesis per unit of population
R = rate of phytoplankton respiration
G = rate of grazing loss to zooplankton

Let us consider first the estimation of P, the gross primary productivity, which is expressed as grams of carbon fixed by photosynthesis per day per gram of carbon in the surface standing crop of phytoplankton. When nutrients are not limiting, and light is, the rate of photosynthesis is simply

$$P = pI$$

where

P = rate of photosynthesis
I = solar radiation in g cal/cm^2/min
p = a constant of conversion (2.5 approx.)

At any depth z, the light is attenuated by the geometric equation

$$I_z = I_0 e^{-kz}$$

where

I_z = solar radiation at depth z
I_0 = solar radiation at surface of sea
e = 2.71828...
k = extinction coefficient (Figure 248)

Consequently the rate of photosynthesis is

$$P_z = pI_0 e^{-kz}$$

where P_z is the rate of photosynthesis at depth z. The mean rate of photosynthesis is obtained by summing this equation over all the depths in the lighted zone to the maximum depth of photosynthesis (z_1). This summation produces an equation,

$$P = \frac{pI_0}{kz_1}(1 - e^{-kz_1})$$

which describes the rate of photosynthesis as a function of incoming light and the clearness of the water only.

Riley (1946) suggested that this simple model was not sufficient because in the summer months photosynthesis was reduced by nutrient shortages. A simple model for this nutrient effect can be constructed. Whenever nutrients become limiting (in Riley's example when phosphate ≤ 0.55), reduce the above equation by a factor N, defined as

$$N = \frac{\text{observed nutrient concentration}}{\text{limiting nutrient concentration}}$$

For the Georges Bank data, the phosphate limitation was

$$N = \frac{\text{observed mg-atoms phosphorus per cubit meter}}{0.55}$$

Our equation for phytoplankton production rate is now

$$P = \frac{pI_0}{kz_1}(1 - e^{-kz_1})(N)$$

A second factor was introduced into this model to cover vertical mixing losses. During the winter months a great deal of vertical turbulence moves the phytoplankton down from the surface of the sea to deep areas with no light. A simple term to cover this factor is

$$V = \frac{\text{depth of photosynthesis}}{\text{depth of mixed layer}}$$

and this is applied only in winter, when the mixed layer is deeper than the depth of photosynthesis (z_1).

Thus we obtain a simple model for phytoplankton production rate:

$$P = \frac{pI_0}{kz_1}(1 - e^{-kz_1})\,(N)\,(V)$$

which takes into account the amount of light, clearness of the water, amount of nutrients, and vertical mixing. Figure 278 illustrates the prediction for this model for the Georges Bank phytoplankton.

Respiration will reduce the photosynthetic production shown in Figure 278. Riley assumed that the respiration rate of the phytoplankton was dependent only on temperature and that this relationship was geometric also:

$$R_T = R_0 e^{rT}$$

where

R_T = respiration rate at temperature T
  (mg carbon consumed/day/mg of phytoplankton carbon)
R_0 = respiration rate at 0°C
r = rate of increase of respiration rate with temperature (a constant)

Riley estimated $R_0 = 0.0175$ from some field measurements, and $r = 0.069$.

Finally, grazing by zooplankton will remove some of the primary production. Since zooplankton are mostly filter-feeding organisms, Riley assumed a simple model of grazing:

$$G = gZ$$

where

G = rate of grazing
  (g of phytoplankton carbon consumed/g of zooplankton carbon)
g = a constant of conversion
Z = quantity of zooplankton (g carbon/sq. m)

FIGURE 278

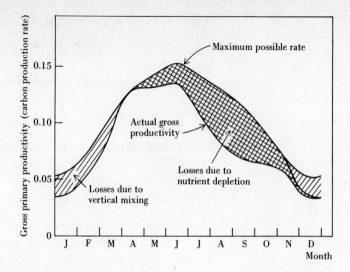

Rate of primary production for phytoplankton of Georges Bank, Atlantic Ocean. The maximum possible rate is determined by solar radiation and water transparency. (After Riley 1946.)

This model assumes that the zooplankton filter a constant volume of water in a unit time and is obviously oversimplified.

We can now return to our original equation for the phytoplankton community:

$$\frac{dx}{dt} = x(P - R - G)$$

which we can expand to

$$\frac{dx}{dt} = x\left[\frac{pI_0}{kz_1}(1 - e^{-kz_1})\,(N)\,(V) - R_0 e^{rT} - gZ\right]$$

where

x = phytoplankton biomass (carbon) per square meter of ocean surface
t = time
p = constant of light conversion in photosynthesis
I_0 = solar radiation at sea surface
z_1 = maximum depth of photosynthesis
k = extinction coefficient for light
N = nutrient limitation factor
V = vertical mixing factor
R_0 = respiration rate at 0°C
r = constant of respiration increase with temperature
T = temperature (°C)
g = constant for grazing rate
Z = biomass of zooplankton (carbon) per square meter of ocean surface

Figure 279 illustrates the result of this model for the Georges Bank phytoplankton, and Figure 280 compares the predictions of this model with the observed phytoplankton population over an annual cycle. The measurement of a few simple environmental parameters has allowed a good estimate to be constructed of the phytoplankton community changes.

Zooplankton feed on phytoplankton and in turn are fed on by carnivores

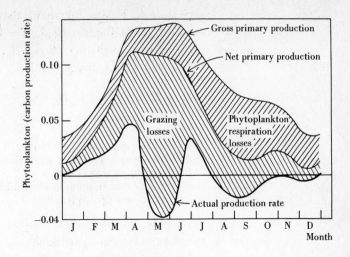

FIGURE 279

Estimated rates of production and consumption of carbon for the phytoplankton of Georges Bank. The curve at the top is the photosynthetic rate. By subtracting the respiratory rate the second curve is obtained, which is the phytoplankton production rate. From this is subtracted the zooplankton grazing rate, yielding the curve at the bottom, which is the estimated rate of change of the phytoplankton. (After Riley 1946.)

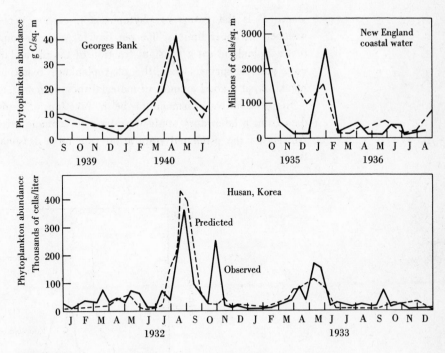

FIGURE 280

Comparison of observed seasonal cycles of marine phytoplankton (solid lines) with theoretical cycles (dashed lines) computed according to Riley's model, as described in the text. (After Riley 1963.)

such as fish. Figure 281 shows the seasonal cycles of phytoplankton and
zooplankton on Georges Bank. The timing of the spring pulses suggests a
predator–prey oscillation. Riley (1947) described the population changes of
zooplankton with a simple equation:

$$\frac{dH}{dt} = H(A - R - C - D)$$

where

H = herbivore population biomass
A = rate of assimilation of phytoplankton by the zooplankton
R = respiration rate
C = rate of consumption of zooplankton by their predators
D = death rate of zooplankton

The theory, though simple, is beyond the available data, and so Riley was
forced to make some approximations.

The assimilation rate is defined as the grams of carbon taken into the
zooplankton tissues per day per gram of carbon in the zooplankton population. Riley found that the assimilation rate was approximately defined by

$$A = 0.0075P$$

where P is the grams of phytoplankton carbon per square meter. Riley
assumed an upper limit of 8% per day for assimilation. The model assumes
that zooplankton eat a constant fraction of the phytoplankton population per
day, and in spring, when the phytoplankton reach high levels, the zooplankton eat a good amount of material they do not assimilate (Figure 282).

Respiration was assumed to be a function of temperature alone, and
data from a laboratory study were used to estimate this relationship. Figure
282 shows the estimated respiration rate on a seasonal basis for Georges
Bank.

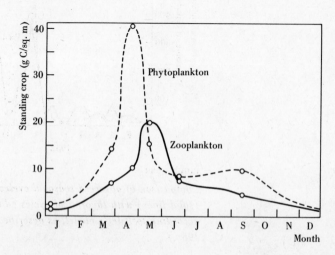

FIGURE 281

*Seasonal cycles of phytoplankton
and zooplankton on Georges Bank.
(After Riley 1947.)*

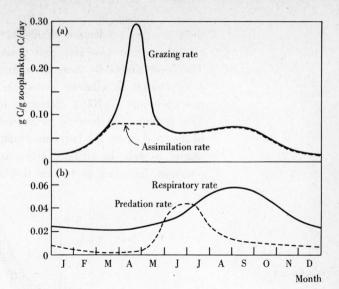

FIGURE 282

Process of accumulation and loss of organic matter by Georges Bank zooplankton: (a) estimated rates of consumption and assimilation of phytoplankton food, (b) estimated rates of respiration and consumption of zooplankton by its predators. (After Riley 1947.)

Predation was assumed to be a constant effort on the part of the predators, and this was described by a simple equation:

$$C = cS$$

where

C = rate of consumption of zooplankton
c = a constant (0.0016)
S = number of predators

The most important predators of zooplankton on Georges Bank are sagittae (*Sagitta elegans*), which reach peak numbers in June and July (Figure 282). Death rate due to other causes was assumed to be constant (0.006) and contributed very little to the total changes in zooplankton numbers.

These factors were all incorporated into an estimate of the seasonal changes in zooplankton of Georges Bank. Figure 283 shows that changes in the zooplankton community of this region can be ascribed to gains caused by high phytoplankton food supply in spring and then losses caused by high predation in summer.

All the models constructed so far have dealt almost exclusively with the plankton, and there are serious difficulties in extending this type of analysis to marine fish at higher trophic levels (Riley 1963).

Fish production in the sea

We can use the information we have on ecological efficiencies and trophic structure to obtain an approximate estimate of the potential fish production of the oceans (Ryther 1969).

The ocean may be subdivided into three broad zones which differ in their primary production (Table 32). Production of phytoplankton is highest in areas of upwelling, but these comprise a small part of the oceans. The food chains in these three zones are quite different. As one moves from coastal to offshore areas, the size of the producers changes from microplankton (>100 μ diameter) to nannoplankton (5 to 25 μ diameter). This is important because in general the larger the plant cells at the start of the food chain, the fewer the trophic levels required to convert the organic matter to fish. In offshore areas nannoplankton are fed on by microzooplankton, including protozoans and small larvae of crustaceans. The micro-

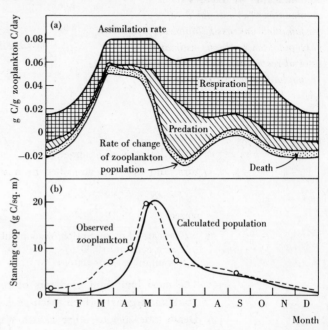

FIGURE 283

Seasonal cycle of zooplankton on Georges Bank. (a) Summation of growth processes. Upper curve is postulated seasonal cycle of the coefficient of assimilation. From it the coefficients of respiration, predation, and natural death are successively subtracted. The remainder, the lowest curve, is the estimated rate of change of the zooplankton population. (b) The observed seasonal cycle in relation to the predicted seasonal cycle from the rate curve in (a). (After Riley 1947.)

TABLE 32

Estimates of primary production and fish production in three zones of the ocean

Zone	Percentage of ocean	Mean primary productivity (g C/m²/yr)	Total primary production (billions of tons C/yr)	No. trophic levels	Efficiency of energy transfer	Fish production (tons wet weight)
Open ocean	90	50	16.3	5	10	0.16×10^7
Coastal zone[a]	9.9	100	3.6	3	15	12.0×10^7
Upwelling areas	0.1	300	0.1	1 or 2	20	12.0×10^7
Total			20.0			24.16×10^7

[a] Includes some offshore areas of high productivity.

SOURCE: After Ryther (1969).

zooplankton are in turn preyed upon by carnivorous zooplankton, many of which have always been thought of as herbivores. Second-order carnivores, such as chaetognaths, feed on the zooplankton, so three trophic levels above the primary producers the animals are still only 1 to 2 cm long. At least one or two additional trophic levels must intervene before we reach the level of fish such as the tunas.

In areas of upwelling, food chains are the shortest. This is primarily because of the large size of the phytoplankton, many of which form colonies several millimeters in diameter. These large colonies of green plants can be eaten directly by large fish. Many of the fish that are abundant in areas of upwelling, like the sardines and anchovies, are herbivores.

Lindeman's efficiency of energy transfer from one trophic level to the next probably lies in the 10 to 20% range for an average value. Ryther (1969) suggests that lower ecological efficiencies will obtain in areas of lower production.

Primary production, number of trophic levels, and Lindeman's efficiency are combined in Table 32 to provide an estimate of total fish production in the sea. Note that the open ocean is a "desert" for fish production, producing about 0.7% of the total for the sea, even though it occupies 90% of the ocean area. Upwelling areas provide about half of the world's fish production.

If the ocean produces 240 million tons of fish per year, how much can man harvest? Clearly not all of this, because there are other predators which live on the fish, and some of the production must be used to sustain reproduction and growth. Ryther estimates that we could harvest about 100 million tons/yr as a maximum sustained yield. The total world fish landing in 1969 was 63 million tons and has been increasing at 8% per year. Clearly the ocean fish resources are not infinite and may reach the point of full exploitation within 10 years.

SUMMARY

The capital of organic matter produced by green plants is used by a food web of herbivores and carnivores. A great deal of the matter and energy that animals eat is lost in feces and in maintenance metabolism. In warm-blooded vertebrates often 98% of the energy taken in is used for maintenance. Invertebrates and fish seem less wasteful.

Succeeding trophic levels take in about 20% of the net production of the previous level and in general about 90% of the energy is lost in the transfer from one trophic level to the next. This loss means that in terms of energy flow and nutrient cycles, animals that feed on living plants are a negligible component of the globe. Many of the animal species in the community that we as humans think are "important" are a small component of the energy flow. Few studies of secondary production have concentrated on the flow of nutrients.

Secondary production may be limited by a variety of interacting factors. Four case studies are presented to illustrate how this problem can be studied in natural systems and in theoretical models. Until we understand the factors that limit primary and secondary production we cannot predict the impact on the community of a change in the environment. At present there is not a single community for which this understanding has been worked out.

SELECTED REFERENCES

EFFORD, I. E. 1969. Energy transfer in Marion Lake, British Columbia; with particular reference to fish feeding. *Verh. Int. Verein. Limnol.* 17:104–108.

ENGELMANN, M. D. 1966. Energetics, terrestrial field studies, and animal productivity. *Advances Ecol. Res.* 3:73–115.

KOZLOVSKY, D. G. 1968. A critical evaluation of the trophic level concept. I. Ecological efficiencies. *Ecology* 49:48–60.

MACFADYEN, A. 1967. Methods of investigation of productivity of invertebrates in terrestrial ecosystems. pp. 383–412 in *Secondary Productivity of Terrestrial Ecosystems*, ed. by K. Petrusewicz. Warsaw.

MANN, K. H. 1969. The dynamics of aquatic ecosystems. *Advances Ecol. Res.* 6:1–81.

ODUM, E. P. 1968. Energy flow in ecosystems: a historical review. *Amer. Zool.* 8:11–18.

RYTHER, J. H. 1969. Photosynthesis and fish production in the sea. *Science* 166: 72–76.

STEELE, J. H. (ed.). 1970. *Marine Food Chains*. University of California Press, Berkeley.

QUESTIONS AND PROBLEMS

1 Ryther's estimate of fish production in the ocean (Table 32) has been criticized by Alverson, Longhurst, and Gulland (1970). Read this criticism and analyze this controversy. Vary some of the estimates in Table 32, such as the efficiency of energy transfer, and see what effect these changes would have on estimated fish production.

2 Odum (1968; p. 14) states: "Many of the controversies about food limitation, weather limitation, competition, and biological control could be resolved if we had accurate data on energy utilization by the populations in question." Review Chapters 15 and 17 and discuss this claim.

3 In discussing the usefulness of community metabolism studies, Engelmann (1966, p. 77) states: "If the community is real, then energy flow within community boundaries will be much greater than across community boundaries. Therefore, the tool for more certainly delimiting and defining communities may be within the ecologist's grasp." Discuss this claim.

4 In discussing the reality of trophic levels, Murdoch (1966a, p. 219) states:

Unlike populations, trophic levels are ill-defined and have no distinguishable lateral limits; in addition tens of thousands of insect species, for example, live in more than one trophic level either simultaneously or at different stages of their life histories. Thus trophic levels exist only as abstractions, and unlike populations they have no empirically measurable properties or parameters.

Discuss.

5 Compile a list of the efficiency of some of our common physical machines, such as automobiles, electric lights, electric heaters, and bicycles.

6 How would it be possible to have an inverted Eltonian pyramid of numbers in which, for example, the standing crop of herbivores is larger than the standing crop of plants? In what types of communities could this occur? Survey the ecological literature on those communities and find out if inverted pyramids do, in fact, occur.

7 On page 482 we discussed a case in which an organism was very important in the functioning of the community but was involved in only a very small fraction of the energy flow. Discuss the converse possibility: Are there organisms that contribute a large fraction of the energy flow in a community but are "unimportant" in the functioning of the community? Begin with an operational definition of "unimportant."

8 How does the question asked in this chapter, What limits secondary production in a community? differ from the question asked in Chapter 14, What factors control population changes?, if this question is repeated for all the dominant animal species in the community?

23   *Species diversity*

Ecological communities do not all contain the same number of species, and one of the currently active areas of research in community ecology is the study of species richness or diversity. A. R. Wallace (1878) recognized that animal life was on the whole more abundant and varied in the tropics than in other parts of the globe, and the same applies to the plants. Other patterns of variation have long been known on islands; small or remote islands have fewer species than large islands or those nearer continents (MacArthur and Wilson 1967). The regularity of these patterns for many taxonomic groups suggests that they have been produced in conformity with a set of basic principles rather than being the accidents of history. How can we explain these trends in species diversity?

MEASUREMENT OF SPECIES DIVERSITY

The simplest measure of species diversity is to count the *number of species*. In such a count one should include only resident species, not accidental or temporary immigrants. It may not always be easy to decide which species are accidentals: Is a bottomland tree species growing on a ridge top an accidental species or a resident one?

There are two principal drawbacks to using species counts as a measure of diversity. First, they fail to take account of species abundance patterns. A community with two species might be divided in two extreme ways:

	Community 1	Community 2
Species A	99	50
Species B	1	50

The second community would seem intuitively to be more diverse than the first. Second, species counts depend on sample size. Adequate sampling can usually get around this difficulty, particularly with vertebrate species, but this difficulty may be important with insects and other arthropods, in which species counts cannot be complete.

Two different strategies have been adopted to deal with these problems. First, a variety of statistical distributions can be fitted to data on the relative abundances of species. One very characteristic feature of communities is that they contain comparatively few species that are common and comparatively large numbers of species that are rare. Since it is relatively easy to determine for any given area the *number of species* on the area and the *number of individuals* in each of these species, a great deal of information of this type has accumulated (Williams 1964). The first attempt to analyze data of this type was made by Fisher, Corbet, and Williams (1943).

In many faunal samples the number of species represented by a single specimen is very large, species represented by two specimens are less numerous, and so on until only a few species are represented by many specimens. Fisher, Corbet, and Williams (1943) plotted data of this type and found that it fitted a "hollow curve" (Figure 284). Fisher concluded that the data available were best fitted by the logarithmic series, which is an integer series with a finite sum whose terms can be written

$$\alpha x, \frac{\alpha x^2}{2}, \frac{\alpha x^3}{3}, \frac{\alpha x^4}{4}, \dots$$

where

αx = number of species represented in the catch by *one* individual

$\frac{\alpha x^2}{2}$ = number of species represented by *two* individuals, etc.

The sum of the terms in the series is equal to the total number of species in the catch. The logarithmic series for a set of data is fixed by two variables, the *number of species* in the sample and the *number of individuals* in the sample. The relationship between these is

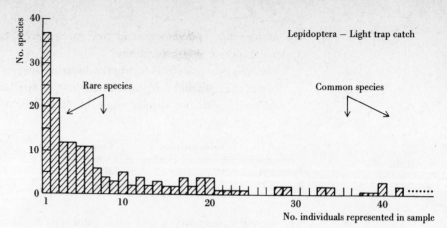

FIGURE 284

*Relative abundance of Lepidoptera (butterflies and moths) captured
in a light trap at Rothamsted, England, in 1935. Not all the abundant
species are shown. There were 37 species represented in the catch
by only a single specimen (rare species); one very common species
was represented by 1799 individuals in the catch. A total of 6814
individuals were caught, representing 197 species. Six common species
comprised 50% of the total catch. (After Williams 1964.)*

$$S = \alpha \log_e\left(1 + \frac{N}{\alpha}\right)$$

where

S = number of species in sample
N = number of individuals in sample
α = index of diversity

The constant α is an expression of species diversity in the community. It is
low when the number of species is low and high when the number of species
is high. Fisher reported that the index of diversity was independent of
sample size. This is an important attribute of any measure we may wish to
take of community organization; it must allow comparisons between different investigators in different areas.

The logarithmic series implies that the greatest number of species have
minimal abundance, that the number of species represented by a single
specimen is always maximal. This is not the case in all communities. Figure
285 shows the relative abundance of breeding birds in Quaker Run Valley,
New York. The greatest number of bird species are represented by 10
breeding pairs and the relative abundance pattern does not fit the hollow-
curve pattern of Figure 284. Preston (1948) suggested expressing the
X axis (number of individuals represented in sample) on a geometric
(logarithmic) scale rather than an arithmetic scale. One of several geo-

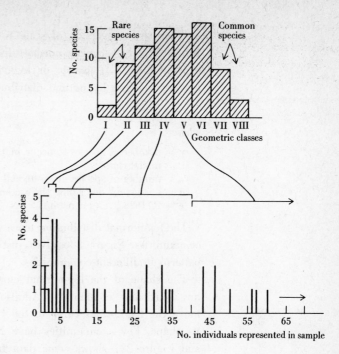

FIGURE 285

Relative abundance of nesting bird species in Quaker Run Valley, New York. The lower figure shows the distribution on an arithmetic scale, and the upper figure shows the same data on a geometric scale with ×3 size groupings (1, 2–4, 5–13, 14–40, 41–121, etc.). (After Williams 1964.)

metric scales can be used, since they differ only by a constant multiplier; a few scales are indicated in Table 33.

TABLE 33

Groupings of arithmetic scale units into geometric scale units for three types of geometric scales[a]

Geometric scale no.	Arithmetic numbers grouped according to:		
	× 2 scale[b]	× 3 scale[c]	× 10 scale[d]
1	1	1	1–9
2	2–3	2–4	10–99
3	4–7	5–13	100–999
4	8–15	14–40	1,000–9,999
5	16–31	41–121	10,000–99,999
6	32–63	122–364	100,000–999,999
7	64–127	365–1,093	—
8	128–255	1,094–3,280	—
9	256–511	3,281–9,841	—

[a] This type of grouping is used in Figures 285, 286, 287, and 288.

[b] Octave scale of Preston (1948), equivalent to log₂ scale.

[c] Equivalent to log₃ scale.

[d] Equivalent to log₁₀ scale.

When this conversion of scale is done, relative abundance data take the form of a bell-shaped, normal distribution, and because the X axis is expressed on a geometric or logarithmic scale, this distribution is called *log normal*. The log-normal distribution is described by the formula

$$y = y_0 e^{-(aR)^2}$$

where

    y = number of species to occur in the Rth octave* to the right or left of the modal class
   y_0 = number of species in the modal octave (the largest class)
    a = a constant describing the amount of spread of the distribution
    e = 2.71828 . . . (a constant)

The log-normal distribution fits a variety of data from surprisingly diverse communities. Figure 286 gives just a few examples of relative abundance patterns in different communities.

The shape of the log-normal curve is supposed to be characteristic for any particular community. Additional sampling of a community should move the log-normal curve to the right along the abscissa but not change its shape. Few communities have been sampled enough to test this idea, and Figure 287 shows some data from moths caught in light traps which suggests that additional sampling moves the curve out toward the right. Since we cannot collect one-half or one-quarter of an animal, there will always be some rare species that are not represented in the catch. These rare species appear only when very large samples are taken.

Preston (1962) showed that data from log-normal curves for biological communities commonly took on a particular configuration which he called

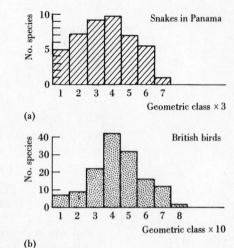

FIGURE 286

Log-normal distribution of relative abundances in some diverse communities: (a) snakes in Panama, (b) British birds. (Data from Williams 1964.)

* An *octave* is a section of the $\log_2$ scale defined in Table 33.

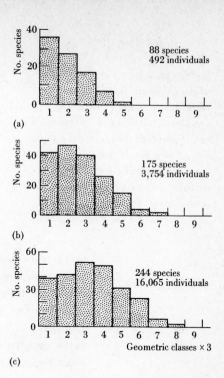

FIGURE 287

Log-normal distributions of the relative abundances of Lepidoptera insects captured in light traps at Rothamsted Experimental Station, England, in periods ranging from (a) ⅛ year to (b) 1 year to (c) 4 years. Note that the log-normal distribution slides to the right as the sample size is increased. (After Williams 1964.)

the *canonical distribution*. The log-normal equation has three basic parameters: y_0, the number of species in the modal (peak) class ("height" of the curve); a, the constant measuring the spread of the distribution; and the position of the curve along the X axis, which depends on the number of individuals in relation to the number of species in the sample. Preston showed that for many cases these three parameters were interrelated, so if we know the number of species in the whole community we can specify the entire equation for the log-normal curve. This implies that species diversity can be measured by counts of the number of species and that relative abundance is not a significant component of species diversity.

Note that when the species abundance distribution is log normal, it is possible to estimate the total number of species in the community, including rare species not yet collected. This is done by extrapolating the bell-shaped curve below the class of minimal abundance and measuring the area. Figure 288 illustrates how this can be done. This can be a useful property for communities where all the species cannot readily be seen and tabulated.

Two difficulties occur in using the log-normal distribution to study species abundance patterns. First, there is no theoretical justification for the log-normal curve as a "law" of relative abundance. At present it appears to be only a convenient form of description. Second, the canonical log normal may also be suspect because it assumes stable equilibrium conditions. We do not know how much the communities of the glaciated regions of the tem-

FIGURE 288

Species abundances in a collection of moths caught in a light trap. Data from Preston (1948). The log-normal distribution is truncated at the point where species are represented by a single individual. More intensive sampling would cause the distribution to move to the right and would unveil the hidden sector of rare species. (After Preston 1948.)

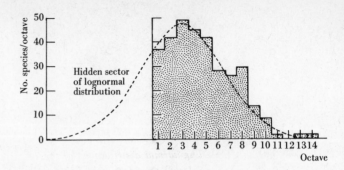

perate zone have been displaced from an equilibrium configuration, and little tropical work has so far been done (Preston 1962). In spite of these difficulties, there is something very compelling about the log-normal distribution. The fact that moths in England, freshwater algae in Spain, snakes in Panama, and birds in New York all have a similar type of species abundance curve suggests that there might be a law underlying all this, if only we could figure it out.

A second approach can be adopted to surmount the relative abundance problem. This approach is independent of any hypothetical distribution such as the log normal and involves the use of information theory for an analysis of community organization. The main objective of information theory is to try to measure the amount of *order* (or disorder) contained in a system (Margalef 1958). Four types of information might be collected regarding *order* in the community: (1) the number of species, (2) the number of individuals in each species, (3) the places occupied by individuals of each species, and (4) the places occupied by individuals as separate individuals. In most community work only data of types (1) and (2) are obtained.

Information theory, Margalef suggested, provides one way to escape some of the difficulties of the log-normal curve and the logarithmic series. We ask the question: How difficult would it be to predict correctly the species of the next individual collected? This is the same problem faced by communication engineers interested in predicting correctly the name of the next letter in a message. This uncertainty can be measured by the Shannon–Wiener function*:

$$H = -\sum_{i=1}^{s}(p_i)(\log_2 p_i)$$

H = information content of sample (bits/individual) = index of species diversity
S = number of species
p_i = proportion of total sample belonging to *i*th species

* This function was derived independently by Shannon and Wiener and is sometimes mislabeled the Shannon–Weaver function.

Information content is a measure of the amount of uncertainty, so the larger the value of H, the more uncertainty. A message such as *bbbbbbb* has no uncertainty in it, and $H = 0$. For our example of two species of 99 and 1 individuals,

$$\begin{aligned} H &= -(p_1)(\log_2 p_1) + (p_2)(\log_2 p_2) \\ &= -[0.99(\log_2 0.99) + 0.01(\log_2 0.01)] = 0.081 \text{ bit/individual} \end{aligned}$$

For a sample of two species with 50 individuals in each,

$$\begin{aligned} H &= -[0.50(\log_2 0.50) + 0.50(\log_2 0.50)] \\ &= 1.00 \text{ bit/individual} \end{aligned}$$

This agrees with our intuitive feeling that the second sample is more diverse than the first sample.

Strictly speaking, the Shannon–Wiener measure of information content should be used only on random samples drawn from a large community in which the total number of species is known. Pielou (1966) discusses information measures appropriate to other circumstances.

Two components of diversity are combined in the Shannon–Wiener function: (1) number of species and (2) equitability or evenness of allotment of individuals among the species (Lloyd and Ghelardi 1964). A greater number of species increases species diversity, and a more even or equitable distribution among species will also increase species diversity measured by the Shannon–Wiener function. Equitability can be measured in several ways. The simplest approach is to ask: What would be the species diversity of this sample if all S species were equal in abundance? In this case,

$$H_{\max} = -S\left(\frac{1}{S} \log_2 \frac{1}{S}\right) = \log_2 S$$

where $H_{\max}$ = species diversity under conditions of maximal equitability
S = number of species in the community

Thus, for example, in a community with two species only,

$$H_{\max} = \log_2 2 = 1.00 \text{ bit/individual}$$

as we observed above. Equitability can now be defined as the ratio

$$E = \frac{H}{H_{\max}}$$

where

E = equitability (range 0–1)
H = observed species diversity
$H_{\max}$ = maximum species diversity = $\log_2 S$

Table 34 presents a sample calculation illustrating the use of these formulas.

Other measures of diversity can be derived from probability theory. Simpson (1949) suggested this question: What is the probability that two

TABLE 34

Sample calculations of species diversity and equitability through the use of the Shannon–Wiener function[a]

Tree species	Proportional abundance (p_i)	$-(p_i)(\log_2 p_i)$[b]
Hemlock	0.521	0.490
Beech	0.324	0.527
Yellow birch	0.046	0.204
Sugar maple	0.036	0.173
Black birch	0.026	0.137
Red maple	0.025	0.133
Black cherry	0.009	0.061
White ash	0.006	0.044
Basswood	0.004	0.032
Yellow poplar	0.002	0.018
Magnolia	0.001	0.010
Total	1.000	$H = 1.829$

$$H_{\max} = \log_2 S = \log_2 11 = 3.459$$

$$\text{Equitability} = E = \frac{H}{H_{\max}} = \frac{1.829}{3.459} = 0.53$$

[a] A virgin forest in northwestern Pennsylvania, composition of large trees (>70 ft tall).

[b] $\log_2 x = \dfrac{\log_e x}{\log_e 2} = \dfrac{\log_{10} x}{\log_{10} 2}$

Note that there is no special theoretical reason to use $\log_2$ instead of $\log_e$ or $\log_{10}$. The $\log_2$ usage gives us information units in "bits" (binary digits) and is preferred by information theorists. See Pielou (1969, p. 229).

SOURCE: Hough (1936).

specimens picked at random in a community of infinite size are the same species? If one went into the boreal forest in northern Canada and picked two trees at random, there is a fairly high probability that they would be the same species. If one went into the tropical rain forest, by contrast, two trees picked at random would have a low probability of being the same species. We can use this approach to determine an index of diversity:

Simpson's index of diversity = probability of picking two organisms at random that are different species
= 1 − (probability of picking two organisms that are the same species)

If a particular species i is represented in the community by p_i (proportion of individuals), the probability of picking two of these at random is the joint probability $[(p_i)\ (p_i),\ \text{or}\ p_i{}^2]$. If we sum these probabilities for all the i species in the community, we get Simpson's diversity (D):

$$D = 1 - \sum_{i=1}^{s}(p_i)^2$$

where

$D = $ Simpson's index of diversity

$p_i = $ proportion of individuals of species i in the community

For example, for our two-species community with 99 and 1 individuals,

$$D = 1 - [(0.99)^2 + (0.01)^2] = 0.02$$

Simpson's index gives relatively little weight to the rare species and more weight to the common species. It ranges in value from 0 (low diversity) to a maximum of $(1 - 1/S)$, where S is the number of species.

In practice it seems to matter very little which of these different measures of species diversity one uses, and the combination of two measures—(1) of the number of species in the sample, and (2) of the relative abundance patterns $(\alpha,\ H,\ \text{or}\ D)$—summarizes most of the biological information on diversity.

SOME EXAMPLES OF DIVERSITY GRADIENTS

Tropical habitats support a larger number of species of plants and animals, and this diversity of life in the tropics contrasts starkly with the impoverished faunas of temperate and polar areas. A few examples will illustrate this global gradient. The tropical rain forest in Malaya may contain up to 227 species of trees on a plot of 4 acres and 375 tree species on a plot of 57 acres (Richards 1969). A deciduous forest in Michigan will contain 10 to 15 species on a plot of 4 acres.

Ants are much more diverse in the tropics (Fischer 1960):

	No. ant species
Brazil	*222*
Trinidad	*134*
Cuba	*101*
Utah	*63*
Iowa	*73*
Alaska	*7*
Arctic Alaska	*3*

There are 293 species of snakes in Mexico, 126 in the United States, and 22 in Canada. Figure 289 shows the number of breeding land-bird species in different parts of North America.

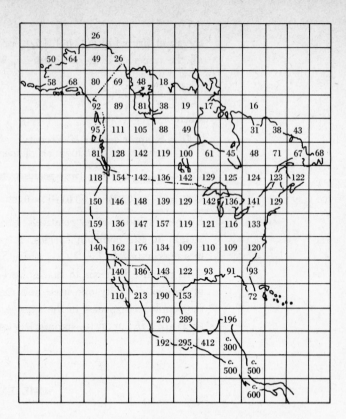

FIGURE 289

Numbers of breeding land-bird species in different parts of North America. (After MacArthur and Wilson 1967.)

Freshwater fishes are much more diverse in tropical rivers and lakes. Over 1000 species of fishes have been found in the Amazon River in South America, and exploration is still incomplete in this region. By contrast, Central America has 456 fish species, and the Great Lakes of North America have 172 species (Lowe-McConnell 1969). Lake Tanganyika alone has 214 fish species, and all of Europe has only 192 species.

Marine invertebrates also have high diversity in the tropics. Figure 290

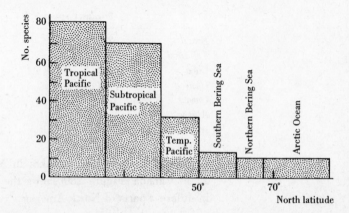

FIGURE 290

Tropical to polar gradient in species diversity for the calanid copepods of the upper 50 m of the Pacific Ocean. (After Fischer 1960.)

shows that calanid copepods (planktonic crustaceans) are most diverse in the tropical Pacific and least diverse in the Bering Sea and Arctic Ocean.

Species diversity patterns of North American mammals were analyzed in detail by Simpson (1964). Figure 291 shows that the number of land mam-

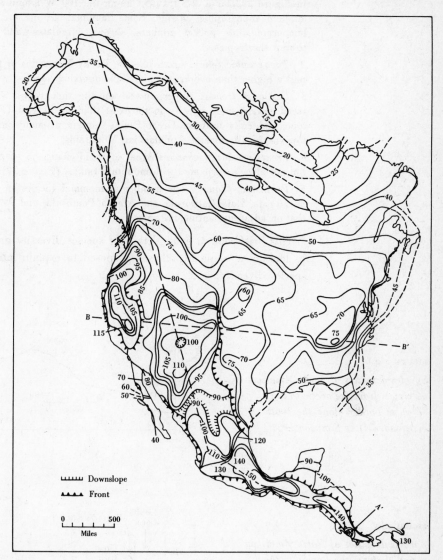

FIGURE 291

Species density contours for Recent mammals of continental North America. The contour lines are isograms for numbers of continental (nonmarine and noninsular) species in quadrats 150 miles square. The "fronts" are lines of exceptionally rapid change that are multiples of the contour interval for the given region. (After Simpson 1964.)

mal species increases from 15 in northern Canada to over 150 in Central America. Simpson recognizes five notable features of this pattern:

1 North-south gradient: The north-south gradient is not smooth, as illustrated in Figure 292 for a N-S transect along the 100°W longitude meridan, which has minimal topographic change. Some mammal groups are most diverse in the temperate zone—pocket gophers, shrews, ungulates—and became less diverse toward the tropics.

2 Topographic relief: Areas like the Rocky Mountains or the Appalachians support a higher than average number of mammal species.

3 East-west trends: Superimposed on the topographic variation is a general trend toward more species in the west than in the east (Figure 293). Thus the topographically uniform Great Plains contain as many mammal species as the topographically diverse Appalachian Mountains.

4 Fronts of abrupt change: Areas of rapid change in species diversity are often but not always associated with mountain ranges (Figure 291).

5 Peninsular "lows": The number of mammal species on peninsular areas such as Florida, Baja California, the Alaska Peninsula, and Nova Scotia is less than that on adjacent continental areas.

This brief look at some details of species diversity gradients can assist us in looking at some hypotheses proposed to explain latitudinal gradients in species diversity.

FIGURE 292

Species densities of North American mammals from the arctic to the Mexican border along the 100th meridian. (After Simpson 1964.)

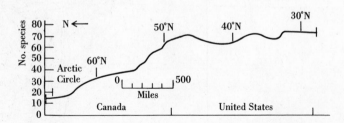

FIGURE 293

Species densities of North American mammals from the Pacific to the Atlantic along line B—B' of Figure 291. The section is a straight line on the projection used, approximately through the western and eastern species density highs in the United States. (After Simpson 1964.)

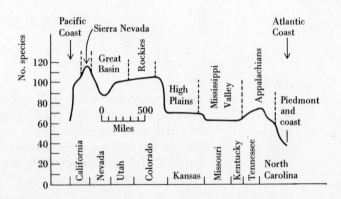

Six more or less distinct hypotheses have been proposed to explain polar–tropical diversity gradients. Let us consider each of these hypotheses (Pianka 1966b).

Time hypothesis   This idea, proposed chiefly by zoogeographers and paleontologists, is a historical hypothesis with two main components. First, biotas in the warm, humid tropics are likely to evolve and diversify more rapidly than those in the temperate and polar regions (Figure 294). This is caused by a constant favorable environment and a relative freedom from climatic disasters like glaciation. Second, biotic diversity is a product of evolution and is therefore dependent on the length of time through which the biota has developed in an uninterrupted fashion (Fischer 1960). Tropical biotas are examples of mature biotic evolution, whereas temperate and polar biotas are immature communities. In short, all communities diversify in time, and thus older communities have more species than younger ones.

The time theory may operate on ecological or evolutionary time scales. The ecological time scale is a shorter time scale, operating over a few gen-

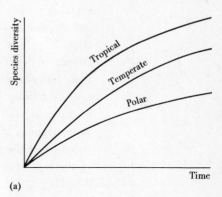

(a)

FIGURE 294

Time hypothesis: (a) Hypothetical increase in species diversity in tropical to polar habitats if there were no interruptions; (b) actual pattern of change in species diversity of a temperate or polar habitat subjected to glaciation and climatic variations. (After Fischer 1960.)

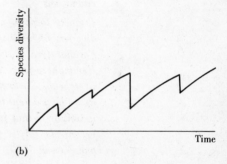

(b)

erations or a few tens of generations. Ecological time would involve situations where a given species could occupy an environment but has not had time to disperse there. The evolutionary time scale is a longer time scale, operating over hundreds and thousands of generations. Evolutionary time applies to cases where a position in the community exists but is not occupied because of insufficient time for speciation and evolution to have occurred.

Lake Baikal in the U.S.S.R. is a particularly striking illustration of the role of time in generating species diversity. Baikal is an ancient lake, one of the oldest in the world, yet is situated in the temperate zone. Baikal contains a very diverse fauna (Kozhov 1963). For example, there are 580 species of benthic invertebrates in the deep waters of Lake Baikal. A comparable lake in glaciated northern Canada, Great Slave Lake, contains only 4 species in this same zone (Sanders 1968).

Some paleontological data support the time hypothesis. The fossil record shows that planktonic foraminifera of the Northern Hemisphere have shown a gradient in diversity from the equator to the pole for at least 270 million years (Figure 295). Consequently, these diversity gradients must be equilibrium conditions and not historical results of recent development. The rate of formation of new species is faster in tropical communities and slower in temperate and polar communities. This rate can be measured by finding the geological time of first appearance of genera or species and thus measuring the "age structure" of fossil communities. If genera and species are evolving rapidly, new taxonomic groups should appear and disappear quickly and the fossil record should have few groups that go far back in geological time. If genera and species are evolving slowly, taxonomic groups should remain in fossil assemblages for long periods of geological time. In planktonic foraminifera from the Cretaceous, tropical genera are "young" (median age 15 million years) and polar genera are "old" (median age over 25 million years). Consequently, evolution seems to be occurring more quickly in the tropical habitats.

Note that the species diversity of a community will be a function not only of the rate of addition of species through evolution but also of the rate of

FIGURE 295

Tropical to polar gradient in species diversity of fossil planktonic Foraminifera of the Northern Hemisphere from a period in the Cretaceous, 70 to 80 million years ago. The gradient in species diversity is similar to that found in living organisms. (After Stehli, Douglas, and Newell 1969.)

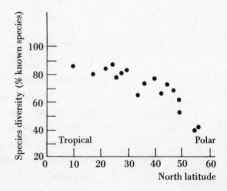

loss of species through extinction or emigration. Thus compared with polar communities, the tropics could have a more rapid rate of evolution and also a lower rate of extinction, and these two rates act together to determine species diversity.

If we accept the time hypothesis as an explanation of latitudinal gradients in diversity, we are then pushed back to a second problem: Why is the rate of evolution more rapid in the tropics, or the rate of extinction lower? The five other theories to be discussed try to answer these questions.

There is also some evidence in favor of the time theory on a shorter time scale. Trees that are abundant and established for a long time in a region tend to have more insect species associated with them (Southwood 1961). Figure 296 shows the relation between "history" and insect species diversity for common British trees. Introduced trees have especially low numbers of associated insects, even if other species of the same genus are native; for example, in the oaks

Species	Status in Britain	Associated insect species
Quercus robur	Native	284
Quercus ilex	Introduced in 1580	2

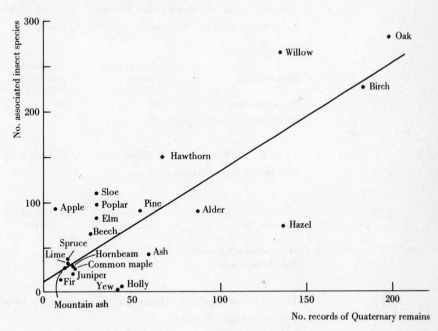

FIGURE 296

Relationship between the history of a tree species and the number of associated insect species in Britain. The Quaternary includes the Pleistocene and Recent periods, approximately the last million years. (After Southwood 1961.)

Historical factors thus have some influence on the species diversity of the insect community of trees.

In general, the time theory is difficult to assess because it involves geological time scales and is not amenable to direct experimentation.

Theory of spatial heterogeneity

There could be a general increase in environmental complexity as one proceeds toward the tropics. The more heterogeneous and complex the physical environment becomes, the more complex the plant and animal communities supported and the higher the species diversity. This theory can be considered on a macro and on a micro scale.

Topographic relief, or macrospatial heterogeneity, certainly has a strong effect on species diversity. Simpson (1964) has shown that the highest diversities of mammals in the United States occur in the mountain areas (Figure 291). The explanation for this seems quite simple; areas of high topographic relief contain many different habitats and hence more species. Also, mountainous areas produce more geographic isolation of populations and so may promote speciation.

MacArthur (1965) suggests that one should recognize two components in trying to analyze latitudinal gradients in species diversity: *within-habitat* diversity, and *between-habitat* diversity. We can illustrate this distinction by two simple schemes to explain tropical diversity:

Scheme A	Temperate country	Tropical country
No. species per habitat	*10*	*10*
No. different habitats	*10*	*50*

Thus all the increase in tropical diversity is caused by between-habitat diversity in this hypothetical scheme.

Scheme B	Temperate country	Tropical country
No. species per habitat	*10*	*50*
No. different habitats	*10*	*10*

In this oversimplified scheme all the increase in tropical diversity is due to within-habitat diversity.

Can the factor of topographic relief provide some explanation for the latitudinal variation in species diversity? There is some evidence that this is part of the reason that the tropics are so rich in species. MacArthur (1969a) showed that for land birds 5 acres of Panama forest supported 2.5 times as many bird species as 5 acres of Vermont forest. But larger areas in the tropics support proportionately even more species. Ecuador has 7 times the number of birds species as New England, even though the areas are both approximately 100,000 square miles. Therefore, for land birds there are both more species per habitat in the tropics and also more habitats per square mile.

Microspatial heterogeneity refers to a local scale of organism-sized objects such as rocks and vegetation. The most difficult problem here is to determine which of the many things we as humans see in a habitat are really important to the particular organisms under study. Birds have been studied more in this regard than other groups. MacArthur and MacArthur (1961) measured bird-species diversity on a series of study areas and attempted to relate this to two aspects of the vegetation: *plant-species* diversity and *foliage-height* diversity. Foliage-height diversity is a measure of stratification and evenness in the vertical distribution of vegetation; highly stratified communities will have high foliage-height diversities with dense growth of branches and leaves at all levels from the ground to the top of the canopy. It does not matter whether the strata are contributed by a variety of species or by a variety of age classes of one species. MacArthur found that bird-species diversity was not correlated so much with plant-species diversity as it was with foliage-height diversity (Figure 297). This suggests that one can predict the bird-species diversity on an area without any knowledge of the

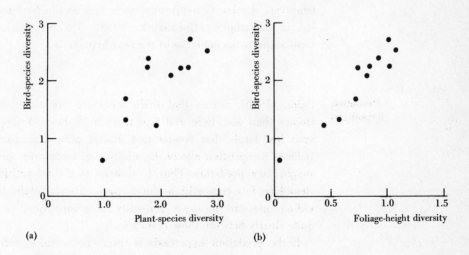

(a)   (b)

FIGURE 297

Bird-species diversity in deciduous forest plots of eastern United States in relation to the plant-species diversity and the stratification of the plant community: (a) plant species, (b) vegetative structure. (After MacArthur and MacArthur 1961.)

plant species that make up the community. Vegetation structure, or stratification, seems to be more important to birds than plant-species composition.

Tropical habitats would contain more bird species if there were more foliage-height diversity in tropical areas and if birds recognized the same vegetation layers as in temperate habitats. But birds in Panama seem to recognize more layers of vegetation, and this allows finer habitat subdivision and hence more species to exist in tropical habitats. Stratification is pronounced in tropical rain forests (Richards 1969), and this increased vegetation structure increases bird diversity.

What are the ecological mechanisms that permit a large number of species to make a living in tropical habitats? Is it simply a case of more food being available? Is competition between species more intense? If it is true that spatial heterogeneity can be used to predict species diversity, we must still determine the ecological machinery behind this prediction.

Competition hypothesis

This hypothesis begins with the suggestion that natural selection in the temperate and polar zones is controlled mainly by the physical factors of the environment, whereas biological competition becomes a more important part of evolution in the tropics. Because of this, animals and plants are more restricted in their habitat requirements and animals have a more restricted diet. Competition is "keener" in the tropics and niches are "smaller." Tropical species are more highly evolved and possess finer adaptations than do temperate species. Consequently, more species can be fitted into a given habitat in the tropics (Dobzhansky 1950). The competition hypothesis is in some respects the converse of the next hypothesis.

Predation hypothesis

Paine (1966) argues that there are more predators and parasites in the tropics than elsewhere and that these hold down their prey populations to such low levels that competition among prey organisms is reduced. This reduced competition allows the addition of more prey species, which in turn support new predators. Thus, in contrast to the competition hypothesis, there should be *less* competition among prey animals in the tropics. Hence, providing one can measure "intensity of competition," one can distinguish quite clearly between these two ideas.

If the predation hypothesis is true, one would expect an increased proportion of predators in more diverse communities, and this has been found in some cases. The Sargasso Sea contains a very rich zooplankton population of at least 268 species, whereas the adjacent waters of the continental shelf of eastern North America contain only 81 species (Grice and Hart 1962). More carnivorous forms occur in the Sargasso Sea fauna:

Group	Continental shelf (%)	Sargasso Sea (%)
Salps (herbivores)	9	—
Copepods (mostly herbivores)	57	50
Chaetognaths (carnivores)	15	19
Siphonophores (carnivores)	—	18
Amphipods (carnivorous)	1	2
Euphasiids (omnivores)	2	5

Thus about 65% of the zooplankton species were herbivores in the coastal waters, but only 50% were herbivorous in the more diverse Sargasso Sea.

Paine (1966) supported his ideas using some experimental manipulations of rocky intertidal invertebrates of the Washington coast. The food web of these areas on the Pacific Coast is remarkably constant:

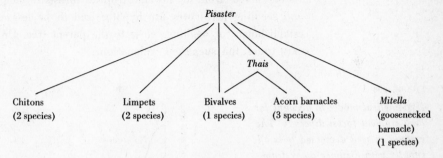

Paine removed the starfish *Pisaster* from a section of the shore and observed a *decrease* in diversity from a 15-species system to an 8-species system. A bivalve *Mytilus* has tended to dominate the area, crowding out the other species. "Succession" in this instance is toward a simpler community. The starfish by continual predation prevent the barnacles and bivalves from monopolizing space. Thus local species diversity on intertidal rocky zones appears to be directly related to predation intensity.

For the predation hypothesis to operate on a broad scale the predators involved must be very efficient at regulating the abundance of their prey species. In terrestrial food webs predators are usually very specialized and in some cases do not seem to regulate prey abundance (Chapters 13 and 15). Note that the predation hypothesis cannot be a sufficient explanation for tropical species diversity unless it can be applied to all trophic levels. If the species diversity of the herbivore trophic level is determined by the predators, we are left with explaining the diversity of the primary producers. Key species, such as the starfish *Pisaster*, should be more common in tropical communities, but at the moment there is no evidence about this. Little information is available on tropical communities.

The predation hypothesis can be extended to the primary producer level. Tropical lowland forests contain many species of trees and a corresponding low density of adult trees of each species. Most adult trees of a given species are also spread out in a regular pattern in the tropical forests, and Janzen (1970) suggests that these characteristics of tropical trees can be explained by the predation hypothesis, the species that eat seeds or seedlings being analogous to the predators discussed above. Figure 298 shows schematically the interaction of seed production and dispersal from the parent tree and the activity of seed and seedling eaters. Many insects that eat seeds and fruits in the tropics are host specific and will therefore tend to congregate around a source of seeds. The probability that a seed or small seedling will be overlooked by these specific herbivores is thus increased as they move farther and farther from the parent tree and are surrounded more and more by other tree species with their own specific herbivores. Each tree thus casts a "seed shadow," in which survival of its own kind is reduced. As one moves from the lowland tropical forests to temperate forests the seed and seedling herbivores are hypothesized to be less efficient at preventing establishment of seedlings close to the parent tree. Unfortunately, few data exist to test this suggested explanation.

FIGURE 298

Hypothetical model to account for high tropical forest diversity. The amount of seed dispersed falls off rapidly with distance away from the parent tree, and the activity of host-specific seed and seedling herbivores is most evident near the parent tree. The product of these two factors determines a recruitment curve with a peak at the distance from the parent tree where a new adult tree is likely to appear. (After Janzen 1970.)

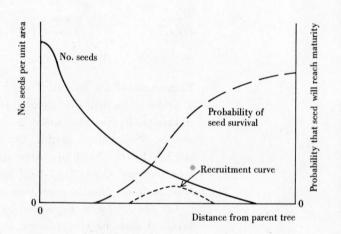

The role of predation in affecting species diversity is unclear, just as the role of predation in regulating population density (Chapters 13 and 15). An increase in predation may cause an increase in prey-species diversity, but this may be more a local effect than a global explanation for latitudinal gradients in species diversity.

Theory of environmental stability

This theory states that the more stable the environmental parameters, the more species will be present. According to this hypothesis, regions with stable climates allow the evolution of finer specializations and adaptations than do areas with erratic climates. This results in "smaller" niches and more species occupying a unit space of habitat. Species should have more flexibility in temperate and polar areas and be more specialized in the tropics.

Evidence that tropical species have more restricted habitat requirements than temperate species would support three hypotheses: competition, predation, and climatic stability. Work along these lines has not progressed very far to date.

A good deal of discussion but relatively little work so far has revolved about the idea that niche "size" might help explain these species-diversity gradients. Since there are, in fact, more tropical species and since by definition each species occupies a niche, it follows that (1) niches in the tropics are more numerous, or (2) more fully occupied, or (3) more frequently overlapped by other niches. Simpson (1964) suggests that (1) is clearly true for mammals, mainly because of greater plant diversity, and that (2) and (3) are hard to evaluate quantitatively. Niches can be defined only in retrospect, because the niche of any species has biotic dimensions determined by evolution (Connell and Orias 1964). It is impossible to look at a vacant habitat and to determine the number of "potential niches." To argue that the tropics have higher diversity because the organisms have narrower niches is to argue in a circle.

The theory of climatic stability can be combined with the time hypothesis, with which it has much in common. The *stability–time* hypothesis (Sanders 1968) emphasizes the role of all environmental parameters—temperature, moisture, salinity, oxygen, pH—in permitting diversity. Low diversity habitats may be either *severe* or *unpredictable*, or both. Severe environments such as hot springs or Great Salt Lake, Utah, can be very predictable (physical conditions constant from day to day) but have low species diversity. A desert environment with irregular rainfall would be an example of an unpredictable and severe environment. Figure 299 illustrates the stability–time hypothesis. Sanders (1968) applied the hypothesis to the marine fauna of muddy bottoms. The deep sea represents a stable environment of long time span, and the diversity of bivalve and polychaete species in bottom samples in the deep sea was almost equal to that in tropical shallow-water areas. This surprising diversity in deep-sea-bottom organisms is difficult to reconcile with other hypotheses. Figure 299 illustrates a transect across a marine area of upwelling in which the bottom water is low in oxygen and shows that fewer species are found in more stressful environments.

Productivity hypothesis Connell and Orias (1964) have presented this next idea, blended with the theory of climatic stability. The productivity hypothesis in its pure form states that greater production results in greater diversity, everything else being equal. The data available do not support this idea. For example,

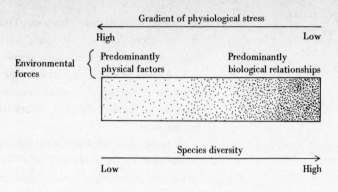

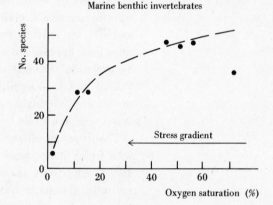

FIGURE 299

Stability–time hypothesis of Sanders (1968). The numbers of species (stippling) will decrease continuously along a stress gradient. The lower figure illustrates this idea for marine invertebrates of a bottom transect off Southwest Africa. The area of oxygen stress is in the center of an upwelling area. (After Sanders 1968.)

Whiteside and Harmsworth (1967) found that species diversity of Chydorids *decreases* with higher production rates in a series of Danish and Indiana lakes (Figure 300). Obviously, in pure form the productivity hypothesis is untenable.

A common modification of the productivity hypothesis is the idea of increased temporal partitioning in the tropics. The main argument is that the longer growing season of tropical areas allows the component species to partition the environment temporally as well as spatially, thereby permitting the coexistence of more species. This idea combines the stability hypothesis with the productivity hypothesis, suggesting that the stability of primary production is a major determinant of the species diversity in a community. One way this idea can be tested is by looking at primary production in different communities over an annual cycle. Another way of testing this idea is to look at the way organisms make a living in different communities.

More bird species occur in tropical forests than in temperate ones because they can find completely new ways of making a living in the productive

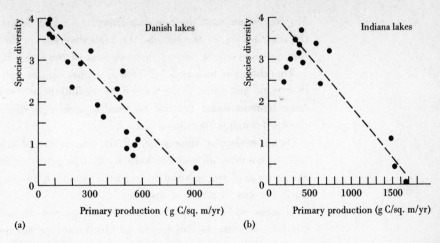

FIGURE 300

Species diversity of Chydorid Cladocera in relation to primary productivity in (a) 20 Danish lakes and (b) 14 northern Indiana lakes. The results are exactly the opposite predicted by the productivity hypothesis. Species diversity was measured by the Shannon-Wiener function. (After Whiteside and Harmsworth 1967.)

tropical forests (Orians 1969a). Temperate-zone forests have no obligate fruit-eating birds like parrots, or birds of prey that eat reptiles only, or birds that follow ant swarms, or birds that sit quietly in trees and watch for insect prey. These are "new niches" that appear only in the tropics, in part because of the stability of primary and secondary production.

There is considerable room for overlap among these six different hypotheses, and several may act together in any particular situation. Pianka (1966b) has suggested some ways of testing the six major hypotheses, but they are not easy to distinguish empirically. Much more work will have to be done on specific latitudinal gradients before we can evaluate the importance of each of these contributing factors.

TWO CASE STUDIES

Desert lizard communities
Deserts are relatively simple communities and yet support a surprising diversity of animal species. What are the ecological variables that control diversity in this environment? Lizards have been studied particularly thoroughly in the United States and in Australia in an attempt to answer this question (Pianka 1967, 1969).

Twelve species of flatland desert lizards occur in western North America in a region spanning the northern Great Basin desert (a cold desert), the

Mojave Desert, and the Sonoran Desert (a warm desert). Figure 301 shows the distribution of the lizards, the high diversity in the southern areas, and the low diversity in the northern deserts of the Great Basin.

The different numbers of lizard species in the northern and southern deserts do not seem to be caused by evolutionary history. Lizards seem to have had an equal amount of time to evolve in the cold and the warm deserts (roughly 10 million years).

On an ecological time scale, all the lizards except one have had adequate time to colonize all suitable habitats in this desert region. The one possible exception is *Uma*, a sand-dune lizard, which may not occur in the Great Basin because of a lack of dispersal.

Climatic stability may promote lizard species diversity. One measure of climatic stability is the length of the frost-free season, and lizard-species diversity is strongly associated with the length of the growing season (Figure 302). Another measure of climatic stability in a desert is the variability in annual rainfall. In the southwest rainfall is most variable in the Mojave, intermediate in the Sonoran, and least variable in the Great Basin. Thus

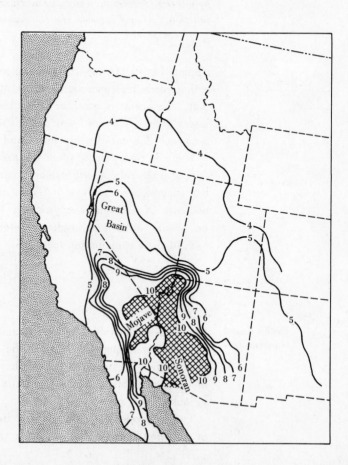

FIGURE 301

Contour map of the number of species of flatland desert lizards of southwestern United States. The region of maximum diversity is shaded. (After Pianka 1967.)

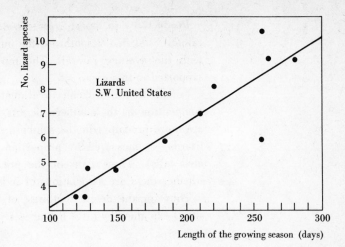

FIGURE 302

*Total number of lizard species
plotted against the average length
of the frost-free period or the
"length of the growing season" for
southwestern United States. (After
Pianka 1967.)*

the least variable area supports the *lowest* number of species, contrary to what the theory of climatic stability predicts.

Spatial heterogeneity seems to be one of the strongest determinants of species diversity in the desert southwest. Both the plant-species diversity and the amount of structural heterogeneity were measured, and the number of lizard species could be predicted by the amount of vegetation structure, not by the plant-species diversity (Figure 303). Lizards seem to respond more to the structure of the habitat than to exactly what plant species are present.

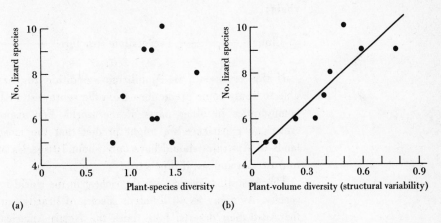

(a) (b)

FIGURE 303

*Number of flatland lizard species of southwestern United States in
relation to the diversity of the plant species and the structure of
the desert vegetation: (a) plant species, (b) vegetative structure.
Species diversity seems more related to vegetation structure than to
the species of plants present. Compare with Figure 297. (After
Pianka 1966a.)*

Productivity in desert areas can be determined very simply by measuring rainfall, and in the southwest the number of lizard species is not associated with the average rainfall. The pure productivity hypothesis thus is not supported in this case.

Competition is difficult to evaluate, but there is no indication of more competition in the southern deserts, where species diversity is high. There are more predators in the southern deserts and more signs of predation on lizards (as measured by proportion of specimens with broken or regenerated tails). These data fit the predation hypothesis, but it is not clear whether these are associations of independent events or causal effects.

Thus for the desert southwest of the United States, lizard-species diversity is explained by three hypotheses:

Hypothesis	Probable explanation
Time	
Evolutionary	— (?)
Ecological	*1 species*
Spatial heterogeneity	*8 species*
Competition	—
Predation	— (?)
Stability	*2 or 3 species*
Productivity	—

Most of the variation in lizard species diversity is determined by the causal chain:

$$\text{Climate} \longrightarrow \text{vegetation structure} \longrightarrow \text{lizard diversity}$$

If this represents an equilibrium condition for lizards, we ought to be able to apply some predictions from the southwestern United States to lizard communities in other parts of the world. For example, from our North American experience we might predict that the most complex desert flatlands of Australia should have only about 10 species of lizards. Let us move to Australia and see if this is true.

The Australian deserts are the richest in the world in the number of lizard species. As many as 40 different species of lizards can be found together in the Australian deserts, four times the North American maximum (Pianka 1969). Our prediction based on North American lizards is thus grossly in error. What causes the high species diversity in Australian lizards?

Four factors produce a high lizard diversity in Australia:

1 In Australian deserts lizards usurp the ecological roles played by other groups in North America. There are insectlike, wormlike, snakelike, and mammal-like lizards.

2 The milder and more stable Australian climate has apparently allowed the lizards to partition the environment in *time* as well as space. Most North American deserts support no nocturnal species of lizards, whereas 32 to 44% of the Australian lizards are nocturnal.

3 Some species groups of Australian lizards are more narrowly specialized than comparable North American lizards. The "narrow" niches of the Australian forms are evidenced by restricted food habits, special foraging techniques, and limited movement patterns.

4 There are more habitats in Australian deserts than in North American deserts, that is, more spatial heterogeneity. Some lizard species can specialize on a single habitat in Australia.

The explanation of high lizard diversity in Australia thus contains a large historical (evolutionary) element. A desert flat, structurally identical to the Great Basin desert, will contain 18 species in Australia, only 5 in North America. In a meaningful sense Australian lizards "see" more habitats in a given area than North American lizards would "see."

The role of historical developments in the evolution of Australia's lizards is significant because Australian deserts are among the youngest deserts on earth, probably dating from the last million years or less (Pianka 1969). If this is true, speciation and evolutionary adjustments must have occurred rather quickly.

If historical factors account for the general level of species diversity in a group of organisms, we will not be able to make quantitative predictions about species diversity that will apply to all continents. Species may be more tightly "packed" in some faunas than in others, but each fauna may still be saturated with species. This "packing" could be measured by the ease of inserting a new species into a community.

Eastern deciduous forests of North America

Plant-species diversity could be related to the same ecological mechanisms we have discussed with regard to animals. Figure 304 gives tree-species diversity for forest stands in eastern North America. The highest diversity values (up to $H = 3.40$ bits/individual) occur in the Cumberland and Allegheny mountains, which Braun (1950) called the mixed mesophytic forest region. This region has been postulated as the ancestral community from which all the other sections of the eastern deciduous forests arose. Tree diversity decreases as one moves north into colder areas and west into dryer areas.

Within smaller areas of the deciduous forest there is considerable variation in species diversity. Monk (1967) sampled 162 stands from north-central Florida and measured species diversity of adult trees, saplings, and seedlings in each stand. Most of the variation in species diversity could be related to the successional stage of the forest stand. The general pattern of

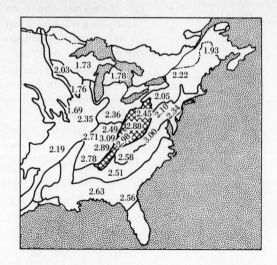

FIGURE 304

Tree-species diversity (measured by H) within the eastern deciduous forest of North America. All data except for northern Florida are based on 326 stands from Braun (1950). The mixed mesophytic forest region is shaded. (After Monk 1967.)

succession is toward a mixed hardwood forest dominated by oaks. Figure 305 shows that tree species diversity tends to increase through succession; consequently, one of the factors determining the species diversity of a plot is its successional status in time.

Two environmental components seem to be associated with these succes-

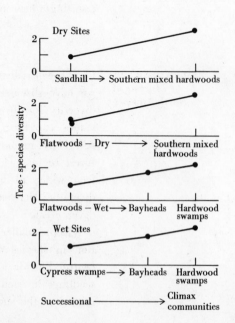

FIGURE 305

Tree-species diversity in deciduous forests of northern Florida. Species diversity depends on the successional stage and increases during succession, regardless of whether succession starts from a very wet site or a dry site. (After Monk 1967.)

sional variations in species diversity: soil moisture and soil calcium levels. Stands with more calcium have more tree species:

Soil calcium (ppm)	Average no. tree species per sample	Tree species diversity, H
<100	9.9	} 2.23
101–300	12.9	
>300	14.1	} 2.74

Moisture was not as significant, but dry sites contained fewer species of trees:

Soil moisture	Tree species diversity, H
Dry	1.98
Mesic	2.78
Wet	2.70

Thus mesic sites with calcareous soil support the highest tree-species diversity.

Finally, the geographical location of the forest stand affects tree-species diversity in a way that is not understood. Stands in eastern Florida averaged 8.9 tree species per sample, while stands in central and western Florida averaged 12.8 species. This may be a historical element that is part of the diversity gradient of the eastern deciduous forests.

Thus the stability–time hypothesis (Figure 299) might be the best explanation for the variation in tree diversity in the eastern deciduous forests of North America. Time can enter as a part of the succession variable, and stability or "favorability" of habitat can enter through variables such as soil moisture and nutrients.

Note that plant-species diversity cannot always be related to the superficial "favorableness" of the environment, as Figure 299 might suggest. Whittaker (1960) showed, for example, that more plant species were found on the very poor soil of serpentine areas in the Siskiyou Mountains of Oregon than on the more fertile quartz diorite soils:

No. species	Soil parent material	
	Quartz diorite	Serpentine
Trees	17	9
Shrubs	13	18
Forbs	46	73
Grasses	8	16
Total	84	116

These comparisons are complicated in plants by the responses of different fractions of the community. What is "favorable" for the tree strata may be "unfavorable" for the herb strata. Serpentine areas are low in tree diversity but high in herb diversity in this example.

THE SPECIAL CASE OF ISLAND SPECIES

Islands are a special kind of trap that catch species able to disperse there and colonize successfully. Since Darwin's visit to the Galapagos Islands, biologists have been using islands as microcosms to study evolutionary and ecologic problems.

The number of species on an island is related to the area of the island. This can be seen most easily in a group of islands like the Galapagos (Figure 306). The relationship between species and area can be described by the simple equation

$$S = cA^z$$

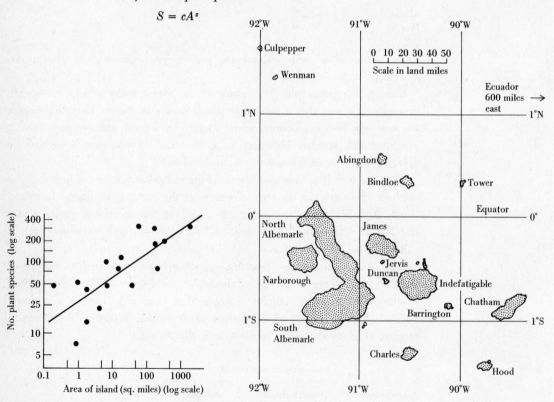

FIGURE 306

Number of land-plant species on the Galapagos Islands in relation to the area of the island. The islands range in area from 0.2 to 2249 sq. miles and contain from 7 to 325 plant species. (After Preston 1962.)

or, taking logarithms,

$$\log S = (\log c) + z(\log A)$$

where

    S = number of species
    c = a constant measuring the number of species on a 1 sq. mile area of island
    A = area of island (in square miles)
    z = a constant measuring the slope of the line relating S and A

For the Galapagos land plants,

$$S = 28.6A^{0.32}$$

The species–area curve, as this relationship is called, is a fundamental one for both plants and animals. Figure 307 illustrates this basic principle for the amphibian and reptile fauna of the West Indies, where the relationship is

$$S = 3.3A^{0.30}$$

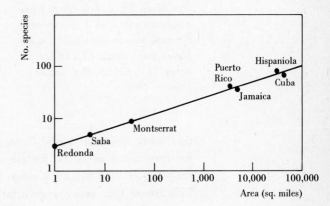

FIGURE 307

Species–area curve for the amphibians and reptiles of the West Indies. (After MacArthur and Wilson 1967.)

Preston (1962) noted that the slope of the species–area curve (z) tended to be around 0.3 for a variety of island situations, from beetles in the West Indies, ants in Melanesia, and vertebrates on islands in Lake Michigan, to land plants on the Galapagos. This raises an interesting question: What is the species–area curve for continental areas? Is it the same in slope as that for islands, and is z some sort of ecological constant?

The number of species increases with area on continental areas as well as on islands. Figure 308 shows the species–area curve for flowering plants of England and Figure 309 for the breeding birds of North America. Note that the species–area curve is not a single straight line. At very small areas the slope is greater, and the same occurs at very large areas. But there is a range from approximately 10 acres to about 1,000,000 acres or more, which is a straight line of the form

$$S = 40A^{0.17}$$

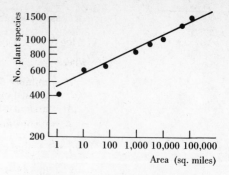

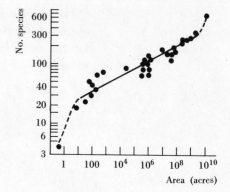

FIGURE 308

Species–area relationship for flowering plants in England. The smallest plot is 1 sq. mile in Surrey and the largest plot is the whole of England (87,417 sq. miles). (After Williams 1964.)

FIGURE 309

Species–area curve for North American birds. The points range from a 0.5-acre plot with 3 species in Pennsylvania to the whole United States and Canada (4.6 billion acres) with 625 species. (After Preston 1960.)

for North American birds. Preston (1962) noted that species–area curves for continental areas, or for *parts* of large islands, had slopes (z) which ranged from 0.15 to 0.24, a range below the z values found in island studies. This means that as we sample larger and larger areas, we add fewer new species if we are sampling a continental area than if we are sampling a series of islands. The explanation for this is that islands are *isolates* with reduced immigration and emigration, while continental areas are under continual flux of immigrants and emigrants. Thus each sample area on the continent will probably contain some transient species from adjacent habitats, which acts to lower the slope of the species–area curve.

The number of species living on any plot, whether an island or an area on the mainland, is a balance between immigration and extinction. If the immigration of new species exceeds the extinction of old species already present, the plot or island will gain species over time. We can thus treat the problem of species diversity on islands by an extension of the approach used in population dynamics (Chapter 9), in which changes in population size were produced by the balance between immigration and births on the one hand and emigration and deaths on the other hand. Figure 310 shows the simplest model. MacArthur and Wilson (1967) discuss this approach in detail.

FIGURE 310

Equilibrium model of a biota of a single island. The equilibrial species number ($\hat{S}$) is reached at the intersection point between the curve of rate of immigration of new species, not already on the island, and the curve of extinction of species from the island. (After MacArthur and Wilson 1967.)

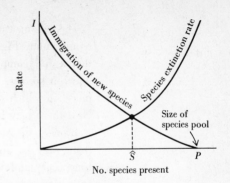

The immigration rate is expressed as number of new species per unit time. This rate falls continuously because as more species become established on the island, most of the immigrants will be from species already present. The upper limit of the immigration curve is the total fauna for the region. The extinction rate (number of species per unit time) rises because the chances of extinction depend on the number of species already present. The point where the immigration curve crosses the extinction curve is by definition the equilibrium point for the number of species on the island.

The shape of the curves of immigration and extinction is critical for making any predictions about island situations. Assume for the moment that the only effect of distance will be on the immigration curve; near islands will receive more dispersing animals than will far-distant islands. Assume also that small islands will differ from large islands in their extinction rate so that the chances of going extinct are greater on small islands. Figure 311 illustrates these assumptions. By graphically estimating the equilibrium points for small and large, near and distant islands (or by doing some algebra) we can come up with a prediction that is not immediately obvious: *The species–area curve should rise more rapidly on distant islands than on near islands.* There are insufficient data at present to test this prediction very carefully.

FIGURE 311

Equilibrium models of biotas of several islands of varying distances from the principal source area and of varying size. An increase in distance (near to far) lowers the immigration curve; an increase in island area (small to large) lowers the extinction curve. (After MacArthur and Wilson 1967.)

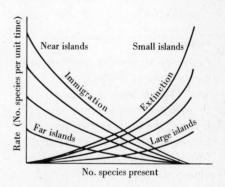

The colonization of an island may go through several phases of species equilibrium (Figure 312). The initial colonization may occur rapidly enough that a full complement of species exists before there is serious interaction between species. The noninteractive phase may be followed by an interactive phase in which competition and predation may reduce the species diversity. Next there may be an assortative phase in which species are replaced through a process of succession, and this may lead to higher diversity. Finally, there may be an evolutionary trend in diversity which operates on a long time scale and which results in genetic adaptation and a lowering of the extinction-rate curve.

An experimental approach to island species diversity can be used to test some of the general aspects of the equilibrium theory of MacArthur and Wilson (1967). Simberloff and Wilson (1970) fumigated six islands of mangrove off the Florida Keys in 1966–1967 and followed the subsequent history of colonization of these islands. The fauna of the mangroves is mostly insects and spiders, along with scorpions, isopods, and other arthropods. The species pool for the area is about 1000 species, but at any given moment only 20 to 40 species occur on each mangrove island, which are 11 to 18 m in diameter.

The colonization curves for four of the mangrove islands are shown in Figure 313. In each case the colonization curve rose rapidly in 8 to 9 months to a high level and then declined slightly to an equilibrium number of species which was near the original species number. The nearest island to the mainland (2 m away) reached a higher equilibrium level than the distant island (533 m away). Both these findings agree with the general predictions of the equilibrium theory.

Unfortunately the turnover of insect species was so fast that immigration and extinction curves could not be estimated for the mangrove islands.

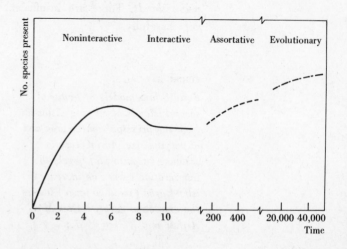

FIGURE 312

Postulated sequence of equilibria in a community of species through time. The time scale is imaginary, supplied here only to convey the notion of the vastly greater time periods required for shifts to states beyond the initial interactive equilibrium. (After Wilson 1969.)

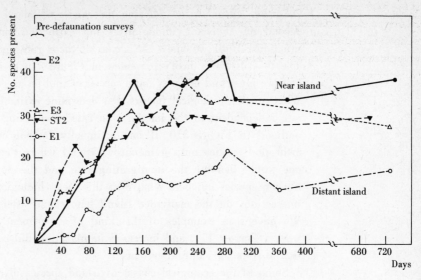

FIGURE 313

Colonization curves of four small mangrove islands in the lower Florida Keys, whose entire faunas, consisting almost solely of arthropods, were exterminated by methyl bromide fumigation. The figures shown are the estimated numbers of species present. The number of species is an inverse function of the distance of the island to the nearest source of immigrants. This effect was evident in the predefaunation censuses and was preserved when the faunas regained equilibrium after defaunation. Thus the near island E2 has the most species, the distant island E1 the fewest, and the intermediate islands E3 and ST2 intermediate numbers of species. (After Simberloff and Wilson 1970.)

Species could have died out and recolonized in the time interval between sampling. Immigration and extinction rates must be high for the islands of mangrove, because the species composition changes remarkably from year to year:

Comparison	Species present in both censuses (%)
Before vs. 1 year later	19
Before vs. 2 years later	30
One year later vs. 2 years later	41

Whether the species composition of the mangroves will converge to those present before the experiment remains to be seen.

Further advances in analyzing the causes of island species diversity will depend on analyzing immigration and extinction curves in a variety of situations. Until we know the shape of these rate curves, we shall not be able to utilize the theory presented in Figure 310 to much advantage. Second, we must find out why more species cannot be accommodated on islands. What are the biological factors that determine extinction? Is the extinction rate independent of the immigration rate? According to the simple theory outlined in Figure 310, if one artificially introduced some of the 1000 arthropod species onto a mangrove island where they did not occur yet, one would increase the immigration rate and therefore increase the equilibrium species number. What does this mean biologically about the species interactions on the mangrove island before and after these introductions? We have seen examples of this kind of experiment in biological control work (Chapter 17), and increased immigration did cause increased extinction in some agricultural systems.

Some of the ecological causes of island species diversity may be studied more easily in well-known groups such as the birds. Ireland, for example, supports only 60% of the British bird fauna, but this is clearly not caused by lack of dispersal, since all but 6 of the 171 British species have been recorded in Ireland. Lack (1969) suggests that the Irish bird fauna is impoverished for ecological reasons; but for many bird species that have been reasonably well studied, no one knows why they avoid Ireland. A few cases are simple—the short-eared owl is absent because there are no field voles in Ireland. Other cases are ascribed to "competition" without any supporting evidence.

SUMMARY

Species diversity can be measured by simply counting all the species in a collection or by weighting each species by its relative abundance. Several measures have been proposed based on statistical distributions, information theory, or probability theory, and each measurement technique has its strong and weak points.

Tropical environments support more species in almost all taxonomic groups than temperate and polar areas. The mammal fauna of North America illustrate the complexity of species diversity gradients, which are not always smooth, steady trends from the equator to the poles.

Six hypotheses have been proposed to explain variation in species diversity. The time hypothesis is historical and emphasizes the time available for speciation and dispersal. Spatial heterogeneity is a second factor that may influence diversity through the number of habitats available per unit of area. Vegetation structure seems important in some groups in determining local diversity. The competition hypothesis states that there is more competition in the tropics and hence niches are "narrow": organisms are specialized and hence more can coexist. The predation hypothesis states the converse—that predators regulate diversity by holding down prey numbers and reducing competition in the tropics. A fifth hypothesis emphasizes environmental stability as a necessary condition for high diversity, and a sixth hypothesis suggests that high productivity is necessary for high diversity. These ideas have been combined in various ways and are not easy to distinguish. A study of desert lizards emphasized the role of historical factors in determining diversity. In the eastern deciduous forests of North America tree-species diversity is highest in climax stages and may be related to soil moisture and soil nutrients. Few case studies on diversity have been completed, and although the patterns are clear, the explanations are not.

Islands are special systems that illustrate the importance of area (and its ecological correlates) in determining diversity. Species numbers increase with area both on islands and on the mainland. Diversity may be viewed as a balance between immigration and extinction, but we know relatively little about what determines immigration and extinction rates on islands.

SELECTED REFERENCES

CONNELL, J. H., and E. ORIAS. 1964. The ecological regulation of species diversity. *Amer. Naturalist* 98:399–414.

HARPER, J. L. 1969. The role of predation in vegetational diversity. *Brookhaven Symp. Biol.* 22:48–62.

JANZEN, D. H. 1970. Herbivores and the number of tree species in tropical forests. *Amer. Naturalist* 104:501–528.

MacARTHUR, R. H., and E. O. WILSON. 1967. *The Theory of Island Biogeography.* Princeton University Press, Princeton, N.J.

PIANKA, E. R. 1966. Latitudinal gradients in species diversity: a review of concepts. *Amer. Naturalist* 100:33–46.

PIELOU, E. C. 1966. The measurement of diversity in different types of biological collections. *J. Theoret. Biol.* 13:131–144.

PRESTON, F. W. 1962. The canonical distribution of commonness and rarity. *Ecology* 43:185–215, 410–432.

QUESTIONS AND PROBLEMS

1 The species–area curve rises continually as area is increased, and this implies that there is no limit to the number of species in any community. Is this a correct interpretation? Discuss the implications of the species–area curve for the problem of community definition (Chapter 19).

2 Calculate Simpson's index of diversity and the Shannon–Wiener index of diversity for the following sets of hypothetical data:

	Proportion of species in community			
Species	W	X	Y	Z
1	0.143	0.40	0.40	0.40
2	0.143	0.20	0.20	0.20
3	0.143	0.15	0.15	0.15
4	0.143	0.10	0.10	0.10
5	0.143	0.05	0.025	0.01
6	0.143	0.05	0.025	0.01
7	0.143	0.05	0.025	0.01
8			0.025	0.01
9			0.025	0.01
10			0.025	0.01
11				0.01
12				0.01
13				0.01
14				0.01
15				0.01
16				0.01
17				0.01
18				0.01
19				0.01
	1.00	1.00	1.00	1.00

What do you conclude about the sensitivity of these measures? Compare your results with those of Berger and Parker (1970) on planktonic Foraminifera communities.

3 Ferns are well known for being extremely free from insect attack in both the juvenile and the adult stages (Janzen 1970). Obtain information on species diversity gradients in ferns from floras of tropical and temperate areas, and suggest some explanations for the diversity changes you find.

4 In discussing the concept of predation, Janzen (1970, p. 503) states: "The act of a fox seeking out and eating mice differs in no significant way from a lygaeid bug seeking out and eating seeds, or a paca seeking out and eating seedlings." Discuss with respect to the predation hypothesis for species diversity.

5 Recher (1969, p. 75) measured bird-species diversity in Australia. In two areas he obtained the following census information:

Area CS-1: 1,2,3,1,2,6,2,4,4,5 birds in 10 species (30 individuals)
Area CS-2: 1,3,2,4,4,3,1,1,28,1 birds in 10 species (48 individuals)

He estimated foliage-height diversity for the three layers to be CS-1, 0.68; CS-2, 0.47. Plot these data on Figure 297. Do they agree with the North American data? How can you explain this? Suppose the outcome had been the opposite.

How could you explain this result? Read Recher's paper and discuss his interpretation.

6 The number of vascular-plant species for the islands off California and the geographic parameters for each island are given by Johnson, Mason, and Raven (1968, p. 300) as follows:

Island	Area (sq. miles)	Maximum elevation (ft)	Latitude (°N)	Distance from mainland (miles)	No. plant species
Cedros	134	3950	28.2	14	205
Guadalupe	98	4600	29.0	165	163
Santa Cruz	96	2470	34.0	20	420
Santa Rosa	84	1560	34.0	27	340
Santa Catalina	75	2125	33.3	20	392
San Clemente	56	1965	32.9	49	235
San Nicolas	22	910	33.2	61	120
San Miguel	14	830	34.0	26	190
Natividad	2.8	490	27.9	5	42
Santa Barbara	1.0	635	33.4	38	40
San Martin	0.9	470	30.5	3.5	62
San Geronimo	0.2	130	29.8	6	4
South Farallon	0.1	360	37.7	27	12
Ano Nuevo	0.02	60	37.1	0.25	40

Make four plots of the number of plant species versus (1) area, (2) elevation, (3) latitude, and (4) distance from mainland. Do these on arithmetic scales and repeat on logarithmic scales (log–log plot). What variable is most closely related to species numbers? Estimate graphically the slope of the species–area curve for this ensemble of islands and compare it with those given in the text.

7 As an exercise in historical ecology and the pathways of science, trace the development and demise of the broken-stick model of species abundance patterns from MacArthur (1957) to MacArthur (1966) and finally to Hairston (1969).

8 Dice (1952, p. 383) states: "In the climax community all the possible niches available to those species that live in the region may be assumed to be already filled. The invasion of another species, therefore, would be practically impossible." Discuss with reference to the idea that "empty niches" do not exist in climax communities.

24 Community organization

Dominant species in a community exert a powerful control over the occurrence of other species, and the concept of dominance has long been engrained in community ecology. It is, however, an elusive concept because dominance can be achieved in two quite different ways. A rare species may, in fact, be a very important "keystone" species for the community. An example might be the starfish *Pisaster* studied by Paine (1966), which is not the most abundant or the most productive species in the intertidal community, yet through its predatory activities seems to permit the community to exist as a diverse assemblage (see page 519). On the other hand, a numerically abundant species may determine the nature of the community. For example, the sugar maple forms part of the climax forest in eastern North America and by its abundance determines the physical conditions of the forest community. This second form of dominance is what we shall discuss here.

Dominance is related to the concept of species diversity, and some of the measures of species diversity discussed in Chapter 23 (such as Simpson's index) could also be considered as measures of dominance. We can define a simple community dominance index as follows (McNaughton 1968):

Community dominance index = percentage of abundance contributed
by the two most abundant species

$$= 100 \times \frac{y_1 + y_2}{y}$$

where

y_1 = abundance of most abundant species
y_2 = abundance of second most abundant species
y = total abundances for all species

Abundance may be measured by density, biomass, or productivity. Dominance, defined by the community dominance index, is inversely related to diversity. Figure 314 illustrates this relationship for annual grassland in California and Figure 315 for trees of the eastern deciduous forest of North America.

FIGURE 314

Relationship of dominance and species diversity in California annual grasslands. Dominance is defined as the percentage of the peak standing crop contributed by the two most abundant species. (After Mc-Naughton 1968.)

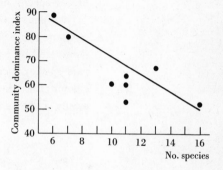

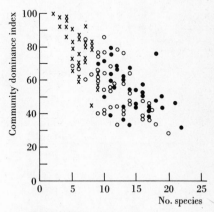

FIGURE 315

Relationship between species diversity and dominance for trees of the eastern deciduous forest of North America. (Data from Braun 1950.)

● Mixed mesophytic forests, climax stands

○ Mixed mesophytic forests, subclimax stands

× Hemlock—white pine—northern hardwoods forest, Great Lakes sector

The degree of dominance in a plant community may be related to the position of the community on a physical or chemical gradient. Figure 316 shows that for North Dakota grasslands the maximum diversity and minimum dominance occurs in mesic sites, not too wet or too dry. The mesic sites support tall-grass prairie dominated by the grasses *Andropogon scoparius*, *Stipa spartea*, and *Sporobolus heterolepis*, which form the classic "climax" of the eastern Great Plains.

If dominance is always closely related to diversity, we can forget it as a concept and talk about diversity alone. There is some evidence that dominance is not closely tied to diversity. Fager (1968) studied the invertebrate community of decaying oak logs on the floor of an oak forest in England. The typical oak log contained two *abundant* species, which contributed 50% of the individuals, and three *common* species, which contributed an additional 25%. Logs with high numbers of total individuals had high numbers of total species as well, but these additional species were in the uncommon species group, and there was only a slight tendency for higher species diversity to be associated with lower dominance (Figure 317).

Dominant species in a community are usually assumed to be ecologically constant. Thus, for example, a deciduous forest in Ohio is expected to be dominated by beech and sugar maple, and botanists would be surprised if a rare species such as black walnut or white ash became dominant. In some communities the dominant species seems to be largely a matter of chance events. For example, the oak logs Fager (1968) studied in England always

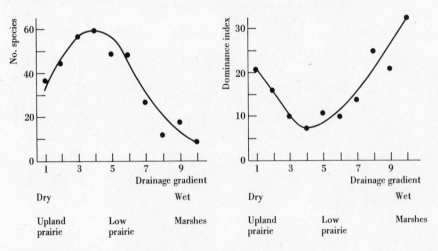

FIGURE 316

Species diversity and degree of community dominance in relation to the moisture gradient in the prairie of east-central North Dakota. Note that the diversity and dominance curves are the reverse images of one another. (After Dix and Smeins 1967.)

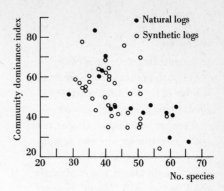

FIGURE 317

Relationship between dominance and species diversity in the invertebrate community of decaying oak logs in Wytham Woods, England. There is a slight tendency for dominance to be low when diversity is high, but the relationship is not very tight. (After Fager 1968.)

had a couple of dominant invertebrate species, but what particular species would be dominant in any one log could not be predicted. Of 108 invertebrate species in the oak logs, 46 species were dominant at least once, but none was dominant in every log. Thus a species could be dominant in one log and very rare in an adjacent log. The suggestion Fager made was that what determined the dominant species was very much a question of who gets there first and so contains a large random component for decaying logs.

The nutrient enrichment of lakes changes the dominance structure of the phytoplankton community. Dickman (1968) showed this effect by artificial fertilization of small enclosures in Marion Lake, British Columbia. Artificial fertilization did not affect the common species in the phytoplankton, but instead a rare species usually increased rapidly until it was the dominant member of the phytoplankton. The number of species in the phytoplankton community did not change during the nutrient experiment but stayed around 50 species in each 200-cc sample. There was no way to predict which of the rare species would become dominant upon nutrient addition. Twenty-three different species of algae were recorded as increasing during one or more of the 24 experiments. Figure 318 summarizes the sequence of events after artificial fertilization with nitrogen or phosphorous.

One possible explanation for the unpredictability of the dominant species is that these communities are not stable but are changing because of succession to a new community type. This leads us to ask about the concept of community stability.

STABILITY

Stability is a dynamic concept that refers to the ability of a system to bounce back from disturbances. If a brick is raised slightly from the floor and then released, it will fall back to its original position. This is the

FIGURE 318

Schematic diagram of the changes in the phytoplankton community of Marion Lake, British Columbia, after artificial enrichment with nitrogen or phosphorus. One or two of the rare species increase rapidly to form a "bloom" and then die back to their former status. Exactly which species will "bloom" cannot be predicted. (After Dickman 1968.)

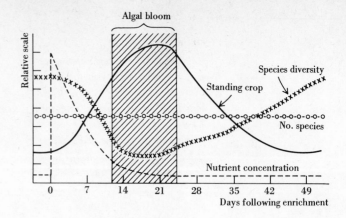

physicists' concept of *neighborhood stability* or local stability. The system will respond to temporary slight disturbances by returning to its original position. Thus, for example, a rabbit population may show neighborhood stability to hunting pressure if it returns to its normal density after hunting is prohibited.

Physicists discuss stability in terms of small perturbations, but ecological systems are subject to large disturbances. To deal with these, we must introduce a second type of stability, *global stability*. A region of local stability shows global stability only if the system returns to the same point after large disturbances. This does not always happen, and one of the problems of ecology is to map out the limits of global stability for various communities (Lewontin 1969). Figure 319 illustrates the ideas of stability in a simple way. Note that the shape of stability "basins" need not be circular in cross section. There may be great stability to disturbances in one direction but little stability to disturbances in other directions.

Stability has a similar meaning when it is used by population ecologists to mean the absence of fluctuations. Thus the African migratory locust (Figure 158) is unstable, whereas the tawny owl maintains a stable population (Figure 146). In this sense we can measure stability by the amount of fluctuation over a long time period, and we can transfer this concept to the community level and define a community as being stable if its constituent populations show little fluctuation. This form of stability is usually considered over many years and excludes seasonal variations in numbers within a single year.

We can use either of these two concepts of stability to refer to a number of biological attributes of communities: Stability of numbers, stability of relative abundance patterns, stability of dominance, and stability of species composition are five such types that might be judged significant to study.

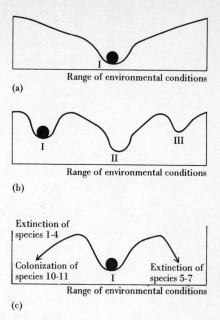

FIGURE 319

*Local and global stability concepts.
The community is represented as a
black ball on a topographic surface
which is a range of environmental
conditions. In (a) the community is
both locally and globally stable
because after all perturbations it
will return to configuration I. In
(b) the community is locally stable,
but if perturbed beyond a certain
critical range it will move to a new
configuration of relative abundances
(II or III). In some cases (c) large
disturbances will cause extinctions
of some species in the community
and colonization by new forms.*

Thus the simple word *stability* may mean many different things and should
not be used without a qualifying description.

One of the hallowed tenets of modern community ecology is that *diversity
causes stability*. Elton (1958) suggested several lines of circumstantial evidence that support this conclusion:

1 Mathematical models of simple systems show how difficult it is to achieve
numerical stability (Chapters 12 and 13).

2 Gause's laboratory experiments on protozoa confirm the difficulty of achieving
numerical stability in simple systems.

3 Small islands are much more vulnerable to invading species than are
continents.

4 Outbreaks of pests are most often found on cultivated land or land disturbed
by man.

5 Tropical rain forests do not have insect outbreaks like those common to
temperate forests.

6 Pesticides have caused outbreaks by the elimination of predators and parasites
from the insect community of crop plants.

These lines of evidence suggest that stability should increase as the number
of links in the food web increases. Thus stability might be achieved by a
large number of species each with a restricted diet, or a smaller number
of species each with a wider diet (MacArthur 1955). Is there any evidence
from field or laboratory experiments that would confirm this?

Few experiments have been done on stability and diversity, and these
suggest that the simple view of diversity causing stability must be modified.

Small laboratory microcosms of bacteria and protozoa were analyzed by Hairston et al. (1968). The microcosms had two or three trophic levels:

Trophic level	Organisms	No. species studied
First	bacteria	1–3
Second	*Paramecium*	1–3
Third	*Didinium* and *Woodruffia* (predatory protozoa)	2

Stability was measured in two ways: (1) persistence in time of all species (so less stability = more extinctions), and (2) evenness of species abundance patterns.

Experiments with the first and second trophic level showed that more diversity at the first trophic level led to more stability at the second trophic level. After 20 days, fewer extinctions of *Paramecium* occurred when the bacteria were diverse:

Experiment	% of cultures showing no extinctions of *Paramecium* after 20 days
1 species of bacteria	32 (less stability)
2 species of bacteria	61
3 species of bacteria	70 (more stability)

We can ask a second question—whether diversity within one trophic level increases stability within that trophic level. This was not true in the *Paramecium* trophic level, because the effect of adding a third *Paramecium* species to two others depended on which particular species was being added to which other two. This means that species-specific quirks can modify diversity–stability relations, and that all species are not equal and interchangeable at the same trophic level.

When a third trophic level was added to the bacteria and *Paramecium* there was a general decrease in stability of the whole system because the *Paramecium* were usually driven extinct (see Figure 135). And it did not matter whether two or three species of *Paramecium* were present, or whether there were one or two predator species. Thus in simplified laboratory communities, diversity does not automatically lead to stability, and the addition of higher trophic levels may reduce community stability.

Since 1936 the Canadian Forest Insect Survey has been monitoring the abundance of several hundred species of forest Macrolepidoptera (moths and butterflies) and other forest insect species that attack trees. K. E. F. Watt (1964, 1965) has analyzed some of these data in order to test the diversity–causes–stability concept. The Survey has estimated the variations in abundance, or "stability," of each species of Macrolepidoptera. Before we look at the data, let us consider what might increase the stability of these insect populations. If the number of links in the food web determines stability, we could increase stability in two ways:

1 Species with a wide diet (many host trees) should be more stable than species with a restricted diet.

2 Species with many competing species on the same trophic level should be more stable than species with few competitors.

Figure 320 shows the data from the Canadian Forest Insect Survey which are relevant to mechanism 1. Note that gregarious species of Lepidoptera are on the average more abundant and less stable than solitary species, so we must treat these two groups separately. The result in Figure 320 is just the opposite of what we predicted; in fact, species with broad diets are more *unstable*. Watt (1965) suggests that the important ecological variable here is the *proportion of the environment filled with usable food*. Species with a broad diet thus find it easier to locate suitable food. An important example is the spruce budworm (Chapter 15), which is unstable but has a very restricted diet. But since the spruce budworm lives in forests dominated almost exclusively by its two food plants, balsam fir and white spruce, a large fraction of its environment is filled with usable food.

The number of competitor species can be measured very crudely by the number of insect species that eat the same food plant. Figure 321 summarizes these data for 414 species of forest Macrolepidoptera and suggests that mechanism 2 is correct for these species. Watt (1965) concluded that

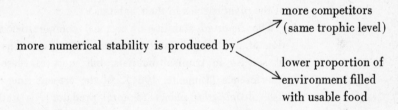

FIGURE 320

Relationship between population stability of forest Macrolepidoptera and the dietary breadth of the species. If diversity causes stability, species with a wide diet should be more stable in numbers over time. These data from the Canada Forest Insect Survey cover 414 species of Lepidoptera from across Canada and do not support the hypothesis. (After Watt 1965.)

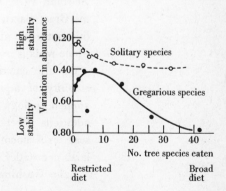

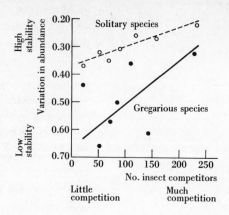

FIGURE 321

Relationship between population stability of Canadian forest Macrolepidoptera and the number of competing insect species (species that feed on the same host tree). If diversity causes stability, species with many competitors should be more stable in numbers. These data support this hypothesis. (After Watt 1965.)

There are some practical consequences of these conclusions, if they are correct for other systems. Agricultural and forestry monocultures greatly increase the proportion of the environment filled with usable food, and so may induce outbreaks of insect pests.

The stability of whole communities has rarely been studied in detail in spite of the great number of perturbations caused by man. We have already discussed for a rocky intertidal community the effect of removing the top predator, *Pisaster*. This community is unstable in species diversity with respect to the removal of the starfish (page 519). In contrast, we would expect that temperate bird communities (Figure 297) and desert lizard communities (Figure 303) would be unaffected by the removal of many of the plant species in their habitats.

The reported stability of tropical communities may be largely a reflection of the lack of data on tropical organisms. There are some "outbreaks" of species in tropical habitats, but most of these are blamed on human interference (Pimentel 1961). At the present time the crown-of-thorns starfish, *Acanthaster planci* (a coral predator), is undergoing an outbreak on tropical coral reefs in many parts of the central Pacific (Chesher 1969, Newman 1970, Paine 1969), and in the process is destroying large parts of the Great Barrier Reef of Australia and other island reefs. What has caused this outbreak of *Acanthaster* and what will stop it short of destruction of whole reefs is not known.

Aquatic communities have been disturbed by man's pollution, and the stability of aquatic systems under pollution stress is a critical focus of applied ecology today. We have already seen an example of how nutrient additions affect the phytoplankton in a lake (Figure 318). A much-larger-scale experiment has been performed by the diversion of sewage into large lakes near cities. Let us examine one such instance.

Lake Washington was a large unproductive lake in Seattle, Washington, which had been used for sewage disposal until recently. In the early phases of development Lake Washington was used for raw sewage disposal, but this practice was stopped between 1926 and 1936 (Figure 322). However, with additional population pressure, a number of sewage-treatment plants built between 1941 and 1959 began discharging sewage into the lake in increasing amounts. By 1955 it was clear that the sewage was destroying the clear-water lake, and a plan to divert sewage from the lake was voted into action. More and more sewage was diverted to the ocean from 1963 through 1968, and almost all was diverted from March 1967 onward (Figure 322). The recent history of Lake Washington thus consists of two pulses of nutrient additions, followed by a complete diversion.

What happened to the organisms in Lake Washington during this time? Some information can be obtained by looking at the sediments in the bottom of the lake (Figure 323). After sewage had been added to the lake, the sedimentation rate rose to about 3 mm/year. The organic content of this sediment has progressively increased since the early 1900s, which suggests an accelerated rate of primary production. The recent lake sediments also have a greater amount of phosphorus in them (Figure 323). Since phosphorus is one of the two main nutrients added by sewage, this is a parallel change to the organic matter. The composition of the diatom community in Lake Washington has also changed. The "shells" of diatoms are made of silica and are preserved well in sediments. Stockner and Benson (1967) showed that a group of species of diatoms (the Araphidinae) varied in abundance in association with the sewage history and consequently can be used as *indicator species* of pollution in this lake.

Since the diversion of sewage began in 1963, Edmondson (1970) has recorded the changes in Lake Washington in detail. Figure 324 shows the rapid drop in phosphorus in the surface waters and the closely associated drop in the standing crop of phytoplankton. Nitrogen content of the water has dropped very little, which suggests that phosphorus is a limiting nutrient to phytoplankton growth. The water of the lake has become noticeably

FIGURE 322

Sewage history of Seattle's Lake Washington. Raw sewage was diverted from the lake gradually over the period 1926 to 1936, but then treated sewage was added at an increasing rate until a second diversion was made from 1963 to 1967. (After Edmondson 1969.)

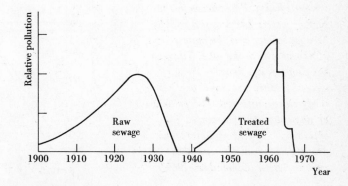

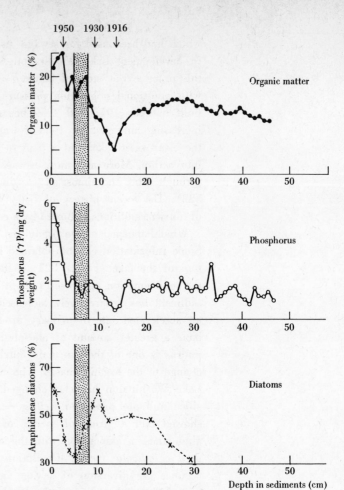

FIGURE 323

Historical changes in Lake Washington as revealed by the sediments in the lake bottom. These core data were taken in 1958. The shaded area represents the approximate position in the core of the time period 1930 to 1940 when nutrient pollution from sewage was temporarily halted. (After Edmondson 1969.)

FIGURE 324

Recovery of Lake Washington from 1963 to 1970 after diversion of sewage effluent. Phosphorus in the surface waters has dropped rapidly because sewage was the main source of phosphorus to the lake. Nitrogen has dropped less because the surface waters feeding the lake are relatively rich in nitrogen. The amount of phytoplankton (measured by chlorophyll content of water) has dropped in parallel to the phosphorus. (After Edmondson 1969.)

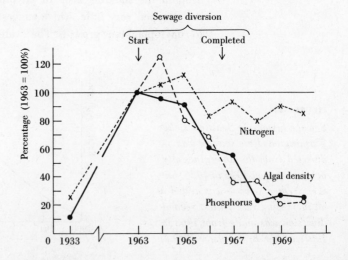

clearer since the sewage diversion. Apparently the phosphorus tied up in the lake sediments is released back into the water column rather slowly.

The Lake Washington experiment is of considerable interest because it suggests that detrimental changes in lakes might be *stopped and reversed* if the input of nutrients can be stopped. That is, the Lake Washington system shows a considerable amount of global stability.

COMMUNITY DEVELOPMENT DURING SUCCESSION

Can we relate the attributes of communities—productivity, diversity, dominance, and stability—together in a unified theory of ecosystem development? Two attempts have been made to do this, and we now examine these.

Margalef's approach   The concept of *maturity* is central to the ideas about ecosystems proposed by Margalef (1963, 1968). Maturity is a dynamic concept related to structural complexity and organization, and we begin with the suggestion that *maturity increases with time in any undisturbed ecosystem.* Maturity can thus be related to succession, and successional changes in a community lead in the direction of more maturity. But maturity can also be measured across different climaxes, so we may consider a deciduous forest climax as a more mature ecosystem than a grassland climax.

How do we measure *maturity*? In the present stage of knowledge about ecosystems, we can best approach this in a qualitative manner by asking about the characteristics of "more mature" versus "less mature" ecosystems. Table 35 will be used to record these characteristics.

The *structure* of the community can be used as one indication of maturity. The standing crop is usually much larger in more mature communities than it is in less mature communities. Examples of this are clearly seen in forest successions (discussed in Chapter 20). The species diversity, or "information content," of the community also increases with maturity, and this typically leads to a more complex spatial structure, evidenced by the stratification seen in plant communities.

The *energy relations* of communities can also be used to measure their maturity. The food chains of less mature communities are typically short; those in more mature communities are long and complex. For a given standing crop, the gross and net primary productivity is very low in mature communities, and the ratio of production to biomass (P/B) is the most important single measure of maturity in an ecosystem. Energy in a complex, highly mature system is shunted into maintenance of order, and less is used for production of new materials.

TABLE 35

Characteristics of more mature and less mature ecosystems according to Margalef's theory

	Ecosystem condition	
Characteristic	Less mature	More mature
Structure		
Biomass	Small	Large
Species diversity	Low	High
Stratification	Less	More
Energy flow		
Food chains	Short	Long
Primary production per unit of biomass	High	Low
Individual populations		
Fluctuations	More pronounced	Less pronounced
Life cycles	Simple	Complex
Feeding relations	Generalized	Specialized
Size of individuals	Smaller	Larger
Life span of individuals	Short	Long
Population control mechanisms	Abiotic	Biotic
Exploitation by man		
Potential yield	High	Low
Ability to withstand exploitation	Good	Poor

The implications of the structural and energetic attributes of a mature community can be followed to the level of individual species populations. Fluctuations in populations should be more pronounced in less mature systems, and hence stability is directly related to maturity. Species in less mature communities should have relatively simple life cycles, small body size, and short life spans. Specialization should be characteristic of mature systems. Margalef suggests that physical factors will have a strong influence on organisms in less mature systems, and climatic stress can prevent a community from progressing to a higher level of maturity.

Finally, the maturity of an ecological community will determine the possible exploitation by man. Potential yield is high only in immature ecosystems, which have a high production/biomass ratio. If a community of high maturity is exploited by man, a shift in maturity is produced toward a lower level.

Margalef suggests that if two ecosystems are adjacent, the system with more maturity tends to cannibalize the system with less maturity. Thus energy will flow from the less mature system into the more mature system. Margalef draws the analogy from human populations: Energy flows from the rural areas (less mature systems) to the cities (more mature systems).

Diversity, stability, and productivity can all be incorporated into a dynamic ecosystem model (Margalef 1969). Figure 325 shows an approximate pattern in which productivity falls with increasing diversity, and, at any given diversity level, more stable communities are less productive. Thus, for example, a plankton community may have the same species diversity (4.5 bits per individual) as a forest community, but a forest has more stability and is less productive per unit biomass. Margalef suggests that the relationship in Figure 325 is logarithmic with respect to productivity. This means that a small change in diversity when diversity is low causes a large change in productivity. On the other hand, when diversity is very high, small changes in productivity are linked with large changes in diversity.

Margalef's theory of ecosystem development provides a broad theoretical framework for community ecology studies. At the present time there is no set of data on community development by which to test Margalef's generalizations.

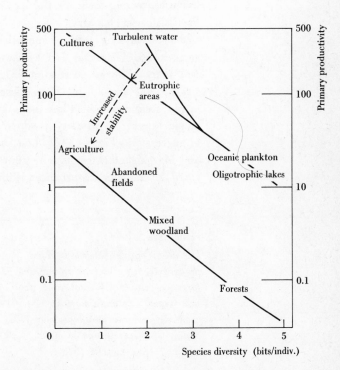

FIGURE 325

Approximate relationship between primary productivity (per square meter per year) and species diversity (H) in a number of typical ecosystems. Stability affects the position of the curve. Oligotrophic lakes are unproductive, clear-water lakes. Eutrophic lakes are very productive. (After Margalef 1969.)

Odum's Approach Ecosystem development is basically a study of ecological succession, in Odum's (1969) view, and the "strategy" of succession is to increase homeostasis of the community by providing more and more protection from environment. Succession thus increases homeostasis of the community by providing more and more protection from environmental variation.

Ecosystem development in Odum's view is very similar to the concept of maturity suggested by Margalef. A few measures of development differ. The ratio of gross photosynthesis/community respiration (*P/R* ratio) is high in the early stages of succession and low, approaching 1, in the climax stage. As long as gross production is greater than respiration, standing crop must accumulate in the community. The *P/R* ratio is thus an excellent index of the relative maturity of the community.

The net result of succession is increased symbiosis between species, nutrient conservation, an increase in information content, and an increase in stability. But this process does not go to completion in all ecosystems. Disturbances may hold a system arrested at an intermediate stage of development. Estuaries, for example, are maintained in a fertile state by the tides and the daily variations in water levels. Freshwater marshes such as the Everglades of Florida are maintained by seasonal changes in water levels, and if the water level is stabilized this community may be destroyed rather than preserved. Fire has been an important agent in maintaining some communities, among them the California redwoods, the African grasslands, and the California chaparral.

Succession may lead a community into a *less* mature configuration in some cases. Wisconsin forests show a decrease in species diversity after 100 years of forest succession (Figure 326). The low tree seedling diversity of 200-year-old stands is caused by a complete domination by sugar maple seedlings, which are very shade tolerant. Replacement with sugar maple lowers the primary production in Wisconsin after about 180 years of succession (Figure 327). Loucks (1970) suggests, in contrast to Odum and Margalef, that community characteristics are wavelike phenomena triggered by random disturbances, with intervals of 30 to 200 years between

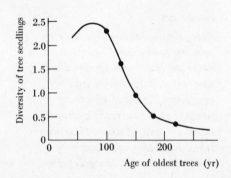

FIGURE 326

Decline in species diversity (H) of the tree seedling layer in the upland forests of southern Wisconsin as the stand ages. The understory is gradually taken over almost completely by the seedlings of sugar maple. (After Loucks 1970.)

FIGURE 327

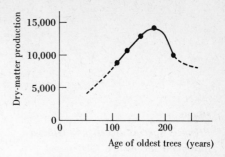

disturbances (fires) in the Wisconsin forest example. Figure 328 illustrates this idea, which has implications for the management of natural landscapes.

The Glacier Bay successional sequence seems to provide an ideal situation to test some of the predictions of the Odum and Margalef models. In the succession on glacial moraines in southeastern Alaska (discussed in Chapter 20) the spruce–hemlock forest is gradually replaced by the muskeg, or *Sphagnum* bog, which would seem a clear contradiction to the patterns proposed by Margalef (Table 35). Muskeg is a one- or two-layered community which contrasts with the multilayered forest that it replaces. Unfortunately, critical data on production/biomass or production/respiration ratios are not yet available for the successional stages in this Glacier Bay sequence, but Reiners, Worley, and Lawrence (1971) have obtained data on species-diversity changes over sites spanning 1500 years of succession. Figure 329 shows that species diversity rises to a plateau in the course of succession and does not fall in the muskeg stage. The diversity of trees and large shrubs drops in the muskeg stage (1500 years), but this is compensated by a rise in herb and low-shrub diversity. The drop in diversity in the 33-year-old *Dryas* site is caused by the extreme dominance of this mat plant, and a detailed picture of diversity changes might show superimposed waves of low diversity associated with successional stages dominated by *Dryas*, then by alder, and then by spruce. The replacement of forest by muskeg does not result in a reduction in community diversity, contrary to what one

FIGURE 328

Hypothetical model to show the pattern of response of tree seedling diversity in southern Wisconsin forests to a series of random perturbations in the form of fires. The wavelike changes shown in Figure 326 would not go to completion until fires were controlled by man. (After Loucks 1970.)

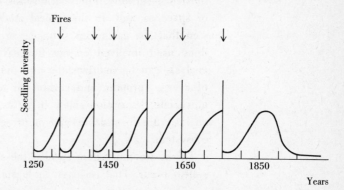

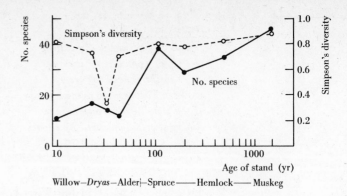

FIGURE 329

Trend in species diversity in Glacier Bay plant succession. (After Reiners, Worley, and Lawrence 1971.)

might expect from a visual assessment of forest versus muskeg. Species diversity of vegetation at Glacier Bay thus varies little between 100 and 1500 years of age.

SYSTEMS ANALYSIS

Another approach to the problem of community organization is through systems analysis, which is the attempt to determine which variables are important to a system and to analyze them with a mathematical model. Four phases may be recognized in systems analysis (Dale 1970).

First, we must choose the parts that comprise the system. The common belief is that these parts are self-evident, but the arguments over the nature of the community (Chapter 19) show that in ecology the parts are seldom clear. We can choose parts on the basis of taxonomic categories, structural categories (such as trees, shrubs, herbs), or functional categories (such as trophic levels). The choice of parts is in many respects the critical decision when starting a systems analysis, and it is not clear at present which categories are best for describing and comparing ecosystems.

Second, we must define the relationships between the parts of the system. These relationships are often concerned with energy or materials (water, nutrients, carbon), but relationships could be defined on the basis of time or space as well. In the typical study of community metabolism, we have seen that the categories defined were trophic levels and that the relationships used involved energy flow. Note that the relationships in systems analysis can be multivariate, and the description of an ecosystem in terms of energy, protein, and carbon all together might be more useful than a univariate description solely in terms of energy. The difficulties of such an analysis are formidable, and at present no one has attempted it for a real ecosystem.

Third, we must now specify the mechanisms by which changes in the system occur. That is, given the parts and the properties we wish to analyze for an ecosystem, we must now specify a mathematical model of how these interact. This model of the system may apply over a limited range of environments only, in which case it may be possible to make a simple model faithfully represent a complex ecosystem. By contrast, a model that would faithfully predict the results of all possible environmental changes would be hopelessly complex and impossible to produce for any biological system.

The mechanisms behind changes in communities are not simple, as all of population ecology suggests, and to describe the relationships between the herbivores and plants, for example, in terms of energy may be difficult. In communities an additional complexity is added because changes in the community are determined in part by the previous states of the system; the system has a "history" or "memory." Evolutionary changes may occur to complicate systems models still further, and assumptions about stationary states of ecological systems may be in error for some predictive purposes.

Fourth, we must now analyze the systems model we have produced and validate it by comparing the predictions derived from the model with data from the real world. This is a point where computers and computer technology can be helpful. A common mistake at this stage is to try to validate a model with the same data used to construct the model in the first place. Obviously a set of independent data are required for testing, but at the present time relatively few systems have been studied enough to be adequate tests for complex mathematical systems models.

We have already seen a simple example of a systems model for an ecosystem (Figure 260). The International Biological Program (IBP) is now working on a worldwide basis to gather data and design systems models of ecological processes in a range of habitats from the tropics to the polar zone. The principal difficulty that faces an ecological systems analyst is this: The mathematics and computer techniques already available are so sophisticated, while the ecological data and understanding are so impoverished and primitive, that one is severely tempted to build premature models of ecosystems and to confuse these with reality. A systems approach may someday produce powerful ecological insights, but it cannot do so by compounding computers and complex mathematics with primitive ecological information.

SUMMARY

Communities are organized around dominant species. In many communities dominance and diversity are negatively related, so that, for example, the tropical rain forest would have high diversity and little dominance. Dominant species in temperate communities may not be predictable. Any number of insect species may be dominant in rotting logs, and this depends on who gets there first. By contrast, in temperate forests the dominant species are predictable.

Stability means persistence in the face of disturbances, and also means lack of fluctuations in populations. One of the tenets of community ecology is that diversity causes stability, so diverse communities are less prone to destructive outbreaks. Laboratory experiments do not support this simple view, and the attributes of particular species may be more significant than diversity in general. Field data suggest further modifications of the diversity—causes—stability hypothesis. Forest insects are more stable in numbers when they have many competitors and when only a small part of the environment is filled with useful food plants. Aquatic ecosystems are unstable under pollution but in some cases recover quickly if the nutrient input is stopped.

Community development can be described by the concept of *maturity* (Margalef) or *succession* (Odum). Maturity increases with time in an undisturbed ecosystem, and a high degree of maturity is indicated by complex structure and a low production/biomass ratio. Succession (closely related to maturity) leads in the direction of high species diversity, increased homeostasis of the community, and more stability.

Few data are available to indicate how natural communities actually develop, and the trends in community structure and energetics suggested by Odum and Margalef are hypotheses to be tested by future work. Data from Wisconsin forests suggest that succession may ultimately lead to less diversity and less productivity unless fire interrupts the succession and starts it again.

Community organization could be most effectively studied by systems analysis, in which we build a mathematical-computer model of an ecological system. Systems analysis is a powerful technique, but its use in ecology is presently restricted by inadequate ecological data about communities and the primitive state of understanding of ecological interactions in field populations.

SELECTED REFERENCES

ARON, W. I. and S. H. SMITH. 1971. Ship canals and aquatic ecosystems. *Science* 174: 13–20.

DALE, M. B. 1970. Systems analysis and ecology. *Ecology* 51:2–16.

HAIRSTON, N. G., et al. 1968. The relationship between species diversity and stability: an experimental approach with protozoa and bacteria. *Ecology* 49: 1091–1101.

MacARTHUR, R. 1955. Fluctuations of animal populations, and a measure of community stability. *Ecology* 36:533–536.

MARGALEF, R. 1963. On certain unifying principles in ecology. *Amer. Naturalist* 97:357–374.

ODUM, E. P. 1969. The strategy of ecosystem development. *Science* 164:262–270.

PIMENTEL, D. 1961. Species diversity and insect population outbreaks. *Ann. Entomol. Soc. Amer.* 54:76–86.

WATT, K. E. F. 1965. Community stability and the strategy of biological control. *Can. Entomol.* 97:887–895.

QUESTIONS AND PROBLEMS

1 Elton (1958, p. 147) claims that natural habitats on small islands are much more vulnerable to invading species than natural habitats on continents. Find what evidence you can which is relevant to this assertion and evaluate its importance for the question of community stability.

2 Watt (1968, p. 50) states:

From the standpoint of community energetics, a short and simple trophic pyramid constitutes the best way to use the biosphere; community-organization theory shows us that such trophic-web simplicity would lead to a wildly fluctuating system. By trading stability for productivity, we could produce a system with high average-productivity values, but there would be such violent oscillations around the long-term mean that ... massive famine would result.

Is this analysis correct? Discuss, listing all the assumptions Watt makes.

3 Discuss the management of "natural areas" in relation (1) to the Margalef and Odum model and (2) to the Loucks model (Figure 328) for community development. Apply this general discussion to a particular type of natural area in your geographical region.

4 Margalef (1968, p. 27) states: "In ecology, succession occupies a place similar to that of evolution in general biology." Discuss.

5 In discussing the distribution of mobile animals, Margalef (1963, p. 368) states: "Animals tend to spend their adult lives in the more mature systems, but to reproduce in the less mature ones and send larvae or reproductive elements into them." Make a list of some animal species that move freely across ecosystem boundaries and discuss the application of this idea to each species.

6 Figure 320 shows that gregarious species of Canadian forest Macrolepidoptera are less stable in numbers than solitary species. Watt (1965) provides references for these data. What are the biological mechanisms responsible for this difference between solitary and gregarious forms?

7 In discussing community organization, Hairston (1964, p. 238) states: "It would be possible, presumably, to build a picture of community organization by separate complete studies of each species present, but such an approach would be comparable to describing an organism cell by cell." Is this a proper analogy?

8 Compare and contrast the statements of the evolutionist and the ecologist about species diversity and stability of biological communities:

a Simpson (1969, p. 175) states: "If indeed the earth's ecosystems are tending toward long-range stabilization or static equilibrium, three billion years has been too short a time to reach that condition."

b Recher (1969, p. 79) states: "The avifaunas of forest and scrub habitats in the temperate zone of Australia and North America have reached equilibrium and are probably saturated."

25 *Evolutionary ecology*

In one sense biology *is* evolution and evolution *is* biology, but in another sense there are certain problems that are particularly evolutionary in focus. We gather a few examples of these here under the aegis of evolutionary ecology.

Evolutionary questions are of two types: (1) How did a particular characteristic of an organism arise? (2) What are the forces which keep that characteristic in existence? Everything an organism is or does can be raised as a problem in evolution, but we shall consider here only a few general problems on the interface between ecology and evolution.

DEFENSE MECHANISMS IN PLANTS

The world is green, and there are two possible explanations for this. First, some herbivore populations may evolve self-regulatory mechanisms to prevent them from destroying their food supply (Chapter 14). Or other control mechanisms, such as predation, may hold herbivore abundance down. Second, all that is green may not be edible. Plants have evolved an array of defenses against herbivores, and this has set up a coevolution game with plants and herbivores trying to outwit each other in evolutionary time.

Plants may discourage herbivores by structural adaptations, as anyone who has tried to prune a rosebush will attest, but they may also use a variety of chemical weapons which we are only just starting to appreciate (Whittaker and Feeny 1971). Plants contain a variety of chemicals which have always puzzled plant physiologists and biochemists. These chemicals are found in some plants only and not in others, and have been called *secondary plant substances*. These substances are by-products of the primary metabolic pathways in plants, and Figure 330 gives a simplified view of the origin of some of the major chemical groups of secondary plant substances. Some of these substances are familiar to us already. Juglone (page 42) is an acetogenin produced by walnut trees. The characteristic spices cinnamon and cloves are phenylpropanes found in some herbs. Peppermint oil and catnip are terpenoids. Nicotine is an alkaloid found in tobacco plants. Morphine and caffeine are other alkaloid secondary plant substances.

Two views have developed about the function of secondary plant substances. One view is that these compounds are primarily waste products of plant metabolism and that the evolutionary origin of secondary plant substances can be understood from the viewpoint of autointoxication (Muller 1970). Excretion is a necessary part of metabolism, and in plants takes forms much different from excretion in animals. According to this view, plants have evolved numerous ways of eliminating toxic organic chemicals by volatilization or leaching and other ways of rendering toxic substances harmless by chemical alterations within the plant. This done, the plant may now be in a position to use these substances for its benefit in one of two ways. First, by releasing chemicals into its immediate environment, a plant may be able to suppress competitors, which are poisoned by the excretory products. This produces *allelopathic effects* (Chapter 4). Second, by accumulating some chemicals in its leaves or stem, a plant may become toxic or distasteful to herbivores.

FIGURE 330

Metabolic relationships of the major groups of plant secondary substances (shown in boxes) to the primary metabolism of plants. (After Whittaker and Feeny 1971.)

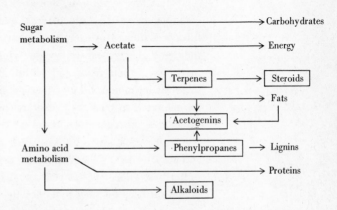

A somewhat different view of the origin of secondary plant substances is that they are chemicals specifically evolved by plants to thwart herbivores (Ehrlich and Raven 1964). Few secondary plant substances are really needed by plants as excretory products, and most substances are actively produced at a metabolic cost to the plant. Only because plants that produce secondary substances are at a selective advantage is there such a chemical variety in different plant groups. Thus, if all animals could be removed from the community, secondary substances would not be produced by plants.

These two views are not completely exclusive hypotheses, and both agree that secondary plant substances may be used to keep herbivores from eating plants. Herbivores do not, of course, sit idly by while plants evolve defense systems (Pimentel 1968). Animals circumvent plant defenses either chemically, by evolving enzymes to detoxify plant chemicals, or by timing the herbivore's life cycle to avoid the noxious chemicals of the plants. The coevolution of animals and plants can thus occur, and we shall examine three cases to illustrate this.

Cardiac glycosides in milkweed

A milkweed (*Asclepias curassavica*) grows abundantly in Costa Rica and other areas in Central America, but cattle will not eat it. This milkweed contains secondary plant substances called cardiac glycosides, which affect the vertebrate heartbeat and are consequently poisonous to mammals and birds. But certain insects are able to eat milkweeds without harmful effects, and among these are the danaid butterflies, including the familiar monarch and queen butterflies. The danaid butterflies are known to be distasteful to insect-eating birds and serve as models in several mimicry complexes. This evidence suggests that the danaid butterflies have developed biochemical mechanisms for feeding on milkweeds containing cardiac glycosides, and then storing this poison in their tissues, so that the insects acquire chemical protection from the plants they eat (Brower 1969).

To test this hypothesis, monarch butterflies were raised on cabbage (which contains no cardiac glycosides) and found to be completely acceptable to bird predators. However, birds that fed on monarch butterflies raised on the milkweed *A. curassavica* became violently ill within 12 minutes, vomited the insects and then recovered within 30 minutes. Such birds learned quickly to reject all monarch butterflies on sight. This rapid learning by birds allows the monarch to trick its predators, because not all milkweeds contain cardiac glycosides. For example, three of the common milkweed species of eastern North America are nontoxic, and monarchs raised on these milkweeds are edible. However, if a vertebrate predator learns to avoid eating monarch butterflies after one unpleasant experience, the edible monarchs escape predation because they look exactly like toxic monarchs. This has led to the evolution of mimicry in other species as well. Thus the defense mechanism of plants can be exploited in turn by animals and turned into a complex network of ecological interactions between predators and their prey.

Tannins in oak trees The common oak (*Quercus robur*) is a dominant tree in the deciduous forests of western Europe and is attacked by the larvae of over 200 species of Lepidoptera, more species of insect attackers than any other tree in Europe. The attack of insects is concentrated in the spring (Figure 331), with a smaller peak of feeding in the fall. One of the most common oak insects is the winter moth, whose larvae feed on oak leaves in May and drop to the ground to pupate in late May. Why is insect attack concentrated in spring? One possibility is that oak leaves change with age to become less suitable insect food (Feeny 1970).

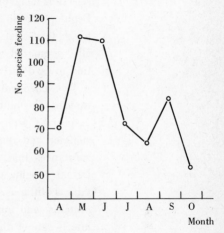

FIGURE 331

Number of Lepidoptera species feeding as larvae on oak leaves in Britain from April to October. (After Feeny 1970.)

If winter moth larvae are fed "young" oak leaves they grow well, but if larvae are fed slightly "older" leaves they grow very poorly:

Winter moth larvae fed on:	Mean peak larval weight (mg)
May 16 oak leaves—natural diet ("young")	*45*
May 28–June 8 leaves ("old")	*18*

No adults emerged from the larvae fed older leaves. Thus some change occurs very rapidly in oak leaves in spring to make them less suitable for winter moth larvae. The most obvious change in oak leaves during the spring is a rapid darkening color and an increase in toughness. The thin oak leaves of May become thick and more difficult to tear by early June (Figure 332). If leaf toughness is a sufficient explanation for the feeding pattern of oak insects in spring, grinding up the older leaves should provide an adequate diet. But if chemical changes have occurred as well as toughening, ground-up older leaves should still be inadequate as a larval diet. Ground-up leaves seem to be an adequate diet:

Winter moth larvae fed on ground-up leaves from:	Mean peak larval weight (mg)
May 13 ("young" leaves)	37
June 1 ("old" leaves)	35

If mature oak leaves can provide an adequate diet, why was there not selection in favor of insect mouthparts able to cope with tough leaves? Some Lepidoptera do feed on summer oak leaves, so it is possible to feed on tough leaves. If mature oak leaves in summer are relatively poor nutritionally, compared with young spring leaves, this would produce natural selection toward early feeding.

Two chemical changes in oak leaves seem to be significant for feeding insects. The amount of tannins in the leaves increases from spring to fall (especially after July), and the amount of protein decreases from spring to summer and remains low from June onward. Tannins are secondary plant substances that may act to reduce palatability and discourage herbivores. Larval weights of winter moths are significantly reduced if their diet contains as little as 1% oak-leaf tannin. Tannins act by forming complexes with proteins, and may act in oak leaves by tying up proteins in complexes that insects cannot digest and utilize.

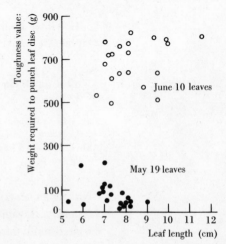

FIGURE 332

Toughness of "young" oak leaves collected May 19 and "old" oak leaves collected June 10. (After Feeny 1970.)

Nevertheless, some insects have evolved ways of minimizing the effect of tannins. Insects that feed on oak leaves in the summer and fall tend to grow very slowly, which may be an adaptation to a low-nitrogen diet. Table 36 shows that many of the late-feeding insects on oak overwinter as larvae and complete their development on the spring leaves. Many others are leaf miners, which may avoid tannins by feeding on leaf parts that contain little tannin.

TABLE 36

Larval feeding habits of early-feeding and late-feeding Lepidoptera species on leaves of the common oak in Britain[a]

	Percentage of:	
Feeding habit	Early-feeding species[b]	Late-feeding species[c]
Larvae complete growth on oak leaves in one season	92	42
Larvae complete growth on low herbs after initial feeding on oak leaves	3	11
Larvae overwinter and complete growth in following year	4	38
Larvae bore into leaf parenchyma (leaf miners)	3	26

[a] Early-feeding larvae are in May and June. Some species exhibit more than one of the feeding habits, so the columns do not add to 100%.
[b] Total of 111 species.
[c] Total of 90 species.
SOURCE: After Feeny (1970).

Thus the oak tree has defended itself against herbivores by the use of tannins as chemical defenses and by leaf texture (toughness) as structural defense. Herbivores have compensated by concentrating feeding in the early spring on young leaves and by altering life cycles in summer and fall.

Ants and acacias A mutualistic system of defense has been achieved by the swollen-thorn acacias and their ant inhabitants in the New World tropics. The ants depend on the acacia tree for food and a place to live, and the acacia depends on the ants for protection from herbivores and neighboring plants. Not all acacias (*Acacia* spp.), approximately 700 species, depend on ants in the New World tropics and not all the acacia ants (*Pseudomyrmex* spp.), 150 species or more, depend completely on acacia. In a few cases a high degree of mutualism has developed, described in detail by Janzen (1966).

Swollen-thorn acacias have large, hollow thorns in which the ants live (Figure 333). The ants feed on modified leaflet tips of the acacia, called Beltian bodies, which are the primary source of protein and oil for the ants, and also on enlarged nectaries, which supply sugars. Swollen-thorn acacias maintain year-round leaf production, even in the dry season, to provide food for the ants. If ants are removed from swollen-thorn acacias, the trees are quickly destroyed by herbivores and crowded out by other plants. Janzen (1966) showed that acacias without ants grew less and were often killed:

	Acacias with ants removed	Acacias with ants present
Survival rate over 10 months (%)	*43*	*72*
Growth increment		
May 25–June 16 (cm)	*6.2*	*31.0*
June 16–August 3 (cm)	*10.2*	*72.9*

Swollen-thorn acacias have apparently lost (or never had) the chemical defenses against herbivores found in other trees in the tropics.

The acacia ants continually patrol the leaves and branches of the acacia tree and immediately attack any herbivore that attempts to eat acacia leaves or bark. The ants also bite and sting any foreign vegetation that touches an acacia, and they clear all the vegetation from the ground beneath the acacia tree. Thus the swollen-thorn acacia often grows in a cylinder of space virtually free of all foreign vegetation (Figure 333). Some of the species of ants that inhabit acacia thorns are obligate acacia ants and cannot live elsewhere.

The ant–acacia system is thus a model system of the coevolution of two species in an association of mutual benefit. The ants reduce herbivore destruction and competition from adjacent plants and thus serve as a living defense mechanism.

CLUTCH SIZE IN BIRDS

Pigeons lay one or two eggs, gulls typically lay 3 eggs, the Canada goose 4 to 6 eggs, and the American merganser 10 or 11 eggs. What determines clutch size in birds? We must distinguish two different aspects of this question. The *proximate factors* that determine clutch size are those physiological factors controlling ovulation and the environmental factors that modify

(a)

(b)

FIGURE 333

(a) Acacia collinsii *growing in open pasture in Nicaragua. This tree had a colony of about 15,000 worker ants and was about 4 m tall.* (b) *Area cleared over past 10 years around a growing* Acacia collinsii *in Panama by ants chewing on all vegetation except the acacia. Machete in photo is 20 in. long. The area was not disturbed by other animals.* (c) *Swollen thorns of* Acacia cornigera *on a lateral branch. Each thorn is occupied by 20–40 immature ants and 10–15 worker ants. All the thorns on the tree are occupied by one colony. An ant entrance hole is visible in the left tip of the fourth thorn up from the bottom. (Photos courtesy of D. H. Janzen)*

(c)

egg laying. Clutch size may be modified by the age of the female, spring weather, population density, and habitat suitability. The *ultimate factors* that determine clutch size are the requirements for long-term (evolutionary) survival. Clutch size is viewed as an adaptation under the control of natural selection, and we seek the selective forces that have shaped the reproductive rates of birds. We shall not be concerned here with the proximate factors determining clutch size, which are reviewed by Klomp (1970).

Natural selection will favor those birds which leave the most descendants to future generations. At first thought we might hypothesize that natural selection might favor a clutch size which is the physiological limit the bird can lay. We can test this hypothesis by taking eggs from nests as they are laid. When we do this we find that some birds, such as the common pigeon, are *determinate layers*; they lay a given number of eggs no matter what. The pigeon lays two eggs; if you take away the first, it will incubate the second egg only. If you add a third egg, it will incubate three. But many other birds are *indeterminate layers*; they will continue to lay eggs until the nest is "full." If eggs are removed as they are laid, these birds will continue laying. This subterfuge has been played on a mallard female, which continued to lay eggs until she had laid 100 of them. In other experiments herring gull females laid up to 16 eggs, a yellow-shafted flicker female 71 eggs, and a house sparrow 50 eggs (Klomp 1970). This evidence suggests that most birds do not lay their physiological limit of eggs, but that ovulation is stopped long before this limit is reached.

The next hypothesis we might suggest is that the clutch size of birds is limited by the maximum number of eggs a bird can cover with its brood-patch. This may be the case for a few birds that lay many eggs. But in many cases the brooding capacity can be shown experimentally to be larger than the actual clutch size. For example, the partridge in England typically lays 15 eggs, but up to 20 eggs can be successfully hatched (Jenkins 1961). The gannet lays one egg but will incubate two eggs successfully if one is added (Nelson 1964). Clutch size in most birds is probably not limited by brooding capacity.

No organism has an infinite amount of energy to spend on its activities. The reproductive rate of birds can be viewed as one sector of a bird's energy balance, and the needs of reproduction must be maximized within the constraints of other energy requirements. The total requirements involve metabolic maintenance, growth, and energy used for predator avoidance, competitive interactions, and reproduction. In 1947 David Lack suggested that the clutch size of birds that feed their young in the nest was adapted by natural selection to correspond to the largest number of young for which the parents can provide enough food. This has been a very fertile hypothesis in evolutionary ecology because it has stimulated a variety of experiments. According to Lack's hypothesis, if additional eggs are placed in a bird's nest, the whole brood will suffer from starvation, so that, in fact, fewer young birds will fly from nests with larger numbers of eggs. Let us look at a few examples to test this idea.

In England the swift normally lays a clutch of two or three eggs. What would happen if swifts had a brood of four? Perrins (1964) artificially created broods of four by adding a chick at hatching and found that the survival of the young swifts in broods of four was poor (Figure 334). Swifts feed on airborne insects and apparently cannot feed four young adequately, so the young starve. Consequently, it would not pay a swift in the evolutionary sense to lay four eggs, and the results agree with Lack's hypothesis.

On Mandarte Island, British Columbia, the glaucous-winged gull normally lays a clutch of two or (usually) three eggs. Vermeer (1963) added eggs and chicks to nests to increase brood size artificially to four, five, and six "supernormal" broods. Figure 335 shows that the number of young fledged per nest increased with larger brood size, contrary to what Lack's hypothesis predicts. Clearly, glaucous-winged gulls could produce more young than they typically do. What might cause this? Lack (1966, p. 247) suggests that these gulls are now in the midst of a large food excess because they feed on garbage dumps. Hence the results of Figure 335 may be atypical.

FIGURE 334

*Production of young swifts (*Apus apus*) in relation to brood size in England. The normal clutch size is two to three, and broods were increased to four artificially. Note that the production of flying young peaks, so larger broods do not necessarily produce more young. (After Perrins 1964.)*

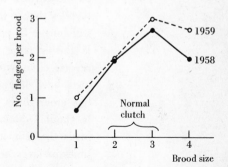

FIGURE 335

Production of young glaucous-winged gulls in relation to brood size, Mandarte Island, British Columbia. The normal clutch size is two or three, and broods were increased up to six artificially. The production of young continues to rise in "supernormal" broods, contrary to Lack's hypothesis. (After Vermeer 1963.)

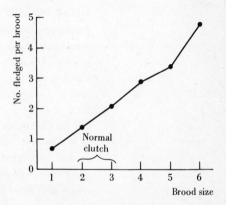

One way to see if Lack's explanation is correct for the glaucous-winged gull is to study gull colonies that are in undisturbed areas far from garbage dumps. Drent and Ward (personal communication) repeated the study both on Mandarte Island (garbage gulls) and on Cleland Island off the west coast of Vancouver Island, where gulls feed only on fish from the sea. Figure 336 shows that on both islands parents were able to raise more chicks than the normal three. The next line of defense for Lack's hypothesis is to say that even though more young were raised, the young from supernormal broods of four, five, and six would suffer high mortality as juveniles. This seems to be true for the garbage gulls of Mandarte Island; 39% of the normal brood juveniles were seen alive in their first winter of life in 1969–1970, but only 15% of the supernormal brood juveniles were seen alive. This was expected because on Mandarte Island the supernormal broods have poor growth rates and fledge at low weights compared with normal broods. On Cleland Island, however, supernormal broods grow no less well than normal broods, and one would predict equal juvenile survival. Thus the glaucous-winged gulls of Cleland Island seem to be clearly a contrary instance to Lack's hypothesis.

Other lines of evidence suggest that Lack's hypothesis is inadequate. Clutch size increases from the tropics to temperate and polar areas. Figure 337 illustrates this trend for three groups of birds. Lack argues that this increase is explicable because daylength is longer in temperate regions (and still longer in polar areas), so parents have more time to feed their young. If this argument is correct, nocturnal birds such as owls should have a reverse cline with larger clutches nearer the equator. But this is not so, and owls have larger clutches in temperate areas than in tropical areas, just like other birds. In temperate Europe during the breeding season daylength is about 1½ times that in the tropics (12 to 18 hours), but in passerine birds the temperate species in Europe have clutches that average 2 to 2.5 times as large as their tropical relatives. This suggests that the trends shown

FIGURE 336

Production of young glaucous-winged gulls in relation to brood size on Mandarte Island (M) off the east coast of Vancouver Island and on Cleland Island (C) off the west coast of Vancouver Island, British Columbia. Normal brood size is two or three. Mandarte gulls can feed at garbage dumps, but Cleland gulls must feed at sea. (After Drent and Ward, personal communication.)

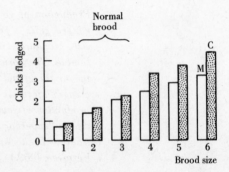

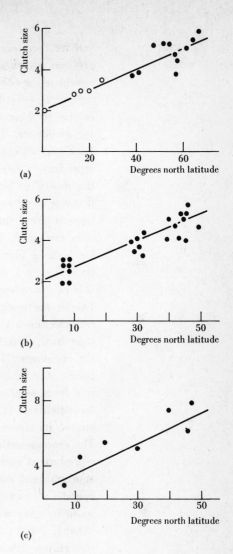

FIGURE 337

Trends in clutch size in the Northern Hemisphere: (a) in the genus Emberiza *(buntings) in Africa (open circles) and Eurasia (closed circles), (b) in the species of the family* Icteridae *in North America, (c) in the genus* Oxyura *(stiff-tailed ducks) in Europe and America. (After Cody 1966.)*

in Figure 337 are not solely a function of change in daylength (von Haartman 1954).

Tropical birds usually lay small clutches, and Skutch (1967) argued that this was an adaptation against nest predators. If the intensity of nest predation increases with the number of parental feeding visits to the nest, natural selection would favor a reduced clutch size. Relatively little work has been done with tropical birds to test this suggestion.

Temperature regulation is an important component of the development of young birds and may have a bearing on clutch size. Small broods will not have the added warmth of the huddling that occurs in large broods, and consequently much energy may be used by nestlings in small broods just for thermoregulation (Royama 1969). In very large broods the opposite problem, overheating, may occur. Thermoregulation is thus another component of reproduction that may place some restraint on clutch size.

Natural selection would seem to operate to maximize reproductive rate, subject to the constraints imposed by thermoregulation, feeding, and predator avoidance. This is called the *theory of maximum reproduction* and Lack's hypothesis is part of this theory. An alternative view suggests that reproductive rates need not be maximal, and this hypothesis can be called the *theory of adjusted reproduction* (Skutch 1967). This theory suggests that the reproductive rate is determined by the annual mortality rate. In tropical areas the annual loss of birds is relatively low, and hence clutch sizes are small. In arctic areas which support migratory birds the annual loss will be high, and hence clutch size must be high or the species would become extinct. Reproductive rate need not be maximal under this hypothesis.

How can a species evolve a lower reproductive rate than the maximum? This is the critical unanswered question. Critics of the theory of adjusted reproduction argue that natural selection cannot operate to produce a lower reproductive rate, a rate below the limits set by feeding ability and predator avoidance. Wynne-Edwards (1962) has suggested that group selection is one way of achieving this kind of evolutionary change. Group selection is a form of selection operating on whole groups of organisms rather than on individuals (Lewontin 1965b), but most evolutionary biologists are dubious of its significance in nature (Williams 1966, Maynard Smith 1964). The group-selection argument is that *populations* of a species which do not reproduce at maximal rates and consequently do not exploit the food supply at a maximal rate will be at an advantage over local populations that do operate at maximal rates. This argument is reasonable but needs to be tested in many more cases (see Figure 336), especially among tropical birds (Skutch 1967).

A major difficulty of the work done to date on the clutch-size problem is that all the information available covers one part (*) of the life cycle:

adults → clutch size $\overset{*}{\to}$ fledged young → breeding adults

The critical variable is the breeding adults that emerge from a given size of clutch, and this is missing from most studies because the fledged young ⟶ adult stage cannot be easily studied. We must assume that more fledged young = more breeding adults for the studies reported, and this may not be correct. A second problem is the genetic basis of clutch-size differences, on which little information is available. If clutch size is variable only because of environmental influences, the studies reported here are less meaningful. If clutch size is variable in part because of genetic variation, we can reasonably ask whether adults of different "clutch-size genotypes" give rise to equal numbers of adults in the next generation.

The long-billed marsh wren population near Seattle, Washington, contains about 30% polygamous males and 70% monogamous males. The same species in eastern Washington divides 50:50, and in the salt marshes of coastal Georgia 3% of the males are polygynous and 97% monogamous (Verner 1964). Why should this variation occur within a single species? What evolutionary factors determine the mating systems of birds and mammals?

Four types of mating systems can be defined:

1 *Monogamous*: a pair bond between one male and one female

2 *Polygynous*: a male simultaneously maintains more than one pair bond with females

3 *Polyandrous*: a female simultaneously maintains more than one pair bond with males

4 *Promiscuous*: no lasting pair bond, multiple copulations of one sex or both

Sexual selection operates because the acceptance of one mate precludes the acceptance of another in many cases. This is true in all monogamous systems and true for females in polygynous situations. In birds and mammals the female puts much more effort into reproduction than does the male. Males produce large numbers of gametes while females produce small numbers of gametes with greater energy cost. Thus a male should always try to mate with numerous females because the more mating he does, the more offspring he should leave. But females must be more discriminating. Natural selection penalizes females much more than males for mistakes in reproduction. A female that mates with a sterile male may lose a whole breeding season's reproductive effort. Thus *sexual selection and mating systems in birds and mammals are largely a product of female choice* (Orians 1969b).

Female choice of mates can be made on the basis of male size, shape, color, and behavior, and this has led to many forms of sexual selection. But females can also choose on the basis of the male's property, if the species defends spatial territories. Let us discuss the territorial case to illustrate the problem.

A female entering an area will choose a mate with the best possible habitat for rearing her young. As the habitat begins to fill with females, each new female must decide whether she would do better by being monogamous and mating with an unmated male on the periphery in poorer habitat, or would do better by being polygynous with a male in the best habitat. If the male helps with the feeding of the young, the polygynous female will be at a relative disadvantage compared with a monogamous female (Verner

1964). This suggests two factors that will determine the balance of the advantages and disadvantages of polygynous mating systems:

1 Variation in suitability among different territories
2 Role of male in affecting reproductive success

Orians (1969b) has suggested seven conclusions from this model for the evolution of mating systems:

1 *Polyandry should be rare among all species.* This follows from the great amount of reproductive effort a female must undertake. A female could probably increase her reproductive output if several males could be induced to care for her offspring. But it would be difficult for a male to maximize his production of offspring in a polyandrous system. This conclusion seems true for birds and mammals. A few polyandrous species, often with sexual-role reversal in birds, are known, but they have not been studied in detail.

2 *Monogamy should be rare in mammals but common in birds.* Since the male can do very little for the young in mammals, there should be little selection for monogamy. This is true for the mammals, where few cases of monogamy have been described. Among birds about 92% of all species are monogamous (Lack 1968).

3 *Polygynous mating systems should be more common in birds that do not feed their young after hatching.* If the young can search for their own food immediately after hatching, the male's role in parental care is reduced. This prediction is not fulfilled in many cases (Orians 1969b). For example, ducks and geese do not feed their young but are almost all monogamous, and the reasons for this mating system are not known. In most ducks the female alone cares for the young.

4 *Polygynous mating should be more common in marsh-nesting species.* Verner and Willson (1966) found that 8 of the 14 polygynous bird species in North America are marsh nesters, and suggest this is due to the great variation in suitability of marsh territories from very poor to very good. A female may leave more progeny by being polygynous with a male in a good territory than by being monogamous with a male in a poor territory.

5 *Polygyny should be more prominent among species inhabiting early stages of succession.* This prediction is based on a presumed variability of sites within an early successional stage, so the arguments of point 4 also apply here. At least 2 of the 14 North American bird species may be polygynous for this reason, but this situation has not been studied (Orians 1969b).

6 *Species that have restricted nesting sites and widespread feeding areas should tend to be polygynous.* If a male holds several nest sites, which are in short supply, it should be advantageous for a female to mate with him rather than accept an inferior site or none at all. Weaverbirds in Africa nest in trees but feed in grasslands and are polygynous in grassland–savannah habitats (where there are few trees) and monogamous in forest habitats (Crook 1964). The northern fur seal is polygynous on its restricted breeding grounds of the Pribilof Islands. However, many sea birds have restricted nesting sites but are monogamous.

7 *Polygyny should be more prevalent among species in which clutch size is strongly affected by factors other than the maximum number of offspring that can be fed by the parents successfully.* In this situation the male is often superfluous.

Thus tropical birds that raise reduced clutches as an adaptation against nest predation should tend to be polygynous. There is little information on this at present.

The analysis of mating systems in birds and mammals is only a small part of the larger problem of social organization in animals. At the present time only general, vague conclusions can be stated rather than rigorous quantitative predictions, and we must be content with after-the-fact analysis rather than prediction. Thus we can provide reasonable explanations for species X having a polygynous mating system after we know that it is polygynous; but we are unable to predict what the mating system of an unstudied species Y will be like. Lack (1968), for example, shows that 93% of the birds that feed their young are monogamous, whereas 83% of the birds that do not have to feed their young after hatching are monogamous. From this we might suspect that the help provided by the male in feeding young is an important advantage of monogamy. This is certainly a reasonable conclusion, but few experiments have been done, and what seems reasonable is not always right. Hypotheses about mating systems have not been fruitful in suggesting experiments, in contrast to hypotheses about clutch-size determination.

EVOLUTION OF LIFE CYCLES

Pacific salmon grow to adult size in the ocean and return to fresh water to spawn once and die. We may call this *big-bang reproduction*. Oak trees may become mature after 10 to 20 years and drop thousands of acorns for 200 years or more. We call this *repeated reproduction*. How have these life cycles evolved? What advantage might be gained by producing salmon that breed more than once? Why do oak trees not drop one set of seeds and die, like annual plants?

The population consequences of life cycles were explored by Cole (1954), who asked a simple question: What effect does repeated reproduction have on the innate capacity for increase (r_m)? Assume that we have an annual species that produces b offspring at the end of the year and then dies. Let us assume a simple survivorship of 0.5 per year and a fertility rate of 20 offspring, so the life table appears as follows:

Age, x	Proportion surviving, l_x	Fertility, m_x	Product, $l_x m_x$
0	1.000	0.0	0.0
1	0.500	20.0	10.0
2	0.0	—	0.0
			$R_0 = 10.0$

The net reproductive rate (R_0) is 10.0, which means that the species could increase tenfold in 1 year. We can determine r_m from the formula (Chapter 10)

$$\sum_0^\infty e^{-r_m x} l_x m_x = 1$$

from which we determine

$$r_m = 2.303$$

for the annual species with big-bang reproduction. What advantage could this species gain by continuing to live and reproduce at years 2, 3, . . . , ∞? Let us assume the most favorable condition, no mortality after age 1 and survival to age 100. The life table now becomes

Age, x	Proportion surviving, l_x	Fertility, m_x	$l_x m_x$
0	1.00	0	0
1	0.50	20.0	10.0
2	0.50	20.0	10.0
3	0.50	20.0	10.0
4	0.50	20.0	10.0
5	0.50	20.0	10.0
.	.	.	.
.	.	.	.
.	.	.	.
99	0.50	20.0	10.0
100	0.00	0.0	0.0

$$R_0 = \sum l_x m_x = 990.0$$

In the manner outlined in Chapter 10, we determine

$$r_m = 2.398$$

for the perennial species with repeated reproduction. Thus we raise the innate capacity for increase only about 4%:

$$\frac{2.398}{2.303} = 1.04$$

if we adopt repeated reproduction in our hypothetical organism.

Now let us work backward. What fertility rate at 1 year would equal the r_m of the perennial (2.398)? We can solve this problem algebraically (Cole

1954) or by trial and error. Increase the birth rate by one individual. The annual life table is now

Age, x	Proportion surviving, l_x	Fertility, m_x	$l_x m_x$
0	1.00	0	0
1	0.50	21.0	10.50
2	0.0	—	0

$$R_0 = 10.50$$

$$\sum_0^2 e^{-r_m x} \, l_x m_x = 1$$

$$r_m = 2.351$$

This is almost the gain achieved by repeated reproduction. If we increase the fertility rate by two individuals, we get $r_m = 2.398$, equal to the r_m for the perennial. This is obviously an ideal case, since we assume no mortality after age 1 in the perennial form. Cole (1954) generalized this ideal case to a surprising conclusion: *For an annual species, the maximum gain in the innate capacity for increase (r_m) which could be achieved by changing to the perennial reproductive habit would be equivalent to adding one individual to the effective litter size ($l_x m_x$ for age 1).* Cole assumed for his ideal case perfect survival to reproductive age. In our hypothetical example we assumed that half of the organisms would die before reaching reproductive age.

Why, then, do species bother to have repeated reproduction? The answer seems to be that repeated reproduction is an adaptation to something other than achieving maximum r_m. Repeated reproduction may be an evolutionary response to uncertain survival from zygote to adult stages (Murphy 1968). The greater the uncertainty, the higher the selection for a longer reproductive life. This may involve channeling more energy into growth and maintenance and less into reproduction. We can thus recognize a simple scheme of possibilities:

	Long life-span	Short life-span
Steady reproductive success	?	*Possible*
Variable reproductive success	*Possible*	*Not possible*

Murphy (1968) analyzed data from marine fishes that support this idea, and Figure 338 shows that species with great variations in reproductive success are long lived.

FIGURE 338

Relationship between reproductive uncertainty and reproductive lifespan in schooling, plankton-feeding marine fishes (herrings, sardines, and anchovy). Variation in spawning success is measured by highest/lowest spawning. (After Murphy 1968.)

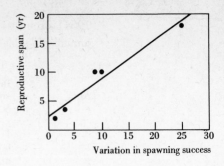

The problem of life-history strategy may be viewed as that of optimum allocation of an organism's energy among growth, maintenance, and reproduction (Gadgil and Bossert 1970). In evolutionary terms an organism will devote energy to growth and maintenance only if this increases its reproductive contribution to future generations. Growth is important in many species because fecundity increases with size, and competition for territories may favor larger males. We can construct a simple model to describe the allocation of energy.

We begin with the idea of *reproductive effort* at each age of a species lifespan. This effort may be measured by the fraction of time and energy at a given age that is devoted to reproduction. Reproductive effort thus is measured on a scale of 0 to 1. A spawning salmon has a reproductive effort of 1 because it expends all its energy in the spawning run and then dies. Immature salmon living in the ocean, by contrast, devote no energy to reproduction (reproductive effort = 0).

Reproductive effort at any given age can be associated with a biological *cost* and a biological *profit*. The biological cost derives from the reduction in growth or survival which occurs as a consequence of using energy to reproduce. For example, as much as 50% of the production of the perch (*Perca fluviatilis*) is used for reproduction (LeCren 1962). Spawning in barnacles reduces growth (Barnes 1962). Adult female carabid beetles survive better in years of little reproduction and worse in years of intensive reproduction (Murdoch 1966b). The biological profit is measured in the number of descendants left to future generations, which will be affected by the survival rate and the growth rate. The hypothetical organism must ask at each age: *Should I reproduce this year or would I profit more by waiting until next year?* Obviously if the mortality rate is high, it would be best to reproduce as soon as possible. But if mortality is low, it may pay an organism to put its energy into growth and wait until the next year to reproduce.

If we could determine the profit and cost for any amount of reproductive effort, we could predict the type of life cycle that should evolve (Gadgil and Bossert 1970). If we subtract the cost from the profit, we can determine the biological balance (Figure 339). Big-bang reproduction will occur when this balance is at a maximum only when the reproductive effort = 1. Repeated reproduction will occur when the (profit–cost) balance is maximum at some intermediate range of reproductive effort between 0 and 1. Figure 339 gives some illustrations.

Big-bang reproducers can operate only at reproductive efforts of 0 or 1, and the problem of optimum strategy for this kind of organism is to determine the best age for reproduction. This will be fixed by the growth rate of the species and the mortality schedule in relation to the number of offspring that could be produced at each age.

Repeated reproducers must decide in an evolutionary sense to increase, decrease, or hold constant their reproductive effort with age. In every case analyzed so far reproductive effort increases with age (Williams 1966, Gadgil and Bossert 1970), and this may be a general evolutionary trend in organisms.

Another way of describing the evolution of life cycles takes us back to the logistic curve (Chapter 11). In some environments organisms exist near the asymptotic density (K) for much of the year, and these organisms are subject to K selection. In other habitats organisms rarely approach the asymptotic density, but remain on the rising sector of the curve for most of the year; these organisms are subjected to r selection (MacArthur and Wilson 1967). The simplest illustration of these two extremes might be organisms in tropical (K selection) versus polar environments (r selection). All organisms reach some sort of compromise between these two extremes, and

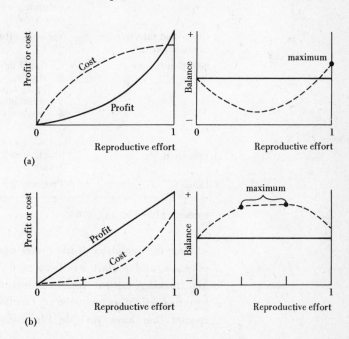

FIGURE 339

Hypothetical illustration of the evolution of life cycles: (a) big-bang reproduction, (b) repeated reproduction. A biological cost and a biological profit can be determined for every level of reproductive effort from 0 (no energy devoted to reproduction) to 1 (all energy devoted to reproduction). The balance (profit minus cost) will fix the reproductive strategy of the organism. Only two hypothetical patterns are shown here; many others could be postulated. (After Gadgil and Bossert 1970.)

we recognize these as the ends of a continuum. Some of the attributes of K and r selection are listed in Table 37. Pianka (1970) suggests that we can recognize whole groups, such as the terrestrial vertebrates, as being K selected, and other groups, such as the insects, as being r selected. Because of the repeatability of environmental changes on an annual basis the critical breakpoint may be when the generation time exceeds 1 year. Perennial organisms must suffer a shift toward K selection, and annual species are dominated by r selection.

TABLE 37

Some of the correlates of r and K selection

	r selection	*K* selection
Climate	Variable and/or unpredictable; uncertain	Fairly constant and/or predictable; more certain
Mortality	Often catastrophic, nondirected, density independent	More directed, density dependent
Survivorship	Often type III (see Figure 69)	Usually types I and II (see Figure 69)
Population size	Variable in time, nonequilibrium; usually well below carrying capacity of environment; unsaturated communities or portions thereof; ecologic vacuums; recolonization each year	Fairly constant in time, equilibrium; at or near carrying capacity of the environment; saturated communities; no recolonization necessary
Intra- and interspecific competition	Variable, often lax	Usually keen
Selection favors	*1* Rapid development *2* High r_m *3* Early reproduction *4* Small body size *5* Single reproduction	*1* Slower development *2* Greater competitive ability *3* Delayed reproduction *4* Larger body size *5* Repeated reproductions
Length of life	Short, usually less than 1 year	Longer, usually more than 1 year
Leads to	Productivity	Efficiency

SOURCE: After Pianka (1970).

Thus the evolution of life cycles can be discussed qualitatively in a variety of ways, and a start has been made in suggesting quantitative predictions and making critical measurements on the cost of reproduction. Further progress might come from a careful analysis of life-cycle adaptations in species that have variable life cycles. General comparisons are available for some plants that have annual and perennial races (Stebbins 1965). The problem of the evolution of the life cycle thus leads us into the general problem of the characteristics of "successful" and "unsuccessful" species (Baker 1965, Carson 1965) and links together ecology and evolution.

SUMMARY

Evolutionary ecology is concerned with the adaptations that affect distribution and abundance of plants and animals. We discuss only four examples for illustration; many others could be included but are not.

Plants have evolved a variety of defense mechanisms which render them less susceptible to herbivore injury. Some chemical defense mechanisms utilize secondary plant substances, and herbivores respond by evolutionary adjustments that attempt to circumvent the plant's defenses. This game of coevolution can lead to elaborate, specialized adaptations.

Clutch size in birds is a model system for analyzing the evolution of reproductive rates. The theory of maximum reproduction states that birds reproduce at rates that are maximal in relation to the parent's ability to take care of the feeding, protection, and sheltering of their young. The theory of adjusted reproduction suggests that birds can evolve reproductive rates lower than the maximal rates. Most of the evidence covers only the nestling stages, and whether clutches larger than average would produce more subsequent breeding adults is not known for any species.

Mating systems in birds and mammals may be monogamous, polygynous, polyandrous, and promiscuous. Most mammals are polygynous but most birds are monogamous. Female choice seems to dictate the type of mating system, and some general conclusions can be derived about conditions under which one would expect different mating systems.

The evolution of life cycles can be approached quantitatively by asking what advantages accrue to single, big-bang reproduction versus repeated reproduction. The innate capacity for increase is increased relatively little by repeated reproduction, and species evolve repeated reproduction as a response to uncertain survival during the juvenile stages. The problem of the evolution of life cycles leads to the general evolutionary problem of what makes for a "successful" species.

SELECTED REFERENCES

BIRCH, L. C., and P. R. EHRLICH. 1967. Evolutionary history and population biology. *Nature* 214:349–352.

KLOMP, H. 1970. The determination of clutch-size in birds. A review. *Ardea* 58: 1–124.

LACK, D. 1965. Evolutionary ecology. *J. Anim. Ecol.* 34:223–231.

MURPHY, G. I. 1968. Pattern in life history and the environment. *Amer. Naturalist* 102:391–403.

ORIANS, G. H. 1969. On the evolution of mating systems in birds and mammals. *Amer. Naturalist* 103:589–603.

SKUTCH, A. F. 1967. Adaptive limitation of the reproductive rate of birds. *Ibis* 109: 579–599.

WHITTAKER, R. H., and P. P. FEENY. 1971. Allelochemics: chemical interactions between species. *Science* 171:757–770.

QUESTIONS AND
PROBLEMS

1 Birds living on oceanic islands tend to have a smaller clutch size than the same species (or close relatives) breeding on the mainland (Klomp 1970, p. 85). Explain this on the basis of Lack's hypothesis and then explain it on the basis of the hypothesis of adjusted reproduction. How could you decide which was correct?

2 In discussing plant species diversity, Whittaker (1969, p. 190) states:

I conclude that species diversity of plant communities is an evolutionary product, subject to self-augmentation through time. There is no ceiling or saturation level for the diversity which results; the chemical differentiation of the higher plants implies virtually unlimited potentialities for the addition of different species with different interactions with predators and seedling soil requirements. It is thus that plants and insects may differ from birds. The niche responses of birds are not to chemistry but to community structure and broad food categories, in which possibilities of niche division are limited. Bird communities can thus be saturated, determinate in their evolution of diversity; but plant and insect communities may show indefinite, indeterminate evolutionary increase in diversity.

Plant chemical interactions are reviewed by Whittaker and Feeny (1971, p. 757). Discuss and evaluate the evidence that is important to Whittaker's conclusions.

3 In a discussion of the relationship between ecology and evolution, Birch and Ehrlich (1967, p. 350) state:

When an ecologist investigates a species he may ask: given the existing characteristics of the species... what determines the distribution and numbers of the species in the world? In order to answer that question we do not need to know how the species evolved its particular characteristics. The phylogenetic question is interesting in itself but it is not relevant to the investigation of the question of distribution and abundance. How the species acquired its present adaptive characteristics is a second and independent question.

Do you agree? Discuss.

4 Perrins and Wynne-Edwards (1964, p. 1147) take the very same data on clutch size and fledging rates in the swift (Figure 334) and come to opposite conclusions with respect to whether the data support the theory of maximum reproduction or not. Read their analyses and discuss the controversy.

5 Marijuana is a secondary plant substance (a terpene) produced by *Cannabis sativa* (Hollister 1971, p. 21). From information available in the literature write an essay on the biological role of marijuana in this plant.

6 In discussing the evolution of reproductive rates, Skutch (1967, p. 598) states:

The general evolutionary trend in the Metazoa is toward producing fewer offspring and taking better care of them. This would hardly be possible if the more prolific genotype always prevails over those which raise smaller families and in consequence can attend their young somewhat better.

Discuss.

7 Royama (1969, p. 562) gives the following data for the European robin from different countries from North Africa to Scandinavia:

North latitude	Average brood size	Mean temp. in May (°C)	Daylength on May 21 (hr)
28°	3.6	19.4	13.58
36°	4.2	18.0	14.17
38°	4.7	—	14.33
40°	4.9	14.5	14.50
52°	5.1	11.9	15.92
57°	5.5	9.6	16.75
48°	5.6	12.9	15.33
51°	5.8	12.6	15.75
47°	5.9	10.9	15.17
52°	5.9	11.2	15.92
47°	5.9	13.9	15.17
50°	6.0	13.2	15.58
61°	6.3	7.6	17.83
62°	6.3	7.8	17.83

Plot the average brood size against (1) latitude, (2) temperature, and (3) daylength. Which relationship is closest?

8 Royama (1970, pp. 641–642) states:

Natural selection favors those individuals in a population with the most efficient reproductive capacity (in terms of the number of offspring contributed to the next generation), which means that the present-day generations consist of those individuals with the highest level of reproduction possible in their environment.

Is this correct? Discuss.

PART FIVE

HUMAN ECOLOGY

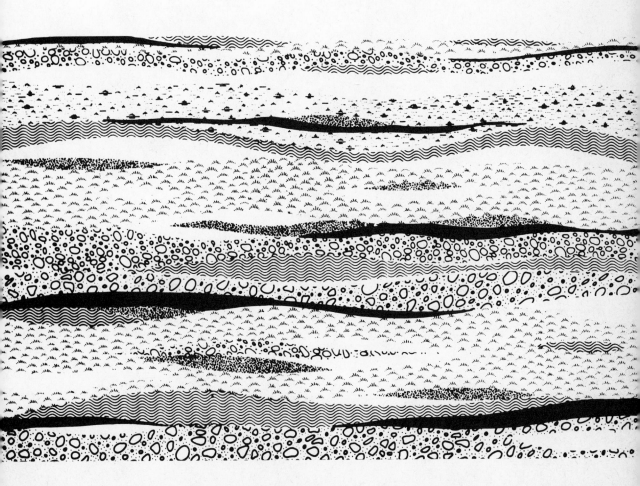

26   *Human population*

The human population problem with all its complex ramifications is the most important and most serious of all the problems confronting man. The increasing human population and its attendant problems of pollution begin as biological problems, but quickly become enmeshed in economic questions, social issues, and moral and religious evaluations. There is an increasing flood of books specifically on these problems, and I shall discuss here only a few of the more ecological aspects of the population problem.

WORLD POPULATION

Paradoxically, the size of the world population is not known accurately. Before 1650 only rough estimates are available, and even today the *Demographic Yearbook of the United Nations* warns us that all their population data are subject to a substantial margin of error. The population of the world in 1971 was about 3.7 billion people. Figure 340 shows that for almost all of the first million years of man's existence there were less than 0.5 billion people on earth. Since A.D. 1650 the human population has doubled, redoubled, and almost redoubled again in an ever-quickening pace. The human population seems to have responded to three revolutions by increas-

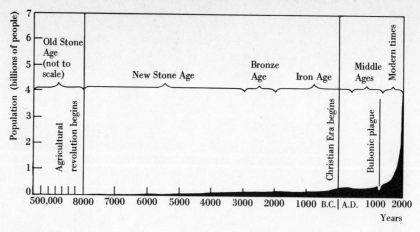

FIGURE 340

*Growth of human numbers for the past 0.5 million years. If the Old
Stone Age were in scale, its base line would extend about 18 ft to
the left. (After* Population Bulletin, *Vol. 18, No. 1.)*

ing in size. The *cultural revolution* was a long-term evolution of early man
in small groups, which began to accumulate a culture. This revolution set
man apart from other animals in the transmission of information by social
means. The *agricultural revolution* began around 9000 B.C. and changed
man from hunting and gathering to farming. This made larger settlements
possible and caused a period of population growth. The *industrial revolution*
began around 1750 in Europe and later in other countries. It resulted in an
increased standard of living, and this was further augmented by the advent
of modern medicine.

The world population has been increasing, as Figure 340 shows, but the
most disturbing aspect of this is that it is *increasing at an increasing rate.*
The estimates of rates of increase for the world are as follows:

Time period (yr)	Finite rate of increase (%/yr)	Doubling time (yr)
1,000,000–8000 B.C.	*0.002*	*34,658*
8000 B.C.–A.D. *0*	*0.012*	*5,545*
A.D. *0–1650*	*0.04*	*1,650*
1650–1750	*0.3*	*231*
1750–1850	*0.5*	*139*
1850–1910	*0.6*	*116*
1910–1950	*1.0*	*70*
1950–1960	*1.7*	*41*
1960–1970	*1.9*	*37*
1970	*2.0*	*35*

In order to understand why the population has increased in such a pattern, we cannot analyze the world as a unit but must look at separate sub-

populations. Table 38 gives the most recent data for different continents. The highest rates of population growth are found in Africa, Central and South America, and South Asia. The lowest rates of population growth are found among the industrialized nations of western Europe.

TABLE 38

Estimates of total human population (1969), annual rate of population increase (% per year, 1963–1969), birth rate per thousand, death rate per thousand, and density (persons per square kilometer of area, 1969) for different continents and regions of the earth

Area	Midyear population (millions)	Annual rate of increase (%)	Birth rate	Death rate	Density
Africa	345	2.5	45	21	11
North America	224	1.2	19	9	10
Central and South America	276	2.9	40	11	13
East Asia (including Japan and China)	901	1.5	32	17	77
U.S.S.R.	240	1.1	19	7	11
South Asia (including India)	1087	2.6	41	15	69
Europe	460	0.8	18	10	93
Oceania[a]	18.9	2.0	25	10	2

[a] Australia, New Zealand, Melanesia, Polynesia, and Micronesia.
SOURCE: After *Demographic Yearbook of the United Nations* 1969.

Within each continent there are further variations in population parameters. A few individual countries can be paired to illustrate different rates of population increase:

	1969 population	Rate of increase (%/yr)	Density per square kilometer
Algeria	*13,349,000*	*3.0*	*6*
Angola	*5,430,000*	*1.3*	*4*
Mexico	*48,933,000*	*3.5*	*25*
United States	*203,216,000*	*1.2*	*22*
Argentina	*23,983,000*	*1.5*	*9*
Ecuador	*5,890,000*	*3.4*	*21*
China	*740,000,000*	*1.4*	*77*
India	*536,984,000*	*2.5*	*164*
Western Germany	*58,707,000*	*1.0*	*237*
Eastern Germany	*16,010,000*	*−0.1*	*149*

Except for a few countries of Europe, there are no nations in which the population is declining. The geometric growth pattern of human population is completely exceptional in the ecological world and cannot continue for very long.

One of the difficulties of thinking about the world population is the immense size of the numbers we must deal with. In 1970 the world population grew by about 2%, and gained nearly 73 million people. This is a gain of 200,000 people per day, or 8333 per hour. If it continues growing at the present rate, the world population will reach 4 billion by 1975, 5 billion by 1986, and 6 billion by 1995.

DEMOGRAPHIC TRANSITION

The industrial nations of western Europe have passed through a series of demographic changes that have been described as the *demographic transition*. About 150 years ago countries like Sweden and England had high birth rates and high death rates. Obviously this is one possible stable con-

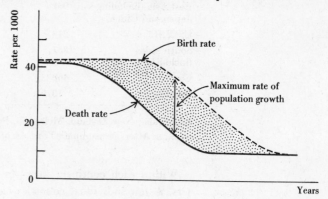

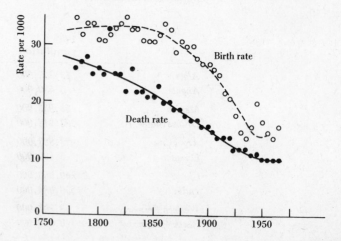

FIGURE 341

Theoretical demographic transition from high birth and death rates to low rates, and data for Sweden, 1778–1967. (After Keyfitz and Flieger 1968.)

figuration, and a population could reach a plateau with this configuration. But about 1800 the death rate began falling slowly from high values (about 40 per 1000 per year) to low values (approximately 10 per thousand per year). The birth rate remained high until about 1850 and then began a slow fall from 40 to 50 per thousand down to 10 to 20 per thousand in 1950. This sequence of changes is shown in Figure 341 and is illustrated with data from Sweden. The maximum rate of population growth occurs near the middle of the transition. The demographic transition leads to increased population size, no matter how quickly or slowly it is achieved. This is an important point to note for countries that have not yet achieved the transition: *The change from a high birth rate–high death rate demographic configuration to a low birth rate–low death rate configuration must lead to substantial increase in population size, if the death rate is decreased first.*

The demographic transition has not occurred in all countries. Figure 342 shows the changes in birth and death rates in Chile (increasing at 2.4% per year in 1969) and Costa Rica (3.4% per year), two underdeveloped countries. There are two things to note about these countries. First, the death rate has fallen very rapidly over a period of 25 to 50 years. In Sweden by contrast, the death rate fell slowly over 150 to 200 years. Consequently, the demographic transition of the death rate has been much more rapid in the underdeveloped countries. Second, birth rates have remained high,

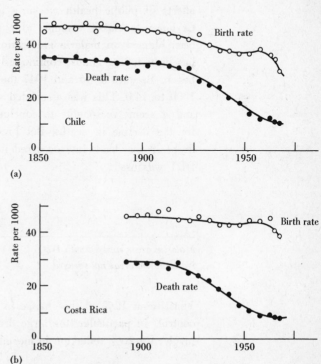

FIGURE 342

Changes in birth and death rates in two of the underdeveloped countries: (a) Chile, (b) Costa Rica. (After Collver 1965 and Demographic Yearbook of the United Nations.)

with only the slightest hint of falling off in the late 1960s. In Sweden the fall in birth rate from high to low values took place over 100 years. In the underdeveloped countries the birth rate must fall much more rapidly from high to low values if it is to mimic the rapid drop in the death rate.

The demographic transition is a descriptive concept and not a "law of nature," and it is important to inquire why the death rate has fallen and why in some countries the birth rate also falls to low levels. What determines the birth and death rates in human populations? We would think that the answer to this question would be well known, since man has been studied so much relative to other animals and plants, but no one knows the answer to this simple question.

Premedical students might like to think that modern medicine has been a major factor in reducing the death rate. This reasonable idea does not entirely agree with the historical record. The European population began to increase rapidly about 1750, long before modern medicine (Dubos 1965). The population of China began to increase about the same time, from 150 million in 1750 to 300 million in 1850 to 600 million in 1950. The role of modern medicine in determining death rates may be rather less than we would like to think, at least in the long run.

Public health can be cited as another area that may reduce death rates, and the advances in sanitary engineering and disease eradication through pesticides may also contribute to a reduction in death rates. Again, the effects of public health measures are not always clear or straightforward. Ceylon is a classic example of a country whose population explosion has been blamed on malaria eradication with DDT. But the Ceylon death rate has been falling almost continuously since 1905, long before DDT spraying began. Between 1946 and 1947 the death rate in Ceylon fell from 19.8 per 1000 to 14.0. This was associated with a start of malarial control by DDT, and it seems reasonable to conclude that malarial control was responsible for the decline in deaths. But Frederiksen (1970) points out that similar drops in the death rate occurred in nonmalarial areas of Ceylon, where no DDT was used:

	Change in death rate from 1944 to 1954 (%)
Malarial areas sprayed with DDT	*−57*
Nonmalarial areas not sprayed	*−45*

Thus about 12% of the change in death rate can be attributed to malarial control. In particular, the large drop in death rate between 1945 and 1946 involved a 26% reduction in mortality in the sprayed areas and 24% reduction in the nonmalarial areas. The decline in death rates on Ceylon seems to be determined by more general factors associated with nutrition and health services and not by specific agents, such as malaria.

The simplest analysis we can make of the fall in death rates is that it is associated with general economic progress in a population, including nutrition, housing, sanitation, public health measures, and medicine.

Why does the birth rate fall, and what determines birth rates in human societies? This is a critical question because if we wish to accelerate the drop in birth rate in countries like Costa Rica (Figure 342), we need to know what policies to adopt. Unfortunately there seems to be even less agreement about the factors affecting the birth rate than about those affecting the death rate. Social and psychological factors predominate, and I can only make a general statement about these. First, before the birth rate is lowered, one needs to create a genuine desire for smaller numbers of children. There is a fundamental impasse here, because the poorer the community, the more important the role played by children in its daily life. As long as children constitute the only hope of reward and the only source of emotional satisfaction, it will be difficult to reduce the birth rate.

The availability of contraception and of abortion have been put forth as major factors determining the human birth rate, but this may be a case of the cart before the horse. Davis (1967) discusses the case of Taiwan, which has responded favorably to a highly organized campaign of family planning begun in 1963. The birth rate has been falling rapidly on Taiwan, but this decline began about 1951, long before the family-planning program.

Almost none of the developed countries have completed the demographic transition to the point of low birth rates *equal* to low death rates, the state of "zero population growth." The birth rate must fall still further to achieve this. There have been large fluctuations in the birth rates of the developed countries in the last 75 years, and these fluctuations cannot be explained on the basis of available food, knowledge of contraception, or religious beliefs. Population growth cannot be checked by family-planning programs, because these programs assume existing reproductive goals (Davis 1967). The maximum impact of family-planning programs will be the difference between actual family size and desired family size. If desired family size is 3.0 children and zero population growth requires a family size of 2.1 children, *family planning will not achieve population control* (Figure 343). We must somehow motivate people to reduce desired family size to that required for zero population growth. We must move beyond family planning (Berelson 1969).

There is a basic division of opinion on whether the underdeveloped countries can pass through the demographic transition successfully or not. The neo-Malthusian school (the "pessimists") present two economic models for

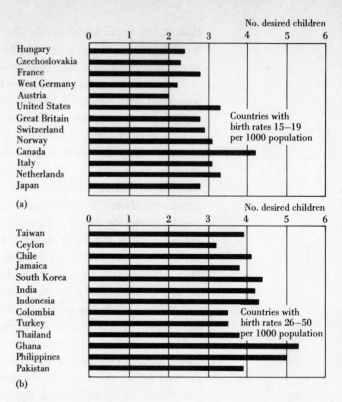

No. desired children

Hungary
Czechoslovakia
France
West Germany
Austria
United States
Great Britain
Switzerland
Norway
Canada
Italy
Netherlands
Japan

Countries with
birth rates 15–19
per 1000 population

(a)

No. desired children

Taiwan
Ceylon
Chile
Jamaica
South Korea
India
Indonesia
Colombia
Turkey
Thailand
Ghana
Philippines
Pakistan

Countries with
birth rates 26–50
per 1000 population

(b)

FIGURE 343

Desired family size in (a) some nations with low birth rates and (b) some countries with high birth rates. (Population Reference Bureau, 1970.)

the demographic transition, which depend on the ability of a society to increase production rapidly enough so that it can accumulate capital (Figure 344). The neo-Malthusians suggest that countries such as Costa Rica cannot achieve a demographic transition because of too rapid a population growth. Countries such as Sweden could achieve a demographic transition because of their slow rate of population growth (Frederiksen 1969).

An alternative model of the demographic transition stresses that a drop in the mortality rate is necessary for the solution to the population problem (Figure 345). A reduction in mortality is viewed as a necessary condition for a subsequent drop in fertility. The critical difference between this model and the neo-Malthusian model is in the relationship between fertility and mortality. The neo-Malthusian model postulates no necessary connection between fertility and mortality rates; the alternative model suggests that low mortality is a necessary cause leading to low fertility rates. The problem thus returns to the question of what determines birth rates in human populations.

Figure 346 summarizes the changes in birth and death rates for the industrialized nations and the underdeveloped countries. The paradoxical fact is that the great increase in the world's population during the past 50 years has coincided with great epidemics, two world wars, several minor wars, and deep disruptions in social and economic life. Population trends have persisted, and the critical aim of the years from 1970 to 2000 must be for countries to complete the demographic transition to a stable configuration of low birth rates that equal low death rates.

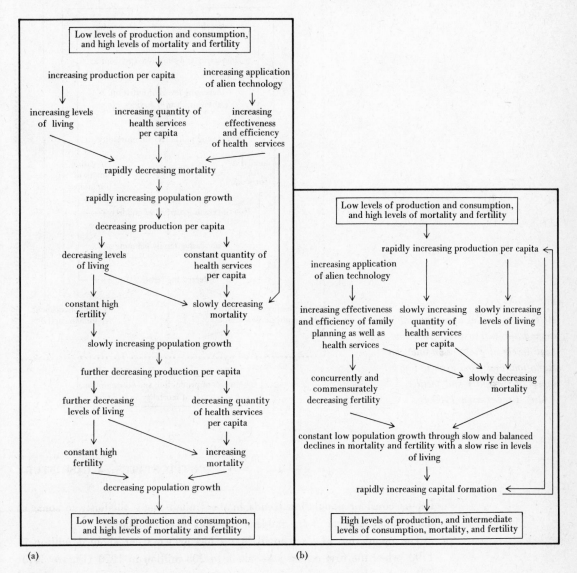

(a)   (b)

FIGURE 344

Neo-Malthusian model of (a) failure of demographic transition and (b) successful demographic transition. Underdeveloped countries supposedly follow the (a) model, industrialized nations the (b) model. (After Frederiksen 1969.)

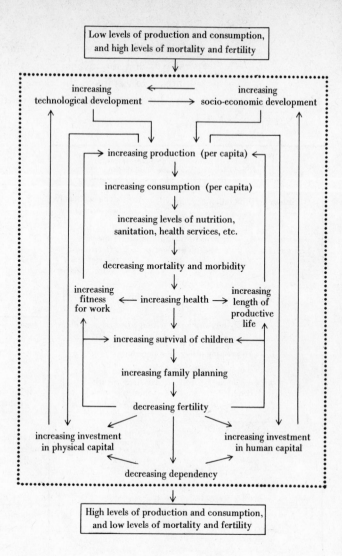

┌───┐
│ Low levels of production and consumption, │
│ and high levels of mortality and fertility │
└───┘

increasing   increasing
technological development ──▶ socio-economic development

increasing production (per capita)

increasing consumption (per capita)

increasing levels of nutrition,
sanitation, health services, etc.

decreasing mortality and morbidity

increasing   increasing
fitness   ◀── increasing health ──▶ length of
for work   productive
                                    life

increasing survival of children

increasing family planning

decreasing fertility

increasing investment   increasing investment
in physical capital   in human capital

decreasing dependency

┌───┐
│ High levels of production and consumption, │
│ and low levels of mortality and fertility │
└───┘

FIGURE 345

Alternative model of successful demographic transition from low to high levels of production and consumption, and from high to low levels of mortality and fertility. (After Frederiksen 1969.)

UNITED STATES: A CASE STUDY

Let us consider population trends in the United States to illustrate some of the detailed aspects of the modern dilemma over population.

The population of the United States has grown from about 4 million in 1790, when the first census was taken, to 205 million in 1970 (Figure 347). There is only a rough estimate of population trends during the colonial period from 1630 to 1790 because there was no formal enumeration in any of the colonies. There were about 4600 people in the colonies in 1630, and this leaped to 27,000 in 1640. The population doubled every 10 to 20 years after that under the influence of heavy immigration from Europe and a

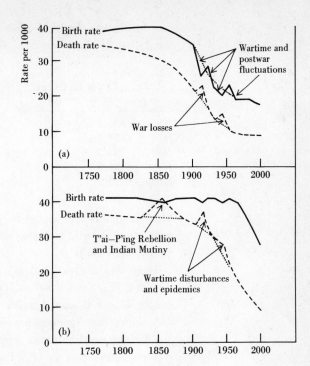

FIGURE 346

Estimated and conjectured trends in birth rate and death rate, 1750–2000, for (a) the more developed regions and (b) less developed regions of the world. (United Nations 1971.)

FIGURE 347

Population growth in the United States, 1790–1970. (Data from Statistical Abstract of the United States *1970.)*

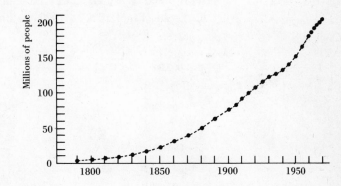

very high birth rate (probably about 55 per thousand). The population reached about 1 million in 1745 and 2 million in 1767. Immigration as a factor contributing to population growth was very important until 1670, but most of the subsequent population growth from 1680 to 1840 was due to excess births.

The United States in 1800 was in the same demographic configuration as Costa Rica and India are today—very high birth rate and very low death rate. Birth rates began declining about 1800, and there was a steady decline throughout the nineteenth century:

	Crude birth rate per thousand
1820	*55.2*
1840	*51.8*
1860	*44.3*
1880	*39.8*
1900	*32.3*

This trend was interrupted by the Civil War (1860–1865), and the rate of population growth has fluctuated both because of birth-rate changes and immigration shifts.

There was a great deal of social and economic disorder associated with the Civil War from 1860 to 1865. The birth rate fell sharply from approximately 43 per thousand to 35 or less, and the death rate also rose. Figure 348 shows that immigration was reduced during the Civil War, and the population growth rate was temporarily slowed.

Immigration rose to very high levels after the Civil War and reached a peak around 1910, when over 1 million immigrants per year were entering the United States. The birth rate was falling steadily during this time. World War I caused a halt in immigration and a temporary drop in the birth rate. From 1922 to 1929 the birth rate fell rapidly during a period of

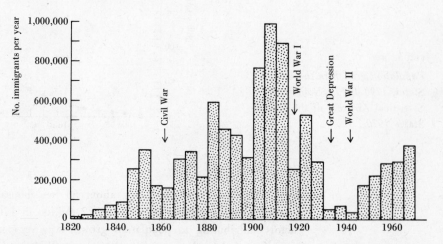

FIGURE 348

Immigration to the United States, 1820–1970. Number of immigrants per year averaged over 5-year intervals. (Data from U.S. Bureau of the Census 1970.)

great prosperity (Figure 349), and worry was expressed that the population would not reproduce itself. The low birth rate plus the immigration restrictions of 1924 caused a slowing down of population growth.

The Great Depression from 1929 to 1940 was a period of severe economic hardship. Birth rates continued to decline until 1933 and remained at a low level during most of the 1930s. Immigration declined to nearly zero at this time, and the population growth was small during the 1930s.

In 1940 the birth rate began to rise rapidly until 1944, when the effects of the war became evident. After the war ended in 1945 the birth rate increased dramatically to a high level of 26.5 per thousand in 1947 and remained at a high plateau for about 10 years (Figure 349). The immigration of refugees after the war also added a substantial number of people to the population of the United States.

Since 1957 the birth rate has been drifting downward from about 25 per thousand in 1957 to 18 per thousand in 1969. This decline again took place in a period of high prosperity and resembled the decline during the 1920s. Immigration has continued at a moderate rate in the 1960s of about 200,000 to 400,000 immigrants per year (Figure 348).

Figure 350 summarizes this discussion by showing the two components of population growth—births and immigration—for the United States from 1630 to 1960. Except for the early colonial period, the great bulk of the population growth has been contributed by excess births.

Changes in the death rate in the United States, although significant, have been modest compared with the variations in births and immigrations. From

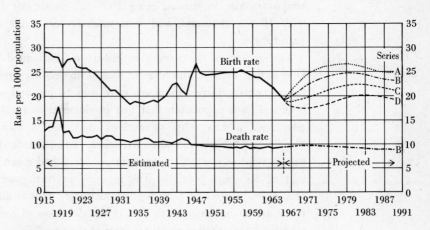

FIGURE 349

Birth and death rates for the United States, 1915–1990. The projected birth rate is based on four different assumptions about future fertility. Recent data have fallen between series C and series D. See page 601 for an explanation of series A to D. (After U.S. Bureau of the Census 1968.)

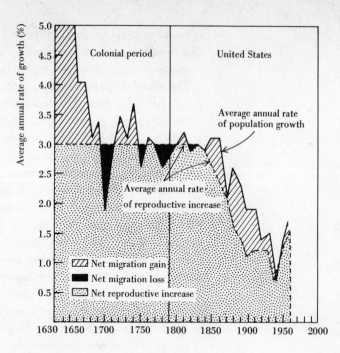

FIGURE 350

Components of population growth rate in the territory of the United States from 1630 to 1960. Most of the population growth has come from excess births except in the early colonial period. (After Bogue 1969.)

1800 to 1850 the death rate was around 20 to 25 per thousand, and from 1850 to 1890 it was fluctuating around 20 per thousand. About 1890 the death rate began to fall slowly and steadily from 20 per thousand to 10 per thousand in 1950 (Figure 349). The influenza epidemic of 1918 caused a temporary rise in deaths. Since 1950 the death rate has stabilized around 9 to 10 per thousand, and it is unlikely to decline much further in the near future.

Two aspects of the population history of the United States are surprising. One is that most of the historic decline in fertility took place in the 1800s, before contraceptive techniques were easy to use and widely available. This occurred in a population that was predominately rural, with a low level of education, and a religious outlook that was a blend of predestination, "God's will be done," and mysticism. By contrast, the highly educated, urban, relatively wealthy population of 1970 had a birth rate about equal to that of 35 years previous. The increase in birth rate from 1940 to 1957 is a second aspect of U.S. population history that is difficult to explain; yet if we are to influence birth rate in the direction of zero population growth, we must know what causes these sorts of changes.

What is in store for the future? In order to make any guesses we must assume no large-scale catastrophes such as nuclear war. Clearly the death rate will not change greatly, and even if lung cancer becomes a serious epidemic and air pollution causes "killer smogs" in large cities, the death rate would probably change only slightly for the nation as a whole. For example, with a population of 205 million, there would have to be 205,000 extra deaths in 1 year to raise the crude death rate from 9.0 to 10.0 per thousand. Second, the immigration rate has to be assumed, and the simplest assumption is that it will be unchanged from the present rate of 400,000 per year. This could be changed by law, however, at any time.

The big unknown in forecasting the future trend of the United States population is the birth rate. The U.S. Bureau of the Census uses a range of values they hope will cover the future trends; these are as follows:

	Total children per female	Median age of mothers (yr)
Series B	3.100	25.8
Series C	2.775	26.4
Series D	2.450	27.2
Series E	2.110	27.2

Series A was a higher estimate (3.35 children) used in the 1960s but later dropped because it appeared too high, and series E was added. Series E is a zero-population-growth series in which there is exact replacement ($R_0 = 1.0$) after the age structure reaches a stationary form. A final series, series X, has been added; it is series E but with zero immigration allowed.

Figure 351 summarizes the population projections for the United States from 1970 to 2015 based on these assumptions about birth rates. There is very little divergence in the estimates during the first five years, so it is difficult to tell in the short run which series is being followed. But as time progresses, there are sharp differences in the projections. For example, in the year 2000 series B projects 321 million and series E 266 million, a very large difference of 55 million people. Series X, the zero-population-growth series with no immigration, reaches an asymptote of 276 million in 2037. (Note that it would take this long to reach a stationary age distribution.)

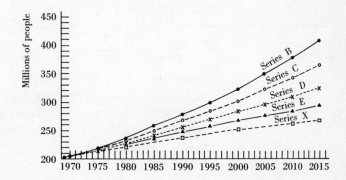

FIGURE 351

Projections of the population of the United States, 1970–2015. Series B to E are based on different fertility rates from high to low. Series E is replacement fertility, 2.11 children per female (net reproductive rate = 1.0). Series X is series E without any immigration allowed. (After U.S. Bureau of the Census 1970.)

All the other series continue to rise because of immigration plus excess births.

The surge in birth rates after World War II has sent a surge through the age distribution, and this has some significant consequences for planning. One example will illustrate this. Figure 352 shows the school enrollment figures for elementary, high school, and college. There is uncertainty in these projections for two reasons: The future birth rate is uncertain and the percentage of people attending higher education may change. The elementary school population has reached a plateau in the late 1960s and is actually declining in 1971. If the series D birth rates prevail (and 1971 evidence suggests that this series is nearly correct for the moment), the elementary school population will decline sharply from a high of 36.5 million in 1969 to 32 million in 1979. The obvious consequence is that fewer elementary school buildings will be needed and fewer teachers. High school enrollment will peak out in the late 1970s and then also decline slightly. If the population moves toward zero population growth, the percentage of young people in the population will drop, and the percentage of older people will grow. The demographic changes in birth rates thus have very great impacts on social and economic planning for the future.

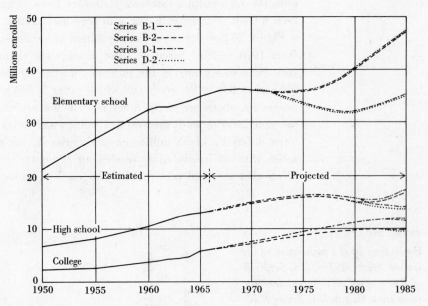

FIGURE 352

Fall school enrollments, 1950–1985. The projected trends depend on the birth rate (see Figure 349) and the percentage of persons attending school. Recent birth rates have suggested that series D is a more accurate predictor than series B. (After U.S. Bureau of the Census 1968.)

SOLUTIONS TO THE WORLD POPULATION PROBLEM

We begin with one certainty: *The world population cannot continue increasing indefinitely.* Consequently, we must reach a stage of zero (or negative) population growth. There are essentially two ways of doing this: there can be high birth rates and high death rates (the *death-rate solution*), or there can be low birth rates and low death rates (the *birth-rate solution*). Let me emphasize that this is not a hypothesis or a theory or a radical proposal; it is a statement of fact. Disagreements arise over two things: (1) whether we will have the birth or the death solution, and (2) how we can influence populations in one direction or the other.

No one seems to be a proponent of the death-rate solution directly, although those who exclude on some grounds the possibility of the birth-rate solution automatically become proponents of the death-rate solution. The humanitarian thrust of civilization has moved in halting fashion toward low death rates, and it would require a major change in our outlook to suggest a return to higher death rates. The principal danger in this connection is that we will inflict higher death rates on ourselves by cigarette smoking, air pollution, and pesticide poisoning.

The birth-rate solution will require strong measures to reduce the birth rate and keep it low. This requires social motivation and is not something that can be imposed easily by governmental regulation. Delay in the age of marriage must be encouraged; in countries with low birth rates females marry about 5 years later than they do in countries with high birth rates. Other changes to encourage people to remain single must be set up. Information about the entire gamut of contraception technology must be made available so that people motivated to reproduce at replacement levels will, in fact, be able to do so. One of the tenets of Western civilization has been that people be given maximum freedom of choice. To retain this humanitarian ideal while solving the population problem will be an important task in the next 50 years.

SUMMARY

The human population has increased rapidly since about A.D. 1650 and this increase has been geometric. Although it took about 1 million years to produce a human population of 1 billion (1850), the second billion was produced in only 80 years, and the third billion in 30 years. The rate of population increase is not uniform, and the underdeveloped nations are increasing more rapidly than the industrialized nations.

The industrialized nations of western Europe passed through a *demographic transition* from high birth and death rates to low birth and death rates. This began around 1750 and was completed in 150 to 200 years. Since the death rate falls first, the demographic transition is always accompanied by population growth. The underdeveloped countries started through the demographic transition in the twentieth century and death rates have fallen very rapidly in less than 50 years. Birth rates, however, have fallen only slightly, and population growth is rapid.

There is a basic division of opinion as to whether the underdeveloped countries will be able to pass through the demographic transition successfully. The neo-Malthusians believe that rapid population growth will prevent the underdeveloped countries from increasing production and accumulating capital. An alternative view believes that the rapid drop in death rate will entail a rapid drop in birth rate. The critical question is what determines the human birth rate and thus how it can be influenced by social and economic policies.

The United States is discussed as a case study in population changes. The interplay of steadily declining birth and death rates and changes in immigration have led to population increase culminating in 205 million people in 1970. A great spurt in the birth rate in the 1940–1957 period has resulted in a pulse in the age distribution. Predicted trends in the U.S. population are largely a function of what birth rate one assumes, and this in turn has economic and social repercussions because of changes in age structure.

The world population increase will stop in the near future either because the birth rate is reduced to equal the low death rate, or because the death rate increases because of large-scale famine and disease. No one seems to prefer the death-rate solution, and this means that strong efforts will be necessary to reduce the birth rate to the replacement level necessary for zero population growth.

SELECTED REFERENCES

BERELSON, B. 1969. Beyond family planning. *Science* 163:533–543.

BLAKE, J. 1971. Reproductive motivation and population policy. *BioScience* 21(5): 215–220.

BOGUE, D. J. 1969. *Principles of Demography*. Wiley, New York.

DAVIS, K. 1967. Population policy: will current programs succeed? *Science* 158: 730–739.

EHRLICH, P. R., and A. H. EHRLICH. 1970. *Population, Resources, Environment: Issues in Human Ecology*. W. H. Freeman, San Francisco.

HARDIN, G. 1968. The tragedy of the commons. *Science* 162: 1243–1248.

1 Hardin (1971, p. 527), in discussing the cyclone that struck East Bengal in November 1970, states:

Early dispatches spoke of 15,000 dead, but the estimates rapidly escalated to 2,000,000 and then dropped back to 500,000.... Pakistani parents repaired the population loss in just 40 days, and the world turned its attention to other matters.

The population of Pakistan at this time was about 137 million. The annual rate of population increase is 3.25% (United Nations, 1971). Is Hardin's statement correct?

2 Crude birth and death rates for France are given below along with the net reproductive rate (R_0).

	Crude rates per 1000		Net reproductive rate
	Birth	Death	
1801–1810	*32*	*28*	—
1811–1820	*31*	*26*	—
1821–1830	*31*	*25*	—
1831–1840	*29*	*25*	—
1841–1850	*27*	*23*	—
1851	*27*	*22*	*0.97*
1854–1858	*26*	*25*	*0.90*
1861	*27*	*23*	*0.97*
1864–1868	*26*	*23*	*1.00*
1871	*22*	*32*	*0.73*
1872	*27*	*22*	*1.05*
1874–1878	*26*	*22*	*1.06*
1879–1883	*25*	*22*	*1.03*
1884–1888	*24*	*22*	*0.98*
1889–1893	*23*	*23*	*0.94*
1894–1898	*22*	*21*	*0.96*
1899–1903	*22*	*21*	*0.98*
1904–1908	*21*	*20*	*0.98*
1909–1913	*19*	*19*	*0.93*
1920–1922	*20*	*17*	*0.97*
1924–1928	*19*	*17*	*0.93*
1929–1933	*18*	*16*	*0.91*
1934–1938	*16*	*16*	*0.88*
1945–1947	*19*	*14*	*1.16*
1949–1953	*20*	*13*	*1.30*
1954–1958	*18*	*12*	*1.25*
1959–1963	*18*	*11*	*1.32*
1965	*18*	*11*	*1.33*
1966	*17*	*11*	
1967	*17*	*11*	

SOURCE: Keyfitz and Flieger (1968).

Plot the demographic transition for France. How can the net reproductive rate be below 1.0 when the crude birth rate exceeds the crude death rate?

3   Canada is a country closely tied to the United States economically but with somewhat different social conditions. Obtain the birth-rate changes for Canada for the past 50 years from *Historical Statistics of Canada* and the *Canada Year Book*, and compare these with the pattern of change in the United States (Figure 349).

4   From *Current Population Reports* of the U.S. Bureau of the Census, obtain information on the birth and death rates of white and nonwhite segments of the population. What effect will these rates have on the composition of the future U.S. population?

5   Write a list of all the variables you think you would need to know to project the future population of any nation of the world. Then check a textbook of demography such as Bogue (1969) or the *Current Population Reports* to see what variables are in fact used to make projections.

6   Suppose a population exists at a "high birth rate equal to high death rate" configuration (A) of approximately 50 per thousand. The death rate drops, then the birth rate, until the population exists at a "low birth rate equal to low death rate" configuration (B) of approximately 10 per thousand. The transition from configuration A to B will entail population increase. Is this increase temporary or permanent? What factors will determine the size of this increase? Is the increase the same if the transition occurs over 50 years as if it occurs over 200 years?

7   From the *Demographic Yearbook of the United Nations* obtain data on the changes in birth rate in Japan since World War II. Discuss the impact of legalized widespread abortion on the birth rate in Japan. In 1948 abortion was legalized, and sterilization was authorized, along with the public sale of contraceptives. Taeuber (1960) discusses some aspects of this question.

8   Discuss the effects of the demographic transition on the age structure of the population.

27 Food production

We can view the human population problem in the same framework we used when discussing plant and animal populations (Chapter 14), and ask which factors will limit population increase. It could be extrinsic factors such as disease or food shortage, or intrinsic factors such as physiological and mental stresses, aggression (war), and genetic deterioration. Unlike other organisms, rational man has the potentiality for avoiding most limiting factors except shortage of food, and although we may be unable to avoid disastrous plagues or wars, our most immediate problem is that of food production.

HUMAN FOOD REQUIREMENTS

General nutritional requirements for humans include 45 chemical compounds and elements falling into five categories: carbohydrates, fats, proteins, vitamins, and minerals. Four groups of foodstuffs should be eaten daily to provide adequate nutrition:

1 Milk and dairy products (calcium, protein, vitamins, minerals)

2 Meat, fish, poultry, and eggs (protein, fats, vitamins)

3 Grains and starchy vegetables (carbohydrates, vitamins, some protein)

4 Fruits and vegetables (carbohydrates, vitamins, minerals, some protein)

There is general agreement that humans need sufficient bulk of a balanced diet to grow up strong and healthy. It is perhaps surprising that there is no agreement on the more quantitative aspects of what forms a balanced diet. Part of the difficulty is that many factors influence dietary needs. Young people need more food than older people, heavy people more food than light people. Temperature affects metabolic requirements, so people in tropical areas require less food than those in polar regions. Physical laborers need more food than office workers.

One simple way of describing human diets is to measure their *energy* in terms of calories consumed per day. Figure 353 shows the average caloric value of the diet of people in 24 different countries. The rich nations have diets containing 3000 calories per person per day; the poor nations have diets ranging from 1800 to 2500 calories. On the average about 2350 calories per person per day are required for a satisfactory diet (President's Science Advisory Committee, 1967). Figure 353 shows that a substantial number of underdeveloped countries do not achieve the *average* caloric requirements. When we combine this with the observation that even in the United States a substantial number of people suffer from malnutrition (Kotz

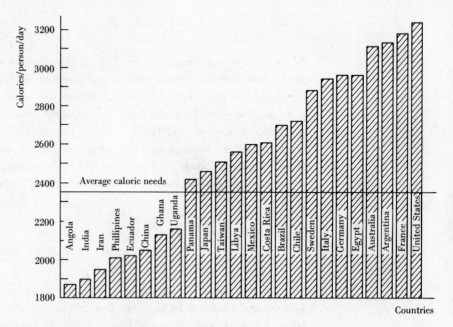

FIGURE 353

Average caloric value of diet for various countries in the late 1960s. (Data from FAO 1970a.)

1970), we can begin to see the magnitude of the malnutrition problem. Not everyone eats the "average diet" even in rich countries.

Perhaps a better way of measuring dietary adequacy is through protein intake. The world population consumes about 85 million metric tons* of protein annually. About two-thirds of this protein comes from plant products, mostly from cereals and legumes (Borgstrom 1967). Animal products contribute only one-tenth of the world's consumption of calories but one-third the protein. Figure 354 shows the protein intake of people in 24 different countries and the proportion of animal and plant protein in the diet. Protein from plant sources is usually inferior to protein from animal sources because of amino acid deficiencies. Corn, for example, is low in the amino acids lysine and tryptophan, which are required by humans in the diet. Animal proteins are more digestible than plant proteins.

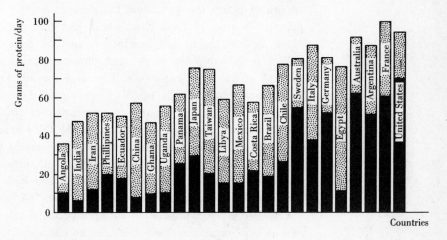

FIGURE 354

Average protein intake (grams per person per day) for various countries in the late 1960s. Countries ranked in same order as in Figure 353. Solid area is animal protein, stippled area is plant protein. (Data from FAO 1970a.)

Deficiency diseases of various kinds are the indicators of inadequate diets. *Kwashiorkor* is a protein-deficiency disease common in young children in underdeveloped countries and is serious even if the number of calories is ample. Growth is retarded, the skin becomes discolored, and a potbelly develops in mild cases. *Marasmus* is a similar disease caused by protein and caloric deficiency and is particularly serious in very young children. *Anemia* is another common disease associated with malnutrition. Various vitamin

* A metric ton is 1,000,000 g, or 2205 lb.

deficiencies are also widespread in association with malnutrition: beriberi (B_1), rickets (D), scurvy (C), pellagra (niacin), and vitamin A deficiency are some of the more common diseases.

The effects of malnutrition are not always reversible. Protein deficiencies, for example, can have permanent stunting effects on mental and physical development of young children (Young 1970). This means that future development may be jeopardized by present malnutrition, and that if the world could eliminate malnutrition tomorrow, there would be a time lag of at least a generation before the effects of past nutrition would disappear.

HISTORICAL CHANGES IN FOOD PRODUCTION

Since the agricultural revolution began about 9000 B.C., man has used many species of plants for agriculture but depends on only a few plants for his principal sources of food. Rice, wheat, and corn are the "big three," and about 50% of the world's farmland is used for these three crops.

Rice is probably the single most important plant, since it is the basic food of almost 2 billion people. Rice is a tropical and subtropical plant, and most of the world's supply is grown in Asia. Wheat is almost as important as rice but is mainly a temperate-zone plant. Corn is grown in both temperate and tropical areas and is the third great crop of the world.

Grains are relatively rich in protein and far surpass the other staple crop, the potato, which is largely water (75%) with little protein (1 to 4%). Legumes, such as soybeans and peanuts, have a high protein content and thus may be important components of the diet.

Changes in food production of agricultural plants can be achieved in one of two ways: (1) More land can be cultivated, or (2) plants can be improved by selecting genetic strains for higher yields or by supplying critical nutrients in fertilizer. Figure 355 shows the changes in yield of corn per acre in the United States since 1866. The yield is essentially constant for 70 years, from 1866 to 1936, at approximately 26 bushels per acre. Hybrid corn was introduced in the early 1930s; by 1938 15% of the corn planted was hybrid corn, and by 1948 this had risen to 76%. Associated with the introduction of hybrids was the increased use of fertilizers, and these two factors have increased U.S. corn yields to an average of 84 bushels per acre in 1969. From 1866 to 1932 corn production was increased by cultivating more and more acreage. Thirty million acres had been harvested in 1866, and this increased over threefold, to 111 million acres, in 1932. Rapidly increasing yields have allowed a reduction in acreages since the 1930s to half the 1932 figure; in 1969 55 million acres were planted in corn in the United States.

Yields of major grain crops have not increased everywhere during the

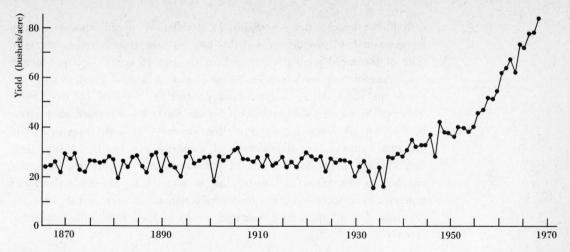

FIGURE 355

Corn production in the United States, 1866–1969. Hybrid corn was introduced in the 1930s and the yield (in bushels per acre) has increased dramatically since that time. (Data from the Statistical Abstract of the United States *1970.)*

past 50 years. Figure 356 compares yield per hectare of wheat in Europe and Asia since 1940. The increase in European yields can be traced largely to increased fertilizer usage. European farmers used about six times as much fertilizer per unit area as farmers used in Asia in 1968 (Brown 1970a).

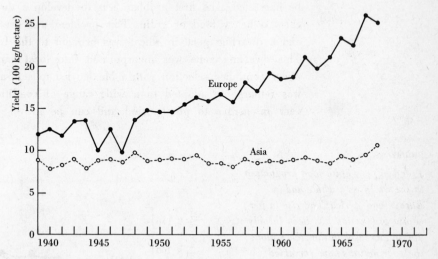

FIGURE 356

Changes in the average yield of wheat in Europe and Asia (excluding China), 1940–1968. Differences in fertilizer use explain most of the trends. (Data from FAO Production Yearbooks.)

Malthus thought that increases in population would always outstrip increases in food production, but this has not been true in recent years. In spite of the rapid population growth of the last 15 years, food production has increased both on a per capita basis and on a total basis. Figure 357 shows the index of per capita food production compiled by the United Nations. Per capita food production for the world has increased about 10% in the past 10 years, but most of this increase has been concentrated in the rich nations; the underdeveloped countries are barely holding their own (Figure 358). As the rate of population growth goes up, obviously one has to run faster and faster just to stand still. The underdeveloped countries have increased their food production at an average rate of 2.7% per year, but all they have managed to do is keep pace with population growth.

THE GREEN REVOLUTION

In 1944 Mexico was a typical underdeveloped country, importing much of its food from the United States. The Rockefeller Foundation assembled a group of four agricultural scientists from the United States to try to improve Mexican agriculture. One purpose was to develop strains of wheat that would grow well in Mexico. The traditional varieties of wheat grew very tall, which was a serious problem where they were fertilized, because the grain became so heavy the wheat stalk broke, or "lodged," before it could be harvested. The first problem was to develop a dwarf strain that could carry a heavy load of grain. This problem was overcome first in Japan, and a dwarfing gene in wheat was brought to the United States in 1947. This dwarfing gene was incorporated into local varieties of wheat, and under continued selection within Mexico led to a dwarf wheat variety that was remarkably adapted to a wide range of conditions. Dwarf wheat is very insensitive to photoperiod and can be grown in tropical and sub-

FIGURE 357

Trend in per capita food production in the world as a whole and in Europe and Africa. The rise in per capita production has been largely due to increases in the rich nations; the poor nations have remained more or less unchanged over the past 10 to 15 years. (Data from the Statistical Yearbook of the United Nations *1969.)*

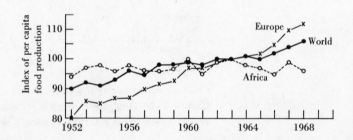

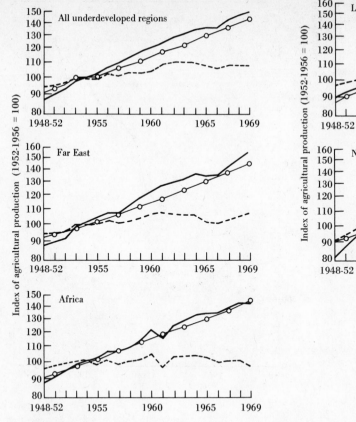
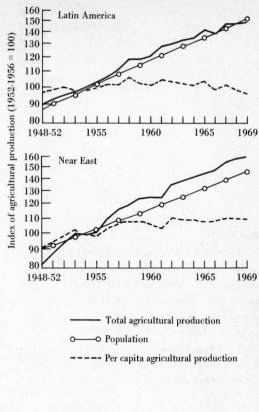

FIGURE 358

Growth in agricultural production and population in the under-developed regions of the world. (After FAO 1970b.)

tropical countries under a range of light conditions. Dr. Norman Borlaug was given the Nobel Peace Prize in 1970 for his work in developing the dwarf wheat (Brown 1970b).

Dwarf wheat is not a miracle plant, however, and to be high yielding must be grown under irrigation (or high rainfall) and with additional fertilizer. Under dryland farming conditions, in which little fertilizer can be used, dwarf wheat is no better than traditional varieties. Figure 359 illustrates the increase in yield that has occurred in Mexico as a result of the combined use of dwarf wheat, irrigation, and increased fertilizer input. In 15 years wheat yields have nearly tripled. Dwarf wheat has recently been introduced to India, Pakistan, and other countries in Asia, and the effects are just beginning to show in increased yields.

Wheat is an important grain, but most of the world lives on rice. In 1962 the Rockefeller and Ford foundations established the International Rice

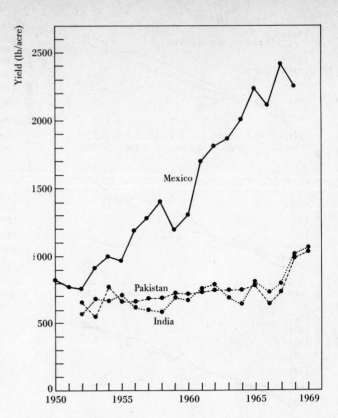

FIGURE 359

Yield takeoff from new varieties of dwarf wheat. Dwarf wheat was developed in Mexico and introduced in the early 1950s, and much of the wheat crop was brought under irrigation between 1950 and 1960. Dwarf wheat was then introduced to India and Pakistan in the mid-1960s. (After Brown 1970c.)

Research Institute at Los Banos in the Philippines, with the object of producing a cosmopolitan dwarf rice strain comparable to dwarf wheat. Ten thousand strains of rice were assembled for crossbreeding. The result was "miracle rice," strain IR-8, which has proved capable of doubling rice yields in Asian countries. Like the wheats, dwarf rice will withstand heavy fertilizer use and will not lodge. The new rice varieties also seem to be more efficient in the use of fertilizer. One pound of nitrogen fertilizer applied to traditional rice produced about 10 additional pounds of grain; with comparable fertilizer IR-8 yields up to 20 additional pounds. The new rice also matures early: IR-8 matures in 120 days, compared with 150 to 180 days for traditional rice. This is important because it then allows a farmer to take multiple crops from the same field within 1 year. One limitation of the dwarf rices is that, in contrast to normal rice, they cannot stand flooding or prolonged submersion. They also require more fertilizer. Dwarf rice can be grown to great advantage in the dry season if irrigation is available.

The yield takeoff for the new rice varieties is still small (Figure 360), owing in part to a lack of fertilizer and irrigation. A farmer in Pakistan must spend five times more on fertilizer with the new strains than with old

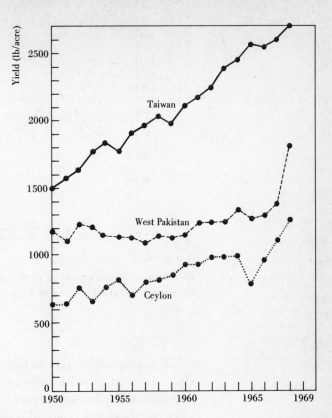

FIGURE 360

Rice yields in West Pakistan, Ceylon, and Taiwan, 1950–1969. New high-yielding strains of rice were introduced to Pakistan and Ceylon starting about 1965. The Taiwan increase is associated with a change from single to multiple cropping in a year, increased fertilizer input, and new genetic strains. (After Brown 1970c.)

varieties. Filipino farmers must use four times as much fertilizer on IR-8 rice as on local varieties. The yield of rice is highly dependent on fertilizer application, even in traditional varieties (Figure 361).

Is there a possibility that the Green Revolution will raise the underdeveloped countries above the level of chronic malnutrition? We now turn to consider possible future trends and needs in food production.

PROGNOSIS FOR FUTURE FOOD PRODUCTION

Two factors must be part of any discussion of future trends in production. First, we must increase per capita consumption in underdeveloped countries and thus raise nutritional standards. Second, we must accommodate to substantial population gains in both the developed and the underdeveloped countries. The Food and Agriculture Organization of the United Nations developed a plan for world agriculture for the 1962 to 1985 period and tried to assess the directions that the food situation would take. The following is a summary of the FAO diagnosis and recommendations.

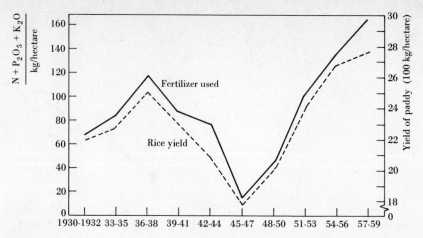

FIGURE 361

Relationship between yield of traditional varieties of paddy rice and the amount of fertilizer used in Taiwan, 1930–1959. (After Doyle 1966.)

The population of the underdeveloped countries was 1.394 billion in 1962 and is projected to increase 80% in 23 years. But per capita food consumption should also increase, if the standard of living can be increased. Table 39 shows the projected increase in demand for food in the under-developed regions. On the average, food production must increase 142% from 1962 to 1985, or 3.9% per year. From 1962 to 1967 the actual increase was only 2.7%, considerably below the required goal (FAO 1969).

TABLE 39

Projected increase in demand for food by regions, 1962 to 1985, underdeveloped countries

Region	Total increase (%)	Proportion of increase due to:	
		Increased population	Increased per capita consumption
Asia, Far East	154	0.64	0.36
North Africa	143	0.74	0.26
Africa south of Sahara	122	0.77	0.23
Latin America	120	0.88	0.12
All Areas	142	0.71	0.29

SOURCE: FAO 1969.

If food production is to be increased, part of the increase might come from farming more land. How much land is currently being cropped? In the underdeveloped countries only a small part of the land is used for crops:

	Total area (%)
Arable land, permanent crops	11
Pasture	21
Forest	28
Not used for agriculture or forestry	40

The distribution of arable land is not uniform, of course, and much more land is usable for crops in Asia and the Far East than in Latin America or the Middle East. Not all the arable land is cultivated each year, and in areas such as Latin America only about half the area is harvested each year.

Arable land can be increased in total acreage provided there are adequate soil- and water-conservation programs. FAO estimates that there are approximately 1,145,000,000 hectares of potential arable land in the underdeveloped regions that could be used for food production. In 1962 there were 512,000,000 hectares in cultivation (45% of potential), and this might be expanded to 600,000,000 hectares in 1985 (53% of potential). This is a modest increase, and two reasons are given for this: (1) The problems of cultivating new areas are substantial, from the economic costs of land clearing to the biological problems of pests, and (2) the best strategy for increasing agricultural production is believed to be by intensifying agriculture on existing cropland. Thus the projected increase in cropland is only 0.7% per year from 1962 to 1985 (FAO 1969).

A large part of the projected increase in food production must come from increased cropping intensity. This can be achieved by the use of high-yield plants and by multiple cropping of land. Irrigation on a large scale seems to be a necessary part of this scheme, since as more fertilizer becomes available, water becomes a limiting factor for crop yields.

A critical factor in improving the nutritional status of people in the underdeveloped countries is the projected increase in cereal production through the use of dwarf wheat and rice. An increased yield in the cereals would allow for more grain to be used in feeding cattle; also land could be released to other crops. The projected increase in demand for cereals is 3.0 to 3.2% per year from 1962 to 1985. The Green Revolution depends heavily on fertilizer input and controlled water supply, both of which can be produced only by large capital investments in agriculture in the underdeveloped countries. Only about 4% of the total rice-growing area in Southeast Asia was planted in "miracle rice" in 1967–1968, and this must be expanded to 39% by 1985. For wheat the corresponding figures were 4 and 16% (FAO 1969).

High-quality seeds, fertilizer, pesticides, and farm machines are all a necessary part of the plan to increase food production. Fertilizer is a key to modern agriculture, and the projected fertilizer requirements are very large:

Index of fertilizer amount needed

1962 (actual)	*100*	*increase = 14.3%/yr*
1975 (projected)	*569*	*increase = 7.8%/yr*
1985 (projected)	*1,210*	

In recent years fertilizer input has been increasing at 12.7% per year, so this rapid increase in fertilizer use may be feasible.

Highly productive agriculture is dependent on a complex industrial base, and this complicates the efforts to increase crop production in the under-developed countries. If all the effort and money is concentrated on food pro-duction in these countries, they will become increasingly dependent on the industrial bases of other countries, with further economic reverberations.

Protein deficiency is the most serious nutritional problem in the world today (United Nations 1968). What are the chances of increasing the pro-duction of animal protein? Efforts to expand animal-protein production in the past few years have met with little success. Livestock production has grown 1.6% per year in the past several years, but this must be increased to at least 3.8% per year by 1985 to meet the rising demand for animal protein. One suggested strategy is to rely on pig and poultry production rather than on beef production, because pigs and poultry have a shorter life cycle and are more efficient at converting plant materials to animal protein.

Ecological constraints operate to influence the protein nutrition of dif-ferent countries. We can divide the countries of the world into seven groups, depending on their source of proteins (Figure 362), and calculate the

---

FIGURE 362

Protein intake and requirements by country, according to type of diet in 1962. List of countries arranged in descending order of total protein intake (left to right):

GROUP 1: *countries whose primary source of protein is animal products; New Zealand, Uruguay, France, Argentina, Finland, Den-mark, Ireland, Canada, United States, Switzerland, Australia, United Kingdom, Austria, Belgium-Luxembourg, Israel, Sweden, Norway, West Germany, Netherlands.*

GROUP 2: *countries whose primary source of protein is wheat; Turkey, Rumania, Greece, Yugoslavia, Poland, Hungary, Italy, U.A.R., Spain, Chile, Afghanistan, Syria, Lebanon, Jordan, Iraq, Morocco, Iran.*

GROUP 3: *countries whose primary source of protein is millet and sorghum; Niger, Chad, Upper Volta, Sudan, Ethiopia, Senegal, Mali, Gambia, Nigeria, Tanzania.*

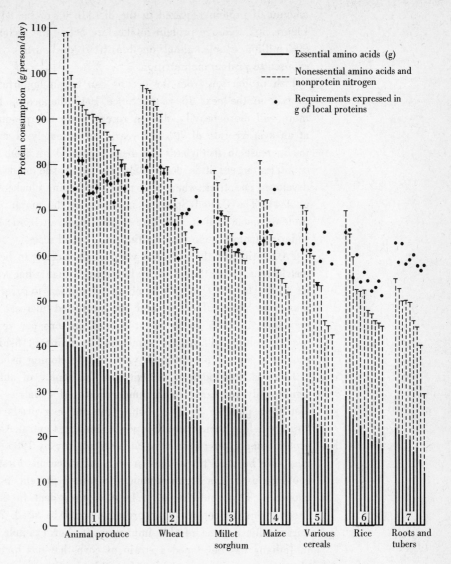

GROUP 4: *countries whose primary source of protein is maize (corn);
South Africa, Mexico, Zambia, Malawi, El Salvador, Guatamala,
Honduras, Dahomey.*

GROUP 5: *countries whose primary source of protein is wheat, maize,
and rice; Paraguay, Brazil, Peru, Venezuela, Costa Rica, Columbia,
Bolivia, Surinam, Ecuador.*

GROUP 6: *countries whose primary source of protein is rice; Japan,
South Korea, Formosa, India, Malaysia, Madagascar, Mauritius,
Thailand, Pakistan, Ceylon, Philippines.*

GROUP 7: *countries on roots, tubers, and plantains; Cameroon,
Ivory Coast, Uganda, Togo, Ghana, C.A.R., Gabon, Congo
(Brazzaville), D.R. of the Congo. (After FAO 1969.)*

amount of protein required in the diet. In 43 of the 84 countries shown in Figure 362, average protein intakes are below the recommended allowance; 900 million people, about one-fourth of the world's population, are thus exposed to protein malnutrition.

Fish production from the oceans can be an important source of animal protein in the next 15 years. Since 1945 the oceans have been exploited more and more heavily, and in recent years fish production has increased at an average rate of 7% per year. Unfortunately, a substantial amount of the increase in fish yields has been siphoned off from the underdeveloped countries, where it is desperately needed, to be used as fish meal in the developed countries, where it is used for feeding chickens (Borgstrom, 1967, p. 354). The United States is now one of the major *importers* of animal protein, much of it in the form of fish meal, an ironic situation in a world suffering from protein malnutrition on a broad scale.

FAO estimated the potential yield of the oceans to be almost 120 million metric tons (an estimate somewhat greater than what we obtained in Chapter 22). The 1969 catch was about 63 million tons, or about 53% of the maximum potential catch, and the projected increase is to 72% of the maximum in 1985, or to about 85 million tons per year. This increase in oceanic fishing will require some modernization of fishing fleets as well as ecological studies on optimum yield for developing fisheries.

There is little hope at present that the supply of animal protein can be significantly increased in the underdeveloped countries by 1985. Increases that seem possible in meat, fish, milk, and egg production will be needed largely to feed their increased population. In Central America and Asia the protein supply per capita may *decrease* slightly by 1985. Two possible strategies may be used to prevent protein malnutrition. First, pork and poultry could be used to a greater extent for animal protein in the underdeveloped countries. This could make at least a small dent in the protein shortage. Second, enrichment of plant proteins could be used. New genetic strains might achieve some of this improvement. For example, Purdue University in Indiana has developed a strain of corn that has high lysine and tryptophan content, two essential amino acids deficient in traditional varieties of corn (Harpstead 1971). This breakthrough makes it possible to grow corn that is almost the protein equivalent of skim milk. If a high-lysine variety of wheat could be developed, this could reduce greatly the protein-malnutrition problems of the next 20 years. Artificial enrichment of plant products could also be used to improve diets. The addition of synthetic amino acids to flour might be used in some cases to supplement the diet. The development of new food sources is difficult, and cultural patterns and traditions must be studied before new sources of protein can be used (Pirie 1967). What works well in one country will not work everywhere.

Thus the prognosis for the world's food needs of the next 15 years is not good. The caloric needs of the underdeveloped nations may be met with the "miracle grains," but protein malnutrition will remain and may grow more serious. An extraordinary effort may improve the diet of people in the underdeveloped countries in the next 15 years, but long-term improvement must depend on a reduction in the rate of population increase. Famine may be averted, but it will not be stopped by words.

SUMMARY

The limitations imposed by food are the most immediate problems facing the world. Humans require a balanced diet of carbohydrates, protein, fats, vitamins, and minerals. One way to quantify these requirements is by *energy* intake, but *protein* intake is probably more critical. Deficiency diseases are the measure of malnutrition and are common in the underdeveloped countries and present even in the United States and Canada.

Food production can be increased by cultivating more land or by increasing yields by fertilizing, irrigating, or producing better varieties of crops. All these factors have been important in the past, but the most striking changes in food production have been determined by technological advances in fertilizer input and new genetic varieties. Hybrid corn in the United States, dwarf wheat in Mexico, and "miracle rice" in the Philippines are three examples of quantum jumps in potential production of food.

The Green Revolution will probably buy the world 15 years in which to reduce population growth. The increased use of high-yielding cereals will increase per capita calories in the diet of the underdeveloped countries by 1985, even in the face of rising population. More serious is protein malnutrition, which cannot be overcome, because the increases in animal protein supplies will barely keep up with population increases to 1985. The protein crisis is critical in the underdeveloped countries, and improvements in protein nutrition can come only by new techniques of increasing the amount and type of protein in cereals and other plant products.

The pessimists predict widespread famine by the mid-1970s in the underdeveloped countries. An extraordinary effort will be required to erase malnutrition, but there are no technical reasons why we cannot prevent famine in the underdeveloped countries.

SELECTED REFERENCES

BORGSTROM, G. 1967. *The Hungry Planet*. Collier Books, New York.

BROWN, L. R. 1970. Human food production as a process in the biosphere. *Sci. Amer.* 223(3):161–170.

BROWN, L. R. 1970. *Seeds of Change. The Green Revolution and Development in the 1970's*. Praeger, New York.

FOOD AND AGRICULTURE ORGANIZATION OF THE UNITED NATIONS. 1969. *Provisional Indicative World Plan for Agricultural Development.* Conference, F.A.O. c69/4, August 1969, 3 vols.

FOOD AND AGRICULTURE ORGANIZATION OF THE UNITED NATIONS. 1970. *The State of Food and Agriculture 1970.* United Nations, Rome.

HOLT, S. J. 1969. The food resources of the ocean. *Sci. Amer.* 221(3):178–194.

PIRIE, N. W. 1967. Orthodox and unorthodox methods of meeting world food needs. *Sci. Amer.* 216(2):27–35.

WHARTON, C. R., JR. 1969. The green revolution: cornucopia or Pandora's box? *Foreign Affairs* 47:464–476.

QUESTIONS AND PROBLEMS

1 Consult the latest publications from the Food and Agriculture Organization of the United Nations, and compare the current world food situation with the predictions discussed in this chapter.

2 Read the Paddock brothers' book *Famine—1975!* (Paddock and Paddock 1967) and discuss their predictions made in the mid-1960s in the light of the current food situation.

3 Brown (1970a, p. 161) states: "Throughout most of man's existence his numbers have been limited by the supply of food." Discuss.

Epilogue

We have progressed from the simple problem of distribution to the complicated applied problems of human ecology. There is a great deal we have omitted in our survey. The applied problems of pesticides and pollution have not been discussed; they are dealt with in a wealth of books specifically oriented toward man and his environment.

In this book I have attempted to sketch the framework of ecology as a pure science, and my purpose is to develop a particular view of the world, an "ecological consciousness." Two possible reasons for studying ecology are (1) to increase one's understanding of the world in which we live, and (2) to provide a basis for practical action on ecological problems. In a world in which many are suffering from poverty and malnutrition, we can justify ecological work on *Paramecium* or flatworms only if such pure research will lead to the solution of practical problems. *Practical problems can be solved only if they can be fitted into a solid theoretical framework.* This belief recurs throughout the book and is emphasized every day in the news media. One example will illustrate the interplay between pure and applied ecology. The Torrey Canyon oil spill was a milestone in pointing out how valuable background research can be when unscheduled calamities occur. When the Torrey Canyon was stranded off the southwest coast of England, none of the work of the Plymouth Laboratory, a research facility of the Marine Biological Association of the United Kingdom, was involved with the effects of oil and detergents on marine life. But because of their background knowledge and work on the local marine organisms, the Plymouth Laboratory could study and evaluate the effects of the Torrey Canyon pollution on marine life (Smith 1968).

The theoretical framework of ecology is beginning to take shape, a halting, slow progression based on many years of work by both theoretical and applied ecologists. The message of ecology today is essentially one of very great complexity, and the problems ecologists are attempting to analyze are as formidable as any in science. We must recognize this complexity but try not to take shelter in it. Most of the ideas of ecology are still hypotheses with an unknown range of applicability. These hypotheses do have consequences, and the job of the ecologist must be to translate these hypotheses into practical suggestions. Some ideas will turn out to be completely wrong; others will stand the practical test. Through all this controversies will flare, contradictions will be published, and tempers will explode. It is all a very human activity, and in some respects a microcosm of the world.

Appendix I   Estimation of the size of the marked population in capture-recapture studies

Data obtained from a multiple census should be cast in the form of a *method B table*. This table is constructed by asking for each individual caught: (1) Was it marked or unmarked when caught? (2) If marked, when was it last captured? The method B table summarizes the answers to these questions:

	Time of capture						
	1	2	3	4	5	6	
Time of last capture 1		10	3	5	2	2	$\leftarrow Z_3$
2			34	18	8	4	
3				33	13	8	$\leftarrow R_3$
4					30	20	
5						43	
Total marked	0	10	37	56	53	77	
Total unmarked	54	136	132	153	167	132	
Total caught	54	146	169	209	220	209	
Total released	54	143	164	202	214	207	

These data are reported in Jolly (1965), and we will use his formulas to estimate the size of the marked population. We use these symbols:

M_i = marked population size at time i
m_i = marked animals actually caught at time i
S_i = total animals released at time i
Z_i = number of individuals marked before time i, not caught in the ith sample but caught in a sample after time i
R_i = number of the S_i individuals released at time i that are caught in a later sample

Some examples from the above table will illustrate these definitions with respect to the method B table:

$m_2 = 10$
$m_5 = 53$
$S_3 = 164$
$S_4 = 202$
$Z_2 = 3 + 5 + 2 + 2 = 12$
$Z_4 = 2 + 2 + 8 + 4 + 13 + 8 = 37$
$R_1 = 10 + 3 + 5 + 2 + 2 = 22$
$R_3 = 33 + 13 + 8 = 54$

The formula to estimate the size of the marked population is

$$M_i = \frac{S_i Z_i}{R_i} + m_i$$

For example,

$$M_3 = \frac{(164)\,(39)}{54} + 37 = 155.4$$

$$M_4 = \frac{(202)\,(37)}{50} + 56 = 205.5$$

From the discussion in Chapter 9, we know that

$$\text{Total population size} = \frac{\text{marked population size}}{\text{proportion of animals marked}}$$

Consequently, we can calculate estimates for:

$$\text{Total population at time 3} = \frac{155.4}{37/169} = 709.8 \text{ animals}$$

$$\text{Total population at time 4} = \frac{205.5}{56/209} = 767.0 \text{ animals}$$

Note that this is only one possible way of estimating the size of the marked population, and it may not be the best technique for all circumstances (Manly 1970).

Appendix II   Instantaneous and

finite rates

The concept of "rates" is critical for quantitative work in ecology, and students may find a brief review useful for the discussions in Chapter 10 especially.

A *rate* is a numerical proportion between two sets of things. For example, the number of rotten apples per bushel might be measured to be 6 rotten apples per bushel. The number of students failing an examination might be 27 of 350, a failure rate of 7.7%. In ecological usage, a rate is usually expressed with a standard time base. Thus if 8 seedlings of 12 die within 1 year, the mortality rate will be 66.7% *per year*. Or if a population grows from 100 to 150 within 1 month, the rate of population increase will be 50% *per month*.

We usually think in terms of *finite rates*, which are simple expressions of observed values. Some ecological examples are

$$\text{Annual survival rate} = \frac{\text{number alive at end of year}}{\text{number alive at start of year}}$$

$$\text{Annual rate of population change} = \frac{\text{population size at end of year}}{\text{population size at start of year}}$$

Rates can also be expressed as *instantaneous rates*, in which the time base becomes very short rather than a year or a month. The general relationship between finite rates and instantaneous rates is:

$$\text{Finite rate} = e^{\text{instantaneous rate}}$$
$$\text{Instantaneous rate} = \log_e \text{finite rate}$$

where $e = 2.71828 \ldots$.

The idea of an instantaneous rate can be explained most simply by the use of compound interest. Suppose we have a population of 100 organisms increasing at a *finite* rate of 10% per year. The population size at the end of year 1 will be

$$100(1 + \tfrac{1}{10}) = 110$$

At the end of year 2:

$$110(1 + \tfrac{1}{10}) = 121$$

At the end of year 3:

$$121(1 + \tfrac{1}{10}) = 133.1$$

Or, in general, for an interest rate of $1/m$ carried out n times,

$$y_n = y_0 \left(1 + \frac{1}{m} \right)^n$$

where

y_n = amount at end of the nth operation
y_0 = amount at start

We can repeat these calculations for a finite interest rate of 5% per half-year. Everyone who has invested money in a savings account knows that 5% interest per half-year is a *better* interest rate than 10% per year. We can see this quite simply. At 6 months our population size will be

$$100(1 + \tfrac{1}{20}) = 105$$

At 1 year

$$105(1 + \tfrac{1}{20}) = 110.25$$

and similarly at 2 years 121.55 and at 3 years 134.01. Compare these values with those obtained above for 10% annual interest.

Biological systems often operate on a time schedule of hours and days, so we may be more realistic in using rates that are instantaneous, rates that break up a year into very many short time periods. Let us repeat the first calculation above with an *instantaneous* rate of increase of 10% per year. If we divide the year into 1000 short time periods with each time period having a rate of increase of 0.10/1000, or 0.0001, we have for the first 1000th of the year,

$$100(1 + 0.0001) = 100.01$$

For the second 1000th of the year,

$$100.01(1 + 0.0001) = 100.020001$$

If we repeat this for all 1000 time intervals, we end with 110.5 organisms at the end of 1 year.

Instantaneous rates and finite rates are nearly complementary when rates are very small. The following table shows how they diverge as the rates become large and illustrates the change in size of a hypothetical population which starts at 100 organisms and increases or decreases at the specified rate for one time period:

Percent change	Finite rate	Instantaneous rate	Hypothetical population at end of one time period
−75	0.25	−1.386	25
−50	0.50	−0.693	50
−25	0.75	−0.287	75
−10	0.90	−0.105	90
−5	0.95	−0.051	95
0	1.00	0.00	100
5	1.05	0.049	015
10	1.10	0.095	110
25	1.25	0.223	125
50	1.50	0.405	150
75	1.75	0.560	175
100	2.00	0.693	200
200	3.00	1.099	300
400	5.00	1.609	500
900	10.00	2.303	1000

	decreases	increases	
0	1.00	$+\infty$	*Finite rates*
$-\infty$	0.0	$+\infty$	*Instantaneous rates*

This illustrates one difference between finite rates (always positive or zero) and instantaneous rates (range from $-\infty$ to $+\infty$).

Mortality rates can be expressed as finite rates or as instantaneous rates. If the number of deaths in a short interval of time is proportional to the total population size at that time, the rate of drop in numbers can be described by the geometric equation

$$\frac{dN}{dt} = iN$$

where

N = population size
i = instantaneous mortality rate
t = time

In integral form we have

$$N_t = N_0 e^{it}$$

or

$$\frac{N_t}{N_0} = e^{it}$$

where

N_0 = starting population size
N_t = population size at time t*

Taking logs, we obtain (if $t = 1$ time unit)

$$\log_e\left(\frac{N_t}{N_0}\right) = i$$

Since N_t/N_o is the finite survival rate by definition, we have obtained

$\log_e$(finite survival rate) = instantaneous mortality rate

We thus obtain the following relationships for expressing mortality rates:

Finite survival rate = 1.0 − finite mortality rate
$\log_e$(finite survival rate) = instantaneous mortality rate
Finite survival rate = $e^{\text{instantaneous mortality rate}}$
Finite mortality rate = 1.0 − $e^{\text{instantaneous mortality rate}}$

Why does one need to use instantaneous rates? The principal reason is that instantaneous rates are easier to deal with mathematically. A simple example will illustrate this property. Suppose you have data on an insect population and know that the mortality rate is 50% in the egg stage and 90% in the larval stages. How can you combine these mortalities? If they are expressed as finite mortality rates, we cannot add them because a 50% loss followed by a 90% loss is obviously not 140% mortality but only 95% mortality. If, however, the mortality is expressed as instantaneous rates, we can add them directly:

	Instantaneous mortality rate
Egg stage (50%)	−0.693
Larval stages (90%)	−2.303
Combined loss	−2.996

We can convert back to a finite mortality rate by the formula given above:

Finite mortality rate = 1.0 − $e^{\text{instantaneous mortality rate}}$
$= 1.0 - e^{-2.996}$
$= 0.950$

and the combined mortality is seen to be 95%.

* Note that instantaneous rates are determined for a specific time base (per year, per month, etc.), even though the rate applies to a very short time interval. The examples on page 633 illustrate this.

Four examples will illustrate some of these ideas, and students are referred to Ricker (1958, Chap. 1) for further discussion.

Example 1 A population increases from 73 to 97 within 1 year. This can be expressed as

a Finite rate of population growth $= 97/73 = 1.329$ per head per year (or the population grew 32.9% in 1 year).

b Instantaneous rate of population growth $= \log_e (97/73) = 0.284$ per head per year.

Example 2 A population decreases from 67 to 48 within 1 month. This can be expressed as

a Finite rate of population growth $= 48/67 = 0.716$ per head per month (or the population decreased 28.4% over the month).

b Instantaneous rate of population growth $= \log_e (48/67) = -0.333$ per head per month.

Example 3 A cohort of trees decreases in number from 24 to 19 within 1 year. This can be expressed as

a Annual survival rate (finite) $= 19/24 = 0.792$.

b Annual mortality rate (finite) $= 1.0 -$ annual survival rate $= 0.208$.

c Instantaneous mortality rate $= \log_e (19/24) = -0.234$ per year.

Example 4 A cohort of fish decreases in number from 350,000 to 79,000 within 1 year. This can be expressed as

a Annual survival rate (finite) $= 79,000/350,000 = 0.2257$.

b Annual mortality rate (finite) $= 1.0 - 0.2257 = 0.7743$.

c Instantaneous mortality rate $= \log_e 0.2257 = -1.488$ per year.

Glossary

Ecological jargon is often carried to extremes in an attempt to confuse the amateur. This book tries to avoid most of this jargon, and the glossary contains words used in the text that might be unfamiliar to students.

abiotic factors characterized by the absence of life; include temperature, humidity, pH, and other physical and chemical influences.

accidental species species that occur with a low degree of fidelity in a community type; not good species for use in community definition; see *characteristic species*.

aestivation condition in which an organism may pass an unfavorable season and in which its normal activities are greatly curtailed or temporarily suspended.

aggregation coming together of organisms into a group, as in locusts.

allele one of a pair of characters that are alternative to each other in inheritance, being governed by genes situated at the same locus in homologous chromosomes.

allelopathy influence of plants, exclusive of microorganisms, upon each other, caused by products of metabolism; "antibiotic" interaction between plants.

association major unit in community ecology, characterized by essential uniformity of species composition.

autecology   study of the individual in relation to environmental conditions.

biogeography   branch of biology that deals with the geographic distribution of plants and animals.

biological control   use of organisms or viruses to control parasites, weeds, or other pests.

biota   species of all the plants and animals occurring within a certain area or region.

biotic factors   environmental influences caused by plants or animals; opposite of *abiotic factors*.

bryophytes   plant in the phylum Bryophyta comprising mosses, liverworts, and hornworts.

canonical distribution   particular configuration of the log-normal distribution of species abundances.

carnivore   flesh eating; organism that eats other animals; contrasted with *herbivore*.

catastrophic agents   term used by Howard and Fiske to describe agents of destruction in which the percentage of destruction is not related to population density; synonymous with density-independent factors.

characteristic species   species that are rigidly limited to certain communities and thus can be used to identify a particular type of community.

climax   kind of community capable of perpetuation under the prevailing climatic and edaphic conditions.

community   group of populations of plants and animals in a given place; ecological unit used in a broad sense to include groups of various sizes and degrees of integration.

compensation point   depth in a body of water at which the light intensity is such that the amount of oxygen produced by a plant's photosynthesis equals the oxygen it absorbs in respiration; the point at which respiration equals photosynthesis so that net production is zero.

competition   occurs when a number of organisms of the same or of different species utilize common resources that are in short supply ("exploitation"); or, if the resources are not in short supply, competition occurs when the organisms seeking that resource harm one another in the process ("interference").

contingency table   frequency distribution for an *n*-way statistical classification.

continuum index   measure of the position of a community on a gradient defined by the species composition.

deme   interbreeding group in a population; also known as local population.

density   number of individuals in relation to the space in which they occur.

deterministic model   mathematical model in which all the relationships are fixed and the concept of probability does not enter; a given input produces one exact prediction as output; opposite of *stochastic model*.

diapause   period of suspended growth or development and reduced metabolism in the life cycle of many insects, in which the organism is more resistant to unfavorable environmental conditions than in other periods.

dilution rate general term to describe the rate of additions to a population from birth and immigrations.

dominance condition in communities or in vegetational strata in which one or more species, by means of their number, coverage, or size, have considerable influence or control upon the conditions of existence of associated species.

dynamic-pool model type of optimum-yield model in which the yield is predicted from the components of growth, mortality, recruitment, and fishing intensity; contrast with *logistic-type model*.

dynamics in population ecology the study of the reasons for *changes* in population size; contrast with *statics*.

ecological longevity average length of life of individuals of a population under stated conditions.

ecosystem biotic community and its abiotic environment; the whole earth can be considered as one large ecosystem.

ecotone transition zone between two diverse communities (e.g., the tundra–boreal forest ecotone).

ecotype subspecies or race that is especially adapted to a particular set of environmental conditions.

elfinwood (Krummholz) scrubby, stunted growth form of trees, often forming a characteristic zone at the limit of tree growth in mountains.

elytron/femur ratio (E/F) ratio of the length of the elytron (outer wing) of locust to the length of the femur (part of hind leg); used to determine morphological phase status of locusts.

environment all the biotic and abiotic factors that actually affect an individual organism at any point in its life cycle.

epidemiology branch of medicine dealing with epidemic diseases.

equitability evenness of distribution of species abundance patterns; maximum equitability occurs when all species are represented by the same number of individuals.

evapotranspiration sum total of water lost from the land by evaporation and plant transpiration.

facultative agents term used by Howard and Fiske to describe agents of destruction which increase their percentage of destruction as population density rises; synonymous with density-dependent factors.

fecundity potential capability of an organism to produce reproductive units such as eggs, sperms, or asexual structures.

fertility actual capability of an organism to produce living offspring.

fidelity degree of regularity or "faithfulness" with which a species occurs in certain plant communities, expressed on a five-part scale: (5) exclusive, (4) selective, (3) preferential, (2) companion, indifferent, (1) accidental, strangers.

food chain figure of speech for the dependence for food of organisms upon others in a series, beginning with plants and ending with the largest carnivores.

genecology study of population genetics in relation to the habitat conditions, the study of species and other taxa by the combined methods, and concepts of ecology and genetics.

genotype entire genetic constitution of an organism; contrast with *phenotype*.

global stability ability to withstand perturbations of a large magnitude and not be affected; compare with *neighborhood stability*.

gradocoen totality of all factors that impinge on a population, including biotic agents and abiotic factors.

gross production production before respiration losses are subtracted; photosynthetic production for plants and metabolizable production for animals.

herbivore organism that eats plants; contrast with *carnivore*.

homeostasis maintenance of constancy or a high degree of uniformity in functions of an organism or interactions of individuals in a population or community under changing conditions, because of the capabilities of organisms to make adjustments.

homeothermic pertaining to "warm-blooded" animals that regulate their body temperature; contrast with *poikilothermic*.

host organism that furnishes food, shelter, or other benefits to another organism of a different species.

hydrophyte plant that grows wholly or partly immersed in water; compare with *xerophyte* and *mesophyte*.

importance value sum of relative density, relative dominance, and relative frequency for a species in the community; scale from 0 to 300; the larger the importance value, the more dominant a species is in the particular community.

index of similarity ratio of the number of species found in common in two communities to the total number of species that are present in both.

indifferent species species occurring in many different communities; not good species for community classification.

innate capacity for increase (r_m) measure of the rate of increase of a population under controlled conditions.

interspecific competition competition between members of different species.

invasion area in locusts the area colonized by swarms during an outbreak; the invasion area cannot support permanent populations of locusts.

isotherm line drawn on a map or chart connecting places with the same temperature at a particular time or for a certain period.

life table tabulation presenting complete data on the mortality schedule of a population.

littoral shallow-water zone of lakes or the sea, with light penetration to the bottom; often occupied by rooted aquatic plants.

logistic equation model of population growth described by a symmetrical S-shaped curve with an upper asymptote.

logistic-type model type of optimum-yield model in which the yield is predicted from an overall descriptive function of population growth without a separate analysis of the components of mortality, recruitment, and growth; contrast with *dynamic-pool model*.

log-normal distribution frequency distribution of species abundances in which the X axis is expressed on a logarithmic scale; X axis is (log) number of individuals represented in sample, Y axis is number of species.

loss rate general term to describe the rate of removal of organisms from a population by death and emigration.

mesic   moderately moist habitat.

mesophyte   plant that grows in environmental conditions that are medium in moisture conditions.

monogamy   mating of an animal with only one member of the opposite sex.

monothetic   positing but one essential element; in classifications, defining groups on the basis of a single key character.

morphology   study of the form, structure, and development of organisms.

multivoltine   refers to an organism that has several generations during a single season; contrast with *univoltine*.

mutualism   interaction between two species in which both benefit from the association and cannot live separately.

neighborhood stability   ability to withstand perturbations of small magnitude and not be affected; compare with *global stability*.

net production   production after respiration losses are subtracted.

niche   role or "profession" of an organism in the environment; its activities and relationships in the community.

obligate predator   (or parasite)   predator that is restricted to eating a single species of prey.

oligochaetes   any of a class or order (Oligochaeta) of hermaphroditic terrestrial or aquatic annelids lacking a specialized head; includes earthworms.

optimum yield   amount of material that can be removed from a population that will maximize biomass (or numbers, or profit, or any other type of "optimum") on a sustained basis.

ordination   process by which plant or animal communities are ordered along a gradient.

outbreak area   in locusts the area that can produce swarms that may then move into the invasion area; outbreak area may be permanently inhabitable by locusts.

parasite   organism that benefits while feeding upon, securing shelter from, or otherwise injuring another organism (the host); insect parasites are usually fatal to their host and behave more like vertebrate predators.

parthenogenesis   development of the egg of an organism into an embryo without fertilization.

phenology   study of the periodic (seasonal) phenomena of animal and plant life and their relations to the weather and climate (e.g., the time of flowering in plants).

phenotype   expression of the characteristics of an organism as determined by the interaction of its genic constitution and the environment; contrast with *genotype*.

photoperiodism   response of plants and animals to the relative duration of light and darkness (e.g., a chrysanthemum blooming under short days and long nights).

photosynthesis   synthesis of carbohydrates from carbon dioxide and water by chlorophyll using light as energy with oxygen as a by-product.

physiological longevity   maximum lifespan of individuals in a population under specified conditions; the organisms die of senescence.

phytoplankton plant portion of the plankton; the plant community in marine and freshwater situations which floats free in the water and contains many species of algae and diatoms.

poikilothermic of or pertaining to "cold-blooded animals"; organisms having no rapidly operating heat-regulatory mechanism; contrast with *homeothermic*.

polyandry mating of a single female with several males.

polygyny mating of one male animal with several females.

polythetic positing many essential elements; in classifications, defining groups on the basis of many characteristics, not just one.

population group of individuals of a single species.

primary production production by green plants.

production amount of energy (or material) formed by an individual, population, or community in a specific time period; see *primary production, secondary production, gross production, net production*.

promiscuous mating system in which males and females are not restricted to one sexual partner.

proximate factors in evolutionary terms the mechanisms responsible for an adaptation with reference to its physiological and behavioral operation; the mechanics of how an adaptation operates; opposite of *ultimate factors*.

recruitment increment to a natural population usually from young animals or plants entering the "adult" population.

respiration complex series of chemical reactions in all organisms by which energy is made available for use; carbon dioxide, water, and energy are the end products.

saprophyte plant that obtains food from dead or decaying organic matter.

secondary production production by herbivores, carnivores, or detritus feeders; contrast with *primary production*.

self-regulation process of population regulation in which population increase is prevented by a deterioration in the quality of individuals that make up the population; population regulation by internal adjustments in behavior and physiology within the population, rather than by external forces such as predators.

senescence process of aging.

seral series of stages that follow one another in an ecological succession.

serotinous cones cones of some pine trees which remain on the trees for several years without opening and require a fire to open and release the seeds.

sessile animal that is attached to an object or is fixed in place (e.g., barnacles).

sigmoid curve S-shaped curve (e.g., the logistic curve).

stability absence of fluctuations in populations; ability to withstand perturbations without large changes in composition.

statics in population ecology the study of the reasons of equilibrial conditions or average values; contrast with *dynamics*.

stenoplastic having little or no modificational plasticity; steno- means narrow; opposite of euryplastic.

steppe extensive area of natural, dry grassland; usually used in reference to grasslands in southwestern Asia and southeastern Europe; equivalent to *prairie* in North American usage.

sterol any of a group of solid, mostly unsaturated polycyclic alcohols, such as cholesterol or ergosterol, derived from plants and animals.

stochastic model mathematical model based on probabilities; the prediction of the model is not a single fixed number but a range of possible numbers; opposite of *deterministic model*.

sublittoral lower division in the sea from a depth of 40 to 60 m to about 200 m; below the littoral zone.

succession replacement of one kind of community by another kind; the progressive changes in vegetation and animal life that may culminate in the climax.

symbiosis in a broad sense the living together of two or more organisms of different species; in a narrow sense synonymous with *mutualism*.

synecology study of groups of organisms in relation to their environment; includes population, community, and ecosystem ecology.

taiga the northern boreal forest zone, a broad band of coniferous forest south of the arctic tundra.

thermoregulation maintenance or regulation of temperature, specifically the maintenance of a particular temperature of the living body.

trace element chemical element used by organisms in minute quantities and essential to their physiology.

triclad any of an order Tricladida of turbellarian platyhelminths, distinguished by having one anterior and two posterior branches of the intestine.

trophic level functional classification of organisms in a community according to feeding relationships; the first trophic level includes green plants; the second trophic level includes herbivores; etc.

tundra treeless area in arctic and alpine regions, varying from bare area to various types of vegetation consisting of grasses, sedges, forbs, dwarf shrubs, lichens, and mosses.

ultimate factors in evolutionary terms the survival value of the adaptation in question; the evolutionary reason for the adaptation; opposite of *proximate factors*.

univoltine refers to an organism that has only one generation per year.

vector organism (often an insect) that transmits a pathogenic virus, bacteria, protozoan, or fungus from one organism to another.

wilting point measure of soil water; the water remaining in the soil (expressed as percentage dry weight of the soil) when the plants are in a state of permanent wilting from water shortage.

xeric deficient in available moisture for the support of life (e.g., desert environments).

xerophyte plant that can grow in dry places (e.g., cacti).

zooplankton animal portion of the plankton; the animal community in marine and freshwater situations which floats free in the water, independent of the shore and the bottom, moving passively with the currents.

Mathematical symbols

All the symbols used in equations in this book are defined here. I have tried to minimize duplication of letters. There is no universal agreement on the use of symbols and other books and papers will not agree with my usage in some cases.

α *1* competition coefficient measuring the effect of species 2 on species 1; converts species 2 into equivalent units of species 1 (page 213)

             2 index of diversity of logarithmic series (page 502)

a *1* in the logistic equation a constant of integration that defines the position of the curve relative to the origin (page 188)

             2 for a log-normal curve a constant measuring the amount of spread (page 504)

A *1* y intercept for a graph of instantaneous death rate (y axis) on population density (x axis) (page 275)

             2 rate of assimilation of phytoplankton by the zooplankton (page 494)

| β | competition coefficient measuring the effect of species 1 on species 2; converts species 1 into equivalent units of species 2 (page 214) |

b instantaneous birth rate (page 186)

B slope of line in a plot of net reproductive rate (y) on population density (x) (page 184)

B_1 and B_2 biomass in the community at time t_1 and time t_2 (page 448)

ΔB biomass change in the community between time t_1 and time t_2 (page 448)

c *1* slope of line for a plot of instantaneous death rate (y-axis) on population density x-axis) (page 275)

     2 constant for conversion of predator numbers to rate of zooplankton consumption (page 495)

C *1* constant measuring the efficiency of the predator (page 246)

     2 rate of consumption of zooplankton by their predators (page 494)

C_x proportion of organisms in the age category x to $x+1$ in a population increasing geometrically; the stable age distribution (page 175)

d instantaneous death rate (page 186)

d_x number of organisms dying in the interval x to $x+1$ in a life table (page 154)

D *1* death rate of zooplankton (page 494)

     2 Simpson's measure of species diversity (page 509)

e_x mean expectation of life for organisms alive at start of age x in the life table (page 154)

E equitability of species abundance patterns (page 507)

F *1* yield to fishery (page 344)

     2 instantaneous fishing mortality rate (page 347)

g *1* reproductive time lag in a time-lag model of population growth (page 202)

     2 constant for converting zooplankton abundance to a rate of grazing loss (page 492)

G *1* generation time; called T by many authors (page 170)

     2 growth in weight of fish in optimum-yield equations (page 344)

3 in production studies biomass losses to consumer organisms (page 448)

4 rate of grazing loss to zooplankton (page 490)

H *1* herbivore population biomass (page 494)

2 species diversity measured by the information content of sample (Shannon-Wiener function) (page 506)

I amount of solar radiation (page 451)

I_z solar radiation at depth z in a water column (page 490)

k extinction coefficient for light passing into water (page 451)

K upper asymptote or maximal density reached by a population growing in a logistic manner (page 188)

K_1 and K_2 *1* in the competition equations upper asymptote for population density of species 1 and species 2 when growing separately (page 212)

2 in predator–prey models K_1 is a constant measuring the ability of the prey to escape predators and K_2 is a constant measuring the skill of the predator in catching prey (page 249)

λ finite rate of increase, equal to $e^r m$ (page 171)

l_x number of survivors at start of age interval x in a life table (page 154)

L *1* in population growth model $L = B \cdot N_{eq}$ (page 186)

2 in production studies biomass losses by death of plants or plant parts (page 448)

L_x stationary age distribution of the life table; number of individuals alive on the average during the age interval x to $x + 1$ (page 156)

m_x fertility table, number of offspring produced per unit of time per female aged x (page 165)

M *1* weight of fish removed by natural deaths (page 344)

2 instantaneous natural mortality rate in yield equations (page 347)

N *1* number of organisms in a population (page 184) may be used with a subscript, N_t = number of organisms at time t (page 182), N_1 = number of organisms of species 1 (page 213)

2 term to measure phosphate limitation for phytoplankton (page 490)

3 in species abundance studies, the number of individuals in a sample (page 502)

N_{eq} equilibrium population size, when $R_o = 1.0$ (page 184)

p constant to convert solar radiation into photosynthesis rate for phytoplankton (page 490)

p_i proportion of the total sample that belongs to the ith species in species abundance studies (page 506)

P *1* population size of predator in predator–prey models (page 249)

        2 rate of photosynthesis per unit of phytoplankton population (page 490)

P_z rate of photosynthesis at depth z in a water column (page 490)

q constant in logistic-type optimum yield equations, conversion factor for converting fishing effort to fishing mortality rate (page 347)

q_x rate of mortality during the age interval x to $x + 1$ in a life table (page 154)

Q constant measuring the efficiency of utilization of prey for reproduction by predators (page 246)

r *1* reaction time lag in a time-lag model of population growth (page 202)

        2 constant measuring the rate of increase of respiration rate with temperature for marine phytoplankton (page 492)

r_m innate capacity for increase in numbers (page 165)

r_1 and r_2 innate capacity for increase of species 1 and species 2 in competition models (page 213)

R *1* maximum reproductive rate of prey in predator–prey models (page 246)

        2 weight of new recruits in optimum-yield equations (page 344)

        3 rate of phytoplankton respiration (page 490)

        4 respiration rate of zooplankton (page 494)

R_0 net reproductive rate (page 166)

R_T respiration rate of phytoplankton at temperature T (page 492)

S *1* maximum reproductive rate of the predator in predator–prey models (page 246)

        2 number of zooplankton predators (page 495)

3   number of species in a sample (page 502)

S_1 and S_2 weight of catchable stock at start of year (S_1) and at end of year (S_2) (page 344)

t time (page 168)

t_c age at which fish enter the fishery (page 348)

T temperature (page 492)

T_x defined as $\sum_x^\infty L_x$ in a life table; measures the remaining life-spans of a life-table cohort in units of (individuals · time units) (page 156)

V term to measure vertical mixing losses of phytoplankton in the sea (page 491)

V_x product of l_x and m_x, called the reproductive function by some authors because it gives the expected number of offspring for a given schedule of natality and mortality (page 167)

W_t average weight of age t fish (page 348)

x 1 subscript to denote age in life tables (page 154)

        2 deviation from equilibrium density $(N - N_{eq})$ (page 184)

        3 phytoplankton population size (page 490)

X amount of fishing effort in logistic-type equation for optimum yield (page 347)

y number of species to occur in the Rth octave to the right or left of the modal class for log-normal distribution (page 504)

y_0 number of species in the modal octave (the largest class) for log-normal distribution (page 504)

Y yield in weight to fishery in optimum-yield equations (page 348)

z_1 maximum depth of photosynthesis (compensation level) (page 490)

Z quantity of zooplankton in water (page 492)

Bibliography

AGNEW, A. D. Q. 1961. The ecology of *Juncus effusus* L. in North Wales. *J. Ecol.* 49:83–102.

ALBRECHT, F. O. 1967. *Polymorphisme phasaire et biologie des acridiens migrateurs.* Masson, Paris.

ALBRECHT, F. O., M. VERDIER, and R. E. BLACKITH. 1959. Maternal control of ovariole number in the progeny of the migratory locust. *Nature* 184:103–104.

ALEXANDER, M. M. 1958. The place of aging in wildlife management. *Amer. Sci.* 46:123–137.

ALLEE, W. C., A. E. EMERSON, O. PARK, T. PARK, and K. P. SCHMIDT. 1949. *Principles of Animal Ecology.* Saunders, Philadelphia.

ALLEN, K. R. 1955. The growth of accuracy in ecology. *Proc. New Zeal. Ecol. Soc.* 1:1–7.

ALLEN, P. H. 1961. Florida longleaf pine fail in Virginia. *J. Forestry* 59:453–454.

ALVERSON, D. L., A. R. LONGHURST, and J. A. GULLAND. 1970. How much food from the sea? *Science* 168:503–505.

ANDERSON, D. J. 1967. Studies on structure in plant communities. IV. Cyclical succession in *Dryas* communities from north-west Iceland. *J. Ecol.* 55:629–635.

ANDREWARTHA, H. G. 1961. *Introduction to the Study of Animal Populations.* University of Chicago Press, Chicago.

ANDREWARTHA, H. G., and L. C. BIRCH. 1954. *The Distribution and Abundance of Animals.* University of Chicago Press, Chicago.

ANON. 1956. Native trees of Canada. *Forestry Branch, Dept. Northern Affairs and National Resources, Ottawa, Bull. 61,* 5th ed. 293 pp.

APPLEGATE, V. C. 1950. Natural history of the sea lamprey, *Petromyzon marinus,* in Michigan. *U.S. Fish Wildl. Ser., Spec. Sci. Rep., Fish., No. 55.* 237 pp.

ARBUTHNOT, K. D. 1944. Strains of the European corn borer in the United States. *U.S. Dept. Agr. Tech. Bull. No. 869.* 20 pp.

ARON, W. I., and S. H. SMITH. 1971. Ship canals and aquatic ecosystems. *Science* 174:13–20.

ASHBY, E. 1948. Statistical ecology. II. A reassessment. *Bot. Rev.* 14:222–234.

AYALA, F. J. 1969. Experimental invalidation of the principle of competitive exclusion. *Nature* 224:1076–1079.

BABCOCK, K. W., and A. M. VANCE. 1929. The corn borer in central Europe. A review of investigations from 1924 to 1927. *U.S. Dept. Agr. Tech. Bull. No. 135.* 54 pp.

BAKER, H. G. 1965. Characteristics and modes of weeds. pp. 147–172 in *The Genetics of Colonizing Species,* ed. by H. G. Baker and G. L. Stebbins. Academic, New York.

BALDWIN, N. S. 1964. Sea lamprey in the Great Lakes. *Can. Audubon Mag.* Nov.–Dec. 1964, pp. 2–7.

BANFIELD, W. M. 1968. Dutch elm disease recurrence and recovery in American elm. *Phytopathol. Z.* 62:21–60.

BARCLAY, G. W. 1958. *Techniques of Population Analysis.* Wiley, New York.

BARCLAY–ESTRUP, P., and C. H. GIMINGHAM. 1969. The description and interpretation of cyclical processes in a heath community. I. Vegetational change in relation to the *Calluna* cycle. *J. Ecol.* 57:737–758.

BARNES, H. 1957. The northern limits of *Balanus balanoides* (L.). *Oikos* 8:1–15.

BARNES, H. 1958. Regarding the southern limits of *Balanus balanoides* (L). *Oikos* 9:139–157.

BARNES, H. 1962. So-called anecdysis in *Balanus balanoides* and the effect of breeding upon the growth of calcareous shell of some common barnacles. *Limnol. Oceanogr.* 7:462–473.

BARTLETT, M. S. 1960. *Stochastic Population Models in Ecology and Epidemiology.* Wiley, New York.

BEALS, E. 1960. Forest bird communities in the Apostle Islands of Wisconsin. *Wilson Bull.* 72:156–181.

BEAUFAIT, W. R. 1960. Some effects of high temperatures on the cones and seeds of jack pine. *Forest Sci.* 6:194–199.

BEILMANN, A. P., and L. G. BRENNER. 1951. The recent intrusion of forests in the Ozarks. *Ann. Missouri Bot. Garden* 38:261–282.

BELL, A. R., and J. D. NALEWAJA. 1968. Competitive effects of wild oat in flax. *Weed Sci.* 16:501–504.

BERELSON, B. 1969. Beyond family planning. *Science* 163:533–543.

BERGER, W. H., and F. L. PARKER. 1970. Diversity of planktonic foraminifera in deep-sea sediments. *Science* 168:1345–1347.

BETTS, E. 1961. Outbreaks of the African migratory locust (*Locusta migratoria migratorioides*, R. & F.) since 1871. *Anti-Locust Mem.* 6:1–25.

BEVERTON, R. J. H. 1962. Long-term dynamics of certain North Sea fish populations. pp. 242–259 in *The Exploitation of Natural Animal Populations*, ed. by E. D. LeCren and M. W. Holdgate. Blackwell, Oxford.

BEVERTON, R. J. H., and S. J. HOLT. 1957. *On the Dynamics of Exploited Fish Populations*. H.M. Stationery Office, London.

BILLINGS, W. D. 1938. The structure and development of old field shortleaf pine stands and certain associated physical properties of the soil. *Ecol. Monogr.* 8:437–499.

BILLINGS, W. D. 1949. The shadscale vegetation zone of Nevada and eastern California in relation to climate and soils. *Amer. Midl. Natur.* 42:87–109.

BILLINGS, W. D. 1950. Vegetation and plant growth as affected by chemically altered rocks in the western Great Basin. *Ecology* 31:62–74.

BILLINGS, W. D. 1952. The environmental complex in relation to plant growth and distribution. *Quart. Rev. Biol.* 27:251–265.

BIRCH, L. C. 1948. The intrinsic rate of natural increase of an insect population. *J. Anim. Ecol.* 17:15–26.

BIRCH, L. C. 1953a. Experimental background to the study of the distribution and abundance of insects. I. The influence of temperature, moisture and food on the innate capacity for increase of three grain beetles. *Ecology* 34:698–711.

BIRCH, L. C. 1953b. Experimental background to the study of the distribution and abundance of insects. III. The relations between innate capacity for increase and survival of different species of beetles living together on the same food. *Evolution* 7:136–144.

BIRCH, L. C. 1957. The meanings of competition. *Amer. Naturalist* 91:5–18.

BIRCH, L. C., and P. R. EHRLICH. 1967. Evolutionary history and population biology. *Nature* 214:349–352.

BJORKMAN, O., and P. HOLMGREN. 1963. Adaptability of the photosynthetic apparatus to light intensity in ecotypes from exposed and shaded habitats. *Physiol. Plant.* 16:889–914.

BLAKE, J. 1971. Reproductive motivation and population policy. *BioScience* 21(5):215–220.

BODENHEIMER, F. S. 1928. Welche Faktoren regulieren die Individuenzahl einer Insektenart in der Natur? *Biol. Zentralbl.* 48:714–739.

BOGUE, D. J. 1969. *Principles of Demography*. Wiley, New York.

BOND, G. 1951. The fixation of nitrogen associated with the root nodules of *Myrica gale* L., with special reference to its pH relation and ecological significance. *Ann. Bot.* 15:447–459.

BOND, R. R. 1957. Ecological distribution of breeding birds in the upland forests of southern Wisconsin. *Ecol. Monogr.* 27:351–384.

BOOTH, W. E. 1941. Revegetation of abandoned fields in Kansas and Oklahoma. *Amer. J. Bot.* 28:415–422.

BORCHERT, J. R. 1950. The climate of the central North American grassland. *Ann. Ass. Amer. Geogr.* 40:1–39.

BORGSTROM, G. 1967. *The Hungry Planet.* Collier Books, New York

BORMANN, F. H., and G. E. LIKENS. 1967. Nutrient cycling. *Science* 155:424–429.

BÖRNER, H. 1960. Liberation of organic substances from higher plants and their role in the soil sickness problem. *Bot. Rev.* 26:393–424.

BOYCE, S. G. 1954. The salt spray community. *Ecol. Monogr.* 24:29–67.

BOYCOTT, A. E. 1927. Oecological notes. X. Transplantation experiments on the habitats of *Planorbis corneus* and *Bithinia tentaculata. Proc. Malac. Soc. London* 17:156–158.

BOYCOTT, A. E. 1936. The habitats of fresh-water Mollusca in Britain. *J. Anim. Ecol.* 5:116–186.

BOYKO, H. 1947. On the role of plants as quantitative climate indicators and the geo-ecological law of distribution. *J. Ecol.* 35:138–157.

BRADSHAW, A. D. 1959. Population differentiation in *Agrostis tenuis* Sibth. I. Morphological differentiation. *New Phytol.* 58:208–227.

BRADSHAW, A. D. 1960. Population differentiation in *Agrostis tenuis* Sibth. III. Populations in varied environments. *New Phytol.* 59:92–103.

BRAUN, E. L. 1950. *Deciduous Forests of Eastern North America.* Hafner, New York.

BRAUN–BLANQUET, J. 1932. *Plant Sociology*, transl. from German by G. D. Fuller and H. S. Conard.

BRAY, J. R. 1963. Root production and the estimation of net productivity. *Can. J. Bot.* 41:65–72.

BRAY, J. R., D. B. LAWRENCE, and L. C. PEARSON. 1959. Primary production in some Minnesota terrestrial communities. *Oikos* 10:38–49.

BRETT, J. R. 1944. Some lethal temperature relations of Algonquin Park fishes. *Univ. Toronto Stud. Biol. Ser.* 52:1–49.

BRETT, J. R. 1956. Some principles in the thermal requirements of fishes. *Quart. Rev. Biol.* 31:75–87.

BRETT, J. R. 1959. *Thermal Requirements of Fish—Three Decades of Study, 1940–1970* (Trans. Second Seminar on Biol. Problems in Water Pollution, April 1959). U.S. Public Health Service, Taft Center, Cincinnati, Ohio.

BRIX, H., and L. F. EBELL. 1969. Effects of nitrogen fertilization on growth, leaf area, and photosynthesis rate in Douglas-fir. *Forest Sci.* 15:189–196.

BROCK, T. D. 1966. *Principles of Microbial Ecology.* Prentice-Hall, Englewood Cliffs, N.J.

BRODY, S. 1945. *Bioenergetics and Growth.* Van Nostrand Reinhold, New York.

BRONGERSMA-SANDERS, M. 1957. Mass mortality in the sea. pp. 941–1010 in *Treatise on Marine Ecology and Paleoecology*, Vol. I, ed. by J. Hedgpeth.

BROOKS, M. G. 1951. Effect of black walnut trees and their products on other vegetation. *West Virginia Univ. Agr. Exp. Sta., Bull. 347.* 31 pp.

BROWER, L. P. 1969. Ecological chemistry. *Sci. Amer.* 220(2):22–29.

BROWN, D. 1954. Methods of surveying and measuring vegetation. *Commonwealth Bureau of Pastures and Field Crops, Bull. 42*, Hurley, Berks, England. 223 pp.

BROWN, L. R. 1970a. Human food production as a process in the biosphere. *Sci. Amer.* 223(3):161–170.

BROWN, L. R. 1970b. Nobel Peace Prize: Developer of high-yield wheat receives award. *Science* 170:518–519.

BROWN, L. R. 1970c. *Seeds of Change. The Green Revolution and Development in the 1970's.* Praeger, New York.

BROWN, R. T., and J. T. CURTIS. 1952. The upland conifer–hardwood forests of northern Wisconsin. *Ecol. Monogr.* 22:217–234.

BUCKNER, C. H., and W. J. TURNOCK. 1965. Avian predation on the larch sawfly, *Pristiphora erichsonii* (Htg.), (Hymenoptera: Tenthredinidae). *Ecology* 46:223–236.

BUFFON, G. L. L., COMPTE DE. 1756. *Natural History, General and Particular.* (translation, W. Creech, Edinburgh, 1780.)

BUMP, G. 1963. History and analysis of Tetraonid introductions into North America. *J. Wildl. Mgmt.* 27:855–867.

BURLEY, J. 1966. Review of variation in slash pine (*Pinus elliottii* Engelm.) and loblolly pine (*P. taeda* L.) in relation to provenance research. *Commonwealth Forestry Rev.* 45:322–328.

BURSELL, E. 1960. The effect of temperature on the consumption of fat during pupal development in *Glossina. Bull. Entomol. Res.* 51:583–598.

CABLE, D. R. 1969. Competition in the semidesert grass-shrub type as influenced by root systems, growth habits, and soil moisture extraction. *Ecology* 50:27–38.

CAIN, S. A. 1944. *Foundations of Plant Geography.* Harper & Row, New York.

CALLAHAM, R. Z. 1964. Provenance research: investigation of genetic diversity associated with geography. *Unasylva* 18(2–3):40–50.

CAMPBELL, I. M. 1962. Reproductive capacity in the genus *Choristoneura* Led. (Lepidoptera: Tortricidae). I. Quantitative inheritance and genes as controllers of rates. *Can. J. Genet. Cytol.* 4:272–288.

Canada Year Book 1969. Dominion Bureau of Statistics, Ottawa, Ontario.

CARLSON, T. 1913. Über Geschwindigkeit und Grösse der Hefevermehrung in Würze. *Biochem. Z.* 57:313–334.

CARSON, H. L. 1965. Chromosomal morphism in geographically widespread species of *Drosophila.* pp. 503–531 in *The Genetics of Colonizing Species*, ed. by H. G. Baker and G. L. Stebbins. Academic, New York.

CAUGHLEY, G. 1966. Mortality patterns in mammals. *Ecology* 47:906–918.

CAUGHLEY, G. 1970. Eruption of ungulate populations, with emphasis on Himalayan thar in New Zealand. *Ecology* 51:53–72.

CAVERS, P. B., and J. L. HARPER. 1967. Studies in the dynamics of plant populations. I. The fate of seed and transplants introduced into various habitats. *J. Ecol.* 55:59–71.

CHAPMAN, R. N. 1928. The quantitative analysis of environmental factors. *Ecology* 9:111–122.

CHARLES, A. H. 1961. Differential survival of cultivars of *Lolium, Dactylis,* and *Phleum. J. Brit. Grass. Soc.* 16:69–75.

CHESHER, R. H. 1969. Destruction of Pacific corals by the sea star *Acanthaster planci. Science* 165:280–283.

CHITTY, D. 1954. Methods of measuring rat populations. pp. 161–226 in *Control of Rats and Mice,* Vol. 1, ed. by D. Chitty. Oxford University Press, New York.

CHITTY, D. 1955. Allgemeine Gedankengänge über die Dicteschwankungen bei der Erdmaus (*Microtus agrestis*). *Zeit. Säugetierk.* 20:55–60.

CHITTY, D. 1960. Population processes in the vole and their relevance to general theory. *Can. J. Zool.* 38:99–113.

CHITTY, D. 1967. What regulates bird populations? *Ecology* 48:698–701.

CHRISTOPHERS, S. R. 1960. *Aedes aegypti* (L.) the yellow fever mosquito; its life history, bionomics and structure. Cambridge University Press, New York.

CLARKE, G. L. 1954. *Elements of Ecology.* Wiley, New York.

CLAUSEN, C. P. 1951. The time factor in biological control. *J. Econ. Entomol.* 44:1–9.

CLAUSEN, C. P. 1956. Biological control of insect pests in the continental United States. *U.S. Dept. Agr. Tech. Bull. No. 1139.* 151 pp.

CLAUSEN, J. 1965. Population studies of alpine and subalpine races of conifers and willows in the California High Sierra Nevada. *Evolution* 19:56–68.

CLAUSEN, J., D. D. KECK, and W. M. HIESEY. 1948. Experimental studies on the nature of species. III. Environmental responses of climatic races of *Achillea. Carnegie Inst. Washington Pub. No. 581.* 129 pp.

CLEMENTS, F. E. 1916. Plant succession: an analysis of the development of vegetation. *Carnegie Inst. Washington Pub. No. 242.* 512 pp.

CLEMENTS, F. E. 1936. Nature and structure of the climax. *J. Ecol.* 24:252–284.

CLEMENTS, F. E. 1949. *Dynamics of Vegetation.* Hafner, New York.

COALE, A. J. 1958. How the age distribution of a human population is determined. *Cold Spring Harbor Symp. Quant. Biol.* 22:83–89.

CODY, M. L. 1966. A general theory of clutch size. *Evolution* 20:174–184.

COLE, L. C. 1954. The population consequences of life history phenomena. *Quart. Rev. Biol.* 29:103–137.

COLE, L. C. 1958. Sketches of general and comparative demography. *Cold Spring Harbor Symp. Quant. Biol.* 22:1–15.

COLE, L. C. 1960. Competitive exclusion. *Science* 132:348–349.

COLLVER, A. O. 1965. *Birth Rates in Latin America* (Inst. International Studies, Research Series 7). University of California Press, Berkeley.

CONNELL, J. H. 1961a. The effects of competition, predation by *Thais lapillus*, and other factors on natural populations of the barnacle, *Balanus balanoides*. *Ecol. Monogr.* 31:61–104.

CONNELL, J. H. 1961b. The influence of interspecific competition and other factors on the distribution of the barnacle *Chthamalus stellatus*. *Ecology* 42:710–723.

CONNELL, J. H. 1970. A predator–prey system in the marine intertidal region. I. *Balanus glandula* and several predatory species of *Thais*. *Ecol. Monogr.* 40:49–78.

CONNELL, J. H., and E. ORIAS. 1964. The ecological regulation of species diversity. *Amer. Naturalist* 98:399–414.

COOKE, M. T. 1928. The spread of the European starling in North America (to 1928). *U.S. Dept. Agr. Circ. No. 40.* 9 pp.

COOLEY, R. A. 1963. *Politics and Conservation. The Decline of the Alaska Salmon.* Harper & Row, New York.

COOPER, W. S. 1939. A fourth expedition to Glacier Bay, Alaska. *Ecology* 20:130–155.

CORMACK, R. M. 1968. The statistics of capture–recapture methods. *Oceanogr. Mar. Biol. Ann. Rev.* 6:455–506 (ed. by H. Barnes, Allen & Unwin, London).

COTTAM, G., and J. T. CURTIS. 1956. The use of distance measures in phytosociological sampling. *Ecology* 37:451–460.

COTTAM, G., and R. P. MCINTOSH. 1966. Vegetational continuum. *Science* 152:546–547.

COWLES, H. C. 1899. The ecological relations of the vegetation on the sand dunes of Lake Michigan. *Bot. Gaz.* 27:95–117, 167–202, 281–308, 361–391.

COWLES, H. C. 1901. The physiographic ecology of Chicago and vicinity. *Bot. Gaz.* 31:73–108, 145–181.

CRISP, D. J. (ed.). 1964. The effects of the severe winter of 1962–63 on marine life in Britain. *J. Anim. Ecol.* 33:165–210.

CRISP, D. J. 1967. Chemical factors inducing settlement in *Crassostrea virginica* (Gmelin). *J. Anim. Ecol.* 36:329–335.

CRISSEY, W. F., and R. W. DARROW. 1949. A study of predator control on Valcour Island. *New York State Conservation Dept., Division of Fish and Game, Res. Ser. No. 1.*

CRITCHFIELD, W. B. 1957. Geographic variation in *Pinus contorta*. *Harvard Univ., Maria Moors Cabot Foundation, Publ. No. 3.* 118 pp.

CROCKER, R. L., and J. MAJOR. 1955. Soil development in relation to vegetation and surface age at Glacier Bay, Alaska. *J. Ecol.* 43:427–448.

CROMBIE, A. C. 1945. On competition between different species of graminivorous insects. *Proc. Royal Soc. London* Ser. B, 132:362–395.

CROOK, J. H. 1964. The evolution of social organisation and visual communication in the weaver birds (Ploceinae). *Behaviour Suppl.* 10:1–78.

CROWELL, K. L. 1968. Rates of competitive exclusion by the Argentine ant in Bermuda. *Ecology* 49:551–555.

CRUTCHFIELD, J. A. (ed.). 1965. *The Fisheries: Problems in Resource Management*. University of Washington Press, Seattle.

CULVER, D. C. 1970. Analysis of simple cave communities. I. Caves as islands. *Evolution* 24:463–474.

CUMMINS, K. W. 1964. Factors limiting the microdistribution of larvae of the caddisflies *Pycnopsyche lepida* (Hagen) and *Pycnopsyche guttifer* (Walker) in a Michigan stream (Trichoptera: Limnephilidae). *Ecol. Monogr.* 34:271–295.

CUNNINGHAM, W. J. 1954. A nonlinear differential-difference equation of growth. *Proc. Nat. Acad. Sci. U.S.* 40:708–713.

CURTIS, J. T. 1959. *The Vegetation of Wisconsin*. University of Wisconsin Press, Madison.

DAHL, K. 1919. Studies of trout and troutwaters in Norway. *Salmon Trout Mag.* 18:16–33.

DALE, M. B. 1970. Systems analysis and ecology. *Ecology* 51:2–16.

DARWIN, C. 1859. *The Origin of Species By Means of Natural Selection*. Reprinted by The Modern Library, Random House, New York.

DAUBENMIRE, R. F. 1943a. Soil temperature versus drought as a factor determining lower altitudinal limits of trees in the Rocky Mountains. *Bot. Gaz.* 105:1–13.

DAUBENMIRE, R. F. 1943b. Vegetation zonation in the Rocky Mountains. *Bot. Rev.* 9:325–393.

DAUBENMIRE, R. F. 1947. *Plants and Environment*. Wiley, New York.

DAUBENMIRE, R. 1954. Alpine timberlines in the Americas and their interpretation. *Butler Univ. Bot. Stud.* II:119–136.

DAUBENMIRE, R. 1956. Climate as a determinant of vegetation distribution in eastern Washington and northern Idaho. *Ecol. Monogr.* 26:131–154.

DAUBENMIRE, R. 1966. Vegetation: identification of typal communities. *Science* 151:291–298.

DAVIS, E. F. 1928. The toxic principle of *Juglans nigra* as identified with synthetic juglone, and its toxic effects on tomato and alfalfa plants. *Amer. J. Bot.* 15:620.

DAVIS, K. 1967. Population policy: will current programs succeed? *Science* 158:730–739.

DEBACH, P. (ed.). 1964. *Biological Control of Insect Pests and Weeds*. Chapman & Hall, London.

DEBACH, P., and R. A. SUNDBY. 1963. Competitive displacement between ecological homologues. *Hilgardia* 34:105–166.

DEEVEY, E. S., JR. 1947. Life tables for natural populations of animals. *Quart. Rev. Biol.* 22:283–314.

DELONG, K. T. 1966. Population ecology of feral house mice: interference by *Microtus*. *Ecology* 47:481–484.

Demographic Yearbook of the United Nations, 1968. New York, Statistical Office of the United Nations, 1969.

Demographic Yearbook of the United Nations, 1969. New York, Statistical Office of the United Nations, 1970 (published annually by the U.N.).

DEMPSTER, J. P. 1963. The population dynamics of grasshoppers and locusts. *Biol. Rev.* 38:490–529.

DEVLIN, R. M. 1969. *Plant Physiology*. Van Nostrand Reinhold, New York.

DICE, L. R. 1952. *Natural Communities*. Univ. Michigan Press, Ann Arbor.

DICKMAN, M. 1968. The relation of freshwater plankton productivity to species composition during induced successions. Ph.D. thesis, Dept. Zoology, Univ. British Columbia, 115 pp.

DICKMAN, M. 1969. Some effects of lake renewal on phytoplankton productivity and species composition. *Limnol. Oceanogr.* 14:660–666.

DILLER, J. D., and R. B. CLAPPER. 1969. Asiatic and hybrid chestnut trees in the eastern United States. *J. Forest.* 67:328–331.

DIRSH, V. M. 1951. A new biometrical phase character in locusts. *Nature* 167: 281–282.

DIX, R. L. 1957. Sugar maple in forest succession at Washington, D.C. *Ecology* 38:663–665.

DIX, R. L., and F. E. SMEINS. 1967. The prairie, meadow, and marsh vegetation of Nelson County, North Dakota. *Can. J. Bot.* 45:21–58.

DIXON, A. F. G. 1970. Quality and availability of food for a sycamore aphid population. pp. 271–287 in *Animal Populations in Relation to Their Food Supply*, ed. by A. Watson. Blackwell, Oxford.

DOBZHANSKY, T. 1950. Evolution in the tropics. *Amer. Sci.* 38:209–221.

DODD, A. P. 1940. *The Biological Campaign Against Prickly-pear*. Commonwealth Prickly Pear Board, Brisbane. 77 pp.

DODD, A. P. 1959. The biological control of prickly pear in Australia. pp. 565–577 *in Biogeography and Ecology in Australia (Monographiae Biologicae*, Vol. VIII). W. Junk, The Hague.

DOUBLEDAY, T. 1841. *The True Law of Population Shewn To Be Connected with the Food of the People*. Smith, Elder, London.

DOUTT, R. L. 1964. The historical development of biological control. Chap. 2, pp. 21–42 in *Biological Control of Insect Pests and Weeds*, ed. by P. DeBach, Chapman & Hall, London.

DOYLE, J. J. 1966. The response of rice to fertilizer. *FAO Agricultural Studies No. 70*. 69 pp.

DREW, J. V., and R. E. SHANKS. 1965. Landscape relationships of soils and vegetation in the forest–tundra ecotone, Upper Firth River Valley, Alaska–Canada. *Ecol. Monogr.* 35:285–306.

DUBLIN, L. I., and A. J. LOTKA. 1925. On the true rate of natural increase as exemplified by the population of the United States, 1920. *J. Amer. Statist. Ass.* 20:305–339.

DUBOS, R. 1965. *Man Adapting*. Yale University Press, New Haven.

DURRANT, S. D. 1946. The pocket gophers (genus *Thomomys*) of Utah. *Univ. Kansas Pub. Mus. Nat. Hist.* 1:1–82.

DYMOND, J. R. 1955. The introduction of foreign fishes in Canada. *Verh. Int. Ver. Limnol.* 12:543–553.

EDMINSTER, F. C. 1939. The effect of predator control on ruffed grouse populations in New York. *J. Wildl. Mgmt.* 3:345–352.

EDMONDSON, W. T. 1944. Ecological studies of sessile Rotatoria. Part I. Factors limiting distribution. *Ecol. Monogr.* 14:31–66.

EDMONDSON, W. T. 1969. Cultural eutrophication with special reference to Lake Washington. *Mitt. Int. Verein. Limnol.* 17:19–32.

EDMONDSON, W. T. 1970. Phosphorus, nitrogen, and algae in Lake Washington after diversion of sewage. *Science* 169:690–691.

EDWARDS, C. A., and G. W. HEATH. 1963. The role of soil animals in breakdown of leaf material. pp. 76–84 in *Soil Organisms*, ed. by J. Doiksen and J. van der Drift. North-Holland, Amsterdam.

EFFORD, I. E. 1969a. Egg size in the sand crab, *Emerita analoga* (Decapoda, Hippidae). *Crustaceana* 16:15–26.

EFFORD, I. E. 1969b. Energy transfer in Marion Lake, British Columbia; with particular reference to fish feeding. *Verh. Int. Verein. Limnol.* 17:104–108.

EFFORD, I. E. 1970. Recruitment to sedentary marine populations as exemplified by the sand crab, *Emerita analoga* (Decapoda, Hippidae). *Crustaceana* 18:293–308.

EFFORD, I. E. 1971. *An Interim Review of the Marion Lake Project.* UNESCO IBP Symposium on Productivity Problems of Freshwaters, Poland, May 1970.

EGERTON, F. N., III. 1968a. Ancient sources for animal demography. *Isis* 59:175–189.

EGERTON, F. N., III. 1968b. Studies of animal populations from Lamarck to Darwin. *J. Hist. Biol.* 1:225–259.

EGERTON, F. N., III. 1969. Richard Bradley's understanding of biological productivity: a study of eighteenth-century ecological ideas. *J. Hist. Biol.* 2:391–410.

EHRLICH, P. R., and A. H. EHRLICH. 1970. *Population, Resources, Environment: Issues in Human Ecology.* W. H. Freeman, San Francisco.

EHRLICH, P. R., and P. H. RAVEN. 1964. Butterflies and plants: a study in coevolution. *Evolution* 18:586–608.

ELLIS, J. A., and W. L. ANDERSON. 1963. Attempts to establish pheasants in southern Illinois. *J. Wildl. Mgmt.* 27:225–239.

ELSON, P. F. 1962. Predator–prey relationships between fish-eating birds and Atlantic salmon. *Bull. Fish. Res. Bd. Can. No. 133.* 87 pp.

ELTON, C. 1927. *Animal Ecology.* Sidgwick and Jackson, London.

ELTON, C., and M. NICHOLSON. 1942. The ten-year cycle in numbers of the lynx in Canada. *J. Anim. Ecol.* 11:215–244.

ELTON, C. S. 1958. *The Ecology of Invasions by Animals and Plants.* Methuen, London.

ELTON, C. S. 1966. *The Pattern of Animal Communities.* Methuen, London.

ENGELMANN, M. D. 1966. Energetics, terrestrial field studies, and animal productivity. *Advances Ecol. Res.* 3:73–115.

ENNIK, G. C. 1960. The competition between white clover and perennial rye-grass with differences in light intensity and moisture supply. *Jaarb. Inst. Biol. Scheik. Onderz. Landb. Gew.* 1960:37–50.

ERRINGTON, P. L. 1956. Factors limiting higher vertebrate populations. *Science* 124:304–307.

ERRINGTON, P. L. 1963. *Muskrat Populations.* Iowa State University Press, Ames.

EVANS, F. C. 1956. Ecosystem as the basic unit in ecology. *Science* 123:1127–1128.

EYLES, D. E. 1944. A critical review of the literature relating to the flight and dispersion habits of Anopheline mosquitoes. *U.S. Public Health Service, Public Health Bull. No. 287.* 39 pp.

EYRE, S. R. 1963. *Vegetation and Soils: A World Picture.* Aldine, Chicago.

FAGER, E. W. 1957. Determination and analysis of recurrent groups. *Ecology* 38:586–595.

FAGER, E. W. 1968. The community of invertebrates in decaying oak wood. *J. Anim. Ecol.* 37:121–142.

FARR, W. 1843. Causes of mortality in town districts. *Fifth Annual Rept. Reg. Gen. of Births, Deaths and Marriages in England* (2nd ed.), pp. 406–435.

FARR, W. 1875. A letter to Reg. Gen. on mortality in the registration districts of England during the years 1861–1870. *Suppl. to 35th Ann. Rept. Reg. Gen. of Births, Deaths and Marriages in England for Year 1872.*

FEENY, P. 1970. Seasonal changes in oak leaf tannins and nutrients as a cause of spring feeding by winter moth caterpillars. *Ecology* 51:565–581.

FERGUSON, T.P., and G. BOND. 1953. Observations on the formation and function of the root nodules of *Alnus glutinosa* (L.) Gaertn. *Ann. Bot.* 17:175–188.

FISCHER, A. G. 1960. Latitudinal variations in organic diversity. *Evolution* 14:64–81.

FISHER, J., and R. M. LOCKLEY. 1954. *Sea-birds.* Collins, London.

FISHER, J., and H. G. VEVERS. 1944. The breeding distribution, history and population of the North Atlantic Gannet (*Sula bassana*). Part 2. *J. Anim. Ecol.* 13:49–62.

FISHER, R. A., A. S. CORBET, and C. B. WILLIAMS. 1943. The relation between the number of species and the number of individuals in a random sample of an animal population. *J. Anim. Ecol.* 12:42–58.

Fishery Statistics of the United States. Washington, D.C. Bureau of Commercial Fisheries. U.S. Dept. of the Interior, Published annually.

FLEW, A. 1957. The structure of Malthus' population theory. *Australasian J. Phil.* 35:1–20.

FOERSTER, R. E. 1954. On the relation of adult sockeye salmon (*Oncorhynchus nerka*) returns to known smolt seaward migrations. *J. Fish. Res. Bd. Can.* 11:339–350.

FOERSTER, R. E., and W. E. RICKER. 1941. The effect of reduction of predaceous fish on survival of young sockeye salmon at Cultus Lake. *J. Fish. Res. Bd. Can.* 5:315–336.

FOOD AND AGRICULTURE ORGANIZATION OF THE UNITED NATIONS. 1969. *Provisional Indicative World Plan for Agricultural Development.* Conference, F.A.O. c69/4, August 1969, 3 vols.

FOOD AND AGRICULTURE ORGANIZATION OF THE UNITED NATIONS. 1970a. *Production Yearbook,* 1969, Vol. 23. United Nations, Rome.

FOOD AND AGRICULTURE ORGANIZATION OF THE UNITED NATIONS. 1970b. *The State of Food and Agriculture 1970.* United Nations, Rome.

FORBES, E. 1844. Report on the Molluscs and Radiata of the Aegean Sea, and on their distribution considered as bearing on geology. *Rep. Brit. Ass. Adv. Sci.* 13:130–193.

FORBES, S. A. 1887. The lake as a microcosm. *Bull. Peoria Sci. Ass.* 1887:77–87 (reprinted in *Bull. Illinois Nat. Hist. Surv.* 15:537–550, 1925).

FORD, E. B. 1931. *Mendelism and Evolution.* Methuen, London.

FORD, E. B. 1967. *Moths,* 2nd ed. Collins, London.

FORMAN, R. T. T. 1964. Growth under controlled conditions to explain the hierarchical distributions of a moss, *Tetraphis pellucida. Ecol. Monogr.* 34:1–25.

FORSKÅL, P. 1775. *Descriptiones animalium, avium, amphibiorum, piscium, insectorum, vermium; quae in itinere orientali observavit P. Forskatl, post mortem auctoris edidit, Carsten Niebuht.* Hauniae, Moelleri (pt. 3).

FOSTER, B. A. 1971. On the determinants of the upper limit of intertidal distribution of barnacles (Crustacea: Cirripedia). *J. Anim. Ecol.* 40:33–48.

FRAENKEL, G., and D. L. GUNN. 1940. *The Orientation of Animals: Kineses, Taxes, and Compass Reactions.* Oxford University Press, New York.

FREDERIKSEN, H. 1969. Feedbacks in economic and demographic transition. *Science* 166:837–847.

FREDERIKSEN, H. 1970. Malaria eradication and the fall of mortality. *Population Stud.* 24:111–113.

FRY, F. E. J. 1951. Some environmental relations of the speckled trout (*Salvelinus fontinalis*). *Proc. N.E. Atlantic Fish. Conf.,* May 1951, 1–29.

FRYER, G. 1959. The trophic interrelationships and ecology of some littoral communities of Lake Nyasa and a discussion of the evolution of a group of rock-frequenting Cichlidae. *Proc. Zool. Soc. London* 132:153–281.

GADGIL, M., and W. H. BOSSERT. 1970. Life historical consequences of natural selection. *Amer. Naturalist* 104:1–24.

GARB, S. 1961. Differential growth-inhibitors produced by plants. *Bot. Rev.* 27:422–443.

GAUSE, G. F. 1931. The influence of ecological factors on the size of population. *Amer. Naturalist* 65:70–76.

GAUSE, G. F. 1932. Experimental studies on the struggle for existence. I. Mixed population of two species of yeast. *J. Exp. Biol.* 9:389–402.

GAUSE, G. F. 1934. *The Struggle for Existence.* Hafner, New York. (Reprinted 1964.)

GAUSE, G. F. 1935. Experimental demonstration of Volterra's periodic oscillation in the numbers of animals. *J. Exp. Biol.* 12:44–48.

GENTLE, W., F. R. HUMPHREYS, and M. J. LAMBERT. 1965. An examination of a *Pinus radiata* phosphate fertilizer trial fifteen years after treatment. *Forest Sci.* 11:315–324.

GERKING, S. D. 1962. Production and food utilization in a population of bluegill sunfish. *Ecol. Monogr.* 32:31–78.

GESSEL, S. P. 1962. Progress and problems in mineral nutrition of forest trees. pp. 221–235 in *Tree Growth*, ed. by T. T. Kozlowski. Ronald, New York.

GIBB, J. A. 1950. The breeding biology of the great and blue titmice. *Ibis* 92: 507–539.

GIBB, J. A., and M. M. BETTS. 1963. Food and food supply of nesting tits (Paridae) in Breckland pine. *J. Anim. Ecol.* 32:489–533.

GLASGOW, J. P. 1963. *The Distribution and Abundance of Tsetse*. Pergamon, Elmsford, N.Y.

GLEASON, H. A., and A. CRONQUIST. 1964. *The Natural Geography of Plants*. Columbia University Press, New York.

GODFREY, P. J., and W. D. BILLINGS. 1968. Factors determining the lower limits of alpine vegetation in southeastern Wyoming. *Bull. Ecol. Soc. Amer.* 49(2):68.

GOLDMAN, C. R. 1960a. Molybdenum as a factor limiting primary productivity in Castle Lake, California. *Science* 132:1016–1017.

GOLDMAN, C. R. 1960b. Primary productivity and limiting factors in three lakes of the Alaska Peninsula. *Ecol. Monogr.* 30:207–230.

GOLDMAN, C. R. 1968. Aquatic primary production. *Amer. Zool.* 8:31–42.

GOLLEY, F. B. 1960. Energy dynamics of a food chain of an old-field community. *Ecol. Monogr.* 30:187–206.

GOLLEY, F. B. 1961. Energy values of ecological materials. *Ecology* 42:581–584.

GOLLEY, F. B. 1965. Structure and function of an old-field broomsedge community. *Ecol. Monogr.* 35:113–137.

GOOCH, B. C. 1967. Appraisal of North American fish culture fertilization studies. *FAO Fisheries Repts.* 44(3):13–26.

GOOD, N. F. 1968. A study of natural replacement of chestnut in six stands in the Highlands of New Jersey. *Bull. Torrey Bot. Club* 95:240–253.

GOOD, R. 1964. *The Geography of the Flowering Plants*. Longmans, London.

GOODALL, D. W. 1963. The continuum and the individualistic association. *Vegetatio* 11:297–316.

GRAHAM, M. 1935. Modern theory of exploiting a fishery, and application to North Sea trawling. *J. Conseil Perm. Int. Explor. Mer* 10:264–274.

GRAHAM, M. 1939. The sigmoid curve and the overfishing problem. *Rapp. Conseil Explor. Mer* 110:15–20.

GRANT, A., and V. GRANT. 1956. Genetic and taxonomic studies in *Gilia*. VIII. The cobwebby Gilias. *Aliso* 3:203–287.

GRAUNT, J. 1662. *Natural and Political Observations Mentioned in a Following Index, and Made upon the Bills of Mortality*. Roycroft, London.

GRAY, J. S. 1966. The attractive factor of intertidal sands to *Protodrilus symbioticus*. *J. Mar. Biol. Ass. U.K.* 46:627–645.

GRAY, R., and J. BONNER. 1948. An inhibitor of plant growth from the leaves of *Encelia farinosa*. *Amer. J. Bot.* 35:52–57.

GREIG-SMITH, P. 1964. *Quantitative Plant Ecology*, 2nd ed. Butterworth, London.

GRICE, G. D., and A. D. HART. 1962. The abundance, seasonal occurrence and distribution of the epizooplankton between New York and Bermuda. *Ecol. Monogr.* 32:287–307.

GRIGGS, R. F. 1934. The edge of the forest in Alaska and the reasons for its position. *Ecology* 15:80–96.

GRIGGS, R. F. 1938. Timberlines in the northern Rocky Mountains. *Ecology* 19:548–564.

GRIGGS, R. F. 1946. The timberlines of northern America and their interpretation. *Ecology* 27:275–289.

GRIME, J. P. 1965. Comparative experiments as a key to the ecology of flowering plants. *Ecology* 46:513–515.

GRIME, J. P. 1966. Shade avoidance and shade tolerance in flowering plants. pp. 187–207 in *Light as an Ecological Factor*, ed. by R. Bainbridge. G. C. Evans, and O. Rackham. Blackwell, Oxford.

GRIME, J. P., and J. G. HODGSON. 1969. An investigation of the ecological significance of lime-chlorosis by means of large-scale comparative experiments. pp. 67–99 in *Ecological Aspects of the Mineral Nutrition of Plants*, ed. by I. H. Rorison. Blackwell, Oxford.

GRIMM, W. C. 1967. *Familiar Trees of America*. Harper & Row, New York.

GRODZINSKI, W., and A. GORECKI. 1967. Daily energy budgets of small rodents. pp. 295–314 in *Secondary Productivity of Terrestrial Ecosystems*, Vol. I, ed. by K. Petrusewicz. Warsaw.

GROSS, J. E. 1969. Optimum yield in deer and elk populations. *Trans. N. Amer. Wildl. Conf.* 34:372–386.

GULLAND, J. A. 1955. Estimation of growth and mortality in commercial fish populations. *U.K. Ministry Agr. Fish., Fish. Invest. Ser. 2*, 18(9):1–46.

GULLAND, J. A. 1962. The application of mathematical models to fish populations. pp. 204–217 in *The Exploitation of Natural Animal Populations*, ed. by E. D. LeCren and M. W. Holdgate. Blackwell, Oxford.

GUNN, D. L. 1952. The red locust. *J. Roy. Soc. Arts* 100:261–284.

GUNN, D. L. 1960. The biological background of locust control. *Ann. Rev. Entomol.* 5:279–300.

GUNN, D. L., and P. HUNTER-JONES. 1952. Laboratory experiments on phase differences in locusts. *Anti-Locust Bull.* 12:1–29.

HAARTMAN, L. VON. 1954. Der Trauerfliegenschnäpper. III. Die Nahrungsbiologie. *Acta Zool. Fennici* 83:1–96.

HAARTMAN, L. VON. 1956. Territory in the pied flycatcher *Muscicapa hypoleuca*. *Ibis* 98:460–475.

HABECK, J. R. 1958. White cedar ecotypes in Wisconsin. *Ecology* 39:457–463.

HAGEN, D. W. 1967. Isolating mechanisms in threespine sticklebacks (*Gasterosteus*) *J. Fish. Res. Bd. Can.* 24:1637–1692.

HAIRSTON, N. G. 1964. Studies on the organization of animal communities. *J. Anim. Ecol.* 33(Suppl.):227–239.

HAIRSTON, N. G. 1969. On the relative abundance of species. *Ecology* 50:1091–1094.

HAIRSTON, N. G., F. E. SMITH, and L. B. SLOBODKIN. 1960. Community structure, population control, and competition. *Amer. Naturalist* 94:421–425.

HAIRSTON, N. G., et al. 1968. The relationship between species diversity and stability: an experimental approach with protozoa and bacteria. *Ecology* 49:1091–1101.

HALL, E. R., and K. R. KELSON. 1959. *The Mammals of North America*. Ronald, New York. 2 vols.

HAMILTON, W. J., III. 1962. Reproductive adaptations of the red tree mouse. *J. Mammal.* 43:486–504.

HARDIN, G. 1960. The competitive exclusion principle. *Science* 131:1292–1297.

HARDIN, G. 1968. The tragedy of the commons. *Science* 162:1243–1248.

HARDIN, G. 1971. Nobody ever dies of overpopulation. *Science* 171:527.

HARPER, J. A., and R. F. LABISKY. 1964. The influence of calcium on the distribution of pheasants in Illinois. *J. Wildl. Mgmt.* 28:722–731.

HARPER, J. L. 1961. The evolution and ecology of closely related species living in the same area. *Evolution* 15:209–227.

HARPER, J. L. 1968. The regulation of numbers and mass in plant populations. pp. 139–158 in *Population Biology and Evolution*, ed. by R. C. Lewontin. Syracuse University Press, Syracuse, N.Y.

HARPER, J. L. 1969. The role of predation in vegetational diversity. *Brookhaven Symp. Biol.* 22:48–62.

HARPER, J. L., and R. A. BENTON. 1966. The behavior of seeds in soil. II. The germination of seeds on the surface of a water supplying substrate. *J. Ecol.* 54: 151–166.

HARPSTEAD, D. D. 1971. High-lysine corn. *Sci. Amer.* 225 (2):34–42.

HARRIS, G. A. 1967. Some competitive relationships between *Agropyron spicatum* and *Bromus tectorum. Ecol. Monogr.* 37:89–111.

HARRIS, V. T. 1952. An experimental study of habitat selection by prairie and forest races of the deer mouse, *Peromyscus maniculatus. Contrib. Lab. Vert. Biol., Univ. Michigan,* 56:1–53.

HART, J. S. 1952. Geographic variations of some physiological and morphological characters in certain freshwater fish. *Univ. Toronto Biol. Ser. No. 60.* 79 pp.

HARTLEY, W. 1950. The global distribution of tribes of the Gramineae in relation to historical and environmental factors. *Aust. J. Agr. Res.* 1:355–373.

HASKINS, C. P., and E. F. HASKINS. 1965. *Pheidole megacephala* and *Iridomyrmex humilis* in Bermuda—equilibrium or slow replacement? *Ecology* 46:736–740.

HASTINGS, J. R., and R. M. TURNER. 1965. *The Changing Mile.* University of Arizona Press, Tucson.

HEED, W. B., and H. W. KIRCHER. 1965. Unique sterol in the ecology and nutrition of *Drosophila pachea. Science* 149:758–761.

HELMS, J. A. 1965. Diurnal and seasonal patterns of net assimilation in Douglas-fir, *Pseudotsuga menziesii* (Mirb.) Franco, as influenced by environment. *Ecology* 46:698–708.

HEPHER, B. 1962. Primary production in fishponds and its application to fertilization experiments. *Limnol. Oceanogr.* 7:131–136.

HESLOP-HARRISON, J. 1964. Forty years of genecology. *Advances Ecol. Res.* 2:159–247.

HESSE, R., W. C. ALLEE, and K. P. SCHMIDT. 1951. *Ecological Animal Geography*, 2nd ed. Wiley, New York.

HEUTS, M. J. 1956. Temperature adaptation in *Gasterosteus aculeatus* L. *Pubbl. Staz. Zool. Napoli* 28:44–61.

HIESEY, W. M., and H. W. MILNER. 1965. Physiology of ecological races and species. *Ann. Rev. Plant Physiol.* 16:203–216.

HILDEN, O. 1965. Habitat selection in birds: a review. *Ann. Zool. Fennici* 2:53–75.

HOAR, W. S. 1966. *General and Comparative Physiology*. Prentice-Hall, Englewood Cliffs, N.J.

HOCKER, H. W., JR. 1956. Certain aspects of climate as related to the distribution of loblolly pine. *Ecology* 37:824–834.

HOCKING, B. 1953. The intrinsic range and speed of flight of insects. *Trans. Roy. Entomol. Soc. London* 104:223–346.

HOLLING, C. S. 1959. The components of predation as revealed by a study of small-mammal predation of the European pine sawfly. *Can. Entomol.* 91:293–320.

HOLLING, C. S. 1965. The functional response of predators to prey density and its role in mimicry and population regulation. *Mem. Entomol. Soc. Can. No. 45.* 60 pp.

HOLLISTER, L. E. 1971. Marihuana in man: three years later. *Science* 172:21–29.

HOLLOWAY, J. K. 1964. Host specificity of a phytophagous insect. *Weeds* 12:25–27.

HOLMQUIST, C. 1959. Problems on marine-glacial relicts on account of investigations on the genus *Mysis*. Berlingska Boktrycheriet, Lund. 270 pp.

HOLT, S. J. 1969. The food resources of the ocean. *Sci. Amer.* 221(3):178–194.

HOOPER, F. F., R. C. BALL, and H. A. TANNER. 1953. An experiment in the artificial circulation of a small Michigan lake. *Trans. Amer. Fish. Soc.* 82:222–241.

HORN, H. S. 1971. *The Adaptive Geometry of Trees*. Princeton Univ. Press, Princeton, N.J.

HOUGH, A. F. 1936. A climax forest community on East Tionesta Creek in northwestern Pennsylvania. *Ecology* 17:9–28.

HOWARD, L. O., and W. F. FISKE. 1911. The importation into the United States of the parasites of the gipsy-moth and the brown-tail moth. *U.S. Dept. Agri., Bur. Entomol., Bull. 91.*

HOWARD, W. E. 1959. The European starling in California. *Calif. Dept. Agr., Dept. Bull. 48*, pp. 171–179.

HOWELL, A. B. 1926. Voles of the genus *Phenacomys*. II. Life history of the red tree mouse (*Phenacomys longicaudus*). *N. Amer. Fauna* 48:39–64.

HUFFAKER, C. B. 1957. Fundamentals of biological control of weeds. *Hilgardia* 27:101–157.

HUFFAKER, C. B. 1958. Experimental studies on predation: dispersion factors and predator–prey oscillations. *Hilgardia* 27:343–383.

HUFFAKER, C. B. 1959. Biological control of weeds with insects. *Ann. Rev. Entomology* 4:251–276.

HUFFAKER, C. B., and C. E. KENNETT. 1959. A ten-year study of vegetational changes associated with biological control of Klamath weed. *J. Range Mgmt.* 12:69–82.

HUFFAKER, C. B., and C. E. KENNETT. 1969. Some aspects of assessing efficiency of natural enemies. *Can. Entomol.* 101:425–447.

HUFFAKER, C. B., and P. S. MESSENGER. 1964. The concept and significance of natural control. Chap. 4, pp. 74–117 in *Biological Control of Insect Pests and Weeds*, ed. by P. DeBach. Chapman Hall, London.

HUFFAKER, C. B., K. P. SHEA, and S. G. HERMAN. 1963. Experimental studies on predation: complex dispersion and levels of food in an acarine predator–prey interaction. *Hilgardia* 34:305–330.

HULL, A. C., JR., and J. F. PECHANEC. 1947. Cheatgrass—a challenge to range research. *J. Forest.* 45:555–564.

HURLBERT, S. H. 1969. A coefficient of interspecific association. *Ecology* 50:1–9.

HUSTICH, I. 1953. The boreal limits of conifers. *Arctic* 6:149–162.

HUTCHINS, L. W. 1947. The bases for temperature zonation in geographical distribution. *Ecol. Monogr.* 17:325–335.

HUTCHINSON, G. E. 1958. Concluding remarks. *Cold Spring Harbor Symp. Quant. Biol.* 22:415–427.

HUTCHINSON, G. E. 1961. The paradox of the plankton. *Amer. Naturalist* 95:137–145.

HUTCHINSON, G. E. 1970. The chemical ecology of three species of *Myriophyllum* (Angiospermae, Haloragaceae). *Limnol. Oceanogr.* 15:1–5.

HUTCHINSON, G. E., and E. S. DEEVEY, JR. 1949. *Ecological Studies on Populations* (Survey of Biol. Progress, Vol. I, pp. 325–359). Academic Press, New York.

HUTCHINSON, J. B. 1965. Crop plant evolution: a general discussion. pp. 166–181 in *Essays on Crop Plant Evolution*, ed. by J. B. Hutchinson. Cambridge University Press, New York.

HYNES, H. B. N. 1954. The ecology of *Gammarus duebeni* Lilljeborg and its occurrence in fresh water in western Britain. *J. Anim. Ecol.* 23:38–84.

ISTOCK, C. 1966. Distribution, coexistence, and competition of whirligig beetles. *Evolution* 20:211–234.

ISTOCK, C. 1967. Transient competitive displacement in natural populations of whirligig beetles. *Ecology* 48:929–937.

JACKSON, C. H. N. 1939. The analysis of an animal population. *J. Anim. Ecol.* 8:238–246.

JAEGER, R. G. 1970. Potential extinction through competition between two species of terrestrial salamanders. *Evolution* 24:632–642.

JAEGER, R. G. 1971. Moisture as a factor influencing the distributions of two species of terrestrial salamanders. *Oecologia* 6:191–207.

JANZEN, D. H. 1966. Coevolution of mutualism between ants and acacias in Central America. *Evolution* 20:249–275.

JANZEN, D. H. 1970. Herbivores and the number of tree species in tropical forests. *Amer. Naturalist* 104:501–528.

JARVIS, M. S. 1963. A comparison between the water relations of species with contrasting types of geographical distribution in the British Isles. pp. 289–312 in *The Water Relations of Plants*, ed. by A. J. Rutter and F. H. Whitehead. Blackwell, London.

JAYNES, R. A. 1968. Progress with chestnuts. *Horticulture* 46(12):16–17, 48.

JENKINS, D. 1961. Population control in protected partridges (*Perdix perdix*). *J. Anim. Ecol.* 30:235–258.

JEWELL, M. E. 1939. An ecological study of the fresh-water sponges of Wisconsin. II. The influence of calcium. *Ecology* 20:11–28.

JOHNSON, M. P., L. G. MASON, and P. H. RAVEN. 1968. Ecological parameters and plant species diversity. *Amer. Naturalist* 102:297–306.

JOHNSON, S. 1971. Thermal adaptation in North American Sturnidae. Ph.D. thesis, Dept. Zoology, University of British Columbia.

JOHNSTON, M. C. 1963. Past and present grasslands of southern Texas and northeastern Mexico. *Ecology* 44:456–466.

JOLLY, G. M. 1965. Explicit estimates from capture–recapture data with both death and immigration: stochastic model. *Biometrika* 52:225–247.

JORDAN, R. C., and S. E. JACOBS. 1947. The effect of temperature on the growth of *Bacterium coli* at pH 7.0 with a constant food supply. *J. Gen. Microbiol.* 1:121–136.

JOWETT, D. 1959. Adaptation of a lead-tolerant population of *Agrostis tenuis* to low soil fertility. *Nature* 184:43.

JOWETT, D. 1964. Population studies on lead-tolerant *Agrostis tenuis*. *Evolution* 18:70–81.

KEEVER, C. 1950. Causes of succession on old fields of the Piedmont, North Carolina. *Ecol. Monogr.* 20:229–250.

KEEVER, C. 1953. Present composition of some stands of the former oak–chestnut forest in the southern Blue Ridge Mountains. *Ecology* 34:44–54.

KEITH, L. B. 1963. *Wildlife's Ten-year Cycle.* University of Wisconsin Press, Madison.

KENNEDY, J. S. 1956. Phase transformation in locust biology. *Biol. Rev.* 31:349–370.

KERSHAW, K. A. 1960. Cyclic and pattern phenomena as exhibited by *Alchemilla alpina*. *J. Ecol.* 48:443–453.

KERSHAW, K. A. 1964. *Quantitative and Dynamic Ecology.* Edward Arnold, London.

KESSEL, B. 1953. Distribution and migration of the European starling in North America. *Condor* 55:49–67.

KEY, K. H. L. 1950. A critique on the phase theory of locusts. *Quart. Rev. Biol.* 25:363–407.

KEYFITZ, N., and W. FLIEGER. 1968. *World Population: An Analysis of Vital Data.* University of Chicago Press, Chicago.

KITCHING, J. A., and F. J. EBLING. 1961. The ecology of Lough Ine. XI. The control of algae by *Paracentrotus lividus* (Echinoidea). *J. Anim. Ecol.* 30:373–383.

KITCHING, J. A., and F. J. EBLING. 1967. Ecological studies at Lough Ine. *Advances Ecol. Res.* 4:197–291.

KLEIBER, M. 1961. *The Fire of Life*. Wiley, New York.

KLEIN, D. R. 1968. The introduction, increase, and crash of reindeer on St. Matthew Island. *J. Wildl. Mgmt.* 32:350–367.

KLEIN, D. R. 1970. Food selection by North American deer and their response to over-utilization of preferred plant species. pp. 25–46 in *Animal Populations in Relation to Their Food Resources*, ed. by A. Watson. Blackwell, Oxford.

KLEMMEDSON, J. O., and J. G. SMITH. 1964. Cheatgrass (*Bromus tectorum* L.). *Bot. Rev.* 30:226–262.

KLOMP, H. 1962. Influence of climate and weather on the mean density level, the fluctuations and the regulation of animal populations. *Arch. Neerl. Zool.* 15:68–109.

KLOMP, H. 1970. The determination of clutch-size in birds. A review. *Ardea* 58:1–124.

KLOPFER, P. 1963. Behavioural aspects of habitat selection: the role of early experience. *Wilson Bull.* 75:15–22.

KLUYVER, H. N. 1951. The population ecology of the Great Tit, *Parus m. major* L. *Ardea* 38:1–135.

KLUYVER, H. N. 1966. Regulation of a bird population. *Ostrich* 6:389–396.

KORRINGA, P. 1957. Water temperature and breeding throughout the geographical range of *Ostrea edulis. Ann. Biol.* 33:1–17.

KORSTIAN, C. F. 1921. Effect of a late spring frost upon forest vegetation in the Wasatch Mountains of Utah. *Ecology* 2:47–52.

KORSTIAN, C. F., and T. S. COILE. 1938. Plant competition in forest stands. *Duke Univ. School Forestry Bull.* 3:1–125.

KOTZ, N. 1970. *Let Them Eat Promises: The Politics of Hunger in America*. Prentice-Hall, Englewood Cliffs, N.J.

KOZHOV, M. 1963. Lake Baikal and its life. *Monogr. Biol.* XI:1–344.

KOZLOVSKY, D. G. 1968. A critical evaluation of the trophic level concept. I. Ecological efficiencies. *Ecology* 49:48–60.

KOZLOWSKI, T. T. 1949. Light and water in relation to growth and competition of Piedmont forest tree species. *Ecol. Monogr.* 19:207–231.

KRAMER, P. J., and J. P. DECKER. 1944. Relation between light intensity and rate of photosynthesis of loblolly pine and certain hardwoods. *Plant Physiol.* 19:350–358.

KREBS, J. R. 1970. Regulation of numbers in the great tit (Aves: Passeriformes). *J. Zool. London.* 162:317–333.

KREBS, J. R. 1971. Territory and breeding density in the great tit, *Parus major* L. *Ecology* 52:2–22.

KRIEBEL, H. B. 1957. Patterns of genetic variation in sugar maple. *Ohio Agr. Exp. Sta. Res. Bull.* 791. 56 pp.

KRUCKEBERG, A. R. 1951. Intraspecific variability in the response of certain native plant species to serpentine soil. *Amer. J. Bot.* 38:408–419.

KRUCKEBERG, A. R. 1967. Ecotypic response to ultramafic soils by some plant species of northwestern U.S. *Brittonia* 19:133–151.

LACK, D. 1933. Habitat selection in birds with special references to the effects of afforestation on the Breckland avifauna. *J. Anim. Ecol.* 2:239–262.

LACK, D. 1937. The psychological factor in bird distribution. *Brit. Birds* 31:130–136.

LACK, D. 1944. Ecological aspects of species-formation in Passerine birds. *Ibis* 86:260–286.

LACK, D. 1945. The ecology of closely related species with special reference to cormorant (*Phalacrocorax carbo*) and shag (*P. aristotelis*). *J. Anim. Ecol.* 14:12–16.

LACK, D. 1954. *The Natural Regulation of Animal Numbers.* Oxford University Press, New York.

LACK D. 1958. A quantitative breeding study of British tits. *Ardea* 46:91–124.

LACK, D. 1964. A long-term study of the great tit (*Parus major*). *J. Anim. Ecol.* 33(Suppl.):159–173.

LACK, D. 1965. Evolutionary ecology. *J. Anim. Ecol.* 34:223-231.

LACK, D. 1966. *Population Studies of Birds.* Oxford University Press, New York.

LACK, D. 1968. *Ecological Adaptations for Breeding in Birds.* Methuen, London.

LACK, D. 1969. The numbers of bird species on islands. *Bird Stud.* 16:193–209.

LACK, D. 1971. *Ecological Isolation in Birds.* Blackwell, Oxford.

LAMBERT, J. M., and M. B. DALE. 1964. The use of statistics in phytosociology. *Advances Ecol. Res.* 2:59–99.

LANGFORD, A. N., and M. F. BUELL. 1969. Integration, identity and stability in the plant association. *Advances Ecol. Res.* 6:83–135.

LANGFORD, R. R. 1948. Fertilization of lakes in Algonquin Park, Ontario. *Trans. Amer. Fish. Soc.* 78:133–144.

LANGLET, O. 1959. A cline or not a cline—a question of Scots pine. *Silvae Genet.* 8:13–22.

LARKIN, P. A. 1956. Interspecific competition and population control in freshwater fish. *J. Fish. Res. Bd. Can.* 13:327–342.

LA ROI, G. H. 1967. Ecological studies in the boreal spruce–fir forests of the North American taiga. I. Analysis of the vascular flora. *Ecol. Monogr.* 37:229–253.

LARSEN, J. A. 1965. The vegetation of the Ennadai Lake area, N.W.T.: studies in subarctic and arctic bioclimatology. *Ecol. Monogr.* 35:37–59.

LAWLER, G. H. 1965. Fluctuations in the success of year-classes of whitefish populations with special reference to Lake Erie. *J. Fish. Res. Bd. Can.* 22:1197–1227.

LAWRENCE, D. B. 1958. Glaciers and vegetation in Southeastern Alaska. *Amer. Sci.* 46:89–122.

LAWRENCE, D. B., R. E. SCHOENIKE, A. QUISPEL, and G. BOND. 1967. The role of *Dryas drummondii* in vegetation development following ice recession at Glacier Bay, Alaska, with special reference to its nitrogen fixation by root nodules. *J. Ecol.* 55:793–813.

LAZENBY, A. 1955. Germination and establishment of *Juncus effusus* L. II. The interaction effects of moisture and competition. *J. Ecol.* 43:595–605.

LEA, A. 1968. Natural regulation and artificial control of brown locust numbers. *J. Entomol. Soc. S. Africa* 31:97–112.

LECREN, E. D. 1962. The efficiency of reproduction and recruitment in freshwater fishes. pp. 283–296 in *The Exploitation of Natural Animal Populations*, ed. by E. D. LeCren and M. W. Holdgate. Blackwell, Oxford.

LEFEBVRE, C. 1970. Self-fertility in maritime and zinc mine populations of *Armeria maritima* (Mill.) Willd. *Evolution* 24:571-577.

LEROUX, E. J. 1971. Biological control attempts on pome fruit (apple and pear) in North America, 1860–1970. *Can. Entomol.* 103:963–974.

LESLIE, P. H. 1966. The intrinsic rate of increase and the overlap of successive generations in a population of guillemots (*Uria aalge* Pont.) *J. Anim. Ecol.* 35:291–301.

LESLIE, P. H., and J. C. GOWER. 1960. The properties of a stochastic model for the predator–prey type of interaction between two species. *Biometrika* 47:219–234.

LESLIE, P. H., and R. M. RANSON. 1940. The mortality, fertility and rate of natural increase of the vole (*Microtus agrestis*) as observed in the laboratory. *J. Anim. Ecol.* 9:27–52.

LEWIS, J. R. 1964. *The Ecology of Rocky Shores*. English University Press, London.

LEWONTIN, R. C. 1965a. Selection for colonizing ability. pp. 77–94 in *The Genetics of Colonizing Species*, ed. by H. G. Baker and G. L. Stebbins. Academic, New York.

LEWONTIN, R. C. 1965b. Selection in and of populations. pp. 299–311 in *Ideas in Modern Biology*, ed. by J. A. Moore. Doubleday, Garden City, N.Y.

LEWONTIN, R. C. 1969. The meaning of stability. *Brookhaven Symp. Biol.* 22:13–24.

LEWONTIN, R. C., and L. C. BIRCH. 1966. Hybridization as a source of variation for adaptation to new environments. *Evolution* 20:315–336.

LINDSEY, C. C. 1964. Problems in zoogeography of the lake trout, *Salvelinus namaycush. J. Fish. Res. Bd. Can.* 21:977–994.

LIVINGSTON, B. E., and F. SHREVE. 1921. The distribution of vegetation in the United States, as related to climatic conditions. *Carnegie Inst. of Washington Publ. No. 284.* 590 pp.

LLOYD, M. 1967. 'Mean crowding.' *J. Anim. Ecol.* 36:1–30.

LLOYD, M., and R. J. GHELARDI. 1964. A table for calculating the 'equitability' component of species diversity. *J. Anim. Ecol.* 33:217–225.

LOTKA, A. J. 1907. Studies on the mode of growth of material aggregates. *Amer. J. Sci.* 24:199–216.

LOTKA, A. J. 1913. A natural population norm. *J. Wash. Acad. Sci.* 3:241–248, 289–293.

LOTKA, A. J. 1922. The stability of the normal age distribution. *Proc. Nat. Acad. Sci. U.S.* 8:339–345.

LOTKA, A. J. 1923. Contribution to the analysis of malaria epidemiology. Summary. *Amer. J. Hyg.* 3 (Jan. Suppl.):113–121.

LOTKA, A. J. 1925. *Elements of Physical Biology*. (Reprinted in 1956 by Dover Publications, New York.)

LOUCKS, O. L. 1970. Evolution of diversity, efficiency, and community stability. *Amer. Zool.* 10:17–25.

LOWE-McCONNELL, R. H. 1969. Speciation in tropical freshwater fishes. *Biol. J. Linn. Soc.* 1:51–75.

LUND, J. W. G. 1950. Studies on *Asterionella formosa* Hass. II. Nutrient depletion and the spring maximum. *J. Ecol.* 38:1–35.

LUND, J. W. G. 1965. The ecology of the freshwater phytoplankton. *Biol. Rev.* 40:231–293.

LUTZ, H. J. 1930. The vegetation of Heart's Content, a virgin forest in northwestern Pennsylvania. *Ecology* 11:1–29.

LUTZ, H. J. 1945. Vegetation on a trenched plot twenty-one years after establishment. *Ecology* 26:200–202.

MACAN, T. T. 1963. *Freshwater Ecology.* Longmans, London.

MacARTHUR, R. 1955. Fluctuations of animal populations, and a measure of community stability. *Ecology* 36:533–536.

MacARTHUR, R. H. 1957. On the relative abundance of bird species. *Proc. Nat. Acad. Sci. U.S.* 43:293–295.

MacARTHUR, R. H. 1958. Population ecology of some warblers of northeastern coniferous forests. *Ecology* 39:599–619.

MacARTHUR, R. H. 1965. Patterns of species diversity. *Biol. Rev.* 40:510–533.

MacARTHUR, R. H. 1966. Note on Mrs. Pielou's comments. *Ecology* 47:1074.

MacARTHUR, R. 1968. The theory of the niche. pp. 159–176 in *Population Biology and Evolution,* ed. by R. C. Lewontin. Syracuse University Press, Syracuse, N.Y.

MacARTHUR, R. H. 1969a. Patterns of communities in the tropics. *Biol. J. Linn. Soc.* 1:19–30.

MacARTHUR, R. 1969b. Species packing, and what interspecies competition minimizes. *Proc. Nat. Acad. Sci. U.S.* 64:1369–1371.

MacARTHUR, R. and J. CONNELL. 1966. *The Biology of Populations.* Wiley, New York.

MacARTHUR, R. H., and J. W. MacARTHUR. 1961. On bird species diversity. *Ecology* 42:594–598.

MacARTHUR, R. H., and E. O. WILSON. 1967. *The Theory of Island Biogeography.* Princeton University Press, Princeton, N.J.

McCOWN, R. L., and W. A. WILLIAMS. 1968. Competition for nutrients and light between the the annual grassland species *Bromus mollis* and *Erodium botrys. Ecology* 49:981–990.

MACFADYEN, A. 1967. Methods of investigation of productivity of invertebrates in terrestrial ecosystems. pp. 383–412 in *Secondary Productivity of Terrestrial Ecosystems,* ed. by K. Petrusewicz. Warsaw.

McINTOSH, R. P. 1967. The continuum concept of vegetation. *Bot. Rev.* 33:130–187.

McKELL, C. M., E. R. PERRIER, and G. L. STEBBINS. 1960. Responses of two subspecies of orchardgrass (*Dactylis glomerata* subsp. *lusitanica* and *judaica*) to increasing soil moisture stress. *Ecology* 41:772–778.

MC LEOD, J. H., B. M. MC GUGAN, and H. C. COPPEL. 1962. A review of the biological control attempts against insects and weeds in Canada. *Commonwealth Inst. Biol. Control, Tech. Comm. No. 2.* 216 pp.

MC MILLAN, C. 1954. Parallelisms between plant ecology and plant geography. *Ecology* 35:92–94.

MC MILLAN, C. 1959. The role of ecotypic variation in the distribution of the central grassland of North America. *Ecol. Monogr.* 29:285–308.

MC MILLAN, C. 1965. Ecotypic differentiation within four North American prairie grasses. II. Behavioral variation within transplanted community fractions. *Amer. J. Bot.* 52:55–65.

MC NAUGHTON, S. J. 1968. Structure and function in California grasslands. *Ecology* 49:962–972.

MC PHERSON, J. K., and C. H. MULLER. 1969. Allelopathic effects of *Adenostoma fasciculatum*, "Chamise," in the California chaparral. *Ecol. Monogr.* 39:177–198.

MAGUIRE, B., JR. 1963. The passive dispersal of small aquatic organisms and their colonization of isolated bodies of water. *Ecol. Monogr.* 33:161–185.

MAJOR, J. 1958. Plant ecology as a branch of botany. *Ecology* 39:352–363.

MAJOR, J. 1963. A climatic index to vascular plant activity. *Ecology* 44:485–498.

MALTHUS, T. R. 1798. *An Essay on the Principle of Population.* (Reprinted by Macmillan, New York.)

MANLY, B. F. J. 1970. A simulation study of animal population estimation using the capture–recapture method. *J. Appl. Ecol.* 7:13–39.

MANN, K. H. 1965. Energy transformations by a population of fish in the River Thames. *J. Anim. Ecol.* 34:253–275.

MANN, K. H., 1969. The dynamics of aquatic ecosystems. *Advances Ecol. Res.* 6:1–81.

MARGALEF, R. 1958. Information theory in ecology. *Gen. Syst.* 3:36–71.

MARGALEF, R. 1963. On certain unifying principles in ecology. *Amer. Naturalist* 97:357–374.

MARGALEF, R. 1968. *Perspectives in Ecological Theory.* University of Chicago Press, Chicago.

MARGALEF. R. 1969. Diversity and stability: a practical proposal and a model of interdependence. *Brookhaven Symp. Biol.* 22:25–37.

MARPLES, T. G. 1966. A radionuclide tracer study of arthropod food chains in a *Spartina* salt marsh ecosystem. *Ecology* 47:270–277.

MARR, J. W. 1948. Ecology of the forest–tundra ecotone on the east coast of Hudson Bay. *Ecol. Monogr.* 18:117–144.

MARSHALL, D. R., and S. K. JAIN. 1969. Interference in pure and mixed populations of *Avena fatua* and *A. barbata*. *J. Ecol.* 57:251–270.

MASSEY, A. B. 1925. Antagonism of the walnuts (*Juglans nigra* L. and *J. cinerea* L.) in certain plant associations. *Phytopathology* 15:773–784.

MAYNARD, L. A., and J. K. LOOSLI. 1956. *Animal Nutrition,* 4th ed. McGraw-Hill, New York.

MAYNARD SMITH, J. 1964. Group selection and kin selection. *Nature* 201:1145–1147.

MAYNARD SMITH, J. 1968. *Mathematical Ideas in Biology.* Cambridge University Press, New York.

MAYR, E. 1954. Change of genetic environment and evolution. pp. 157–180 in *Evolution as a Process,* ed. by J. Huxley, A. C. Hardy, and E. B. Ford. Allen and Unwin, London.

MAYR, E. 1963. *Animal Species and Evolution.* Harvard University Press, Cambridge, Mass.

MAYR, E. 1964. The nature of colonization in birds. pp. 29–43 in *The Genetics of Colonizing Species,* ed. by H. G. Baker and G. L. Stebbins. Academic, New York.

MEADOW, P. M., and S. J. PIRT. 1969. *Microbial Growth. Nineteenth Symposium of the Society for General Microbiology.* Cambridge University Press, New York.

MEDAWAR, P. B. 1957. Old age and natural death. Chap. 1, pp. 17–43, in *The Uniqueness of the Individual.* Methuen, London.

MENZEL, D. W., and J. H. RYTHER. 1961a. Nutrients limiting the production of phytoplankton in the Sargasso Sea, with special reference to iron. *Deep Sea Res.* 7:276–281.

MENZEL, D. W., and J. H. RYTHER. 1961b. Annual variations in primary production of the Sargasso Sea off Bermuda. *Deep Sea Res.* 7:282–288.

MERRELL, M. 1947. Time-specific life tables contrasted with observed survivorship. *Biometrics* 3:129–136.

MERRIAM, C. H. 1898. Life zones and crop zones. *U.S. Dept. Agr. Div. Biol. Surv. Bull. No. 10.* 79 pp.

MERTZ, D. B. 1970. Notes on methods used in life-history studies. pp. 4–17 in *Readings in Ecology and Ecological Genetics,* ed. by J. H. Connell, D. B. Mertz, and W. W. Murdoch. Harper & Row, New York.

MILLER, C. A. 1963. The spruce budworm, pp. 12–19 in *The Dynamics of Epidemic Spruce Budworm Populations,* ed. by R. F. Morris, Mem. Entomol. Soc. Canada No. 31.

MILLER, R. B. 1949. The status of the hatchery. *Can. Fish. Cult.* 4, No. 5.

MILLER, R. S. 1957. Observations on the status of ecology. *Ecology* 38:353–354.

MILLER, R. S. 1964. Ecology and distribution of pocket gophers (Geomyidae) in Colorado. *Ecology* 45:256–272.

MILLER, R. S. 1967. Pattern and process in competition. *Advances Ecol. Res.* 4:1–74.

MILNE, A. 1943. The comparison of sheep-tick populations (*Ixodes ricinus* L.). *Ann. Appl. Biol.* 30:240–250.

MILNE, A. 1958. Theories of natural control of insect populations. *Cold Spring Harbor Symp. Quant. Biol.* 22:253–271.

MILNE, A. 1962. On a theory of natural control of insect population. *J. Theoret. Biol.* 3:19–50.

MILNER, C., and R. E. HUGHES. 1968. *Methods for the Measurement of the Primary Production of Grassland* (Int. Biol. Program Handbook No. 6). Blackwell, Oxford. 70 pp.

MÖBIUS, K. 1877. *Die Auster und die Austernwirtschaft.* Wiegundt, Hempel and Parey, Berlin. (Translation: *Rept. U.S. Comm. Fish.,* 1880:683–751.)

MOHR, C. O. 1943. Cattle droppings as ecological units. *Ecol. Monogr.* 13:275–298.

MOIZUK, G. A., and R. B. LIVINGSTON. 1966. Ecology of red maple (*Acer rubrum* L.) in a Massachusetts upland bog. *Ecology* 47:942–950.

MONK, C. D. 1967. Tree species diversity in the eastern deciduous forest with particular reference to north central Florida. *Amer. Naturalist* 101:173–187.

MOOK, L. J. 1963. Birds and the spruce budworm. pp. 268–271 in *The Dynamics of Epidemic Spruce Budworm Populations,* ed. by R. F. Morris, *Mem. Entomol. Soc. Can. No. 31.*

MOONEY, H. A. 1963. Physiological ecology of coastal, subalpine, and alpine populations of *Polygonum bistortoides. Ecology* 44:812–816.

MOONEY, H. A., and W. D. BILLINGS. 1961. Comparative physiological ecology of arctic and alpine populations of *Oxyria digyna. Ecol. Monogr.* 31:1–29.

MOORE, B. 1926. Influence of certain soil and light conditions on the establishment of reproduction in northeastern conifers. *Ecology* 7:191–220.

MOORE, H. B. 1958. *Marine Ecology.* Wiley, New York.

MORAN, R. J., and W. L. PALMER. 1963. Ruffed grouse introductions and population trends on Michigan islands. *J. Wildl. Mgmt.* 27:606–614.

MOREAU, R. E. 1935. A critical analysis of the distribution of birds in a tropical African area. *J. Anim. Ecol.* 4:167–191.

MOREY, H. F. 1936. A comparison of two virgin forests in northwestern Pennsylvania. *Ecology* 17:43–55.

MORGAN, E. 1970. The effect of environmental factors on the distribution of the amphipod *Pectenogammarus planicrurus*, with particular reference to grain size. *J. Mar. Biol. Ass. U.K.* 50:769–785.

MORISITA, M. 1965. The fitting of the logistic equation to the rate of increase of population density. *Res. Population Ecol.* 7:52–55.

MORRIS, R. F. 1957. The interpretation of mortality data in studies on population dynamics. *Can. Entomol.* 89:49–69.

MORRIS, R. F. (ed.) 1963. The dynamics of epidemic spruce budworm populations. *Mem. Entomol. Soc. Can. No. 31.* 332 pp.

MORRIS, R. F., and C. A. MILLER. 1954. The development of life tables for the spruce budworm. *Can. J. Zool.* 32:283–301.

MORRIS, R. F., W. F. CHESHIRE, C. A. MILLER, and D. G. MOTT. 1958. The numerical response of avian and mammalian predators during a gradation of the spruce budworm. *Ecology* 39:487–494.

MOUTIA, L. A., and R. MAMET. 1946. A review of twenty-five years of economic entomology in the island of Mauritius. *Bull. Entomol. Res.* 36:439–472.

MUIRHEAD-THOMSON, R. C. 1951. *Mosquito Behaviour in Relation to Malaria Transmission and Control in the Tropics.* Edward Arnold, London.

MULLER, C. H. 1953. The association of desert annuals with shrubs. *Amer. J. Bot.* 40:53–60.

MULLER, C. H. 1966. The role of chemical inhibition (allelopathy) in vegetational composition. *Bull. Torrey Bot. Club* 93:332–351.

MULLER, C. H. 1970. Phytotoxins as plant habitat variables. *Recent Advances Phytochem.* 3:105–121.

MULLER, C. H., R. B. HANAWALT, and J. K. MCPHERSON. 1968. Allelopathic control of herb growth in the fire cycle of California chaparral. *Bull. Torrey Bot. Club* 95: 225–231.

MURDOCH, W. W. 1966a. "Community structure, population control, and competition"—a critique. *Amer. Naturalist* 100:219–226.

MURDOCH, W. W. 1966b. Population stability and life history phenomena. *Amer. Naturalist* 100:5–11.

MURDOCH, W. W. 1970. Population regulation and population inertia. *Ecology* 51:497–502.

MURIE, A. 1944. *The Wolves of Mount McKinley.* Fauna of the National Parks of the U.S., Fauna Series No. 5, Washington, D.C. 238 pp.

MURPHY, G. I. 1966. Population biology of the Pacific sardine (*Sardinops caerulea*). *Proc. Calif. Acad. Sci.* 34:1–84.

MURPHY, G. I. 1967. Vital statistics of the Pacific sardine (*Sardinops caerulea*) and the population consequences. *Ecology* 48:731–736.

MURPHY, G. I. 1968. Pattern in life history and the environment. *Amer. Naturalist* 102:391–403.

NARISE, T. 1965. The effect of relative frequency of species in competition. *Evolution* 19:350–354.

NATIONAL CENTER FOR HEALTH STATISTICS. 1968. *United States Life Tables: 1959–61*, Vol. I, Nos. 1–6. Public Health Service Pub. No. 1252, Washington, D.C.

NATIONAL CENTER FOR HEALTH STATISTICS. 1969. Vital Statistics of the United States, 1967, Vols. I and II. U.S. Public Health Service, Washington, D.C.

NELSON, J. B. 1964. Factors influencing clutch-size and chick growth in the North Atlantic gannet, *Sula bassana. Ibis* 106:63–77.

NELSON, T. C. 1955. Chestnut replacement in the Southern Highlands. *Ecology* 36:352-353.

NEWBOULD, P. J. 1967. *Methods for Estimating the Primary Production of Forests.* (Int. Biol. Program Handbook No. 2). Blackwell, Oxford.

NEWMAN, W. A. 1970. *Acanthaster*: a disaster? *Science* 167:1274–1275.

NEWSON, R. 1963. Differences in numbers, reproduction and survival between two neighboring populations of bank voles (*Clethrionomys glareolus*). *Ecology* 44:110–120.

NEYMAN, J., T. PARK, and E. L. SCOTT. 1956. Struggle for existence. The *Tribolium* model: biological and statistical aspects. pp. 41–79 in *Proceedings of the Third Berkeley Symposium on Mathematical Statistics and Probability.* Vol. IV, University of California Press, Berkeley.

NICHOLSON, A. J. 1933. The balance of animal populations. *J. Anim. Ecol.* 2: 132–178.

NICHOLSON, A. J. 1954a. Compensatory reactions of populations to stress, and their evolutionary significance. *Aust. J. Zool.* 2:1–8.

NICHOLSON, A. J. 1954b. An outline of the dynamics of animal populations. *Aust. J. Zool.* 2:9–65.

NIELSEN, E. STEEMANN, and E. A. JENSEN. 1957. Primary oceanic production. pp. 49–136 in *Galathea Report*, Vol. 1. Copenhagen.

NIERING, W. A., R. H. WHITTAKER, and C. H. LOWE. 1963. The saguaro: a population in relation to environment. *Science* 142:15–23.

NOLTE, D. J. 1967. Phase transformation and chiasma formation in locusts. *Chromosoma* 2:123–139.

NOVICK, A. 1955. Growth of bacteria. *Ann. Rev. Microbiol.* 9:97–110.

NUTTONSON, M. Y. 1955. *Wheat-Climate Relationships and the Use of Phenology in Ascertaining the Thermal and Photo-thermal Requirements of Wheat.* Amer. Inst. Crop Ecology, Washington. 388 pp.

ODUM, E. 1963. *Ecology.* Holt, Rinehart & Winston. New York.

ODUM, E. P. 1964. The new ecology. *BioScience* 14(7):14–16.

ODUM, E. P. 1968. Energy flow in ecosystems: a historical review. *Amer. Zool.* 8:11–18.

ODUM, E. P. 1969. The strategy of ecosystem development. *Science* 164:262–270.

OLSON, J. S. 1958. Rates of succession and soil changes on southern Lake Michigan sand dunes. *Bot. Gaz.* 119:125–170.

OOSTING, H. J., and W. D. BILLINGS. 1942. Factors affecting vegetational zonation on coastal dunes. *Ecology* 23:131–142.

OOSTING, H. J., and P. J. KRAMER. 1946. Water and light in relation to pine reproduction. *Ecology* 27:47–53.

ORIANS, G. H. 1969a. The number of bird species in some tropical forests. *Ecology* 50:783–797.

ORIANS, G. H. 1969b. On the evolution of mating systems in birds and mammals. *Amer. Naturalist* 103:589–603.

ORIANS, G. H., and G. COLLIER. 1963. Competition and blackbird social systems. *Evolution* 17:449–459.

ORIANS, G. H., and M. F. WILLSON. 1964. Interspecific territories of birds. *Ecology* 45:736–745.

OVERLAND, L. 1966. The role of allelopathic substances in the "smother crop" barley. *Amer. J. Bot.* 53:423–432.

OVINGTON, J. D. 1962. Quantitative ecology and the woodland ecosystem concept. *Advances Ecol. Res.* 1:103–192.

OVINGTON, J. D. 1965. *Woodlands.* English University Press, London.

PADDOCK, W., and P. PADDOCK. 1967. *Famine—1975!* Little, Brown, Boston.

PAINE, R. T. 1966. Food web complexity and species diversity. *Amer. Naturalist* 100:65–75.

PAINE, R. T. 1969. A note on trophic complexity and community stability. *Amer. Naturalist* 103:91–93.

PALMER, W. L. 1962. Ruffed grouse flight capability over water. *J. Wildl. Mgmt.* 26:338–339.

PARENTI, R. L., and E. L. RICE. 1969. Inhibitional effects of *Digitaria sanguinalis* and possible role in old-field succession. *Bull. Torrey Bot. Club* 96:70–78.

PARK, T. 1948. Experimental studies of interspecies competition. I. Competition between populations of the flour beetles, *Tribolium confusum* Duval and *Tribolium castaneum* Herbst. *Ecol. Monogr.* 18:265–307.

PARK, T. 1954. Experimental studies of interspecies competition. II. Temperature, humidity, and competition in two species of *Tribolium. Physiol. Zool.* 27:177–238.

PARK, T. 1962. Beetles, competition, and populations. *Science* 138:1369–1375.

PARK, T., P. H. LESLIE, and D. B. MERTZ. 1964. Genetic strains and competition in populations of *Tribolium. Physiol. Zool.* 37:97–162.

PARK, T., D. B. MERTZ, and K. PETRUSEWICZ. 1961. Genetic strains of *Tribolium*: their primary characteristics. *Physiol. Zool.* 34:62–80.

PARK, T., D. B. MERTZ, W. GRODZINSKI, and T. PRUS. 1965. Cannibalistic predation in populations of flour beetles. *Physiol. Zool.* 38:289–321.

PARKER, J. 1950. Planting loblolly pine outside its natural range. *J. Forestry* 48:278–279.

PARKER, J. 1952. Environment and forest distribution of the Palouse Range in northern Idaho. *Ecology* 33:451–461.

PARKER, J. 1955. Survival of some southeastern pine seedlings in northern Idaho. *J. Forestry* 53:137.

PARKER, J. 1963. Cold resistance in woody plants. *Bot. Rev.* 29:123–201.

PARKER, J. 1969. Further studies of drought resistance in woody plants. *Bot. Rev.* 35:317–371.

PAULEY, S. S., and T. O. PERRY, 1954. Ecotypic variation of the photoperiodic response in *Populus. J. Arnold Arboretum* 35:167–188.

PEARL, R. 1922. *The Biology of Death.* Lippincott, Philadelphia.

PEARL, R. 1927. The growth of populations. *Quart. Rev. Biol.* 2:532–548.

PEARL, R. 1928. *The Rate of Living.* Knopf, New York.

PEARL, R. 1930. *Introduction to Medical Biometry and Statistics.* Saunders, Philadelphia.

PEARL, R., and J. R. MINER. 1935. Experimental studies on the duration of life. XIV. The comparative mortality of certain organisms. *Quart. Rev. Biol.* 10:60–79.

PEARL, R., and L. J. REED. 1920. On the rate of growth of the population of the United States since 1790 and its mathematical representation. *Proc. Nat. Acad. Sci. U.S.* 6:275–288.

PEARL, R., L. J. REED, and J. F. KISH. 1940. The logistic curve and the census count of 1940. *Science* 92:486–488.

PEARSON, G. A. 1936. Why the prairies are treeless. *J. Forestry* 34:405–408.

PEARSON, O. P. 1964. Carnivore-mouse predation: an example of its intensity and bioenergetics. *J. Mammal.* 45:177–188.

PEARSON, O. P. 1966. The prey of carnivores during one cycle of mouse abundance. *J. Anim. Ecol.* 35:217–233.

PERRINS, C. 1964. Survival of young swifts in relation to brood-size. *Nature* 201: 1147–1149.

PERRINS, C., and V. C. WYNNE-EDWARDS. 1964. Survival of young swifts in relation to brood-size. *Nature* 201:1147–1149.

PERRINS, C. M. 1965. Population fluctuations and clutch-size in the great tit, *Parus major* L. *J. Anim. Ecol.* 34:601–647.

PERRY, T. O., and W. C. WU. 1960. Genetic variation in the winter chilling requirement for date of dormancy break for *Acer rubrum*. *Ecology* 41:790–794.

PETIPA, T. S., E. V. PAVLOVA, and G. N. MIRONOV. 1970. The food web structure, utilization and transport of energy by trophic levels in the planktonic communities. pp. 142–167 in *Marine Food Chains*, ed. by J. H. Steele. University of California Press, Berkeley.

PETRIDES, G. A., and W. G. SWANK. 1966. Estimating the productivity and energy relations of an African elephant population. *Proc. Ninth Int. Grass. Cong., San Paulo, Brazil*, pp. 831–842.

PETRUSEWICZ, K., and A. MACFADYEN. 1970. *Productivity of Terrestrial Animals— Principles and Methods* (IBP Handbook No. 13). Blackwell, Oxford.

PHARIS, R. P., and W. K. FERRELL. 1966. Differences in drought resistance between coastal and inland sources of Douglas fir. *Can. J. Bot.* 44:1651–1659.

PHILLIPS, E. A. 1959. *Methods of Vegetation Study*. Holt, Rinehart & Winston, New York.

PHILLIPS, J. 1934–1935. Succession, development, the climax, and the complex organism: an analysis of concepts. *J. Ecol.* 22:554–571; 23:210–246, 488-508.

PHILLIPS, J. C. 1928. Wild birds introduced or transplanted in North America. *U.S. Dept. Agr. Tech. Bull. No. 61.* 63 pp.

PIANKA, E. R. 1966a. Convexity, desert lizards, and spatial heterogeneity. *Ecology* 47:1055–1059.

PIANKA, E. R. 1966b. Latitudinal gradients in species diversity: a review of concepts. *Amer. Naturalist* 100:33–46.

PIANKA, E. R. 1967. On lizard species diversity: North American flatland deserts. *Ecology* 48:333–351.

PIANKA, E. R. 1969. Habitat specificity, speciation, and species density in Australian desert lizards. *Ecology* 50:498–502.

PIANKA, E. R. 1970. On *r*- and *K*-selection. *Amer. Naturalist* 104:592–597.

PICKERING, S. 1917. The effect of one plant on another. *Ann. Bot.* 31:181–187.

PIELOU, E. C. 1966. The measurement of diversity in different types of biological collections. *J. Theoret. Biol.* 13:131–144.

PIELOU, E. C. 1969. *An Introduction to Mathematical Ecology*. Wiley-Interscience, New York.

PIJL, L. VAN DER. 1969. *Principles of Dispersal in Higher Plants*. Springer, Berlin.

PIMENTEL, D. 1961. Species diversity and insect population outbreaks. *Ann. Entomol. Soc. Amer.* 54:76–86.

PIMENTEL, D. 1963. Introducing parasites and predators to control native pests. *Can. Entomol.* 95:785–792.

PIMENTEL, D. 1968. Population regulation and genetic feedback. *Science* 159: 1432–1437.

PIMENTEL, D., W. P. NAGEL, and J. L. MADDEN. 1963. Space–time structure of the environment and the survival of parasite–host systems. *Amer. Naturalist* 97:141–167.

PIRIE, N. W. 1967. Orthodox and unorthodox methods of meeting world food needs. *Sci. Amer.* 216(2):27–35.

PITELKA, F. A., P. Q. TOMICH, and G. W. TREICHEL. 1955. Ecological relations of jaegers and owls as lemming predators near Barrow, Alaska. *Ecol. Monogr.* 25:85–117.

PLATT, J. R. 1964. Strong inference. *Science* 146:347–353.

PONTIN, A. J. 1961. Population stabilization and competition between the ants *Lasius flavus* (F.) and *L. niger* (L.) *J. Anim. Ecol.* 30:47–54.

PONTIN, A. J. 1969. Experimental transplantation of nest-mounds of the ant *Lasius flavus* (F.) in a habitat containing also *L. niger* (L.) and *Myrmica scabrinodis* Nyl. *J. Anim. Ecol.* 38:747–754.

POORE, M. E. D. 1956. The use of phytosociological methods in ecological investigations. IV. General discussion of phytosociological problems. *J. Ecol.* 44:28–50.

POPPER, K. R. 1963. *Conjectures and Refutations*. Routledge & Kegan Paul, London.

POPULATION REFERENCE BUREAU, INC. 1970. World population data sheet. Washington, D.C. April 1970.

POSEY, C. E. 1967. Natural regeneration of loblolly pine within 230 miles of its native range. *J. Forest.* 65:732.

POTTER, L. D., and D. L. GREEN. 1964. Ecology of ponderosa pine in western North Dakota. *Ecology* 45:10–23.

PRATT, D. M. 1943. Analysis of population development in *Daphnia* at different temperatures. *Biol. Bull.* 85:116–140.

PRESIDENT'S SCIENCE ADVISORY COMMITTEE—Panel on the World Food Supply. 1967. *The World Food Problem*, 3 vols. Washington, D.C.

PRESTON, F. W. 1948. The commonness and rarity of species. *Ecology* 29:254–283.

PRESTON, F. W. 1960. Time and space and the variation of species. *Ecology* 41:611–627.

PRESTON, F. W. 1962. The canonical distribution of commonness and rarity. *Ecology* 43:185–215, 410–432.

PROEBSTING, E. L. 1950. A case history of a "peach replant" situation. *Proc. Amer. Soc. Hort. Sci.* 56:46–48.

PROVOST, M. W. 1957. The dispersal of *Aedes taeniorhynchus*. II. The second experiment. *Mosquito News* 17(3):233–247.

QUETELET, A. 1835. *Sur l'homme et le developpement de ses facultes or essai de physique sociale.* Bachelier, Paris. 2 vols.

RABB, R. L., and F. E. GUTHRIE (eds.). 1970. *Concepts of Pest Management.* Proceedings of a Conference, North Carolina State University, Raleigh.

RAINEY, R. C. 1963. Meteorology and the migration of desert locusts. *Anti-Locust Mem.* 7:1–115.

RASMUSSEN, D. I. 1941. Biotic communities of Kaibab Plateau, Arizona. *Ecol. Monogr.* 3:229–275.

RAWSON, D. S. 1943. The experimental introduction of smallmouth black bass into lakes of the Prince Albert National Park, Saskatchewan. *Trans. Amer. Fish. Soc.* 73:19–31.

RAWSON, D. S. 1945. The failure of rainbow trout and initial success with the introduction of lake trout in Clear Lake, Riding Mountain Park, Manitoba. *Trans. Amer. Fish. Soc.* 75:323–335.

RECHER, H. F. 1969. Bird species diversity and habitat diversity in Australia and North America. *Amer. Naturalist* 103:75–80.

The Registrar General's Statistical Review of England and Wales for the Year 1967. Part I. Tables, Medical. H.M. Stationery Office, London, 1968.

REINERS, W. A., I. A. WORLEY, and D. B. LAWRENCE. 1971. Plant diversity in a chronosequence at Glacier Bay, Alaska. *Ecology* 52:55–69.

RENNIE, P. J. 1957. The uptake of nutrients by timber forest and its importance to timber production in Britain. *Quart. J. Forestry* 51:101–115.

REYNOLDSON, T. B. 1958. Triclads and lake typology in northern Britain: qualitative aspects. *Verh. Int. Ver. Limnol.* 13:320–330.

REYNOLDSON, T. B. 1964. Evidence for intra-specific competition in field populations of triclads. *J. Anim. Ecol.* 33(Suppl.):187–201.

REYNOLDSON, T. B. 1966. The distribution and abundance of lake-dwelling triclads —towards a hypothesis. *Advances Ecol. Res.* 3:1–71.

REYNOLDSON, T. B., and R. W. DAVIES. 1970. Food niche and co-existence in lake-dwelling triclads. *J. Anim. Ecol.* 39:599–617.

REYNOLDSON, T. B., and J. O. YOUNG. 1966. The relationship between the distribution of *Dendrocoelum lacteum* (Mull.) and *Asellus* in Britain and Fennoscandia. *Verh. Int. Ver. Limnol.* 16:1633–1639.

RICE, E. L. 1968. Inhibition of nodulation of inoculated legumes by pioneer plant species from abandoned fields. *Bull. Torrey Bot. Club* 95:346–358.

RICE, E. L., W. T. PENFOUND, and L. M. ROHRBAUGH. 1960. Seed dispersal and mineral nutrition in succession in abandoned fields in central Oklahoma. *Ecology* 41:224–228.

RICHARDS, O. W. 1928. Potentially unlimited multiplication of yeast with constant environment, and the limiting of growth by changing environment. *J. Gen. Physiol.* 11:525–538.

RICHARDS, O. W. 1939. An American text-book. (Book review of A. S. Pearse, *Animal Ecology.*) *J. Anim. Ecol.* 8:387–388.

RICHARDS, P. W. 1969. Speciation in the tropical rain forest and the concept of the niche. *Biol. J. Linn. Soc.* 1:149–153.

RICKER, K. E. 1959. The origin of two glacial relict crustaceans in North America, as related to Pleistocene glaciation. *Can. J. Zool.* 37:871–893.

RICKER, W. E. 1934. An ecological classification of certain Ontario streams. *Univ. Toronto Stud. Biol. Ser.* No. 37:1–114.

RICKER, W. E. 1954. Stock and recruitment. *J. Fish. Res. Bd. Can.* 11:559–623.

RICKER, W. E. 1958. Handbook of Computations for Biological Statistics of Fish Populations. *Fish. Res. Bd. Can., Bull. No. 119.* 300 pp.

RICKETTS, E. F., and J. CALVIN. 1968. *Between Pacific Tides*, 4th ed., revised by J. W. Hedgpeth. Stanford University Press, Stanford, Calif.

RIGLER, F. H. 1964. The contribution of zooplankton to the turnover of phosphorus in the epilimnion of lakes. *Can. Fish. Cult.* 32:3–9.

RILEY, G. A. 1946. Factors controlling phytoplankton populations on Georges Bank. *J. Mar. Res.* 6:54–73.

RILEY, G. A. 1947. A theoretical analysis of the zooplankton population of Georges Bank. *J. Mar. Res.* 6:104–113.

RILEY, G. A. 1963. Theory of food-chain relations in the ocean. pp. 438–463 in *The Sea*, Vol. 2, ed. by M. N. Hill. Wiley-Interscience, New York.

RITCHIE, J. C. 1959. The vegetation of northern Manitoba. III. Studies in the subarctic. *Arctic Inst. N. America Tech. Paper No. 3.* 56 pp.

RODIN, L. E., and N. I. BASILEVICH. 1968. *Production and Mineral Cycling in Terrestrial Vegetation*, trans. by G. E. Fogg. Oliver & Boyd, Edinburgh.

ROSENZWEIG, M. L. 1968. Net primary productivity of terrestrial communities: prediction from climatological data. *Amer. Naturalist* 102:67–74.

ROSENZWEIG, M. L., and R. H. MACARTHUR. 1963. Graphical representation and stability conditions of predator–prey interactions. *Amer. Naturalist* 97:209–223.

ROSS, H. H. 1957. Principles of natural coexistence indicated by leafhopper populations. *Evolution* 11:113–129.

ROSS, R. 1908. *Reports on the Prevention of Malaria in Mauritius*. Waterloo, London.

ROSS, R. 1911. *The Prevention of Malaria*, 2nd ed. London.

ROUNSEFELL, G. A. 1958. Factors causing decline in sockeye salmon of Karluk River, Alaska. *Fish. Bull. (U.S.)* 58(130):83–169.

ROWE, J. S. 1961. The level-of-integration concept and ecology. *Ecology* 42:420–427.

ROWE, J. S. 1966. Phytogeographic zonation: an ecological appreciation. pp. 12–27 in *The Evolution of Canada's Flora*, ed. by R. L. Taylor and R. A. Ludwig. University of Toronto Press.

ROYAMA, T. 1969. A model for the global variation of clutch size in birds. *Oikos* 20:562–567.

ROYAMA, T. 1970. Factors governing the hunting behaviour and selection of food by the great tit (*Parus major* L.). *J. Anim. Ecol.* 39:619–668.

RUSSELL, E. S. 1931. Some theoretical considerations on the "overfishing" problem. *J. Con. Perm. Int. Exp. Mer* 6:3–27.

RUSSELL, P. F., and T. R. RAO. 1942. On relation of mechanical obstruction and shade to ovipositing of *Anopheles culicifacies*. *J. Exp. Zool.* 91:303–329.

RYDBERG, P. A. 1913. Phytogeographical notes on the Rocky Mountain region. I. Alpine region. *Bull. Torrey Bot. Club* 40:677–686.

RYTHER, J. H. 1954. Inhibitory effects of phytoplankton upon the feeding of *Daphnia magna* with reference to growth, reproduction and survival. *Ecology* 35:522–533.

RYTHER, J. H. 1956. Photosynthesis in the ocean as a function of light intensity. *Limnol. Oceanogr.* 1:61–70.

RYTHER, J. H. 1963. Geographic variation in productivity. pp. 347–380 in *The Sea*, Vol. 2, ed. by M. N. Hill. Wiley-Interscience, New York.

RYTHER, J. H. 1969. Photosynthesis and fish production in the sea. *Science* 166:72–76.

RYTHER, J. H., and W. M. DUNSTAN. 1971. Nitrogen, phosphorus, and eutrophication in the coastal marine environment. *Science* 171:1008–1013.

RYTHER, J. H., and C. S. YENTSCH. 1957. The estimation of phytoplankton production in the ocean from chlorophyll and light data. *Limnol. Oceanogr.* 2:281–286.

SALISBURY, E. 1961. *Weeds and Aliens*. Collins, London.

SALISBURY, E. J. 1926. The geographical distribution of plants in relation to climatic factors. *Geogr. J.* 67:312–342.

SALISBURY, E. J. 1942. *The Reproductive Capacity of Plants. Studies in Quantitative Biology*. G. Bell & Sons, London.

SALT, G., and F. S. J. HOLLICK. 1944. Studies of wireworm populations. I. A census of wireworms in pasture. *Ann. Appl. Biol.* 31:52–64.

SANDERS, H. L. 1968. Marine benthic diversity: a comparative study. *Amer. Naturalist* 102:243–282.

SANG, J. H. 1950. Population growth in *Drosophila* cultures. *Biol. Rev.* 25:188–219.

SATCHELL, J. E. 1955. Some aspects of earthworm ecology. pp. 180–201 in *Soil Zoology*, ed. by D. K. McE. Kevan. Butterworth, London.

SAUER, C. O. 1969. *Agricultural Origins and Dispersals*, 2nd ed. M.I.T. Press, Cambridge, Mass.

SCHAEFER, M. B. 1968. Methods of estimating effects of fishing on fish populations. *Trans. Amer. Fish. Soc.* 97:231–241.

SCHEFFER, V. B. 1951. The rise and fall of a reindeer herd. *Sci. Monthly* 73:356-362.

SCHMIDT-NIELSEN, K., and B. SCHMIDT-NIELSEN. 1953. The desert rat. *Sci. Amer.* 189(1):73–78.

SCHNEIDERHAN, F. J. 1927. The black walnut (*Juglans nigra* L.) as a cause of the death of apple trees. *Phytopathology* 17:529–540.

SCHOONHOVERN, L. M. 1968. Chemosensory bases of host plant selection. *Ann. Rev. Entomol.* 13:115–136.

SCHWERDTFEGER, F. 1941. Über die Ursachen des Massenwechsels der Insekten. *Z. Angew. Entomol.* 28:254–303.

SELIGER, H. H., J. H. CARPENTER, M. LOFTUS, and W. D. MCELROY. 1970. Mechanisms for the accumulation of high concentrations of dinoflagellates in a bioluminescent bay. *Limnol. Oceanogr.* 15:234–245.

SHEAR, C. L., N. E. STEVENS, and R. J. TILLER. 1917. *Endothia parasitica* and related species. *U.S. Dept. Agr. Bull. No. 380.* 82 pp.

SHREVE, F. 1910. The rate of establishment of the giant cactus. *Plant World* 13:235–240.

SHREVE, F. 1911. The influence of low temperatures on the distribution of the giant cactus. *Plant World* 14:136–146.

SILLIMAN, R. P., and J. S. GUTSELL. 1958. Experimental exploitation of fish populations. *Fish. Bull.* (*U.S.*) 58(133):215–252.

SIMBERLOFF, D. S., and E. O. WILSON. 1970. Experimental zoogeography of islands. A two-year record of colonization. *Ecology* 51:934–937.

SIMMONDS, F. J. 1956. The present status of biological control. *Can. Entomol.* 88:553–563.

SIMPSON, E. H. 1949. Measurement of diversity. *Nature* 163:688.

SIMPSON, G. G. 1969. Species density of North American Recent mammals. *Syst. Zool.* 13:57–73.

SIMPSON, G. G. 1969. The first three billion years of community evolution. *Brookhaven Symp. Biol.* 22:162–177.

SIMPSON, G. G., A. ROE, and R. C. LEWONTIN. 1960. *Quantitative Zoology*. Harcourt Brace Jovanovich, New York.

SINCLAIR, W. A. 1964. Comparisons of recent declines of white ash, oaks and sugar maple in northeastern woodlands. *Cornell Plantations* 20:62–67.

SKELLAM, J. G. 1955. The mathematical approach to population dynamics. pp. 31–46 in *The Numbers of Man and Animals*, ed. by J. B. Cragg and N. W. Pirie. Oliver & Boyd, Edinburgh.

SKUTCH, A. F. 1967. Adaptive limitation of the reproductive rate of birds. *Ibis* 109:579–599.

SLOBODKIN, L. B. 1961. *Growth and Regulation of Animal Populations*. Holt, Rinehart & Winston, New York.

SLOBODKIN, L. B. 1964. Experimental populations of Hydrida. *J. Anim. Ecol.* 33 (Suppl.):131–148.

SMALLEY, A. E. 1960. Energy flow of a salt marsh grasshopper population. *Ecology* 41:672–677.

SMITH, F. E. 1963. Population dynamics in *Daphnia magna* and a new model for population growth. *Ecology* 44:651–663.

SMITH, F. E. 1970. Analysis of ecosystems. pp. 7–18 in *Analysis of Temperate Forest Ecosystems*, ed. by D. Reichle. Springer, Berlin.

SMITH, H. S. 1935. The role of biotic factors in the determination of population densities. *J. Econ. Entomol.* 28:873–898.

SMITH, J. E. (ed.) 1968. 'Torrey Canyon' Pollution and Marine Life. Cambridge Univ. Press, London.

SOKAL, R. R., and P. H. A. SNEATH. 1963. Principles of Numerical Taxonomy. W. H. Freeman, San Francisco.

SOUTHERN, H. N. 1970. The natural control of a population of tawny owls (Strix aluco). J. Zool. London 162:197–285.

SOUTHWARD, A. J. 1958. Note on the temperature tolerances of some intertidal animals in relation to environmental temperatures and geographical distribution. J. Mar. Biol. Ass. U.K. 37:49–66.

SOUTHWOOD, T. R. E. 1961. The number of species of insect associated with various trees. J. Anim. Ecol. 30:1–8.

SOUTHWOOD, T. R. E. 1966. Ecological Methods with Particular Reference to the Study of Insect Populations. Methuen, London.

SPARROW, R. A. H., P. A. LARKIN, and R. A. RUTHERGLEN. 1964. Successful introduction of Mysis relicta Loven into Kootenay Lake, British Columbia. J. Fish. Res. Bd. Can. 21:1325–1327.

SPENCE, D. H. N. 1967. Factors controlling the distribution of freshwater macrophytes with particular reference to the lochs of Scotland. J. Ecol. 55:147–170.

STALEY, J. M. 1965. Decline and mortality of red and scarlet oaks. Forest Sci. 11:2–17.

Statistical Abstract of the United States. 1970. U.S. Bureau of the Census. Washington, D.C.

Statistical Yearbook of the United Nations, 1969. New York, Statistical Office of the United Nations, 1970. (Published annually by the U. N.)

STEBBINS, G. L. 1965. Colonizing species of the native California flora. pp. 173–195 in The Genetics of Colonizing Species, ed. by H. G. Baker and G. L. Stebbins. Academic Press, New York.

STEELE, J. H. (ed.). 1970. Marine Food Chains. University of California Press, Berkeley.

STEENBERGH, W. F., and C. H. LOWE. 1969. Critical factors during the first years of life of the saguaro (Cereus giganteus) at Saguaro National Monument, Arizona. Ecology 50:825–834.

STEHLI, F. G., R. G. DOUGLAS, and N. D. NEWELL. 1969. Generation and maintenance of gradients in taxonomic diversity. Science 164:947–949.

STEWART, G., and A. C. HULL. 1949. Cheatgrass (Bromus tectorum L.)—an ecologic intruder in southern Idaho. Ecology 30:58–74.

STOCKNER, J. G., and W. W. BENSON. 1967. The succession of diatom assemblages in the recent sediments of Lake Washington. Limnol. Oceangr. 12:513–532.

STONE, M. H. 1944. Soil reaction in relation to the distribution of native plant species. Ecology 25:379–386.

STORTENBEKER, C. W. 1967. Observations on the population dynamics of the Red Locust, Nomadacris septemfasciata (Serville), in its outbreak areas. Inst. for Biol. Field Res. (ITBON), Mededeling No. 84. 118 pp.

SUTCLIFFE, D. W. 1967a. Sodium regulation in the amphipod *Gammarus duebeni* from brackish-water and fresh-water localities in Britain. *J. Exp. Biol.* 46:529–550.

SUTCLIFFE, D. W. 1967b. Sodium regulation in the fresh-water amphipod, *Gammarus pulex. J. Exp. Biol.* 46:449–518.

SUTCLIFFE, D. W. 1967c. A re-examination of observations on the distribution of *Gammarus duebeni* Lilljeborg in relation to the salt content in fresh water. *J. Anim. Ecol.* 36:579–597.

SWAN, H. S. D. 1965. Reviewing the scientific use of fertilizers in forestry. *J. Forestry* 63:501–508.

SYMMONS, P. 1959. The effect of climate and weather on the numbers of the red locust, *Nomadacris septemfasciata* (Serv.), in the Rukwa Valley outbreak area. *Bull. Entomol. Res.* 50:507–521.

TADROS, T. M. 1957. Evidence of the presence of an edapho-biotic factor in the problem of serpentine tolerance. *Ecology* 38:14–23.

TAEUBER, I. B. 1960. Japan's demographic transition re-examined. *Population Stud.* 14:28–39.

TANSLEY, A. G. 1935. The use and abuse of vegetational concepts and terms. *Ecology* 16:284–307.

TANSLEY, A. G. 1939. *The British Islands and Their Vegetation.* Cambridge University Press, Cambridge.

TAYLOR, M. C., and T. B. REYNOLDSON. 1962. The population biology of lake-dwelling *Polycelis* species with special reference to *P. nigra* (Mull.) (Turbellaria, Tricladida). *J. Anim. Ecol.* 31:273–291.

TAYLOR, T. H. C. 1955. Biological control of insect pests. *Ann. Appl. Biol.* 42:190–196.

TEAL, J. M. 1962. Energy flow in the salt marsh ecosystem of Georgia. *Ecology* 43:614–624.

TERBORGH, J. 1971. Distribution on environmental gradients: theory and a preliminary interpretation of distributional patterns in the avifauna of the Cordillera Vilcabamba, Peru. *Ecology* 52:23–40.

THOMAS, A. S. 1960. Changes in vegetation since the advent of myxomatosis. *J. Ecol.* 48:287–306.

THOMAS, A. S. 1963. Further changes in vegetation since the advent of myxomatosis. *J. Ecol.* 51:151–183.

THOMPSON, W. R. 1929. On natural control. *Parasitology* 21:269–281.

THORNTHWAITE, C. W. 1948. An approach toward a rational classification of climate. *Geogr. Rev.* 38:55–94.

TOMANEK, G. W., and F. W. ALBERTSON. 1957. Variations in cover, composition, production, and roots of vegetation on two prairies in western Kansas. *Ecol. Monogr.* 27:267–281.

TOUMEY, J. W., and R. KIENHOLZ. 1931. Trenched plots under forest canopies. *Yale Univ. School Forestry Bull. No. 30.* 31 pp.

TRANSEAU, E. N. 1935. The prairie peninsula *Ecology* 16:423–437.

TURESSON, G. 1922. The species and the variety as ecological units. *Hereditas* 3:100–113.

TURESSON, G. 1925. The plant species in relation to habitat and climate. *Hereditas* 6:147–236.

TURESSON, G. 1930. The selective effect of climate upon the plant species. *Hereditas* 14:99–152.

TURNBULL, A. L., and D. A. CHANT. 1961. The practice and theory of biological control of insects in Canada. *Can. J. Zool.* 39:697–753.

TURNER, R. M., S. M. ALCORN, and G. OLIN. 1969. Mortality of transplanted saguaro seedlings. *Ecology* 50:835–844.

TURNER, R. M., S. M. ALCORN, G. OLIN, and J. A. BOOTH. 1966. The influence of shade, soil, and water on saguaro seedling establishment. *Bot. Gaz.* 127:95–102.

UDVARDY, M. D. F. 1959. Notes on the ecological concepts of habitat, biotope, and niche. *Ecology* 40:725–728.

UDVARDY, M. D. F. 1969. *Dynamic Zoogeography with Special Reference to Land Animals.* Van Nostrand Reinhold, New York.

UNITED NATIONS. 1968. *International Action to Avert the Impending Protein Crisis.* New York. 106 pp.

UNITED NATIONS. 1971. A concise summary of the world population situation in 1970. *Dept. Economic and Social Affairs, Pop. Studies No. 48.* 35 pp.

U.S. BUREAU OF THE CENSUS. 1968. Summary of demographic projections. *Current Population Rept., Series P-25, No. 388.* U.S. Gov't. Printing Office, Washington, D.C.

U.S. BUREAU OF THE CENSUS. 1970. Projections of the population of the United States, by age and sex (interim revisions): 1970 to 2020. *Current Population Rept., Series P-25, No. 448.* U.S. Gov't Printing Office, Washington, D.C.

UTIDA, S. 1957. Cyclic fluctuations of population density intrinsic to the host-parasite system. *Ecology* 38:442–449.

UVAROV, B. P. 1921. A revision of the genus *Locusta* with a new theory as to the periodicity and migration of locusts. *Bull. Entomol. Res.* 12:135–163.

UVAROV, B. P. 1928. *Grasshoppers and Locusts.* Imperial Bureau of Entomology, London.

UVAROV, B. P. 1931. Insects and climate. *Trans. Entomol. Soc. London* 79:1–247.

UVAROV, B. P. 1961. Quantity and quality in insect populations. *Proc. Roy. Entomol. Soc. London, C,* 25:52–59.

VALLENTYNE, J. R. 1965. Net primary productivity and photosynthetic efficiency in the biosphere. pp. 309–311 in *Primary Productivity in Aquatic Environments,* ed. by C. R. Goldman. University of California Press, Berkeley.

VARLEY, G. C. 1949. Population changes in German forest pests. *J. Anim. Ecol.* 18:117–122.

VARLEY, G. C. 1970. The concept of energy flow applied to a woodland community. pp. 389–405 in *Animal Populations in Relation to Their Food Resources,* ed. by A. Watson. Blackwell, Oxford.

VAUGHAN, T. A. 1967. Two parapatric species of pocket gophers. *Evolution* 21: 148–158.

VAUGHAN, T. A., and R. M. HANSEN. 1964. Experiments on interspecific competition between two species of pocket gophers. *Amer. Midl. Naturalist* 72:444–452.

VERHULST, P. F. 1838. Notice sur la loi que la population suit dans son accroissement. *Corresp. Math. Phys.* 10:113–121.

VERMEER, K. 1963. The breeding ecology of the glaucous-winged gull (*Larus glaucescens*) on Mandarte Island, B.C. *Occ. Papers of B.C. Provincial Museum No. 13*. 104 pp.

VERNBERG, F. J., and W. B. VERNBERG. 1970. *The Animal and the Environment*. Holt, Rinehart & Winston, New York.

VERNER, J. 1964. Evolution of polygamy in the long-billed marsh wren. *Evolution* 18:252–261.

VERNER, J., and M. F. WILLSON. 1966. The influence of habitats on mating systems of North American Passerine birds. *Ecology* 47:143–147.

VOLLENWEIDER, R. A. 1969. *A Manual on Methods for Measuring Primary Production in Aquatic Environments*. (Int. Biol. Program Handbook No. 12). Blackwell, Oxford.

VOLTERRA, V. 1926. Fluctuations in the abundance of a species considered mathematically. *Nature* 118:558–560.

WAGNER, R. H. 1964. The ecology of *Uniola paniculata* L. in the dune-strand habitat of North Carolina. *Ecol. Monogr.* 34:79–96.

WALKER, R. B. 1954. The ecology of serpentine soils. II. Factors affecting plant growth on serpentine soils. *Ecology* 35:259–266.

WALLACE, A. R. 1878. *Tropical Nature and Other Essays*. Macmillan, New York.

WALLACE, B. 1960. Influence of genetic systems on geographical distribution. *Cold Spring Harbor Symp. Quant. Biol.* 24:193–204.

WALOFF, Z. 1966. The upsurges and recessions of the desert locust plague: an historical survey. *Anti-Locust Mem.* 8:1–111.

WALSHE, B. M. 1948. The oxygen requirements and thermal resistance of chironomid larvae from flowing and from still waters. *J. Exp. Biol.* 25:35–44.

WANG, J. Y. 1960. A critique of the heat unit approach to plant response studies. *Ecology* 41:785–790.

WANGERSKY, P. J., and W. J. CUNNINGHAM. 1956. On time lags in equations of growth. *Proc. Nat. Acad. Sci. U.S.* 42:699–702.

WARDLE, P. 1965. A comparison of alpine timber lines in New Zealand and North America. *New Zeal. J. Bot.* 3:113–135.

WARING, R. H., and J. MAJOR. 1964. Some vegetation of the California coastal redwood region in relation to gradients of moisture, nutrients, light and temperature. *Ecol. Monogr.* 34:167–215.

WARMING, J. E. B. 1895. *Plantesamfundgrundträk af den ökologiska plantegegrefi.* Copenhagen.

WARMING, J. E. B. 1896. *Lehrbuch der ökologischen Pflanzengeographie*. Berlin. (English transl.:1909, *Oecology of Plants*. Oxford University Press, New York.)

WARMING, J. E.B. 1909. *Oecology of Plants*. Oxford University Press, New York.

WARREN, C. E., and G. E. DAVIS. 1967. Laboratory studies on the feeding, bioenergetics, and growth of fish. pp. 175–214 in *The Biological Basis of Freshwater Fish Production*, ed. by S. D. Gerking. Blackwell, Oxford.

WARREN, C. E., J. H. WALES, G. E. DAVIS, and P. DOUDOROFF. 1964. Trout production in an experimental stream enriched with sucrose. *J. Wildl. Mgmt.* 28:617–660.

WATERS, T. F. 1957. The effects of lime application to acid bog lakes in northern Michigan. *Trans. Amer. Fish. Soc.* 86:329–344.

WATSON, A., and R. MOSS. 1970. Dominance, spacing behaviour and aggression in relation to population limitation in vertebrates. pp. 167–218 in *Animal Populations in Relation to Their Food Resources*, ed. by A. Watson. Blackwell, Oxford.

WATT, A. S. 1940. Contributions to the ecology of bracken (*Pteridium aquilinum*). I. *New Phytol.* 39:401–422.

WATT, A. S. 1947a. Contributions to the ecology of bracken (*Pteridium aquilinum*). IV. The structure of the community. *New Phytol.* 46:97–121.

WATT, A. S. 1947b. Pattern and process in the plant community. *J. Ecol.* 35:1–22.

WATT, A. S. 1955. Bracken versus heather, a study in plant sociology. *J. Ecol.* 43:490–506.

WATT, A. S. 1964. The community and the individual. *J. Ecol.* 52(Suppl.):203–211.

WATT, K. E. F. 1964. Comments on fluctuations of animal populations and measures of community stability. *Can. Entomol.* 96:1434–1442.

WATT, K. E. F. 1965. Community stability and the strategy of biological control. *Can. Entomol.* 97:887–895.

WATT, K. E. F. 1968. *Ecology and Resource Management*. McGraw-Hill, New York.

WEAVER, J. E. 1968. *Prairie Plants and Their Environment*. University of Nebraska Press, Lincoln.

WEAVER, J. E., and F. W. ALBERTSON. 1956. *Grasslands of the Great Plains*. Johnsen Publishing Co., Lincoln, Nebr.

WEBB, D. A. 1954. Is the classification of plant communities either possible or desirable? *Bot. Tidsskr.* 51:362–370.

WEBB, L. J., J. G. TRACEY, and K. P. HAYDOCK. 1967. A factor toxic to seedlings of the same species associated with living roots of the non-gregarious subtropical rain forest tree *Grevillea robusta*. *J. Appl. Ecol.* 4:13–25.

WECKER, S. C. 1963. The role of early experience in habitat selection by the prairie deer mouse, *Peromyscus maniculatus bairdi*. *Ecol. Monogr.* 33:307–325.

WECKER, S. C. 1964. Habitat selection. *Sci. Amer.* 211(4):109–116.

WEISER, C. J. 1970. Cold resistance and injury in woody plants. *Science* 169:1269–1278.

WELLINGTON, W. G. 1957. Individual differences as a factor in population dynamics: the development of a problem. *Can. J. Zool.* 35:293–323.

WELLINGTON, W. G. 1960. Qualitative changes in natural populations during changes in abundance. *Can. J. Zool.* 38:289–314.

WELLINGTON, W. G. 1964. Qualitative changes in populations in unstable environments. *Can. Entomol.* 96:436–451.

WELLINGTON, W. G. 1965. Some maternal influences on progeny quality in the western tent caterpillar *Malacosoma pluviale* (Dyar.). *Can. Entomol.* 97:1–14.

WELLS, B. W., and I. V. SHUNK. 1938. Salt spray: an important factor in coastal ecology. *Bull. Torrey Bot. Club* 65:485–492.

WELLS, P. V. 1965. Scarp woodlands, transported grassland soils, and concept of grassland climate in the Great Plains region. *Science* 148:246–249.

WENT, F. W. 1942. The dependence of certain annual plants on shrubs in southern California deserts. *Bull. Torrey Bot. Club* 69:100–114.

WESTING, A. H. 1966. Sugar maple decline: an evaluation. *Econ. Bot.* 20:196–212.

WESTLAKE, D. F. 1963. Comparisons of plant productivity. *Biol. Rev.* 38:385–425.

WETZEL, R. G. 1965. Nutritional aspects of algal productivity in marl lakes with particular reference to enrichment bioassays and their interpretation. pp. 137–157 in *Primary Productivity in Aquatic Environments*, ed. by C. R. Goldman. University of California Press, Berkeley.

WETZEL, R. G., and H. L. ALLEN. 1971. Functions and interactions of dissolved organic matter and the littoral zone in lake metabolism and eutrophication in *Productivity Problems of Freshwaters*, Proceedings of IBP–UNESCO Symposium, Poland, May 1970, ed. by Z. Kajak and A. Hillbricht-Ilkowska, Warsaw.

WHARTON, C. R., JR. 1969. The Green Revolution: cornucopia or Pandora's box? *Foreign Affairs* 47:464–476.

WHITE, H. C. 1939. Bird control to increase the Margaree River salmon. *Bull. Fish. Res. Bd. Can. No. 58.* 30 pp.

WHITESIDE, M. C., and R. V. HARMSWORTH, 1967. Species diversity in Chydorid (Cladocera) communities. *Ecology* 48:664–667.

WHITTAKER, R. H. 1953. A consideration of climax theory: the climax as a population and pattern. *Ecol. Monogr.* 23:41–78.

WHITTAKER, R. H. 1954. The ecology of serpentine soils. I. Introduction. *Ecology* 35:258–259.

WHITTAKER, R. H. 1956. Vegetation of the Great Smoky Mountains. *Ecol. Monogr.* 26:1–80.

WHITTAKER, R. H. 1960. Vegetation of the Siskiyou Mountains, Oregon and California. *Ecol. Monogr.* 30:279–338.

WHITTAKER, R. H. 1962. Classification of natural communities. *Bot. Rev.* 28:1–239.

WHITTAKER, R. H. 1967. Gradient analysis of vegetation. *Biol. Rev.* 42:207–264.

WHITTAKER, R. H. 1969. Evolution of diversity in plant communities. *Brookhaven Symp. Biol.* 22:178–196.

WHITTAKER, R. H. 1970. *Communities and Ecosystems.* Macmillan, New York.

WHITTAKER, R. H., and P. P. FEENY. 1971. Allelochemics: chemical interactions between species. *Science* 171:757–770.

WICKLOW, D. T. 1966. Further observations on serpentine response in *Emmenanthe*. *Ecology* 47:864–865.

WIEGERT, R. G., and F. C. EVANS. 1967. Investigations of secondary productivity in grasslands. pp. 499–518 in *Secondary Productivity of Terrestrial Ecosystems*, ed. by K. Petrusewicz, Polish Acad. Sciences, Warsaw.

WILLIAMS, C. B. 1964. *Patterns in the Balance of Nature and Related Problems in Quantitative Ecology*. Academic, New York.

WILLIAMS, G. C. 1966. *Adaptation and Natural Selection*. Princeton University Press, Princeton, N.J.

WILSON, E. O. 1969. The species equilibrium. *Brookhaven Symp. Biol.* 22:38–47.

WILSON, R. E., and E. L. RICE. 1968. Allelopathy as expressed by *Helianthus annuus* and its role in old-field succession. *Bull. Torrey Bot. Club* 95:432–448.

WISHART, G. 1947. Further observations on the changes taking place in the corn borer population in western Ontario. *Can. Entomol.* 79:81–83.

WIT, C. T. DE 1960. On competition. *Versl. Landbouwk. Onderzoek.* No. 66,8. Wageningen, Netherlands. 82 pp.

WIT, C. T. DE 1961. Space relationships within populations of one or more species. pp. 314–329 in *Mechanisms in Biological Competition*, (Symp. Soc. Exp. Biol. No. 15), ed. by F. L. Milthorpe. Cambridge University Press, New York.

WOLFSON, A. 1964. Animal photoperiodism. Chap. 12, p. 1–49, in *Photophysiology*, Vol. II, ed. by A. C. Giese. Academic, New York.

WOODWELL, G. M. and R. H. WHITTAKER. 1968. Primary production in terrestrial ecosystems. *Amer. Zool.* 8:19–30.

WRIGHT, H. E., JR. 1968. The roles of pine and spruce in the forest history of Minnesota and adjacent areas. *Ecology* 49:937–955.

WRIGHT, R. D. 1970. Seasonal course of CO_2 exchange in the field as related to lower elevational limits of pines. *Amer. Midl. Naturalist* 83:321–329.

WRIGHT, R. D. and H. A. MOONEY. 1965. Substrate-oriented distribution of bristlecone pine in the White Mountains of California. *Amer. Midl. Naturalist* 73:257–284.

WYNNE–EDWARDS, V. C. 1962. *Animal Dispersion in Relation to Social Behaviour*. Oliver & Boyd, Edinburgh.

YOUNG, H. B. 1970. Effects of nutrition on growth and performance. *Agr. Sci. Rev.* 8(2–3):1–8.

YOUNG, J. A., R. A. EVANS, and R. E. ECKERT, JR. 1969. Population dynamics of downy brome. *Weed Sci.* 17:20–26.

YOUNG, J. O., and T. B. REYNOLDSON. 1966. A quantitative study of the population biology of *Dendrocoelum lacteum* (Muller) (Turbellaria, Tricladida). *Oikos* 15:237–264.

Species index

Species names and common names are listed here for organisms discussed in this book. Page entries are under the Latin names. References to general groups such as "ants" are given in the Subject Index.

Abies balsamea, 333, 338, 390, 405, 406, 547
Acacia spp., 326, 565–567
Acacia ants. *See Pseudomyrmex* spp.
Acacias. *See Acacia* spp.
Acanthaster planci, 548
Acer rubrum, 95, 120, 397
  saccharum, 75, 76, 119–120, 396, 397, 407, 423, 431, 540, 554
Achillea borealis, 112, 114, 115
  lanulosa, 112, 113
  spp., 111–114, 115
Adelina spp., 223, 224
Adenostoma fasciculatum, 47
Aedes aegypti, 62–63
  taeniorhynchus, 26
African migratory locust. *See Locusta migratoria*
Agelaius phoeniceus, 53
  tricolor, 53
Agropyron spp., 313, 314

Agrostis tenuis, 118, 135, 385
Alchemilla alpina, 436
Alder. *See Alnus* spp.
Alnus glutinosa, 95
  spp., 418, 419
Alpine sorrel. *See Oxyria digyna*
Ambystoma gracile, 486–488
Ameiurus nebulosus, 58, 62
American beech. *See Fagus sylvatica*
American chestnut. *See Castanea dentata*
American elm. *See Ulmus americana*
American oyster. *See Crassostrea virginica*
Ammophila breviligulata, 382, 385, 421-423
Anchovy. *See Engraulis mordax*
Andropogon littoralis, 102
  scoparius, 382, 385, 422, 426–428, 542
  virginicus, 424

Anopheles culicifacies, 30, 34
  gambiae, 30
  maculatus, 30
  spp., 26
Anthoxanthum odoratum, 228
Anthus pratensis, 31
  trivialis, 31
Aonidiella aurantii, 236
Aphytis chrysomphali, 236, 237
  lingnanensis, 236, 237
  melinus, 236
  spp., 236, 238
Aplopappus tenuisectus, 241
Apus apus, 569, 582
Arbutus menziesii, 72, 394
Arctostaphylos spp., 432, 433
Argentine ant. *See Iridomyrmex humilis*
Aristida oligantha, 426–428
Armeria maritima, 118
Artemisia californica, 46

House fly. *See Musca domestica*
House mouse. *See Mus musculus*
Hyalella azteca, 485–487
Hydra littoralis, 227
Hypericum perforatum, 40, 369–371

Icerya purchasi, 366–367
Iridomyrmex humilis, 238
Ixodes spp., 153

Jack pine. *See Pinus banksiana*
Juglans nigra, 42
Juncus effusus, 71, 386–388, 393, 409
spp., 71

Kangaroo rats. *See Dipodomys* spp.
Klamath weed. *See Hypericum perforatum*
Knotweed. *See Polygonum bistortoides*
Kokanee, 486, 488

Lake trout. *See Salvelinus namaycush*
Lamprey. *See Petromyzon marinus*
Larus glaucescens, 569–570
Lasius flavus, 238
niger, 238
Leafhopper. *See Erythoneura* spp.
Lebistes reticulatus, 354–356
Lepomis macrochirus, 150, 151, 483
Lepus americanus, 265, 266
Linum usitatissimum, 240
Little bluestem. *See Andropogon scoparius*
Littorina irrorata, 442, 443
Loblolly pine. *See Pinus taeda*
Locusta migratoria, 289, 292, 294, 296, 302, 304, 544
Lodgepole pine. *See Pinus contorta*
Lolium perenne, 229, 244
Long-billed marsh wren. *See Telmatodytes palustris*
Lophocereus schottii, 40
Lucilia cuprina, 353
Lynx canadensis, 265, 266

Malacosoma pluviale, 304, 321
Marijuana. *See Cannabis sativa*
Marram grass. *See Ammophila breviligulata*
Masked shrew. *See Sorex* spp.
Meadow mice. *See Microtus* spp.
Meadow pipit. *See Anthus pratensis*
Mesquite. *See Prosopis glandulosa*
Micropterus dolomieu, 62
Microtus agrestis, 177, 472
californicus, 240, 259
Milkweed. *See Asclepias* spp.
Mosquitoes. *See Anopheles* spp., *Aedes* spp.
Mountain hemlock. *See Tsuga mer-*

tensiana
Mule deer. *See Odocoileus* spp.
Mus musculus, 240
Musca domestica, 255
Muskrat. *See Ondatra zibethicus*
Myrica gale, 95
Myriophyllum spp., 101
Mysis relicta, 22
Mytilus edulis, 35–38
spp., 519

Nasonia vitripennis, 255
Neodiprion sertifer, 260, 267
Nomadacris septemfaciata, 289–291, 293, 301
North Atlantic gannet. *See Sula bassana*
Nothofagus spp., 79

Oaks. *See Quercus* spp.
Oats. *See Avena* spp.
Odocoileus spp., 268
Oenanthe oenanthe, 31
Oncorhynchus nerka, 257, 258, 351, 359
Ondatra zibethicus, 259
Operophtera brumata, 443, 563
Opuntia spp., 367–369
Orchard grass. *See Dactylis glomerata*
Orchelimum fidicinium, 472, 473
Oryzaephilus spp., 226
Ostrea edulis, 124
Ostrinia nubilalis. *See Pyrausta nubilalis*
Ovis dalli, 162, 163
Oxyria digyna, 116–117

Pacific madrone. *See Arbutus menziesii*
Papaver spp., 25
Paracentrotus lividus, 38–39, 56
Paramecium aurelia, 190, 220, 221, 227, 546
bursaria, 227
caudatum, 190, 220, 221, 250–252
Parus caeruleus, 314–317, 444
major, 314–321, 444, 482
spp., 314
Pectenogammarus planicrurus, 97
Perca fluviatilis, 578
Perch. *See Perca fluviatilis*
Peromyscus maniculatus, 32–34, 262
Perennial rye grass. *See Lolium perenne*
Petromyzon marinus, 39, 260, 261
Phagocata vitta, 100
Phalacrocorax aristotelis, 233
carbo, 233
Phasianus colchicus, 23–24
Pheidole megacephala, 238
Phenacomys longicaudus, 41

Phleum pratense, 228, 229
Picea glauca, 390, 405, 406, 547
mariana, 405, 407
Pinus aristata, 96
banksiana, 105, 396, 397, 422
contorta, 120–122
echinata, 425, 426
jeffreyi, 95
murrayana, 79
ponderosa, 82, 83, 95, 106, 107
pungens, 395
radiata, 465
rigida, 395
strobus, 41, 397, 422
sylvestris, 120, 121, 276, 467
taeda, 59, 93, 102
virginiana, 395
Pisaster spp., 519, 540, 548
Plaice. *See Pleuronectes platessa*
Planorbis corneus, 21, 22
Plantago maritima, 111
Plethodon cinereus, 53–54
richmondi, 53–54
Pleuronectes platessa, 153, 348–353
Polycelis felina, 100
hepta, 100
nigra, 100, 306–311
tenuis, 100, 306–308, 310, 311
Polygonum bistortoides, 117
Ponderosa pine. *See Pinus ponderosa*
Poppies. *See Papaver* spp.
Populus deltoides, 422
tremuloides, 397, 405, 406
trichocarpa, 119
Porcellio scaber, 29
Port Orford cedar. *See Chamaecyparis lawsoniana*
Prickly pear. *See Opuntia* spp.
Prokelisia marginata, 442, 443
Prosopis glandulosa, 106, 326, 327
Protodrilus symbioticus, 98
Prunella vulgaris, 115
Prunus pumila, 422
Pseudomyrmex spp., 565
Pseudotsuga menziesii, 41, 82, 83, 394, 447, 465
Pteridium aquilinum, 434, 436
Pycnopsyche guttifer, 98
lepida, 98
Pyrausta nubilalis, 29, 126, 271, 371

Quercus coccinea, 75, 76
ellipsoidalis, 396, 397
robur, 443, 467, 563
rubra, 75, 93, 397
velutina, 75, 422, 423

Rainbow trout. *See Salmo gairdneri*
Rana aurora, 486
Rangifer spp., 196, 197
Red locust. *See Nomadacris septemfaciata*

Red maple. *See Acer rubrum*
Red oak. *See Quercus rubra*
Red-osier dogwood. *See Cornus stolonifera*
Red tree mouse. *See Phenacomys longicaudus*
Redwing blackbird. *See Agelaius phoeniceus*
Reindeer. *See Rangifer* spp.
Rhizopertha dominica, 172, 173, 221, 222, 226
Ribes spp., 41
Ringed-neck pheasant. *See Phasianus colchicus*
Rodolia cardinalis, 366–367
Ruffed grouse. *See Bonasa umbellus*
Rumex acetosella, 115
  crispus, 24

Saccharomyces cervisiae, 218–220
Sagebrush. *See Artemisia tridentata*
Sagitta elegans, 495
Sagittae. *See Sagitta elegans*
Saguaro. *See Carnegiea gigantea*
St. John's wort (Klamath weed). *See Hypericum perforatum*
Salix spp., 417, 418, 422
Salmo clarkii, 488
  gairdneri, 23, 486–488
  salar, 23, 256, 257
Salt marsh grasshopper. *See Orchelimum fidicinium*
Salvelinus fontinalis, 61
  namaycush, 39, 260, 261
Salvia leucophylla, 46, 47
Sand cherry. *See Prunus pumila*
Sand crab. *See Emerita analoga*
Sand reed grass. *See Calamovilfa longifolia*
Sardinops caerulea, 356, 578
Scarlet oak. *See Quercus coccinea*
Schistocerca gregaria, 289, 290, 293–295, 297
Schizosaccharomyces kephir, 218–220
Scotch pine. *See Pinus sylvestris*
Sea lamprey. *See Petromyzon marinus*
Sea oats. *See Uniola paniculata*
Sea urchin. *See Paracentrotus lividus*

Senita cactus. *See Lophocereus schottii*
Shag. *See Phalacrocorax aristotelis*
Sheep blowfly. *See Lucilia cuprina*
Sheep tick. *See Ixodes* spp.
Shortleaf pine. *See Pinus echinata*
Short-tailed vole. *See Microtus agrestis*
Shrews. *See Sorex* spp.; *Blarina* spp.
Smallmouth black bass. *See Micropterus dolomieu*
Snowshoe hare. *See Lepus americanus*
Sockeye salmon. *See Oncorhynchus nerka*
Solidago virgaurea, 118
Sorex spp., 261, 262
Spartina alterniflora, 442
Sphaerotilus natans, 489
Speckled trout. *See Salvelinus fontinalis*
Sphagnum spp., 95, 418, 449
Spizella passerina, 32, 267
Sporobolus heterolepis, 542
Spruce budworm. *See Choristoneura fumiferana*
Spruce sawfly. *See Diprion hercyniae*
Starfish. *See Heliaster* spp.; *Pisaster* spp.
Starling. *See Sturnus vulgaris*
Stipa spartea, 542
Strix aluco, 263–265, 544
Sturnus cristatellus, 132–133
  vulgaris, 17–19, 131–133
Sugar maple. *See Acer saccharum*
Sula bassana, 197, 568
Sunflower. *See Helianthus annuus*
Sweet vernal grass. *See Anthoxanthum odoratum*
Swift. *See Apus apus*

Taricha granulosa, 486, 487
Tawny owl. *See Strix aluco*
Telmatodytes palustris, 573
Tetraphis pellucida, 83–85
Thomomys bottae, 51, 52
  talpoides, 51, 52
Three-spined stickleback. *See Gas-*

terosteus aculeatus
Thuja occidentalis, 122, 123
Timothy. *See Phleum pratense*
Tree pipit. *See Anthus trivialis*
Trembling aspen. *See Populus tremuloides*
Tribolium castaneum, 194, 222–226
  confusum, 194, 209, 222–226
  spp., 193, 222
Tricolored blackbird. *See Agelaius tricolor*
Trifolium repens, 229, 244
Tsetse. *See Glossina* spp.
Tsuga canadensis, 89, 90, 92, 396, 397
  mertensiana, 394, 418
Typhlodromus occidentalis, 253, 254

Ulmus americana, 28
Uniola paniculata, 102

Vedalia. *See Rodolia cardinalis*

Western tent caterpillar. *See Malacosoma pluviale*
Wheatear. *See Oenanthe oenanthe*
Wheatgrass. *See Agropyron* spp.
Whirligig beetles. *See Dineutes* spp.
White cedar. *See Thuja occidentalis*
Whitefish. *See Coregonus clupeaformis*
White pine blister rust. *See Cronartium ribicola*
White pine (eastern). *See Pinus strobus*
White spruce. *See Picea glauca*
Willows. *See Salix* spp.
Winter moth. *See Operophtera brumata*
Woodruffia spp., 546

Xanthocephalus xanthocephalus, 53

Yarrow. *See Achillea* spp.
Yeast, 190–192. *See also Saccharomyces* and *Schizosaccharomyces*
Yellow-headed blackbird. *See Xanthocephalus xanthocephalus*

Subject index

Abortion, 593, 606
Absolute density, 141
Abundance, 9. *See also* Density
Accidental species, 386
Actual rate of increase, 164
Adaptation, 110–134
Age distribution, 174–178, 331, 346, 357, 602
   dominant year classes, 177, 179, 358
   life-table, 156, 176
   stable, 167, 169, 175, 177, 194
   stationary, 176, 177, 474, 601
Agricultural revolution, 588
Agriculture, 464, 466. *See also* Food production
Alaska salmon fishery, 359–361
Algae, 26, 38, 235, 427, 442, 456, 485, 543
Allelopathic agents, 41–47, 415, 427–428, 561
Altitudinal distribution. *See also* Timberline
   lower limits, 80–82
   upper limits, 75–81
Anemia, 609
Ants, 509

and acacias, 565–567
   competition in, 238
Aquatic plants, 93, 100, 485
Arable land, 617
Arctic tree line, 80–81. *See also* Timberline
Aristotle, 4
Assimilation, 471, 477, 494, 495
Association
   detection of, 386
   plant, 379
   between species, 381, 387
Australian deserts, 526–527
Autecology, 12

Bacteria, 95, 191, 195, 427, 428, 442, 480, 486, 489, 546
Balance of nature, 4, 6, 272, 274, 276
Barnacles, 63–66, 140, 155, 441, 442, 519, 578
Basal metabolic rate, 471–472, 476
Behavior
   and population regulation, 284
   territorial, 259, 320
Bermuda, 238
Between-habitat diversity. *See* Species diversity

Big-bang reproduction, 575
Biocoenosis, 8
Biogeography, 17, 27
Biological control, 7, 365
   attributes of agents, 373
   percentage of successes, 372
Biological cost, 578–579
Biological profit, 578–579
Biomass, 195, 228, 344, 354, 445, 448, 472, 489
Biosphere, 10
Biotic school, 273, 276, 283
Birds
   colonization in, 22, 28
   competition in, 52–53, 410
   habitat selection in, 31–32
   population control in, 279–280
   species abundance and diversity, 503, 504, 510, 517, 518, 522–523, 539
Birth rate, 144, 146–148, 151, 152, 165, 202, 206, 207
   in human societies, 589–596
   instantaneous, 186, 205, 274
   in Japan, 606
Boreal forest, 393, 394, 405–407, 508
Bradley, R., 7

Buffon, 5
Bunchgrass, 426, 428, 429

Caddisflies, 98
Calcium, 24, 99, 100, 118, 311, 445, 446, 457, 463, 529
Caloric value of the diet, 608
Canadian Forest Insect Survey, 546–548
Cannibalism, 212
  in flour beetles, 224, 225
Canonical distribution, 505
Capture-recapture methods, 144–148, 348, 627–628
Carbon dioxide, 446, 447
Cardiac glycosides, 562–563
Carnivores, 212, 268, 440, 444
Catastrophic agents, 270, 275
Catch curves, 150–151
Cattle
  effects on range deterioration, 327–328, 333
  grazing on grasses, 306, 313
Caves, 109
Census techniques. See Population density, estimation of
Chaparral, 45, 554
Characteristic species, 386
Chemical materials, 445
Chironomids, 104, 105
Chi-squared test, 382
Cichlidae, 235
Classification of communities. See Communities
Clements, F. E., 8, 392, 417
Climate, 59, 71, 73, 81, 106, 129, 224, 276, 280, 315, 417, 430, 513, 520, 524, 526, 580
  effects on range deterioration, 328–330
  school of population regulation, 271, 277
Climatic climax, 417, 422
Climatic release, 337
Climax adaptation numbers, 396, 398
Climax communities, 381
  definition, 429
  operational criterion, 431
  productivity of, 463, 552
Climax-pattern hypothesis, 430
Clutch size in birds, 316, 566–572, 582
Coefficient of association, 383
Cohort life tables, 159–161
Colonization, 26, 27, 131, 534
Common-property resources, 361
Communities
  characteristics of, 380–381
  classification of, 411–413
  development of, 417, 551
  measurements of species groupings, 381–389

relative importance of species, 401, 445
Community dominance index, 541
Compartment of an ecosystem, 461–462
Compensation point, 437, 446
Compensatory reactions, 353
Competition
  in birds, 233–235, 283
  in different taxonomic groups, 242
  in experimental laboratory populations, 218–230
  as factor limiting distributions, 48–54, 57, 244, 410
  for food or space, 212, 283, 486–487
  as an input–output problem, 215–217, 227–230
  interspecific and intraspecific, 211, 580
  mathematical models of, 212–217
  in natural populations, 230–242, 273, 358, 547
  in plants, 212, 215, 313, 401
Competition hypothesis. See Species diversity, explanations of gradients, competition
Competitive exclusion principle, 230–232
Components of the environment, 278
Comprehensive theory of natural control, 271, 277
Consumers, 444
Consumption efficiency, 478, 480, 482
Contingency table, 381
Continuity and discontinuity of stands, 393
Continuum, 393, 430
Continuum index, 398, 399
Contraception, 593, 600, 603
Controlling factor, 272
Convergent oscillations. See Oscillations
Corn (maize), 42, 609–611, 619–620
Cotton, 124
Cow droppings, 420
Cowles, H. C., 8, 417
Crop plants, 123–124. See also Corn, Wheat, Rice
Cultural revolution, 588
Cyclic vegetation changes, 416, 432–437

Danaid butterflies, 562
DDT, 336, 366, 367, 592
Death rate, 144, 146–147, 151, 152, 165, 202, 206, 207, 281, 282
  in human populations, 180, 589–596
  instantaneous, 186, 205, 274, 275, 347

Deciduous forest, 71, 74, 402, 404, 509
  species diversity of, 527–529, 541
Decomposers, 442, 480
Defense mechanisms in plants, 560–566
Demes, 139
Demographic transition. See World population problem, demographic transition
Density, 140. See also Population growth
Density-dependent factors, 275, 278, 280, 282, 284, 317, 351
Density-independent factors, 275, 278, 281, 282
Desert, 71, 73, 326, 329, 521, 523
Desert grassland, 325, 327, 328
Desert lizard communities, 523–527, 548
Destruction and control compared, 273
Determinate layers, 568
Deterministic models, 204
Detritus, 442, 443, 480, 484, 486
Diatoms, 26, 140, 549
Dieback declines, 75
Digestible energy, 470
Dilution rate, 147, 151. See also Birth rate
Disclimax, 429
Diseases, 41, 75, 271, 336, 369
Dispersal, 17, 50, 129, 151, 279, 304, 323, 324, 334, 335, 339, 351, 369, 427, 520
Distribution
  and abundance, 9
  genetic adaptation and limits of, 110–111, 127
  methods of explaining, 16
Distributional relations of species, 402
Divergent oscillations. See Oscillations
Diversity-causes-stability concept, 545–548
Diversity gradients. See Species diversity
Dominance, 380, 401, 413, 433, 540–543
Dominance type, 413
Doubleday, T., 5–6
Doubling time, 186–187
Drought, 60, 75, 81–82, 120, 304–306
Dutch elm disease, 28
Dwarf wheat, 612–613
Dynamic integration in a community, 410
Dynamics, 339, 340

Earthworms, 101

Eastern deciduous forest of North America. *See* Deciduous forest
Ecological consciousness, 623
Ecological efficiencies
between trophic levels, 478–480, 482
within a trophic level, 477, 478
Ecological longevity, 150
Ecological time scale, 255, 513
Ecology
basic problems of, 8–9
defined, 3–4
descriptive vs. functional, 8–9
plant vs. animal ecology, 12
theoretical framework, 11, 623–624
Ecosystem, 10, 466, 551–554, 556–557
Ecotype, 111, 135
E/F ratio, 302
Efficiencies between trophic levels. *See* Ecological efficiencies
Efficiency of utilization of sunlight, 450, 484
Elfinwood, 79–80, 135
Eltonian pyramids, 483, 499
Emigration, 140, 151, 152, 254, 284, 320, 321, 473, 474, 515, 532
Empty niches. *See* Niches
Energy, 445, 551, 556, 568
Energy-flow
in marine food chains, 489–497
in Marion Lake, 484–487
role of bacteria, 480, 482
in a sucrose-enriched stream, 487–489
and systems analysis, 556
Environmental factors, 165, 278, 566
Environmental gradients, 394, 395, 410, 414, 430
Equilibrium density, 184, 202, 215–217, 245, 274, 278
Equitability, 507
Errington, P. L., 259
European titmice, 314
Eutrophic lake, 451
Evapotranspiration, 71
and net primary production, 463
Evolution, 104, 110, 139, 281, 284, 513–515, 520, 527, 557, 560
of life cycles, 575–581
in predator–prey systems, 255, 372
Evolutionary time scale, 513–514
Exploitation, 211, 344–346, 354, 355, 552
Extinction, 206–207, 232, 355, 515, 536, 546
Extinction coefficient, 451
Extinction rate, 533–536
Extrinsic factors, 281, 284, 340

Factors limiting primary produc-

tivity. *See* Primary production
Facultative agents, 270, 275
Family planning, 593
Famine, 621
Farr, W., 6
F/C ratio, 297
Fecal energy, 470, 474, 476
Fecundity, 149, 338
Ferns, 538
Fertility, 149
Fertility table, 165–166
Fertilizers, 434, 458, 459, 465, 543, 611, 613–618
Fidelity, 386
Finite rates, 171, 629–633
Finite rate of increase, 171, 175
Fire, 45, 46, 105, 120, 313, 328, 431, 554
Fishponds, 458
Fish production
maximum harvest, 497, 620
in the sea, 496, 498
Florida Keys, 534–535
Floristic provinces, 402, 403
Flour beetles, 193, 209, 222–227
Fluctuations in numbers, 194, 249, 269, 282, 321, 544, 552
Foliage-height diversity, 517
Food chains, 440–444, 551
and community stability, 545
mathematical model of, 489–495
in ocean, 489, 496–497
size of organisms in, 444
Food production, 607, 610–612
Food supply, 280, 283, 307, 309–312, 318, 320, 321, 336, 337, 486, 488, 560
Food webs, 440, 519. *See also* Food chains
Foraminifera, 514, 538
Forbes, E., 8
Forbes, S. A., 8
Forest-prairie boundary, 105–108, 117, 393
Forestry, 333, 343, 465, 617
Fossil communities, 514
Freshwater communities, 457–463
Freshwater fishes, 510
Frost drought, 73
Functional response, 260–264
Fundamental niche. *See* Niches
Fundamental-unit assumption, 391–392

Gause, G. F., 190, 218–221, 230–231
Gause's hypothesis. *See* Competitive exclusion principle
Genecology, 111
Generation time, 166, 170–171, 580
Genetic feedback mechanism, 284, 288
Genetic strains of *Tribolium*,

225–227
Genetics, 32, 33, 127–128, 139, 282, 285, 303, 338
Genotypic, 111, 281
Geometric population growth. *See* Population growth, geometric
Geometric scales, 503
Global stability. *See* Stability, global
Gradations, 276
Gradient analysis, 393, 430
criticism of, 400
of Wisconsin forest stands, 395–400
Gradocoen, 277
Grasshoppers, 289, 304
Graunt, J., 5
Grazing, 306, 485, 486, 492, 493. *See also* Cattle
Grazing pressure on saguaro, 330–333
Great Salt Lake, 521
Great Slave Lake, 514
Gregaria, 296–299, 302, 303
Green Revolution, 612–615
Gross energy intake, 470, 476
Group selection, 572
Growth efficiency, 477, 478
Growth of populations. *See* Population growth

Habitat selection, 29–34, 370
Haeckel, Ernst, 3
Herbivores, 212, 268, 440, 442, 444, 477–479, 486, 560, 564, 566
Hierarchical classification, 412
History of ecology, 4–8
Holling, C. S., 260–263
Homeostasis, 380, 554
Human food requirements, 607–610
Human population problem, 587. *See also* World population problem
Hummock-and-hollow cycle, 433
Hybrid corn, 610–611
Hydrophytes, 70

Immigration, 140, 151–152, 252–254, 284, 319, 321, 500, 532, 598
Immigration rate, 533–536
Importance value, 396
Indeterminate layers, 568
Index of diversity. *See* Species diversity
Index of similarity, 402, 405, 407
Indicator species, 549
Indifferent species, 386
Industrial revolution, 588
Information theory, 506
Innate capacity for increase, 164–174, 186, 188, 274, 347, 575–577

72 73 74 75 76   9 8 7 6 5 4 3 2 1